AF352736

The History of
Modern Japanese Philosophy

The History of
Modern Japanese Philosophy

FUJITA MASAKATSU

Translated by
ROBERT CHAPESKIE

Cover credit: *White, Silence, Sea, Rock 14*, Nathan Wirth, https://sliceofsilence.com/photography/.

Published by State University of New York Press, Albany

EU GPSR Authorised Representative:
Logos Europe, 9 rue Nicolas Poussin, 17000, La Rochelle, France
contact@logoseurope.eu

For information, contact State University of New York Press, Albany, NY
www.sunypress.edu

Library of Congress Cataloging-in-Publication Data

Names: Fujita, Masakatsu, 1949– author. | Chapeskie, Robert, translator.
Title: The history of modern Japanese philosophy / Masakatsu Fujita ;
    translated by Robert Chapeskie.
Description: Albany : State University of New York Press, [2026]. | Series:
    SUNY series in transcontinental philosophy | Includes bibliographical
    references and index.
Identifiers: LCCN 2025041170 | ISBN 9798855806106 (hardcover : alk. paper) |
    ISBN 9798855806137 (epub) | ISBN 9798855806120 (PDF)
Subjects: LCSH: Philosophy, Japanese.
Classification: LCC B5241 .F7613 2026
LC record available at https://lccn.loc.gov/2025041170

Contents

Part II
The Era of Formation—The Philosophy of the Taishō and Early Shōwa Periods

Part III
The Period of Development—Postwar Philosophy

Translator's Note

Round parentheses are present in the original text or quotation. Square brackets have been added by the translator in the case of the main text or by the author or translator in the case of quotations, with all such additions having been approved by the author.

Titles of Japanese texts are given in translation in the body of the text, with the original Japanese titles provided in the footnotes or bibliography. For certain words, phrases, and names, the original Japanese has been given in a footnote. Japanese names are written in the order used in Japanese (family name followed by given name).

Introduction

Japanese "Philosophy" and the "History of Philosophy" in Japan

1. How Should We View "Philosophy"?

(1) What Is Philosophy?

When discussing the "history of Japanese philosophy," the first question we must answer is "what is philosophy?" If we take the perspective of the Western tradition that began in ancient Greece, the answer may seem self-evident. When it comes to philosophy in Japan, however, it is not nearly so straightforward. In Japan, politics underwent a radical transformation after the Meiji Restoration in 1868, and in the academic domain, too, there was a fundamental shift toward forms of scholarship favored in the West. Philosophy was a field of inquiry adopted at this time, along with other subjects such as physics and law. But this adoption was not simply a project of importing something that had already been created. This newly introduced philosophy was placed on the foundation of a worldview that had already been formed and achieved acceptance through becoming intermixed with it. This having been the case, can what was adopted and eventually given the name *tetsugaku* (哲学, the current Japanese word for "philosophy") truly be called "philosophy" in the Western sense? And can all that served as its foundation rightly be considered *tetsugaku* as well? If not, then the question of what should be placed under this rubric naturally arises. From the perspective of those who have received and incorporated it into their own tradition, the question of what "philosophy" is cannot easily be separated from such conundrums.

Today we use the term *tetsugaku* in Japanese without any sense of incongruity, but this translation itself was first formulated on the basis of traditional thought. When they learned of the existence of the field of inquiry called "philosophia," "filosofie (wijsbegeerte)," or "philosophy" in the West, Japanese scholars at the start of the Meiji period (1878–1912) were at a loss for how to translate it. This is apparent from the various attempts at coining a Japanese equivalent, such as *kyūrigaku* (究理学, investigation of principles [ri[1]]), *seirigaku* (性理学, study of the principles [ri] of human nature), *rigaku* (理学, study of principles [ri]), *riron* (理論, theory of principles [ri]), *gengaku* (玄学, Chinese *xuanxue*, study of the mysterious), and *chishikigaku* (知識学, study of knowledge), that we find during this period. The use of the terms *kyūrigaku, seirigaku,* and *rigaku* resulted from philosophy being overlaid on *sōgaku* (宋学, also known as *seirigaku* [性理学] and usually referred to as "Neo-Confucianism" in English), a school of thought pioneered by Zhou Dunyi (1017–1073) in Song dynasty China. *Rigaku* was initially the most favored among these tentative translations. Most foreign language dictionaries translated "philosophy" as *rigaku*,[2] as did the translation of John Stuart Mill's *On Liberty* (Nakamura Masanao, 1871) that was widely read at the beginning of the Meiji period.

In contrast to these approaches, Nishi Amane initially used *kitetsugaku* (希哲学, study of the desire for wisdom) and later *tetsugaku* as a more direct translation of "the love of wisdom," the original meaning of "philosophy" or filosofie (wijsbegeerte). This term eventually became widely adopted, and a clue to why Nishi avoided the translation *rigaku* can be found in his essay "Seisei hatsuun" (生性発蘊, To clarify human nature). "While using *seiri* or *riron* would be a direct translation, these often get mixed up with other things, so here I have translated [philosophy] as '*tetsugaku*' and drawn a distinction with the Confucianism of the East."[3] While acknowledging the suitability of *seiri* and *riron* as accurate translations, here he states he has chosen *tetsugaku* because those terms "often get mixed up with other things." When he says "mixed up with other things" he is clearly thinking of their being confused with Confucianism. The reason he sought to avoid this confusion was that he understood philosophy and Confucianism as radically different fields of inquiry. It was in order to highlight this difference that he arrived at the neologism *tetsugaku* (for more on this, see chapter 1, section 1). Nishi did not come up with this translation entirely from scratch; he had in mind the phrase "The holy long for heaven, the wise long for holiness, and the noble long for wisdom"[4] from the "tenth study" of Zhou Dunyi's *Penetrating Writings on The Book of Changes.*[5] Drawing on this text, he hit upon the translation *kitetsugaku.*

This process of arriving at a Japanese name for this new field further demonstrates that the adoption of philosophy was an undertaking begun atop an existing intellectual foundation, an intellectual tradition that organically embedded itself in the history of the adoption and development of philosophy in Japan. What was formed out of this process can be called *tetsugaku,* today's Japanese word for "philosophy."

(2) Is There Such a Thing as the "Core of Philosophy"?

In response to the question of whether this discipline, having been taken up on the basis of its adopters' existing intellectual foundation and developed independently while incorporating traditional thought, can be called *tetsugaku* with the meaning of "philosophy," for some the answer may be that only Western philosophy beginning in ancient Greece should be placed under this heading. Anything beyond the orbit of Western philosophy would, according to this view, be tantamount to a transformation of philosophy as such. But is it really so simple?

At an international symposium held at Kyoto University to commemorate the hundredth anniversary of the publication of Nishida Kitarō's *An Inquiry into the Good,* one of the guests, Lee Kwang Rae of South Korea's Kangwon National University, gave a talk entitled "Dialogue Between Western and Eastern Philosophy: The Core of Philosophy Is Everywhere/Nowhere."[6] The phrase used in the subtitle, "the core of philosophy is everywhere/nowhere," was taken from the writings of Maurice Merleau-Ponty (1908–1961), a leading twentieth-century French philosopher who devoted himself to the development of phenomenology. In the essay *"Partout et Nulle Part"* (Everywhere and nowhere), originally published as the preface to *Les Philosophes Célèbres*[7] and included in a collection of his writings entitled *Signes* (1960), Merleau-Ponty writes, "The center of philosophy is everywhere, its circumference nowhere."[8] Lee's presentation was based on this phrase.

In the preface to this collection of writings by ancient and modern philosophers from the East and the West, Merleau-Ponty begins by discussing the danger of gathering the works of famous philosophers of the past into a single volume. Such efforts tend to produce merely something that resembles a catalogue of various points of view and theories. Writing in the preface before the book's publication, Merleau-Ponty reveals his fear that a catalogue of intellectual portraits of philosophers of the past may give readers the impression of "a vain attempt" in which the disparate notions of these thinkers are simply lined up and no comparison of their mental universes can be made.

We can imagine that when he used the expression "catalogue of various points of view and theories" he had in mind the phrase *Galerie der Narrheiten* (gallery of follies) from Hegel's *Vorlesungen über die Geschichte der Philosophie* (*Lectures on the History of Philosophy*). Hegel's *Lectures on the History of Philosophy* greatly influenced later generations, and what he did in this work, to begin with, was reconsider the requirement, previously taken for granted, that accounts of the history of philosophy be objective. To use Hegel's own words, he cast doubt on the requirement that "history, whatever the subject may be, should state the facts without prejudice," that is, the requirement that one who recounts the history of philosophy must do so while making every effort to suppress "any particular object or end."⁹ This amounts to a rejection of the approach to the history of philosophy found in doxographia from Diogenes Laërtius onward, or, in concrete terms, the history of philosophy as a chronological list of the assertions of philosophers. Regarding this history of philosophy in which the views and assertions of the philosophers of the past are simply lined up like works of art in a gallery, Hegel says that while it may make one learned, this learning is useless; it is merely learning many things that have no use beyond being known, and he dubs this kind of history of philosophy that is nothing more than an assembly of useless knowledge a "gallery of follies."

In Hegel's thought, the history of philosophy is to be not a "collection of haphazardly conceived opinions," that is, a simple collection—lacking necessity—of various assertions, but the necessary development of "the *Idee*" (idea). In other words, it is a process by which the Idea births itself, sublates contradictions, and makes itself concrete. The Idea becomes more concrete as the history of philosophy develops. Seen from this perspective, the various philosophies that appear in the course of the development of the Idea are not simply "follies." They are not merely portraits lined up in a gallery without any connection to each other. Each philosophy is positioned within the entirety of history as a necessary stage in the development of the Idea. Moreover, each is positioned not only as something that was necessary in the past, but as an indispensable moment in the formation of the Idea as a whole. Hegel says that a history of philosophy written from this perspective will be not a "gallery of follies" but a "gallery of the heroes of rational thought."

Merleau-Ponty strongly opposed this kind of Hegelian understanding of the history of philosophy. In such an understanding, the particular vocabulary and concepts of each philosophy are ignored, each is deprived of its particularity and in a sense its soul, and all are subsumed into Hegel's outline of an "absolute system" as its earlier drafts. On the basis of this view, Merleau-Ponty severely criticizes Hegel's optimistic approach in which the philosophies of the past are to be taken beyond themselves and ultimately assembled into an "absolute system."

Merleau-Ponty says that every philosophy of the past—including of course Hegel's attempt at an "absolute system"—was a whole undertaking filled with both truth and folly, and "there is no philosophy that contains all the philosophies."[10] This is the context in which he says, "The center of philosophy is everywhere, its circumference nowhere."

There is an additional meaning within Merleau-Ponty's decentralist declaration that "the center of philosophy is everywhere, its circumference nowhere." This is related to the issue of "philosophy and the East," and here too Hegel's understanding of the history of philosophy is invoked. In his *Lectures on the History of Philosophy*, Hegel begins by discussing the questions of what the history of philosophy is and where philosophy, and therefore the history of philosophy, began. He concludes that philosophy began in Greece without having arisen in the East, and therefore declares that an account of the history of philosophy should begin with Greek philosophy.

Hegel's having excluded Indian and Chinese thought from the history of philosophy was a result of the fact that, according to his understanding, in the East thought had been only subjective and had never risen to the level of objective, substantial inquiry. To put it another way, it was because being had not been viewed as something universal and had not been given a clear definition. Thought had not yet become the "thought of thought." It was Hegel's belief that this "thought of thought" first arose in Europe, and it was thus in Europe that thought first became philosophy.

In contrast to this Hegelian understanding, Merleau-Ponty asserts that Western thought is also a "historical creation." Borrowing from *The Crisis of European Sciences and Transcendental Phenomenology* by Edmund Husserl (1859–1938), in *Signes* he lifts a phrase from Husserl's question of "whether European humanity bears within itself an absolute idea, rather than being merely an empirical anthropological type like 'China' or 'India' "[11] and says that in principle every variety of thought is nothing more than "an anthropological type," none have any special rights or privileges, and as a result European thought, too, has no such special status. While Western thought is indeed remarkable in its conceptual understanding and rigor, Eastern thought is characterized by its striving not to "dominate existence" but rather to "be the echo or sounding board of our relationship with being." Merleau-Ponty says that by engaging with this other thought Western philosophy can "take stock of the possibilities from which we have closed ourselves off in becoming 'Westerners,' and perhaps reopen them."[12]

As is indicated here, adhering to the position that only Western "philosophy" beginning in ancient Greece is philosophy, and all philosophy created in other cultures after encountering Western philosophy is merely a heterogenous transformation of it, will no doubt lead to a closing off of one's field of view. An understanding in which only what is "Western" can be considered philosophy is merely one way of looking at things, or one understanding of "philosophy." Philosophy is fundamentally sustained by the active contemplation of those who engage in it; it has developed while transcending its earlier frameworks, and it will presumably continue to develop in this way in the future. Philosophy that has been placed in a new setting will be taken up by thinkers who begin to engage in contemplation in that place, and it will attain new developments while confronting and fusing with existing worldviews. Indeed, can it not be said that each of these new developments is "philosophy," and that no philosophical tradition or framework has the right to view others as something other than philosophy?

When we take this position, the importance of philosophical "dialogue" emerges. In most cases we are dogged by preconceptions in our way of looking at things, and in philosophy, too, there are assumptions that are hidden or overlooked as obvious. Noticing them and becoming conscious of them, however, is far from easy. We form our thought within a way of looking at things that has been created over a long period of time and engage in contemplation within this framework. When we think about things within this framework, we focus our awareness on the object of our contemplation and are not conscious of the framework itself. It never occurs to us that we are engaging in contemplation within a particular framework, and we never look closely at the assumptions that have formed it. It is when we encounter thought with a different framework that we become aware of our own hidden assumptions. As is true of culture in general, when it encounters another way of thinking and discovers in it something lacking in itself, a particular philosophical approach can also become aware of its own limitations and enrich itself by developing beyond its old framework.

In *The Structure of Scientific Revolutions*,[13] Thomas Kuhn (1922–1996), known as a historian and philosopher of science, asserted that while there can be meaningful dialogue and mutual criticism when learning is pursued on the basis of the same paradigm, this becomes impossible when the paradigms of the parties involved differ. In opposition to this "theory of paradigms," Karl Popper (1902–1994) wrote an essay entitled "The Myth of the Framework" in which he criticized Kuhn's relativistic understanding as a rejection of the rationality and objectivity of science. Popper writes that the more someone was faced with an understanding whose framework differed from their own, or, in other words, "the more interesting and difficult questions they were asked . . . the more they were shaken in their opinions, and the more they could see things differently after the discussion—in short, the more their intellectual horizons were extended."[14]

Is it not indeed when we engage in dialogue with thinkers who have different assumptions, rather than those who share our own, that we are able to transcend our existing framework and engage in creative thought? And are we not then able to open up the possibility of new learning that could never arise within a closed environment? It would seem that it is not by excluding what grows in a different intellectual soil but rather by actively engaging with it that we become able to bring philosophy to a new horizon. This is the wide sense in which I would like to view "philosophy."

(3) Can Intellectual Undertakings Prior to the Meiji Period Be Called "Philosophy"?

If the adoption of philosophy in Japan involved using an existing worldview as a base and combining it with this new mode of thought, the question then becomes whether this foundation that preceded contact with Western philosophy can be called "philosophy (*tetsugaku*)" or not, and if not, then how exactly it should be described. What first comes to mind when considering this question are the words of Nakae Chōmin: "Here in Japan, from the past to the present there has been no philosophy (*tetsugaku*)."

Nakae is known for having introduced Jean-Jacques Rousseau's idea of the social contract and theory of popular sovereignty to Japan in his *Translation of Du Contrat Social in Chinese with Commentary*[15] (1882–1883) and for having provided a theoretical foundation for the Freedom and People's Rights Movement, but he also wrote many works dealing with philosophy, including *Digging Up the Hidden and Profound Truths of Philosophy*[16] and

The History of Philosophy[17] (both published in 1886). As these titles indicate, Nakae used *rigaku* as the translation of the foreign term "philosophy" for quite a long time. In *A Year and a Half*[8] (1901), completed just before his death, Nakae writes as follows.

> Here in Japan, from the past to the present there has been no philosophy (*tetsugaku*). People like Motoori [Norinaga] and [Hirata] Atsutane are no more than a kind of archaeologist, exploring old tombs and studying ancient texts. . . . Recently, people like Katō [Hiroyuki] and Inoue [Tetsujirō] have proclaimed themselves "philosophers," and while the general public may accept this, the truth is that they directly import theories they have studied in various Western sources; they are like those who "swallow the fruit without tasting it" and do not reach the level of "philosopher."[19]

Here Nakae clearly expresses his view that while there had been people who investigated old ruins and studied old texts, and from the start of the Meiji period there had been people who introduced philosophy, from the past to his present there had not been anyone who could be called "a philosopher" in Japan, and therefore philosophy had never existed in his country.

If this was indeed the case, the question becomes what is it that *had* existed? What has generally been used in answer to this question is the term "thought" (*shisō* [思想]). *Shisō*, like *tetsugaku*, is not an old word, having only come into widespread use in the Meiji period. It seems to have been employed as an equivalent for the English "thought," and generally referred to a certain way of looking at life and society. In *Dictionary of Philosophy* (*Tetsugaku Jii*), edited by Inoue Tetsujirō and others, "thought" is translated as *shisō*.

In general, the writings of figures such as Kūkai and Shinran, or Zeami and Motoori Norinaga, were referred to as "thought" rather than "philosophy," and this became established practice. The field of "the history of Japanese thought" also established a foothold in academia through the work of Muraoka Tsunetsugu, who taught a course on cultural history at Tōhoku University for many years. When compared to academic discourse in other countries, however, this approach to "the history of Japanese thought" can be said to have taken quite a distinctive form. In Europe this area of inquiry was traditionally covered by philosophy and the history of philosophy. Philosophy was a wide-ranging field that included not only ontology and epistemology but also disciplines such as practical philosophy, the philosophy of history, political philosophy, the philosophy of art, and the philosophy of religion, but nothing corresponding to "the history of Japanese thought" had been formed either as a discipline within philosophy or as a separate field.

In China, the word 哲学 (Japanese *tetsugaku*, Chinese *zhexue*) began to be used as the translation of "philosophy" in accordance with the practice in Japan, and today this term is standard. It is said to have first come into use around the end of the nineteenth century. There seems to have been some debate at the time about whether or not it was appropriate, but in the twentieth century its use very quickly became widespread, and people began to write about "the history of Chinese philosophy" (examples of this include Hu Suh's *Overview of the History of Chinese Philosophy*[20]). In such cases its scope naturally included the thought of Laozi and Zhuangzi as well as that of Confucius and Mencius. Of course, neither Confucius nor Laozi presented their thought in the framework of "philosophy," but there seems to have been an understanding that the matters they discussed could be overlaid on Western philosophy in terms of their content. In other words, it was understood that treatments of ethics, political philosophy, and logic existed within traditional Chinese thought. The term *zhexue* (Japanese *tetsugaku*) came to be widely used on the basis of this kind of understanding.

In contrast to these developments in China, why were no books covering ancient and medieval thought and modern philosophy written under the heading "the history of Japanese *philosophy*" in Japan?[21] Why do we refer to the "thought of Kūkai" and the "thought of Zeami" but not the "philosophy [*tetsugaku*] of Kūkai" or the "philosophy of Zeami"? A clue to thinking about this question can be found in Watsuji Tetsurō's *The History of Japanese Ethical Thought*.[22] In order to distinguish between the "history of ethical thought" and the "history of ethics," Watsuji describes the relationship between ethical principles (*rinri*), ethical thought (*rinrishisō*), and ethics as a field of inquiry (*rinrigaku*) as follows. "Ethical principles" are the universal laws that are found throughout humanity, both at the level of the individual and that of society. These universal laws, however, do not exist as universals within society; they are subject to historical and social strictures and exist on the basis of specific rituals. What is more, they are not unwittingly instilled in the individual and unconsciously manifested as behavior, but rather are connected to words, that is, to "logos," from the start. Through the power of logos, they then develop into organized intellectual expression. This is "ethical thought." Its chief characteristic is that it is subject to the strictures of its era and society. The field of "ethics," in contrast, is formed by transcending the framework of sociohistorical constraints possessed by "ethical thought," addressing them from a universal perspective, and questioning their rational basis.

Even this field of "ethics," however, cannot completely avoid sociohistorical constraints and changes from era to era. This is because while it is indeed an effort to pursue universal ethical principles, it is not these universal ethics themselves. As a result, there is a history of ethics. For Watsuji, both histories were possible: a "history of ethics" that traces the history of "ethics" and a "history of ethical thought" that studies the history of ethical thought that takes shape and dynamically evolves within a sociohistorical framework. As evidenced by the title of his book, *The History of Japanese Ethical Thought*, Watsuji chose to pursue the latter approach. This decision stemmed from his view that there was almost nothing "that can be called 'ethics' in a strict sense" in Japanese history.[23] Watsuji believed that "skepticism about teachings" was a necessary premise for the formation of ethics. Both Buddhism and Confucianism, however, fundamentally reject any skepticism regarding the doctrines of their founders. It was also influenced by Nakae's not having recognized "archeologists" who explored ruins and studied ancient texts as philosophers. In other words, while "archeologists" were discoverers, and perhaps even interpreters and explainers, of ancient texts, they were not people who questioned or thoroughly investigated the validity of these texts from a universal perspective. What was considered absolute truth not being sufficiently doubted and closely examined from a rational perspective seems to have made some Japanese thinkers reluctant to use the word "philosophy." "Thought" was perhaps more acceptable than "philosophy" when adopting the stance of first affirming the existence of that which is subject to sociohistorical constraints and then considering its characteristics and significance.

There is another angle from which I would like to consider the question of why traditional thought was not called "philosophy (*tetsugaku*)." Within philosophy there is a field called "the philosophy of art." If asked whether the philosophy of art existed in Japan prior to the adoption of Western learning, one hesitates to reply in the affirmative. Of course, there is no doubt that from ancient times there had been contemplation of beauty. In most cases, however, the fundamental question "what is beauty?" was not raised. The nature of beauty was mostly considered in connection with actual activities of creation or expression and thought on beauty was developed in this context. Zeami's theory of *Noh* drama can be cited as one example of this. His writings were fundamentally a theory of *Noh* as a guide to training or practice that was only meant to be directly conveyed to his successor. Of course, the question "what is beauty?" does arise within them, but their original purpose was to present a course of training.

I have noted that contemplation tied to instances of actual practice was built up over time, and it can also be pointed out that underlying this state of affairs was the fact that within Japan's intellectual landscape there was a tradition of emphasizing practice over logic or wisdom. When such a perspective is adopted, logic and wisdom become meaningless on their own and only acquire significance when they are tied to actual practice, secular or religious. This way of thinking can be seen as having been deeply entrenched in Japan and throughout East Asia.

In sum, on the one hand it can be said that there was indeed content within Japanese thought that overlapped that found in fields such as the philosophy of art, ethics, and political philosophy, and philosophy that existed even prior to the modern era. On the other hand, it can also be pointed out that posing the question "what is beauty?" was rare, as was interrogating the rational basis for claims made regarding it. The absence of philosophy was presumably discussed with a focus on this facet of Japanese thought, and it seems to have been for this reason that the term "thought" was preferred.

This was the basis for the widespread use of the expression "history of Japanese thought" and the establishment of this subject as a field of academic inquiry. On the one hand, this can of course be said to have been an inquiry that aimed to take up the thought that had developed in places of actual practice directly (in all its richness). In this sense one can say there was ample reason for the contemplation of the "history of Japanese thought." However, one can also note that if it goes no further than grasping these concrete facts and ends up lacking in fundamental principles, this kind of "thought" will never be capable of replacing philosophy.

The question examined above of whether the thought that formed the foundation upon which the new field of "philosophy" was adopted was also philosophy (*tetsugaku*) in its own right is directly related to the question of where a book on the history of Japanese philosophy should begin its account. Should it include the history of pre-Meiji "thought," or should it restrict itself to tracing the development of philosophical inquiry from the point that Japanese thinkers encountered and began incorporating Western philosophy?

While traditional Japanese "thought" may have been lacking in the contemplation of fundamental principles, it goes without saying that in terms of its content there were places in which it overlapped Western philosophy; it cannot simply be characterized as something of a completely different nature. And even if one emphasizes the differences between the two approaches, the adoption of philosophy from the Meiji period onward was based on the intellectual foundation that preceded it and incorporated this earlier tradition. To give a concrete example of this, Nishida Kitarō was influenced in the formation of his thought not only by Western philosophy but also by Zen and Neo-Confucianism, and these traditions were incorporated into his philosophy. This being the case, the history of philosophy from the Meiji period onward can only be fully understood or grasped at a deeper level on the basis of an account of the traditional thought that preceded it.

What was undertaken by James Heisig and his coeditors in *Japanese Philosophy: A Sourcebook*,[24] that is, an attempt to give an account of the history of Japanese philosophy by tracing its development all the way from Shōtoku Taishi's "Seventeen Article Constitution" (604 CE) to modern thought, is a viable approach. But a history that confines itself to the questions of how Western philosophy was addressed and adopted in Japan after its introduction and how Japanese philosophers then developed their own original thought also seems possible, and undertaking such a history may indeed allow for a more focused, tightly woven account. In this book I adopt this latter approach, albeit mainly for reasons related to my own ability and expertise.

2. What Is the History of Philosophy?

Next, I would like to consider the meaning of the phrase "the history of philosophy." The answer to the question "what is the history of philosophy?" may seem self-evident, but this is by no means the case. For example, should accounts of the history of philosophy aim to relate historical facts as objectively as possible, or should historians of philosophy engage with the philosophy of the past as philosophers in their own right? In other words, should they adopt a particular perspective from which to select what content should be addressed and perform their own evaluation of it? The question of how philosophy and the history of philosophy relate to each other then arises. Can the pursuit of the history of philosophy be described as directly equivalent to the undertaking of philosophy itself? Anyone who attempts to give an account of the history of philosophy will inevitably come face to face with these questions.

(1) The Reception of the History of Philosophy in Japan

Before addressing these questions, I would like to begin by first examining how histories of philosophy written in the West were received in Japan beginning in the Meiji period and what kind of role they went on to play.

At the start of the Meiji period, perhaps the most widely read text of Western philosophy was J. S. Mill's *On Liberty*. Published in London in 1859, by 1871 (the fourth year of the Meiji period) it had already been translated into Japanese by Nakamura Masanao under the title *The Principles of Liberty*.[25] The theory of evolution had been successfully introduced, and in the early Meiji period the writings of Herbert Spencer were also being widely consumed. These works were not read as purely philosophical or scientific texts, but rather in relation to the demands of contemporary society. In other words, readers sought in these texts, whether by Mill or by Spencer, pillars of intellectual support for the Freedom and People's Rights Movement that criticized the authoritarian rule of the Meiji government and called for a government that would guarantee the freedom and rights of each individual citizen. The content of Spencer's *Social Statics* (1851), for example, does not seem at all radical today, but as is evident from the fact that its Japanese translation was published under the title *Social Equal Rights Theory*[26] (translated by Matsushima Kō, 1881–1884), and from the fact that Itagaki Taisuke called it "a textbook for people's rights," it had a great influence on those sympathetic to the Freedom and People's Rights Movement.

Eventually, however, attention turned to philosophy itself as something separate from the demands and pressing issues of Japanese society. Partly as a result of the establishment of the university system, philosophy gradually became something found mainly within the academy. The "history of philosophy" as a subject of inquiry was the key to understanding what kind of inquiry philosophy itself had been up to that point and what kind of inquiry it was engaged in at the time of this transition. Many works on the history of philosophy were translated from the beginning to the middle of the Meiji period. Eventually the history of Western philosophy came to be lectured on and written about by such figures as Inoue Enryō, Miyake Setsurei, Kiyozawa Manshi, Ōnishi Hajime, and Hatano Seiichi.[27]

What appears to have been the first course on the history of philosophy offered in Japan was given by Nishi Amane. Nishi taught this course, entitled Hyakugaku Renkan (Network of All Studies),[28] starting in 1870 (third year of the Meiji period) at a private school (Ikueisha). "Network of all studies" was a translation of "encyclopedia," and as this phrase's literal meaning suggests, this course addressed not only philosophy but academic inquiry as a whole and was not a detailed course in philosophy. It did, however, provide outlines of the various domains within philosophy, such as "logic"[29] and "ontology,"[30] and at the same time gave an overview of "the history of philosophy." It can be described as the first introductory course on philosophy or the history of philosophy given in Japan.

In *To Clarify Human Nature*,[31] a text written while he was teaching this course (it is noted in the draft that corrections were completed in June 1873), after touching on the history of philosophy in the West from ancient Greece to his own era, Nishi then went on to discuss the content of Auguste Comte's *Cours de philosophie positive* (1830–1842) in detail. In doing so he drew upon two works by British philosopher and theater critic G. H. Lewes: *A Biographical History of Philosophy*[32] and *Comte's Philosophy of the Sciences*.[33] The history of Western philosophy was thus introduced to Japan through Lewes's works on the subject.

"Network of All Studies" was the first overview of philosophy or course on the history of philosophy created in Japan, but it did no more than provide a simple introduction to each field of inquiry as an academic domain, and its audience was limited. Much more significant in terms of its lasting influence was the course on the history of philosophy given by Ernest Francisco Fenollosa (1853–1908) as a foreign lecturer at the University of Tokyo. I will discuss the role Fenollosa played in the history of philosophy in Japan in detail in chapter 2, but in this course he lectured on the history of philosophy from Descartes to Hegel and Spencer, drawing on the English translation[34] of Albert Schwegler's *Geschicte der Philosophie im Umriß*,[35] Lewes's *A Biographical History of Philosophy*, and Francis Bowen's *Modern Philosophy from Descartes to Schopenhauer and Hartmann*[36] (Bowen had been one of Fenollosa's instructors at Harvard University). Through this course, modern German philosophy from Kant to Hegel was introduced in detail for the first time at the University of Tokyo and indeed anywhere in Japan.

This course of Fenollosa's can be described as a key milestone in the reception of Western philosophy in Japan, and following it several works on the history of philosophy written in the West were translated into Japanese. Bowen's book was one of the earliest of these texts on the history of philosophy to be published in Japanese. It was translated by Ariga Nagao, who had studied the history of philosophy under Fenollosa, and it was published in 1884 and 1885 (seventeenth and eighteenth year of the Meiji period) under the title *Translation of Modern Philosophy with Commentary*.[37] Also in 1884, Takekoshi Yosaburō, who had studied at Keio Gijyuku, translated *Cours de l'histoire de la philosophie moderne*[38] by leading nineteenth-century French philosopher Victor Cousin (1792–1867), drawing on its English translation[39] and publishing it as *General History of Modern Philosophy*[40] (volume 1). Takekoshi's lectures that relied heavily on the English translation[41] of *Historische Entwickelung der speculativen Philosophie von Kant bis Hegel* (*Historical Survey of Speculative Philosophy from Kant to Hegel*)[42] were also published in the same year under the title *The Excellence of German Philosophy*.[43] Two years later, in 1886, Nakae published *The History of Philosophy*.[44] This was a translation of Alfred Fouillée's *Histoire de la Philosophy*[45] and was published by the publishing office of the Ministry of Education.

The introduction of the history of Western philosophy thus began with translations of foreign texts, but eventually Japanese scholars began to write about this subject themselves. Suematsu Kenchō's *A Part of Ancient Greek Philosophy*[46] (1883) and Inoue Tetsujirō and Ariga Nagao's *Lectures on Western Philosophy*[47] (1883–1885) can be cited as two of the first such works, but they dealt only with ancient philosophy. As a text that provides an overview from antiquity to modern times, Inoue Enryō's *Key Points in Philosophy, Part One*[48] (1886) belongs to the earliest period. This *Key Points in Philosophy* is characterized by having brought together a history of philosophy and an overview of philosophy (in *Part Two*), and by providing a history of philosophy composed of both Western and Eastern philosophy rather than restricting itself to the former. In contrast to its detailed account of ancient Greek philosophy, however, its account of philosophy from other times and places was quite simplistic.

The first detailed discussion of modern Western philosophy can be found in Miyake Setsurei's *Philosophical Trifles*.[49] In his explanatory notes, Miyake states that he drew on the accounts of Schwegler and Kuno Fischer (1824–1907), and the texts to which he is referring are presumably the *Geschichte der Philosophie im Umriß*, which was used by Fenollosa in his course at the University of Tokyo, and *Geschichte der neuern Philosophie*.[50] In contrast to Miyake Setsurei's work, which was limited to modern philosophy, the course in Western philosophy taught at Shinshū Buddhist Seminary from 1890 to 1893 by Kiyozawa Manshi[51] dealt with everything from the ancient to the modern, right up to such figures as Lotze, Comte, and Spencer, and in terms of both the breadth of its field of view and the depth of its understanding was the era's best example of a history of philosophy, albeit one that was never officially published. It seems to have been based on works by historians of philosophy such as Schwegler, Bowen, and Lewes, but far from simply paraphrasing their accounts, Kiyozawa fully digested them and appended his own critiques.

(2) What Is the History of Philosophy?

If Miyake Setsurei's *Philosophical Trifles* was the first proper history of modern Western philosophy produced in Japan, Ōnishi Hajime's *The History of Western Philosophy*[52] illustrates the success of the reception of the history of Western philosophy in the Meiji period as the first (published) work that traced the history of Western philosophy in detail from ancient Greece to the contemporary era. This text was first published in the course records of Ōnishi's place of employment, Tokyo Vocational School[53] (the school that would later become Waseda University), and later as *Complete History of Western Philosophy*.[54] Ōnishi died of illness in 1900, and his writings were published as *Complete Writings of Professor Ōnishi*[55] beginning in 1903. His *Complete History of Western Philosophy* comprises volumes 3 and 4 of this collection.

This history of Western philosophy by Ōnishi is worthy of special mention both for its thorough account of ancient philosophy and for its having been the first such work to take up medieval philosophy in detail, and it also provided an extremely thoroughgoing account of Kantian philosophy, a topic in which Ōnishi's interest was profound. Not content to merely engage in a detailed description of Western philosophy, he always had in mind the meta-level question of what sort of inquiry the history of philosophy should be as he developed these accounts. This is where the defining characteristic of Ōnishi's history of philosophy is to be found.

In the introduction to this work, on the one hand he writes that "even though a historian of philosophy may have their own deeply held beliefs about philosophy, if they render judgement on all theories with this as their sole criterion they will have a tendency to be biased." On the other hand, he also avers that "not employing criticism at all can be described as a dereliction of one's duty as a historian,"[56] thereby highlighting the essential difficulty in the work of illuminating the history of philosophy. Ōnishi does not discuss this issue any further there, but even earlier, in 1903—four years after having graduated from Tokyo University—he had published an article entitled "What Is the History of Philosophy?" in volume 15 of *Rikugō Journal*[57] and was already engaged in a profound consideration of this topic.

This question of the nature of the history of philosophy had been one of immense significance for historians of philosophy since Hegel. Historians of philosophy active from the middle of the nineteenth century to the beginning of the twentieth century, such as the previously mentioned Schwegler, K. Fischer, and Wilhelm Windelband, were faced with the problem of how to evaluate Hegel's understanding of the history of philosophy. This meant answering the question of what the history of philosophy is or ought to be.

In Hegel's understanding, as mentioned in the first section, the history of philosophy is not "a jumble of haphazardly assembled views" but a "system of the development of the Idea" and something that possessed "an inevitable connection." Of course, the things that appear in actual history cannot avoid a "haphazard character." They emerge cloaked in randomness in particular circumstances and particular places. If this covering is stripped away, however, various stages of the Idea (that is, the Idea described in Hegel's *Logic*) can be discerned in the form of logical concepts. In other words, if external elements are taken away, we are able to see that the "sequence of philosophical moments in history" and the development of the Idea on a logical level overlap one another.[58]

To study and describe the history of philosophy, therefore, means to grasp and elucidate the concrete process by which the Idea is realized. In other words, studying the history of philosophy is itself a philosophical undertaking. From this point of view Hegel asserts that "the study of the history of philosophy is the study of philosophy itself."[59]

According to Hegel, the history of philosophy, which is itself the "system of the development of the Idea," is also a process by which the Idea becomes something real or concrete. Conversely stated, the newest philosophy is the "most developed, richest, and deepest philosophy."[60] Taking it one step further, the completion of the logical stipulation of the Idea means the conclusion of philosophy. If the various philosophies in the history of philosophy are a single ring, ultimately a giant circle will be drawn that includes all of them as parts of its circumference.[61] It can presumably be said that in Hegel's understanding it was his own philosophy and history of philosophy that ultimately closed this circle.

For historians of philosophy who came after Hegel and had to describe post-Hegelian philosophy, it was impossible to write about the history of philosophy without making clear their stance regarding this understanding. Schwegler begins his *Geschicte der Philosophie im Umriß* with a chapter entitled "The Concept of the History of Philosophy" in which he reveals strong doubts about the phrase "the completion of philosophy." According to him, philosophy is "the philosophical expression of the overall way of life of an era" and can only exist in the form of "various philosophies of the times [*Zeitphilosophien*][62] arising one after the other"; it is inconceivable to him that something of this sort could ever be completed or perfected. Schwegler explicitly criticized Hegel's thesis that the progression of philosophical systems found in history is consistent with the progression of logical categories found in logic, writing that "this way of looking at things is wrong in principle, and cannot be maintained in the light of history."[63]

In his *Lehrbuch der Geschichte der Philosophie*, Windelband points out that Hegel, along with falling into the "error of a structure that attempts to philosophically systematize the history of philosophy," often "forcibly twisted historical events."[64] Historians of philosophy must first and foremost precisely determine the facts. But the work of these historians does not stop there. They must also explain a given theory in terms of its relationship to the theories that precede it, its relationship to the culture, that is, the religion, art, politics, science, and so on of its era, and its relationship to the personal characteristics and educational background of the philosopher who asserted it. On top of this, they must clarify what kind of contribution the theory in question made within the history of philosophy as a whole. Windelband understands the history of philosophy as a field that must take up these three tasks.

Various such doubts and criticisms concerning Hegel's approach to the history of philosophy that emphasized logical development were thus displayed in post-Hegelian philosophy, and diverse arguments surrounding the form the history of philosophy should take were put forward. Drawing on these arguments, Ōnishi Hajime addressed the question "what is the history of philosophy?" directly.

Ōnishi pointed out that establishing and explaining historical facts is essential to any account of the history of philosophy, and in "What Is the History of philosophy?"[65] he writes as follows.

> To merely describe events and lay out theories in the form of so-called chronological history should of course not be said to fulfill the duty of the history of philosophy, nor should explaining the relationships that arise between these events and theories be considered sufficient. Without looking at the traces of the progress and regress of philosophy in the rising, falling, and transforming of these theories, our undertaking cannot be described as a deep contemplation and study of the history of philosophy.[66]

As his use of the phrase "progress or regress" here attests, Ōnishi empha-sized that a history of philosophy should include a critical evaluation of the theories of the past. He then continues as follows.

> Moreover, when the idea of progress is thoroughly pursued, it includes within itself a philosophical viewpoint. To say that there are elements of progress in this world and to specify what they are you must have a definite viewpoint on philosophy that gives you your own perspective. To say that something is progressive or something is regressive we need to know more than merely what comes before and after its era. We must glean the criteria for this from the philosophical position we ourselves adopt.[67]

Along with asserting that we must have our own philosophical standpoint in order to undertake critical evaluation, Ōnishi notes that here a kind of circle arises. You cannot be a historian of philosophy if you are not a phi-losopher, but you cannot be a philosopher unless you learn from the history of philosophy. Thus, "The one and the other must be studied in tandem. Philosophy must be completed to complete the history of philosophy, and the history of philosophy must be completed to complete philosophy."[68]

As Ōnishi acknowledges, however, this kind of completion of both philosophy and the history of philosophy is "not to be expected." Accordingly, one may think that the history of philosophy should limit itself to simply stating facts and should not engage in critical evaluation. Ōnishi responds to this counterargument as follows.

> Is it not the case that things are discovered while pursuing a critique of the history of philosophy from an incomplete phil-osophical standpoint? Is it not the case that this philosophical standpoint is moved forward, and along with this the study of the history of philosophy also progresses? Even if it can be said there is no hope of the history of philosophy based on philosophy, and philosophy based on the history of philosophy, ever being completed, are they not nevertheless undertakings that should advance in collaboration with each other?[69]

In other words, the fact that the history of philosophy will always involve incompleteness is acknowledged at the start. The provisional conclusion Ōnishi puts forward is that, through the cooperation of philosophy based on the history of philosophy and the history of philosophy based on philosophy, a path is cleared on which both philosophy and the history of philosophy can gradually overcome their incompleteness. This of course leads to the difficult question of how, in concrete terms, this cooperation is to be promoted. In any case, it can be recognized as an argument for a certain heading or approach. It is notable that within only a few years of Japanese thinkers beginning to write about philosophy, the question "what is the history of philosophy?" was already being consciously raised and profoundly addressed. The fact that most later writings on the history of philosophy do not touch on this issue illustrates the tremendous incisiveness of Ōnishi's insight as a historian of philosophy.

We too, as Ōnishi believed, can only write about the history of philosophy by having taken up our own point of view; without it we cannot choose what to write about or decide how to explain and evaluate what we have chosen to examine. If we bring this standpoint to the foreground, as for example Kiyozawa Manshi does in his previously mentioned course on the history of Western philosophy, it takes the form of adding a "critique" after presenting the theories of each philosopher. I did not always have the space to do so in this book, but this is essentially how the history of philosophy ought to be pursued.

Of course, this does not mean incorporating the philosophy of the past within your own philosophical system in the manner conceived by Hegel. Just as no fixed center exists anywhere in philosophy, neither does it have a "completion." As was maintained by historians of philosophy after Hegel, greater emphasis must be placed on historicity. As Windelband and Ōnishi claimed, the history of philosophy requires first the establishment of precise facts and then explanations of them. There is then a need to clarify what kind of role the theories in question played in the history of philosophy. This kind of evaluation is only possible on the basis of the philosophical stance of the person talking about the history of philosophy. A critical reexamination is always required, both regarding this stance itself and regarding the history of philosophy described from it. It is through such criticism that the history of philosophy manages to take its next step forward.

I mentioned Hegel's assertion that "the study of the history of philosophy is the study of philosophy itself," and here I would like to say a few words about what we are to make of the relationship between philosophy and the history of philosophy when we adopt the understanding described above. If the task of the history of philosophy is only to reflect on events and accurately describe them, then the history of philosophy cannot be described as the same thing as philosophy itself. It is nothing more than the traces left by philosophy. But what is demanded of the historian of philosophy is to engage in their own rumination and reflection on the issues raised by the philosophers of the past, and, on the basis of this consideration, at the same time to evaluate the role played by the philosophy in question. This evaluation can naturally be assumed to contribute to the development of philosophy. From this perspective, the history of philosophy is not merely what philosophy leaves behind. On the contrary, it can be described as the practice of philosophy itself.

(3) The Methodology of the History of Philosophy

Next, I would like to consider the methodology of studying and giving an account of the history of philosophy. As mentioned above, along with establishing the facts, Windelband also emphasized explaining them. He considered it the job of the history of philosophy to explain the relationship of a given philosophical theory to those that preceded it and its relationship to other factors such as the religion, art, politics, and science of its era. The former is to clarify the formation and characteristics of a given theory diachronically, that is, in a form that follows a temporal axis, while the latter clarifies what kind of significance a given theory possessed and what kind of role it played in its era synchronically, that is, by focusing on a particular era.

The "history of ideas" conceived by Arthur O. Lovejoy (1873–1962) can be thought of as an approach that focuses on temporal/chronological changes as in the first method. It is a history of concepts or ideas, but in addition it is also a study undertaken from a diachronic perspective; it is a history of influence that studies what kind of effect a given theory or concept had on the philosophy that came after it and a history of adoption that clarifies, for example, how the dialectic was received after having been introduced in Japan in the Meiji period. The history of the development of philosophy—for example, clarifying how the phenomenology Husserl advocated later developed—is another instance of this approach.

In *Iwanami Ethics Course*[70] (1940–1941), a work in the editing of which he was deeply involved, Watsuji Tetsurō authored two articles, "The Thought of Revering the Emperor and Its Heritage"[71] and "The Ethics of Self-Sacrificing Service and Its Heritage,"[72] that followed a temporal axis diachronically, or, to put it another way, that examined thought revering the emperor and the ethics of self-sacrifice from the perspective of the history of these topics. Interestingly, in *The History of Ethics in Japan*[73] (1952), a text published after the war, while drawing on the same materials, Watsuji nevertheless employed a different approach. Here he emphasized the horizontal axis, that is, he undertook his account while viewing the various eras as a whole. There is good reason to expect many things that cannot be seen from a diachronic perspective will be revealed through the carrying out of this kind of examination from a synchronic perspective. In this sense, this approach that cuts across different eras can also be described as an important methodology in the study of the history of philosophy.

One of Hegel's famous phrases is that philosophy is a "son of its time" (*Sohn der Zeit*).[74] In other words, Hegel claimed that philosophy is not something that emerges outside of its era and unrelated to it; on the contrary, it is the era that gives birth to philosophy. In the introduction to *The History of Western Philosophy*, Ōnishi Hajime asserts that philosophy is formed under the influence of the society of its era: "Philosophy is surely something that should never be completely separated from a time and a society, that is, from the overall tendencies, hopes, and beliefs in the minds of the people of a particular era."[75] If so, the argument that separating a philosophy that is a child of its times from its era and examining it on its own is a one-sided approach is quite persuasive.

This being the case, the style of the history of philosophy should change depending on the scope of what is being examined. First, we can compare one philosophy to others formed in the same era and circumstances. Doing so enables us to find commonalities between the philosophies in question, and conversely also to bring into relief their differences or distinctiveness. Second, we can focus on the relationship between the politics, culture, and thought of a given era. Far from being an isolated undertaking, philosophy is formed and constrained within the political, cultural, and intellectual circumstances of its era. By clarifying such relationships, it is possible to examine how philosophers took up the intellectual challenges of their day, how they reflected these issues in their thought, and what kind of influence they had on their era. Third, we can turn our attention to the relationship between the philosophy in question and its socioeconomic foundation or background. This is related to the issue of the "base" (*Basis*) and "superstructure" (*Überbau*) Marx discusses in *Zur Kritik der Politischen Ökonomie* (*A Contribution to the Critique of Political Economy*). Since philosophy is not formed in isolation from the socioeconomic foundation and political background of its era, the examination of such relationships is presumably also required.[76]

Regarding a given philosophical claim or theory, whether you address its formation and development diachronically or compare it to other philosophical ideas of the same era and discuss it synchronically, when you give an account of the history of philosophy you are also faced with the question of whether to limit your inquiry to the philosophical theory in question or also include within it the life of the philosopher who formulated it, that is, their activities apart from philosophy.

Sueki Takehiro raises this issue in connection with the study of the philosophy of Nishida in *The Philosophy of Nishida Kitarō: His Philosophical System*.[77] In his introduction to volume 1 of this work, Sueki declares that its purpose is "to trace the internal context of Nishida's writings." The "internal context" of which Sueki speaks is the "semantic association of words and phrases" seen in a philosopher's writings. This is contrasted with "external context," in other words, "the relationship between a work and its external environment." In concrete terms, this includes "the psychological states and life circumstances of the author, the social circumstances (political, economic, class, and historical circumstances) in which the work is placed, its linguistic circumstances, and so on."[78]

The methodology adopted by Sueki was to ignore these external relationships, to exclude them to the greatest extent possible from his inquiry, and to focus his attention on describing the internal context of Nishida's thought. Sueki based this approach on the idea that to clumsily jam external context into internal context leads to smuggling things into the work in question that did not originally belong to it, thereby altering its nature. As an example of this he mentions the interpretation of *An Inquiry into the Good*[79] as an expression of Nishida's experience of Zen Buddhism. According to Sueki, such an interpretation is not necessary in order to follow the internal context of *An Inquiry into the Good*, and on the contrary the introduction of this kind of external context runs the risk of distorting it. With such concerns in mind, Sueki declares he will adopt a "purely internal analysis."

It is by no means the case, however, that the "external context" Sueki talks about is of no significance whatsoever to the study of the history of philosophy. For example, in *Nishida Kitarō: The Life of a Man*[80] Ueda Shizuteru focuses on "the life of a man" as he traces the path of Nishida's thought. Ueda views Nishida's "life" in terms of three overlapping aspects. The first is his "biographical life," the second his "sociohistorical life," and the third his "way of life." His "biographical life" refers to the things that happened in his life, the people he met, what he thought, and what he did. His "sociohistorical life" refers to the life he lived within a particular society or particular era. His "way of life" does not refer to his psychological attitude or way of getting by in the world at particular points in time. In Ueda's own words, it was "a 'way of life' that included a determination of how to 'live his life' as a whole; a 'way of life' in which a 'way of living' and 'way of dying' are one."[81] It is inconceivable that a person's "life" made up of these three layers could be unrelated to their thought or philosophy. On the contrary, there is a sense in which a thought or a philosophy is a crystallization of a person's "life." Interpreting a philosophy from this kind of perspective is also a very meaningful undertaking.

In the study of the history of philosophy, the question of whether to limit one's inquiry to "internal context" or to also consider "external context" is not one that is easily answered, and it is perhaps impossible to say that either one of these methodologies is correct. We might say instead that two approaches to the history of philosophy are possible. The issue being addressed itself may demand either an inquiry limited to "internal context" or the consideration of "external context." In this book I intend to set the focus of my examination in accordance with what is called for in each case.

Similarly, when it comes to the previously mentioned question of whether to undertake a diachronic or synchronic examination, here too I do not think we should limit ourselves to one approach. To take the philosophy of Nishida Kitarō as an example, his late thought was formed on the basis of elements such as the theory of "pure experience" found in *An Inquiry into the Good* and the theory of "place" developed in his middle period, and surely it cannot be properly understood without being considered in connection with them. However, it was also formed in relation to the politics, society, and culture of the 1930s and 1940s, and was closely tied to the issues of its era. It can be said to have been at the same time constrained by these issues and an attempt to address them. Bearing such factors in mind, in this book I aim to examine philosophical theories from an appropriate perspective in accordance with the demands of what is being discussed.

Part I

The Era of Reception from the West— Philosophy in the Meiji Period

Chapter 1

Early Meiji Philosophy

1. Early History of the Reception of Philosophy

(1) THE FIRST "PHILOSOPHY" COURSE IN JAPAN

When was the first "philosophy" course taught in Japan? This may seem an obscure, unanswerable question, but fortunately a specific date has emerged out of the study of Christianity in Japan. Surprisingly, it was in 1583, more than 430 years ago. In 1580, Japan's first Jesuit "Collegio" was established as an institution of higher learning in the City of Funai (now Ōita City) in Bungo Province (roughly corresponding to today's Ōita Prefecture on the island of Kyūshū) and a course in the humanities was begun that same year. A philosophy course for theology students who had completed the humanities course was then begun on October 21, 1583. The text used in this course was an explanation of Aristotle's logic by Francisco de Toledo, a teacher of philosophy and theology at the Collegio Romano, a school of theology located in Rome. This course was given in Latin, however, and its attendees were five Portuguese theology students.[1] In this sense it perhaps cannot be said to have been the true start of philosophy being taught in Japan.[2]

The first recorded use of words for "philosophy" or "philosopher" in Japan are also found in Christian writings. These were the so-called "Christian press" texts printed by the Society of Jesus from the end of the sixteenth century to the beginning of the seventeenth century using the first letterpress printing machine brought to Japan. The oldest of these documents still extant, *Excerpts from Hagiographies*,[3] was published in 1591 in the city of Kazusa in Shimabara Province, and in it we find the words "philosophia" and "philosopho" (philosopher) being used in passages such as the following.

> Seneca praised the words of Stilpon. After the place where this *philosopho* lived was sacked by an enemy army, Stilpon was brought before Demetrius I, a great general. When the general asked him what he had lost in the turmoil, Stilpon replied, "Nothing." His view was that if what he valued was *philosophia*, then what he valued could never be lost.[4]

As is reflected in this English translation, the Portuguese word *philosopho* is not translated but simply transliterated as *firozoho* in the original Japanese text. This is the first example of its use in Japan.

(2) The People Who Encountered Philosophy

One example of a text that described the nature of philosophical inquiry and touched on its basic content is *The Writings of Okamoto Sanemon*,[5] a record left by an Italian missionary named Guiseppe Chiara (1602–1685). Chiara attempted to sneak into Japan in defiance of its *sakoku* policy banning foreigners, but was arrested, tortured, and ultimately "fell" (renounced his faith). He then adopted the Japanese name Okamoto Sanemon. In 1674 he wrote a text on Christianity entitled *Religious Writings*[6] at the behest of a public official. This three-volume work is believed to have discussed not only religion but also the politics and institutional systems of various European countries, including even their systems of education, but it has been lost and its contents cannot be confirmed today. *The Writings of Okamoto Sanemon*, however, has been preserved in the Cabinet Library.[7] In these writings Chiara includes a chapter entitled "On Various Forms of Academic Inquiry"[8] in which he provides brief explanations of various branches of inquiry in Europe, from subjects in the humanities such as *guramachika* (grammar) and *retorika* (rhetoric) to navigational techniques and the natural sciences. Regarding *hirosohiya* (philosophia), he begins by defining it as "study that illuminates the principles [*ri*] of all things" and then adds the following explanation: "*Philosophia* is an inquiry that asks and answers questions to refine our wisdom regarding the meaning of the world. It does not address the afterlife."[9]

Arai Hakuseki (1657–1725) was a Neo-Confucian scholar deeply involved in the politics of the shogunate in the mid-Edo period, but is also widely known as the author of *An Account of the West*[10] (1715), a text based on his interrogation of Giovanni Battista Sidotti (1668–1715), an Italian who had smuggled himself into Japan and attempted to engage in missionary activities in spite of the ban on Christianity. Before questioning Sidotti, Arai had prepared himself by reading Chiara's three volumes on Christianity. Written on this basis, *An Account of the West* includes detailed descriptions of Christian doctrine and faith, along with information on the geography and history of the world. There is no mention of philosophy, but Arai writes that Sidotti's knowledge was vast and that he understood sixteen of the many forms of Western learning, so it seems likely that their discussions also involved philosophy and logic. On the one hand he finds that Western learning "is unsurpassed when it comes to astronomical and geographical matters." On the other hand, however, he states that "when it comes to the preaching of [religious] doctrine, there is nothing close to the teachings of Confucius, and it is as though I were listening to two people, one wise the other stupid, who suddenly changed places. What I learned here of the nature of their studies is that they are very precise regarding form and matter, but only understand the so-called 'physical,' and there is not yet any understanding of the metaphysical. It is thus not surprising that they say there is something [God] that created heaven and earth."[11]

His impression seems to have been that while the rigorous natural science of the West was marvelous, its Christian worldview or cosmology was quite shoddy when compared to the *taiji*[12] philosophy of Neo-Confucianism. This comparison can also be thought of as having influenced the "Eastern morality, Western technology" doctrine of Sakuma Shōzan (1811–1864) in the late Edo period and the slogan "Japanese spirit, Western knowledge" that became influential in the Meiji period.

Japanese scholars capable of undertaking an overview of European learning as a whole emerged in the late Edo period, and leading examples of such figures include Watanabe Kazan (1793–1841) and Takano Chōei (1804–1850). Takano Chōei was originally a doctor who studied medicine under Philipp Franz von Siebold and a scholar of *rangaku* (Dutch, and by extension Western, learning), but in addition to medicine his writings also covered other subjects such as chemistry, and his *Jottings on Things Seen and Heard, Part One*,[13] which can be described as notes on his readings, includes a section on "Teachings of Western *Gakushi* [master of learning, teacher]."[14] (The original work was untitled. It is believed to have been written in 1835.) The word *gakushi* is thought to have been a translation of the Dutch word "wijsgeer" (philosopher), and in this text Takano presents a history of philosophy from Thales and Pythagoras to the eighteenth century. While it goes no further than a simple introduction and is mostly concerned with natural philosophy, it can indeed be described as the first overview of Western philosophy written in Japan. Concerning Socrates, for example, Takano writes as follows.

> There was a man called "Socrates." He culled the bad and col-lected the good from traditional views and founded a school of thought through which he opened the way to politics and learning. . . . those who came after hailed him as the father of philosophers [*gakushi*]. He emphasized moderation in behavior, for example, in eating and drinking (he said nothing should be done to an excessive degree), was constantly seeking more wisdom [a reference to his motto "love wisdom"] without ever being satisfied with his progress, and exercised self-restraint regarding material desires. He became a model for later generations.[15]

Takano closes by undertaking a classification of different fields of inquiry. According to this breakdown, "The places from which the types of learning emerge, from a broad perspective, are no more than five in number." In other words, learning can be divided into five categories. First there is *redenkunde*, "a method of positing rules pertaining to the source of the natural workings of things, and finding out whether they are true or false, fact or fiction." This corresponds to logic, called *ronrigaku*[16] in modern Japanese, but Takano appends the translation *chirigigaku*[17] (the study of knowledge of what is right). Next comes *zedenkunde*. This is ethics, called *rinrigaku*[18] in today's Japanese, but Takano translates it as *hōkyō*[19] (law [moral principle] teachings). After that comes *natuurkunde*. This corresponds to the study of nature and is provisionally translated into Japanese as *kakubutsu kyūrigaku*[20] (study of the essence and principles of all things). Fourth comes *bovennatuurkunde*. This is metaphysics, and Takano describes it as "the study of the knowledge of the various qualities not perceived using the five organs of sense (ears, eyes, mouth, nose, and body)." Last comes *wiskunde*, mathematics, which is translated as *sūgaku*[21] (the study of numbers), the term used in today's Japanese.[22]

Regarding metaphysics, Takano held it was made up of general meta-physics (*metaphysica generalis*), that is, ontology, and special metaphysics (*metaphysica specialis*), which included psychology, cosmology, and theology, but his understanding does not seem to have extended to the substance of these fields of inquiry. Attempts at translating "philosophy" and a concrete knowledge of this field can be said to have begun with the undertakings of Nishi Amane, Tsuda Mamichi, and their contemporaries.

(3) The Translation of the Word "Philosophy"

As I mentioned in the introduction, the word *tetsugaku*[23] as a translation of "philosophy" was coined by Nishi Amane, but here I would like to go a bit further and give a brief account of the process by which this translation became established. The word "philosophia" was directly transliterated in *Excerpts from Hagiographies*, and the *Latin-Portuguese-Japanese Dictionary*[24] (1595) published by the Jesuits in Amakusa includes entries for both *Philosophia* and *Philosophor*, the former being defined (in Japanese written in the Latin alphabet) as "the love of learning, or learning that illuminates the principles [*ri*] of all things" and the latter as "to undertake the inquiry known as 'philosophy,' or to engage in debate in the manner of such scholars." "The love of learning" is presumably a translation of the Greek root of the word "philosophy," while "learning that illuminates the principles of all things" can be seen as an attempt at describing what philosophy actually does. At this point, however, no Japanese term corresponding to "philosophy" had been created.

In a draft history of Western philosophy presumably written before he went to study at Leiden University in 1861, or perhaps while en route to the Netherlands, Nishi Amane refers to "philosophy" as *hirosohi*, a phonetic transcription of "philosophy." Describing it, he writes, "Sages who practiced this discipline proclaimed themselves 'sophists,' a very proud title meaning 'people of great wisdom'; Socrates humbly called himself a 'philosopher,' meaning 'one who loves wisdom and virtue,' which should be considered equivalent to what is called the 'desire for wisdom.'"[25]

On the other hand, in an afterword to Tsuda Mamichi's "Philosophical Theory"[26] Nishi translates "philosophy" using the Chinese characters "希哲学" with superscript indicating this word is to be pronounced *hirosohi* (the Chinese characters would normally be read *kitetsugaku* and literally mean something like "desire for wisdom studies"). He writes, "Regarding the learning of Western lands, which has already been conveyed to us for more than a hundred years, there are people who have studied its various fields such as physics, chemistry, geography, and machines, but in the case of the subject called 'philosophy' no such figures have emerged . . . [the study of this subject] has begun from the only such person to be found, namely, my friend Tengai Nyorai [a pen name of Tsuda Mamichi]."[27] This *kitetsugaku*[28] can be considered the first Japanese translation of "philosophy."

This translation, as is noted in Nishi's "Network of All Studies" (Encyclopedia) lectures[29] and *To Clarify Human Nature*,[30] was based on the expression "the holy long for heaven, the wise long for holiness, and the noble long for wisdom"[31] from the "tenth study" of Zhao Dunyi's *Penetrating Writings on The Book of Changes*.[32] In his essay *Monolog of Tengai (Tsuda)*,[33] thought to have been written between 1860 and 1861, Tsuda Mamichi uses the term *kyūseigaku* (search for holiness studies),[34] which he indicates is to be pronounced as the transliteration *hirosohi*, and in "Theory of the Principles of Reality and Human Nature" he employs the phrase "one who commits to the path and desires holiness."[35] This translation also seems to have been inspired by the language of Zhou Dunyi's *Penetrating Writings*. It is reasonable to assume that these translations *kitetsugaku* and *kyūseigaku* were not hit upon by Nishi and Tsuda separately but arose instead as the result of discussions that took place between them.

Another reason this phrase from Zhou Dunyi's *Penetrating Writings* occurred to both Nishi and Tsuda when translating *filosofie* or *philosophy* may have been that the word *wijsbegeerte* (desire for wisdom), a literal Dutch translation of the original Greek meaning of "philosophy," was being used alongside these terms.[36]

Various other translations were also tried in addition to Nishi's and Tsuda's *kitetsugaku* and *kyūseigaku* from the end of the Edo period to the beginning of the Meiji period. As noted in the introduction, the most influential of these was *rigaku* (the study of principles).[37] This translation was presumably favored because philosophy was understood by being overlaid on and combined with Neo-Confucianism. Zhū Xī understood the *taiji* (great pole) spoken of by Zhōu Dūnyí, the founder of Neo-Confucianism, as "*ri*," that is, the ontological grounding of individual phenomena (energy and yin-yang) or universal principles underlying individual entities, and with this *ri* as his foundation he undertook a new development of Confucianism. It was because of this focus on underlying principles (*ri*) that Neo-Confucianism was also referred to as *seirigaku* (study of the principles [*ri*] of human nature)[38] or simply *rigaku* (study of principles [*ri*]). Scholars seem to have seen a commonality between this *seirigaku* or *rigaku* and Western "philosophy" and adopted the former as translations of the latter.[39]

Nishi Amane, however, did not employ this *rigaku* in his translations. Sticking closely to the original meaning of "love of wisdom," he rendered "philosophy" first as *kitetsugaku* and then eventually as *tetsugaku*. As far as can be surmised from his surviving writings, Nishi's first use of *tetsugaku* as a translation of "philosophy" was in his *Reflections on a Certain Person*,[40] written in 1870 (the third year of the Meiji period). This has been described as a critique of the approach taken by Ōkuni Takamasa, a scholar of Japanese thought and literature active at the end of the Edo period and beginning of the Meiji period who, like Nishi, hailed from Tsuwano, and his disciples. In this text Nishi writes, "It seems the path of Mencius and Confucius is not so different from Western philosophy (*tetsugaku*); East and West, in spite of being independent traditions, somehow tally with each other." In his "Network of All Studies" (Encyclopedia) lectures begun the same year, he says that "it can also be [translated as] *kikengaku* [study that seeks intelligence],"[41] but ultimately he adopts the translation *tetsugaku*.

Nishi's first public use of *tetsugaku* in print was in *A New Theory That Unites All Theories*,[42] published in 1874. "Unites all theories" referred to Nishi's assertion that "if we consider the essential parts of a hundred theories, they all come back to the same main ideas," with "theories" here referring not to religion but to "the theories of correct human behavior" as "tools for controlling oneself," or, in other words, morals. Here Nishi developed the idea that while morals may differ from country to country, what lies at their core is the same. At the end of *A New Theory That Unites All Theories*, Nishi writes as follows.

> It is "philosophy," which translates as "*tetsugaku*,"[43] that considers various states of affairs ["the principles of matter," "the principles of nature,"] and reflects on the principles of the mind, elucidates the ways of nature and humanity, and establishes a method of scholarship. In the West there has long since been a discourse on this study.[44]

This translation of "philosophy" as *tetsugaku* seems to have gradually spread and taken hold. The decisive moment in its adoption was the establishment of the Department of History, Philosophy (*tetsugaku*), and Politics within the Faculty of Letters of the University of Tokyo at its founding in 1877. The term *tetsugaku* was presumably chosen over terms such as *rigaku* in order to distinguish this department from the Faculty of Science (*Rigaku-bu*).[45]

Dictionary of Philosophy (*Tetsugaku Jii*) (1881),[46] edited by Inoue Tetsujirō and his collaborators, contributed greatly to the establishment of philosophical terminology in Japanese, and as its title indicates this work fundamentally adopts *tetsugaku* as the translation of *philosophy*. Interestingly, however, the translation *rigaku* is also employed alongside it; "critical philosophy" is translated as *hihyōrigaku*,[47] for example, and "practical philosophy" as *jissenrigaku*.[48] In 1886 Nakae Chōmin, whom I will discuss later, published *The History of Philosophy*[49] (a translation of Alfred Fouillée's *Histoire de la Philosophie*) and *Digging Up the Hidden and Profound Truths of Philosophy*,[50] an overview of Western philosophy. In both works he translates "philosophy" as *rigaku*, another indication that both translations (*tetsugaku* and *rigaku*) coexisted for an extended period.

(4) "Philosophy" as Something Distinct from Confucianism

As we have seen, sticking closely to the original meaning of "love of wisdom," Nishi Amane translated "filosofie" and "philosophy" as *kitetsugaku* and eventually *tetsugaku* rather than *rigaku*. Considering the tradition of Confucianism in Japan and Nishi's own education, *rigaku* seems an equally plausible choice, but as it turned out Nishi preferred *tetsugaku*. Why?

In *To Clarify Human Nature* Nishi, while acknowledging the suitability of *rigaku* or *riron* (the theory of principles [*ri*])[51] as direct translations, explains that he chose to translate philosophy as *tetsugaku* in order to avoid it being confused with Confucianism.[52] Why was he concerned about this kind of confusion? Before answering this question, I would first like to examine what sort of undertaking Nishi understood Western philosophy to be. We have seen that prior to this, in 1870's *Reflections on a Certain Person*, Nishi had asserted that the approach of Mencius and Confucius was not so different from Western philosophy, and that the independent traditions of East and West in some sense overlapped. His claim was that despite not having had any influence on each other, Confucianism and Western philosophy had the same basic content. More or less the same assertion is made in *Introductory Exegesis*.[53] "In the East this is called 'Confucianism,' while in the West it goes by the name 'philosophy.' Both illuminate the ways of heaven and establish the poles of humanity, and in effect become one."[54] Insofar as they both elucidate the laws that run through all that exists and establish the roots and principles of morality, both philosophy and Confucianism amount to the same thing.

In his "Network of All Studies" (Encyclopedia) lectures begun in November of 1870, however, Nishi emphasized that philosophy was a field of inquiry particular to the West and distinct from Confucianism. He states, for example, "In my explanations [e.g., the section of the course on theology] I have covered Japan, China and the West in that order, but in the section on philosophy I start with the West because there is little in our country that can be called 'philosophy,' nor is there anything comparable to Western philosophy in China."[55]

Of course, it was not as though Nishi believed the two traditions had nothing whatsoever in common. Particularly in regard to the study of ethics and morality, translated as *meikyōgaku* (the study of morality as the way of humanity),[56] he acknowledged that their content overlapped. "The major elements of *meikyōgaku* [Western ethical philosophy] are the same as those of Chinese Confucianism, and the minor elements differ only slightly."[57] As we have already seen, in *A New Theory That Unites All Theories*, too, Nishi says that when it comes to "the teachings of the way of humanity" their content "comes back to the same main ideas" regardless of whether they are pursued in the East or in the West. In the case of ethics, his understanding was that while minor differences could indeed be found, the content of this field of inquiry was fundamentally the same in both traditions.

Regarding other fields of inquiry, however, Nishi asserted there was nothing in the East comparable to what was found in the West. The "principles" spoken of in Neo-Confucianism address the source or grounding of all that exists and indeed seem quite comparable to the content of Western philosophy. Why then did Nishi say, "There is no comparison with [the philosophy of] the West"?

In his "Network of All Studies" (Encyclopedia) lectures Nishi expresses what he saw as the fundamental difference between the inquiry undertaken in the East and that in the West.

> Regarding philosophy in what is referred to as "Confucianism"
> in the East, the source of this Confucianism is Confucius and
> Mencius. Scholars that came later inherited and continued this
> school of Confucius without radical change, but scholars in the
> West, while they can be said to have continued their inquiry
> from ancient times, are constantly developing and renewing their
> inquiry; they have each taken up the task of tearing down the
> theories of their predecessors through their own innovations and
> keeping only what is unassailable.[58]

Nishi finds the defining characteristic of Confucianism first and foremost in its placing "truth" in the teachings of its founders, Confucius and Mencius, and seeking to carry on this tradition in succeeding generations. To give one example, this view of truth in Confucianism is clearly evident in the words of Itō Jinsai: "One book, *The Analects of Confucius*, lays out the laws and precepts of morality for eternity. Its words are most right and most just."[59]

In stark contrast to this approach, "truth," according to Nishi, was addressed in a fundamentally different way in Western learning. Of course, there is a sense in which academic inquiry cannot exist without a connection to tradition. But at the root of this inquiry in the West is a view of truth that holds that it is only by criticizing and verifying tradition, rather than directly adopting it as a starting assumption or premise, that we can arrive at the true nature of things. We might say that in this view truth is always in the midst of being developed.

Through this contrast with philosophical inquiry in the West, Nishi finds the fundamental limitation of Confucianism in its stance of striving to adhere to the doctrines of those who have come before. This is expressed, for example, by the phrase "mired in the past" when he writes that "Chinese Confucianism not reaching the pinnacle of excellence can be summed up in the phrase 'mired in the past.' "[60] We might say that Nishi saw something incompatible with the spirit of academic inquiry in the stance of looking for the standards of truth in the teachings of the founders of Eastern traditions. Based on this understanding, he drew a sharp line between philosophy and Confucianism. He seems to have coined the new term *tetsugaku* rather than use *rigaku* when translating philosophy in order to highlight this difference.

Of course, this does not mean that Nishi sought to completely reject Confucianism. After stating that "Chinese Confucianism not reaching the pinnacle of excellence can be summed up in the phrase 'mired in the past,' " he goes on to say, "When this old view is subjected to rigorous criticism [Eastern thought] will surely attain a parity of development and become comparable with the West."[61] Nishi acknowledged Confucianism's potential to become the equal of Western philosophy by critically examining the teachings of its founders, rather than regarding them as laws and precepts as had been the practice up to that point, and directing its efforts toward discovering new truth.

2. The Reception of Philosophy by Nishi Amane

(1) Dividing Meiji Philosophy into Periods

Inoue Tetsujirō (1850–1944) entered the first class of the University of Tokyo's newly established Department of Philosophy in 1877. After having studied abroad in Germany, in 1890 he became a professor at this university, a position he would continue to hold until 1923. He was thus a scholar whose career placed him directly in the middle of the process of philosophy being received and taking hold in Japan. Late in his life Inoue published an essay entitled "Reflections on the World of Meiji Philosophy" (1932).[62] In this work he divides Meiji philosophy into three periods. The first was the "period of enlightenment" running from the start of the Meiji period to 1890. During this period, British, American, and French thought concerning freedom, independence, and civil liberties was introduced and extolled. The second period, stretching from 1890 to 1905, was the period following the promulgation of the Constitution of the Empire of Japan[63] and the end of the active role of the civil liberties movement. Inoue notes that this was the period during which German philosophy was introduced and its study came to occupy a particularly prominent position in university education. The third period began with the increase in nationalism and the predominance of ideas of national supremacy sparked by the start of the Russo-Japanese War in 1904, but Inoue characterizes it as a period of remarkable awareness of the individual that produced many figures greatly concerned with social issues, along with the birth of a global spirit.[64]

In terms of this division, what I address in this chapter belongs to the first period. This corresponds to the period before philosophy found its place within the university system and was developed in that context. During this period, philosophy was taken up not as a subject of study within the university framework but rather in society as a whole. As I noted in the introduction, philosophical writings were read more in relation to the demands and issues of the day than as purely academic texts. It can be described as a period during which the light of philosophy illuminated the way forward toward a new era.

In his essay "My Teacher Nishida Kitarō,"[65] Karaki Junzō, who studied under both Nishida and Tanabe Hajime, recalls a visit to Nishida during which his mentor recommended he study the Meiji period, remarking that "the first twenty years of the Meiji Period are interesting."[66] What exactly Nishida was referring to as "interesting" is not recorded, but I think it was likely related to what I have just discussed. I suspect he was urging Karaki to study the intriguing remnants of the debates and discourse of those who first encountered European philosophy and ideas about liberty and tried to put them into practice in Japanese society.

(2) Nishi Amane's Studies in the Netherlands

Nishi Amane (1831–1897) initially studied Confucianism, but after coming to Edo to study Western learning his ability in this regard was recognized, and in 1857 he was hired as an assistant professor at the Institute for the Study of Barbarian Books,[67] an educational institution of the Tokugawa Shogunate. Along with Tsuda Mamichi (1829–1903), a colleague from this institute, in 1862 he accompanied a delegation sent to the Netherlands by the shogunate to place an order for two warships and continued his studies overseas. Arriving in Hellevoetsluis, his party was welcomed by J. J. Hoffmann, a professor of Sino-Japanese studies at Leiden University. A document written in Dutch survives that is thought to have been written by Nishi while at sea and handed to Hoffman in person. Addressed "to whom it may concern," it describes Nishi's intentions regarding studying abroad as follows.

> In order to improve our internal affairs or institutions and relations with European countries, a greater level of learning is required, and while this must be sought in fields such as statistics, law, economics, political science, and diplomacy, these sorts of learning are still unknown in Japan. . . . In addition to the above, I would also like to study the field of inquiry called "philosophy" or "love of wisdom studies." This is the form of inquiry advocated by the likes of Locke, Hegel, and Kant, and is different from the study of theology that is banned under the laws of my country.[68]

In response, Hoffmann introduced Nishi and Tsuda to his colleague Simon Vissering, a professor of statistics and economics who ended up tutoring them personally at his home.

Vissering taught Nishi and Tsuda five subjects—"natural law," "international law," "constitutional law," "economics," and "statistics"—over a period of two years. Before beginning this instruction, Vissering is said to have told them, "First, I will explain natural law, which forms the foundations of various laws. Next, I will explain international and constitutional law, which expand on natural law and regulate the interactions of countries externally and the laws of a nation internally. Later I will also explain economics, which tells us how to make the nation wealthy and the people secure. Finally, I will explain statistics, a technique for thoroughly assessing the actual state of the nation."[69] Vissering thus taught subjects related to law and economics by beginning with their most fundamental aspects and progressing in order of relevance. We can assume that not only the content of this teaching but also its method had a powerful influence on Nishi's understanding of Western learning.

After returning to Japan, Nishi set out to pass on what he had learned from his studies in the Netherlands to young people at a private school called Ikueisha in a series of lectures he called Network of All Studies (Encyclopedia).[70] In these lectures he attempted to convey the nature of Western learning as a whole, rather than as a set of individual subjects such as economics or international law.

Japan in the nineteenth century was a country that has been closed off from other nations and suddenly encountered a civilization that was not only very different but highly developed. As in any such encounter, one of the tasks—and this is indeed a truly mammoth undertaking—that must be taken up by such a country's intellectuals is to compare this different civilization, or the knowledge underpinning it, to what had been the dominant form of knowledge in their own country up to that point, and to describe what sort of knowledge it is and what sort of system of knowledge it creates when taken as a whole. Among Japanese thinkers at the time, it was perhaps Nishi Amane who took up this task most directly. Of course, during that period the introduction of individual fields of study such as law and economics as discrete subjects of inquiry was also an important task, and Nishi himself published Vissering's course on international law under the title *International Law by Mr. Vissering*[71] (1865) and a translation of Joseph Haven's *Mental Philosophy* (1857) entitled *Study of the Principles [ri] of the Mind*[72] (in three volumes, 1875–1876). Nevertheless, Nishi took clarifying how this newly encountered learning differed in its essential character from traditional Japanese learning when considered as a whole to be a more important task. By making this his mission, Nishi can be said to have played an outsized role among Japanese intellectuals of the early Meiji period.

(3) Western Academic Inquiry as an "Intellectual System"

How Nishi viewed Western learning is manifested in his use of the term "network" in the title of his lecture series Network of All Studies (Encyclopedia). In other words, he viewed it not as simply an accumulation of results obtained in individual disciplines, but rather as a single entity in which various branches of inquiry were organically connected to each other. In Nishi's understanding, Western academic inquiry was essentially a single system in which individual forms of learning were interconnected. How did he acquire this kind of systematic or synthetic perspective? The instruction he received from Vissering was no doubt deeply connected to the formation of his point of view. It was presumably through this instruction that he learned to see Western academic inquiry not as an assemblage of various disciplines but as a single "intellectual system."

Nishi's having encountered the thought of Auguste Comte (1789–1857) when he was studying in the Netherlands can be posited as another reason for his having arrived at this perspective. He not only studied law and economics with Vissering but continued to have an interest in philosophy, and during his time in the Netherlands he read voraciously on the subject.[73] While he had already acquired some knowledge of Descartes and Kant before studying abroad, it was not their philosophy but new intellectual trends, such as the positivism of Comte, the most influential thinker in the Netherlands at the time, and the utilitarianism of John Stuart Mill (1806–1873), that he found most stimulating. In *On the Three Treasures of Life*[74] (1875), an essay published in the *Meiji 6 Journal*, he writes, "Since the emergence of this positivism (through France's Auguste Comte), the world has come to see things in a new way, and many of the teachings of great thinkers have at last acquired a foundation in reality."[75] In his Network of All Studies (Encyclopedia) lectures he is recorded as having said, "Through today's Mr. Mill, all learning is enjoying great development."[76]

In the manuscript of *To Clarify Human Nature*,[77] which is thought to have been written in parallel to Network of All Studies (Encyclopedia) (it is noted in the clean copy that proofing was completed in June of 1873), Nishi discusses the revolution caused by Comte's philosophy. According to his account, the greatest problem facing the academic inquiry of the day was its subdivision into specific disciplines. Nishi writes that academic inquiry found itself in a state in which, with no one able to present an acceptable judgment concerning how the various subdivided disciplines should be positioned within this inquiry as a whole, there was an effort to leave this task up to philosophers; philosophers, however, lacked the concrete knowledge of science required to carry it out successfully. In the midst of this quagmire, it was Comte's positive philosophy, specifically the philosophy developed in *Cours de Philosophie Positive* (6 vols., 1830–1842), that had provided a "unified perspective"[78] of the results obtained from each scientific discipline and sparked a revolution in academic inquiry.

Nishi's attempt to present Western philosophy as a single "intellectual system" when introducing it in Japan can be seen as owing to his having had this kind of understanding of Comte and a strong sympathy with his perspective. This approach to the introduction of philosophy reveals much about how Nishi saw the questions of what Meiji Japan needed and what ought to be incorporated into its society. He seems to have believed that what was required was not lifting elements from individual disciplines here and there and merging them with existing forms of study like grafting bamboo onto a tree, but rather beginning with an understanding of the nature of Western learning as a whole and then undertaking a fundamental reform of existing learning based on this perspective. It is here that the true quality of Nishi's insight becomes apparent.

(4) A Focus on Positive Knowledge and Induction

One of the major characteristics of Nishi Amane's philosophy is his interest in the methodology of academic inquiry. I have already noted that Nishi saw the elucidation of how Western learning taken as a whole differed from the learning of the past as an important task to be undertaken. What he focused on from this perspective was induction as a method of inquiry. In *To Clarify Human Nature*, Nishi explicitly states that induction is the methodological stance upon which his inquiry is based. "Right now, what I consider most important and what forms the foundation of my inquiry is the method of induction of Britain's John Stuart Mill, who has recently become a prominent figure, an approach originating in the positivism of France's Auguste Comte."[79]

This went hand in hand with Nishi's critique of the old form of inquiry that relied on Confucianism. In the "General Remarks" section of his Network of All Studies (Encyclopedia) lectures, after stating that the method used by Confucianism is the "method of deduction" in which "those who study the Confucian texts place great weight on them, and . . . draw all of their various reasonings out of these favored writings," he then continues as follows.

> Learning is generally divisible into deduction and induction, and because learning in the past was deduction, as I have said before it had a single foundation from which everything began. In the end, therefore, it was unable to escape from this enclosure, and became stubbornly stuck in its ways. In other words, it is a learning wholly reliant on books without positive knowledge; unable to use books, on the contrary it is used by them and becomes a slave.[80]

Nishi saw the inadequacy of Eastern thought in its being rooted in the deductive method of beginning from a foundation of assumptions and then trying to derive everything from that starting point; it was not so much using its texts as being used by them, and ultimately ensnared itself in a stubborn adherence to tradition. Nishi saw this as an inquiry that had ended up far removed from "positive knowledge."

Nishi's repeated reference to Comte's law of three stages of development in his writings was a result of this understanding. In the same "General Remarks" he writes as follows.

> In the discourse recently put forward by the Frenchman Auguste Comte, all things, no matter what they are, do not proceed smoothly from start to finish. To be accomplished they must go through what he calls "stages." There are three stages, and things go from the first to the second and stop at the third. He says that the first stage is the "theological stage,"[81] that is, theologians, the second is the "metaphysical stage," that is, ideologists, and the third is the "positive stage," that is, positivists, and it is only here that things stop. Everything goes like this, spending a long or short time in the first and second stages before sooner or later arriving at the third stage—the positive stage. Nothing can arrive at the third stage without having gone through the first and second stages.[82]

Human culture and society, and indeed academic inquiry, advance from a stage founded on a mythical worldview, reach a stage based on a metaphysical worldview, and complete their development when they arrive at a final stage grounded in positive knowledge. Nishi situates Western rationalism and Confucianism in the second (metaphysical) stage. In the manuscript of "Introductory Exegesis," thought to have been written near the beginning of his career,[83] Nishi was already writing, "I would say that Confucianism and Rationalism, while their ideas come and go, appear quite similar, but the positivism put forward recently by Auguste Comte that will greatly enhance the learning of the future has not yet been discovered in Asia."[84]

Here "Rationalism" of course refers to modern rationalist philosophy from Descartes to Hegel, and Nishi saw something in common between this kind of philosophy and Confucianism. He turned away from both because, to use the language of Network of All Studies (Encyclopedia), their assertions were grounded in "prejudice" and "superstition."[85] Nishi's philosophy was undergirded by the idea that the label of truth should not be given to "metaphysical" conclusions based on such "prejudice" and "superstition"—about which he writes, "however grandiloquent their assertions and detailed their arguments, how useful are they?"—but instead to what is obtained by investigation on the basis of "actual things" and accumulation of "positive knowledge," or, in other words, to "positive principles" derived inductively on the basis of the "empirical method." Nishi is saying that having passed through the "metaphysical" stage, by means of the philosophy of Comte and J. S. Mill we are arriving at the "positive" stage. Interestingly, however, in "Introductory Exegesis" Nishi adds, "This philosophy has emerged only recently with the sudden rise to prominence and widespread acclaim of [John] Stuart Mill, and its being brought to fruition through the expansion of its scope and fleshing out of its details will be the duty of those who come later."[86] Here it is apparent that Nishi viewed the establishment of this new method of discovering truth and the construction of a philosophy based on it as a task to be taken up in his own era.

3. Fukuzawa Yukichi and Modern Japanese Academic Inquiry

(1) The Meiji 6 Society (Meirokusha)

To borrow a phrase from Maruyama Masao's "Opening of the Country,"[87] when Japan opened itself up and brought itself face to face with Western civilization at the end of the Edo period and beginning of the Meiji period, "Various cultural elements that had developed in Europe over a long period of time . . . were piled together and came rushing in all at once as a great conglomeration called 'the West.'"[88] Faced with the choice of surrendering to this "conglomeration" or rejecting it, Japan chose the former path. Thus began, under the overwhelming influence of this "conglomeration," an undertaking of radical change not only in politics and economics but also in culture, academic inquiry, and all other aspects of society. While under overpowering assault from the modern Western view of humanity, way of looking at things, and various systems constructed on this basis (or, to put it more concretely, from an understanding of human beings as subjects of liberty and rights, a rationalistic approach to thought, and a progressivist view of history, and the political systems, economic systems, technology, and industry supported by these ideas), an effort was launched to internalize these elements amid conflict with tradition and to achieve self-transformation.

The Meiji 6 Society (Meirokusha), which counted Nishi Amane among its members, was a group dedicated to laying the intellectual foundations for this self-transformation and thus took on the role of providing the theoretical underpinnings for this "civilization and development."[89] Named after the year of its founding, it was a scientific society set up in 1873 (the sixth year of the Meiji period) by Mori Arinori and Nishimura Shigeki, the former having recently returned from America where he had been dispatched as a chargé d'affaires. Mori was its president, and in addition to Nishimura its members included Fukuzawa Yukichi, Nishi Amane, Tsuda Mamichi, Nakamura Masanao, and Katō Hiroyuki. Mori Arinori expresses the intentions behind its establishment as follows.

> In America scholars create academic societies in each area of study, collaborate on scientific research, and give talks to benefit the general public. Japanese scholars are all isolated, with no back-and-forth between them, and as a result are of very little benefit to the world. It is therefore desirable that Japanese scholars form academic societies and gather to engage in research and discussion like scholars in that country [America].[90]

Through their society's publication, *Meiji 6 Journal*,[91] and the hosting of talks and lectures, they strove to spread the enlightened ideas of the West. We find the following words in an article by Nishimura Shigeki published in the first issue of this journal: "Today marks the first time a group of those involved in science and letters has been formed in this country. . . . With their profound learning and brilliant discourse, I pray that these scholars, by awakening the ignorant and foolish from their slumber and presenting a model of the world, will ensure the hopes of the learned and insightful are not dashed."[92] The phrase "awakening the ignorant and foolish from their slumber" neatly expresses the intentions of the members of this society; they were "proponents of enlightenment" in every sense of the phrase.

Their activities, however, would not continue for very long. The *Meiji 6 Journal* itself could not avoid being shut down under the restriction of civic political discourse carried out through the Press Regulations and Defamation Law passed in the eighth year of the Meiji period (1875). At a meeting of the Meiji 6 Society after the promulgation of the Press Regulations and Defamation Law, Fukuzawa presented a "Proposal to cease publication of the *Meiji 6 Journal*" that included the following passage.

Only here in Japan . . . do eight or nine out of ten matters involve the government when it comes to human affairs. This can be said to be a set of intractable circumstance or customs that cannot be changed overnight. But it can nevertheless also be said that today's Japan is a Japan of the government and not a Japan of the Japanese people. In practice, scholars living in this country pursue their own work while avoiding anything connected to politics, watching their every word, considering their every phrase, and choosing their path carefully with every step they take. Is this how it ought to be?[93]

The members of the Meiji 6 Society were therefore forced to arrive at a difficult conclusion. "We cannot compromise our principles. But neither can we freely express our views. Our only recourse is thus to simply cease publication of the journal." It was in the context of this kind of power struggle that the process of "modernization" was carried out, a process in which self-transformation was accomplished in the midst of conflict with tradition while absorbing the impact of the West.

(2) Fukuzawa Yukichi and the Task of Becoming "Civilized"

Fukuzawa Yukichi was one of those caught up in the chaos in the places where this "modernization" was being carried out. Not only was he in the thick of the turmoil, but perhaps more than anyone else Fukuzawa can be said to have addressed the impact of the West thoughtfully (not merely as a shock, but as something connected to necessary change), and engaged in extensive discourse regarding this transformation, in particular regarding its ideas and the route it would take.

We do not, of course, find the word "modernization" in Fukuzawa's writings. In Fukuzawa "modernization" in today's sense of the word was expressed with the phrase "becoming civilized," that is, "plotting the ongoing advancement of civilization in our country." In *An Outline of a Theory of Civilization*,[94] published in 1875, perhaps more than in any other of his numerous writings Fukuzawa lays out clearly and in one place the elements at the core of his thought, and as the title of this work implies its subject was "civilization" or "becoming civilized." Fukuzawa can indeed be described as someone who never stopped extolling the necessity of this process of "becoming civilized."

The distinctive characteristic of Fukuzawa's understanding of "civilization" lies in his having distinguished between "external civilization" and "internal civilization." External civilization was the visible manifestation of the results of civilization, and internal civilization was the way of looking at things that gave rise to it and its basic operating principles. Fukuzawa clearly distinguished these two phenomena, and it was his fundamental belief that in order to realize civilization we must prioritize internal civilization over external civilization.

This was clearly the assertion that lay behind Fukuzawa's harsh criticism of the ongoing adoption of all things Western. He criticized the stance of superficial civilization promoters who merely attempted to transplant externally observable aspects of Western civilization such as clothing, food, dwellings, and even legal and social systems without paying any heed to what supported this "external civilization" from within, claiming that "in many cases this is not only useless, but actually harmful."[95]

A hint to grasping what Fukuzawa understood to be the concrete basis of "internal civilization" can be found in the following passage from chapter 2 of his *An Outline of a Theory of Civilization*.

> Even after having gained mastery of all things between heaven and earth within a framework of laws, if, while observing these laws, we do not rest but continue in our own activities, galvanize the spirits of the people without being stupefied by old customs, take charge of ourselves, cultivate our own morals, and make our learning deeper and more accurate without relying on the praise or deferring to the authority of others, avoid complacency and plot a great future without either yearning for the past or being satisfied with the present, and, moving ever forwards and never backwards, pursue this achievement without stopping—if all of this is realized, the path of academic inquiry will by no means be empty or useless. If this is done, scholarship will serve as the foundation of invention, allow the business of manufacturing and commerce to grow with each passing day, and deepen the wellspring of happiness.[96]

Fukuzawa believed that the Japanese people freeing themselves from the fetters of the authority of rulers, old ways of looking at things, and the patterns of behavior that had become customary to engage in their own activities, autonomously tend to their own morals, and polish their own wisdom and intellect would create the "spiritual foundation" for the process of "becoming civilized."

Here he uses the expression "galvanize their spirits without being stupefied by old customs," and phrases such as "the stupefaction of old customs" and "the stupefaction of the fetters of old customs" are found throughout Fukuzawa's writings. Here "stupefaction" refers to a state in which we are in the grip of ways of thinking or ways of looking at things that have become customary and are therefore unable to see anything else. Viewed from a different perspective, "stupefaction" is a way of being in which we live comfortably with fixed principles and values and abandon the subjectivity of thinking for ourselves and making our own judgments. This is a trap into which it is often easy for people to fall, but what Fukuzawa is addressing is not the capturing of consciousness that occurs in such individuals each time this occurs, but rather what results when this loss of individual awareness eats its way deep into a people's way of looking at things and is normalized. Fukuzawa thought that what made this stupefaction not merely temporary but rather something that rose to the level of national character or spirit in the case of Japan was the "imbalance of power." He writes, "Comparing the civilization of our country to Western civilization, the difference in its character should be seen in particular in its imbalance of power."[97]

This "imbalance of power" must not be understood as the differences between human beings that exist as facts in the world. "Regarding such categories as highborn and lowborn, rich and poor, wise and foolish, and strong and weak, there is of course no limit to the number of degrees of these conditions. While the existence of these gradations should not be an impediment to human relationships and interactions, in most cases in the past rights have also differed in accordance with these differences in condition. This is called an 'imbalance of power.'"[98] According to this explanation, an "imbalance of power" comes into being when differences in actual circumstances are solidified as differences in rights, and this then leads to the subservience of those of lower rank to those of higher rank on this basis and in turn to their psychological subordination.

This "imbalance of power" creates a climate in which "human beings act in accordance with the minds [will, ideas] of others even when it is irrational to do so and are discouraged from expressing their own thoughts and opinions"[99] and produces people who live comfortably within fixed principles and values. Fukuzawa maintains that this kind of stupefaction is a phenomenon that can be widely seen arising not only out of the relationship between those of higher and lower rank but also in the domains of politics, academic inquiry, and religion.

(3) Wide-Ranging Debate and a Skeptical Spirit

How to emerge from this "stupefaction" and realize freedom was the most important issue Fukuzawa attempted to address in his *An Outline of a Theory of Civilization*. There were two things Fukuzawa believed were essential to this end. One was a "questioning mind," and the other was a diversity of thoughts, opinions, and values.

In *An Encouragement of Learning*[100] (1872–1876), Fukuzawa claims it is indeed questioning or doubt that is the wellspring of civilization.

> As for where the progress of civilization originates, its source is the detailed examination and discovery of the truth about the workings of all things between heaven and earth, both objects with concrete form and formless aspects of human affairs. If we want to find the source behind the civilization that has been achieved today by the people of the countries of the West, we need look no further than this questioning of all things.[101]

New laws and truths are discovered by questioning and reconsidering ways of looking at things that have become fixed as customs and the assertions and arguments of our predecessors, and without this doubting of existing views the progress of civilization cannot possibly occur. Fukuzawa emphasized, however, that this must be "autonomous questioning."

> When we inquire as to the reason that even in our own minds we have come to question the customs we [Japanese] have maintained for thousands of years, if it is because we have opened our country for the first time and encountered the countries of the West, and seeing the state of their civilization have put our faith in this splendor, this cannot be called autonomous questioning. This is merely adopting a new faith in place of the old, a shifting of our hearts and minds from the old belief in the East to a new belief in the West, and does not offer any guarantee that we are correct in our determination of what we should believe and what we should doubt, what we should adopt and what we should discard.[102]

Questioning that comes from a stance of simply copying what is new lacks reflection on basic principles regarding what should be believed and what should be doubted, and cannot be questioning in the true sense of the word.

Along with this skeptical spirit, Fukuzawa also focused on diversity of thought, opinions, and values as another premise necessary for "civilization" and the realization of liberty. He expresses this, for example, in the following paradoxical phrase: "If you defend a single doctrine, even if this doctrine is pure and good it will never give rise to a climate of liberty. We must understand that a climate of liberty only arises amid 'wide-ranging debate.' "[103]

How can a "pure and good" opinion or assertion run counter to liberty? Why does a climate of liberty arise when many opinions and assertions confront and compete with each other? Fukuzawa does not answer this question directly, but we can flesh out his assertion as follows. A platform for debate is formed when various opinions and assertions are permitted, the grounds for each are considered, and the best ideas are chosen. Conversely, domination by a single doctrine prevents the formation of this kind of space for debate. It also prevents the maturation of the technique of debate. It is when the kind of platform for debate described above is formed that a climate of free argument and the pursuit of truth is created.

Fukuzawa describes a paradox in which it is not by suppressing differing opinions but through different assertions competing with each other and taking each other to task that liberty arises.

> When it comes to civilized liberty, the liberty of others is not to be squandered or obtained for ourselves. It only exists when we accept the rights of other people, allow them to obtain benefits, accept various opinions, develop the capacity of each individual, and in this way strike a balance between ourselves and others. It can thus be said that liberty arises when there is an absence of liberty [that is, when we accept the liberty of others and thereby limit our own].[104]

Fukuzawa grasped with perfect clarity the paradox of liberty being accompanied by or arising through the absence of liberty.

(4) Changes in Academic Inquiry

Fukuzawa did not adopt the approach of distinguishing between external civilization and internal civilization and emphasizing the importance of the latter simply to criticize the climate of unreflective adoption of the former prevalent in his era. At the same time—and indeed more fundamentally—this approach was also taken in order to criticize the way of thinking expressed by the slogan "Eastern morality, Western technology." Criticizing the notion of keeping Japan's traditional worldview or morality unchanged and grafting Western technological civilization onto it can indeed be described as the core of Fukuzawa's theory of civilization. His theory of modernization was clearly connected to the issue of changes in academic inquiry.

This view is perhaps most plainly stated in the following passage from Fukuzawa's *Autobiography* (1899).[105]

> If we compare the Confucianism of the East and the civilization
> of the West, we see that what is absent in the East is mathe-
> matics and natural science [particularly physics] regarding that
> which has form, and an independent mind regarding that which
> is formless. . . . Here in Japan little attention has been paid to
> this important understanding that human beings, in all matters,
> cannot avoid mathematics and natural science, and our thought
> must erect itself on the basis of independence. This is entirely
> the fault of the teachings of the Chinese classics.[106]

This passage provides an important clue to understanding what Fukuzawa was advocating and aiming to achieve through his *An Outline of a Theory of Civilization*, and here he identifies "mathematics and natural science" and an "independent mind" as essential elements of civilization not present in the East. An "independent mind" can be thought of as referring to the mental or spiritual foundation supporting the previously addressed "external civilization." In *An Encouragement of Learning*, Fukuzawa uses the expression "the impetus of people's independence." Here "mathematics and natural science" can also be thought of as referring to the fundamental inquiry that supports rational thought more broadly. This passage clearly indicates that Fukuzawa considered the adoption of this kind of inquiry to be an essential premise of civilization.

It must be noted that Fukuzawa's aim was not to introduce this inquiry, which was "absent in the East," alongside the old form of inquiry or to graft it onto the roots of this existing scholarship. Judging only from the phrase "what is absent in the East is mathematics and natural science regarding that which has form," it is of course possible to interpret Fukuzawa's claim to be merely that mathematics or physics does not exist as a field of study in the East. But Fukuzawa did not accept the old inquiry as it was and take issue only with the absence of a particular field of study; he clearly asserted that there were elements of the old learning—which was primarily Confucianism—that stood in the way of civilization. As Fukuzawa puts it, "Both Confucianism and Buddhism have performed important functions in their own domains and enabled this country to attain the civilization it has today, but neither can escape the disease of aspiring to the past."[107]

As is explicitly stated here, Fukuzawa acknowledges that in some respects Confucianism has supported Japanese civilization. In particular, he recognizes the role it has played in the domain of personal morality; in concrete terms, it has "disciplined people's minds and made them pure and refined."[108] At the same time, however, Fukuzawa also points out that Confucianism has a fundamental flaw. In chapter 9 of *An Outline of a Theory of Civilization*, "The Origins of Japanese Civilization," he writes as follows.

> To believe in and aspire to the things of the past without making any effort of your own [to pursue truth] is to be a "mental slave." Devoting oneself to the ways of the past, falling under the sway of people of the past while living in the present, continuing to accept this domination while seeking to rule the world of today—introducing such stagnant or inactive elements to human beings and throughout all of society can be said to have been the fault of Confucianism.[109]

Perhaps drawing on J. S. Mill's *On Liberty*, Fukuzawa thus expresses the flaw of "Confucianism" with the phrase "mental slavery." This mental state of "believing in and aspiring to the things of the past" is deeply connected to the study of teachings that had been established—not merely begun but developed in a complete manner—in ancient times forming the core of academic inquiry. In concrete terms these were the Confucian teachings of "control oneself, bring stability to the people"[110] and "control oneself, bring order to one's family,"[111] or, in other words, the study of the "way"[112] human beings ought to live in a Confucian sense. Other fields of inquiry were developed on the basis of this core learning (and thus its classicism), and the fundamental character of this central learning had a pivotal influence on the state of mind of those living in this society. This is what Fukuzawa regards as "the fault of Confucianism."

As Maruyama Masao argues in "The 'Practical Learning' Turn in Fukuzawa: An Introduction to the Philosophy of Fukuzawa Yukichi,"[113] what Fukuzawa was trying to realize through this theory of civilization was a shift in the learning that formed the core or "prototype" of academic inquiry from the Confucian study of the "way" to the study of mathematics and natural science. As Maruyama emphasizes, however, to view this turn as simply a shift in the focus of academic interest is to misunderstand Fukuzawa's intentions.[114] Nor, as I have already mentioned, was his aim merely to augment existing learning with mathematics and natural science. What Fukuzawa truly intended to accomplish was a change in the fundamental character of academic inquiry. Precisely speaking, his aim was to alter its underlying spirit.

While discussing the question of the progress of academic inquiry in *An Outline of a Theory of Civilization*, Fukuzawa writes as follows about the character of the inquiry that must be constructed anew.

> Human learning is steadily advancing, and what was success yesterday becomes failure today. What was considered correct last year is deemed mistaken this year. We harbor doubts about each and every object, view every phenomenon with suspicion, investigate everything, examine everything closely, make new discoveries, and improve on what has been done in the past. Children and younger brothers become better than their fathers and older brothers, and those who come later advance further than those who have come before. Inquiry progresses with each passing year, and looking back a century from now there are many things that will be considered of no use to civilization and elicit only a wry smile—such is the progress of civilization and the advancement of academic inquiry.[115]

From this passage it is clear that what Fukuzawa demanded in a new form of academic inquiry was, first and foremost, a stance or attitude of questioning and closely examining all things—including, therefore, everything that had been considered unshakeable truth up to that point. I have already noted that what Fukuzawa extolled as the primary premise required in order to escape stupefaction was a "questioning mind," and when it came to the construction of a new academic inquiry this skeptical spirit was again his main focus.

Another point of note in the passage quoted above is that Fukuzawa says we are to "investigate everything, examine everything closely, make new discoveries, and improve on what has been done in the past." What he is addressing here is the verification of theory through comparison with concrete phenomena. Rather than absolutizing theory, he saw constantly holding it up against reality and carefully assessing its validity as a premise necessary to the progress of academic inquiry.

Fukuzawa also emphasized the importance of "tests" in regard to the concrete policy to be adopted for the realization of civilization. For example, in chapter 3 of *An Outline of a Theory of Civilization*, "To Consider the Purpose of Civilization," he writes, "The sole aim of humanity is to attain civilization. There are various means by which to do so. We thus try one approach, improve it, and through countless tests make some amount of progress. A person's thoughts must therefore not become biased in one direction."[116] Here the word "test" is being used in a broader context, but it seems clear that one of Fukuzawa's fundamental ideas was that academic inquiry, too, can only progress through concrete verification against reality.

As we have seen, what Fukuzawa tried to argue was the necessity of an inquiry grounded in skepticism and the verification of theory. Returning to the phrase "what is absent in the East is mathematics and natural science regarding that which has form, and an independent mind regarding that which is formless" from his autobiography, Fukuzawa understood "mathematics" and natural science not merely as a single domain of academic inquiry but as something closely connected to "an independent mind," the other element cited as being "absent in the East." "Mathematics and natural science" were understood as being closely tied to a state of mind in which, without being constrained by traditional thought or theories, one engages in subjective examination and consideration and constantly strives to discover new truths. What Fukuzawa advocated was the introduction of mathematics and natural science in the sense just described, and ultimately what he aimed to achieve was the construction—or complete reconstruction—of academic inquiry based on this kind of mentality.

Fukuzawa also turned his attention to another issue in relation to the question of the construction of a new academic inquiry. I have already mentioned the trait of an "imbalance of power." I have noted that in Japan relationships of superiority/inferiority in the context of professions or social status governed the entirety of human relations and created relationships of psychological dependence. This trait had created human beings who were powerfully influenced by a traditional sense of value, and at the same time had exerted a strong influence on academic inquiry. Thinking of the Edo period in particular, Fukuzawa writes as follows.

> What was the difference [between the inquiry of the West and that of the East]? It was that when the era of constant warfare ended and an effort was made to develop academic inquiry, in Western countries this inquiry arose among the general population, while here in Japan it arose within the government. In Western countries academic inquiry was something pursued by scholars. There was no distinction between officials and ordinary citizens in this undertaking; inquiry was positioned within the world of scholars. In Japan, on the other hand, it was positioned within the world of rulers, and was nothing more than a part of the government.[117]

Here Fukuzawa states that academic inquiry could only exist in the world of governing officials and had established itself by serving these rulers. He can be seen as asserting that the establishment of an inquiry grounded in skepticism and the verification of theories could only be achieved through liberation from such fetters—something that was inseparable from liberation from an "imbalance of power" in the mindset of the population as a whole.

(5) Nishimura Shigeki's Theory of Morality

Nishimura Shigeki (1828–1902) was another thinker who devoted his efforts to the establishment of the Meiji 6 Society and published essays such as "A Theory of Three Types of Government"[118] and "An Explanation of Twelve Foreign Words"[119] in the *Meiji 6 Journal*. He too was one of the promoters of enlightenment active at the start of the Meiji period, but unlike Fukuzawa he pursued a path of reevaluating Confucianism. In 1887 he published *A Theory of Japanese Morality*[120] and presented the world with a unique vision of morality.

According to this view, because "Confucian morality" had been discarded after the Meiji Restoration, a situation had arisen in which "people with a middle-class or better upbringing have lost the foundation of their morality. . . . The force that tied people's minds together is slackening, and there are signs that the morality of the people is in gradual decline."[121] Nishimura believed that when "the teaching of morality has declined in the country as a whole, and people's manners and customs are dying out" in this way, the only possible salvation is the study of morality. In his view there are two forms of moral persuasion: worldly teachings and extraworldly teachings. Worldly teachings are teachings that instruct us to master ourselves and seek to realize peace in our country or society, while extraworldly teachings are the teachings of religion that focus mainly on the world after death. Nishimura held that Confucianism and philosophy belonged to the former and Buddhism and Christianity to the latter. Which approach should be taken depended on the country in question, and since in Japan those in the upper ranks of society had traditionally sought to improve themselves through Confucianism and established the nation's legal system on this basis, Nishimura believed that in this country it would make sense to base morality on worldly teachings.

By that point in time, however, it was impossible to construct a morality based solely on Confucianism. This intellectual system presented many serious problems, such as the fact that it contained many aspects that could not be reconciled with the refined results of Western academic inquiry and that it had a strong tendency toward affirming the past and rejecting the present. Philosophy, in contrast, had developed such that "its inquiry gradually becomes deeper and more refined" by "making principles one's teacher, rather than a particular person." This approach is inadequate when it comes to morality, however, insofar as it "emphasizes engaging in discourse on *theory* and neglects to discuss *practice*." Based on this way of thinking, Nishimura writes, "The policy at which I have arrived is to distill the best parts and discard the dregs of each of these two teachings [Confucianism and philosophy]; in other words, I have adopted the spirit of each while discarding their external trappings."[122] Here we see another form of the reception of philosophy.

4. Nakae Chōmin—Philosophy as "the Study of Principles [*Rigaku*]"

(1) NAKAE CHŌMIN'S VIEW OF ACADEMIC INQUIRY

Nakae Chōmin (1847–1901) was the son of an infantryman (*ashigaru*) in what was then known as the Tosa Domain (today's Kōchi Prefecture). After studying French in Nagasaki and Edo (Tokyo), in 1871 (the fourth year of the Meiji period), he went to study in France as a Justice Ministry scholar. There he absorbed learning in a variety of fields, including law, philosophy, history, and literature. In 1874 he returned to Japan, opened a school called Furansu Gakusha (France School) (later renamed Futsugaku Juku [France Studies School]) in his own home in Tokyo, and gathered a large number of students. In 1882 Futsugaku Juku's journal, *Writings on Political Theory*,[123] published a serialized translation into Classical Chinese of Rousseau's *Du Contrat Social* with explanatory notes.[124] Later publications included *History of Philosophy [Rigaku]*[125] (1886), a translation of Alfred Fouillée's *Histoire de la Philosophie*, and *Digging Up the Hidden and Profound Truths of Philosophy [Rigaku]*[126] (1886), the first overview of Western philosophy published in Japan.

As the titles of these texts indicate, Nakae continued to use *rigaku*[127] (the study of principles [*ri*]) as the translation of "philosophy" even after *tetsugaku* had become the standard term. At the beginning of *Digging Up the Hidden and Profound Truths of Philosophy [Rigaku]*, Nakae writes, " 'Philosophy' is Greek, and is generally translated as '*tetsugaku*.' This is of course not incorrect. I myself translate it as '*rigaku*' based on the word '*kyūri*'[128] that appears in the *Yì Jīng*,[129] but the meaning is the same."[130] While he says that the meaning is the same, Nakae makes a point of using *rigaku* instead of *tetsugaku*, which had already started to become the established translation. As this passage indicates, he seems to have done so because he preferred to base his translation on the existing term *kyūri*, which originates in the *Yì Jīng* and plays an important role in Neo-Confucianism. Of course, he did not believe that "philosophy" had exactly the same content as the *kyūri* spoken of in the *Yì Jīng* ("Investigate the principles [*ri*] of all things, master human nature, and by doing so attain knowledge of the mission of heaven")[131] or the *kakubutsu kyūri* (seeking the essence of all things and investigating their principles)[132] of Neo-Confucianism. He maintained, however, that using this sort of concept rooted in tradition as a handhold would make it easier to understand and adopt ideas that had been developed in a different culture. He was convinced this was possible because he believed in the existence of universal elements running through both Eastern and Western thought.

What should be noted here to begin with is that Nakae's view of academic inquiry was clearly different from that of other early Meiji promoters of enlightenment thought, such as Nishi Amane and Tsuda Mamichi, who belonged to the Meiji 6 Society. As we have already seen, Nishi expressed the contrasting character of Eastern and Western learning with the phrase "*kūri* [empty principles][133] and *jitsuri* [positive principles]."[134] Confucianism is said to "rarely hit upon the truth" because from start to finish it is merely the interpretation of texts, and is thus a set of "empty principles" lacking in "empirical observation."[135] Tsuda also characterizes Eastern and Western learning with the terms *kyogaku* (empty learning)[136] and *jitsugaku* (positive or practical learning)[137] in his "Discourse on Methods of Advancing Enlightenment."[138]

Assertions that are refined and expansive but empty and lacking in content, merely empty teachings, the doctrine of five elements [the doctrine that everything is created or changes through the five elements of wood, fire, earth, metal, and water], the doctrine of the principle of nature [which holds that human nature and the principles of heaven are one and the same] or the doctrine that we are born with the ability to determine what is good and to realize it—these [Confucian teachings] are empty learning. Academic inquiry, such as the modern Western fields of astronomy, physics, chemistry, medicine, economics, and philosophy, which examines these things [the fundamental principles of all things and the nature and abilities of human beings] on the basis of reality and phenomena that actually occur, is real or practical learning. The result of this practical learning spreading widely within the country and individuals following its logic can be described as a truly civilized society.[139]

Of course, there is no doubt that Nishi and Tsuda had extensive knowledge of the Chinese classics and adopted Western thought on the foundation of this learning. They nevertheless explicitly classified the Eastern worldview and morality of Buddhism and Confucianism not based on concrete experience as "empty theory," and Western learning that had been built on concrete grounds as "definite principles." In order to "advance enlightenment," they began by clearly contrasting these two approaches.

Nakae, on the other hand, did not hold only one approach in high regard or view one as absolute. For him, academic inquiry was not something that could be neatly organized into the dichotomy of "empty studies versus real or practical studies." He believed that Eastern and Western inquiry were not two systems that ought to have a clear dividing line between them, but rather two approaches that each ought to contribute to the development of learning from its own perspective.

At the same time, Nakae was of course cognizant of the inadequacy of Eastern thought. In a draft manuscript ("Offering Solutions")[140] thought to have been written around 1875, he writes, "Are France and Britain superior to us [Japan] when it comes to fathers and children loving each other and brothers sharing a close bond? They are not at all superior. Are France and Britain superior to us when it comes to courtesy between those of higher and lower rank or status? They are not at all superior. The only points on which they are superior to us are technology and theoretical knowledge."[141] As noted in the introduction, in *A Year and a Half*[42] (1901a) Nakae asserts that "here in Japan, from the past to the present there has been no philosophy (*tetsugaku*)."[143] This absence of philosophy could also be said to reflect an inadequacy in the theorization of experience.

When it came to overcoming this absence of philosophy in Japan, Nakae saw European philosophy as an instructive model. His having translated not only *Du Contrat Social* but also works such as Fouillée's *Histoire de la Philosophie* and Eugene Véron's *L'Esthétique*[144] can be seen as having been based on this understanding. But Nakae did not unconditionally affirm European philosophy. Interestingly, in his final work, *A Year and a Half Continued*,[145] Nakae turned a critical eye to the philosophy of positivism that Nishi Amane had praised as an approach that would "greatly enhance the learning of the future because of its certainty grounded in evidence and clear argumentation."

> The views of this faction (the positivists) seem very certain and reliable, but because they are too devoted to reality, they utterly reject everything that cannot be grounded in empirical experiments, even perfectly clear logic,[146] box themselves in, and fall into a stiff, inflexible stance. The malign effects of this greatly distort our intellectual capabilities, and cause them to be underestimated.[147]

Nakae believed there are some convictions that are unshakeable or that must be accepted on the basis of logical reasoning even if they cannot be scientifically verified, and held that if we reject all such convictions we improperly narrow the scope of human capabilities.

Nakae was able to criticize positivist philosophy in this way because he did not organize Eastern and Western philosophy into a dichotomous framework of "empty studies versus real or practical studies" in which one approach was to be rejected. On the contrary, he positioned his own perspective in a place where this framework had been stripped away, and consistently adopted an approach of simply praising what ought to be praised. Having taken this stance, for Nakae there was no need to worry about Western thought getting "mixed up with other things," and there was indeed no need to create a new word, *tetsugaku*, for this "philosophy" in Japanese.

(2) NAKAE AND ROUSSEAU

Early Meiji-period proponents of enlightenment thought and the movement for civil liberties relied mainly on British ideas of natural law and utilitarianism and the theories of liberty and politics that had been developed from these perspectives. By introducing French political thought in contrast to this approach, Nakae provided a new theoretical foundation for the civil liberties movement. Rousseau's thought concerning the social contract and popular sovereignty, in particular, gave a greater impetus to the burgeoning movement for civil rights. Nakae's specific focus on the theory of popular sovereignty within Rousseau's thought can be seen in the phrases "what Rousseau considered most important was people being allowed to govern themselves and not being oppressed by the state, and this is why later generations have praised him and elevated him to the highest rank"[148] and "[Rousseau's] book on the social contract held nothing back in its assault on the politics of its era, and made it clear that rights are to belong to the people"[149] from his *Annotated Translation of* Du Contrat Social. The specific character of this understanding of Rousseau is also apparent in Nakae's choice of words in his translation. For example, he translates *république* not as *kyōwakoku* (jointly ruled country),[150] the standard Japanese translation of "republic" today, which had already come into use at that time, but as *jichi no kuni* (self-governing country).[151] This was because *république* referred to a state of affairs in which "the people are the masters of the state, and regard nothing as being above themselves," and it was not possible to derive this meaning from *kyōwakoku*.

By introducing Rousseau's theory of popular sovereignty in this way, Nakae had a great influence on people active in the movement for civil rights who had previously relied on the theories of liberty and representative government of Mill and Spencer. But it was only after the *Eastern Liberty* newspaper,[152] with Saionji Kinmochi at its helm and Nakae as its chief writer, began being published in 1881 that he took center stage in the Freedom and People's Rights Movement. This was a cause that benefited greatly from the power of his pen. In the "Blessing" published in the first edition of this newspaper, Nakae put Rousseau front and center. "Aren't these words of Rousseau magnificent? 'A person without the right to liberty is not a person.'"[153] At the root of Rousseau's theory of popular sovereignty was the understanding that people are in essence free beings. This is shown in the phrase with which he begins *Du Contrat Social*, "Man is born free, and everywhere he is in chains," and again in chapter 4 when he writes, "To renounce liberty is to renounce being a man, to surrender the rights of humanity and even its duties."[154] These are presumably the words that inspired Nakae in his "Blessing."

Moreover, what Rousseau believed people obtained through the social contract was not simply political or civil liberty but also moral liberty (*liberté morale*) (book 1, chapter 8). Nakae draws on this conception in his editorial in the first edition of the *Eastern Liberty* newspaper when he discusses two liberties. "There are two senses of liberty: *liberté morale* (liberty of the mind) and *liberté politique* (liberty of action)."[155] In contrast to *liberté politique*, which signifies political liberty, including such things as freedom of speech, freedom of assembly, freedom of association, and freedom of action, *liberté morale* signifies the liberty of mental activity. In more concrete terms he describes this as follows: "*Liberté morale* means that a person's mind and thoughts are in no way restricted by anyone else, and as such are allowed to completely develop and reach their full potential."[156] "Liberty of the mind" means our mental activities not being fettered in any way and developing in a complete form. It was the latter, developmental aspect that Nakae emphasized. With the former aspect as a premise, it was the mind attaining comprehensive development and engaging fully in activities that constituted *liberté morale*.

Rousseau himself did not discuss *liberté morale* in detail in *Du Contrat Social*, but this kind of subjective understanding of liberty undoubtedly originates in his thought. In chapter 8 of book 1, Rousseau describes the benefits obtained through the transition to this civil state as follows: "His [humanity's] faculties are so stimulated and developed, his ideas so extended, his feelings so ennobled, and his whole soul so uplifted."[157] *Liberté morale* refers to this elevated state of humanity.[158]

Of course, *liberté morale* can also be understood in connection with morality. In *Du Contrat Social* Rousseau writes that "the mere impulse of appetite is slavery, while obedience to a law which we prescribe to ourselves is liberty."[159] Rousseau saw the essence of *liberté morale* in autonomy. While drawing on this understanding of Rousseau's, Nakae took it a step further by reading Confucian ethics into this conception of liberty. Citing Mencius, in an editorial in the *Eastern Liberty* newspaper he writes, "This [*liberté morale*] is also looking within yourself and not finding guilt or shame, reflecting on yourself and being upright."[160] That a Confucian ethical perspective lay at the foundation of Nakae's thought can be seen elsewhere in the same editorial where he writes, "Counselor Inoue's speech is nothing but a fleeting falsehood." In response to an address given by Inoue Kaoru (1835–1915), the gist of which was "the creator of all things created humanity for the purpose of giving it pleasure,"[161] Nakae in contrast presents an ascetic, Confucian view of ethics.

> Surely Heaven did not create humanity merely so that it could seek its own pleasure. . . . if my actions are in line with the way, happiness will come without my seeking it. As Confucius

says, "Do what is difficult first, and get something for it later." In the words of the *Yi Jing*, "For a family that has accumulated good deeds, there is always good fortune that will be obtained through their virtue."[162]

It is presumably because this ethical perspective was so firmly rooted in Nakae that he not only distinguished *liberté morale* from *liberté politique*, but emphasized, more than Rousseau, the significance of this form of liberty as a grounding, or indeed as the "radical foundation"[163] of human activity as a whole.

By introducing this view of liberty, Nakae had a large influence on the civil liberties movement, and the venue for this discourse was *Writings on Political Theory*, the journal of the Futsugaku Juku (France Studies School). In total more than eighty essays and other writings were translated and published in this journal. What brought it renown, however, was Nakae's *Annotated Translation of Du Contrat Social*. It was the publication of this text that led to his being dubbed the "Rousseau of the East." Given his deep sympathy for Rousseau's thought, this can perhaps be considered an apt moniker. Nakae clearly took up Rousseau's understanding of liberty and the theory of popular sovereignty. But he did not simply try to transplant Rousseau's thought to Japan without alteration. On the contrary, he was explicitly critical of Rousseau's radicalism. "[Rousseau] was born with a strong, intense character, and through the addition of confidence in his own abilities and pride in his own fortitude, this made him unhappy to follow in the footsteps of others. He was thus not without a propensity to sometimes go too far."[164]

Nakae was on the one hand an idealist who never surrendered his ideals. On the other hand, he knew that in actuality these ideals could only be realized in the presence of certain conditions. He did not speak only of ideals and ignore the actual circumstances in which he found himself. In this sense Nakae was a thoroughgoing realist. This is well demonstrated by his theory of "joint rule by the monarch and the people." He prioritized the "actual benefits" of self-rule by the people and was not particularly concerned about the existence of a monarch. On the contrary, he recoiled from people who got carried away by the "name" of new ideas and enthusiastically pursued progressivism.

Credulous people are often blinded by a name and do not investigate the reality [of its referent]. Such people are taken in by the connotations of the word "kyōwa" ["joint rule," used in the Japanese translation of "republic"], and, having been riled up by it, may well engage in the kind of actions seen in France long ago [the French Revolution] and attempt to change this country's form of government. It cannot be said that such people do not exist in Japan.[165]

Rather than pressing forward with a progressivism that aimed at the perfect realization of his ideals, Nakae thus strove instead to plot their greatest possible realization within the circumstances in which he had been placed. This was one of the defining characteristics of his thought.

Another characteristic of his thought that can be gleaned from what I have already presented is his always having kept the Eastern intellectual tradition in mind when he discussed Western thought. The most straightforward example of this is the editorial in the *Eastern Liberty* newspaper quoted above. In it Nakae equates *liberté morale* and Mencius's "feeling of expansiveness that attaches to reason and morality."[166] Nakae understood the "capaciousness"[167] of the mind of a person who does not merely act on their own desires but creates their own laws and acts in accordance with them in terms of this "feeling of liberation" that naturally accompanies reason and morality.

Here, of course, Nakae was not merely referencing traditional ideas as an expedient method of helping Western thought take root in Japan. He did so because of his unshakeable conviction that there were genuine commonalities between the intellectual traditions of the West and the East. In *Offering Solutions*, he writes, "The morality of the West originates in two Greeks, Socrates and Plato. The discourse of these thinkers by no means excludes human righteousness and honesty [as discussed by Confucius]. When I was in Europe and read their works, I realized that morality is indeed fixed and unchanging, be it in ancient times or today, in places nearby or far away."[168] Here this is asserted only in regard to morality, but it was not only in their discourse on morality that Nakae saw commonalities between the West and the East. In *A Year and a Half*, a text written near the end of his life, Nakae claims that the idea of civil rights, too, was not something found only in the West.[169]

One of the defining characteristics of Nakae's thought is that he focused his attention on what was universal and common to both traditions, rather than merely understanding Western and Eastern thought within their separate contexts.[170] For Nakae, turning his gaze toward Western thought did not mean one-sidedly accepting it, but rather focusing on what was universal and ran through both the thought of the East that of the West, both of which were indeed distinct, particular traditions. On this point, Nakae can be said to have adopted a stance that clearly differed from that of the other promotors of enlightenment in the Meiji-6 Society.

(3) Nakaeism

In the spring of 1901, Nakae was diagnosed with cancer of the larynx and told he had a year and half to live. While undergoing treatment he wrote *A Year and a Half* and *A Year and a Half Continued.*

We have already seen that Nakae placed great importance on philosophy and morality, but what he emphasized most strongly in *A Year and a Half* was the importance of "principles [*ri*]"[171] and "reason and justice [*rigi*]"[172] He employs the term "reason and justice" in multiple senses, but to begin with he uses it to mean "Confucian moral rectitude." Contrasting "the beauty of material things" and "the good of reason and justice," he writes as follows.

> No matter how deep his learning, how powerful his influence, and how great his reputation, if a man mistreats his father as a son, causes suffering to his wife as a husband, deceives his friends, or engages in other bad acts, what are we to think of him? No matter how strong our nation and how weak our neighbors, if we deploy our soldiers to a neighboring country without reason, how are we to be judged? Ultimately, other things cannot triumph over reason and justice. Because there is a difference between the roots of a tree [what is of import] and the tips of its leaves and branches [what is inconsequential]. When I put it like this, today's "high-collar" types [followers of Western fashion, i.e., the latest trends] will surely say my words are "timeworn and insufferable." [I would reply,] "Indeed, all words that express reason and justice are timeworn." While saying such things is timeworn, putting them into practice is quite novel.[173]

Of course, this need not necessarily be viewed as simple traditionalism. It also incorporates a sympathy for Rousseau's moralism.

"Reason and justice" is also used with the sense of "principles or theories that implement reason."

> People in this country have a clear understanding of their interests but remain in the dark when it comes to reason and justice. They like to conform to things [current trends] but are not fond of thinking [for themselves]. . . . consequently, they are superficial in their actions and cannot go far enough to get to the heart of things. What our country needs going forward are not great men of action but great philosophers.[174]

While on the one hand acknowledging their adapting themselves to their circumstances and avoiding pointless disputes as a strength of the Japanese people, on the other hand Nakae also saw that this was the flipside of an even greater weakness. He strongly criticized the "capricious frivolity" of Japanese people who did not pursue reason themselves and thus did not possess any fundamental principles for acting on a rational basis. This Japanese flaw of being "in the dark" when it came to reason and justice was inevitably reflected in their academic inquiry. It was also deeply related to the fact that "here in Japan, from the past to the present there has been no philosophy [*tetsugaku*]."

After the publication of *A Year and a Half*, it was clear to Nakae that he had very little time left, but in order to leave behind an outline of his own philosophy he took up his pen once more. He seems to have done so out of a desire to not merely lament the lack of philosophy but leave behind something that could serve as the cornerstone of a new, original philosophy. It can perhaps even be said that it was his dream to die a "philosopher." *A Year and a Half Continued* was written in only ten days, in a state in which "breathing is a struggle, and my entire body is [as fragile] as a crane."

Nakae explicitly declares that he has adopted the stance of materialism, expressing his own approach as one of "no god and no soul." As in *Digging Up the Hidden and Profound Truths of Philosophy* [*Rigaku*], however, he does not discuss the content of the natural sciences but rather begins by engaging in a critique of positivism before going on to develop his own epistemology.

In Nakae's thought, positivism (the realist school), which is grounded in facts and emphasizes experience, stands above the spiritual school, which develops its theories based on "poetic imagination." As I have already noted in section 1, however, to him the realist school is not absolutely correct either, and it indeed has a major flaw: there are countless indubitable facts that can be known without being verified. To exclude all such knowledge is nothing other than "narrow-minded dogma." Nakae thus moves away from positivism, writing that "we must ask ourselves why realists [positivists] are so frightened of inference."[175]

Nakae then proceeds to develop an epistemology from a materialist perspective. He rejects an idealism that tries to dissolve things in the external world into ideas, and on the contrary grounds ideas in the experience of external things. He views ideas as arising through the copying of various things that exist independently of consciousness. ("The external world actually exists, and images of it are projected in our minds.")[176] It is of course possible to criticize this understanding. Here perception is viewed as a direct reflection of external objects in consciousness. No attention is paid to the active aspects of human perception, nor is there any focus on its historical and social nature. However, Nakae's intention in *A Year and a Half Continued* was to lay the foundation for the formation of independent philosophy in Japan. The concrete construction of this philosophy was left to those who would follow him. Nakae ends the book with a plea for this kind of undertaking. "The author's deepest desire would be satisfied if one day someone created a system of 'Nakaeism' out of his writings."[177]

Chapter 2

Philosophy Within the University System (Academic Philosophy)

1. Fenollosa's Philosophy Courses at the University of Tokyo

(1) ESTABLISHMENT OF THE UNIVERSITY OF TOKYO AND ITS FACULTY OF LETTERS

At the beginning of the Meiji period philosophy was taken up within Japanese society as a whole as something that would point the way forward for the nation, and there was vigorous debate surrounding its development. Eventually it was given a more concrete position with the establishment of the university system, undergoing a process in which it was placed within the framework of academic inquiry that was pursued and studied at universities.

In 1877 (the tenth year of the Meiji period), the University of Tokyo was established through the merging of the Tokyo Kaisei School and the Tokyo Medical School.[1] The Tokyo Kaisei School was reorganized into the three faculties of law, science, and letters, and the Tokyo Medical School became the Faculty of Medicine. Kato Hiroyuki (1836–1916) was put in charge of the faculties of law, science, and letters. In the Faculty of Letters, two departments were established at the start, the Department of History, Philosophy (*tetsugaku*) and Politics and the Department of Japanese and Chinese Literature. In 1887 the first of these departments was remade into the Department of Philosophy, Politics, and Economics, and in 1881 the faculty was once again reorganized into three departments, the Department of Philosophy, the Department of Politics and Economics, and the Department of Japanese and Chinese Literature.

Prior to the Meiji Restoration, Katō Hiroyuki, the first head of the three faculties of law, science, and letters, had worked in the bakufu's Institute for the Study of Barbarian Books and had been the first person to study German in Japan. After the Meiji Restoration he served the new government in various positions, including as "University *Taijō*."[2] In *Tree Peony*,[3] which was written in 1861 but not published at the time, and *Summary of the Constitutional System*,[4] published in 1868, he introduced Western constitutional thought to Japanese readers. In 1870 he published *Outline of the True Politics*[5] and introduced the theory of innate human rights. He then published *New Theory of the National Body*[6] in 1874. In this work he championed popular sovereignty, writing that "the greatest meaning of the nation is attained in the sovereign and government viewing the people as most important, in particular making the pursuit of the people's security and happiness their goal and existing only for the sake of realizing this aim," and reiterated his theory of innate rights: "The right to liberty is innate, and is the greatest tool in the pursuit of security and happiness."[7]

Katō can also be described as the first major figure in Japan to devote his attention to freedom and civil rights theory. When he took charge of the University of Tokyo in 1881, however, he came to view the idea of innate rights as clearly mistaken, even appealing to the government for *Outline of a True Politics* and *New Theory of the National Body* to be taken out of print. In the following year he published *A New Doctrine of Human Rights*[8] and undertook a critique of civil rights thought from the perspective of social Darwinism. Those who are superior will always triumph, those who are inferior will be defeated, and only the former will survive—this was an "eternal, unchanging law of nature," and society, too, had evolved in accordance with this law of survival of the fittest. He claimed that proponents of the theory of innate rights who asserted that all human beings are born with the rights of freedom and equality were nothing more than "advocates of delusion."[9] Behind this change in Katō's views was presumably the gradual shift toward conservatism in the political environment following the release of the petition for the establishment of a popularly chosen assembly[10] in 1874, and it can also be supposed that he had become more acutely aware of the position in which he himself had been placed.

(2) Fenollosa and Spencerian Philosophy

The first course related to philosophy at the University of Tokyo was taught by Edward W. Syle (1817–1890). Born in Britain, Syle had emigrated to America and evangelized in both China and Japan as a missionary of the

Episcopal Church. In 1874 he became an instructor at Tokyo Kaisei School, where he taught morality and history. In his courses on morality, he used Mark Hopkins's *Theory of Man* and Joseph Haven's *Mental Philosophy* as his textbooks.[11] When the University of Tokyo was created through the merging of Tokyo Kaisei School and Tokyo Medical School in 1877, he continued teaching history and moral science at the newly established university, but he did not have a strong influence on his students. In an "Addendum" to Inoue Tetsujirō's *Reflections on the World of Meiji Philosophy*,[12] Miyake Yūjirō (1869–1945, pen name "Miyake Setsurei"), who entered the fourth class at the University of Tokyo in 1879, wrote, "There was a lot of theology and not much philosophy; he didn't refer to philosophy enough to say that we encountered philosophy [in his course]."[13]

The first to properly introduce Western philosophy at the University of Tokyo was Ernest Francisco Fenollosa (1853–1908). After studying at Harvard University, at the age of twenty-five Fenollosa was given a position teaching politics, economics, and the history of philosophy at the University of Tokyo in 1878, having been recommended by Edward Morse, who at the time was teaching zoology there. He later focused his teaching mainly on philosophy. He taught at the University of Tokyo for eight years before moving to the Ministry of Education in 1886 and later to the Tokyo School of Art, and during his time at the university he played an important role in the education of many students, including Inoue Tetsujirō.

According to his "Declaration" included in the *Tokyo University Faculties of Law, Science, and Literature Annual Report* and the *Tokyo University Faculties of Law, Science, and Literature List* for academic years 1878 and 1879, in his course on the history of philosophy for second year students, Fenollosa, as was noted in the introduction, drew on texts such as Albert Schwegler's *Geschicte der Philosophie im Umriß*, George Henry Lewes's *A Biographical History of Philosophy*, and Francis Bowen's *Modern Philosophy from Descartes to Schopenhauer and Hartmann* in presenting the history of modern philosophy from Descartes to Hegel and Spencer. Through this course, modern German philosophy from Kant to Hegel was introduced in detail for the first time in Japan. Miyake Setsurei, who attended these lectures on philosophy in 1880–1881, later wrote about the impression they made on him in a book entitled *Universities Then and Now*.[14]

In August of 1878, an American called Fenollosa arrived and began teaching economics at the preparatory school and philosophy at the university. In this period in which the Department of Philosophy was not independent, Fenollosa's classes were very interesting and captured students' attention. Philosophy had previously been taught by Professor Toyama [Masakazu], who had focused mainly on Spencer's *First Principles* [1862], but Fenollosa simply and eloquently laid out thinkers from Descartes to Kant, Fichte, Schelling and Hegel, introducing German philosophy within a short time frame. There were aspects [of what he taught] that had been largely unknown to the British scholar [Edward W. Syle, who had taught at the University of Tokyo prior to Fenollosa's arrival] and to society at large, things that sparked one's interest, sounded novel to our ears, and gave us the sense of having only then discovered what sort of inquiry philosophy was.[15]

At Harvard, Fenollosa had been most strongly influenced by Spencer's evolutionary philosophy, which was tied to Darwin's theory of evolution and had been extremely influential at the time. Spencer's evolutionary philosophy had been welcomed more warmly in America than in his native Britain, and around 1880 it sparked an unprecedented "Spencer boom" in the United States. Fenollosa had been a student during the height of this boom. According to the recollections of his wife, Mary, Fenollosa had devoted considerable effort to the formation of the "Spencer club" when he was a student a Harvard.[16]

Given this academic background, it was natural that Fenollosa would promote philosophy based on the theory of evolution at the University of Tokyo. When he died in 1908, the following passage was included in an article entitled "Former Professor Fenollosa Passes Away" published in the "Miscellaneous Records" section of the *Journal of Philosophy*[17] (no. 260), the journal of the University of Tokyo's Society of Philosophy.

Edward S. Morse took up a teaching position in [the faculty of] science, and greatly promoted the theory of evolution. At almost the same time Dr. Toyama [Masakazu] returned from abroad and espoused the theory of evolution alongside others such as Yatabe [Ryōkichi] in [the faculty of] science. Mr. Fenollosa then arrived, and he too advocated the theory of evolution; the intellectual world of the Imperial University was brimming with evolutionary discourse.

In the introduction, I noted that Spencer's *Social Statics* was published in translation under the title "Social Equal Rights Theory"[18] and had a strong influence on those sympathetic to the freedom and civil rights movement.

Parallel to this, Spencer's evolutionary philosophy was also being heavily promoted by educators at the University of Tokyo such as Fenollosa and Toyama Masakazu during the second decade of the Meiji period. It is generally said that Spencer's thought contains a combination of two aspects. One is the natural law and individualism aspect seen in his early works such as *Social Statics*. The other is the organic conception of society that comes to the fore in his later works such as *The Principles of Sociology* (1876–1896). In America it was mainly his later thought that found acceptance under the influence of dominant, conservative social forces, but in Japan both aspects of his thought were taken up separately. Fenollosa had undergone his intellectual formation in America during the peak of the adoption of Spencerian thought, with a focus on the organic theory of society, and it was from this perspective that he gave talks and lectures on Spencer's philosophy. In a report to the Minister of Education submitted shortly after arriving in Japan, Fenollosa argued that it was necessary to establish "fundamental principles of society" as a subject within the Faculty of Letters of the University of Tokyo and to teach students that society was an organism. He also gave lectures along these lines. The content of these addresses was translated by Inoue Tetsujirō and published under the title "Theory of the Advancement of the State of Society"[19] in *Arts and Sciences Review*,[20] the journal of the faculties of law, science, and letters of the University of Tokyo, in 1880. Beginning in 1881, Fenollosa also gave lectures on "state of society studies [sociology]"[21] as an official subject at the University of Tokyo.

Fenollosa's introduction of Spencerian thought focusing on the organic theory of society brought about a major transformation in the acceptance of Spencer in Japan. Takahashi Akira writes about this in an essay entitled "The Formation of Social Psychology in Japan."[22]

> Fenollosa urged a reconsideration of the trend toward radicalism in the interpretation of Spencer, and by pointing out the "moderation" in Spencer's theory of social change laid the groundwork for the transformation in interpretation from "Spencer as a textbook for the theory of people's rights" to "Spencer as a manual for the theory of state power" that would eventually occur.[23]

In fact, in his lectures published as "Theory of the Advancement of the State of Society," while on the one hand talking about "innate freedom," on the other hand Fenollosa also said, "If to begin with a despotic government had not emerged, bent the barbarous people to its will, taught and guided them, and created a spirit of obedience, then an era in which this freedom demonstrates the power to actively expand would surely never have arisen. It is therefore not wrong to say that despotic government is the swaddling clothes of freedom."[24] In Fenollosa's view, first despotic government is established and then freedom is realized; it is impossible to circumvent this order.

(3) Fenollosa's German Philosophy Course

During his student years, Fenollosa's attention was first captured by Spencer's evolutionary philosophy, but eventually he encountered Hegelian philosophy via such sources as the lectures of Francis Bowen (1811–1890), who possessed a profound understanding of German philosophy, and the *Journal of Speculative Philosophy*, a journal published by the St. Louis Philosophical Society that played a major role in the reception of Hegelian philosophy in America, and seems to have been powerfully drawn to this school of thought.[25] Based on this interest, he taught a course focusing mainly on modern German philosophy and Hegel in particular at the University of Tokyo. Kiyozawa Manshi, who attended Fenollosa's course on the history of philosophy in the 1884 academic year and who would himself later go on to teach the history of Western philosophy at Shinshu University, stated in one of his own lectures, "At the University of Tokyo, Mr. Fenollosa praises Hegel effusively, and has said that from now on philosophy will be nothing more than the development of Hegel's philosophy."[26]

Fenollosa was thus someone influenced by evolutionary philosophy on the one hand and Hegelian philosophy on the other, and we can glean what he thought about the relationship between these two branches of philosophy from the records of his lectures. According to notes on his history of philosophy course taken by Sakatani Yoshirō (a student in the fifth class at the University of Tokyo), after discussing the philosophy of Spencer and Hegel, Fenollosa said the following.

> If I can unite the doctrine of Spencer's Evolution and Hegel's philosophy, we will have a complete philosophy, and we believe this will be done within next thirty or forty years. Only the weakness of Hegel is his scanty knowledge of science. Two supplement one another. Spencer's Evolution supplies the deficiency of mechanical evolution. Though Spencer and Hegel seem to be quite different, but in reality most closely connected. Indeed, without the doctrine of Hegel, Spencer's Evolution is utterly inconceivable.[27]

As the words of Miyake Setsurei quoted above indicate, Fenollosa's course on German philosophy, the first such course ever given in Japan, greatly stimulated his students' interest. But his higher-year courses did not always satisfy them. In *Universities Then and Now*, Miyake himself writes, "Even Fenollosa, while he was instructive and interesting when he taught the introduction to philosophy, later [in higher-year courses] stuck only to literal readings of the works of Hume and English translations of Kant and Hegel without adding anything of particular note."[28]

One year, Fenollosa used Hegel's *Wissenschaft der Logik* (*Science of Logic*) as a text in his course, but his decision to use an English translation was not welcomed by students who had worked very hard to learn German. It can be surmised that his courses not being able to satisfy more advanced students was the result of factors such as his having had to teach courses in a wide range of fields, including politics, economics, and sociology, while himself still a young scholar, and the fact that while he had developed an interest in German philosophy, he had not studied it as a specialist. As I will discuss in part 5 of this chapter, it may also have had something to do with the fact that his own interest became drawn more toward Japanese art.

There is no doubt, however, that Fenollosa opened a new page in the history of the teaching of philosophy in Japan. Students who attended his classes included Ariga Nagao, Miyake Setsurei, Tsubouchi Shōyō, Inoue Enryō, Tokunaga (Kiyozawa) Manshi, Sawayanagi Masatarō, and Ōnishi Hajime.[29] After graduating, most of these students would go on to lecture in this field and make their own mark on the history of philosophy. In this sense it is no exaggeration to say that Fenollosa's courses were the starting point of the reception of the history of Western philosophy in Japan.

2. The Identity of Phenomenon and Reality—
The Philosophy of Inoue Tetsujirō and Inoue Enryō

(1) Inoue Tetsujirō's "Philosophy of Phenomenon-Reality Identity"

In the early days of the University of Tokyo's Faculty of Letters, an extraordinarily diverse group of people emerged from the Department of History, Philosophy (*tetsugaku*) and Politics (later subdivided into the Department of Philosophy and the Department of Politics and Economics). Examples of such figures include Inoue Tetsujirō, Okakura Tenshin, Kanō Jigorō, Miyake

Setsurei, Tsubouchi Shōyō, Inoue Enryō, and Sawayanagi Masatarō. I would like to begin by discussing Inoue Tetsujirō, a long-standing pillar of the study and teaching of philosophy in the academy. After studying philosophy under Fenollosa in the inaugural class at the University of Tokyo, Inoue went abroad to study in Germany, and upon his return to Japan in 1890 immediately became a professor in the University of Tokyo's Faculty of Letters. While in Germany he studied under Kuno Fischer at the University of Heidelberg and Wilhelm Wundt at the University of Leipzig. Later he took up a position as a teacher of Japanese at the University of Berlin's newly established School of Eastern Languages. After returning to Japan, he devoted himself to introducing students to German philosophers such as Kant and Schopenhauer.

One of Inoue's greatest achievements occurred prior to his time studying abroad: he played a leading role in compiling and publishing Japan's first philosophical dictionary, *Dictionary of Philosophy*[30] (University of Tokyo Three Faculties Printing, 1881). This dictionary did not explain the meaning of philosophical jargon, providing only Japanese terms corresponding to foreign words, but it played a major role in determining the technical language that would be used in discussing Western philosophy in Japanese. Most of the academic jargon that became standard in Japanese was coined by Nishi Amane, but Inoue is credited with having come up with the Japanese equivalents of words like "ethics,"[31] "linguistics,"[32] "absolute,"[33] "wordview,"[34] and "personality."[35]

Inoue made other diverse contributions, but most notable when it comes to the later development of philosophy in Japan was his attempt to work out an original approach he called the "Philosophy of Phenomenon-Reality Identity."

In his "Main Points of the Philosophy of Phenomenon-Reality Identity,"[36] published in the *Journal of Philosophy* in 1897, while on the one hand rejecting the stance that the world emerges only from phenomena, or the view that what truly exists are the concepts of reality obtained within consciousness, on the other hand Inoue also rejects the approach that divides the world into reality and phenomena, maintaining that an unchanging underlying reality is the basis of phenomena and that phenomena are nothing more than its derivative manifestations. He describes his own stance as the "philosophy of phenomenon-reality identity." He explains this approach as follows.

> Reality and phenomena are in the end the same world; it is not that phenomena emerge out of reality, but rather that phenomena are themselves reality. We abstract [parts of this unity] and make

a distinction between reality and phenomenon, but these are merely two ways of being of what is essentially a single entity; in essence they are identical and inseparable. Fundamentally they are not different things; there is no reality separate from phenomena, and there are no phenomena separate from reality. Together they form a unity that creates the world.[37]

Inoue's understanding was that although phenomena and reality are indeed distinguished when we focus on different aspects, in fact phenomena are reality, and as a unity both compose the world.

In Inoue's later years, he once again discussed his "philosophy of phenomenon-reality identity" in his "Reflections on the World of Meiji Philosophy," distinguishing between what he called "monistic, superficial realism," "dualistic realism," and the "philosophy of phenomenon-reality identity." "Monistic, superficial realism" is a realism in which phenomena are straightforwardly real just as they are. "Dualistic realism," in contrast, is a stance in which phenomena and reality are clearly distinguished, and a world of reality that differs from the world of phenomena is thought to exist behind it. The "philosophy of phenomenon-reality identity" is of course Inoue's own approach, and here he explains it using the Buddhist concept of discrimination and equality. In one aspect, the world is made up of phenomena that appear to have their own distinct forms, or in other words through discrimination. Running through all of these phenomena, however, is something they have in common. In other words, there is also an aspect of equality. As concepts they are distinguished, but in fact they are unified. This aspect of discrimination and aspect of equality, or, to put it another way, phenomena and reality, are fused; in other words, the main idea of Inoue's "philosophy of phenomenon-reality identity" is that "phenomena accompany reality, and reality penetrates phenomena."[38]

In his "Main Points of the Philosophy of Phenomenon-Reality Identity," Inoue says of his "philosophy of phenomenon-reality identity" that "as this worldview adopts the perspective of 'perfect fusion and mutual identity,'[39] it can also be called the 'philosophy of perfect interfusion of reality,' "[40] and here we can see the influence of the idea of "perfect fusion and mutual identity," spoken of in particular in the Tiantai and Huayan schools of Buddhism, which hold that while contrasting things are distinct from one another, at the same time they are also identical and interpenetrating. The Buddhist concept of "perfect fusion" can be said to lie at the root of Inoue's idea of "phenomenon-reality identity."

Inoue's encounter with Buddhist thought at the University of Tokyo came through the lectures of Hara Tanzan[41] (1819–1892), a monk of the Sōtō school of Zen Buddhism (at the time Inoue attended his lectures, Hara had been temporarily deprived of his monkhood). At the request of Katō Hiroyuki, supervisor of the faculties of law, science, and letters, as a lecturer in the Department of Japanese and Chinese Literature in the Faculty of Letters, Hara took charge of a "Buddhist writings course" set up outside of the department's formal subjects in which he lectured on classic Buddhist texts such as *Awakening of Faith in the Mahāyāna* (in 1882 this course was renamed "Indian Philosophy"). The establishment of this course can be seen as having been a bold decision given the circumstances in which Buddhism had been placed following the anti-Buddhist movement known as *haibutsu kishaku* (abolish Buddhism and destroy Shākyamuni). It was of great significance not only in terms of the reevaluation of Buddhism but also in regard to the formation of Japanese philosophy.

In both his *Reminiscences*[42] and *Autobiography*,[43] Inoue writes that it was through Hara's lectures on Buddhist texts that he first learned the subtleties of Mahāyāna Buddhism, and from that point onward he continued to study this religion. He focused in particular on the concept of "suchness"[44] described in *Awakening of Faith in the Mahāyāna*. In "The Relationship Between Cognition and Reality," published in 1901, Inoue stated that existence cannot be expressed as a concept that is only valid in the phenomenal world of being/nonbeing, and the quality of "suchness" described in *Awakening of Faith in the Mahāyāna*, which "stands apart from speech and from names" and "is neither being nor nonbeing,"[45] was more fitting.

Interestingly, in the *Dictionary of Philosophy* Inoue gives *shinnyo*, the Japanese word for the Buddhist term "suchness," along with *jittai* (actual body) as a translation of "reality." He refers readers to the following phrase in *Awakening of Faith in the Mahāyāna*: "One should know that truth cannot be spoken or thought—that is why it is called 'suchness.'"

In *Awakening of Faith in the Mahāyāna* it is said that there are two aspects to all beings, the "suchness mind" and the "arising and disappearing mind." In its true essence the mind transcends vain distinctions and goes beyond arising and disappearing, but in practice it is captivated by passions and desires and is itself repeatedly arising and disappearing. But these two aspects are not separate entities; *Awakening of Faith in the Mahāyāna* describes arising and disappearing being nonarising and nondisappearing, since "nonarising and nondisappearing are in harmony with arising and disappearing; they are neither identical nor distinct." When Inoue asserts that reality and phenomena, while in one aspect distinct from each other, are in essence identical and inseparable and fused together create the world, this can be seen as having been based on this understanding of "suchness" in *Awakening of Faith in the Mahāyāna*.[46]

Before going abroad to study in Germany in 1884, Inoue taught "the history of Eastern philosophy" for one year as an assistant professor in the University of Tokyo's Faculty of Letters (Inoue Enryō and Miyake Setsurei were among his students), and his having been greatly influenced by Hara Tanzan and having maintained a strong interest in Buddhism are reflected in the taking up of this topic. Even after returning to Japan and becoming a professor at the University of Tokyo, Inoue continued to be interested in Eastern philosophy along with Western philosophy and gave lectures on Indian philosophy. He later also lectured on topics such as various schools of Japanese Neo-Confucianism and Shinto. These lectures were collected in *The Philosophy of the Japanese Yangming School*[47] (1900), *The Philosophy of the Japanese Ancient Learning School*[48] (1902b), and *The Philosophy of the Japanese Shushi [Zhu Xi] School*[49] (1905). In these works, Inoue organized the thought of Edo-period philosophers in line with Western categories of academic inquiry (cosmology, psychology, ethics, and so on) and attempted to highlight the existence of these distinct "schools." Together with Kanie Yoshimaru he edited *The Compendium of Japanese Ethics* (Ikuseikai, 1901–1902), which organized Edo-period Confucianism into five schools with the addition of the Compromise School[50] and the Independent School[51] to the three schools already mentioned and published their texts and related historical materials. Inoue's framework for understanding Edo-period Confucianism strongly influenced later studies of Japanese thought.

In "Reflections on the World of Meiji Philosophy," Inoue criticized the "lack of philosophical spirit" of the status quo in which Western philosophy was simply taken up and repeated and Eastern philosophy, when it was addressed at all, was merely studied out of philological interest, and argued that the task for thinkers of his era was to "construct more advanced philosophical thought"[52] by comparing Eastern philosophy to Western philosophy. From these words it is clear that Inoue was not focused exclusively on Western philosophy but also studied Eastern philosophy extensively and was keenly aware of the need to combine the two traditions and develop them conjointly. This stance of Inoue's also influenced others such as Inoue Enryō and Miyake Setsurei. Here we can find one of the main characteristics of Meiji-period philosophers.

Inoue Tetsujirō strove to hammer out a distinctive philosophical stance through his "philosophy of phenomenon-reality identity," but as Funayama

Shin'ichi pointed out in *Studies in the History of Meiji Philosophy*,[53] prior to his own scholarship this undertaking had not received sufficient recognition in the study of Meiji-era philosophy. Funayama's observation that the history of Meiji philosophy up until that point had been drab and shallow because it had failed to portray Inoue as the "peak determiner of the character of Meiji philosophy" is apt. His claim that Nishida Kitarō's philosophy of "pure experience," while of course in one sense possessing a unique character not found in the "philosophy of phenomenon-reality identity," in another sense took up this philosophy and "developed and made it great" can also be said to have raised an important point.

Addressing the interactions between subjectivity, objectivity, and existence in "The Relationship Between Cognition and Existence," for example, Inoue writes, "Reality does not exist separately and distinctly from subjectivity and objectivity and occupy the position of a third party (tertium quid); in 'reality' (Wesen) there is no distinction between subjectivity and objectivity."[54] It does indeed seem possible that this understanding showed Nishida, who studied under Inoue, a direction in which to form and develop his thought. When he championed this fusion of phenomenon and reality Inoue did not sufficiently explain how it was formed. Regarding this point it was not a fully worked out theory, but Nishida seems to have been intrigued by this concept.

In this sense, examining Nishida's assertions in *An Inquiry into the Good*[55] that " 'reality' is only our phenomena of consciousness that are facts of direct experience" and "in the facts of direct experience there is neither opposition of subject and object nor distinction between mental and physical; there is only a single reality of mind that is thing and thing that is mind" in connection with Inoue's "philosophy of phenomenon-reality identity"[56] is an important undertaking. The many notes Nishida set down while writing *An Inquiry into the Good* have been collected as "Fragments Concerning Pure Experience,"[57] and among them is a fragment entitled "Fundamental Principles of Buddhism."[58] It is also interesting that in this context he writes, "Mahāyāna Buddhism is a philosophy of phenomenon-reality identity. It is a philosophy of concrete monism. Suchness and creation/destruction are the same thing, just like water and waves. Distinction that is nondistinction, nondistinction that is distinction—eventually the three marks of the dharma return to a single, true mark."[59] This indicates that Nishida was aware of the fact that Inoue had put forward his "philosophy of phenomenon-reality identity" on the basis of *Awakening of Faith in the Mahāyāna*.

(2) Inoue Enryō's "Philosophy of Phenomenon-Reality Identity"

The "philosophy of phenomenon-reality identity" did not belong to Inoue Tetsujirō alone. Inoue Enryō (1858–1919), who was a student in the sixth class at the University of Tokyo and thus Inoue Tetsujirō's junior, was also a proponent of this way of thinking. While he did not refer to his own approach as the "philosophy of phenomenon-reality identity," Inoue Enryō in fact presented this idea before Inoue Tetsujirō; it can already be seen in *An Evening of Philosophical Conversation*,[60] published in 1886. In the first part of this text, "On the Relationship Between the World of the Mind and the World of Things," Inoue Enryō begins by retreating from materialism, which "holds that the world is only things without the mind," and idealism, which "holds that the world is only in the mind, and there are no things existing outside it," as one-sided, biased ways of thinking. He also rejects a rationalism that asserts that a "nonthing, nonmind principle" that combines things and the mind constitutes fundamental reality and "holds that there are neither minds nor things outside of this principle" as a position that is biased toward principle. Here he presents the idea that principle is not something separate from things and the mind; on the contrary, "principle contains things and the mind, and things and the mind are furnished by principle; the two are different, but neither can be separated from the other. They cannot be separated, but they are not without distinction. This is the middle path of philosophy."[61] This can be described as the first time the perspective that has been called the "philosophy of phenomenon-reality identity" was expressed and given a concrete form.[62]

Inoue Enryō was a philosopher, but at the same time he was also a Buddhist and considered it his mission to revive a Buddhism that had lost its vitality. He wrote many works from this perspective, one of which was *An Introduction to a Discourse to Revitalize Buddhism*[63] (1887). In it he uses the term "suchness" to describe what is referred to as principle (*ri*) in *An Evening of Philosophical Conversation*. Borrowing the metaphor of waves and water (Inoue Enryō too had attended Hara Tanzan's "Lectures on Mahāyāna Buddhism"), he explains the relationship between suchness and relative existence as follows.

> Water is like absolute suchness, waves are like all things relative; all things not having one shape is like the many particular shapes of waves, the fundamental substance of suchness being

> equal and universal is like the substance of water being without
> distinction . . . the reason for the inseparability of suchness and
> all things is shown by there being no water separate from waves
> and no waves separate from water.[64]

He then concludes that "in short, the relationship between suchness and all things is sameness that is different, and difference that is the same. One that is two, and two that are one. In Buddhism this is called 'perfect fusion and mutual identity.' "[65]

In 1909, twenty-three years after publishing *An Evening of Philosophical Conversation*, Inoue Enryō penned a work entitled *A New Conception of Philosophy* in which he once again presented his own stance and attempted to work out an original philosophy through the "synthetic formation" of Western and Eastern philosophy. In this text he engaged in highly systematic thought, but his fundamental stance was the "philosophy of phenomenon-reality identity" he had been pursuing since *An Evening of Philosophical Conversation*.

Here Inoue Enryō distinguishes material phenomena and the material suchness that is their substance from mental phenomena and the mental suchness that is their substance, but according to him the two are in essence one. They are in a relationship of "things that are neither one nor two but contain each other." He also asserts that this relationship exists in regard to material suchness and mental suchness, expressing this with the phrase "mutual inclusion of suchnesses." He also states that there is at the root of the world of things and the world of the mind something that unifies these two worlds, and he describes this with the terms "singular suchness," "original suchness," and "true origin." He then adds the following statement regarding the relationship between these worlds of things and the mind and the singular suchness that is their substance.

> While in the substance of singular suchness all forms and all
> perceptions are put in place, embraced, incorporated, included
> and made to manifest both the world of things and the world
> of the mind, at the same time all forms and all perceptions put
> singular suchness that is the true origin in place, embrace it,
> incorporate it, and include it, and this interrelatedness extends
> without limit; within each thing, each particle, and each element
> the singular suchness that is the true origin is subsumed, within
> each mind and each perception the singular suchness that is the

true origin is incorporated, and this interrelatedness also extends without limit.[66]

From this perspective, along with asserting that the truth of the universe can be expressed as "phenomena and suchness include each other, [material] suchness and [mental] suchness include each other,"[67] Inoue Enryō describes the position at which he ultimately arrived as follows. "Observation that takes as its starting point the world of things, reasoning based on the world of the mind, an approach that focuses on experience and emphasizes cognition—there is a certain logic to all of these ways of thinking, and the way of thinking at which I arrived was a theory of infinite mutual inclusion that comprehensively compiles all of these views."[68] His ultimate philosophical stance can be described as a "theory of mutual inclusion that brings together all arguments and views."[69]

Inoue Enryō's main contribution to philosophy is thus to be found in his attempt to work out a "philosophy of phenomenon-reality identity" together with Inoue Tetsujirō. With the endorsement of figures such as Katō Hiroyuki and Nishi Amane, together with Inoue Tetsujirō and Miyake Setsurei he also organized the Society of Philosophy[70] and founded the *Journal of Philosophy*. In addition to these undertakings, in order to make philosophy accessible to older students, those without many resources, and those unable to read foreign languages, Inoue Enryō also established the Philosophy Academy (now Tōyō University),[71] published the lectures given there as the "Record of Philosophy Academy Lectures,"[72] and created opportunities for people to encounter philosophy outside of the Philosophy Academy. These activities played a major role in philosophy transcending the framework of the university and extending its roots more broadly in society.

Attention has also been paid to the fact that Inoue Enryō, like Inoue Tetsujirō, adopted a stance of attempting to combine Eastern and Western philosophy and develop them together. This outlook is featured in *Key Points of Philosophy* (books 1 and 2),[73] published in 1886–1887. Book 1 is the first history of philosophy, providing an overview from ancient to modern times written by a Japanese thinker, and its main features are its linking of the history of philosophy to an outline of philosophical thought (book 2) and the fact that the history of philosophy it presents is not limited to Western philosophy but also includes the philosophy of the East. Of course, Inoue Enryō clearly acknowledges the superiority of Western philosophy as philosophy. He sees this superiority in the emphasis placed on supporting logic using facts and in various theories constantly competing to establish truth and falsehood as they strive to develop. His decision to nevertheless compose his history in two parts, including both Western and Eastern philosophy, was the result of his belief that Western philosophy was not perfect and his hope that in the future Eastern philosophy might be able to contribute to its development. This view is evident in a text entitled "On the Need for Philosophy and the History of This Society"[74] he wrote for the *Journal of Philosophy*, the journal of the Society of Philosophy that had been established in the University of Tokyo's Faculty of Letters in 1887.

> We in the East have a distinctive philosophy studied since ancient times that has not been examined in the West. New perspectives can naturally be found within it. Today I am studying this here in Japan and contrasting it with Western philosophy, and if someday I am able to extract the best from both traditions and create a new school of philosophy this will be a great honor not only for me but for the entire nation of Japan.[75]

This passage further demonstrates the broad overview of the history of philosophy Inoue Enryō maintained while engaging in his own philosophical thought.

3. The Reception of Philosophy Through Writings on the History of Philosophy—Miyake Setsurei and Kiyozawa Manshi

(1) MIYAKE SETSUREI'S *PHILOSOPHICAL TRIFLES*

As I noted in the introduction, the discourse on the history of philosophy played an important role in the reception of philosophy in Japan. From the beginning to the middle of the Meiji period a great number of foreign texts on the history of philosophy were translated into Japanese, and eventually thinkers such as Miyake Setsurei, Kiyozawa Manshi, Ōnishi Hajime, and Hatano Seiichi began to lecture and publish their own writings on this subject. Through their work, philosophy came to be established as a branch of academic inquiry. Particularly influential in this process was Miyake Setsurei's *Philosophical Trifles*, published in 1889 (the twenty-second year of the Meiji period).[76]

Miyake (1860–1945) was a student in the fourth class admitted to the University of Tokyo and was taught by the likes of Fenollosa and

Toyama Masakazu. He would go on to work as an independent journalist and critic, but in the early part of his career he devoted his energies to the formation of the Society of Philosophy and publication of the *Journal of Philosophy* (along with Inoue Tetsujirō, Inoue Enryō, and others), and with *Philosophical Trifles* published the first proper history of early modern and modern philosophy by a Japanese scholar.

As is stated in the explanatory notes to the text, most of the materials upon which this book was based were drawn from the writings on the history of philosophy by the Hegelian historians of philosophy Albert Schwegler (1819–1857) and Kuno Fischer (1824–1907). Following Fischer, Miyake divided early modern and modern philosophy into three categories: "dogmatic philosophy"[77] (subdivided into empiricist and rationalist schools), "skeptical philosophy"[78] (the philosophy of thinkers such as Berkeley and Hume), and "critical philosophy"[79] (the philosophy of German idealism from Kant to Hegel). It was the last of these categories, "critical philosophy," that Miyake described in greatest detail, writing of Hegel that he "truly produces a denouement for philosophy."[80] In comparison to Nakae Chōmin's *History of Philosophy*, for example, Miyake's history of philosophy is characterized by a much more detailed account of German philosophy after Kant, particularly that of Hegel, and a high regard for this branch of philosophy. Here we can see the influence of Fenollosa and of the view of the history of philosophy espoused by the Hegelian school. The most significant aspect of Miyake's work is that the view of the history of Western philosophy he presented established the framework for the understanding of this history in Japan from that time forward.

One of the points worth noting in *Philosophical Trifles* is that it included the first use of what would become the Japanese translation of the technical term "dialectic."[81] Miyake actually used this word only for Kant's "transzendentale Dialektik" and preferred a different translation for Hegel's dialectic,[82] but it would eventually become the standard translation of this term as well. He describes Hegel's dialectic as follows.

> To illustrate the form of reasoning of the dialectic, first, when there is an original thesis "A," a contradictory thesis "not-A" will necessarily arise. When "A" and "not-A" are already in opposition, while they of course contradict each other, at the same time there is always a reasoning that reconciles them, and a new thesis "B" that synthesizes them will arise. When this happens, "A" is called the "thesis," "not-A" is called the "antithesis" and "B" is called the "synthesis."[83]

Here it is notable that the dialectic is understood extremely schematically as a formula in which "A" and "not-A" are synthesized by "B."[84] This characteristic is also seen in the approach of Kiyozawa Manshi, and I will touch on it again when I discuss him later in this section.

Another point worth noting in *Philosophical Trifles* is that before beginning his account of the history of Western philosophy, Miyake includes a chapter entitled "Eastern Philosophy and Western Philosophy" in which he argues against the view that Western culture is unambiguously superior to Eastern culture. Following the path of thinkers such as Inoue Tetsujirō and Inoue Enryō, he formulated a synthesis of Eastern and Western philosophy. Of course, Miyake was not unaware of the weakness of Eastern philosophy. Informed by the understanding of Nishi Amane, in concrete terms he saw Eastern philosophy's flaw as its having "stopped at merely interpreting the words of the founders in every school and every discourse."[85] He points out that Eastern philosophy ultimately fell into exegetical interpretation of the statements of its founding figures without examining them objectively and scientifically, creating a situation in which only devotees took any interest in it, and declares that "Eastern philosophy exists [nominally] but does not exist [substantially]." The reason that Miyake remained interested in Eastern philosophy despite this flaw was that in his understanding philosophy included, or ought to include, the three domains of knowledge, sentiment, and will. He believed that while Western philosophy had indeed demonstrated overwhelming superiority in the field of knowledge, in Eastern philosophy knowledge was deeply connected to practice, and on this point there was much that Eastern philosophy could contribute. (From this perspective Miyake focused on Wang Yangming, known for his doctrine of the integration of knowledge and action, and published a book entitled *Wang Yangming*[86] in 1893.)

Miyake thus adopted a stance of using what should be used and discarding what should be discarded in regard to philosophy. Based on this approach, at the conclusion of *Philosophical Trifles* he writes as follows.

> Confucianism came to our country a long time ago. As did Buddhism. If Western philosophy is injected here, mixes and combines with these traditions, and further evolves and develops anew, then the East may come to dominate philosophy in the world of the twentieth century.[87]

He expected new possibilities to open up through the traditions of Confucianism and Buddhism and the precise argumentation of Western philosophy coming into contact with each other.

(2) Kiyozawa Manshi's *Lectures on the History of Western Philosophy* and the Reception of Hegel's Dialectic

Kiyozawa Manshi (1863–1903) chose the path of religion rather than scholarship after graduating from the University of Tokyo, and as a result did not leave behind many achievements in the field of philosophy. He nevertheless won considerable renown in his own era for books such as *Skeleton of a Philosophy of Religion*[88] (1892). For example, in the chapter entitled "The Meiji World" in his *Lectures on the History of Japanese Literature*,[89] Fujioka Sakutarō (1870–1910) writes, "The names Ōnishi Hajime and Kiyozawa Manshi figured prominently in the intellectual milieu of the day, and must not be omitted from any discussion of Meiji philosophy and religion."[90] Fujioka was a scholar of Japanese literature, and not particularly familiar with the world of philosophy. But Nishida Kitarō, when he was invited to give a lecture at a meeting commemorating the twenty-fifth anniversary of Kiyozawa Manshi's death, is also reported to have said that "while in the past there were quite a few Japanese scholars of philosophy, it is Ōnishi Hajime and Kiyozawa Manshi who should be called Japanese philosophers."[91] While there were many who could be called "scholars of philosophy," in Nishida's eyes only these two merited the title "philosophers," having been thinkers who took their own stance and did not merely introduce Western philosophy.

Kiyozawa lectured on the history of Western philosophy at Shinshū Daigakuryō (a school that later became Ōtani University) from 1890 to 1893.[92] Unlike *Philosophical Trifles*, his lectures covered everything from ancient to modern philosophy, right up to figures such as Lotze, Comte, and Spencer, and while they were not published at the time they constituted the best history of philosophy that had been presented in Japan up to that point, both in terms of broadness of perspective and depth of understanding. While he drew on works by scholars such as Schwegler, Bowen, and Lewes that he had encountered when studying under Fenollosa, rather than simply paraphrasing these texts Kiyozawa added his own "critique" of their content after thoroughly digesting them and summarizing their main points.

In the chapter on Hegel in *Lectures on the History of Western Philosophy*, Kiyozawa writes, "At the University of Tokyo Fenollosa praises Hegel highly, and says that in the future philosophy will only be the development of Hegel's thought."[93] He also praises Hegel himself, writing that "there is no disputing that Hegel's philosophy does indeed take the correct approach."[94] This included Hegel's dialectic, which he viewed as an essential element of Hegel's philosophy and characterized as its "law of the development of principles." But his understanding, like that of Miyake, was extremely schematic. He writes, "Where there is a thesis and an antithesis, there is always a synthesis"[95] and appends the following diagram.

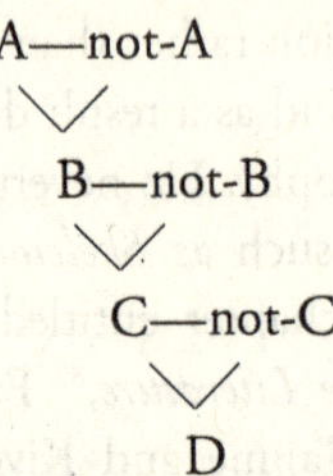

This schematic understanding of the dialectic did not stop with Miyake and Kiyozawa. Similar approaches are also found in Inoue Enryō's *Key Points of Philosophy: Book 1* (1886), Kuwaki Gen'yoku's *Overview of Philosophy* (1900), and Tanabe Hajime's *Outline of Philosophy* (1933). Kuwaki (1874–1946), for example, explains Hegel's dialectic as follows with the aid of a diagram, clearly demonstrating an understanding of the dialectic as a highly mechanical process of development.

> When there is a thesis, an antithesis must inevitably distinguish itself and emerge from within it. When thesis and antithesis oppose each other, both must themselves be synthesized. In other words, the two operations of analysis and synthesis are carried out in sequence.[96]

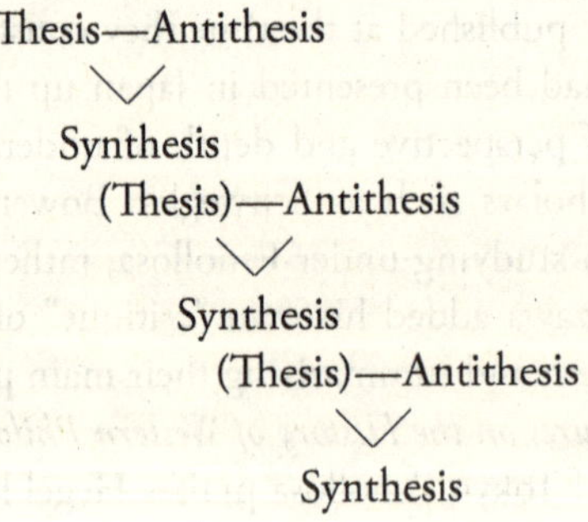

This kind of schematic understanding, in which the opposition between A and not-A is synthesized through B, or the opposition between thesis and antithesis is synthesized by a synthesis, is not found in the writings of Hegel himself. Why this kind of understanding was nevertheless taken up and handed down by early Meiji-period philosophers is an interesting question, and the origins of this approach, as Sakai Osamu points out, can be found in Fenollosa.[97]

Various notes taken by students in Fenollosa's lectures on the history of philosophy at the University of Tokyo have been preserved. One such document was recorded by Sakatani Yoshio in 1881. According to Sakatani's lecture notes, Fenollosa said that "trichotomy" had been discovered by Fichte in the practical domain and had later formed the foundation of Hegel's thought and to a certain extent that of Spencer. He explained trichotomy using the following diagram.[98]

$$A - \text{not } A$$
$$\vee$$
$$A'$$

According to notes recorded by Kiyozawa Manshi, when Fenollosa lectured on Hegel's dialectic he drew the following diagram.[99]

$$A - \text{not } A$$
$$\vee$$
$$A' - \text{not } A'$$
$$\vee$$
$$A'' - \text{not } A''$$
$$\vee$$
$$A'''$$

This presentation seems to have been informed by passages such as the following in Schwegler's *Geschicte der Philosophie im Umriß*. "This Fichtian method (Thesis, Antithesis, Synthesis), like that of Hegel after it, is a combination of the analytic and synthetic methods. Fichte has the merit of having been able, by means of this method, to be the first to deduce all the philosophical fundamental notions from a single point, and to bring them into connection."[100] It is believed that Fenollosa used the previous diagram to explain Fichte's trichotomy and this diagram to explain Hegel's dialectic. There are clear commonalities between this diagram of Fenollosa's and the diagram Kiyozawa Manshi includes in his *Lectures on the History of Western Philosophy*. I have already noted that Fenollosa's lectures became a focal point for the reception of Western philosophy in Japan, and this schematic understanding can also be seen as having been first presented in

Fenollosa's lectures at the University of Tokyo and then taken up by his students. A schematic understanding of the dialectic is not unique to Japan, but the primary cause of its having taken root so firmly here can thus be found in Fenollosa.

(3) KIYOZAWA MANSHI'S PHILOSOPHY OF RELIGION

One of Kiyozawa Manshi's main contributions was laying the foundations of the philosophy of religion in Japan. His profound interest in religious issues was quite natural given that he had studied at the University of Tokyo as a visiting student from Higashi-Hongan Temple and following his graduation had served as principal of Kyoto Prefecture's Jinjō Middle School, in the running of which Higashi-Hongan Temple was deeply involved. His only book published in his lifetime was *Skeleton of a Philosophy of Religion* (1892), in which he addressed issues involving religion and Buddhism but not from within what might be called a "religious" framework. Writing from a new perspective based on the Western system of academic inquiry, he tried to construct his thought as a field of inquiry in Japan. To put it another way, he asked the questions "What is religion?" and "Why does religion exist?" while adopting the standpoint of philosophy or academic inquiry.

As chapter 1, "Religion and Academic Inquiry," of *Skeleton of a Philosophy of Religion* indicates, for Kiyozawa this meant examining the relationships between religion and academic inquiry and between faith and reason. From this perspective, on the one hand he writes, "Why should those who believe in sudden enlightenment, prompt rebirth in the Pure Land, and the existence of an infinite being take up the hard work of philosophical discourse?"[101] and asserts that for those able to directly apprehend an infinite being and acquire faith in religion there is no need to undertake philosophical inquiry. On the other hand, however, he says that reason is something faith cannot do without. When taken literally, there are many things in the teachings of religion that appear contradictory. Faced with these contradictions, doubt emerges about how they are to be understood. Kiyozawa believed that when such doubt arises, we should rely on reason.

> When there is a conflict between faith and what reason tells us, we should discard faith and adopt the teachings of reason. This is the case because while true reason and true faith will ultimately be consistent with each other, reason has the means to correct itself but faith does not.[102]

When there is a conflict between faith and reason, Kiyozawa's view was that we should adopt the stance of reason, which has the capacity to correct itself, and attempt to resolve it. He believed that when there is a conflict between one religion and another, this too should be mediated by reason.

Kiyozawa's having attempted to take a philosophical stance and address issues of religion is also clearly manifested in his viewing the relationship between the finite and the infinite as the issue at the core of religion. According to Kiyozawa, everything that exists, "all things and all changes,"[103] contrasts with every other thing. There are distinctions between them. They do not exist independently but rather in dependence on each other and are imperfect and finite. In contrast to this interdependence, the whole that includes "all things and all changes" is an absolute that has neither limits imposed on it from the outside nor anything to which it should be opposed or contrasted. It is independent, does not rely on anything else, and has no limits; in other words, it is infinite.

Kiyozawa expresses the relationship between the finite and the infinite with the term "duality in the same body."[104] In other words, Kiyozawa's fundamental understanding was that the finite and the infinite were not separate entities but indeed one and the same.

> Are the infinite and the finite the same thing or different things? Let me put it like this. If they are different things, then the finite must exist outside of the infinite. This contradicts the meaning of the infinite. It must not be the case, therefore, that the finite exists outside of the infinite. In other words, the infinite and the finite must be one and the same thing.[105]

If the infinite and the finite are different things, then the finite must exist outside of the infinite. But this would mean that the infinite has limits. The infinite would be something contracted with the finite, and thus would itself become a finite thing. This would contradict the meaning of the infinite. This is Kiyozawa's theory of "duality in the same body." Kiyozawa's theory of the infinite and the finite reexamined the Buddhist worldview from the perspective of philosophy and was underpinned by Hegel's theory of "infinity," that is, his discourse regarding "true infinity" as distinguished from "bad infinity." *Skeleton of a Philosophy of Religion* can be described as a work formed at the intersection of this kind of philosophical reasoning and traditional Buddhist thought.

4. The Formation of Critical/Rational Thought— Ōnishi Hajime and Kanō Kōkichi

(1) The Study of Logic in the Meiji Period

As I mentioned in the introduction, Ōnishi Hajime (1864–1900) was a first-rate scholar of the history of philosophy, but his accomplishments do not stop there. After leaving the University of Tokyo, in 1891 he became an instructor at the Tokyo Specialist School[106] where he lectured on subjects such as philosophy, psychology, logic, aesthetics, and the history of Western philosophy. These lectures were made public as records of this institution. *The History of Western Philosophy*[107] was one of these texts, as was *Logic*,[108] which played a major role in the study of logic in Japan.

Logic was one of the first branches of Western philosophy received in Japan. It dealt with the form of thought and was considered easy to accept. Nishi Amane was also interested in logic from a very early stage. This is evident from an 1869 (second year of the Meiji period) draft explaining Western logic entitled "Logic (manuscript)."[109] In *Network of All Studies* he gives a simple introduction to logic, writing, "What is called 'logic' today deals with what is 'subjective;' it is a field that deals with [the workings of] subjective reasoning before things [objects] are addressed."[110] Nishi had the conviction that it was "positive principles" derived inductively from "positive knowledge" that were worthy of being called "true principles," and here he contrasts deduction and induction as follows.

> In the past logic was all about deduction, but in the system of logic devised by Mill induction is seen as the most important part of this field of inquiry, and this has led to significant developments in its study. Every scholar must rely on this method of induction.[111]

In 1874 he published *Logical Enlightenment*[112] on the basis of his "Logic (manuscript)." Most of this work is devoted to explanations of "old logic" based on deduction, but at the end he speaks of the need for this to be supplemented by a "new logic" based on induction.

Nishi initially used the terms *gakugen* (origin of learning)[113] and *chichigaku* (attained knowledge studies)[114] as translations of "logic," and he first used *ronrigaku* (study of the principles of argument), which became the standard translation in use today, in a speech about whether or not foreigners should be allowed to travel within Japan entitled "Domestic Travel" (1874, published in *Meiji 6 Journal* no. 23). This did not become the standard term right away, however, and following its introduction various other translations continued to be used. *Ronrigaku* seems to have become established as the standard translation of "logic" around the twentieth year of the Meiji period (1887).

Many Western books on logic were translated and published in the second and third decades of the Meiji period. Examples of such texts include Chambers' *Logic* (a translation of the entry on logic in *Chambers' Encyclopædia* by Tsukamoto Shūzō published in 1878) and Jevons's *Logic* (translated by Toda Kindō and published in 1879). As for original Japanese texts, the politician Ozaki Yukio published *Logic of Deduction*[115] in 1882, and the following year saw the publication of works such as Kiyono Tsutomu's *Philosophy of Logic (Introduction)* and Tsuboi Kumezō's *Logic Lectures*.[116] Later Miyake Setsurei and Takayama Chogyū also published books entitled *Logic*.[117]

Stimulated by the vigorous reception of Western logic, there were others who actively sought to advance the study of the traditional Buddhist form of logic called *inmyō* (*hetuvidyā*).[118] A leading representative of those who took this approach was Kira Kōyō (1831–1910), a monk of the Jōdo Shinshū (Ōtani) School[119] who founded the Society for the Study of *Inmyō*.[120] He published many works of scholarship, including *Outline of Inmyō (Hetuvidyā)*[121] (1881), *Insights into Inmyō*[122] (1884), and *Lectures on the Introduction to the Logic of Inmyō*[123] (1893). Murakami Senshō (1851–1929), another Shinshū Ōtani School monk who would go on to teach the first course on Indian studies at the University of Tokyo in 1917, published works such as *Complete Collection of Practical Lectures on Inmyō Logic*[124] (1891) and *Outline of the Study of Inmyō*[125] (1897).

In *Studies in the History of Meiji Philosophy*,[126] Shin'ichi Funayama summarizes the history of the study of logic in the Meiji period as follows: "If Meiji logic was founded by Nishi, it was firmly established by Kiyono and brought to fruition by Ōnishi."[127] In addition to the previously mentioned *Philosophy of Logic (Introduction)*, Kiyono Tsutomu also wrote other books such as *Inductive Logic: Philosophy of the Study of Truth*[128] (1889) and *Inductive Logic and Harsh Opinions on Politics and Economics*[129] (1890), and in these works he gave a detailed explanation of induction, a topic that had not been adequately introduced in the past. In emphasizing the importance of induction to academic inquiry, Kiyono played an important role in the history of logic.

As for Ōnishi Hajime, his lectures on "logic" given at the Tokyo Specialist School were published as lecture records of this school in addition to being serialized in *Waseda Literature*[130] and the *Journal of Philosophy*.[131] Following Ōnishi's death, the *Complete Writings of Ōnishi Hajime, Volume 1: Logic*[132] was published in 1903 based on these lectures. This text is composed of three parts: part 1, "Formal Logic," part 2, "Outline of *Inmyō*" and part 3, "Outline of Induction." As can be seen from this structure, Ōnishi's intention was to give a systematic account of logic in its entirety. Along with pointing out the significance and problematic aspects of deduction (formal logic) and induction, he also introduced *inmyō* and undertook a detailed consideration of this form of reasoning. In contrast to Kira and Murakami, who were Buddhists, Ōnishi was a believer in Christianity and focused on the logical meaning of *inmyō* unrelated to religious belief. In contrast to most scholars of Western philosophy at the time who showed little interest in *inmyō*, Ōnishi acknowledged its significance and placed it alongside Western formal logic and induction in his attempt to create a complete logical system.

"*Inmyō*" was one of the *pañcavidyā*, the five branches of knowledge in ancient India, and simply stated was the study of the relationship between assertions and the reasons behind them. It is subdivided into "old-*inmyō*" and "new-*inmyō*," the point of division being the emergence of Dignāga, who was active from around the end of the fifth century to the middle of the sixth century. Reasoning of the following sort is conducted in new-*inmyō*:

Claim: All S are P.

Reason: Because they are M.

Example: All M are P. Such as e, for instance.

According to Ōnishi, new-*inmyō* has some of the character of induction and in this sense differs from Western formal logic (syllogism), but fundamentally it is deductive reasoning. Insofar as it has an argumentative or rhetorical character, however, it is quite different from formal logic. As Ōnishi puts it, "*Inmyō* is a kind of logic, but its main concern is not to present a method for each of us to pursue the truth; put plainly, it is not logic as a method of investigation but rather learning that exclusively concerns methods of making another person understand the things I want to assert."[133] It is not a method of pursuing the truth on your own, that is, a logic of "self-enlightenment," but rather a set of techniques for persuading someone with an opposing view, that is, a logic of "other-enlightenment." As a result, *inmyō* begins by adopting the structure of positing an assertion not accepted by the other party as a "claim," and then positing a "reason" and "example" that the other party would also accept, thereby winning them over to your assertion.[134] Possessing this other-enlightening aspect is one of the major characteristics of *inmyō*, but on the other hand its self-enlightening aspect is quite weak, and Ōnishi saw this as its greatest flaw. Moreover, *inmyō*, as I have already mentioned, has aspects that are partially inductive, and in this respect differs from formal logic. This induction remains at a "painfully rough level" and in this sense represents another serious deficiency.[135] Ōnishi seems to have attempted to make up for this failing through his discussion of inductive logic in part 3.

(2) Ōnishi Hajime's Critical Philosophy

In contrast to Nishimura Shigeki and Inoue Tetsujirō, who engaged in gradually rehabilitating feudal traditions (in his *Explanation of Imperial Edicts*,[136] Inoue explains the "Imperial Edict on Education"[137] from a perspective that places loyalty to one's sovereign and parents at the foundation of ethics), the defining characteristic of Ōnishi's thought was his having developed it from the perspective of the individual.

Ōnishi's sympathy for Kant's philosophy can be seen as underlying this approach. Regarding Ōnishi's place in the history of philosophy in the Meiji period, in his *History of Meiji Thought* Kōsaka Masaaki writes, "Can it not perhaps be said that it was in Ōnishi Hajime that the spirit of Kantian criticism was first transplanted to Japan?" What Kōsaka meant by "Kantian criticism" can be gleaned from the following passage.

> In contrast to [Inoue] Enryō and [Miyake] Setsurei's loose eclecticism and fanciful metaphysics that employs analogical thinking as a weapon, [Ōnishi's approach] demands philosophy be a strict inquiry that eschews compromise and is mediated by a critique of knowledge [Erkenntniskritik]. Regarding the positivism and evolutionary theory of the kind advocated by Katō Hiroyuki, it emphasizes that a distinction should be made between natural laws and normative laws, that is, we cannot derive "ought" from "is."[138]

Kōsaka thus asserts that these two pillars of Kant's philosophy, the establishment of a strict form of inquiry based on the critique of knowledge and the drawing of a sharp distinction between what is and what should be, were first properly understood and taken up by Ōnishi Hajime.

"Criticism" in this sense can indeed be said to lie at the foundation of Ōnishi's thought. Ōnishi himself expresses his own stance using a slightly different Japanese term that also translates as "criticism" but includes a character with the nuance of "evaluate" rather than "judge."[139] He discusses this concretely in an essay entitled "The Duty of the Intellectual World Today."[140]

> Occidentalism, Japanism, radicalism, conservatism—all of these see only one side of things. In the intellectual world, there must be an approach that stands above these various perspectives and integrates them. I think criticism occupies this position. To me, the first important duty of the intellectual world in this country is to compare, distinguish, and criticize all aspects of Eastern and Western thought, and thereby elucidate their tendencies and values.[141]

In this way Ōnishi understands the term "criticism" not within the narrow framework of Kant's critical philosophy but in a broader sense as an approach that aims to "gather all forms of thought, old and new, Eastern and Western, and illuminate them in the light of our reason to discover their value." When Ōnishi emphasizes that what this requires more than anything else is "fair and impartial examination" by means of "our reason," however, it is clear that "criticism" in the Kantian sense described above lies at the foundation of Ōnishi's "criticism."

This phrase "fair and impartial public examination" comes from a Japanese translation of the preface to the first edition of Kant's *Critique of Pure Reason*. In "The Duty of the Intellectual World Today," after quoting Kant's assertion that "religion because it is holy and the law because it is stately, tend to want to stand outside of criticism, but if they stand outside of it in this way . . . our reason should not give religion or the law genuine respect,"[142] Ōnishi states that "the first important duty of the intellectual world in our country is to subject all things to a 'fair and impartial examination.' "[143]

This examination was of course also directed toward the politics and thought of the day. Ōnishi focused his criticism on the upsurge in nationalism following the Sino-Japanese War and the movement seeking to regulate education based on Confucian tradition and strengthen moral education in opposition to the burgeoning movement for freedom and civil rights. In

"On the Spirit of the Age of Enlightenment," an essay published just before he left to study abroad, he strongly criticizes this movement.

> While the [Japanese] enlightened thought that suddenly arose at a certain point in time has not yet achieved half of what it ought to achieve, people have already turned to historical reflection, asserting that there is nothing more calamitous than breaking the chain of history and forming the misapprehension that insistence on [maintaining the connection to] history is loyalty to the nation. This misapprehension, in recent years, has in our country's educational sphere had the bad effect of an obstinate fixation on what are old, narrow, and biased ways of thinking.[144]

While Kant's criticism lay at the foundations of Ōnishi's thought, his contemplation was by no means confined to the framework of Kantian critical philosophy. In the previously cited *History of Meiji Philosophy*, Kōsaka Masaaki also states that Ōnishi, unsatisfied with Kant who sharply distinguished reason from impulses, sought to establish a "Greenian idealistic metaphysics."[145] His discourse on "conscience," a major part of his work, can also be considered to have been related to this kind of "idealistic metaphysics." In his *On the Origins of Conscience*,[146] Ōnishi asserts that all of the "ideals" we are conscious of in our daily lives arise from our having a "true purpose" and working to attain it, and it is the "special impulse" we feel in regard to these ideals, that is, "the impulse of obligation, the awareness that we should, should not, or must do something" that is our conscience. The conscience he describes is nothing other than "a kind of impulse or tendency that sends us toward an ideal and draws us closer to it."[147] In Kant, conscience is the "faculty of moral judgment" that determines whether we have actually carried out the actions we believe to be correct. Ōnishi views it instead as an "impulse" that inevitably points us toward ideals.

(3) Kanō Kōkichi's Ethics and Philosophy of History

Ōnishi Hajime went to Europe in 1898 and studied under Rudolf Eucken (1846–1926) and Wilhelm Wundt. At the same time, having been promised the position of the first dean of the College of Humanities at the newly established Kyoto University, he also undertook the inquiries this position required. The following year he fell ill and returned to Japan, however, and he passed away in 1900 without having been able to take up the position at

Kyoto University as planned. His replacement as the first dean of the College of Humanities was Kanō Kōkichi (1865–1942). Kanō had originally studied mathematics in the Faculty of Science at the University of Tokyo, but he later reenrolled in the College of Humanities and studied philosophy. After graduating, he took up various positions, including teacher at the Number Five High School, and from 1898 he served for eight years as the principal of the Number One High School. Tanabe Hajime and Abe Yoshishige thus had the opportunity to make his acquaintance.[148]

During this period, Kanō published an essay entitled "On Moral Education."[149] In it he describes the state of contemporary politics and society as one in which "people rush about trying to produce results without any understanding or purpose, neither defending what is unbiased and correct nor avoiding devious manipulations. While such an approach can lead to temporary achievements that seem to make people happy, forgetting about correct foundations will cause one harm after another, and their accumulation will ultimately drag the world into decline." He asserts that if "a long-term plan for the improvement of the nation is to be achieved" then it must rely on a form of education whose chief aim is the inculcation of morality.[150] Perhaps because of the acclaim this essay received, in 1906 Kanō became the professor in charge of ethics at the University of Kyoto, and at the same time also served as dean of the College of Humanities. In the latter role Kanō is said to have demonstrated particular competence and judgment in regard to personnel. Kōda Rohan and Naitō Konan were invited to Kyoto University from the private sector, and while ultimately nothing came of it, Kanō tried to arrange for the novelist Natsume Sōseki, whom he had known as a student in the class below him at the University of Tokyo, to become a professor of English literature. In later years these personnel choices were widely praised, but at the time the lack of an academic record in the case of people like Naitō led to intense clashes with the Cabinet Legislation Bureau. Such issues are thought to be the reason that Kanō served as dean of the College of Humanities for only two years before resigning,[151] never to hold another position in the public sector. In the latter part of his life he studied Edo period thinkers and scientists while becoming involved in the buying and selling of old books and the appraisal of antiques.

Within this scholarship, the discovery of Andō Shōeki, a Meiji period doctor who was also an extraordinary thinker, can be counted among Kanō's greatest accomplishments. He realized the value of the ideas (for example, "direct cultivation by all people," an approach that criticized the feudal system and social hierarchy and held that every person should take up the hoe and cultivate fields directly) he found in a manuscript of *The Way of the Enterprise of Natural Truth*[152] he acquired by chance around 1899, and in 1928 he published the essay "Andō Shōeki." Had he not done so, Andō Shōeki would probably have remained forever in obscurity.

In "Andō Shōeki" Kanō says that "no more precise knowledge could be desired than that of physics, and someday even the science of the mind will submit to it,"[153] and in "The Three Great Delusions of Humanity" he is recorded by Watanabe Daitō as asserting that "values such as truth, goodness, and beauty are of course not absolute. . . . something like a system based on values is [nothing more than] a secondary or tertiary phenomenon derived from the forces of nature."[154] As is evident from such statements, scientific rationalism and a materialist worldview lay at the foundation of Kanō's thought.

What sort of ethics did Kanō develop from this standpoint? Manuscripts of lectures on ethics he gave at Kyoto University from September 1906 to June of the following year remain, and in them he asserts that in ethics "free will is invoked out of the blue, but [whether it exists] in actuality should be viewed with skepticism."[155] Regarding the existence of God, immortality of the soul, and free will that are given by Kant as postulates of practical reason, in "Three Great Delusions of Humanity" he writes, "In fact, [these three postulates] should be described as the three great delusions that have confused humanity, and in the past they have often led people into error throughout the world."[156] It was Kanō's belief that "free will" was merely something dreamt up in connection with the concept of "responsibility" that is necessary for community living, and ethics had to be constructed on a more certain foundation. Here Kanō turned to "conscience," but unfortunately did not get as far as giving a sufficient explanation of how this could serve as the foundation of ethics.

Kanō also constructed a philosophy of history in an essay entitled "The Concept of History"[157] (included in Kawai Eijirō, ed., *Students and History*[158]) published in 1940. In this essay, along with thinking of that which composes our world and our universe as "facts," Kanō considers these facts as interacting with each other and constraining one another, expressing this with the term "network of facts." The fields of thought that have worked to understand and interpret this "network of facts" from ancient times are religion, philosophy, science, and history. In contrast to religion, which relies on faith, philosophy tries to undertake rational explanation, but its approach is inadequate because it is built on the "illusion of taking ideals to be reality." For its part, science limits itself to particular objects of study and endeavors to discover similar structures and laws among them. Its interpretations avoid subjectivity, but its perspective is limited to the "microscopic." "History," on the other hand, takes a "macroscopic" view in which each fact in the network "is closely connected to others in ways big and small, pulsates without for a moment becoming static, constantly gives rise to changes . . . and transforms into new states"[159] and tries to accurately grasp this situation as a whole. Here Kanō argues that in this sense "history" acquires the character of a "cosmology that synthesizes all knowledge."

5. Fenollosa's and Okakura Tenshin's Understanding of Aesthetics and Art History

(1) Fenollosa's "True Theory of Art"

Nishi Amane's "Aesthetics"[160] (thought to have been written around 1877) marked the introduction of the field of aesthetics proper in Japan. In it he writes, "There is a kind of philosophy called 'aesthetics.' It is related to so-called 'fine art,' and seeks to elucidate its principles."[161] He then states that these "principles," in other words, the fundamental elements that give rise to beauty, are beauty possessed by the thing itself (*birei*[162]) and the human imagination that aids in its perception. Nishi's understanding is character- ized by his view of the human capacity to perceive beaty and ugliness as being deeply connected to the moral capacity to distinguish good and evil and the legal capacity to distinguish right and wrong, and by his belief that through this connection it is possible to "elevate the human world to a higher plane."[163]

However, this "Aesthetics" exists only in the form of a manuscript and was first published in *Collected Philosophical Writings of Nishi Amane* (1933),[164] edited by Asō Yoshiteru. It was Fenollosa's "True Theory of Art,"[165] published in 1882 (the fifteenth year of the Meiji period), that played the greatest role in laying the foundations of aesthetics in Japan. Fenollosa had come to Japan to teach political science, economics, and the history of phi- losophy at the University of Tokyo, but he immediately became fascinated by Japanese art, particularly the paintings of the Kanō School,[166] which he began to collect. Behind this interest lay the influence of the "art history" lectures given by Charles E. Norton (1827–1908) that he had attended while in graduate school at Harvard University, and the fact that at one point he had even considered making a living as an art educator or critic.[167]

Perhaps because of his having displayed a strong interest in Japanese art from such an early period, Fenollosa was often asked to give lectures on the subject. "True Theory of Art," delivered in 1882 to the Ryūchi Association, a group created by Sano Tsunetami and Kuki Ryūichi for the cultivation of Japanese art, was one such talk. Ōmori Ichū, a member of this group, transcribed this lecture and published it under the same title. Fenollosa opens this talk with a serious discussion of the nature of art, its essence and role, and in relation to this praises traditional Japanese art, which at the time was very seldom given serious consideration. He then presents concrete proposals regarding the administration of Japanese art. Regarding these points it was a very significant lecture.

Fenollosa begins "True Theory of Art" with the claim that "calligraphy and pictures are needed because they are good and beautiful and elevate people's emotions and quality." He sees the meaning of works of art in their "goodness and beauty," and in their improving people's grace and refinement through these properties. This "goodness and beauty" exists within a work of art itself and not in relation to anything else, and moreover its elements "depend on each other, are bound together as one, and can never be separated." This creates "a completely unique sensation," and he uses the word "idea" to express that which gives rise to this feeling. For example, we can think of an aesthetic ideal that painters have inside themselves when they paint a picture. Fenollosa states that "the essential property that creates the qualifications for a work of art to be called good or beautiful is the 'idea' that work possesses,"[168] and maintains that a work of art is not a work of art without this kind of idea.

Taking this perspective, the matter Fenollosa seeks to address is whether the current circumstances of Japanese painting, that is, a state of affairs in which "since the introduction of [Western] oil paintings in Japan, people of high status, finding them novel, have praised them to no end, while conversely looking down on Japan's distinctive paintings and shunning the painters of traditional schools,"[169] should be accepted. He presents the various characteristics of both Western and Japanese painting and critiques them both from the perspective outlined above. In concrete terms, he compares them in terms of five elements—whether they reproduce real objects, whether they have shadows, whether they have outlines (*kōroku*), whether their colors are rich, and whether their composition is simple or complicated—and reaches the conclusion that Japanese paintings are better suited than Western paintings to the expression of ideas, writing that "to throw away Eastern paintings and say that today they are crude or childish—I think this must be considered the greatest of errors."[170]

In "True Theory of Art," Fenollosa thus takes a dim view of Western painting and emphasizes the superiority of traditional Japanese painting, but doubts remain about whether these were his genuine beliefs and whether he actually said these things in his lecture. For example, in *The Dawn of Aesthetics: The Study of Art in Modern Japan*[171] Kanbayashi Tsunemichi discusses the possibility that Fenollosa's intended meaning was not properly understood by his audience. In "True Theory of Art," Fenollosa repeatedly talks about "true painting," and "most of those listening to his lecture undoubtedly understood 'true painting' to be Japanese traditional painting represented by the Kanō School. But as was indicated by the title it was given, 'True Theory of Art,' what Fenollosa was trying to explain through this lecture as a whole was the nature of 'true painting' that transcended the distinction between East and West, that is, the nature of ideal painting."[172] A deep concern regarding the state of the Japanese art world can indeed be found in Fenollosa. But it seems safe to say that his intention was not to reject Western painting itself.

In *Fenollosa: A Life Devoted to the Enhancement of Japanese Culture*[173] Yamaguchi Seiichi further examines the question of whether "True Theory of Art," having been recorded by Ryūchi Association member Ōmori Ichū and published as an imprint of this association, accurately reflected the content of the lecture Fenollosa gave to the Ryūchi Association in 1882. Based on evidence such as documents kept at Harvard University's Fogg Museum in which Fenollosa does not claim Western painting is comprehensively inferior to Japanese painting and on the contrary also points out the weak points of the latter, Yamaguchi presents the following view. "The main thrust of Fenollosa's discourse on art was to lament the decline of Japanese painting and encourage Japanese painters. In line with the purpose of its founding, the Ryūchi Association embellished this into an extreme rejection of Western painting, and promoted it as a Westerner's 'true theory' of art."[174]

That Fenollosa did not see Japanese art as something unique to Japan is evident, for example, from a lecture entitled "A Talk for the Gentlemen of Nara" given when he visited that city in 1888 as part of a survey of the treasures of ancient temples and shrines in western Japan. Pointing out that the influence of culture from the West caused by Alexander the Great's invasion of the East can be seen in Japanese Buddhist art, he states as follows.

That the purity of the artistic thought of the ancient Japanese was the same as the purity of Greek art is evident from the elaborateness of the bronze sculptures that remain today. These sculptures directly express the nature and thought of the person in question, and it is plain to see that [Japanese] art was in no way inferior to European art at the time.[175]

Linking Japanese art to the art of ancient Greece, from this perspective he asserts that Japanese art is the equal of European art.

In his posthumously published *Epochs of Chinese and Japanese Art* (1912), which had been left incomplete upon his passing despite his having devoted his later years to its writing, Fenollosa also states that "we are approaching the time when the art work of all the world of man may be looked upon as one, as infinite variations in a single kind of mental and social effort," and "a universal scheme or logic of art unfolds, which as easily subsumes all forms of Asiatic and of savage art and the efforts of children as it does accepted European schools."[176] These words demonstrate that a view of what is universal and runs throughout all kinds of art was deeply rooted in Fenollosa. His aim can perhaps be described as having been to discover the concrete development of a universal scheme in various forms of art and to find a particular value within each of them.

(2) Okakura Tenshin's Views on Art

In addition to his introduction of aesthetics and appraisal of Japanese art, Fenollosa's suggestion that focusing only on Western painting and dismissing the traditional painting of the East was the "greatest of errors" also had a large, multifaceted impact at the time. This can be seen, for example, in Tsubouchi Shōyō's having referenced these lectures in his *The Essence of the Novel*.[177] Fenollosa's lectures also had a strong influence on the policies of the Meiji government. Kuki Ryūichi, who was at the center of cultural administration as the junior vice-minister of culture, had already shown an inclination toward emphasizing traditional culture, but following Fenollosa's lectures both the Ministry of Culture and the Ministry of the Imperial Household made even greater efforts to promote traditional Japanese art. Beginning in 1880 (the thirteenth year of the Meiji period), Fenollosa repeatedly visited Kyoto and Nara to conduct surveys of Buddhist art, and after becoming a member of the Ministry of Culture's Art Survey Committee in 1884 he actively participated in or directed the Ministry of Culture's survey of ancient shrines and temples.

On the other hand, "True Theory of Art" drew a strong negative reaction from artists who painted in the Western style. They saw Fenollosa's book as a rejection of oil painting. For example, Koyama Shōtarō,[178] a Western-style painter and painting teacher at Tokyo Teachers' College,[179] showered Fenollosa, and those such as Kuki Ryūichi who stood behind him in actively promoting the resurgence of Japanese-style painting, in intense criticism. In his "Draft on Examples of the Rejection of Western Techniques and the Protection of Art,"[180] Koyama asserted that the people who ought to be protecting art were attempting to unilaterally reject Western techniques and was sharply critical of the bias in the administrative policy toward art at the time.

> [The protection of art] must be undertaken with an appropriate mentality that looks on everyone with equal favor. One must not inject one's own likes or dislikes to treat some well and others coldly. Protecting doesn't mean getting one's own ideas through or obtaining one's own joy or pleasure. We must not forget that [protecting art] means allowing artists to freely display their ideas, and by doing so cause the beautiful culture of this country to shine even brighter.[181]

Okakura Kakuzō (also known as Okakura Tenshin, 1863–1913) studied under Fenollosa at the University of Tokyo. Along with assisting Fenollosa in his collecting of art and his survey of ancient temples and shrines in Western Japan, after working at the Ministry of Culture following graduation he also collaborated with Kuki in his efforts to revitalize traditional painting and sculpture. The debate between Okakura and Koyama can be described as one act in the struggle for leadership between the factions promoting Western-style and Japanese painting. Immediately after Koyama published "Calligraphy Is Not Art"[182] in *Eastern Art and Science*[183] in 1882, Okakura responded with a piece entitled "Reading 'Calligraphy Is Not Art'"[184] in the same magazine, and the debate was joined. Okakura's high regard for calligraphy was a result of his view, also expressed in the lecture "The History of Japanese Art" (originally entitled "Art, or the History of Art")[185] given at the University of Tokyo, that calligraphy was the "foundation of Eastern painting," and Eastern painting and calligraphy went hand in hand. In response to Koyama's having considered calligraphy useless for reasons such as that it cannot be exported for a high price and does not inspire other undertakings, in "Reading 'Calligraphy Is Not Art'" Okakura criticizes him for understanding development and art in connection with matters of "the lust for profit," and argues "the development of the lust for profit means the destruction of morality, and will ruin the refined emotions. It will make the human body merely a profit-seeking machine."[186] Okakura understood art as separate from utilitarian aims, seeing it instead as something that is based on morality and expresses refined feelings.

This piece of writing is interesting not only in the context of Okakura's argument with Koyama but also from the perspective of what sort of thing he understood art to be. While from a slightly later period, Okakura's "Artist's Resolution,"[187] an address given at a gathering of Western-style painters called the "20th Day [of the month] Assembly" in 1903, is also an important text when it comes to understanding Okakura's view of art. In it he states that in recent years the art world, while vibrant on the surface, was at its core in a state of decline or even imminent extinction. He argues that while many Western-style painters had emerged and exhibitions of a kind that had not existed in the past were flourishing, painters created their art while thinking only about what was good or bad from the perspective of whether their work would be accepted for exhibitions or sell well and spiritually had become completely corrupt.

> In the past, artists in the East and West were respected because, like religious figures and writers, they were leaders at the forefront of their civilization. Today's artists, however, lack this resolve, and do not practice the discipline it requires. It is therefore natural that people have come to look upon them with contempt.[188]

In other words, it was Okakura's understanding that the meaning of art lay in its being on the cutting edge of its era. As he puts it, "The only reason artists are to be respected is that they have an innate talent for grasping the direction in which society should head, opening the gate to the world of beauty, giving people comfort in their lives, and leading people to a higher level of refinement. When it comes to ordinary artisans and factory workers, is there any reason to give them particular respect?"[189] Here he is saying that art has meaning insofar as it leads people to greater refinement, that artists must be the "world's trailblazers," and that it is precisely in this regard that artists are to be distinguished from artisans and craftspeople. These words give us a good sense of how Okakura understood art.

Of course, this was not a view unique to Okakura, and in a sense can be widely seen among thinkers of the Meiji period. It was expressed, for example, in the passage from Nishi cited above where he says that the meaning of art lies in its serving to "elevate the human world to a higher level." Moreover, the influence of Fenollosa's understanding of art should not be overlooked. As we have seen, his fundamental idea was that "calligraphy and pictures . . . are needed because they are good and beautiful and elevate people's emotions and quality." In an address entitled "Do Japanese Arts and Crafts Fit the Requirements of the West?" given to the Painting Appraisal Society,[190] an organization whose aims included the appraisal of ancient paintings, the training of Japanese painters, and the study of art theory, Fenollosa puts it as follows.

> Art is a tool with which, by having them look at something beautiful, people's spirits are refined and they are brought to a sublime state; it is by no means a mere toy to fill the idle hours of the old and wealthy. In the West art is seen as an important tool for governing the world, and is talked about on the same level as religion, morality and science.[191]

Here Fenollosa's idea that art exists for the purpose of leading the human spirit to a "sublime state" is given clear expression.

It is striking that in one of the passages quoted above Okakura clearly distinguishes artists, who are the "world's trailblazers," from "ordinary artisans and factory workers," and says of the latter "is there any reason to give them particular respect?" But this too is based on Fenollosa's thought as expressed in "The True Theory of Art," in which he writes, "It is completely inappropriate to see artists as being on the same level as regular artisans, or to view them like humble workers with inferior capabilities who are put to work by other people."[192]

Okakura displayed a strong interest in the surveying of ancient Japanese art, emphasized the significance of Japanese painting, and clashed with Koyama Shōtarō, but it was not as though he focused solely on the art of the past and attempted to completely eliminate Western-style painting. The primary mission of the Tokyo Art School, established through the efforts of Okakura and Fenollosa, was indeed the promotion of art that was distinctly Japanese, and at its founding in 1889 its only three departments were Japanese-style painting, wood carving, and metal carving. However, even in the "Introduction" to his "History of Japanese Art," a course he taught at the Tokyo Art School for a period of three years beginning in 1890, Okakura states, "The need for the study of the history of art does not stop at merely recording the past. It must also lay the foundations for the art of the future,"[193] and "Looking at this in the light of history, if we simply imitate [the art of] the people of the past, [art] will inevitably cease to exist. While protecting tradition, we must study the things of the past and strive to take a step beyond them. We must also draw on Western-style painting in an appropriate manner. In this case, too, it is important that we move forward with ourselves as subjects."[194] As is evident in the latter passage, Okakura emphasized the necessity of also drawing on Western-style painting and creating new art. Previously, in an essay entitled "Are We to Sit and Wait for the Extinction of Japanese Art?" that appeared in *Great Japan New Art Bulletin*[195] in 1885, Okakura had written, "Today . . . the only way to promote art is to apply the truths of Western art, and encourage steady progress in the correct manner,"[196] and it is clear that he had intended to make Western art the foundation of his promotion of art in Japan.

Another interesting point is Okakura's understanding regarding the propagation of civilization. I have noted that Fenollosa discussed the eastward transmission of Greek culture and believed that evidence of this could be found in Nara's ancient sculptures. It was his conviction that "no national or racial art is quite an isolated phenomenon."[197] Presumably influenced by this understanding, in his "History of Japanese Art" lectures Okakura also discussed the influence of Greek art on India and China, saying, "It is as though the art of the Tenpyō period [729–749][198] emerged through a mixing together of the art of the Suiko period [593–628] and art in the style of Greece and India."

Later, in a course entitled "History of Eastern Arts and Crafts"[199] given at the University of Tokyo in 1910, Okakura also discussed the art of China and Japan within this broad perspective. Watsuji Tetsurō, who attended this course, recorded his impression of it. "During my time as a student I was most deeply impressed by this course [Okakura's 'History of Eastern Art'] and Prof. Ōtsuka Yasuji's 'History of Modern [Western] Literature.' . . . Prof. Okakura's lectures were equally passionate, but they inspired in us a love of art rather than a fondness for scholarship . . . simply put, the professor fanned the flames of the love for art within us. . . . he truly had an extraordinary talent."[200] The gaze toward Greece in Watsuji's *Ancient Temple Pilgrimage*[201] should perhaps be thought of as having been cultivated by this course.

6. The Contributions of Ludwig Busse and Raphael von Koeber to the Study of Philosophy in Japan

(1) THE RECEPTION OF GERMAN PHILOSOPHY

In "Reflections on the World of Meiji Philosophy," Inoue Tetsujirō states that German philosophy was introduced during the second period of the reception of Western philosophy in Japan (1890 to 1905), and the study of this field came to occupy a particularly important position in the context of university education. Inoue himself returned from Germany in 1890, but in 1887 the German philosopher Ludwig Busse (1862–1907) had already arrived in Japan and replaced Fenollosa as instructor of philosophy at the University of Tokyo, a role in which he was succeeded by another scholar from a German university, Raphael von Koeber (1848–1923), in 1893.

Behind this shift toward inviting foreign instructors from Germany lay a major change in the political circumstances at the time. Amid the growing movement for freedom and civil rights, there was lively debate surrounding the establishment of a constitution, but following what is known as the "Meiji Fourteen (1881) Political Crisis" Ōkuma Shigenobu, who had been considering a constitution based on the British parliamentary cabinet system, left power, and the discussion in government shifted sharply toward an approach modeled on Bismarck's imperial constitution. This inclination toward Germany (Prussia) in the political sphere also had an influence on the academic domain. This is well attested by the "Advice to Ministers" that Inoue wrote for the chancellor of the realm[202] and the ministers of left and right.[203] In this text Inoue Kowashi, who was a member of the Cabinet Legislation Bureau that had been created after the "Meiji Fourteen Political Crisis," proposes "encouragement of German studies" as one policy to deal with the movement for freedom and civil rights. Reflecting on the fact that the "spirit of revolution" had been born out of the flourishing of British and French studies, he recommended the introduction of German studies alongside a revival of Chinese studies as its remedy.

> In the Kingdom of Prussia, the government is ultimately the government of the royal family. . . . today, in order to create a reasonably conservative character in the hearts and minds of the people [of Japan], we must exclusively promote Prussian academic inquiry, so that several years from now Prussian learning will have won out in the academic domain and the overwhelming influence of British learning will have been extinguished.[204]

This is the context in which Busse was invited to Japan. He was a disciple of Hermann Lotze (1817–1881), a philosopher who had taught at the University of Göttingen and the University of Berlin and had occupied a prominent position in Germany before the Neo-Kantian School emerged around the middle of the nineteenth century. Lotze had studied both medicine and philosophy, and in his thought he attempted the integrations of natural science and metaphysics and of mechanical philosophy and teleology. Busse can be seen as having carried on this approach. Nishida Kitarō attended his lectures, and in an essay entitled "Tokyo University Faculty of Letters Extra-curricular Courses, 24th and 25th Years of the Meiji Period"[205] he writes that "[Busse] was a complete Lotzian. His introductory course on philosophy was nothing more than an overview of Lotzian philosophy."[206]

In addition to logic and *shinbigaku* (a term sometimes used for "aesthetics," in this case it is thought to have been a unique course focusing on sculpture and architecture), Busse gave detailed lectures on the history of Western philosophy at the University of Tokyo, and in his seminar focused mainly on reading Kant's *Critique of Pure Reason* with his students. The study of philosophy in Japan based on close textual analysis can be said to have begun with Busse. In his *Philosophical Community in the Meiji Period*[207] (1943a), Kuwaki Gen'yoku writes as follows.

> Busse allowed the study of the history of philosophy to flourish. I think it might even be fair to say that it was thanks to Busse that philosophy began to be studied in a genuinely historical and academically rigorous manner. Busse, who introduced what was at the time a new academic approach in Germany, can be considered the first to have extolled the thorough application of academic methods to philosophy and to assert that we must study philosophy historically.[208]

One of those most strongly influenced by Busse was Ōnishi Hajime, discussed in section 4 of this chapter, who built a foundation for philosophical research through the meticulous study of the history of philosophy.

Busse worked at the University of Tokyo for six years before returning home to Germany in 1892, and two years later published *Metaphysics and the Critique of Knowledge*.[209] In the introduction to this book, along with stating that it was deeply connected to his lectures and seminars in Japan, he writes, "I was stimulated by the interest Japanese students took in my lectures. In this way they made no small contribution to the advancement of my research."[210]

(2) Koeber as an Educator

Raphael von Koeber came to Japan in 1893 (the twenty-sixth year of the Meiji period) as a replacement for Busse and took charge of the teaching of philosophy at the University of Tokyo. Inoue Tetsujirō was involved in his having been invited. Inoue, who was studying at the University of Berlin, developed a close mentor-disciple relationship with Eduard von Hartmann (1842–1906), an independent scholar who had become well known in Germany following the publication of *Philosophy of the Unconscious*[211] in 1869. When Inoue asked Hartmann's assistance in finding a replacement for Busse, Hartmann recommended Koeber.[212]

Prior to leaving Germany, Koeber had published works such as *Schopenhauer's Theory of Redemption* (1881)[213] and *The Philosophical System of Eduard Hartmann* (1884),[214] but after arriving in Japan his output was modest; he can be said to have demonstrated his abilities more in the domain of education than as a scholar. He taught not only philosophy but also Greek, Latin, the history of Christianity, and German literature, and placed particular emphasis on the Greek classics and the Western intellectual tradition that grew out of them—in other words, on Western art and literature—and wanted his students to understand philosophy not only in its ultimate form but also in terms of its origins and position within a broader cultural tradition. To this end he required they learn not only modern languages but also classical Greek and Latin.

Nishida Kitarō studied under Koeber for a year, and in "Remembering Professor Koeber,"[215] a text written when Koeber passed away, he reflects, "More than for his academic achievements, Professor Koeber should be remembered as someone whose incomparable value lay in the way his deeply cultured and refined character infused his surroundings, just as water that flows through a bamboo grove is cooled or a breeze that blows through trees in bloom acquires their scent."[216] As these words indicate, it was not through his own achievements but rather through the influence he had on the scholarship and character of his disciples that Koeber left a significant legacy.

Koeber taught for twenty-one years until his contract with the University of Tokyo was terminated in 1914, and during this time he sent many accomplished scholars out into the world, including Hatano Seiichi, Tanabe Hajime, Abe Yoshishige, Kuki Shūzō, Watsuji Tetsurō, Abe Jirō, and Fukada Yasukazu. Nishida Kitarō had profound respect for Koeber's character but distanced himself from his educational approach that emphasized *kyōyō*[217] (*Bildung*; personal, cultural, and academic maturation). Succeeding generations that studied longer under Koeber, on the other hand, were strongly influenced by his attitude to philosophy. Watsuji Tetsurō was one of these disciples. In 1946 (although based on lecture manuscripts from the end of the Taishō era) Watsuji published *A Philological Criticism of Homer*,[218] a book in which he discussed the history and current state of philological criticism of Homer's *Iliad* and *Odyssey*. In its preface he writes, "The late Professor Koeber passed away at the beginning of the summer of 1923, and close to the end he said something along the following lines. Philosophy promises a great deal, but in the end he had not been able to get much out of it. *Philologie* (the study of literature) promises nothing, but looking back he realized that he had in fact been able to learn many things from it."

From this quote it is clear that Koeber placed great faith in the fecundity of *philologie*, or the study of literature. This faith was shared by Watsuji. It is what can be said to have guided him toward the study of Homer, and also toward the study of *The Pillow Book*[219] in *On Japanese Intellectual History*[220] and the analysis of stories about the Buddha in *The Practical Philosophy of Primitive Buddhism*.[221] It is also found in Hatano Seiichi and Kuki Shūzō, and it can be said that the "Taishō *kyōyō*-ism" seen prototypically in Abe Jirō flowed out of it as well. This influence illustrates the importance of the role played by Koeber in the history of philosophy in Japan.[222]

Chapter 3

Awareness of the Individual and Interest in the State and Society in the Mid and Late Meiji Periods

1. Reflection on the March Toward Modernization

(1) The State of Thought from the Mid-to-Late Meiji Period

Going beyond the framework of philosophy in universities, in this chapter I will consider what sort of thought emerged in society during the middle and latter part of the Meiji period and influenced people at the time.

Looking at Meiji thought as a whole, a major change can be said to have occurred around the twentieth year of this period (1887). From the start of the Meiji Restoration, the reception of Western civilization and the creation of a modern, Western-style society in Japan had been considered the primary task to be undertaken. After twenty years this society had begun to take shape, as is evidenced by the promulgation of the Constitution of the Empire of Japan in 1889. At that point people began to reexamine this path of modernization (civilizational development) that had brought such results and take stock of its history. The history of modernization had always been a history of Europeanization, but particularly in the latter half of the second decade of the Meiji period the government made a greater push toward Europeanizing policies with the aim of revising unequal international treaties. Strong opposition to this then began to be voiced around the twentieth year of the Meiji period.

Tokutomi Iichirō (pen name Tokutomi Sohō, 1863–1957) emerged as an opinion leader in this movement. Tokutomi's *The Japan of the Future*[1] was published by Keizai Zasshi-sha,[2] a publishing company established by Taguchi Ukichi, in 1886, and garnered attention for its advocacy of the realization of a society in the formation of which every human being takes part equally, that is, the realization of "commonerism,"[3] rather than a society dominated by a group of leaders with special privileges. In 1887 he founded Minyū-sha[4] with the stated aim of realizing the "happiness and benefit of the people as a whole," and began publishing the magazine *Friend of the People*.[5] With submissions from the likes of Nakae Chōmin, Uchimura Kanzō, and Mori Ogai, *Friend of the People* played an influential role in the print media of the day. In 1890 Tokutomi established the newspaper company Kokumin Shimbun-sha[6] and began publishing *The People's Newspaper*.[7] Through these media, Tokutomi attempted to construct a foothold for a "from the bottom up" modernization in contrast to the government's "aristocratic Europeanization," or, in other words, development "from the top down."

On the other hand, there were also those such as Shiga Shigetaka (1863–1927), Miyake Setsurei, and Kuga Katsunan (1857–1907) who strongly advocated the preservation of traditional Japanese culture and the Japanese spirit in the face of the government's Europeanization policies. Shiga, Miyake, and others such as Inoue Enryō established Seikyō-sha,[8] a political and cultural organization of intellectuals, in 1888 and published a magazine called *Japanese People*.[9] They opposed the government's line of uncritical Europeanization and expressed their stance of aiming at the "promotion of the excellent qualities that are particular to Japan" with the term "nationalism" (*kokusuishugi*).[10] Kuga Katsunan had been a civil servant in the Meiji government, but in 1888 he resigned in protest of the government's policies and founded the newspaper the *Tokyo Telegraph*. The following year he moved on and launched another newspaper, *Japan*, and became one of the leading figures in Meiji-period print media. Kuga, too, opposed the "Occidentalism" that took all things Western as its model and sought to imitate them, arguing that on the contrary uniquely Japanese culture was to be preserved and its merits demonstrated. Kuga referred to his stance as "nationalism" (*kokuminshugi*).

The second decade of the Meiji period thus saw a sharp contrast between Europeanizationism and Japanese nationalism and intense debates surrounding politics and the nature of the state. From the third decade of this period onward, however, the focus on political issues waned, and people's attention shifted toward the interior of the individual.

As notable intellectual trends in the decade from 1900 to 1910, in his *History of Meiji Thought* Kōsaka Masaaki cites on the one hand the emergence of a strong individualist tendency to separate oneself from the state, avoid national issues, and focus intently on the interior of the individual, and on the other hand the emergence of thinkers who focused their attention on social issues (social contradictions and issues of peace and harmony).[11]

While his demarcations differ slightly from those given by Kōsaka, in his "Reflections on the World of Meiji Philosophy" (discussed in section 2 of chapter 1), Inoue Tetsujirō also divides trends in Meiji philosophy into three periods. The third of his periods ran from the end of the Russo-Japanese War in 1905 (the thirty-eighth year of the Meiji period) until the end of the Meiji period (although it should perhaps also include the early years of the Taishō period up until the beginning of the First World War in 1914). The start of the Russo-Japanese War that marked the end of the second period sparked an upsurge in nationalism and predominance of state supremacist thought, and the third period was defined as the period following this movement. Regarding the ensuing intellectual environment, Inoue writes, "After the Russo-Japanese War, awareness of the individual came to the fore; there was a sudden awakening from narrow patriotism, a broad, global spirit sprang up, and people began to pay particular attention to social issues."[12] Awareness of the individual, a global perspective, and social issues can be considered the key terms that characterized this period.

(2) Tokutomi Sohō's "Commonerism"

Amid the changes occurring around the twentieth year of the Meiji period (1887), Tokutomi Sohō was a thinker who keenly felt this shift in the zeitgeist. He became well known in the world of letters through his self-published *The Youth of Nineteenth Century Japan and Their Education*.[13] In a chapter added when this book was published again under the title *The Youth of the New Japan*, he called the current leaders in society "the Tenpō elders" (Fukuzawa Yukichi, for example, had been born in the fifth year of the Tenpō period [1834])) and in contrast dubbed his own generation "the Meiji youth." He writes:

> If a society ages as it advances toward civilization, then it must be said that we young people born in the Meiji period are further advanced than elderly people born in the Tenpō period. As a result, the youth born in the Meiji period should not be led by the elders born in the Tenpō period; on the contrary, it is they who should be led by us.[14]

This was a declaration that new leaders were stepping forward to replace those who had been at the forefront of Japanese politics, society, and scholarship since the Meiji Restoration.

In the prospectus printed on the inside cover of volume 5 of *Friend of the People*, after repeating more or less the same declaration, Tokutomi writes, "the era of destruction will at last pass away and an era of construction will come." He was one of those who sought to answer the questions of who should take charge of this "construction" and how this task should be approached. As is noted in texts such as *An Individual View of the Tasks of the Age*[15] (1913) and *Autobiography of [Tokutomi] Sohō*[16] (1935), in this undertaking he drew on the thought of Spencer, particularly his social evolutionary thought regarding the development from "militant" societies to industrial societies presented in *The Principles of Sociology*, and the economic liberalism of the Manchester school advocated by figures such as Richard Cobden (1804–1865) and John Bright (1811–1889). Tokutomi developed his thought on the basis of their assertion that it was through a free economy and free trade that a just and peaceful society could be realized. In *The Japan of the Future*, for example, he writes:

> In countries that have developed military institutions a small number of people have a monopoly on political power, while in countries that have developed industrial institutions [political power] is distributed among many citizens. In the one case people are born for the sake of the state, in the other case the state is created for the sake of the people. . . . Inegalitarianism comes to solely dominate societies that have developed military institutions. Egalitarianism comes to solely dominate societies that have developed industrial institutions. The phenomena of militant societies are therefore all aristocratic phenomena. The phenomena of industrial societies, in contrast, are all commoner phenomena.[17]

The expressions "military institutions" and "industrial institutions" can be seen as having been based on Spencer's conception of "militant societies" and "industrial societies." In societies built around the military, power is concentrated in the hands of a small, privileged elite, and citizens are used for the sake of the state, while in societies built around industry, every person who is involved in production participates equally in the construction of society. It is in the latter scenario that a society is realized in which the common people take hold of real power. As Tokutomi puts it, "This approach focused on trade is pacifist. If so, then as wealth increases so too will peace, but what is wrong with this?"[18] It is through the development of economies and trade that peaceful relationships between nations are formed. Tokutomi declares this process to be "one of the great facts of history." This assertion that the construction of a new era was to be undertaken not by the small elite that had seized power and privilege following the Meiji restoration but by the "common people" involved in productive activities resonated strongly with those critical of the Meiji government's top-down approach to social progress.

Tokutomi's assertions, however, were not based on a firm grasp of politics, the economy, and international relations; they simply juxtaposed an aristocratic society and a commoner society and claimed that the former would transition to the latter through economic and commercial development. This approach was dominated by strong optimism and a simplification of various matters. Eventually Tokutomi himself could not avoid acknowledging this optimism and the inadequacy of his own understanding of politics and the economy. It was presumably this realization that led to the major shift in his position or "betrayal" triggered by the First Sino-Japanese War discussed later in this chapter.

(3) Shiga Shigetaka and Miyake Setsurei's Japanese Nationalism

Figures belonging to the Seikyō-sha cultural organization such as Shiga Shigetaka and Miyake Setsurei called for "nationalism" (*kokusuishugi*) to counter the trend toward Europeanization. In an article entitled "Declaration of the Significance of What 'Japanese People' Hold Dear" published in *Japanese People* no. 2, Shiga argues that it is necessary to preserve good traditions and culture. He thoroughly critiques the "veneerism" that accepts everything about Western culture without adequately digesting it and wears this culture as an external decoration and the "molecular breaking down of Japan" that wholly rejects the traditional culture and spirit of Japan and seeks to replace them with their Western counterparts. In the face of these trends, he asserts the need to preserve Japan's traditions and culture. His "nationalism" or "Japanism," however, did not attack or attempt to drive out Western culture itself. He writes, "We are not people who want to thoroughly preserve every old element unique to Japan and maintain all old components [of Japanese society]. Instead, when it comes to the importing of Western civilization and culture, using Japan's superb organs we aim to masticate and digest these elements and make them a part of the body that is 'Japan.'"[19] As these words indicate, his approach was one that sought to actively incorporate the great achievements of Western civilization. This was to be done, however, by carefully chewing up and digesting these elements on the basis of Japan's traditions before making them a part of Japan's "body."

Miyake Setsurei was not simply "antiforeign" either, and also encouraged Japanese nationalism (*kokusuishugi*) through inquiries presented in *Japanese People*. Miyake and Shiga created their term for "nationalism" by appending the suffix *-shugi* (-ism) to *kokusui*, a word that had originally been used as a translation of the English word "nationality," and in their writings the term "nationalism" was not used with the intention of unilaterally asserting the superiority of their own culture. In his essay "Is Our Insistence on Nationalism Merely Happenstance?," also printed in *Japanese People* no. 2, Miyake emphasizes that "nationalism" is "born from the knowledge and thought of enlightened society" and is by no means an approach of "preserving old things." On the contrary, Miyake explicitly endorsed the active adoption of whatever is useful. "Even if something originates in the West, if using it is beneficial then it should be used; if it is useful to imitate European customs or American habits, what is wrong with importing and adopting them?" What he criticized was "the so-called 'Europeanism' that is pointlessly fixated on the beauty of foreign countries and forgets its own country and its own flesh and blood." He also writes, "Even if we use Western machines and adopt Western knowledge, surely none of us will lose our Japanese spirit,"[20] and the essence of his "nationalism" can perhaps be seen in this preservation of unique spiritual or intellectual values.

The True, Good, and Beautiful Japanese Person[21] (1891) may have been Miyake's most important work. In its explanatory notes he writes:

> When it comes to those who may be called "nationalists," if they seek the flourishing of the power of the nation as a whole, then I agree with them. If they follow certain scholars of German studies, however, and see the existing government as an organization that is to hold all power, then I cannot support them.[22]

The "scholars of German studies" to whom he is referring presumably included the likes of Katō Hiroyuki, and Miyake was by no means either a national supremacist or government supremacist. In the same explanatory notes we also find the following passage.

To devote one's energies to one's own country is to devote one's energies to the world. To display the characteristics of one's own ethnic group is to contribute to the development of humanity. Why should there be any conflict between defending one's own nation and loving humanity?[23]

Miyake claims that displaying the characteristics of one's own ethnic group is deeply connected to the development of humanity as a whole. His nationalist perspective was one in which each nation preserving its agency and developing its own distinct culture (its own truth, goodness, and beauty) did not conflict with different nations respecting each other's cultures and seeking harmony and cooperation. Here too we see that Miyake sought a path to modernization that differed from simply imitating the West.

(4) KUGA KATSUNAN'S CONCEPTION OF "NATIONALISM" (*KOKUMINSHUGI*)

Kokuminshugi,[24] the word used by Kuga Katsunan to express his own stance of "nationalism," was based on a different translation of the English "nationality" (*kokumin*, literally the people or citizenry of a nation). Precisely what he meant by it can be seen from his essays published in the *Tokyo Telegraph* and *Japan* newspapers. For example, in the inaugural remarks included in the first issue of *Japan* released on February 11, 1889, he writes:

> The Japan of recent times has lost its distinctive character and has thrown away the things that are unique to it. This process has reached an extreme, and nearly every member of the citizenry is trying to become Western. Eventually the group of islands called "Japan" will be nothing more than a name on a map. . . . the people of Japan are like people who have lost their roots and are adrift in a whirlpool.[25]

Here he writes that "every member of the citizenry is trying to become Western," and in the essay "A Dark Cloud over the Sea of Politics,"[26] published in the *Tokyo Telegraph* on May 16, 1888, he describes this trend as a form of "Westernism" in which "all things Western are admired and Western ways are imitated." Kuga characterized his own time as "the era of a great collision" between Westernism and Japanese nationalism.[27]

Kuga lays out the purpose of the newspaper *Japan* in his inaugural remarks printed in its first edition.

> *Japan* aims to save this Japan that is drifting without direction and make it a stable nation with a firm foundation; to begin with, our mission is to restore the "national spirit" Japan has lost and give it even greater vigor.[28]

As for what Kuga means by the term "Japanese spirit," this can be seen as referring to the "unique character" he speaks of when he says "the Japan of recent times has lost its unique character and has thrown away the things that are unique to it." In a later essay entitled "Global Ideals and National Ideas" (*Japan* no. 270) he writes as follows.

> Just as I do not wish for the political life of the Japanese people to be unified with [that of] the people of other countries, I do not wish for our cultural life to be made the same as [that of] the people of other countries. I want us to be politically independent, and at the same time I also want us to be culturally independent. As a result, I desire the independence of our language, the independence of our literature, the independence of our handicrafts, the independence of our politics, the independence of our rituals, the independence of our customs, and the independence of our religion.[29]

In contrast to "Westernism" in which "all things Western are admired and Western ways are imitated," Kuga's "nationalism" can be described as an effort to restore this kind of unique culture and the spirit that undergirds it, and to bolster its standing in regard to the outside world.

It is important to note, however, that Kuga's nationalism was not a xenophobic conservatism that steadfastly adhered to traditional values. We have already seen that Miyake took the position that there is no contradiction whatsoever between nationalism and the love of humanity, and in a similar vein Kuga writes as follows in his inaugural remarks in *Japan*.

> We at *Japan* consider it our duty to restore the Japanese spirit and increase its vigor, but we are not ignorant of the good and beautiful aspects of Western civilization. We value its ideas of rights, freedom, and equality, respect its theories of philosophy

and ethics, find some of its customs to our liking, and in particular have the utmost regard and admiration for its science, economy, and industry.[30]

In "Global Ideals and National Ideas," too, the restoration and enhancement of the national spirit is presented as by no means contradicting, and indeed as being fully compatible with, global ideals—in concrete terms, rights, freedom, equality, and the love of humanity.

As Kano Masanao points out in his essay "Subjects, Citizens, Nationality [*kokumin*],"[31] when Kuga named his own position "nationalism" (*kokuminshugi*) based on the term *kokumin*, this was clearly intended to indicate opposition to the mainstream politics of the day. Following the Imperial Decree on the Establishment of a National Diet[32] in 1881, and particularly in the Constitution of the Empire of Japan (1889), the people of Japan were positioned as "subjects" subordinate to a monarch. It was with this broad trend in mind that Kuga focused on the concept of "nationality." In his essay "A Nationality-Based [*kokuminteki*] Conception" printed in the second issue of *Japan*, for example, Kuga writes as follows.

> The foundation of a modern state is to be built neither simply upon the aristocracy, nor simply upon individual people, nor simply upon monarchical authority; instead, it is to be built upon a "nationality" that signifies the union of the monarch and the people. A state constructed atop this conception of a nation gives ample weight to the rights of commoners, does not cause them to conflict with the rights of the monarch, and fully accepts an aristocracy without placing it above the common people. This is because within this conception of "nationality" there is ultimately neither aristocracy nor commoners nor monarchical authority.[33]

In one aspect both versions of nationalism (*kokusuishugi* and *kokuminshugi*) strongly opposed the government's Europeanization policies and advocated the preservation and promotion of the traditional spirit and culture of Japan, but at the same time these movements also opposed the formation of a paradigm of "subjects" by the government and sought a politics based on a conception of "nationality" that did not distinguish between the monarch and the common people. The fact that *Japanese People*, a magazine published by Seikyō-sha, shared these views can be seen in the following passage from an essay entitled "Japanese Nationality Was Born on February 11, 1889."[34]

> It is appropriate to call people living in a state with an absolute monarchy system "subjects," but the people of a state with a constitutional monarchy system should be called a "nationality" (*kokumin*).

In perhaps his most significant work, *A Study of Modern Politics*[35] (1891), Kuga calls his own stance the "nationality faction,"[36] and states that this approach is neither national preservationist nor exclusionist, nor is it reactionary. Here he gives a concise statement of the aims of "nationalism."

> The nationality faction is not a faction that supports the doctrine of exclusion. On the contrary, we uphold the principle of the love of humanity. We are not a conservative but a progressive faction.[37]

(5) From Nationalism to Imperialism

As we have seen, entering the third decade of the Meiji period the awareness of "nationality" increased markedly and a wave of nationalism swept through the intellectual world, but this movement underwent a major change around the time of the First Sino-Japanese War. Simply stated, there was a shift from nationalism to imperialism. "Asia" emerged as a spatial representation loaded with political significance, and "Asianism" took shape as an intellectual trend and political stance.

This change was most clearly displayed in the thought of Tokutomi Sohō. As we saw earlier, Tokutomi was a leading proponent of "commoner-ism," but his political stance underwent a dramatic change triggered by the First Sino-Japanese War. This change is most evident in *On the Expansion of Great Japan*,[38] which was published in 1894—the year the First Sino-Japanese War began. This book was a collection of essays that had been published in *Friend of the People* and *The People's Newspaper*. In it, Tokutomi argued unabashedly to justify imperialistic invasions on the grounds that for the changes of the Meiji Restoration to succeed it was necessary for "the Empire of Japan to complete the process of unification and self-defense, and then turn outward and expand into a Great Japan" and that expansion into China and the Korean Peninsula was "for the sake of bringing the blessed light of civilization to barbarian societies."[39]

The intellectual trend referred to as "Asianism" took various forms, but fundamentally its role was to provide a justification for the invasion of Asia. In his 1881 book *Concerns About Current Events*,[40] Fukuzawa argued that it was necessary to compel the civilization of underdeveloped Asian countries using military force and strengthen these nations to resist the threat of Western invasion, writing that the most important measure to be taken in order to prepare for invasion from Western countries was "to bring civilization" to a stagnant, underdeveloped Asia, and to this end "compelling this progress by force is permissible."[41]

This view was expressed in a more extreme form in the 1883 essay *On Diplomacy*.

> Today the nations of the world are like predators or birds of prey trying to feed on each other, and if the people of civilized nations are the ones eating and the people of uncivilized nations are the ones being eaten, then should our country of Japan position itself as a civilized nation trying to eat well, or should we join the ranks of the ancient countries of Asia who, after several thousand years, have not managed to display sufficient power, and while joining them in protecting old customs be devoured ourselves by civilized people? Should we become a hunter and pursue rabbits and deer, or should we become rabbits and deer and be pursued by hunters? We must choose one or the other.[42]

Tokutomi's *On the Expansion of Great Japan*[43] was written amid the intensifying conflict with Qing dynasty China, and in the same year Takekoshi Yosaburō, who had played a major role in the reception of Western philosophy in Japan as the author of works such as *The Beauty of German Philosophy*[44] and *The History of Modern Philosophy and Religion*,[45] wrote *On China*[46] (1894). In one of its chapters entitled "Civilization Cannot Be Brought to the Qing Nation Without the Ravages of War"[47] he makes the following assertion. While in recent years Qing dynasty China had also begun to import Western weapons, "in the hands of barbarians, the tools of civilization become on the contrary impediments to civilization; the people of our nation must not hesitate. In order to establish Great Japan, . . . in the name of justice, in the name of humanity, and in the name of civilization . . . we truly have no choice but to resolutely take up the sword, exercise our right to attack the Qing nation, and through the ravages of war awaken it from its slumber."[48] Here too imperialistic invasion is being justified under the banners of "justice" and "civilization."

But not everyone supported advances into the Korean Peninsula and Qing dynasty China through military force. Interestingly, "nationalism" advocate Kuga Katsunan presented a more insightful view. After the First Sino-Japanese War had ended and a weakened China had begun to be carved up by the Western powers, the following passage appeared in an editorial in *Japan* (February 1898).

> If today the many nations of Europe, looking beyond Europe's borders, are seeking to realize the brutal ambition of invading external territories, then surely China, Korea, and Japan will become victims. . . . At present Germany, one of the three nations [Russia, Germany, and France], is clearly clamoring for the invasion of the East. Even so, the people of the Eastern nations, seeing nothing wrong with this, applaud the development of their brutal power and are even seeking to follow in its footsteps. . . . Do the Japanese people, who see themselves as belonging to a civilized Eastern nation, welcome an era in which this kind of brutal power dominates? Do we not acknowledge moral struggle outside of this kind of brutal power? For the sake of [Japan being] a civilized Eastern nation, I find this [conflict involving brutal force] shameful.[49]

This statement of Kuga's can be said to display much greater logical consistency than the position taken by his more imperialistic contemporaries.

(6) Okakura Tenshin's "East"

One of the most prominent opinions regarding "the East (Asia)" expressed during the era spanning the late Meiji and Taishō periods was that of Okakura Tenshin. He begins *The Ideals of the East,* which was published in London in English in 1903, with the words "Asia is one," and *Awakening of the East,* another English manuscript written in India the previous year, includes the phrase "Pan-Asian Alliance."

Awakening of the East is said to have been directed toward the people of India suffering under British colonial rule and abounds with expressions of Okakura's profound sympathy and solidarity regarding India's "anguish." Okakura was captivated by the question of how Asia (the East) might respond to the "white peril" created by Europe (the West). This did not stop at military or industrial domination. Okakura was particularly focused on "moral conquest," regarding which he writes as follows.

> The ideals of our ancestors, our family system, our ethics, and our religions grow weaker by the day. Each succeeding generation loses its moral fortitude through contact with Westerners. Grooming and appearance supplant purity, and cleverness supplants manliness.[50]

For Okakura, the issue was how India, and Asia as a whole, could overcome the suffering it was currently experiencing, or, in other words, how a foundation could be built from which to resist European (Western) intellectual and moral domination. It was presumably out of this interest that he spoke of "Eastern ideals." What Okakura considered on this basis was a philosophy of "constantly seeking unity in the midst of diversity," a system of ethics with "benevolence, love for one's compatriots, loyalty, and manners" at its core, a religion that allows for liberation from all worldly desires, and art that expresses what is universal and spiritual in what is particular. These were "ideals" that had been shared throughout the East in the past, that is, the "ideals of our ancestors," but had been lost or were being lost in the process of the "worship and imitation of Europe." In *The Ideals of the East*,[51] Okakura writes that "to feel and revitalize the dormant life of the old Asiatic unity becomes our mission."[52] How could this "dormant life" be awakened? How could it be reinvigorated? How could the intellectual and moral domination of Europe (the West) be confronted? These were the questions posed by Okakura.

Okakura's thought advocating a "pan-Asian alliance" can be described as one form of "Asianism." This Asianism, however, was not an Asianism that concerned itself with the question of how to justify the invasion of Korea and China. Okakura was always conscious of Asia within the dichotomous schema of Europe versus Asia or the West versus the East. In the face of the problem of how to construct a basis upon which to confront Western domination, however, Okakura's thought drew a wide arc. In solving this problem, it converged on the privileged nature of Japan. In *The Ideals of the East*, after discussing the diverse development of Eastern thought, religion, and art, Okakura writes, "It has been, however, the great privilege of Japan to realize this unity-in-complexity with a special clarity."[53] All of the thought and culture of Asia had been conveyed to Japan, which lies on the easternmost edge of this region, and had accumulated there without each element losing its distinctive nature. In other words, Okakura argued that Japan was the beach on which wave after wave of Eastern thought had washed up, leaving permanent traces in the landscape, and as such only Japan could awaken the "dormant life" of the East and create an intellectual basis from which it would be possible to confront Europe (the West). As we saw earlier, there is an aspect in which Okakura was certainly an "Asian," but in *The Ideals of the East* an element of strong Japanese ethnocentrism also reveals itself.

2. Awareness of the Individual

(1) Kitamura Tōkoku's "Theory of Inner Life"

One of the major characteristics of the intellectual climate after the thirtieth year of the Meiji period (1897) was the shifting of attention toward the interior of the individual and away from politics or the state. A tendency to avoid problems of the state and stay cloistered within oneself as an individual can of course be seen even earlier, for example in the work of Kitamura Tōkoku (1868–1894). Kitamura displayed a strong interest in the Freedom and Civil Rights Movement from around the time he entered the Tokyo Specialist School.[54] The Freedom and Civil Rights Movement can be described as a movement that promoted the ideal of a state that guarantees the freedom of the individual, or, in other words, a movement that sought a harmonious union of the state and the individual, but the state that was actually being realized was one that prioritized state stability and prosperity. Under these circumstances, the ideals that had initially been extolled by this movement were gradually forced to seek a place for their realization within the individual, and Kitamura can be characterized as someone whose way of life embodied this trend of the times. Frustrated with political activism, along with being baptized as a Christian he sought to realize his ideals in the "world of ideas."[55]

"Theory of Inner Life,"[56] published in 1893, the year before his death, was Kitamura's best-known essay, and in it he emphasizes the need to turn our attention toward the "inner life" that is our "fundamental life," rather than the everyday life we live within an actual society. He also asserts that this "inner life" is not something human beings create themselves, understanding it instead as a manifestation of the "spirit of the universe." Not only human beings but all of creation (nature) is "a manifestation of the spirit of the universe" and "a representation of the form of God." As a result, human beings feel a sense of awe in the face of creation, and in our "inner lives" we are in "spiritual commune" with some kind of entity. Regarding this "spiritual commune," in "Theory of Inner Life" Kitamura writes as follows.

> What is momentary spiritual commune? It is inspiration. To have this momentary spiritual commune is to be an inspired poet. . . . what is inspiration? It is not necessarily inspiration in a religious sense. If not a single religion exists (as an organization) there can still be inspiration. If not a single philosophy exists there can still be inspiration; inspiration is indeed a kind of commune between the spirit of the universe (God) and the spirit of a human being (inner life).[57]

This immediately calls to mind Schleiermacher's concept of "intuition," and gives the sense of having something in common with Romanticism's efforts to create a self-sufficient space within the self through imagination. In a sense, Kitamura can be said to have lived the entire span of European history from the French Revolution to the Romantic Period in his short, twenty-five-year life.

(2) The "Personal Cultivation" Movement

On the one hand, Kitamura's individualism tied to Romanticism flowed into Takayama Chogyū's theory of a "beautiful life" based on Nietzsche's idea of self-affirmation, but on the other hand his pursuit of ideals within the self also led to a stance of ethical idealism and the movement for personal moral cultivation.

The Teiyū Rinri-kai (Teiyū Ethics Society),[58] established in 1900, was centered on figures such as Ōnishi Hajime and Anesaki Masaharu but also brought together many of the other leading philosophers and thinkers of the era. This organization's "Prospectus" emphasized:

> The foundation of morality is the personal cultivation[59] of character. It is said that loyalty to the sovereign and patriotism are the most important elements of morality for the citizenry, but if in addition an awareness of the fundamental nature of humanity is not roused and an appeal to the depths of the [human] mind is not made, we cannot expect people to lead vibrant lives.

The phrase "loyalty to the sovereign and patriotism"[60] appears, but nationalism is kept at arm's length. That the aim of this organization was "to ethically respect intellectual freedom and demonstrate human values" is also evident from Anesaki's "Purpose of the Event" remarks delivered at the first Teiyū Ethics Society Academic Lecture Meeting.

> From our perspective, the ethics of extreme national supremacism, in other words, education that emphasizes only patriotism, is merely blustering authoritarianism, and this is on the contrary an impediment to appealing to the true feelings of human beings and developing their ethical character.[61]

As Miyakawa Tōru points out in *Issues in Japanese Intellectual History*,[62] the personal cultivation movement sought to secure the autonomy of the inner world of the individual in the face of state coercion, but at the same time this shutting itself within the interior of the individual led to it losing its capacity to criticize the state. Miyakawa argues that as a result "in an objective sense" it could not avoid playing "the role of shaping loyal subjects."[63]

"Character" and "personal cultivation" having been key terms in this era is evinced by the release of special issues of magazines on these topics and the publication of books such as Kihira Tadayoshi's *The Power of Character: A Method of Personal Cultivation*[64] (Dōbunkan, 1906) and Nakajima Rikizō's *Educators' Personal Cultivation of Character*[65] (Meguro Shoten, 1911).

Kitamura's Romantic individualism was not only taken up by this kind of movement for the personal cultivation of character focused on academia, but was also developed in the direction of Kiyozawa Manshi's spiritualism[66] and Tsunajima Ryōsen's understanding of religion based on personal experiences of the divine. In the field of literature its influence can also be seen in naturalism.

(3) Spiritualism

As we saw in chapter 2, Kiyozawa Manshi studied philosophy under Fenollosa at the University of Tokyo and went on to deliver highly regarded lectures of his own on the history of Western philosophy. His greatest contribution, however, lies in his way of life as a man of religion who strove to reform and revitalize a desiccated Buddhism. This effort to reform Buddhism was called the "spiritualism" movement.

At the beginning of "Spiritualism," an essay published in the first issue of the magazine *The Spiritual World*[67] in 1900, Kiyozawa asserts that human beings need "a complete foundation on which to stand" that can only be obtained through "the absolutely infinite," and presents the main aim of "spiritualism" as "seeking satisfaction within one's own spirit" while standing on this kind of foundation. He then states that this is not a worldview like idealism but a keystone to be relied upon in building one's life.

Why did Kiyozawa advocate "spiritualism" in this period? A hint can be found in the words of Andō Shūichi, one of his disciples.

> Sensei [Kiyozawa] said as follows. The activism being undertaken in Tokyo consists of strenuous efforts to obtain money and fame and rash actions for the sake of food and clothing. These things are called "activism." . . . the only way to avoid the harmful influence of this is something called "passivism."[68]

These words make it clear that Kiyozawa's advocacy of spiritualism was strongly connected to the attitudes of people at the time who pursued money and fame, and the climate of an era in which there were constant calls for civilization, progress, and a wealthy and militarily powerful nation. Kiyozawa referred to this attitude and climate taken together as "activism," and maintained that in the end this search for satisfaction and security outside the self would always be in vain; one desire gives rise to another, and the pursuit of satisfaction never ends.

The "passivism" Kiyozawa proposed in response "introspects" the self and seeks the "satisfaction" of the spirit within it. In "Spiritualism and the Three Worlds [a Buddhist term meaning the past, the present, and the future]," another essay published in *The Spiritual World*, Kiyozawa writes as follows.

> Spiritualism views one's own spirit as most important, and holds that we must find a place to live peacefully where this spirit can be satisfied with its current condition and is free to exist as it pleases.[69]

Among the Buddhists of this period, there were also those such as Sakaino Kōyō and Tanaka Jiroku who engaged in efforts to actively reform society while remaining firmly grounded in Buddhism. They criticized Kiyozawa's "spiritualism" as a stance that "simply tries to dissolve external objective reality within a subjective spirit."[70] Kiyozawa himself was well aware of the possibility of this kind of criticism. His spiritualism is in no way opposed to social welfare and on the contrary encourages it, but defends an introspective approach on the grounds that "it is a mistake to try to steady other people without having made sure one's own footing is solid."

(4) Tsunashima Ryōsen

Tsunashima Ryōsen (1873–1907) studied under Ōnishi Hajime at the Tokyo Specialist School. He did important work in the field of ethics, translating the writings of British scholars such as H. Sidgwick and J. S. Mackenzie and penning his own books such as *A History of European Ethical Thought*[71] (1909) and *The History of Ethical Thought in the Spring and Autumn Period in China*[72] (1907). It was his understanding of religion, however, that had a greater influence on people at the time. He had been baptized as a Christian when he was young (fourteen or fifteen years of age), and after having drifted away from this faith once again became deeply devout around 1896. In 1904 he experienced a "vision of God."

Tsunashima writes about the "sorrow" he experienced during this process in an essay entitled "Emphasizing Sorrow"[73] included in *Record of a Period of Illness*[74] (1905).

> Aware of our own finitude, flaws, smallness, weakness, shamelessness, and wretchedness,[75] we look upward with yearning toward something greater than ourselves, something beyond the finite, without knowing precisely where it is.

But eventually he realizes that this sorrow itself is the key to overcoming sorrow.

> Feeling my blood coursing through my veins, I did nothing but fight, move forward, pray through hot tears, and seek. Then I received a kind of divine response. ("The Secret Rite of Sorrow"[76])

It was this response that led Tsunashima toward his "vision of God." He writes about this vision in an essay entitled "My Experience of a Vision of God"[77] included in *Record of a Period of Illness*.

I saw God as He is. I met God as He is. No, the words "see" and "meet" are too superficial or external to properly describe this momentary awareness. It was a fusion of God and myself, a unity; in this moment I melted into the being of God and became I-that-is-God.[78]

Tsunashima influenced many people at the time through his personal religious experience and profound faith that expressed an "ardent yearning" for God. For example, in an essay entitled "[Tsunashima] Ryōsen, [Takayama] Chogyū, the Times, and a New Self"[79] Shimamura Hōgetsu, who is best known as a literary critic and stage director, writes that what might be called "Tsunashima fever" swept over the era.[80] This fever also affected Nishida Kitarō. The year after the publication of *Record of a Period of Illness*, Nishida, who was still working as a teacher at the Number Four High School, wrote to his friend Hori Koretaka, "Regarding Tsunashima's *Record of a Period of Illness*, we cannot imagine his elevated state, but when it comes to [his] thought I agree with every word, and I feel as though he is speaking for me, saying exactly what I would like to say."[81] In part 4, "Religion," of *An Inquiry into the Good*, Nishida asserts that "religion's true intent is to obtain the significance of this union of God and human being," and here he may have had in mind Tsunashima's experience of a "vision of God." Abe Yoshishige writes that the thinkers discussed in this chapter who attempted to delve deep inside the self, including Tsunashima, had a strong influence on students at the Number One High School.

> From the thirty-fifth year of the Meiji period (1902) onwards, under the influence of Takayama Chogyū, and other figures further upstream such as Uchimura Kanzō and Kitamura Tōkoku and downstream such as Kiyozawa Manshi, Chikazumi Jōkan, and Tsunashia Ryōsen, an individualistic trend toward sinking within the self arose, centered in the literature club of the Number One High School.[82]

(5) Uchimura Kanzō's Individualism

While Christianity spread its belief apace amid the active acceptance of Western writings in the first half of the Meiji period, from around the middle of the third decade of this era this religion was put through a great "trial" by the rise of various forms of nationalism. Inoue Tetsujirō's *The Collision of Education and Religion*[83] (1893) is a paradigmatic example of the intense attacks leveled against Christianity. Inoue points out that Christianity is incompatible with the nationalism of the Imperial Edict on Education, and harshly criticizes it for being at its root antinationalist or anationalist. Amid this criticism, figures such as Ebina Danjō (1856–1937) emerged who sought to compromise with nationalism and "Japanicize" Christianity. This can be described as a painful decision taken for the sake of survival.

On the other hand, there were also some who could not accept this kind of compromise. In his *The Formation of Modern Japan and Christianity*[84] (1950), Sumiya Mikio writes that there were three approaches among those who took this path. First, like Uemura Masahisa (1858–1925), there were "people who, by closing themselves off within their church, attempted to preserve the purity of their faith with their church as its core." Second, like Abe Isoo (1865–1949), there were "people who sought new developments in Christianity in combination with social movements." Third, like Uchimura Kanzō, there were those who took "the approach of trying to establish faith within the individual as something truly personal."[85] In his *The Modern Spirit and Its Limits*,[86] in which he discusses the historical significance of Uchimura Kanzō as a modern thinker, Ienaga Saburō sees a "lofty individualism" in Uchimura, and this individualism can perhaps be described as one of the characteristics of Uchimura's faith.

This individualism is particularly evident in Uchimura's "nonchurch" thought. Uchimura had always had a profound interest in social issues. In 1897, at the invitation of its founder, Kuroiwa Ruikō, he became editor-in-chief of the English language section of the *Yorozuchōhō* newspaper and turned his pen to social commentary. There he became associated with the likes of Kōtoku Shūsui (1871–1911) and Sakai Toshihiko (1870–1933) and argued strongly against the Russo-Japanese War. Together with these thinkers he formed an organization called the "Ideals Group"[87] and devoted his energies to social reform. He was also deeply involved in the protest movement that arose in response to the Ashio mining pollution incident.[88]

Eventually, however, Uchimura came to believe that social problems could not be solved through concrete reform movements but rather through each individual's faith in God. From around the time of the establishment of the religious magazines *Bible Studies*[89] (founded in 1900) and *Non-Church*[90] (founded in 1901) his attention turned to the Bible itself and its "study." Looking at writings such as "My Reform Method,"[91] published in *Bible Studies* in 1903, it is clear that even after this shift Uchimura had not by any means lost interest in social betterment. The conviction that to truly better society each individual must establish their own faith nevertheless seems to have taken hold within him.

Uchimura did not, however, view the institution of the church or the words of the Bible as fixed and believe that adherence to them was necessary. His approach to the Bible is well illustrated by the following passage from the essay "Discourse on Truth"[92] (1909) published in *Bible Studies*.

> I don't necessarily preach Christianity; I preach what I believe to be the truth. I do not say that it is the truth because it is written in the Bible; I say it is the truth because it is the truth. I study the Bible, but I do not follow it blindly.[93]

Uchimura's aim was always the pursuit of truth, and it was to this end he endeavored to "study" the Bible.

Uchimura was at his core a proponent of freedom. As can be seen in writings such as "The Decline of Freedom,"[94] which was published in *Bible Studies* in 1909, he did not stop emphasizing the importance of "freedom" even as most of his compatriots were moving toward state authoritarianism. When it came to his handling of the Bible, too, he sought to treat this text as testimony of a living faith rather than dogma. It was also his belief that salvation of the soul was possible only through faith, not through the institution of a church or established sacraments. In "On the Abolition of the Baptism and the Feast,"[95] published in *Bible Studies* in 1901, Uchimura writes, "We are saved by faith; we are not saved by action (ritual). . . . what is important is to believe that the child of God was nailed to a cross and redeemed all our sins; everything else is trivia."[96] He had no need for either church or sacraments. His "nonchurchism" can be said to have been born out of this belief that one can encounter God directly through faith, not as a member of a church but as an individual human being.

3. Looking Toward Peace and Social Paradoxes

(1) The Early Socialist Movement Tied to Christianity

Along with the turn toward the interior of the individual, a strong interest in social issues can be cited as one of the characteristics of the intellectual environment in the latter half of the Meiji period.

Presumably as a result of both changes in industrial structure and an accompanying increase in wage laborers and the government's approach to the expansion of armaments following the end of the First Sino-Japanese War in 1895 (the twenty-eighth year of the Meiji period), there was intensified focus on labor and social issues (including the Ashio mining pollution incident) and issues related to peace (the "antiwar movement" during the Russo-Japanese War, for example). In this context people began to look toward socialism.

Socialist thought had been known in Japan prior to the third decade of the Meiji period. Through articles such as "Labor Unions"[97] and "Workers' Voice"[98] (1890), Tokutomi Sohō's *Friend of the People* had introduced socialist thought and the labor movements of various foreign countries. But these issues had been debated as theoretical questions, and it was only after the end of the First Sino-Japanese War that they were discussed as practical matters. Kōsaka Masaaki records this in *The History of Meiji Thought*, writing, "What had merely been questions of concepts or ideals up until the First Sino-Japanese War have now become practical issues."[99]

One of the characteristics of the early socialist movement was the participation of many Christians. The Socialism Studies Association founded in 1898 was one of the starting points of the socialist movement in Japan, and this association was created by Christians such as Murai Tomoyoshi[100] (1861–1944), Abe Isoo[101] (1865–1949), and Katayama Sen[102] (1859–1933), along with socialists such as Kōtoku Shūsui[103] (1871–1911). Abe, Katayama, Kinoshita Naoe[104] (1869–1937), and Nishikawa Kōjirō[105] (1876–1940) are also listed as founders of the Social Democratic Party, which was formed in 1901 (and immediately ordered disbanded). Its founding declaration extols aims such as the fair distribution of wealth, a guarantee of equal educational opportunities, and the realization of peace. In the early period of socialist activism, this movement was linked to Christian humanitarianism in their mutual pursuit of the realization of social justice and opposition to war.

In Murai Tomoyoshi's *Socialism* (1899),[106] for example, we find the following passage.

Here I can speak from my own experience. In the past I studied early Christianity, and from that starting point I came to recognize the truth of socialism. Conversely, starting from a belief in socialism I then grasped a new significance of Christianity.[107]

Reflecting on his period as a minister in the Okayama Church in *Until I Became a Socialist: The Autobiography of Abe Isoo*[108] (1932), Abe Isoo describes being moved by the sight of a believer from the discriminated-against *buraku* class giving a talk on the Bible at Sunday school in front of other believers that included members of the elite *samurai* class, and records having been drawn to Christianity by its humanitarian, egalitarian, and "commonerist" spirit.[109] It can perhaps be said that Abe, and the many other Christians who embraced socialism, saw the same spirit in both this religion and this political movement.

(2) Kōtoku Shūsui's Socialism

Uchimura Kanzō had a close relationship with Kōtoku Shūsui and Sakai Toshihiko when he was an employee of *Yorozuchōhō*, and he argued strongly against the Russo-Japanese War alongside them in its pages. But as public opinion started to shift toward the outbreak of hostilities, the editorial stance of *Yorozuchōhō* and the opinion of its proprietor, Kuroiwa Ruikō, also turned toward support for the war. As a result of this change, in October 1903 Uchimura, Kōtoku, and Sakai all resigned from this newspaper. The following month Kōtoku and Sakai founded Heimin-sha[110] and established the weekly *Common People* newspaper.[111] In a "Declaration" printed in its first issue, they stated their support of "commonerism" to make freedom complete, socialism to realize equality, and pacifism to truly walk the path of love for humanity.

In 1903 Kōtoku also published *The Essence of Socialism*. Drawing on American economist Richard T. Ely's *Socialism: An Examination of Its Nature, Its Strength and Its Weakness* (1894), he enumerates the core concepts of socialism as follows: "public ownership of land capital"; "public management of production"; "distribution of social income"; and "returning the greater part of social income to the private ownership of individuals."[112] This approach is characterized by not criticizing private ownership (apart from the ownership of land) and on the contrary considering it to be the foundation of freedom.

Following the end of the Russo-Japanese War, the Heimin-sha was forced to dissolve under pressure from the government, but a mass movement was nevertheless developed in various forms. In 1906 Sakai's group joined forces with a group headed by Nishikawa Kōjirō to seek common suffrage and the Japan Socialist Party was formed. This party played an active role in various areas including the common suffrage movement, labor disputes, and the debate over the Ashio mining pollution incident, but eventually cracks began to appear within it. On the one hand, a gulf emerged between socialists and Christians who had come together with the aims of realizing social justice and opposing war. Figures such as Kinoshita Naoe declared that Christianity was incompatible with socialism and shifted their stance. On the other hand, cracks also opened up within the ranks of the socialists themselves. Kōtoku was imprisoned for five months in 1905 after an incident involving his writings in *Common People* newspaper and left for America after his release. After returning to Japan the following year, his focus shifted from parliamentarianism to direct action. In an article entitled "The Change in My Thinking (Regarding Common Suffrage)"[113] published in the daily *Common People* newspaper in 1907 he declared, "The aims of socialism cannot be accomplished by anything other than the direct action of workers united as one"[114] and proceeded to develop a doctrine of direct action based on general strikes.

Within this environment, some socialists turned to terrorism, and there was an incident[115] following which Kōtoku was imprisoned along with many other socialists under suspicion of having been a ringleader in a seditious plot. From that point on the socialist movement suffered an inevitable decline.[116]

(3) Interest in Peace

On October 12, 1903 Sakai Toshihiko and Kōtoku Shūsui issued a joint "Resignation Statement" and severed their ties to *Yorozuchōhō*, which had shifted its stance toward support for war, and on the same day Uchimura Kanzō published "Memorandum to [Kuroiwa] Ruikō on the Occasion of My Resignation"[117] in which he expressed strong opposition to Japan's embarking on the path to war, writing, "I believe that to assent to the initiation of a Russo-Japanese war is to assent to the destruction of Japan."

Uchimura had not always been opposed to war. When the First Sino-Japanese War broke out, he published an article entitled "The Righteousness of the Sino-Japanese War"[118] in *Friend of the People* in which he promoted this conflict as a "righteous war"[119] that aimed to overcome barbarism with civilization. The year after a peace treaty had been signed, however, he published another article in *Friend of the People*, "Observations of the Times."[120] In it he records that "as soon as the war ended, as the victor it was as though [Japan] removed its original aim of the independence of neighboring countries from all consideration, and paying no heed to this issue the attention of all its citizens turned to opening up new territories, expanding into new markets, and obtaining as many of the spoils of war as possible,"[121] and having come to the realization that the ideal of seeking the independence of the Korean Peninsula had been nothing more than a cover for obtaining territory and expanding markets, confesses his own "stupidity and faithlessness."[122]

This understanding presumably led Uchimura toward opposing war. In "On the Abolition of War,"[123] an article published in *Yorozuchōhō* the year before the Russo-Japanese War began, he states, "I am not merely opposed to war with Russia. I am an absolute pacificist. To engage in warfare is to kill human beings. To kill human beings is a grossly evil act. . . . if anything can be described as the most foolish thing in the world, it is to attempt to advance the fate of the nation by the sword."[124] In the same year he published an article entitled "The Gospel of Peace (Absolute Pacificism)" in *Bible Studies* in which he asserts that what the Bible advocates is "absolute peace" and declares that he has adopted the stance of an "absolute pacificist" who refuses to take up the sword no matter what kind of situation may arise.[125]

> A good aim cannot be achieved through evil means. It is nonsensical to speak of creating a permanent peace in Asia by means of murder. Peace can never come through war. [126]

At the start of "War and Morality," an essay published on the eve of the Russo-Japanese War, Kōtoku Shūsui echoes Uchimura in declaring "war is an evil act." While Uchimura appeals to faith in calling war evil, Kōtoku Shūsui does so by appealing to morality. In response to those who say that the abolition of war is an ideal but when it comes to actual international morality conflict is inevitable, Kōtoku writes as follows.

> Regarding the occurrence of war, then, even if this is inevitable, if we know that war is an evil act are we not obligated to oppose it in all circumstances and do everything in our power to prevent it? One should think of low international morality as no different from low personal morality.[127]

Part II

The Era of Formation—
The Philosophy of the Taishō
and Early Shōwa Periods

Chapter 4

Thought in the Taishō and Early Shōwa Periods

1. The Taishō Period

(1) Culture and Cultivation

A clue to grasping Taishō period thought as a whole can be found in the following words by Miki Kiyoshi, from an essay entitled "Reading Wanderings"[1] in his *Reading and Life*[2] (1942).

> While living through the First World War, we were completely indifferent to politics. Or we were able to be indifferent. What eventually came to dominate us was, on the contrary, "cultivation" thought. This was a culturalist way of thinking, an antipolitical or apolitical tendency to look on politics with disdain while emphasizing the importance of culture. This "cultivation" thought was cultural and philosophical. It placed a special emphasis on literature and philosophy, and dismissed fields such as science and technology as belonging to "civilization" rather than "culture." To put it another way, the cultivation thought of the Taishō period arose as a countermovement against the enlightenment thought of the Meiji period.[3]

This passage reveals that in this period people in Japan turned their backs on politics and convenience pursued through science and technology, engaged in cultivation through literature and philosophy, and tried to improve themselves, emphasizing over all else the "culture" that would make this possible. This "culture" and "cultivation" can be said to characterize—although of course not in all respects—the Taishō period (1912–1926).

This inward-looking orientation running through the Taishō period was also reflected in philosophy. In *Studies in the History of Taishō Philosophy*[4] (1965), Funayama Shin'ichi (1907–1994) states that "internal individuality" was the fundamental principle of philosophy in this period. The foundation of Meiji philosophy had been realism and positivism, and philosophy's relationship with the state had always been at issue. In contrast, the foundation of Taishō philosophy was idealism, and it was characterized by its aloofness from politics. Here we can also see the modernity of Taishō philosophy. Funayama, however, sees this shift as double-edged. On the one hand he views philosophy's independence from politics as a positive development, but on the other hand "in the name of philosophy's transcendency of politics, it also had the negative meaning of indifference to politics and a lack of political criticism, and therefore indirectly the affirmation, defense, and even glorification of state authoritarianism."[5]

(2) T. H. Green's Theory of Personality Realization

Of course, the tendency to emphasize culture and cultivation was not something that emerged suddenly in the Taishō period; it had in fact already begun in the Meiji period. This is demonstrated by the popularity of the thought of T. H. Green (1836–1882) in the latter part of the Meiji period. Green was a philosopher and one of the leading figures in British idealism. In contrast to the empiricism of thinkers such as Hume that attempted to explain all experience by reducing human understanding to sensation, Green's philosophy was characterized by his assertion of the active nature of the actions of the mind and the unity of the self. Green's thought was first introduced in Japan by Nakajima Rikizō (1858–1918), who taught ethics at the University of Tokyo after having studied at Dōshisha English School in Kyoto and Yale University in the United States. Nakajima introduced Green's theory of "self-realization" through essays such as "On the British Neo-Kantian School" (1892) and his lectures at the University of Tokyo. This idea was widely disseminated at the time, having a strong influence not only on those who attended his lectures directly, such as Fujii Kenjirō (1872–1931) and Nishi Shin'ichirō (1873–1943), but also the likes of Ōnishi Hajime and Tsunashima Ryōsen.

Nishida Kitarō also had the opportunity to attend Nakajima's lectures at the University of Tokyo. Presumably as a result of their influence, he began to study Green's theory of ethics around the time he graduated, and in 1895 he published a summary of the content of Green's *Prolegomena to Ethics* entitled "An Outline of Green's Ethics." In it he writes, for example, that "the progress and development of humanity is in essence nothing other than the progress and development of individual qualities, that is, it should be said to lie in my perfectly realizing my capacities of perception and understanding and by doing so developing my personality."[6] Drawing on this conception, in *An Inquiry into the Good* (1911) he writes, "the good is the full development of the self (self-realization)"[7] and "the development of our personality is for us the absolute good."

As these examples demonstrate, from the third decade of the Meiji period Green's theory of self-realization was received as a doctrine of "personality development" or "personality realization" and the term "personality realization theory" eventually came into wide use. The Japanese word *jinkaku*[8] was a new term that had been in use since the second decade of the Meiji period. It had originally been suggested to Nakajima as a translation of "personality" by Inoue Tetsujirō, and Nakajima went on to employ it in his essays and lectures. It became widely known in connection with the movement for personal moral cultivation discussed in chapter 3.

It was in this context that through the efforts of Nakajima and others Green's ideas were received as a "personality realization theory." In his *Lectures on Educational Ethics*[9] published in 1911, after presenting hedonism and rationalism as ethical theories that explain what the ultimate good is, Nakajima offers personality realization theory as the final option and asserts that the goal of human life is a personality that is fully realized in both individual and societal aspects.[10]

Underlying Green's thought being received as "personality realization theory" there was the popularity of the concept of "personality" in the late Meiji period, but there was also another reason for this interpretation. Inoue Tetsujirō's having drawn on Green's self-realization theory in his discussion of questions of ethics and morality can be seen, for example, in his five-volume *Middle School Moral Training Textbook*.[11] In chapter 3, "On Ideals," of volume 5 of this series he discusses what should be considered ideal behavior and the purpose of life, and after pointing out the one-sidedness of theories based on hedonism and self-denial, Inoue asserts that the ultimate purpose of life is "to realize and develop personality" and refers to this as "realization theory."[12] He did not call it "self-realization theory" because this can be taken to be individualism. He sought to avoid this term from a perspective that emphasized the nation over the individual. Years later, in an essay entitled

"Remembering Professor Nakajima Rikizō," Inoue writes that he avoided this risk by expressing "self-realization" as "personality realization."[13]

(3) ABE JIRŌ'S PERSONALITY-ISM

Abe Jirō was foremost among those who carried forward into the Taishō period the Meiji period view that the ultimate good was for each individual to demonstrate their abilities to the greatest possible extent and fully develop their personality. Jirō (1883–1959) was a disciple of Raphael von Koeber who became the first professor of aesthetics at Tohoku University. He published a book entitled *Personality-ism*[14] in 1922, in which he defined personality-ism as "an approach that makes the growth and development of personality its highest value, and seeks to establish the meaning and consideration of all other values in relation to this most important value."[15]

As for the definition of personality, Abe describes it as the subject who thinks, feels, and desires. Moreover, rather than being the sum of individual thoughts, feelings, and desires, it is the subject that undergirds these sorts of internal activities and serves as their unifying principle. Personality-ism is an approach that places the greatest value on striving to fully develop this personality through ceaseless effort, and when it comes to what points the way toward this full development Abe focuses on "ideals." As can be seen from book 1 of *Personality-ism* having been entitled "Introduction—Idealism,"[16] personality-ism was deeply tied to idealism.

Abe defines idealism as a stance that "seeks to regulate all thought and action with ideals as guiding principles."[17] In other words, it is a stance in which once ideals have been established they are given "authority to command and govern reality" and considered the fundamental principles of thought and action. Regarding the nature of ideals, Abe gives "love, justice, and the fulfillment of personality values" as concrete examples. But these things are not fixed. They are "reconstructed, re-created, and relearned" in the course of actual lives.

Abe refers to someone who is able to regulate their life with ideals as their guiding principles as a "sovereign person."[18] A "sovereign person" is a "free person in the deepest sense" who can believe in the dignity of their own personality and act according to their own autonomous will. They not only perceive fully fostering the growth of their own personality to be their greatest duty, but also aim to influence those around them and transform society into a union of free personalities. In a society that creates "free people," everyone is "treated equally as someone with a free personality," and "the opportunity to foster and expand their own personality is given to each individual according to their ability."[19] The fulfillment of each personality and the formation of a society through the free personalities thus created binding themselves together as free personalities can be described as the aims of personality-ism. This is one of the main characteristics of Abe Jirō's "personality-ism."

(4) CULTIVATIONISM

For Abe, what made the "growth and development of personality" possible was "cultivation." As he stated in *The Diary of Santarō*,[20] the meaning of "cultivation" was to be found in encountering the universal through the rich culture bequeathed by humanity, "escaping the limits of individual existence," and obtaining "internal freedom of the will and autonomy of the will." This approach is connected to the Meiji-period "self-cultivationism"[21] that aimed at the "cultivation of personality," but rather than training based on a fixed frame or mold it involves the constant pursuit of the universal through wide reading and observation and is characterized by the attempt to secure internal freedom without any sort of constraint. This idealism and personality-ism based approach later came to be called "cultivationism"[22] and was taken up as a philosophical trend particularly among young intellectuals studying at universities and old-system high schools. In the previously cited "Reading Wanderings," Miki Kiyoshi writes, "The concept of 'cultivation' was shaped mainly by students of [Natsume] Sōseki who had been influenced by Professor Koeber. Abe Jirō's *The Diary of Santarō* was a leading example of this, and I too indulged in it by candlelight in my dormitory after lights out."

The concept of "cultivation" thus gradually took shape, and Koeber was part of the backdrop against which it was embraced. Hatano Seiichi (1877–1950) was one of the students who was heavily influenced by Koeber's scholarship and personality, and in an essay entitled "Reminiscences,"[23] written when Koeber passed away, he emphasizes that Koeber always placed great weight on "cultivation" in his guidance of students and was himself someone who engaged in rich and profound cultivation.

Koeber did not produce many writings after coming to Japan, but several of his essays can be found in *Collected Essays of Professor Koeber*.[24] One of these is "Response to the Dean of the Faculty of Letters." It seems to have been a presentation of his own views regarding university reforms in answer to a request from the dean of the Faculty of Letters of the University of Tokyo. In it he writes that "humanistic cultivation" (*humanistische*

Bildung) is the only means by which students can be led toward free and independent academic activity, and the only means by which Japan can stand shoulder to shoulder with the nations of Europe."[25] When it came to the teaching of philosophy, too, Koeber required his students to understand it not simply as a finished product but from its origins and positioned within a wider cultural tradition. This approach was then inherited by those who studied under him.

This Taishō-period cultivationism also continued into the Shōwa period (1926–1989). This is well demonstrated by *Student Library*,[26] a twelve-volume series edited by Kawai Eijirō and published between 1936 and 1941. Its authors include Minobe Tatsukichi (1873–1948), Abe Jirō, Amano Teiyū (1884–1980), Tanikawa Tetsuzō (1895–1989), and Hani Gorō (1901–1983). In the introduction to volume 1, *Students and Cultivation*,[27] Kawai writes, "How should subjectivity itself be? This question has gradually drawn the attention of young people. This long-neglected issue is indeed the most radical issue for us as human beings, and must indeed also form a starting premise when it comes to the analysis and reform of objectivity."[28]

Various criticisms had already been leveled against cultivationism in the Taishō period. A critical eye was turned toward its apolitical stance and aloofness that takes pride in the richness of one's own internal life. Although not published until after the war in 1949, Karaki Junzō's *An Attempt at Modern History*[29] offers the following critique of Taishō-period cultivationism.

> Can we really establish a true inner life through the method
> of reading works by people of the past? To put it another way,
> can we really establish our own core by enriching our cultiva-
> tion or devoting ourselves to cultivation? To read is indeed to
> enjoy and appreciate. Can we really establish our core through
> enjoyment in the library, the quiet enjoyment obtained through
> the printed word?[30]

(5) Culturism

"Culture" is what enables cultivation and elevating oneself, and conversely "culture" is also what is produced by cultivation and a fully matured personality. It is therefore not at all surprising that during the Taishō period personality-ism and cultivationism were proclaimed on the one hand while on the other hand there was also much discussion of culturism. One of the driving forces in this trend was an organization called the Dawn Society.[31] The Dawn Society was an enlightenment organization formed by Yoshino Sakuzō (1878–1933) together with the economist Fukuda Tokuzō (1874–1930) and others such as Miyake Setsurei, Sōda Kiichirō (1881–1927), Tomonaga Sanjyūrō (1871–1951), and Kuwaki Gen'yoku. Its stated aims included "to demonstrate Japan's unique mission in the development of global culture" and "to eradicate dangerous, bigoted thought that runs counter to the majority of the world." Most of its members were scholars who supported the democracy[32] advocated by Yoshino. At its first lecture meeting, held in January of 1919, the Dawn Society presented a talk by Sōda Kiichirō entitled "The Logic of Culturism," and in the same year it also presented a talk by Kuwaki Gen'yoku entitled simply "Culturism." "Culture" was one of its key terms.

In "The Logic of Culturism," Sōda Kiichirō asserts that when we attempt to "purify the values found in the history of human culture," what stands at the end as the ultimate aim of this endeavor are "cultural values," and these can be said to have been understood as the ideals of truth, goodness, and beauty discussed in Neo-Kantianism. Sōda referred to the effort to plot out the realization of these sorts of "cultural values" as "culturism."[33]

Kuwaki asserted that "culture" corresponded to the German *Kultur* and signified progress "in the spiritual, ideal direction" in contrast to "civilization," which signified progress in the material domain. In explaining the aim of culture, he invoked the concept of "personality." The purpose of culture was to develop personality, which is the essence of a person, as richly as possible; in other words, it was "to develop freely all faculties of a person with a personality" without being limited to the domains of academic learning or morality. He then states that "the thought that puts this culture at the center of our daily lives is culturism."[34] Sōda also saw the true meaning of culture in the "self-development and creation of a free personality," and in both cases culturism can be said to have at the same time been "personality-ism."

In the middle of the Meiji period, when Inoue Tetsujirō studied in Europe, studying abroad was limited to a very small number of people, but twenty years later, from the Russo-Japanese War to the First World War, the number of scholars studying overseas grew markedly. In the field of philosophy, scholars such as Hatano Seiichi, Sōda Kiichirō, Kuwaki Gen'yoku, and Tomonaga Sanjyūrō studied in Germany, mainly in Heidelberg. Heidelberg was a focal point of the Neo-Kantian School, which at the time was the most powerful school of philosophy in Germany, and in particular its Southwest School. Sōda and Tomonaga studied there and were greatly influenced by the philosophy of thinkers such as Wilhelm Windelband (1848–1915) and Heinrich John Rickert (1863–1936).

In contrast to the Marburg School of Neo-Kantians such as Hermann Cohen (1842–1918) who developed Kant's criticism in the direction of logicism, the Southwest School sought a grounding for the human and social sciences based on the philosophy of value. Underlying this approach was the rise of scientific materialism and positivism that had accompanied notable advances in the natural sciences and the idea that philosophy had lost sight of the path forward. In this context the Neo-Kantian School, while acknowledging the importance of positivist science, attempted to provide a grounding for it, that is, to elucidate how it was to be made possible. The Southwest School was characterized by not restricting this critique of knowledge to the natural sciences but expanding it more broadly to the humanities and social sciences.

Drawing on Windelband's distinction between natural science and historical science, Rickert finds the defining characteristic of natural science in its discovery of universal conceptual relationships (laws) regarding the existence and occurrence of objects free from value, and in contrast finds that of cultural science in the description of the particularity and individuality of objects that provide meaning and value. The influence of cultural philosophy at the time can be seen from the publication of *LOGOS: Internationale Zeitschrift für Philosophie der Kultur* by Windelband, Rickert, Rudolf Eucken (1846–1926) and Georg Simmel (1858–1918) in 1910 and Simmel's *Philosophische Kultur* in 1911.

This was precisely the era in which the likes of Sōda, Kuwaki, and Tomonaga were studying in Germany, and their having been greatly influenced by the German trend of cultural philosophy led to the abovementioned lectures. Through their activities, for a time cultural philosophy became a major trend in Japan as well. Publications in this vein included Kuwaki's *Culturism and Social Issues*[35] (Shizendō Shoten, 1920), Tsuchida Kyōson (1891–1934)'s *Fundamentals of Culturism*[36] (Naigai Shuppan, 1921), Nomura Waihan (1884–1921)'s *Culturism Studies*[37] (Daidōkan Shoten, 1921), and, from 1922, Kaizōsha's *Cultural Philosophy Series*.[38] Nishida Kitarō also published an essay on Windelband's and Rickert's historical science (cultural science) entitled "Natural Science and Historical Science"[39] in 1913, and Tanabe Hajime (1885–1962) published an essay entitled "The Concept of Culture"[40] in 1922.

(6) Kantian and Neo-Kantian Studies

This culturalism movement was deeply connected to the development of the study of Kantian philosophy. In his *Studies in the History of Taishō Philosophy*, Funayama Shin'ichi asserts that "the primary characteristic of *Taishō* culturism was the development of [Kantian] criticism."[41] Those who played an important role in the development of Kantian studies included Kuwaki Gen'yoku, Sōda Kiichirō, and Tomonaga Sanjyūrō. Behind their work lay their having encountered the rapid development of Kantian studies in Germany while studying overseas and having been greatly influenced by philosophers of the Neo-Kantian School. Their time in Germany coincided with an upsurge in Kantian studies; the centenary of Kant's death was commemorated in 1904 and the bicentenary of his birth in 1920. In Japan, too, *The Collected Writings of Kant*[42] began to be published in 1918, and academic writings on Kant followed in a steady stream. Through works such as Kuwaki Gen'yoku's *Kant and Modern Philosophy*[43] (1917), Tomonaga Sanjyūrō's *Kant's Theory of Peace*[44] (1922), Abe Yoshishige's *Kant's Practical Philosophy*[45] (1924), and Tanabe Hajime's *Kant's Teleology*[46] (1924), the study of Kant in Japan progressed rapidly.

Here I would like to discuss Tomonaga Sanjyūrō's *Kant's Theory of Peace*, which can be thought of has having had great significance in relation to the intellectual trends of the Taishō period. The significance of this text lay, to begin with, in its having introduced Kant's belief that "republican government" was the form of governance most compatible with the idea of the nation and emphasized that this was a premise for securing peace, that is, that "the nations in question having republican governments is an important condition for the advent of perpetual peace."[47] Another important point is that Tomonaga displayed doubt about Kant's having sought concrete measures to realize perpetual peace in a peace alliance (international alliance) that would secure the sovereignty and freedom of each nation. On the one hand, Kant discusses the possibility of all nations abandoning their sovereignty and freedom to create a single international nation (*civitas gentium*) that would ultimately expand into a "global republic" (*Weltrepublik*). But he then points out that the concept of an international nation contradicts the original concept of a nation, and asserts that war should be prevented to the greatest extent possible through international alliances as a passive replacement for this single global republic. In contrast to Kant's view, Tomonaga asserts that the realization of an international nation or global republic "is not only by no means theoretically impossible, however difficult it may be in practice, but is the most thoroughgoing approach by which to usher in a perpetual peace."[48]

This focus on Kant's philosophy in the Taishō period was overlaid with an interest in the Neo-Kantian School. Kuwaki's understanding of Kant was strongly influenced by the realist interpretation advocated by Alois Riehl (1844–1924), under whom he studied at the University of Berlin, and the cultural philosophy of Windelband. After having studied in Germany for ten years, Sōda Kiichirō produced works such as *Issues in Economic Philosophy*[49] (1917) and *Cultural Values and Extreme Concepts*[50] (1922) and poured his energy into the construction of "economic philosophy," and here too the influence of Rickert can be found.

Tanabe Hajime also engaged in the study of the Neo-Kantian School at an early stage. Tanabe's scholarship concerning the Neo-Kantian School—found in essays such as "The Limits of Logicism in Epistemology: A Critique of the Marburg and Freiberg Schools"[51] (1914)—became a major influence on the thought of Nishida Kitarō. During this period Tanabe and Nishida developed their thought regarding the evaluation of the Neo-Kantian School in a relationship of close communication.[52]

(7) The Philosophy of Life / Pragmatism

In Tanabe Hajime's abovementioned "The Concept of Culture" it is pointed out that within the trend of culture or culturism there was "a tendency to emphasize the creative activities of life," and the Taishō period was indeed an era in which the term "life"[53] enjoyed great prominence. For example, Shimamura Hōgetsu (1871–1918), a leader in the New Theater movement who was also active as a critic in the late Meiji and Taishō periods, translated Ibsen's *A Doll's House*, and in the included "Explanation" he writes, "What is emitted from the core of art is the light of life, and the heat of life. Art is the boiling of life itself." Ōsugi Sakae (1885–1923) was a well-known social activist who published essays such as "The Expansion of Life"[54] and "The Creation of Life,"[55] and in the former we find the phrase "the beauty of the pinnacle of life is seen in the expansion of life." In *Santarō's Diary*,[56] Abe Jirō writes, "Emphasizing life, creation, and unity is a welcome intellectual trend"[57] (1913). Focusing on this state of affairs, Suzuki Sadami believed "life" can be "a device for observing the state of thought and culture in this period," and from this perspective employs the term "Taishō life-ism."[58]

As an example of someone who focused on the meaning of "life" in the domain of philosophy, first and foremost there is Nishida Kitarō. In chapter 8, "Nature," of book 2, "Existence," of *An Inquiry into the Good* (1911), which I examine in detail in the next chapter, Nishida asserts that nature is not simply an objective target of observation from the outside but a concrete reality of consciousness that unifies the subjective and the objective, that this nature as a concrete entity is endowed with a unified force, and that this unified force is what makes nature "life."

The period in which the discourse surrounding "life" flourished overlapped with the period in which Henri Bergson's philosophy was introduced and had a powerful influence on Japan's intellectual milieu. Nishida created the opportunity for this trend to arise. In 1910, the year before the publication of *An Inquiry into the Good*, Nishida had taken up a post at Kyoto University (at the time *An Inquiry into the Good* had already been written), and in his work there addressed Bergson, publishing the two essays "Bergson's Philosophical Methodology"[59] (1910) and "Bergson's Pure Duration"[60] (1911). The reason Nishida's interest had been drawn to Bergson's philosophy can be seen in the following passage from "Bergson's Philosophical Methodology."

To describe the inclination of his [Bergson's] thought, in contrast to the view that the method of learning of natural science is paramount and reality cannot be explained without cramming each and every phenomenon into the iron confines of laws of cause and effect, he says that there are creative acts beyond the laws of nature in the depths of our mental life, that to us the world of direct existence is not the world of objects of knowledge but rather this world of activities of the will, and that the explanations of natural science are nothing more than superficial explanations of reality.[61]

This text is also relevant when considering why people's interest turned to "life" in the Taishō period. It shows there was a desire to not simply explain nature from a mechanistic perspective but to attempt to discover "creative acts beyond the laws of nature" in its depths. At the same time, the view that the "world of direct existence" was not simply the world of objects of knowledge but the world of activities of the will also applies to Nishida's understanding of "pure experience," and here it is clear that Nishida saw commonalities with his own thought in Bergson.

Following its introduction in these two essays by Nishida, Bergson's philosophy became very popular at the end of the Meiji period and the beginning of the Taishō period. Many books on it were published, including Nomura Waihan's *Bergson and Modern Thought*[62] (1914) and Nakazawa Rinsen's *Bergson*[63] (1914) and translations such as *Bergson's Philosophy*[64] (1913, a translation of *Introduction à la Métaphysique* by Nishikida Yoshitomi), *Creative Evolution*[65] (1913, translated by Kaneko Umaji and Katsurai Tōnosuke), and *Matter and Memory*[66] (1914, translated by Takahashi Satomi). As Nishida aptly put it, Bergson's philosophy "held sway over our nation's intellectual sphere." Kuki Shūzō studied in Europe for eight years from 1921 to 1929, and while living in Paris published an essay entitled "Bergson au Japon" in *Les Nouvelles Littéraires'* special issue on Bergson. In it he writes, "The main role he played for us was arousing a desire for metaphysics. Our spirits, parched by the critical formalism of German Neo-Kantianism, welcomed the blessed rain of Bergson's metaphysical intuition."[67] The popularity of Bergson's philosophy shows that while Neo-Kantian philosophy wielded overwhelming influence at the time, there were also those who resisted it and turned in the direction of metaphysics.

Starting with Bergson, there were many thinkers whose intellectual importance Nishida recognized and introduced to Japan, one of whom was Dilthey. Nishida first cites Dilthey in 1913 in an essay published in the *Journal of Philosophy* entitled "Natural Science and Historical Science,"[68] and prior to this almost no Japanese thinkers had examined and discussed his philosophy. In this essay, Nishida basically follows Rickert's view and employs his terms "general perspective" and "individual perspective" in distinguishing the methodology of natural science from that of historical science. Here Nishida also states the view that the task of historical science is to reveal the historical phenomenon of "individuality." When the mental activities of human beings are made the object of academic inquiry, he distinguishes between approaches that, like psychology, attempt to address them from a "generalized perspective" and approaches that address human mental activities as "developments of lived individuality," and asserts that Dilthey's concept of "experience" (*Erlebnis*) is an attempt to treat human mental activities as "developments of individuality" in this way. He recognizes Dilthey's distinctiveness in his focusing on the "impulsive power" found in our mental activities and attempting to take our "experiences" as "lived events" that arise, develop, and disappear.

Nietzsche's thought had already been introduced in the 1890s, the middle of the Meiji period, and was touched on in the so-called beautiful life debate sparked by Takayama Chogyū's "Discourse on the Beautiful Life"[69] (1901), but it was Watsuji Tetsurō who pioneered its study in earnest in *Nietzsche Studies*[70] (1913). Watsuji describes the early reception of Nietzsche in Japan as one in which "he [Nietzsche] was showered in all sorts of abuse as a shallow egotist and crude proponent of instinct," but in stating his own contrasting view emphasizes that according to Nietzsche the affirmation of the will was not simply an assertion of egotism but included the negation of the will, and that "Nietzsche's übermenschian affirmation, like the will to power, was in fact a negation of the will that enables life at a higher level."[71] From this perspective, focusing mainly on *The Will to Power*, Watsuji tried to portray Nietzsche as a thinker advocating a "sharply autonomous morality."

Pragmatism had also become well known in Japan by the end of the Meiji period. The psychology of John Dewey (1859–1952) and William James (1842–1910) had been introduced by Motora Yūjirō (1858–1911), who had studied in America and lectured on psychology at the University of Tokyo upon his return to Japan. Among the earliest works to introduce pragmatism were Kihira Tadayoshi's "Mr. Alexander's Truth and Its Characteristics" and "The Division of Academic Inquiry and the Duty of Philosophy" (both published in 1905).[72]

The introduction of pragmatism began in earnest the following year with the publication of Kuwaki Gen'yoku's "Concerning Pragmatism"[73] (1906). After giving a detailed presentation of the doctrines of Charles Sanders Peirce (1839–1914) and F. C. S. Schiller (1864–1937), Kuwaki finds the core of pragmatism in its making the standard of truth "usefulness" or "effectiveness" and its explaining this in terms of society. However, in response to pragmatism's assertion that action is the foundation and root of knowledge, Kuki criticized it for being lax in its consideration of knowledge that is the basis for action, and therefore remaining incomplete as a "pure philosophical doctrine."[74]

This kind of evaluation of pragmatism is widely seen from the end of the Meiji period into the Taishō period, but a more positive assessment was given by Tanaka Kiichi (also known as Tanaka Ōdō, 1868–1932), who had studied under Dewey at the University of Chicago. Tanaka not only introduced pragmatism but also developed original thought based on it in works such as *From the Study to the Streets*[75] (1911), *Thorough Individualism*[76] (1918), and *Creativity and Pleasure*[77] (1921). Dewey's visit to Japan in 1919 also fueled the spread of pragmatism. His series of lectures delivered at the University of Tokyo entitled "The Position of Philosophy at Present: Problems of Philosophic Reconstruction" was later published by Iwanami Shoten as *Reconstruction in Philosophy*[78] (1921).

(8) Taishō Democracy

I have presented Miki Kiyoshi's words "antipolitical or apolitical tendency" as emblematic of the Taishō period, but it is not as though there was no interest in politics at the time. On the contrary, through the development of media such as newspapers and magazines, this was an era during which the general public gained access to a vast quantity of information and came to display great interest in the state of politics and society. And against the backdrop of the rise of democratic movements around the world that began toward the close of the First World War, in Japan, too, a wave of democracy swept through this period as a whole.

In *Studies in the History of Taishō Philosophy*, Funayama Shin'ichi writes that "Taishō democracy and Taishō humanism/cultivationism were parallel phenomena, and there may not have been any interaction between them,"[79] but whether this conclusion can be drawn requires detailed consideration. As I noted above, one of the leading factors in the rise of culturism was the Dawn Society formed by thinkers such as Yoshino Sakuzō and Sōda Kiichirō. As this organization exemplifies, it can be said that Taishō period cultivationism/humanism and Taishō period democracy were connected at their roots.[80]

It is not easy to define what Taishō democracy was, but the definition "a popular movement to democratize the Meiji constitution system in the imperialist stage"[81] can be considered. This presents it as a movement pursuing the realization of democracy in the context of the Meiji constitution system, but when this definition is adopted the question that springs to mind is how to understand the "demos," or, in other words, who is to have the authority to govern the nation. One clear answer to this question is given by Yoshino Sakuzō's "democracy."

Yoshino's understanding of "democracy" is well demonstrated in "On the Essential Meaning of Constitutional Government and the Road to Perfecting Its Beauty"[82] published in *Central Review*.[83] In it he writes that literally democracy means the theoretical assertion that "the authority of the state lies with the people," but this is not amenable to Japan's constitution, which makes the Emperor the overall holder of state authority. It must therefore be understood to mean "the fundamental aim of the activities of state authority must politically lie in the people,"[84] and this is what Yoshino called "democracy." He asserted this "democracy" in order to avoid the question of who has power and clarify that "the fundamental aim of the activities of state authority must politically lie in the people." Yoshino's belief was that the aim of politics should always be "the benefit and well-being of the general public." In accordance with this he asserts that decisions about the direction of the operation of governance, that is, policy decisions, are to depend on "public opinion."[85]

In order to realize this aim, Yoshino called for the adoption of popular elections and a party cabinet system. Regarding foreign affairs, he resolutely criticized Japan's policy of invading Korea and China at a time when nearly everyone else was silent. Immediately after "On the Essential Meaning of Constitutional Government and the Road to Perfecting Its Beauty" Yoshino also published "The Stupor of Japanese Politicians Regarding the Determination of Diplomatic Policy Toward China" and "Examining Manchuria and Korea" in *Central Review*, revealing doubts about Japan's assimilation policy and displaying sympathy toward the nationalism of oppressed people in Korea and China. Matsuo Takayoshi writes that "Yoshino's theory of democracy was established in these three essays."[86]

(9) MARXISM

Following the High Treason Incident of 1910,[87] socialist thought in Japan was for a time enervated, but it once again began to attract widespread interest against the backdrop of the Russian Revolution in 1917 and the formation of the Soviet Union in 1922. Its resurgence also came in the context of domestic developments such as Kawakami Hajime's *Poverty Story*[88] (first serialized in *Osaka Asahi Shimbun*[89] in 1916 and published as a book the following year) becoming a bestseller and its author's later shift toward socialism with the publication of his own journal *Social Problems Studies*[90] (Kōbundō, 1919–1930) and efforts to further its study and promotion.[91] Journals such as Hasegawa Nyozekan and Ōyama Ikuo's *We*[92] and Sakai Toshihiko and Yamakawa Hitoshi's *Socialism Studies*[93] were also published during the same period as Kawakami's *Social Problems Studies*.

Kawakami presented the results of his study of Marxism and the history of economic thought in a rapid-fire series of publications including *On the History of Economic Thought in the Modern Period*[94] (1920), *A Study of Historical Materialism*[95] (1923), and *The Historical Development of Capitalist Economics*[96] (1923), while at the same time receiving a great deal of criticism for these efforts. The critique of Kushida Tamizō (1885–1934), who had studied under Kawakami, is a paradigmatic example of these attacks. In essays such as "The Position of Historical Materialism in the Study of Marx"[97] and "Does Socialism Face the Darkness or Face the Light? One View of Doctor

Kawakami's *The Historical Development of Capitalist Economics*"[98] (included in volume 1 of *The Complete Works of Kushida Tamizō*[99]) Kushida makes the criticism that while Kawakami does indeed address historical materialism, fundamentally he approaches it from a humanitarian perspective and does not understand that at its foundation lies dialectical materialism.

Fukumoto Kazuo (1894–1983), one of the leading theorists of the communist movement in his era, also strongly criticized Kawakami. In works such as *On the Methodology of Economic Criticism*[100] (1926) and *Historical Materialism and the Centrist View of History*[101] (1926), Fukumoto argued that Kawakami's understanding of historical materialism never got beyond the point of shallow formulism and that he excluded dialectical materialism from historical materialism, grasping it only as an economic view of history.[102]

Having received these criticisms, Kawakami realized that his understanding of the philosophical foundations of Marxism was wholly inadequate,[103] and along with once again examining *Das Kapital* he deepened his interactions with philosophers of the Kyoto School in order to come to grips with dialectical materialism. After requesting Nishida's assistance, he began to read Hegel's *Wissenschaft der Logik* with professors and instructors in the faculties of law and economics under the tutelage of Kimura Motomori (1895–1946), one of Nishida's disciples. Apart from these efforts he also organized an association to engage in the fundamental study of Marx's philosophy to which he invited Miki Kiyoshi. Ishikawa Kōji (1892–1976), one of the main members of this group, reports that to address Fukumoto's criticism they read Marx's *Zur Kritik der politischen Ökonomie*. He also notes that Miki suggested making the group an "Association for the Criticism of Economics" and this proposal was accepted.[104]

(10) The Influence of Japanese Philosophy (Thought) on China

When socialism once again began to attract the attention of people in Japan, those drawn to it included Chinese intellectuals studying abroad.

Studies of the influence of Japanese philosophy and thought on Chinese thinkers include "The Dialogue Between Chinese Philosophy and Japanese Philosophy" and "The Significance of Modern Japanese Philosophy in East Asia: Focusing on Meiji Philosophy" by Bian Chongdao (1942–2012), a professor at the Chinese Academy of Social Sciences. In these essays he argues that the thought of figures such as Fukuzawa Yukichi, Kōtoku Shūsui, and Kawakami Hajime played a major role in China's process of modernization. According to Bian, one significance of Japanese philosophy in the Meiji and Taishō periods was that other countries in East Asia such as China and Korea learned about Western philosophy through it, and this was an extremely important development for these other nations.

From around the middle of the nineteenth century, the countries of East Asia had been facing the threat of the Western powers and had realized the necessity of acquiring Western learning in order to overcome it. One method of realizing this was to learn about the West through Japan, which had been quicker to start down the path of modernization. From 1896 in the Qing dynasty through the establishment of the Republic of China and right up until the late 1930s, scholar after scholar was sent to study in Japan. Through the work of these students many books were translated into Chinese. According to Bian's research, 958 works were translated from Japanese between 1896 and 1911. These included Western texts that had played a major role in the intellectual world of the Meiji period, such as Montesquieu's *De l'Esprit des Lois*, Rousseau's *Du Contrat Social*, Spencer's *Representative Government: An Essay*, and Samuel Smiles's *Self-Help*.

This did not simply mean, however, that Western thought, being readily available there, was introduced via Japan. At the same time, it also meant that these Chinese scholars studied how Japan had digested and applied Western culture and thought, or, in other words, Japan's experience of receiving the West. What is particularly notable from this perspective is the translation of many writings by Fukuzawa Yukichi. At the end of the Qing dynasty in 1898—a time when Western powers were increasingly demanding leases from China—the Wuxu Reform was carried out, mainly by intellectuals, in imitation of Japan's Meiji Restoration, and the intellectual foundation of this movement was the enlightenment thought of Fukuzawa. This reform itself failed, but even after it had ended scholars such as Liang Qichao continued to introduce Fukuzawa's thought in China. Fukuzawa's educational thought and implementation of it at the private school Keiō Juku are also said to have been greatly influential in China.

Once again according to Bian, along with or perhaps even more than—Fukuzawa, Kawakami Hajime was also very influential in China. Many of the Chinese intellectuals studying in Japan embarked on the path to revolution through Kawakami's writings, and many people in China encountered socialist thought through their translations of his works. For example, Li Dazhao (1889–1927), who studied at Waseda University and later became one of the founders of the Chinese Communist Party, translated the preface to Marx's *Zur Kritik der Politischen Ökonomie* and Marx and Engels's *The Communist Manifesto*, to which he had been introduced in

Kawakami's writings, into Chinese, and played a major role in introducing Marxism in China. Zhou Enlai (1898–1976) was greatly influenced by Kawakami's *Social Problems Studies* and wanted to study under him but ended up returning to China before he could do so in order to participate in the May Fourth Movement that took place in 1919. Guo Moruo (1892–1978) translated Kawakami's voluminous *Social Systems and Social Revolution*, which he considered to be the pinnacle of early Japanese Marxist theory, into Chinese.[105] These works later had a major influence on the direction of politics in China.

In an essay entitled "Twentieth-Century Chinese-Japanese Cultural Exchange from the Perspective of Translation," Lu Xudong (1958–), another scholar at the Chinese Academy of Social Sciences, also sheds light on the flow of culture between China and Japan from the point of view of translation. In his essay Lu makes the very interesting observation that translations of Japanese scholarship were greatly influential not only through their content itself but also through their effect on ways of thinking and expression in the Chinese language.[106]

2. Thought in the Early Shōwa Era

(1) 1920S EUROPE

Japanese philosophy in the early Shōwa period was not only that of Nishida Kitarō and Tanabe Hajime touched on in the previous chapter; it displayed extremely diverse development in the work of their contemporaries and disciples and produced rich results. The stimulation provided by Nishida and Tanabe was of course great (and led to the formation of what came to be known as the "Kyoto School"), but their having studied in Europe and learned much there was also a major factor.

I have noted that thinkers such as Hatano, Kuwaki, and Sōda studied in Germany at the end of the Meiji period, but in the latter part of the Taishō period and beginning of the Shōwa period many scholars had the opportunity to study in Germany and France. These scholars are too numerous to list in full, but they include Yamauchi Tokuryū, Kuki Shūzō, Abe Jirō, Miki Kiyoshi, Amano Teiyū, Abe Yoshishige, Takahashi Satomi, Mutai Risaku, and Watsuji Tetsurō. After returning to Japan, these scholars created their own original thought on the basis of what they had absorbed in Europe. It is no exaggeration to say that Japanese philosophy in the early Shōwa period was built on their efforts.

The period during which they visited and studied in Europe, the 1920s, was the era in which European philosophy shone brightest. Europe, and in particular Germany, had been thrown into turmoil after the First World War. This era can be characterized with the phrase "postwar uncertainty," but at the same time it was also an era in which traditions were being overturned and bold new experiments were being attempted in various cultural domains. Diverse movements such as Expressionism, Dadaism, and New Objectivism emerged in various fields including painting, literature, theater, music, cinema, design, and photography. The cultural epoch that would later be referred to in Germany as the "Golden Twenties" blossomed.

This vitality found in culture also coursed through the thought of this era. Nearly all of the major currents in twentieth-century philosophy formed or achieved significant development during this period. Tanabe Hajime expressed this as a shift from the "philosophy of science" to the "philosophy of life," and the questions "what is existence?" and "what is a human being?" were reexamined from new perspectives that had never been considered before; rather than considering existence and humanity only from the perspectives of consciousness, knowledge, reason, and logic (identity), the focus turned to that which spills outside this framework, that which is covered up and hidden by it, and that which supports what comes to the surface while lying behind it. The unconscious, the environment/place, emotions, desires, the body, and symbols (reality possessing difference) were brought into view.

The Japanese scholars named above had the opportunity to study abroad during this extraordinarily fecund era. Their work after they returned to Japan was fueled by the stimulation they received from their direct contact with the extremely creative philosophical undertakings of the 1920s. Their original thought could not have emerged without it.

(2) The Neo-Kantian School

The Neo-Kantian School was at the height of its influence over a period of roughly twenty years centered on the turn of the century. By the beginning of the 1920s its influence was rapidly waning, but it still shone with a final burst of light. Most students from Japan chose the University of Heidelberg, where leading Neo-Kantian philosopher Rickert was a professor, as their destination when studying abroad. Rickert moved to the University of Heidelberg from the University of Freiburg in 1915 and taught philosophy there until 1932, during which time his students included Kuki Shūzō, Miki Kiyoshi, Takahashi Satomi (1886–1964), and Mutai Risaku (1890–1974).[107]

Kuki Shūzō stayed in Europe from 1921 to 1929, heading first to Heidelberg. Hermann Glockner (1896–1979), one of Rickert's disciples, later noted in his *Heidelberger Bilderbuch*, a recollection of Heidelberg in this period, that Kuki came to Rickert and asked for private instruction on the *Critique of Pure Reason*,[108] and that Rickert gladly accepted this request.[109]

Miki Kiyoshi began studying in Heidelberg in 1922, and his memories of this time are recorded in his "Reading Wanderings." Regarding Rickert, he writes, "I had read the course materials in advance, so I didn't get much that was new out of the lectures, but seeing the countenance of this elderly professor in person felt like coming face to face with the tradition of philosophy itself, and I enjoyed it very much."[110]

While he was studying in Germany, Tanabe Hajime saw the prevailing trend in philosophy shift from the "philosophy of science" to the "philosophy of life" before his eyes, and this had a powerful effect on him. After returning to Japan, his first publication, *Kant's Teleology*,[111] was an attempt to interpret Kant's teleology that did not stop at Kant's own stance but, in accordance with the demands of the "worldview (*Weltanschauung*) philosophy" that was flourishing in Germany at the time, continued to an orientation running through German idealism. In his 1948 "Introduction to the Reprint," however, Tanabe states that he got no further than "attempting to logicize Kant's teleology on the basis of Cohen's logic, which had been my sole foundation up to that point."[112] From this we also learn that the Marburg School's interpretation of Kant continued to be Tanabe's foundation even after his return to Japan.

Around this time, Tanabe published *Lask's Logic*[113] (1925), in which he examined *The Logic of Philosophy and the Doctrine of Categories*[114] (1911) and *The Doctrine of Judgement*[115] (1912), two works by Emil Lask (1875–1915), a disciple of Rickert's who had died quite young with a promising future still ahead of him. While acknowledging the correctness of Lask's assertion of the super-oppositionality of the objects of judgment from the perspective of logical objectivism, at the same time Tanabe tried to synthesize Lask's approach with that of Rickert, who criticized this bias toward objectivism and insisted on the priority of the subject from the viewpoint of the critique of knowledge. Seemingly responding to this discussion in his essay "Place,"[116] Nishida Kitarō also cites Lask's concept of "the object without opposition" (the object itself before it is changed or destroyed by forms of judgment) and attempts to reposition it from his own perspective of "place," writing that "such an object too must be situated in something."

Translations of *The Doctrine of Judgement* and *The Logic of Philosophy and the Doctrine of Categories* by Kubo (Doi) Torakazu were published in 1929 and 1930, respectively. Lask becoming well known in Japan was also owing to one of his disciples, Eugen Herrigel, having taught at Tohoku University from 1924 to 1929.

(3) PHENOMENOLOGY

As just noted, most Japanese scholars who went to study in Europe in the 1920s headed for Heidelberg where Rickert taught, but right away they seem to have sensed that Neo-Kantianism no longer had the power to lead the tide of the times. Kuki moved to Paris to study under Bergson (and later to Freiburg), Takahashi Satomi and Mutai Risaku went to Freiburg to study under Husserl (Tanabe also moved to Freiburg from Berlin), and Miki went to Marburg to study under Heidegger. What drew most of these students was phenomenology, which was becoming a major movement.

Husserl's phenomenology had already been established during his time at the University of Göttingen from 1901 to 1916, and had become widely known through works such as *Ideas Pertaining to a Pure Phenomenology and to a Phenomenological Philosophy, Book One*[117] (1913), published in the first volume of the *Yearbook for Philosophy and Phenomenological Research*.[118] During his time at the University of Freiburg from 1916 to 1929, along with working to refine phenomenology, Husserl devoted himself to the general advancement of this movement through undertakings such as the founding of the Freiburg Phenomenology Society. After retiring from his post at the university he remained vigorously active, producing works such as *Cartesian Meditations*[119] (1931) and *The Crisis of European Sciences and Transcendental Phenomenology*[120] (1936). Phenomenology established its position in the history of philosophy between the First World War and the Second World War.

Perhaps the first in Japan to focus on Husserl's philosophy was Nishida Kitarō, who did so immediately after taking a position at Kyoto University. As early as "On the Assertions of the Pure Logic School Regarding Epistemology,"[121] published in the same year as *An Inquiry into the Good* (1911), Nishida lumped Husserl and those belonging to the Southwest School of Neo-Kantianism such as Rickert together as the "Pure Logic School" and discussed their criticism of "psychologism." Having just written *An Inquiry into the Good*, Nishida did not view these criticisms from a distance but took them seriously as a critique that necessitated reflection on the psychological character of this work. It is no exaggeration to say that encountering this critique shaped the development of Nishida's thought after *An Inquiry into the Good*.

In his *The Philosophy of Idealism in the Modern Period*,[122] published in 1917, while referencing the *noema-noēsis* concept he would later put to frequent use in explaining his own logic of "place," Nishida also provides an explanation of the essence of the phenomenology Husserl describes in *Ideas Pertaining to a Pure Phenomenology and to a Phenomenological Philosophy*. Yamauchi (Nakagawa) Tokuryū (1890–1982), a disciple of Nishida's from his early period, was deeply involved in the editing of *The Philosophy of Idealism in the Modern Period*, and it was perhaps this process that inspired his interest in Husserl's phenomenology. He studied in Europe from 1920 to 1923, spending most of his time with Husserl in Freiburg. Along with Itō Kichinosuke (1885–1961), a preparatory course instructor at Keiō Gijyuku, Yamauchi was perhaps the first Japanese to study under Husserl.[123] Next to visit Husserl as a student was Tanabe Hajime, who was introduced in the previous chapter. Takahashi Satomi and Mutai Risaku then came to Freiburg in 1926 with an introduction from Tanabe, and along with attending Husserl's lectures received private instruction in phenomenology from him at their residence.[124] Takahashi published "Husserl's Phenomenology: In Particular His Phenomenological Reduction"[125] (1929) immediately after returning to Japan followed by *Husserl's Phenomenology*[126] in 1931. 1929 also saw the publication of Yamauchi Tokuryū's *A Discourse on Phenomenology*[127] and Satō Keiji (1904–1994)'s *Outline of Phenomenology*,[128] and it can thus be said that the foundations of the study of phenomenology in Japan were laid in a period spanning the late 1920s and early 1930s.

Kuki Shūzō's *The Structure of "Iki"* (stylish refinement, chicness)[129] is notable as a work that did not simply introduce Husserl's phenomenology but put its methods to use in developing its author's own ideas. Kuki had moved to Paris out of a desire to study under Bergson, but he returned to Germany in the summer term of 1927 and studied phenomenology under Husserl and Oskar Becker. The strong influence of Heidegger's philosophy can be seen in *The Structure of "Iki,"* and a shift can be observed in its methodology. As can be seen in the draft he began writing in Paris having been given the title "The Essence of 'Iki,'" however, he was also strongly influenced by Husserl's phenomenology.[130]

(4) HEIDEGGER'S PHILOSOPHY

Tanabe Hajime attended Heidegger's Ontology (Hermeneutic of Facticity)[131] course during the summer term of 1923. After returning to Japan, he published an account of the ideas he encountered in this course entitled "A New Turn in Phenomenology: Heidegger's Phenomenology of Life,"[132] the first academic article introducing Heidegger's philosophy, which was still being formed, in Japan. In it he positioned Heidegger's hermeneutic phenomenology as an attempt to surpass Husserl's phenomenology that had failed to obtain the full concreteness required by the "philosophy of life." In other words, it was Tanabe's understanding that Heidegger's hermeneutic phenomenology could be characterized as the "self-understanding or self-interpretation" of "living concrete consciousness, or in other words actual existence—*Dasein*—itself."

Tanabe's focus later shifted to studying the dialectic and constructing the "theory of species," but even in the process of these pursuits he repeatedly referenced Heidegger's philosophy and engaged in a critical confrontation with it. For example, in "Elucidating the Meaning of the Theory of Species"[133] he rejects Heidegger's philosophy as going no further than "the interpretation of potential being that cannot achieve true being" and in opposition to its "theory of self-conscious being" presents a "theory of social being" based on the logic of the negative intermediation of subject and substratum (species). In essays such as "Ontology of Life or Dialectic of Death?"[134] (completed in 1958), toward the end of his life Tanabe worked out a "philosophy of death" and undertook a radical critique of Heidegger's ontology of "being" or "life." It can be said that throughout his life Tanabe viewed Heidegger, along with Nishida Kitarō, as an intellectual rival.

Like Tanabe, Miki Kiyoshi also focused on Heidegger's philosophy from an early period and was strongly influenced by it. In the winter term of 1923 Heidegger moved from Freiburg to Marburg as an extraordinary professor, and Miki moved from Heidelberg to Marburg to be able to attend his lectures. After returning to Japan, in 1927 Miki published "Basic Concepts of Hermeneutic Phenomenology"[135] and introduced Heidegger's fundamental stance presented in *Being and Time*,[136] which would be published the following month. Through this text and Tanabe's essay mentioned above, Heidegger's new undertaking had been introduced in Japan even before the publication of this landmark text.

Miki's first publication after returning to Japan was *The Study of the Human Being in Pascal*[137] (1926), but in *Reading Wanderings* he describes the large role what he had learned from Heidegger played in it: "As I was thinking about the *Pensées*, I felt what I had learned from Professor Heidegger come to life."[138] For example, Miki views the fear, horror, and awe human beings who are intermediaries feel on the basis of their character as intermediary beings not as simply psychological emotions but as the fundamental ontological definition of human beings, or the "stativity" of human existence, and in this we can clearly see Pascal being interpreted through the lens of Heideggerian *Daseinsanalysis*.

When considering the relationship between Heidegger and Japanese philosophers, one important question to be examined is how the latter evaluated the former in the context of his connection to the Nazis. In 1933, the year in which Adolf Hitler came to power, Heidegger became rector of the University of Freiburg and gave an inaugural address entitled "The Self-Assertion of the German University,"[139] on which both Tanabe and Mike commented immediately. The tone of their responses, however, differed substantially. Tanabe's "Philosophy of Crisis or Crisis of Philosophy?" points out the contradiction in Heidegger's approach that on the one hand speaks of service to the nation while on the other hand advocates returning to Aristotle's academic perspective, which does not take an active interest in matters of state. Miki, in contrast, published an essay entitled "Heidegger and the Fate of Philosophy" in November of that year in which he views Heidegger's thought when he speaks of the "blood and soil" of the people as something like Nietzsche's "amor fati," that is, "the emotional affirmation of the pathetic, and thus of the Dionysian," and argues for the need to "restore the power of logos and the authority of reason" in opposition to Heidegger's descent into "the pathetic."[140]

Kuki Shūzō returned to Germany from Paris for the summer term of 1927 and studied under Husserl in Freiburg, but in the winter term he moved to Marburg and attended Heidegger's lectures. This demonstrates how powerfully he was drawn to this youthful philosopher a year younger than himself. As noted above, a strong influence from Husserl can be seen in the draft of *The Structure of "Iki"* written while Kuki was in Paris, but in the version of this text eventually published after his return to Japan he emphasizes the necessity of examining the *existentia* of "iki" rather than its *essentia*, and in terms of methodology he clearly adopts the stance of Heideggerian rather than Husserlian phenomenology. The year he returned to Japan he published an essay entitled "The Problem of Time: Bergson and Heidegger,"[141] and in 1931–1932 he took up the theme of "Heidegger's Phenomenological Ontology" in a special course at Kyoto University. In 1933 he also published various essays including "Heidegger's Philosophy"[142] and "The Philosophy of Existence."[143] "Heidegger's Philosophy," which was published in *Iwanami Course: Philosophy*, profoundly influenced Heideggerian studies in Japan, both as a proper introduction of *Being and Time* and for having established the Japanese translations of many Heideggerian terms such as *Entwurf* (投企), *Geworfenheit* (被投性), and *Dasein* (現存在).

What is interesting from the perspective of interaction between European and Japanese philosophers is that Heidegger also expressed profound interest in his dialogue with Kuki. In the chapter entitled "A Dialogue on Language" in his *On the Way to Language*,[144] Heidegger mentions having often discussed the Japanese term *iki* with Kuki. He raises the question of whether it is necessary or correct for East Asians who live in a tradition completely different from that of Europe to follow European conceptual systems. This question can be said to have great significance even today.

Watsuji Tetsurō studied in Europe slightly later than Tanabe and Kuki, arriving in Berlin in 1927. He read Heidegger's *Being and Time*, published the year he studied abroad, fervently and was greatly influenced by it. His encounter with this text clearly underpins *Climate and Culture* (1935), which can be described as a by-product of his studies overseas, and his own ethical thought. In the preface to *Climate and Culture*, for example, he writes:

> [Heidegger's] attempt to understand the structure of human existence as temporality was extremely interesting to me. But when temporality is used as the structure of this kind of subjective existence, why is spatiality not likewise employed as a fundamental structure of existence? This was a problem for me. . . . Temporality that is not connected to spatiality is not true temporality.[145]

Climate and Culture was an attempt to present this structure of human existence viewed from the perspective of spatiality.

(5) Philosophical Anthropology

One of the central themes of Japanese philosophy in the 1930s was "philosophical anthropology." Max Scheler (1874–1928) initiated the discourse of "philosophical anthropology" toward the end of his life, and his assertion in *The Human Place in the Cosmos*[146] (1928) that the questions of philosophical anthropology were the core issues in philosophy led to various debates in Germany. The same year also saw the publication of Helmuth Plessner (1892–1985)'s *The Levels of Organic Life and the Human*.[147]

In response to this discourse, Nishida Kitarō published an essay entitled "Anthropology"[148] in 1931. As its opening passage, "Recently a faction of philosophers advocating something called 'anthropology' has emerged," indicates, Nishida was clearly aware of the discourse on philosophical anthropology that developed in Germany in the 1920s, but his main focus in this text was Maine de Biran, considered the father of *spiritualisme français*. At its core was Nishida's understanding that philosophy must begin from "awareness that is nothingness[149] and at the same time defines the self." From this perspective, in "The Act of Consciousness as the Self-Limiting of Place,"[150] the essay preceding "Anthropology," he writes, "I think philosophy can have the meaning of a kind of anthropology, or indeed anthropology in its truest sense. But this must be the anthropology of self-aware human beings, the study of *homo interior* rather than *homo exterior*."[151] Nishida found this kind of internal anthropology in Maine de Biran. In "Anthropology" he focuses not only on the aspect of self-awareness but also on the fact that human beings are physical and social-historical entities. That this aspect possessed great significance in the development of Nishida's thought is evident in his writings from *Fundamental Problems of Philosophy*[152] (1933) onward.

The year after Nishida's "Anthropology" appeared in print, Tanabe Hajime published an essay entitled "The Standpoint of Anthropology"[153] in *Thought*.[154] The publication of this work coincided with the period during which Tanabe had begun to criticize Nishida's philosophy, and it can be assumed to have been written with an acute awareness of Nishida's writings on this topic. What is most characteristic of Tanabe's understanding of anthropology is his focus on the physicality of human existence. From this perspective he pointed out the inadequacy of the philosophy of life and Scheler's anthropology, and also of Heidegger's philosophy.

The study of this philosophical anthropology pioneered by Nishida and Tanabe was undertaken in earnest by Miki Kiyoshi. Miki planned to publish *Philosophical Anthropology* as a book in the Iwanami Zensho series in 1933, but while it reached the stage of proofs after multiple rewrites from 1933 to 1937, this manuscript was never published. Chapter 1, "Myth,"[155] of *The Logic of Imagination*[156] was published in the journal *Thought* in May of 1937, and it can be surmised that Miki abandoned any further efforts toward publishing *Philosophical Anthropology* in favor of beginning work on this new book (see chapter 7, section 3).

Miki's *Philosophical Anthropology* thus ended up going unpublished, and it was instead Kōyama Iwao (1905–1993) who first publicly presented anthropological philosophy in an organized form. Kōyama's *Philosophical Anthropology*,[157] published in 1938, is a work that attempts to trace humanity's conscious development, beginning with the fundamental fact of life, proceeding through labor and culture to reason, and then addressing what transcends its limits. It was an attempt at anthropology with original content that differed from the philosophical anthropology of Scheler and Plessner.

In 1938 and 1939 Risōsha published *Anthropology Course*, a series comprised of five volumes, and Kuki Shūzō's "What Is Anthropology?" was included in its first volume, *Human Philosophical Thought*. It can be said that the discourse surrounding philosophical anthropology in Japan reached its peak during this period. Watsuji Tetsurō's assertion in *Climate and Culture* (1935) that human beings must be understood not simply as "people"—as in anthropology—but through the dual natures of "people" and "society" was a jab at this trend.

(6) The Influence of Marxism

The Russian Revolution of 1917 and formation of the Soviet Union in 1922 had enormous significance in world history, and parallel to these developments Marxist philosophy also attracted considerable attention and was pursued through various approaches. On the one hand it was simplified and dogmatized as a theory supporting revolutionary practice, but on the other hand its significance was also examined beyond the framework of dogmatic ideology. György Lukács's *History and Class Consciousness*,[158] for example, was published in 1923, and its theories of "alienation" and "reification" contain a fresh approach to these issues that does not fit within the objective framework of Marxism.

After Marx's death in 1883, the writings of Friedrich Engels (1820–1895), such as *Anti-Dühring*[159] (1878) and *Ludwig Feuerbach and the End of Classical German Philosophy*[160] (1888), were considered authoritative in discussions of Marxist philosophy. Marx's own philosophical writings were published posthumously in the 1920s and 1930s. "Feuerbach," the first chapter of the first volume of *The German Ideology*,[161] coauthored by Engels, was published in 1926, and *Economic and Philosophic Manuscripts of 1844*[162] was first published in 1932. These writings attracted much attention as works displaying Marx's own thought, and it was noted that they overlapped Lukács's understanding of the issues in many respects.

It was during this period that interest in Marxist philosophy increased in Japan, and at the center of this movement was Miki Kiyoshi. It was not during his time studying in Europe from 1922 to 1926 but after he had returned to Japan that Miki displayed an interest in Marxist philosophy. The year after his return, while teaching philosophy at the Number Three High School, with a recommendation from Nishida Kitarō he also supervised the reading of Hegelian texts by Kawakami Hajime, a professor in the Department of Economics, and participated in a study group, the Association for the Criticism of Economics, organized by Kawakami. Around this time he seems to have begun studying Feuerbach's thought and historical materialism. Beginning in 1927, the results of this inquiry were published in a rapid-fire series of essays including "A Marxist Form of Anthropology,"[163] "Marxism and Materialism,"[164] and "Pragmatism and Marxist Philosophy."[165]

In "A Marxist Form of Anthropology" Miki placed the concept of "basic experience" at the center of his consideration. This approach demonstrates that he addressed Marxist philosophy free from naïve realism and reflection theory (*Widerspiegelungstheorie*). According to Miki, "basic experience" was experience that can also be described as the "dark" before "light" has been given through language, that is, before a concrete form has been given through verbalization. To put it another way, it is dynamic experience before *logos* intervenes and subjects it to stabilization. Through logicizing it, that is, by adding our own interpretation of it within ourselves and then giving it universality (publicness) that transcends our own framework, we polish it into theory (ideology), and it was Miki's fundamental understanding that theory is undergirded by "basic experience" in this way.

In the preface to *The Materialistic View of History and Contemporary Consciousness*[166] (1928), in which the above-mentioned essays are included, Miki states that these writings are intended to be a "genealogy of theories" (*Genealogie der Theorien*). Their purpose was to elucidate "how an ideology emerges, develops, collapses, and is then replaced by something new."[167] With this in mind, Miki attempted to explain the formation of Marxist philosophy from "proletarian basic experience." In the essays collected in *The Materialistic View of History and Contemporary Consciousness*, Miki argued that "proletarian basic experience" is the experience, not simply as consciousness but as a sensible being, of those who are constantly acting on the world in actuality, and the theory formed when the self-interpretation of this kind of being is brought into objective publicness is historical materialism.

Miki's having been able to address Marxist philosophy free from naïve realism and reflection theory was presumably largely owing to his having encountered Marx's own writings, which had begun to be published in the 1920s, directly rather than through simplified and dogmatized Marxist philosophy as an ideology supporting revolutionary practice based on the writings of Engels and Lenin.[168] In this sense, Miki's understanding of Marxism was profoundly connected to the circumstances of the 1920s.

This attempt by Miki to provide a foundation for Marxist philosophy had a powerful influence on those around him. Following Miki's return to Japan, Tosaka Jun, together with other alumni of Number One High School who had graduated from or were students at Kyoto University such as Tanikawa Tetsuzō (1995–1989) and Kakehashi Akihide (1902–1996), formed an organization called the Number One High School Philosophy Society where they learned from Miki about the various ideas and schools of thought he had encountered in Europe. They were also greatly stimulated by the activities of Miki himself, who had moved to Tokyo as a professor at Hōsei University and had emerged in the world of critical discourse as a Marxist. Around 1929 Tosaka formed a reading circle on Marx's writings with members such as Amakasu Sekisuke (1906–1975), Kakehashi Akihide, and Mashita Shin'ichi (1906–1985), and began to study historical materialism in earnest. In 1931, the year after Miki Kiyoshi had been arrested on suspicion of having provided financial support to the Japanese Communist Party and resigned from his position as a professor at Hōsei University, Tosaka became a lecturer at this institution and moved the locus of his activities to Tokyo. There he organized a historical materialism study group with members such as Oka Kunio (1890–1971) and Saigusa Hiroto (1892–1963), published *Materialism Studies,*[169] and became a leading figure in the study of materialism in Japan while at the same time also pursuing various other critical activities.

After the publication of Marx's *Economic and Philosophic Manuscripts of 1844* in 1932, in Japan, too, many people's attention turned to the writings of Marx himself, and one of those who moved in this direction was Kakehashi Akihide. He had specialized in sociology at Kyoto University, focusing his studies on Jean Gabriel Tarde, but influenced by Miki and Tosaka he shifted his efforts toward the study of Marxism, and through the examination of the concept of "matter" in particular produced writings such as *A Philosophical Concept of Matter*[170] (1943).

Nishida's disciples' interest in Marxism did not fail to have a significant effect on Nishida himself. He was stimulated by his discussions with these disciples and others such as Kawakami Hajime, read Marx's writings himself, and from *A Self-Aware System of Universals*[171] (1930) onwards began to actively present his own views on Marxist thought. In response, critiques of Nishida's thought were conducted by those in the Marxist camp. For example, in "The Philosophy of the Kyoto School," published in 1932, Tosaka

Jun characterized Nishida's philosophy as "hermeneutic, trans-historical, formalistic, romantic, . . . phenomenological philosophy" and criticized it for being at its roots "bourgeois idealist philosophy."[172] In "Is 'The Logic of Nothingness' a Logic?" published the following year in *Materialism Studies*, he criticized Nishida's philosophy as a philosophy only capable of considering the "logical significance of being" rather than being itself.

Nishida did not respond to this criticism in his writings, but in a letter to Tosaka he praised the critique of "The Philosophy of the Kyoto School."

> I think it is a very good critique with understanding. I am grateful for the many things you pointed out. It is not a stretch to say that what I have written thus far is hermeneutic. I have not yet written about my thinking with a focus on praxis. . . . I think Marxism is *einseitig* [one-sided][173] and in some respects not thorough. But I would like to properly understand Marxism and take from it what should be taken.[174]

That Nishida found this "one-sidedness" in Marxism's understanding of nature, for example, can be seen from his statements in *Fundamental Problems of Philosophy* (1933). In this text he criticizes Marxists for understanding nature from an intellectualist stance as completely objective in opposition to the subjective. This can be described as an indirect response to Tosaka.

Tanabe Hajime published *Kant's Teleology* in 1924, but reflecting on this period in the preface added when it was reprinted after the war he writes as follows.

> The rise of the global revolutionary movement of the proletariat following on from the Soviet revolution was a wave that also hit Japan; Marxist theoretical battles shook the academic world, and everyone involved in academic thought was, to a greater or lesser extent, stimulated by this discourse.[175]

These words clearly demonstrate that Marxist philosophy formed one of the key axes of philosophical discourse in Japan in the 1920s and 1930s.

(7) The 1930s

The Mukden Incident of 1931[176] was a major turning point in Japanese politics. Domestic politics began a broad shift toward the establishment of a fascist system, and Japan's international isolation was deepened by its policy of overseas expansion (it withdrew from the League of Nations in 1933). In accordance with these developments, there was also a major shift in the intellectual environment in Japan. Around the end of the Taishō period and beginning of the Shōwa period a movement to defend constitutional government became active, the common suffrage law was passed, the proletariat class became a powerful force in politics, and social movements were energized. Alongside these developments socialist thought had attracted many adherents and undertakings such as the proletarian literature movement had flourished, but after the Mukden Incident such movements found themselves under pressure. This pressure affected liberal academic inquiry; in 1933 Takigawa Yukitoki (1891–1962) was forced out of his position at Kyoto University, and in 1935 Minobe Tatsukichi's doctrine of the Emperor as an organ of government came under attack. Triggered by the Marco Polo Bridge Incident, in 1937 all-out war between Japan and China began, and the Japanese army expanded the front from the north of China to the central and southern parts of the country. Domestically, the University of Tokyo's Yanaihara Tadao was removed from his position for his criticism of this invasion of China, and university professors belonging to the labor and agriculture faction[177] such as Ōuchi Hyōe (1888–1980) and Arisawa Hiromi (1896–1988) and social activists such as Arahata Kanson (1887–1981) were caught up in a sweep of arrests along with many others on suspicion of organizing a popular front (this is known as the Popular Front Incident[178]).

Seeing the freedom of academic inquiry and the rights of the individual being squashed by the power of the state, several times in his correspondence Nishida Kitarō deplored the return of an era in which books should be put into walls[179] (see, for example, his 1937 letter to Hori Koretaka). Nishida had a deep interest in Japanese politics but was extremely cautious about expressing his views in public. He may have thought that he had no chance of effecting actual change even if he had made his views known. In October of 1935, for example, he wrote to one of his disciples, Hidaka Daishirō, as follows.

> This is a fascist era. Rather than scrupulously fighting against this from the start in rash futility, I believe those who put themselves aside and truly consider the future of our country deeply and at a distance must somehow endure the present moment and dedicate their efforts to gradually returning to a balanced state.

Nishida's fundamental approach seems to have been to endure and wait for the opportunity to eventually "return to a balanced state" rather than fight fascism head-on and be crushed.

The era, however, did not allow Nishida to quietly endure the roiling waves of fascism. The turning point came when Nishida could not avoid appointment as a member of the "Educational Reform Committee"[180] that had been established as an advisory panel for the Ministry of Education in November of 1935. In 1937 he gave a talk entitled "Academic Method" organized by the Committee for the Promotion of Various Academic Disciplines in Japan.[181] The following year he gave a talk entitled "The Characteristics of Eastern Philosophy Seen from Western Philosophy: Is a National Philosophy Conceivable?" at the Shōwa Research Association established by Gotō Ryūnosuke, one of Prime Minister Konoe Fumimaro's key policymakers, and a talk entitled "Problems of Japanese Culture" at Kyoto University. Coinciding with Japan's having expanded the war in China and begun to move in a direction from which it would be difficult to turn back, a desire to seriously consider how the nation and its politics ought to be, and to improve, if only a little, the actual orientation of Japanese politics, seems to have arisen in Nishida. This can clearly be seen in a letter to Watsuji Tetsurō, a former colleague at Kyoto University who had moved to the University of Tokyo, written in November of 1937. "There is a kind of undercurrent[182] flowing at great speed. Sooner or later we are bound to be swept away. Knowing this from the start it would be wise to hang back, but I think it is my duty to enter the arena anyway and fight to the last." This suggests that an awareness of a duty to take up arms in opposition to the current of the times, despite it being an unwinnable fight, was beginning to emerge in Nishida, replacing his stance of quiet forbearance from two years earlier.

One event that symbolized the 1930s was the above-mentioned removal of Takigawa Yukitoki from his academic position that came to be called the "Takigawa Incident (Kyoto University Incident)." This was an incident in which the sale of the books *Criminal Law Course*[183] and *Criminal Law Reader*[184] by Takigawa, a professor in the Faculty of Law of Kyoto University, was prohibited on the pretext of the views they contained concerning criminal insurrection and adultery, and Minister of Education Hatoyama Ichirō demanded Takigawa's dismissal by Kyoto University president Konishi Shigenao. This was opposed by other professors in the Faculty of Law, all of whom offered their resignations, and also by students who supported their professors' protest. At the center of these protest activities were the Faculty of Letters' Nakai Masakazu (1900–1951) and Kuno Osamu (1910–1999).

These protests did not bear fruit, but after the Takigawa Incident Nakai and Kuno published *World Culture* (February 1935–October 1937), a magazine introducing trends in the European antifascist movement, and *Saturday* (July 1936–November 1937), a biweekly cultural magazine aimed at a slightly broader readership whose title was a play on *Friday*, the magazine of the French Popular Front.

On the surface these were movements that took the form of opposition to Hitler's fascism, but indirectly they also implied opposition to Imperial fascism. It was for this reason that Nakai and Kuno were arrested in 1937 for their involvement in these magazines under suspicion of violation of the Peace Preservation Law and the magazines themselves were driven to discontinuation. This can be thought of as interlocking with the Popular Front Incident in which figures such as Ōuchi Hyōei and Arahata Kanson were arrested in 1937–1938. Nakai and Kuno both underwent harsh interrogation before eventually being released, Kuno after two years and Nakai after three.

One of Nakai's major prewar works was "The Logic of Committees"[185] (published in *World Culture* in 1936). Here "committees" are collegial bodies formed for the creation of new things, whether in places of production or in the academic world, and in such bodies the two obstacles of "uncriticalness"[186] and "uncooperativeness"[187] invariably arise. In this essay Nakai addresses how these impediments are to be overcome. Against "uncriticalness" organizational "deliberativeness"[188] must be put in place, and against "uncooperativeness" organizational "representativeness"[189] must be secured. Nakai calls the "logic of practice" found here "the logic of committees." This work was presumably written with the intention of constructing a foundation for opposition to pressure on discourse and thought.

Chapter 5

The Philosophies of Nishida and Tanabe

1. Nishida Kitarō's Early Period

In the Taishō period various ideas were developed and Japanese philosophy entered a new stage, and at the center of this movement were Nishida and Tanabe (the latter having created his own original philosophy while being influenced by the former), whose work I touched on several times in the previous chapter. In this chapter I will follow the development of their thought along a temporal axis from the late Meiji period through the Taishō and early Shōwa periods to elucidate what they examined and what characterized their philosophy.

(1) The Conceptual Foundation of Nishida's Philosophy

In 1911 (the forty-fourth year of the Meiji period), Nishida published his first book, *An Inquiry into the Good.* This work marked the point at which, after nearly forty years of receiving philosophy following its introduction to Japan as an academic discipline at the beginning of the Meiji period, Japanese philosophy began to walk on its own two feet. It was a book that did not aim merely to introduce or summarize Western philosophy, but to think through and present an answer to questions such as what true reality is, what we ought to do, and where peace of mind in a religious sense is to be found. It became an achievement later thinkers aspired to emulate and a signpost for the formation of their thought. In this sense this book and Nishida's thought occupy an important position in the history of Japanese philosophy.

Nishida's thought, however, did not spring up out of nowhere; it was created by receiving, utilizing, and developing the thought of the Meiji period. The ideas of earlier thinkers such as Fukuzawa Yukichi, Kitamura Tōkaku, Kiyozawa Manshi, and Tsunashima Ryōsen, for example, flowed into Nishida's thought.[1] Inoue Tetsujirō's "philosophy of phenomenon-reality identity" can also be seen as having given him significant inspiration.[2]

On the other hand, behind Nishida's work there was also the influence of Zen Buddhism, with which he had wrestled for many years. Interestingly, however, he makes almost no mention of Zen in *An Inquiry into the Good*. It is not difficult to imagine that the understanding of Zen that Nishida had acquired through many years of practice formed part of his foundation when he addressed the questions of reality, the good, and religion taken up in *An Inquiry into the Good*. But Nishida did not, as has often been asserted, aim to translate Zen thought into the language of Western philosophy. His intention was to address philosophical questions purely as philosophical questions. He was therefore careful to avoid referring to Zen in this text. Ever so slightly, however, the world of Zen does allow itself to be glimpsed. How these influences affected Nishida is an interesting topic in its own right. In this chapter, however, I will focus on the nature of the philosophy Nishida tried to work out rather than looking at its relationship to the earlier ideas that formed the foundation of his thought.

(2) The Philosophy of "Pure Experience"

What was the fundamental question Nishida Kitarō sought to address through the contemplation in which he engaged throughout his life? When we try to approach this question directly we face significant changes along with the times in which he lived. Nishida himself wrote about these changes when *An Inquiry into the Good* was reprinted in 1936.

> The perspective of pure experience emerges in *Intuition and Reflection in Self-Awareness*[3] and proceeds, through Fichte's perspective of *Tathandlung*, to the perspective of absolute will. Then, in the latter half of *From That Which Acts to That Which Sees*,[4] I made a sharp turn and arrived at the idea of "place"[5] through the mediation of Greek philosophy. That is where I found the starting point for the logicization of my thought. The idea of "place" is made concrete as the "dialectical universal,"[6] and the perspective of the "dialectical universal" is made direct as the

perspective of "action-intuition."[7] What is described as the world
of direct experience or the world of pure experience in this book
I have now come to think of as the world of historical reality.
It is the world of action-intuition, or the world of poesis, that
is the world of pure experience.[8]

Nishida thus acknowledges a sense in which there were changes in his
thought. On the other hand, however, he also asserts that there was
something in it that remained consistent. When one of his disciples,
Kōyama Iwao, published *Nishida Philosophy*[9] in 1935, Nishida wrote in its
foreword.

My thought since *An Inquiry into the Good* has proceeded neither
from a subjective viewpoint nor from an objective viewpoint,
but instead from a viewpoint prior to the distinction between
subject and object. This remains unchanged even today. In the
midst of my ongoing efforts, however, there have been all sorts
of changes in my thinking regarding how to grasp this direct,
concrete perspective as philosophy and how to then consider
various problems.[10]

As this passage makes clear, Nishida's stance of returning to what is most
direct and concrete, expressed here as "prior to the distinction between
subject and object," and attempting to grasp matters as a whole from this
perspective did not change from the beginning of his career to his final years.
He consistently pursued the question of what is most direct and concrete,
and his answer was that which is "from prior to the distinction between
subject and object." Nishida gave this reality "prior to the distinction between
subject and object" the name "pure experience."

Nishida offers various explanations of this "pure experience" in *An
Inquiry into the Good*. In the opening paragraph of chapter 1 of book 1,
for example, he writes, "Pure experience is identical to direct experience.
When I experience my own state of consciousness directly, knowledge and
its object are completely unified and neither subject nor object yet exists."[11]
He also writes, "without injecting our thought in the slightest, we can turn
our attention to the state of undistinguished subject and object,"[12] and in the
chapter "Intellect and Love," at the end of the book, he adds: "For example,
we get so absorbed in what we love that we are almost unconscious. We
forget ourselves, and a mysterious force outside us operates confidently on

its own. At such moments there is neither subject nor object but a true unity of subject and object."[13]

Nishida's critique of the dualism that places subjectivity and objectivity in opposition to each other is clearly present in phrases such as "neither subject nor object yet exists," "undistinguished subject and object," and "unity of subject and object." Regarding the opposition of subject and object, Nishida writes,

> To look directly at reality is to stand face to face with reality, being wholly in a state of direct experience without any distinction between subject and object. . . . the distinction between subject and object is a relative form that occurs when the unity of experience has been lost, and to view this as a reality that makes them independent of each other is merely an arbitrary judgment.[14]

Considering it to be an "arbitrary judgment," Nishida rejects thinking of the "mind," or more precisely the "internal mind," and "consciousness" that represents the external world on the one hand, and of the "external world" that is represented by consciousness on the other, and viewing each as substantiated. Here he expresses the idea that the opposition of subject and object is something introduced through an act of reflection after the fact, and that in the place of original experience there is no such distinction or opposition. The repeated discussion of experience with "undistinguished subject and object" shows that this kind of critique of the opposition of subject and object was the central theme of *An Inquiry into the Good*.

One conclusion that emerges naturally from the opposition of "consciousness" and the "external world" is that being conscious is an event that occurs entirely within consciousness, and the content of which we are conscious is nothing more than a mental image or representation of objects in the external world. Another conclusion is a state of affairs in which sensations such as color and taste are attributed to consciousness, and the object itself is depicted as the world prior to sensation without color, taste, or smell. These conclusions then lead to a way of thinking in which the content of consciousness emerges as the result of in some sense applying transformations to the object and is not the object itself. Here the question naturally becomes this process of transformation. The history of philosophy tells us that most philosophers began with this assumption and got stuck at the bottleneck of the "mind-body problem."

If the fundamental structure of dualism is one in which the world of sensation is placed in opposition to the object prior to sensation, the two are thought of as though they were spatially separate, and there is seen to be, for example, a relationship of copying and being copied between them, then Nishida's critique of the opposition of subject and object can be said to have highlighted a great discrepancy between this kind of schema and the actual state of our experience.

Borrowing the words of Gustav Fechner (1801–1887), in the preface ("Upon Resetting the Type"[15]) to *An Inquiry into the Good* Nishida expresses the abstractness of the understanding of reality that positions the world of sensation on one hand and objects prior to sensation on the other as "the night view of natural science without color or sound," and contrasts it with the "day view in which just-as-it-is is truth."[16] Standing before flowers and trees, we encounter "flowers and trees equipped with vivid colors and forms" not "purely physical" flowers and trees. Nor do we simply address flowers and trees as objects of perception or knowledge. Along with being the objects of knowledge, flowers and trees are also things that give us pleasure and peace of mind, in other words, "things composed of emotion and volition."[17] Our seeing "vivid colors and forms" or feeling pleasure and peace of mind through flowers and trees is not, according to Nishida, simply something that occurs within consciousness; he rejected positioning mental phenomena inside and physical phenomena outside as an "arbitrary judgment."

Of course, in *An Inquiry into the Good* Nishida asserts that the "phenomena of consciousness" are reality; one of the major theses of this work is that "phenomena of consciousness are the only reality." This is not, however, an assertion that experience is internal to consciousness. Nishida clearly rejects this understanding as erroneous. "Phenomena of consciousness" are not mental phenomena as distinguished from physical phenomena. They are the ascertaining of facts as facts before thought reaches the point of external existence and subjective existence. "If red, then simply red"[18]—this is a phenomenon of consciousness. It is also the direct appearance of the object. When I look at a red flower, a red flower itself is appearing right there. Reality does not exist in some other, separate place. "True reality does not separate the subjective and objective; actual nature is not simply an abstract concept like one-sided objectivity, but a concrete fact of consciousness equipped with both subjectivity and objectivity."[19]

As noted above, we do not see things simply as objects of perception. We find them beautiful or see them as things that give us comfort or fear.

Here things appear directly, and we are not shut away within the interior of our consciousness when our emotions flow. Objects themselves are involved in the arousal of our feelings. When we are moved by sad music, this emotion is not produced by associations or analogies called to mind by the sound; it is the sound of the instruments itself that causes emotions to occur within us.

Nishida believed it is this kind of concrete experience that goes hand in hand with "emotion and volition" that is true reality. "Pure material" that comes before any kind of sensation is something conceived by trying to reposition a concrete fact in a three-dimensional space without any viewpoint, and in this sense it can only be described as "that which is most abstract, that is, that which is furthest from the true landscape of reality."[20]

When it comes to things positioned in three-dimensional space, we can measure them with *public* scales and talk about them with *public* language. But regarding our direct experience of facts itself, in which intellect, emotion, and volition cannot be distinguished, such *public* measurement and *public* discourse are impossible. Nishida expresses this in chapter 4 of book 2, "Reality," of *An Inquiry into the Good*, writing, "The true landscape of reality is something we must simply apprehend by ourselves; it is not something we should reflect on, analyze, or express in words."[21] Nishida's critique of the opposition of subjective and objective was also a critique of the view that measuring with *public* scales and discussion in *public* language is equivalent to understanding the true nature of things.

For example, if I move my arm in a circle or swing my leg back and forth, the position of my arm or leg and the time that passed can be measured, and the nature of this movement can be physically recorded and explained. But this does not explain the continuity or unity of this movement of which I am indeed conscious. Nevertheless, we endlessly divide things that are constantly changing and attempt to understand them by reconstructing the whole out of countless parts that have been singled out and fixed. Or we take a single slice of something that is constantly changing and try to make this cross-section represent the whole. What we actually experience, however, is not a compilation of divided, fixed parts, but something with the character of a continuous motion that rejects division. Such things, in Nishida's words, we can only "apprehend by ourselves." In Bergson's terminology, they are things that can only be "intuited." All we can do is "look deeply into life, and with a kind of mental stethoscope try to take the pulse of the soul."[22]

As mentioned in the previous chapter, the year before the publication of *An Inquiry into the Good*, the same year he took up a position at Kyoto University, Nishida published an essay entitled "Bergson's Philosophical Methodology." In it he describes Bergson's "intuition" as "seeing things from the inside" or "becoming the thing itself and seeing," and asserts that this is the only method by which to "know the true state of things themselves."[23]

In this "true state," things move without stopping even for a moment, and if they are made the object of division or analysis they "dry out, become fixed, lose the spark of life, and become a kind of encoded knowledge."[24] In this essay Nishida clearly rejects as erroneous the stance of fixing this kind of "encoded knowledge" and from that basis attempting to see things as a whole, or, in other words, the method of proceeding from analysis to intuition. He argues that inverting this and beginning with "directly experiencing from the inside" things that change and flow, that is, going from intuition to analysis, is the method of true philosophy. From this perspective Nishida displayed great sympathy for Bergson's understanding of "intuition."

(3) Place

When the development of Nishida Kitarō's thought is divided into early, middle, and late periods, the middle period is represented by the idea of "place." This was expressed in its full form in the essay "Place,"[25] published in 1926. Immediately following its publication, Sōda Kiichirō penned an essay called "Regarding the Method of Nishida Philosophy: Seeking the Teaching of Professor Nishida"[26] in which he mercilessly criticized "place" from a Neo-Kantian perspective, writing that this text "cannot help deepening doubts about whether [Nishida's claims] are academically acceptable."[27] He did not entirely condemn Nishida's philosophy, however, launching his critique only after acknowledging that in this essay and a previous work entitled "The Actor"[28] Nishida had "entered the territory of what can be called the establishment of a system." Sōda's reference to Nishida's thought as "Nishida philosophy," as seen in the title of this essay, was also a result of his having discerned its maturation in these two works. The term "Nishida philosophy" came to be widely used for Nishida's thought following this essay by Sōda.

After "Regarding the Method of Nishida Philosophy" was published, Nishida promptly responded to Sōda's critique in an essay entitled "Responding to Dr. Sōda" (1927). At the beginning of this text he writes,

"At the end of 'Place,' I believe I arrived at an idea somewhat different from what had come before."[29] Here the transition to the perspective of "place" is presented in quite a restrained manner. In "Upon Resetting the Type," the preface to a new edition of *An Inquiry into the Good*, however, he acknowledges that his thought achieved significant development during this period. "In the latter half of *From That Which Acts to That Which Sees*, I made a sharp turn and arrived at the idea of 'place' through the mediation of Greek philosophy. That is where I found the starting point for the logicization of my thought."

The phrase "made a sharp turn" indicates the magnitude of this shift. And as can be seen from this preface, this turn was closely connected to the "logicization" of Nishida's philosophy. In contrast to this new approach, he described the inadequacies his thought had involved up to that point with the phrases "psychologism," "standpoint of consciousness," and "subjectivism." The cause of this kind of "reflection" to which Nishida was led was presumably the critique of so-called psychologism by Husserl and the Neo-Kantians. In his essay "On the Assertions of the Pure Logic School in Epistemology," included in *Thoughts and Experiences* (1911), Nishida lumps together the Neo-Kantians, in particular those belonging to the Southwest School, and Husserl as the "pure logicians" and discusses their critique of "psychologism." Nishida took up their vigorous criticism of the stance of trying to dissolve the problem of knowledge into that which is empirical or temporal as an important critique. Nishida also looked back at his thought after *An Inquiry into the Good* in the preface to *Philosophical Essays Volume 3* published in 1939, acknowledging that his theory of "pure experience" was "tinged with psychologism" and writing, "Having encountered the Southwest School, this perspective had to be thoroughly critiqued. I came to adopt a stance similar to Fichte's self-awareness."[30]

However, the standpoint of "self-awareness" Nishida reached in *Intuition and Reflection in Self-Awareness*[31] (1917), a work that came after *An Inquiry into the Good*, had not completely erased this "psychologistic tinge." To put it another way, the logicality required for the construction of a philosophical system had not been put in place. Here the necessity of the turn toward the standpoint of "place" was indeed evident. Nishida expresses this as follows in his foreword to Kōyama Iwao's *Nishida Philosophy*. "Whether we call it 'pure experience' or 'Tathandlung,' at its root we cannot get away from subjectivism. Through Aristotle's hypokeimenon, my thought at last came to seek a point of departure in what is logical."[32]

As Nishida himself thus acknowledges, his philosophy succeeded in making a major shift by adopting the standpoint of "place." If we look only at the change in Nishida's approach, however, we are left with an incomplete understanding of his thought. We must thoroughly consider the connection of this development to his thought up to that point, because the "logicization" of Nishida's philosophy was by no means a case of his merely applying some other logic he had happened to learn; it was on the contrary an undertaking necessitated by Nishida's thought itself. And as Nishida himself points out in his foreword to Kōyama's *Nishida Philosophy*, the key to this "logicization" was Aristotle's concept of hypokeimenon (ὑποκείμενον). It was from this concept that Nishida obtained the "starting point" for the logicization of his thought.

Nishida first addressed this issue in "On Internal Perception," the fourth essay in *From That Which Acts to That Which Sees*. Citing Bernard Bosanquet (1848–1923)'s *The Essentials of Logic*, at the start of the third section Nishida states that "the subject of perceptual judgment is not the so-called 'logical subject' but reality"[33] and then proceeds to a discussion of Aristotle's concept of hypokeimenon. This assertion corresponds to the following passage from "Remaining Problems of Consciousness," an essay written immediately after "Place."

> As Bosanquet says, when we say the desk is made of oak, the true subject is not the desk but the Reality. It is something like a synthesized whole that truly becomes Aristotle's hypokeimenon.[34]

By introducing these concepts of reality and hypokeimenon, Nishida attempted to connect direct experience to conceptual knowledge. While directly adopting Aristotle's conceptual definition of hypokeimenon as "that which is always subject and never predicate," Nishida writes as follows about the connection between the two.

> Hypokeimenon that is always subject and never predicate must be a unity of countless predicates, that is, that which unifies countless judgments. That which unifies one judgment with another must be something beyond judgment, an object our acts of judgment limitlessly approach but never attain. We can conceive of such a thing intuitively.[35]

The view of it as something intuitive presented here can be considered a characteristic of Nishida's understanding of hypokeimenon. It is not, as Aristotle says, "unique, individual things." Nishida's idea was that at its root there is always "the intuition of something irrational." He also thought that "individual entities" were established by the "conceptualization" of this intuition.

Regarding the relationship between experience and judgment, Nishida offers the following explanation in "The Actor," the sixth essay in *From That Which Acts to That Which Sees*.

> The world of things emerges through the rationalization of the content of our experience. To rationalize experience, experience itself becomes the subject, that is, it becomes hypokeimenon that is subject and not predicate. Experience itself becoming the subject must be experience, as a self-identical, concrete universal, causing judgments to arise within itself by limiting itself.[36]

The rationalization of experience means experience that itself transcends contemplation and judgment is first reexamined as a self-identical—and thus concerning which only identity judgments are possible—universal. In Aristotelean terms, this means for it to be reexamined as "hypokeimenon that is subject and not predicate." "Judgment" then emerges in a universal through this "hypokeimenon that is subject and not predicate," that is, a "concrete universal," "reflecting within itself," or, in other words, "differentiating" that which is identical to itself and "predicating itself."

Nishida views this process of rationalizing experience as "self-awareness." In the essay "On Internal Perception" he writes, "Judgment . . . must be the self-awareness of hypokeimenon without it ever becoming a predicate."[37] Here hypokeimenon is not simply a universal but something "without action" that goes beyond all acting and judgment and is understood as the "I" or "self" at the root of action that makes action possible. This is "hypokeimenon that does not enter into action," and at the same time it is also something that "knows itself" or "sees itself." In other words, it is something that concretizes and maintains the self by "projecting the self within the self." Judgment carries the meaning of the "self-expression" of this kind of hypokeimenon.

Along with focusing on the acting of this kind of "self-awareness" that "projects the self within the self," Nishida also trained his attention on the place where the actions of "self-awareness" arise. He writes, for example, that " 'in the self' must be added to the formation of a self-aware consciousness. Self-awareness occurs when the I that knows, the I that is known, and the place where the I knows itself are one."[38] It was in this passage that Nishida first used the word "place" with his own distinctive meaning. The emergence of the idea of "place" was thus deeply connected to the place-like character of "self-awareness" being addressed. Nishida's reception and distinctive understanding of the concept of hypokeimenon can be thought of as a premise of this inquiry. He expressed this essential nature of self-awareness in which the "I" as "hypokeimenon that does not enter into action" concretizes the self and sees the self by projecting the self within the self as "that which transcends the I and envelops the I is the I itself."[39] When the relationship between "that which transcends the I" and the "I" is viewed as one of "enveloping," attention turning to the place-like quality of self-awareness being "within the self" is inevitable.

I have noted that the reception of Aristotle's concept of hypokeimenon played a major role in the formation of the idea of "place." As I have already discussed, however, Nishida did not accept Aristotle's concept just as it was. His having used the term "place" to express his own thought was also related to this divergence from Aristotle. Nishida's critique of Aristotle's concept of hypokeimenon can be found, for example, in the abovementioned "Remaining Problems of Consciousness."

> In the past Aristotle defined substance (οὐσία)[40] as that which is the subject of judgment and never its predicate. I have not found any better definition of it. . . . If this kind of account can be given, then should it not be possible to invert this and conceive of an even deeper meaning in that which is predicate and never subject? Aristotle sought that which is transcendent and forms the foundation of judgment only in the direction of the subject, but that which is transcendent and forms the foundation of judgment lies not in the direction of the subject but in the direction of the predicate.[41]

As we have seen, Nishida defined hypokeimenon as that which sees itself and knows itself by projecting itself within itself, and in this sense understood it as that which transcends and envelops the "I." In terms of the relationship between subject and predicate in subsumption judgment, it is always sought in the direction of the predicate. Nishida's criticism of Aristotle's concept of hypokeimenon was that it does not address what truly lies at the foundation of judgment in this way.

According to Nishida, hypokeimenon[42] is that which is never objectified even if it objectifies itself. It is not conceptualized and is not defined as a subject. He expresses this in the following terms. "This [the true I] cannot be said to be the same, nor can it be said to be different, nor can it be said to exist or not exist, nor can it be defined in a logical form; it is on the contrary the place that gives rise to logical forms."[43] This is not the content of knowledge but the place where knowledge arises; phrased in terms of the subsumption relationship between subject and predicate, it is the transcendental "predicate plane" ultimately reached when this relationship is pushed as far as it can go—"that which is always predicate and never subject." This itself can never be a subject, or, to put it another way, can never be the content of knowledge, and can only be understood as simply "place."

As we have just seen, the concept of hypokeimenon played an extremely important role in the development of Nishida's theory of "place." Ultimately, however, he used this term "place" rather than "substance" to express his own thought. This was presumably related to the fact that hypokeimenon had originally referred to οὐσία (substance) in its true sense in Aristotle. In contrast, Nishida asserted that "place" was not being but rather "nothingness." However, this was of course not "nothingness" that was distinguished from or opposed to being, because even nothingness that rejects all being can, to the extent that it has something it opposes, still be considered a kind of being. When Nishida expressed place as the "place of nothingness," he meant "that which envelops being/nothingness" and "that which transcends being/nothingness and causes them to arise within it."[44] Nishida expresses this as "simply place"[45] because it can never be the content of knowledge nor can it in any sense be defined as being. It is there, however, that being/nothingness arise through this projecting itself within itself. This twofold nature is embedded in Nishida's concept of "place" or "place of nothingness."

At the root of Nishida's thought was a stance of trying to adopt the viewpoint of things as a whole or, in other words, of reality itself, rather than objectify things and thereby attempt to clarify them. In other words, he did not begin as modern epistemology does with the opposition of subjective and objective, but rather attempted to understand things from the reality itself that comes before this kind of schema is drawn; he understood things not in terms of their relationship to attributes on the basis of having assumed substance, but rather in terms of concrete universals. By doing so Nishida attempted to free us from being captivated by being. He placed that which cannot be viewed as an object, which he called "nothingness," at the foundation of his thought and attempted to understand things from this starting point. To put it in terms of logic, we can think of him as having tried to conceive of a logic centered on the predicate rather than a logic arranged with the subject at its core. If we focus on the "self," Nishida's aim was to understand this not as substance but rather as place. He thus attempted to call into question the premises or framework of our thought. In this sense Nishida's philosophy can be said to have had a truly radical character.

2. The Formation of Tanabe Hajime's Thought and His Critique of Nishida's Philosophy

(1) From the Study of the Philosophy of Mathematics and Science to the Study of Kant and Hegel

Tanabe Hajime was strongly influenced by Nishida Kitarō in the starting point of his own thought. This can be seen in the claim that "pure, inseparable experience" without "distinction between matter and the self" is the foundation of all knowledge made in his first essay, "On Thetic Judgments"[46] (1910). Their relationship was not one-way, however, and as noted in the previous chapter each developed his thought while being influenced by the other. Through this process Tanabe obtained a doctoral degree from Kyoto University for his thesis "A Study of Mathematical Philosophy"[47] (1918, published in 1925) and published works such as *Overview of Science*[48] (1918). No one held this scholarship in higher regard than Nishida Kitarō, and it led to Tanabe being invited to Kyoto University. After arriving there in 1919, Tanabe mainly studied Kant and Hegel. He published *Kant's Teleology*[49] in 1924 and *Hegel's Philosophy and Dialectic*[50] in 1932.

This was a major shift in the focus of Tanabe's scholarship, and it was presumably deeply connected to his having studied abroad, first under Alois Riehl at the University of Berlin in 1922 and then under Husserl at the University of Freiburg for a period of one year beginning in the winter term. Tanabe writes about this in the preface to a reprint of *Kant's Teleology*[51] published after the Second World War.

> Since first engaging in philosophy, up to that point I had focused my efforts exclusively on epistemological methodology, that is, the so-called "scientific critique," and the trigger of the shift in my thought toward the pursuit of a worldview lay in this study of Kant's teleology. What motivated this reorientation at the time

> was my studying overseas under Husserl and realizing the limits
> of scientific philosophy, and, as a positive aspect contrasting this
> negative view, sharing the desire for a worldview philosophy with
> which the post–First World War German philosophical world
> was overflowing at the time.[52]

As he notes here, while in Germany Tanabe was able to witness firsthand
a sea change in German philosophy. In the confusion and instability that
followed the First World War, along with Neo-Kantian philosophy coming
to be seen as a mostly "frivolous undertaking" and losing its influence, he
saw a new trend that focused on the "life" of human beings (which the
Neo-Kantian school had ignored) and attempted to understand it through
direct experience of the emergence of a domain of "life" as a whole, and
through a movement gaining strength that sought to construct a worldview
based on unified metaphysical principles. Sympathy with these philosophical trends shifted Tanabe's interest "from criticism to worldview, and from
mathematical, physical nature to the history of human society."

What is interesting here is that Tanabe did not simply extoll the
"philosophy of life" and the "philosophy of worldview," but also turned
his attention to the limits of these approaches. In "Epistemology and Phenomenology,"[53] published in 1925, a year after he had returned to Japan,
Tanabe emphasizes that for the "philosophy of life" to be more than simply
a product of clever words it must stand atop strict principles as a philosophy. Considering the Neo-Kantian "philosophy of knowledge" (Philosophie
der Wissenschaft) and the "philosophy of life" (Philosophy des Lebens), he
understood the task of contemporary philosophy to be not the expunging
of the former but the synthesis of both approaches. He found an attempt
to do so in Husserl's phenomenology.

At the same time, Tanabe also expressed the opinion that Husserl's
phenomenology was not able to fully satisfy the needs of philosophy. On
the one hand he stated that the "original spirit" of phenomenology is of
course to "eschew the abstract and emphasize concrete objectivity" and displayed a strong sympathy with this approach. On the other hand, he also
concluded that Husserl's phenomenology had not yet reached the "perfect
concreteness" required by the "philosophy of life."[54]

Tanabe arriving at this critical view of Husserl's phenomenology was
presumably owing to his having attended lectures at Freiburg given by
Heidegger, who had served as an assistant under Husserl. Tanabe saw greater
potential in Heidegger's hermeneutic phenomenology than in Husserl's

phenomenology. As noted in the previous chapter, "A New Turn in Phenomenology: Heidegger's Phenomenology of Life,"[55] published immediately after Tanabe's return to Japan, was the first academic article introducing Heidegger's philosophy in Japan, and this introduction came before the publication of *Being and Time* when Heidegger's philosophy was still in the process of formation. At that point, in 1923, Tanabe had already taken notice of the innovativeness and significance of Heidegger's thought.

In "A New Turn in Phenomenology," Tanabe begins by saying that, in contrast to the formalism of the Neo-Kantian School, Husserl's phenomenology is characterized by its reliance on the "evidentiary nature of intuition" as its foundation and asserting that this allows it to engage in a broader development toward an understanding of the domain of "life" as a whole. On the other hand, he also expresses doubt about Husserl's philosophy, asking, "Does it sufficiently demonstrate the concreteness—Sachlichkeit[56]—that is required?"[57] Tanabe believed the response to this need for concreteness was instead to be found in Heidegger. This can be seen in the following passage from this essay.

> Phenomenology is nothing other than the self-understanding or self-interpretation of consciousness of reality. Heidegger refers to phenomenology as this kind of self-interpretation—Selbstauslegung—of consciousness as "hermeneutische Phänomenologie"[58] to distinguish it from Husserl's structural phenomenology.[59]

Tanabe found a new turn and fresh possibilities for phenomenology in Heidegger's hermeneutic approach that pursued the self-understanding or self-interpretation of "living concrete consciousness itself" rather than an analytic account of the structure of consciousness from the perspective of the intuition of essence. This is what Tanabe is referring to with the phrase "New Turn" in the essay's title.

(2) The Study of Hegel's Philosophy and Critique of Nishida's Philosophy

Rather than continuing to pursue Heidegger's thought, however, in 1927 Tanabe began publishing a long essay entitled "The Logic of the Dialectic."[60] Following this he went on to release a series of essays on Hegelian philosophy and dialectic, and in 1932 these were published together as *Hegel's Philosophy and Dialectic*.[61] His thought in this period also marks a major turning point for Tanabe, as it was here he made a sharp change in course toward the dialectic rather than the "philosophy of life" or hermeneutic phenomenology.

Instrumental to this pivot were the current social and intellectual circumstances. The changes in the intellectual circumstances of the day are well expressed in the passage from the preface to the reprint of *Kant's Teleology* quoted in the previous chapter: "Marxist theoretical battles shook the academic world, and everyone involved in academic thought was, to a greater or lesser extent, stimulated by this discourse."[62] Those who were most directly influenced by this discourse were young scholars such as Miki Kiyoshi, Tosaka Jun, and Kakehashi Akihide. In *Hegel's Philosophy and Dialectic*,[63] Tanabe writes that with students beginning to believe in dialectical materialism as an "all powerful theory," these circumstances that did not allow him as a "teacher engaged in logical theory" to sit on the sidelines turned him toward the study of the dialectic. Regarding the perspective or standpoint from which he addressed this topic of the dialectic, Tanabe writes:

> I took the approach of extracting the distinctive character of the dialectic as a theory and analytically critiquing it, illuminating how it transcends a perspective of pure theory and what sort of super-theoretical or irrational elements are required as a foundation for it to arise.[64]

Tanabe initially attempted to show that the dialectic described by Hegel and Marx included among its premises elements that transcended theory or were irrational from the perspective of the pure theory of the Neo-Kantian School; in other words, he tried to show that it went beyond the limits philosophy must observe.

Eventually, however, Tanabe—presumably influenced by the circumstances affecting Japanese politics, scholarship, and discourse having undergone a radical change marked by the Mukden Incident that occurred in 1931—became aware of the importance of addressing issues of actual society, history, and action, and realized that the dialectic could be effectively employed in this undertaking. That this change took place very quickly within him can be seen from the fact that in "Action and History, and the Relationship of the Dialectic to Them"[65] (1929), which was published immediately after "The Logic of the Dialectic,"[66] he was already viewing Marxism in a positive light.

The direct trigger of this shift in Tanabe was the criticism of his thought on the dialectic—the thought presented in the essay "The Logic of the Dialectic"—by figures such as Miki Kiyoshi, Honda Kenzō, and Tosaka Jun. Tanabe writes about the dialectic in his preface to *Hegel's Philosophy and Dialectic*.

> As a result of this [the criticism of Miki and others], I learned the error of beginning from the perspective of logic in my initial approach to the dialectic, and realized the need to think about it from the perspective of the analysis of movement, action, practice, and existence.[67]

In 1931's "Hegel's Philosophy and Absolute Dialectic,"[68] for example, Tanabe emphasized that philosophy was "the self-awareness of the dialectic," and that as such philosophy could not be "contemplation separated from practice and aloof from daily life" and must instead be "reflection rooted in daily life and grounded in practice."[69] "Dialectic" came to be a word used to express Tanabe's own philosophical stance; incorporating a critique of Hegel and Marx, he often described his own approach as "absolute dialectic." He continued to maintain the dialectic as his own philosophical method and fundamental principle from then on, writing in the period of "the logic of species," for example, that "as long as philosophy is not knowledge but the love of knowledge, the dialectic must be its inevitable path."[70]

It was in this period, that is, the period during which he began to express his own standpoint with the word "dialectic," that Tanabe made public his critique of the philosophy of Nishida Kitarō. In 1930, two years after Nishida had reached retirement age and left Kyoto University and immediately after publishing "Action and History, and the Relationship of the Dialectic to Them,"[71] Tanabe released an essay entitled "A Request for Professor Nishida's Thoughts"[72] in which he developed a scathing critique of Nishida's philosophy.

Tanabe had learned much from the dialectic of Hegel and Marx, but at the same time he also offered his own criticism, having by no means blindly accepted their approach. Speaking of Hegel's philosophy, Tanabe began by criticizing its "emanationist" character. As early as "The Logic of the Dialectic" he had criticized Hegel's philosophy for having the "panlogicistic" character of attempting to understand everything through "necessary principles" along with being a philosophy that saw all reality as "emanating from logical universals."[73]

To the extent that one adopts the standpoint of emanationist "pan-logicism," neither reality itself nor history can be understood. This is the case because what makes reality not merely logic but literally something real is its "irrationality that includes freedom and happenstance, incommensurability with concepts, and superfluity to logic."[74] Moreover, this kind of "panlogicism" results in "impractical theoreticality"[75] and "quietism"[76] in regard to history. History is not a necessary process that emerges from what already exists. History "arises in a present that is always moving and is constantly changing its meaning along with this in relation to the future as subjective free potential that is anticipated in each present."[77] History cannot arise without the "free autonomy" of something that acts. As he puts it in "Action and History, and the Relationship of the Dialectic to Them," history is not the movement of a puppet controlled by "cunning reason" described by Hegel, but rather emerges through "the free creation of acts that deliberately alter history," that is, through action based on free autonomy that not only bears the burden of the negatives of the past but also anticipates the free potential of the future.[78]

This critique of Hegelian philosophy and the critique of Nishida's philosophy in "A Request for Professor Nishida's Thoughts" were deeply connected. It seems that while developing his critique of Hegel in the manner outlined above Tanabe realized that the same problem was also present in Nishida's philosophy.

In "A Request for Professor Nishida's Thoughts," Tanabe begins by addressing the fact that Nishida takes the "religious experience" of the "self-awareness of absolute nothingness" as his starting point, establishes this as the fundamental principle of his philosophy, and then attempts to explain everything as its self-determining. Tanabe rejected the approach of positing "absolute totality" as a "given" rather than as an ideal demanded on the other side of the process of the unification of relative things, positioning it as the principium of the system, and from this starting point attempting to assign order to what is relative as following the tracks of Plotinus's doctrine of emanation. If this kind of "emanationist structure"[79] is adopted, will it not lead to philosophy abandoning itself? This is the fundamental question Tanabe poses to Nishida.

If we take this stance, "everything turns into a shadow being."[80] Reality, which stands before us as something irrational and imposes limits on our actions, is characterized as simply a "shadow being." In Nishida's perspective the "irrationality and anti-valuableness of reality" amounts to an inadequacy of self-awareness and has no positive meaning in and of itself. What is sought is not the rationalization of the irrational, but rather the adoption of a "religious self-awareness" in which the anti-valuable does not exist. Everything is "enveloped in the light of detached observation," and "what can be described as raw reality or action completely loses its essential meaning."[81]

Tanabe clearly understood Nishida's understanding of reality or its irrationality, and of action and history, overlaid on that of Hegel. This is evident in these words that follow his critique of Nishida. "Is this not a restoration of what has been attacked as the quietism of Hegel's philosophy? From this perspective I cannot help but harbor doubts in particular about Professor [Nishida]'s view of history and his interpretation of anti-value."[82]

3. The Philosophy of Nishida's Late Period

(1) Nishida and Tanabe's Interest in History and the Real World

Taking up Tanabe's criticism described in the previous section, Nishida shifted his inquiry to issues of history and the real world. This is clearly seen in his *The Self-Aware Determination of Nothingness*,[83] published in 1932. His acute awareness of Tanabe's critique in writing this text is evident in the following passage that opens the preface.

> What can be thought of as reality must have that which can be thought of as thoroughly irrational at its foundations. What is simply rational is not real. However, if what is irrational is to be contemplated, even as irrational, we must clarify how it is to be conceived. If the irrational is to be conceivable, there must be something in the structure of our logical thinking itself that makes this possible.[84]

While acknowledging the validity of Tanabe's argument that we must focus on the irrationality of reality, at the same time Nishida emphasizes the necessity of presenting a foundation for how the irrational is to be contemplated.

Nishida then states, "At the root of what I call the self-determining of the universal, there must be a sense of social or historical determining."[85] The "self-determining of the universal" is addressed in the essays "Self-Determining of the Universal" (September–October 1929) and "General Remarks" (October 1929–January 1930), both of which were included in *Self-Aware System of the Universal* (1930). Along with asserting that the fundamental structure of consciousness is self-awareness, Nishida states that finally, at the ultimate limit of self-awareness that sees the self within the self, there comes a point at which what is seen disappears, or, in other words, there comes a point where we "see absolute nothingness."[86] This "absolute nothingness," according to Nishida, is something that transcends the limits of knowledge, and is not simply nothing at all. At its root there is the "infinite flow of life."[87] Its "deep internal life" determines and expresses itself. This is the "self-determining of the universal." Here Nishida emphasizes that this is not merely the manifestation of internal life, but rather something that signifies "social and historical determining," or, in other words, what is determined here is the "social and historical world."[88] Such statements make it clear that Nishida was indeed aware of Tanabe's critique of his work.

Of course, *The Self-Aware Determination of Nothingness* was not the first time Nishida had addressed issues of history and the world. In "The Self-Determining of the Universal" he had already spoken of what is objectively seen as the determining of "internal life" being "history" in a broad sense. Likening this "internal life" to the "dazzling obscurity" of pseudo-Dionysius, he says it includes "the deeply irrational,"[89] and that history too, by reflecting it, is impregnated with "irrationality."

As though echoing this view, in his "Logic of the Dialectic (Continued)," published in September 1929, Tanabe focused on the "irrationality containing freedom and contingency"[90] found in history. In his "Acts and History, and the Relationship of This to the Dialectic"[91] (November 1929) he discusses history on this basis. "History is by no means the realization of an existing divine plan for the world. It cannot avoid being thoroughly irrational and contingent."[92] It is action that rationalizes and makes necessary this contingent, irrational history in the direction of an aim. Action is not simply a means employed for the sake of history, but indeed the "axis upon which history turns."[93] History, through the creative acts of human beings, is constantly developing and renewing its own meaning. Tanabe emphasized the dialectic as logic that grasps this fact. According to him, however, the dialectic is not a law that stipulates the necessary development of history as an objective entity. The dialectic demonstrates that history is made up and reformed by "the free creation of acts," and through this correlative relationship with action is continuously obtaining new meaning.

(2) The Reception of Hegel's Dialectic

Notable as a work in which Nishida engages in a detailed discussion of "the social and historical world" is his essay "I and You"[94] (1932), which was included in *The Self-Aware Determination of Nothingness*. In this text, the historical world is portrayed as one in which individual things (the individual self) and the environment (society) mutually determine each other. While on the one hand the individual is born in society and lives under its influence, on the other hand individuals also determine themselves independently from these limitations, and even conversely "reform" society. The individual is "the acme of historical and social limitation," and at the same time changes society and moves history. Nishida used the phrase "dialectical process" to describe this process of mutual determining between individual people and society or individual objects and their environment. His focus on action and history meant taking up the dialectic of Marx and at the same time also that of Hegel on which it was predicated.

A positive reception of Hegel's dialectic is demonstrated by Nishida's having placed the "principle of direct intuition of seeing the other in the self" at the foundation of the mutual determining of individual things and the environment. In *The Phenomenology of Spirit*,[95] Hegel determines the element in which truth is developed, that is, the foundation that gives rise to science, as "the pure recognition of the self in what is absolutely outside of the self."[96] It is only as "self-consciousness" that knowledge or consciousness prior to this kind of learning stands in this "home of truth"; this is the case because "self-consciousness" is a consciousness that distinguishes itself from the self, while at the same time also being immediately conscious of the fact that what has been distinguished is not truly distinct. Hegel asserts that it is only when self-consciousness is related to another self-consciousness that it truly becomes self-consciousness in this sense. Self-consciousness first emerges as true self-consciousness when I acknowledge that another person is free and independent like I am, and moreover when this acknowledgment is mutual (and made consciously); in other words, it emerges with the formation of the "I that is we and we that is I."[97]

Through this discourse, Nishida thus depicts the historical world as a world in which one individual and another, you and I, relate and interact. On the one hand, you and I are "that which is absolutely other." On the other hand, however, along with "seeing the absolute other within myself" I also "see myself within the absolute other."[98] I acknowledge you as an individual person, and you likewise acknowledge me as an individual person. Through this kind of "echo of personal action" I know myself and you become conscious of yourself. What makes me me is you, and what makes you you is me. Self-awareness has a fundamentally "social"[99] character.

While on the one hand giving his thought this kind of positive reception, Nishida also clearly distinguished his own stance from that of Hegel. He characterized this approach as the "dialectic of place." According to Nishida, dialectic movement is not simply a continuous process. There an absolute negation must be considered. To use an expression he favored, dialectic movement is based on "absolute death." Its negation, however, is what gives birth to the historical world. In other words, the historical world is formed from the self-determining of the "place of absolute nothingness" that is expressed as "death-that-is-life." And in this place I relate to you; at the root of my being I see the absolute other, and by doing so I know myself. Nishida likens this "place of absolute nothingness" to a "circle that has no periphery and of which every point can be the center."[100] Innumerable circles are determined within this circle without periphery, and history moves forward through the self-determining of these circles.

Nishida criticizes the "process-like" character of Hegel's dialectic from this kind of perspective. In other words, he criticizes Hegel for having viewed dialectic movement as a single continuous process. Of course, in Hegel, too, dialectic movement is thought of as the process of self-realization of the concrete universal. According to Nishida, however, this process does not go beyond thoroughly purposive development. Living, acting individuals that transcend the framework of purposiveness cannot be conceived there, nor can "individual life" that is grounded in nothingness and creatively determines its environment.

Nishida's thought thus achieved great development from *The Self-Aware Determination of Nothingness* onward, and this development can indisputably be said to have been instigated by Tanabe's critique and Nishida's debates with his disciples.

(3) The Dialectical Universal

Nishida's interest thus shifted from the problem of "consciousness" and "the self" to "the world." The turning point came in the essay "I and You." In the preface to his *Fundamental Problems of Philosophy Volume 2*[101] (1934), however, Nishida himself points out that "I and You" was unable to escape the one-sidedness of viewing the world mainly from the perspective of the individual self. It was from the essays collected in *Fundamental Problems of Philosophy* (1933) onward that Nishida came to truly address "the world."

A clear instance of this shift can be found in the following passage from "Prolegomena to Metaphysics"[102] (1933).

> What is properly described as the most concrete true reality is what is thought of as the real world mutually determined by individuals, and this can be said to dialectically determine itself as the self-identity of absolutely opposed things. That is, it can be thought of as dialectical reality. What is thought of as the world of our personal acts can be said to be the most concrete true reality.[103]

Here it is no longer the "phenomena of consciousness" but rather the "real world," in other words, "the world that envelops our individual acts, the world in which we act individually," that is said to be true reality. And as is indicated by the title of the essay "The Logical Structure of the Real World" included in *Fundamental Problems of Philosophy Volume 2*, in his later period Nishida developed his inquiry surrounding this "logical structure" of the world.

It is important to note, however, that in Nishida's focus on "the world" in his late period he by no means ignores the individuals that operate or act within it. As evinced by the phrase "world of our individual acts," Nishida's gaze was on the contrary focused on the human beings who act and operate within the world. This can also be seen in the following passage that opens "The Logical Structure of the Real World."

> What is the real world? The real world does not simply stand in opposition to us; it must be the world in which we are born and in which we die. In the past, philosophy that could not escape the perspective of intellectualism considered the real world to be the so-called "objective world." This was nothing more than the world we see outside ourselves. In relation to this world, we were simply seers. The true real world, however, must be the world that envelops us. It must be the world in which we operate. It must be the world of acts. What is the logical structure of this world?[104]

As can clearly be seen in this passage, this focus on "the true real world" was at the same time a focus on the self; not the self simply as "seer," that is, as the subject of perception, but a self that operates and acts in the real world. We are not "simply seeing eyes" that gaze upon the world from the outside. We are beings who stand in a necessary relationship with things. We have a body, and we act. Nishida's contemplation of "the world" in his late period was also the contemplation of this kind of human being who has a body and who acts.

We have seen that from *Fundamental Problems of Philosophy* to *Fundamental Problems of Philosophy Volume 2*, Nishida focused his attention on the "logical structure" of the real world. What emerged in this process was the concept of "the dialectic universal." From the essay "I and the World" onward, what had been referred to as "the self-determining of absolute nothingness" or "the self-determining of the universal of nothingness" in *The Self-Aware Determination of Nothingness* came to be expressed mainly by the phrase "the self-determining of the dialectic universal." This was related to the real world being viewed as the *identity of those things that stand in absolute opposition and absolute conflict with each other*: the determining of individuals from within individuals themselves (individual determining) and the determining of the universal by the universal itself (universal determining).

Along with on the one hand having thoroughgoing internal unity and determining themselves in the flow of time ("linearly"), on the other hand individuals are also enveloped by the universal and determined from the outside in space or "place" ("circularly"). These two kinds of determining have thoroughly conflicting orientations. Individual determining does not directly become universal determining. However, when individual opposes individual (I oppose you) and individuals engage in mutual interaction, in other words, as the determining of individuals becomes more concrete, this determining comes to acquire a spatial (circular) character. Conversely, the more concrete the determining of individuals by the universal becomes, the more it comes to involve the determining of individuals by individuals themselves. In other words, it acquires a temporal (linear) character. Nishida focused on this structure in which these things that thus absolutely oppose each other (individual determining and universal determining) are, while still opposing each other, at the same time also one, and described it with the phrase "dialectic universal."

(4) Absolutely Contradictory Self-Identity

As something with the kind of structure just described, the real world is expressed with the phrase "self-identity of absolutely conflicting things." Nishida puts it like this because the real world is in one aspect an infinite dialectic process, while at the same time its content is always something given as a single, unified whole. In the essay "Prolegomena to Metaphysics," for example, he writes as follows.

> In one aspect, what we consider to be the concrete world is thought of as existing in the infinite flow of time, but it can also be thought of as a superposition of infinite worlds. In other words, while in one aspect it determines itself linearly, in another aspect it can be said to determine itself circularly.[105]

According to Nishida, the "present" that arises in the real world is not a simple present cut off from the past and future as a single point in dialectic history; infinite past and future, that is, the meaning possessed by each era, are included in it, simultaneously coexisting. They become the concrete content of the present and give it shape. This is expressed by the phrase "superposition of infinite worlds" in the passage quoted above. Past and future, or the various meanings, topics, and tendencies they contain, being simultaneously coexistent means that at the same time the present contains contradictions within itself. An era always contains "self-contradictions" within itself, and therefore "transcends itself from within itself."

As something that is on the one hand an infinite dialectic process, along with on the other hand constituting an infinite superposition of worlds, the world of historical reality has the character of an identity of things that absolutely contradict each other. From *Philosophical Essays III* onward, this relationship of "an identity of things that absolutely contradict each other" is expressed with the phrases "contradictory self-identity" and "absolute contradictory self-identity." These phrases came to be used as technical terms that expressed the core of Nishida's thought. We can see this as one of the fruits of the thought developed in Nishida's late period after he confronted the criticisms that had been brought against his philosophy of "place."

(5) Action-Intuition

I have noted that Nishida's focus on the "true real world" was not simply a focus on the self as "seer" but on a self who operates and acts within the real world. We are not standing outside the world and gazing at it but rather standing inside a necessary relationship to things. We have a body, and we act. In his late period, Nishida attempted to express this manner of existing of human beings with the phrase "action-intuition." How does Nishida define "action-intuition"? In an essay discussing this concept entitled

"The Standpoint of Action-Intuition," he writes, "We see things through action, and we determine things along with things determining us. This is action-intuition."[106]

Examining what Nishida was trying to express with the phrase "see things through action," at its root we find a critique of the perspective that views the real world as simply the world of objects. That is, at the root of the concept of "action-intuition" there is a critique of the "intellectualism" that had come to view human beings as simply cognitive subjects and the world as a world of objects that stands in opposition to them. The development of Nishida's thought surrounding "action-intuition" can be said to have been motivated by this kind of critique.

Here Nishida emphasizes that human beings are not simply cognitive subjects but rather beings with bodies. He believed that human beings are first and foremost physical beings, and consciousness is one aspect of our activities or manifestation. "We do not have consciousness and then have a body, but rather have a body and then have consciousness." Human beings having a body, however, was not simply our having a body in a biological sense. The sort of perspective from which Nishida viewed the human body is clearly expressed in the following passage from "The Standpoint of Action-Intuition." "By 'the body' here I do not mean simply the biological body, but the expressive action body; from another point of view, the historical body."[107] The body is first spoken of in relation to expression. Our being not simply "consciousness" but physical beings means that we are also beings with desires. To such beings, things appear not only as things but as "expressions." In other words, they present themselves to us wearing a "mien." The phrase "see things through action" given as a definition of "action-intuition" means, primarily, things appearing to us expressively in this manner.

Moreover, things are not only filled with various expressions. At the same time, they also affect us profoundly as human beings who are subjects of desire. When a cold glass of water is offered to us, we cannot help but drink it down. In this way things that appear expressively call on us to act. The second meaning of "see things through action" is found in this eliciting of action.

Nishida emphasized that this "action" is not simply a physical movement of the body, but rather something with the character of making things, that is, poiesis (creation). This "making things" or "creation" is where the third meaning of "see things through action" lies. Examples of this presumably include agricultural production and the making of handicrafts as a daily occupation, as well as artistic undertakings such as painting a picture or writing a poem. Here we express ourselves through our bodies, and what we make appears before us once again as an expressive thing. Here "seeing" arises. Creation leads to intuition. For example, a landscape we have painted, as something still inadequate, makes us aware of the need to make further improvements. The fourth meaning of "see things through action" is found in seeing things we have created in this way. This intuition once again moves us to act. The phrase "we see things through action, and we determine things along with things determining us" can be said to refer to this process as a whole, and the body that supports this process can be described as the "expressive action body."

As physical beings, we are moved by expressive things and create expressive things. But "creation" is not simply a response to stimulation. It has "history" behind it. As Nishida puts it, "Human beings can never jettison an infinitely heavy historical ballast." In walking our own path, we act while shouldering the burdens we have created, and while bearing some responsibility for dealing with the issues society as a whole has come to face. In other words, while we make things and act, we do not simply make things and act but make and act while having the question of what to make and how to act posed to us by history. The "historical body" mentioned in the quote above refers to our bodies that carry this kind of historical ballast.

To say that we act while bearing the burden of history is, conversely, also to say that history, or the world itself, is formed by our actions. History takes shape through the actions of individuals. Nishida expresses this relationship as follows. "With our physical selves as creative elements in the historical world, historical life realizes itself through our physical bodies. The historical world forms itself through our physical bodies."[108] The act of making things while being conscious of the tasks given to us by history is not simply an act closed off within me; it is the means by which the historical world forms itself, and it is in this sense that here we are said to be "creative elements" of the historical world.

(6) Nishida's Religious Thought at the End of His Life

Nishida continued to have a deep interest in the problem of religion from his early period until his final years. In *An Inquiry into the Good* he states that religion is "the end of philosophy" and concludes his inquiry with a chapter on religion. We are also told that in his final years he often expressed a desire to write a treatment of religion that would tie together his own system of thought. This was realized in his final essay, "The Logic of Place and the Religious Worldview"[109] (completed in April of 1945). The problem of religion can be described as an axis running through the entirety of Nishida's thought.

In this final essay Nishida writes, "Religious consciousness, as the fundamental fact of our life, must be the foundation of learning and morality. The 'religious mind' must be something lying hidden in the depths of every human mind, not the exclusive possession of a particular person. One who is not aware of this cannot be a philosopher."[110] Nishida emphasizes above all else the claim that religious consciousness is "the fundamental fact of our life" that lies hidden deep in every human mind. It can be said that both the core of Nishida's understanding of religion and its defining characteristic are to be found in this point.

Here too Nishida expresses his conviction that philosophy (learning) that turns its back on our "life" cannot be philosophy. Being based on the "fundamental fact of life," both philosophy and religion stand upon a common foundation. Of course, Nishida does not think of them as simply one and the same thing. In his essay "The Science of Experience" (1939), he describes the difference between them as follows.

> The problem of the historical world is the problem of our own life. This is where the problem of philosophy and religion lies. The point that is the alpha and omega of our selves is the problem of philosophy and religion. Philosophy must be a consideration of the world that proceeds from the standpoint of the self-awareness of the concrete self of poiesis, that is, the standpoint of the whole self. . . . religion remains committed to the depths of contradictory self-identity and understands this self-awaredly.[111] As is stated here, both philosophy and religion require adopting the "standpoint of the whole self." They require being a self that does not look at the world from the outside but rather lives and acts (creates) within it. This must be a self that focuses its gaze on the fundamental fact of life. But while philosophy then concerns itself with the world, religion continues to pursue the self. Religion strives to understand the root source of our selves.

In the passage quoted above, Nishida uses the phrase "something *lying hidden* in the depths of every human mind," and this root fact is not necessarily apparent in our ordinary consciousness. This is our self itself, but we live while looking away from it. If so, in what circumstances do we become conscious of this shrouded self? In "The Logic of Place and the Religious Worldview," Nishida's answer to this question is "when we are conscious of the profound self-contradiction at the root of our self." What sort of thing is this "profound self-contradiction"? He says it is the "awareness of death." This death is not simply physical death or death in a biological sense. The self-contradiction at the root of our self is said to be the awareness of "eternal death."

What is "eternal death"? Nishida writes, "Being aware of the eternal death of the self presumably occurs when our self confronts what is absolutely without limit, that is, the absolute. Through facing absolute negation, we come to know the eternal death of the self."[112] By coming face to face with that which is absolutely infinite, we become aware of "eternal death," and, moreover, "eternal nothingness." What sort of state is being concretely referred to when Nishida says the self is eternally nothing? A clue to this can be found in the religious faith of Shinran, a thirteenth-century Japanese Buddhist monk, to which Nishida often refers in "The Logic of Place and the Religious Worldview."

"Ordinary person of desires and suffering"[113] is a phrase Shinran often used. He had a clear-eyed view of people as foolish beings filled with endless desires and suffering. Shinran himself was no exception. His own condition is laid bare in the chapter on "Faith" in his *On Teaching, Practice, Faith, and Enlightenment*. "Sadly I, foolish Shinran, sink in the vast ocean of lust and become lost in the mountains of fame and wealth."[114] He had a thorough awareness of evil, and this awareness led to despair. In the third section of *Lamentations of Divergences*,[115] a collection of Shinran's sayings recorded by his disciple Yuien, he states, "No matter the practice, we of desires and suffering can never separate ourselves from death and rebirth." The phrase "to know eternal death" signifies this turn toward despair. Consciousness of our "profound self-contradiction," however, is not exhausted by consciousness of our own "nothingness." Following the passage quoted above, Nishida continues, "If this were all, however, I would not yet call it a fact of absolute contradiction. But this knowing my own eternal death is conversely the fundamental reason for my own existence."[116] It is because awareness of my own "nothingness" and my own "eternal death" is at the same time the "fundamental reason for my own existence" that Nishida describes this as a "profound self-contradiction."

What does it mean, then, for awareness of death to also be the "fundamental reason for my own existence"? Presumably this means that by facing death we encounter, conversely, that which allows the self to arise, or, in other words, that which underpins the existence of the self. For example, Nishida writes, "The absolute is something that endlessly envelops our self, that endlessly pursues and envelops our self that betrays and runs from it; in other words, it is infinite mercy."[117] Sinking in the "ocean of lust," lost in the "mountains of fame and wealth," in our despair we encounter something that envelops us. As Shinran puts it, "no matter our practice, we can never separate ourselves from death and rebirth," but we nevertheless encounter Amida-buddha, who "offered mercy and wished to save all of us." He hears the call of Amida-buddha who would save precisely those "evil people" who cannot attain enlightenment no matter how diligently they engage in religious practice.

Nishida believed that religion was an attempt to understand our own "root source," and by this he meant this kind of contradictory self-awareness, that is, the contradictory self-awareness of encountering that which underpins my self precisely when I am conscious of my own "death" and my own "nothingness." Nishida expressed this relationship between the self and that which transcends the self through his own concept of "inverse correspondence."[118] He calls this relationship "inverse correspondence" because, to begin with, the self and that which transcends the self are mutually contradictory and can never directly interact with each other. There is an unbridgeable gap between that which is finite and that which is absolutely infinite. No matter how ardently we pursue the absolutely infinite directly, we can never reach it. Nishida reiterates this with the phrase "there is no path from human beings to the divine." But when we are aware that our self is thoroughly nothing, that is, when we are aware of our own death, we encounter that which makes us live, that is, that which underpins our existence. Through this encounter we are indeed able to transcend our own nothingness. Nishida refers to this paradoxical situation as "inverse correspondence." Nishida often expressed this with a phrase from a Kamakura-period dialogue between Daitō Kokushi, a Rinzai monk, and retired Emperor Hanazono: "separated from each other for eternity, but not separated for even an instant; face to face all day long, but not face to face even for a moment." We encounter the absolutely infinite not when we rely on the power of the self and attempt to face the absolutely infinite directly, but when we are that which is furthest away from the absolutely infinite (nothing).

4. Tanabe Hajime's "Logic of Species"

(1) Toward the Formation of the "Logic of Species"

Nishida responded to Tanabe's criticism by shifting his thought toward issues of the real world and history, but right around the same time Tanabe was also creating his own philosophical perspective. This approach came to be called the "logic of species." This name refers to a philosophical stance developed in a series of essays beginning in 1934, including works such as "The Logic of Social Existence: An Attempt at Philosophical Sociology,"[119] "The Logic of Species and a World Schema: The Path Toward a Philosophy of Absolute Mediation,"[120] and "Elucidating the Meaning of the Logic of Species."[121]

Why did Tanabe start thinking about "species"? What motivated him to create the "logic of species," and what significance did he give it? Several times in his own writings, Tanabe offered the following two factors as motivations behind his proposal of the "logic of species." One is a "practical" motivation, the other a "logical" motivation. Before discussing this in detail, I would first like to briefly touch on Tanabe's thought prior to the "logic of species."[122]

During the period he wrote the essays collected in *Hegel's Philosophy and the Dialectic*, Tanabe not only engaged in criticism of Hegel's and Marx's dialectic and Nishida's philosophy, but at the same time also turned his attention to Heidegger's philosophy, engaging in a critical examination of this thought. In 1931 he published "Synthesis and Transcendence"[123] and "The Standpoint of Anthropology"[124] and in 1932 "From the Schema of 'Time' to the Schema of the 'World.'"[125] All three of these essays were deeply related to Heidegger's philosophy, and in particular to his *Kant and the Problem of Metaphysics*,[126] which had been published in 1929.

In these texts Tanabe criticizes Heidegger from several perspectives, one of which is the latter's excessive emphasis on the supremacy of time in his interpretation of Kant. In "From the Schema of 'Time' to the Schema of the 'World,'" Tanabe asks, "From only time as a root source, how can one introduce space that in its essence cannot be reduced to time?"[127] Tanabe believed that what lay at the root of time and space was itself something with the character of an "oppositional unity of time and space." Tanabe expressed this unity with the word "world" (*Welt*). This was inspired by the understanding of the "world" of Hermann Minkowski (1864–1909), who had provided a grounding for Einstein's special theory of relativity from a mathematical perspective, an understanding that came to be called "Minkowski space (space-time)." From this perspective, in "Synthesis and Transcendence" Tanabe asserts that "the schema of time Heidegger believes is the axis of rational criticism at the core of Kant's thought must be expanded into a schema of the world."[128]

By expanding the "schema of time" to the "schema of the world," Tanabe thus attempted to go beyond Heidegger's one-sidedness, and he also asserted that by doing so Kant's epistemology, which had been limited to the knowledge of nature, might perhaps "be expanded to an understanding of concrete historical social reality."[129] The "logic of species" was presumably conceived through an intertwining of several motivations, but this can be described as one of the ideas that paved the way for its development.

(2) The Practical Motivation Behind the "Logic of Species"

As noted above, Tanabe stated "practical" and "logical" motivations for having proposed the "logic of species," and an example of the former can be found in the following passage from "Answering Criticism of the Logic of Species"[130] (1937). "The first motivation was to examine the coercive power of the state over the individual, and to look for a rational grounding for this coercion."[131] In "Elucidating the Meaning of the Logic of Species," which was published in the same year, he states that the purpose of this undertaking "lay in confronting the state control that constitutes power within the country and seeking a rational principle to govern it."[132]

These passages indicate that the "logic of species" was deeply connected to the circumstances of its era. As noted earlier, Japan's intellectual circumstances underwent a dramatic change in 1931 around the time of the Mukden Incident. Along with Japan adopting a policy of external expansion and its political isolation on the world stage deepening, people's gaze turned inward, and there was a demand for thought that would support this policy. Around 1930, Kihira Tadayoshi (1874–1949)'s *The Japanese Spirit*[133] (1930) and Kanokogi Kazunobu (1884–1949)'s *Philosophy of the Japanese Spirit*[134] were published, and many journals put out special editions focusing on "the Japanese spirit" or "Japanism."[135] Along with this rise in ethnicism and nationalism, discourse and thought became greatly restricted.

These circumstances of the era can be thought of as having turned Tanabe's attention toward the realities of society, but what drew him even more strongly toward these issues was his own firsthand experience of the Takigawa Incident (the firing of a law professor by the Ministry of Education on the grounds of publishing books that "disturbed the peace and order").[136] When he used the phrase "the coercive power of the state over the individual" in "Answering Criticism of the Logic of Species," this incident was presumably at least part of what he had in mind. In the context of this tide of the times, the question of whether control of the individual by the state had a rational basis, and if so what this basis might be, came to occupy a significant position in Tanabe's thought. His interest in these questions is presumably what led him to the topic of "social existence" and the "logic of species."

(3) The Logical Motivation Behind the "Logic of Species"

The other reason Tanabe gives for having come up with the "logic of species" is his "logical motivation." This was his desire to establish a "method of philosophy itself" from a more general perspective, separate from the issue of control of the individual by the state and how this ought to be.

Ultimately this meant Tanabe creating his own original logic, the "logic of absolute mediation." In Tanabe's understanding, the essence of logic is found in deduction, and this cannot be understood when separated from the mediating relationship of genus, species, and individual. The defining characteristic of Tanabe's understanding, however, was his view of genus, species, and individual not simply as a sequence of things that differ from each other quantitatively, but as entities irreducible to anything else that possesses their own unique significance. The individual emerges in contrast to the species, and the genus only comes into being through the negation of the species. At the same time, however, all three are mutually interrelated through the mediation of negation. This relationship in which "one cannot stand without the mediation of the others" is what Tanabe calls "absolute mediation."

What was the particular principle that made Tanabe's thought unique in the period of the "logic of species"? The answer to this question is "the dialectic of absolute mediation." In other words, Tanabe conceived of a dialectic that, rather than positing an absolute and then grounding all things in it, adopts a perspective in which all things—genus, species, and individual—are "mediated" by each other. It was not during this period, however, that Tanabe first used the term "dialectic" to describe his own stance. Even in his earlier works *Hegel's Philosophy and Dialectic* and *An Outline of Philosophy*[137] (1933), Tanabe had, while criticizing the perspectives of Hegel, Marx, and Nishida, described his own approach as "dialectic"—or, more concretely, "absolute dialectic." In these texts, however, he criticized the dialectic of Hegel and Marx and spoke of "absolute dialectic" in terms of reversing it. A distinctive semantic content that could be called "Tanabe's philosophy" was still not sufficiently formed.

For "absolute dialectic" to develop into "dialectic of absolute mediation," "species" had to be positioned at the center of mediation and understood not simply as a logical concept but as something with concrete meaning. Considered from a different perspective, in the "absolute dialectic" as he had conceived of it at the stage of works such as *An Outline of Philosophy*, Tanabe's thought was developed along the two axes of the whole and the individual, or the absolute and the free and autonomous actions of the individual. In contrast to this, in the period of "the logic of species" the problem had become the positioning of "species" between the individual and the whole. Here there can be said to be a clear divide between his thought before and after the "logic of species."

Why did Tanabe come to think not only of the whole and the individual but of this "species" between them? Here we must note that his "practical" and "logical" motivations were not entirely separate and cut off from each other. Tanabe himself says that they "possess a necessary, internal relationship to one another."

Why do these motivations have a necessary relationship to each other? Various irrational things exist in an actual society, and Tanabe understood philosophy as a field of inquiry that, unable to ignore such actual irrationality, must on the contrary actively engage with it. The existence of this kind of irrationality signifies the "limit (*Schranke*) of philosophy," but accepting this limit is nothing other than "the rejection of philosophy." According to Tanabe, philosophy therefore has no choice but to engage with irrationality. As Tanabe puts it, "Logic only becomes capable of absolute mediation by mediating irrational, immediate being that defies logic. Irrational, immediate being is a negative moment that is indispensable for logic as absolute mediation."[138] The "logic of absolute mediation" engages with the irrationality of reality and must be positioned as a mediating term within the whole for rationality to be affirmed (as the negation of a negation).

(4) What Is the "Logic of Species"?

According to Tanabe, the coercive power the state holds over the individual originates in "something tribal,[139] into which individuals are born and inside of which they are embraced,"[140] or, in other words, a "species substrate." What is conceived of here is a clan or people as an "immediate, species unity, bound by blood and soil," and on top of that a "nation-state."[141] Tanabe found the pure form of this in the totem society analyzed by Lucien Lévy-Bruhl (1857–1939). This kind of society is governed by the "law of participation" (*loi de participation*). In other words, a force that unifies individuals into a whole is operating. The individuals that are its members, however, resist this unifying force and assert their independent autonomy.

Their essence is not "participation" but "separation." Borrowing Nietzsche's phrase, Tanabe refers to this free will of the individual that separates itself and tries to oppose the whole as the "will to power." In response, a species society attempts to suppress and reject individuals who seek to separate themselves from this kind of whole and rob it of its unifying power. In Tanabe we can see an awareness of living in an era in which the conflict between these two forces had been radicalized.

Tanabe saw his task as overcoming this oppositional conflict and bringing this blind, closed-off unity of species toward the "absolute liberation of human[142] society as a limitless whole."[143] According to Tanabe, this could only be realized by negating the individual self that is the will to power. But this was not a simple negation; at the same time, it was also an affirmation. The negation of the self as the will to power was also the birth of the individual as a "member of humanity," that is, as a "true individual." Through this absolutely negative turn of negation-that-is-affirmation, a state that forms the individual as a member of humanity, in other words, a "human state," comes into being.

This turn also signifies species as an immediate unified body—the nation-state—obtaining "human universality." Genus society does not arise without a connection to species; it arises by mediating species' immediate unity, that is, it arises with species as its substrate. Through the negation of the individual, this species as substrate achieves transformation into genus. A "species that has become genus" is said to arise. This can only occur on the basis of species as substrate, but on the other hand it can only be realized through the negation of the immediacy of species, and Tanabe is cognizant of the fact that the two must be clearly distinguished.

> While the nation-state is also sublated by the human state, it does not lose its species character; when the immediate unity of species is sublated by the absolutely negative unity of genus they appear in different stages in an affirmation-that-is-negation manner.[144]

As a result, control of the individual remains even in the "human state." However, this control is not simply coercion but is "turned into autonomy by reason." Tanabe can be said to have sought the "rational principle" of the state's coercive power over the individual in this coercion that is at once autonomy.

(5) The "Logic of Species" and Tanabe's Critique of Nishida's Philosophy

In the "logic of absolute mediation," all things—genus, species, and individual—are "mediated" by each other. In other words, nothing is immediately given or made a premise. Regarding something absolute occupying the position of genus in particular, Tanabe says, "While this is called 'absolute,' directly positing it without the mediation of a relation that negates it is impermissible." When he made this kind of statement, what Tanabe undoubtedly had in mind was his understanding of Nishida's "place of nothingness" and "absolute nothingness." In "The Logic of Species and a World Schema," too, Tanabe reiterates that "absolute nothingness," to the extent it is something immediately posited, cannot be accepted from the perspective of the "logic of absolute mediation." The "logical" motivation for proposing the "logic of species" can be said to have been deeply linked to Tanabe's critique of Nishida's philosophy.

Behind Tanabe's assertion of absolute mediation of genus, species, and individual lay his understanding that logic could not be something that leaves outside itself that which is immediate and irrational. He believed logic could only become logic by negating the irrational, mediating it toward the rational, and affirming it. This meant that the immediate and irrational "species" was on the contrary a negative moment indispensable to logic being logic. This was tied to his criticism that this kind of mediation does not arise in Nishida's "logic of place," which is composed of the two moments of "place" and "that which is emplaced"; in other words, there is no room in it for "species."

Relatedly, Tanabe also asserted that Nishida's philosophy could not constitute a logic of history. Of course, as we have already seen, Nishida addressed the topic of history in his essay "I and You." He had also previously written an article entitled "History" (1931) for *Iwanami Course: Philosophy*. In it he writes, "That which changes over time does not constitute history; that which enfolds time constitutes history."[145] Nishida's fundamental idea was that historians look at the content of "that which enfolds time," that is, "that which is eternal"; in other words, history is that which projects "that which is eternal" or its "shadow." From Tanabe's perspective, however, this understanding was nothing more than "religious contemplation that looks at history from the standpoint of the determination of nothingness."[146]

Of course, Nishida did not understand history only in relation to "that which enfolds time." As previously noted, in "I and You" he had spoken of the significance of the "reconstruction of society" by the individual. Influenced by Tanabe's "logic of species," in "The Continuity and Self-Identity of the World,"[147] written immediately after the publication of Tanabe's "The Logic of Social Existence" (1935), Nishida refers to the role played by states and nations in history. For example, he writes that "various states or nations each take on their own orientation in history; each must play its own role, each has its own fate, and each is born onto and off of history's stage."[148]

From Tanabe's perspective, states or nations are not simply entities that project "shadows" of the eternal (ideas) and arrive on the stage of history to take up the particular tasks given to them by the eternal before eventually making their exit. First and foremost, states and nations are entities that limit or suppress the actions of individuals in history. They are "a species-type unity that directly controls the individual."[149] The individual, in contrast, while making the species the womb of its own existence, attempts to seize this power to control or suppress and "separate" itself from its own root source. This "separate" individual, however, then rejects its ego-nature and becomes a "rational individual," and through its negatively mediating the immediate irrationality of species toward universality a concrete unity of both is realized. History is nothing other than this process of absolutely negative turning.

The individual can only become the subject that absolutely negatively converts the irrationality of "species" in this way, however, by mediating this "species" that is its womb and substrate. In this sense Tanabe asserts that it is in fact "species" that is the "subject of history."

> It is the nation as species that truly stands in contrast to the individual person as the substrate of history. It is precisely this species that can be described as the substrate of history. The purely individual person lacks the mediation of substrate as the subject of history.[150]

Tanabe saw abstractness in Nishida's understanding of history that lacked the positioning of "species" in this sense. In his own words, "How is the place of nothingness, in which species that is substrate and individual that is subject are buried together, to form history? The logic of the place of nothingness is not a logic at all."[151]

(6) The Positioning of "Species" in Nishida's Philosophy

The development of the "logic of species" by Tanabe described above and the criticism of Nishida's philosophy from this perspective had a major influence on the development of Nishida's thought from that point onward. This is clearly demonstrated in *Philosophical Essays Volume 2*,[152] published in 1937.

In one of the essays it includes, "Problems of Species Formation and Development"[153] (1937), Nishida states that in order for historical reality to form itself as something with a distinctive character, it requires "numerous species that independently determine themselves." A species is a "form" or "paradigm," but is by no means something fixed. In the "historical present" that forms itself, species "negates itself and forms something individual," and by being an "act of formation that changes the given world," or, in other words, by taking charge of the "direction of the self-determination of historical reality, that is, the direction of the times," it becomes something imbued with life—a "living species." Here Nishida expresses the view that it is through this "living species" that the historical world, while implying contradictions, forms itself in a self-negating manner.

On the other hand, he also argues against Tanabe's assertion that species is the "substrate of history." In "Logic and Life"[154] (1937), Nishida states, "Something that can be thought of as a state or society in the historical world, while indeed specific, surely should not be described as the substrate of history. A particular state or society must be mediated in the historical world."[155] Just as the specific is always specific in relation to the general, a concrete state or society only emerges as specific within the "historical world," and states or societies themselves cannot be seen as the "substrate of history." Nishida believed it is the general that forms itself by mediating the specific that is this substrate, and states and societies can only be specific as "specific to the world."

It was by taking up Tanabe's criticism from the perspective of the "logic of species" in this way that Nishida's concept of the "social and historical world," which was given a prominent position in his thought at the stage of *The Self-Aware Determination of Nothingness*, obtained its concrete content. Here too we can see that Nishida and Tanabe directly addressed the development of each other's ideas and critiques, using them as a springboard for the development of their own thought.

(7) The Question of the State

The "logic of species" took its complete form in "Elucidating the Meaning of the Logic of Species," published in 1937, but given the circumstances of his era Tanabe had no choice but to then discuss its relevance to the "state." "The Logic of the Existence of the State," published in 1939, was particularly focused on this issue.

Of course, this essay was not the first time Tanabe had addressed the question of the state. He had also discussed it in "The Logic of Social Existence" and "Elucidating the Meaning of the Logic of Species." Simply stated, the "logic of species" aimed to transform species into genus through the self-negation of the individual, or, in other words, to form a state that obtained human universality. Here the "nation-state" as an immediate unified body and the "human state" formed through species becoming genus were clearly distinguished as different stages.

This distinction is maintained in "The Logic of the Existence of the State." Here Tanabe strongly opposed the immediate species substrate—the nation-state—being made absolute. He went as far as to say that such a perspective "heralds destruction as the judgment of the world handed down by the history of the world."[156] Moreover, he explicitly notes that "totalitarianism's chorus of praise for wars of raw power aggression is difficult to accept as is."[157] This was an almost unthinkably bold statement at the time.

However, it must be pointed out that here the distinction between the state as an immediate form and the state as species that has been made genus mentioned above is blurred. For example, the state can be described as "the most concrete existence" formed by "social existence and the creation of history [being] mediated by the actions of human beings." The introduction of the concept of "adaptive manifestation"[158] in the same essay made this distinction even harder to see. "Adaptive manifestation" is a Buddhist term referring to buddhas and bodhisattvas revealing themselves in a manner corresponding to the capacities of living beings, but Tanabe uses it to say that the state is an "adaptive manifestation of the absolute." The introduction of this concept clearly involves the possibility of interpreting an actual state as a manifestation of the absolute. This was of course not something directly intended, as can be seen from the passage rejecting the making absolute of species substrate cited above, but it does indeed open the possibility of affirming the existing state in its current form.[159]

After publishing "The Logic of the Existence of the State," throughout 1941 Tanabe continued to publish various essays, such as "The Morality of the State,"[160] "The Way of Intellectual Patriotism,"[161] and "The Development of the Concept of Existence,"[162] but from the outbreak of the Pacific War until its conclusion he published no articles and, with the exception of a handful of lectures, kept silent. We know the circumstances in which Tanabe was placed during this period from the preface to *Philosophy as the Way of Repentance*,[163] published in 1946. There Tanabe states that between on the one hand having the belief that "the government should perhaps be made to reflect on the state's policies regarding academic inquiry through speaking plainly" and on the other hand having the "self-restraint of believing this was impermissible because it would reveal domestic intellectual division in the face of the enemy in wartime," he found himself suffering, "unable to resolve myself in either direction." This dilemma can perhaps be said to have imposed his silence.

Nevertheless, in a lecture entitled "Death and Rebirth"[164] given in front of students at Kyoto University in the May of 1943, for example, Tanabe said, "It is impermissible for us to stand apart from the state. We are to give ourselves to it without hesitation."[165] At the end of that year, the measure for the deferment of the conscription of students in the humanities was halted and these students were in fact sent to the battlefield. Tanabe's remarks thus seem to have foreseen this shift in policy. In a special lecture given at Kyoto University in 1944, Tanabe spoke of the "way of repentance," and after Japan's defeat he published *Philosophy as the Way of Repentance*. This focus on repentance can be said to have arisen out of his reflection on the attitude he had taken toward the war.

Chapter 6

Various Developments in Philosophy in the Era of Nishida and Tanabe

1. Takahashi Satomi

(1) Initial Critique of Nishida's Philosophy

This chapter traces the thought of several philosophers active in the same era as Nishida and Tanabe, the early Shōwa period. The first of these is Takahashi Satomi, who taught for many years at Tōhoku University. In 1912, the year after the publication of Nishida's *An Inquiry into the Good*, Takahashi published "The Fact of Phenomena of Consciousness and Their Significance: Reading Nishida's *An Inquiry into the Good*,"[1] which became the first academic critique of this work. Writing on the one hand that it was the joy of encountering "the first and only philosophical text by a Japanese person since the Meiji period" that made him decide to review Nishida's book, on the other hand he laid out several questions and criticisms regarding its vagueness, particularly in regard to the concept of "pure experience."

Takahashi took issue with three points in particular. First, Nishida defines "pure experience" as the "state of experience just as it is" without the addition of any deliberation, or the completely independent, pure activity of consciousness with neither the opposition of subject and object nor any distinction between intellect, emotion, and volition having yet arisen. At the same time, however, he also views judgment and contemplation as "pure experience," and tried to explain the difference between "pure experience" as a strictly unified state and judgment and contemplation that are also in a sense a single unified operation as "a difference of degree" of unity.

213

Second, noting that while "pure experience" was explained as the "state of experience just as it is" without the addition of any deliberation but at the same time was also viewed as a universal that differentiated itself (and through the process of this differentiation completed and realized itself), he questioned how these two definitions could be reconciled. Third, he took issue with Nishida taking "pure experience" as consciousness in a state of strict unity to be a simple fact while also maintaining that meaning and judgment arise when this unity is broken, for example, when a connection is made to past sensations. According to Takahashi, meaning is not grounded in relation to something else, or in the "great unity" Nishida describes, but rather fact and meaning are distinguished within a single phenomenon of consciousness itself. He suggests that problems surrounding consciousness cannot be resolved unless we take this as our starting point.

In response to these questions and criticisms from Takahashi, Nishida promptly published "Answering the Critique of my *An Inquiry into the Good* by Takahashi (Satomi),"[2] in which he writes that pure experience and non-pure experience are not different types of conscious states that independently oppose each other, but rather "two sides" of a single consciousness, and that "pure experience" is a "concrete totality" that spontaneously develops itself, which moreover is also "meaning that is fact." Nishida did not believe he had sufficiently answered Takahashi's critique, however, and aware of the importance of these issues and the difficulty of resolving them continued to use this as an impetus in the development of his own thought. In this sense Takahashi's critique can be said to have had great significance.

(2) The Philosophy of "Enveloping Totality"

After serving as a teacher at Niigata High School, in 1921 Takahashi became an assistant professor in the Faculty of Science of Tōhoku University, and from 1925 he spent two years studying in Europe. Beginning in the winter term of 1926, for two terms he studied under Husserl at the University of Freiberg. This stay in Freiberg had a major influence on Takahashi's later thought. After returning to Japan, he published a series of essays, including "Husserl's Phenomenology, Particularly Its Phenomenological Reduction"[3] and "Time and the Stream of Consciousness in Husserl,"[4] which were then collected in *Husserl's Phenomenology*,[5] published in 1931. Thanks to this work by Takahashi, and also to the scholarship of Yamauchi Tokuryū, Husserl's phenomenology became widely known in Japan.

Takahashi's stay in Freiberg coincided with a period of transition in Husserl's thought. This was the period during which Husserl was laying the foundations of the "genetic phenomenology" found in his later philosophy. Husserl presumably discussed this topic in his lectures and seminars. Takahashi discussed this idea in his essays before Husserl had presented it in his own writings. From them we see, for example, that at the time Husserl was engaged in tackling the problem of "the consciousness of other selves." After stating that this is one of the most difficult problems in philosophy, Takahashi records that Husserl had introduced the concept of "emotional ingress"[6] and was struggling to find a solution. We can also see that at this stage the problems of "physicality" and "the sensation of movement" (*Kinästhese*) had been brought into the discussion in relation to the problem of the consciousness of other selves.[7]

Takahashi thus blazed a trail for the study of phenomenology in Japan by introducing Husserl's later thought while it was still in formation. He also went on to construct his own thought in works such as *The Standpoint of Totality* (1932),[8] *Experience and Existence* (1936),[9] *History and Dialectic* (1939),[10] and *Enveloping Dialectic* (1942).[11] In *The Standpoint of Totality*, for example, he candidly expresses his doubts about phenomenology. Phenomenology asserts that we must separate ourselves from all points of view through phenomenological reduction, but Takahashi reveals doubts about whether we can actually achieve freedom from all standpoints. His intent, however, was of course not to reject phenomenology, because philosophical inquiry is only possible from a fixed standpoint. Takashi believed that in the end philosophy is nothing other than "an intellectual system of the totality of what we are able to experience moment by moment."[12] This is something that is constantly developing and continuing to expand, but as a totality it never gets beyond being something relative.

Takahashi then tried to take his thought a step further. He believed that when we probe the possibility of infinite development, a "stillness as the totality of development" is to be expected. He asserts that a system of knowledge that is ceaselessly continuing to develop "does not contradict a stillness of high potency as the absolute complete corpus of the experience of infinite development."[13] Takahashi believed it was this totality as a higher-order stillness that "envelops" all things—"enveloping totality"—that was the root source of all beings and their activities.

(3) Second Critique of Nishida's Philosophy

Takahashi then once again turned his attention to Nishida's philosophy. He was clearly conscious of Nishida's philosophy, for example, when he wrote that "absolute nothingness" can be thought of as further underlying "stillness as the totality of activity"[14] in "The Possibility of Phenomenological Reduction: Appendix: The Introduction of Neutrality Modification,"[15] an essay included in *The Standpoint of Totality*. According to Takahashi, "absolute nothingness" is that which envelops all beings as a totality and makes them possible, and he uses this term, which is also employed by Nishida, because its referent is not something to be sought in the domain of existence. It is not the same, however, as Nishida's "absolute nothingness." In 1936, Takahashi penned another essay focusing on Nishida's thought, "On Nishida's Philosophy"[16] (included in *History and Dialectic*), in which he writes, "This is not simply place like [Nishida] sensei's absolute nothingness, but rather that which envelops place as well, nor is it a self-determining creative nothingness like sensei's, but rather that which envelops this kind of nothingness as well."[17]

Takahashi considered Nishida's concept of "absolute nothingness" inadequate because he thought that as a place that envelops things it was seen in correlation to individual objects. This "absolute nothingness" seen in relation to individual objects could not be described as "absolute nothingness" in a true sense. Takahashi's understanding was that "absolute nothingness" must be nothingness that transcends even place as self-determining nothingness and envelops it along with everything else. From this perspective he further criticized as relativization of the absolute and temporalization of the eternal Nishida's attempt to develop the "place of nothingness" as a dialectic world from *Fundamental Problems of Philosophy* onward.

As is clear from this criticism, Takahashi had been constantly mindful of the development of Nishida's thought in the formation of his own philosophy in which it is "enveloping totality" that is the root source of all existence. Takahashi's philosophy can thus be said to have been formed through a confrontation with Nishida's philosophy.

2. Kuki Shūzō

(1) The Development of Kuki's Thought

Kuki Shūzō (1888–1941) entered the University of Tokyo in 1909, and was particularly influenced by Raphael von Koeber, who taught philosophy there as a foreign instructor. Kuki's fascination with various forms of Eastern and Western thought and art both new and old and interest in Japanese culture were presumably cultivated during his time at the University of Tokyo studying under Koeber. After graduating, he studied in Europe from

1921 to 1929, which at the time was a very long stay overseas. He lived in Germany and France for nearly the entire decade of the 1920s, and he was very fortunate to have been able to study abroad in this period during which Europe produced an extraordinary number of intellectual achievements.

The 1920s were a decade that saw the sunset of the Neo-Kantian School, and Kuki chose as his first destination in Germany the University of Heidelberg, where Rickert was a professor. Kuki was not satisfied with the philosophy of the Neo-Kantians, however, and in 1924, enamored with France's Bergson, he moved to Paris. What had drawn Kuki to Paris is revealed in "Bergson au Japon," an essay he published in French while living in France. Here I will quote at greater length from a passage cited in the first section of chapter 4.

> The main role he played for us was arousing a desire for metaphysics. Our spirits, parched by the critical formalism of German Neo-Kantianism, welcomed the "blessed rain" of Bergson's metaphysical intuition. Bergson saw the fundamental error of Kantianism in Kant's having sought to hammer out too strict a distinction between the matter and form of knowledge. . . . To do philosophy is to place oneself inside concrete reality through an effort of intuition. . . . Bergson allowed us to "resuscitate the absolute."[18]

In "Introduction à la Métaphysique," Bergson asserts that reality is apprehended not by fixing and dividing it, that is, by the method of "analysis," but only when we enter deeply into reality itself and "with a kind of mental stethoscope take the pulse of the soul,"[19] that is, through "intuition," and states that the stance of attempting to grasp reality through this approach is both "true empiricism" and "true metaphysics." In Kuki's "Bergson au Japon" we can see strong sympathy for this position.

In "Recollections of Henri Bergson"[20] (1941), Kuki recalls meeting Bergson and praises him highly, writing, "I doubt anyone would disagree that he was the greatest philosopher the world produced in the first half of the twentieth century." This stay in France led Kuki to construct the foundations for the serious study of French philosophy in Japan after his return from abroad. This work fostered the development of many excellent scholars of philosophy such as Omodaka Hisayuki. Along with the introduction of Heidegger discussed below, this was one of the important roles Kuki played in the history of Japanese philosophy.

In the summer term of 1927, Kuki returned to Germany from Paris and studied phenomenology in Freiberg under Husserl and Oskar Becker. In the winter term he moved to the University of Marburg where he also had the opportunity to attend Heidegger's lectures (Heidegger had moved to Marburg from Freiberg in 1923 and did not return to Freiberg as Husserl's successor until the winter term of 1928). Kuki presumably returned to Germany for the same reason he had gone to France; we can assume he saw in Heidegger, an energetic young philosopher a year his junior, "something metaphysical" or "something that will resuscitate the absolute." Over the eight years Kuki spent living and studying overseas, in the end it was France's Bergson and Germany's Heidegger that most strongly influenced him.

(2) Kuki's Theory of "Time"

Kuki's scholarship covered a wide gamut of topics, but his philosophy first began to take concrete form in his theory of time. From June to December of his last year abroad he once again stayed in Paris and gave lectures entitled "La notion du temps et la reprise sur le temps en Orient" and "L'expression de l'infini dans l'art japonais" in nearby Pontigny. These two lectures were published in the same year by Philippe Renouard in Paris under the title *Propos sur le temps*. This was Kuki's first published work.

Presumably conscious of his audience, the question Kuki addresses in "La notion du temps et la reprise sur le temps en Orient" is "Eastern time." Another significant work in the development of Kuki's theory of time was "Metaphysical Time,"[21] included in *Humanity and Existence*[22] (1939). As is clear from the title, this essay addresses the topic of time from a metaphysical perspective. The question addressed in *On Time*,[23] in contrast, was the nature of time in the East. Kuki characterized this with the phrase "recursive time."[24] In other words, in the East time is not thought of as proceeding linearly but rather as something that "repeats."

This can be seen, for example, in the concept of *saṃsāra*[25] (cyclicality). Here Kuki focuses on identity. *Saṃsāra* is of course rebirth or transmigration and originally did not imply any identity. Kuki, however, believed that the cause of a new life is already present in the previous life, and between the two "there is in fact no change whatsoever." If this understanding is adopted, *saṃsāra* then means things existing eternally as the same things. The same things are endlessly reborn. Here there is time that endlessly repeats, or, in other words, recursive time. Kuki then expands this recursive time as "*saṃsāra* of the soul" into "*saṃsāra* of the universe" and discusses universal recursive time (the doctrine of *kalpa*[26] [universal aeon or timescale]).

"Metaphysical Time" also addresses this topic of "recursive time," but here Kuki's starting point is the question of the absolute foundation of time. This is related to the question of whether time is limited or unlimited. If we believe time is limited, we then face the difficult question of how it goes from not existing to existing.

If we believe it is unlimited, two ways of thinking are distinguished. The first is that in which time is viewed as linear, in which case unlimited time inevitably has the fragmentary nature of never attaining wholeness. Kuki calls this kind of infinity "latent infinity." The second is that in which time is viewed as a circle with no beginning or end, that is, as recursive time. Kuki calls this conception of time, an infinity that is not only unbounded but also simultaneously complete, "manifest infinity." *Saṃsāra* is then interpreted as a typical example of this "manifest infinity." As in the Upanishads, *saṃsāra* is likened to a "wheel," and this wheel is both absolutely unitary and continuously, endlessly turning. Here both "absolute identity" and "quantitative diversity" stand without contradiction.

(3) The Structure of *Iki*

Contemplation of *iki* (stylish refinement, chicness) and "contingency" can be said to have formed the core of Kuki's thought. He had already hit upon these ideas during his stay in Europe. After returning to Japan, he gave a lecture entitled "Contingency" in October of 1929, and the following year he published "The Structure of Iki"[27] in the January and February issues of the journal *Thought*. A revised version of this essay was published that November as *The Structure of "Iki."*

The intent behind this work can be seen in the quote from Maine de Biran printed on the back of the title page: "La pensée doit remplir toute l'existence" (Thought must satisfy the whole of existence). As though responding to these words, in the preface to *The Structure of "Iki"* Kuki writes, "Living philosophy must be capable of understanding reality. . . . grasping reality just as it is and logically putting into words experiences that should be savored is the task pursued by this book."[28] It was Kuki's conviction that philosophy must not be confined to the world of logic and must engage with reality and address it just as it is; in this sense it must be a "living philosophy." *The Structure of "Iki"* can be described as a text that directly concretizes this approach.

This still leaves us with the question of how "grasping reality just as it is" is related to addressing *iki*. This question is deeply connected to how Kuki viewed language. Regarding this point, Kuki writes, "A meaning or language is nothing other than the self-expression of the past and present state of being of a people, or the self-disclosure of a particular culture with its own history."[29] He believed that the way of being, history, and culture of a people are directly manifested in the language they speak. In other words, a language is the distillation of the cultural and spiritual undertakings of a people accumulated over vast stretches of time. No element of a language is arrived at simply by chance; a people's way of seeing and thinking about things is vividly reflected in every word.

Even if this is the case, however, it still does not answer the question of why Kuki was concerned with *iki*. If, as Kuki says, every word reflects the culture and way of looking at things of the people that uses it and is tinged with their distinctive coloring, then it should not matter which word is examined. Kuki's response to this would presumably have been something like the following. The degree to which each word reflects the history and culture of a people is not necessarily the same. Just as there are words such as "left" and "right" that have strong universality, that is, words whose equivalents can easily be found in other languages, there are also words with strong particularity, that is, words whose equivalents in other languages cannot easily be found and that furthermore highlight the distinctive characteristics of the culture and traditions of the people in question.

As examples of the latter Kuki offers the French word *esprit* (spirit, wit) and the German word *Sehnsucht* (yearning). Kuki thought that if we were to look for a word in the Japanese language that evoked the characteristics of Japanese culture and traditions in this way, a prime candidate would be *iki*. While there are words in other languages that are close to it in meaning, *iki* nevertheless retains distinctive semantic content that cannot be reduced to any word in another language. The belief that this uniqueness of *iki* could facilitate the elucidation of Japanese people's sense of beauty and values, or more broadly the distinctive character of Japanese culture, lay at the root of Kuki's discourse on *iki*.

If we try to abstract the concrete semantic content of *iki* and extract its essence, however, we will fail to truly grasp this word. To understand *iki* we must grasp it in its immediacy as a phenomenon of consciousness. While thoroughly respecting its concreteness, we must grasp it in its "living form." In other words, we must address not its *essentia* but its *existentia*, that is, its factual or real existence. To use Kuki's term, we must "apprehend"[30] its existence.

Based on this kind of "hermeneutic" method, Kuki extracted three features, or main component factors, from *iki*—"coquetry,"[31] "fortitude,"[32] and "resignation"[33]—and presented a vivid structurization of this phenomenon of consciousness. "Coquetry" forms the base of the whole, through the addition of the idealism of fortitude the directness of coquetry is "spiritualized,"[34] and with the addition of resignation the attachment to reality at the root of coquetry is sublimated and becomes elegant. Kuki calls the "aimless, insouciant autonomous play" that takes shape here, or, in other words, free play that has escaped attachment to reality, *iki*.

Through this kind of analysis, Kuki pulled philosophy, which tends to get shut away in logic or history, back toward living concrete experience and granted Japanese philosophy the kind of rich content and potential it had not had up until that point. Of course, *iki* is only part of the consciousness of value that has been cultivated in the history of Japanese culture. In this sense the results produced by Kuki's discourse on *iki* were indeed limited. Through this analysis, however, Kuki can be said to have demonstrated how close philosophy can get to reality and how much it can enrich itself by doing so. Following the path he had revealed and enriching the content of Japanese philosophy was a task he left for others.

(4) The Philosophy of Contingency

If one text were to be highlighted as Kuki Shūzō's most important work, it would presumably be *The Problem of Contingency*,[35] published in 1935. He addresses the issue of "contingency" not only in this book but also repeatedly in his lectures, and "Contingency" was the title of the dissertation he submitted to Kyoto University. He also wrote several essays on the subject, such as "Various Aspects of Contingency"[36] and "Contingency and the Feeling of Surprise."[37]

At the start of *The Problem of Contingency*, Kuki describes the nature of "contingency" as "existence that includes negation, being that is capable of not being."[38] He also states that it is "the form of nothingness invading being." Along with these sorts of statements, he additionally claims that only metaphysics that is philosophy in the truest sense can address existence or being not as fragments but in relation to nothingness, that is, in its entirety. Kuki thus asserts that while contingency is an issue unique to philosophy, it has never been properly taken up within the philosophical tradition. On the contrary, it has always been shunted outside the mainstream of philosophy; being that is completely cut off from nothingness has occupied the position of its main subject of study. Contingency that arises at the border of being and nothingness has been pushed into "the darkest depths of the intellect." Kuki tried to directly address this issue that had been driven into the shadows. Being is being because of the nothingness that surrounds and eats away at it. In this sense, what Kuki attempted in his contemplation of contingency signified a challenge to Western philosophy.

Kuki divides contingency into three types. At first these were logical contingency, empirical contingency, and metaphysical contingency, but in his book *The Problem of Contingency* they became categorical contingency, hypothetical contingency, and disjunctive contingency. In formal logic, judgments are generally divided into categorical, hypothetical, and disjunctive judgments depending on how the subject and predicate are connected. Kuki ties the problem of these three forms of judgment and their aspects, that is, the problem of necessity and contingency, together, and considers categorical necessity/categorical contingency, hypothetical necessity/hypothetical contingency, and disjunctive necessity/disjunctive contingency.

Taking them in order, categorical necessity is expressed by the proposition "p is p." This is the relationship between p and itself, or the relationship between the concept of p and its essential characteristics. In the case of clover, for example, there are almost always three leaves, and this can be seen as an essential characteristic of clover. In rare instances, however, there are four leaves. In that case a nonessential characteristic of a concept has been realized, and Kuki calls such cases, that is, cases in which a judgement of "p is q" emerges, "categorical contingency." This categorical contingency focuses on the fact that individual things (particularly things that have nonessential rather than essential characteristics) exist by chance, or, in other words, on the "contingency of existence."

"Hypothetical necessity" refers to cases such as "If you drop a glass, it will break" in which there is a necessary connection between cause and consequence, or, in other words, in which identity between cause and consequence can be observed. He expresses this kind of necessity with the proposition "if p then p."[39] "Hypothetical contingency" refers to cases in which this kind of identity between cause and consequence cannot be observed. An example of this would be the wall of a house beside the road I walk every day being blown over by a strong wind and injuring me. In this case a contingent event can be said to have occurred through two unrelated sets of cause and consequence encountering (intersecting with) each other by chance. In this sense this contingency can be said to have the character of the "contingency of chance encounters."

Disjunctive necessity is expressed with the proposition "p is p' or p"." Here p being one of the two disjuncts is necessary, but neither being p' nor being p" is necessary. It is on the contrary contingent. In other words, the relationship one disjunct (part) has to the whole is "disjunctive contingency." This is how Kuki considers "disjunctive necessity" and its opposite "disjunctive contingency" in *The Problem of Contingency*. As noted above, however, at first—in the special lecture "Contingency" delivered at Kyoto University in 1930, for example—he called this "metaphysical contingency." What he was thinking about at the time was not simply "disjunctive contingency." Even in *The Problem of Contingency*, he writes that "disjunctive contingency emerges particularly in relation to the metaphysical absolute" and thinks about this kind of contingency in relation to "the absolute" and "absolute being." In other words, it was considered in connection with the creation of the world by absolute being. From this perspective, we are beings that happen to exist here and now, but we could just as easily not exist. This existing by chance is "metaphysical contingency." In this sense it can be described as contingency related to "being and nothingness."

The above gives us an overview of Kuki's theory of contingency, but what was Kuki ultimately trying to say through this theory? What he was trying to articulate was that in the end our existence has no necessity whatsoever; below it yawns the abyss of nothingness, and our existence thus floats atop nothing. Looking at it from the opposite perspective, what he tried to express was the strangeness of our existence, or, in other words, how unlikely and precious it is.

Concordant with this approach, at the end of the concluding section of *The Problem of Contingency*, Kuki quotes a passage from Vasubandhu's *Discourse on the Pure Land*:[40] "Having seen the power of the Buddha's vow, there is no one who encounters this and lives an empty life." Precisely speaking, Kuki rephrases this as a negative imperative: "Do not encounter this and live an empty life."[41] Kuki tried to confront the "unlikeliness" of my existing here and now despite there being ample chance of my not existing at all, and the "unlikeliness" of my encountering you despite there being ample chance of our never having met.

(5) Concerning Poetry and Rhyme

Kuki Shūzō's thought contained aspects that do not fit within the framework of what is considered "philosophy." This is evident from the poems "Mental Landscape of Paris"[42] and "Windows of Paris"[43] that he sent back to Japan while studying abroad for publication in the magazine *Bright Star*,[44] and from his having taken charge of the newly created "overview of literature" course in the Faculty of Letters of Kyoto University in 1933. In his final years Kuki also devoted himself to the writing of *On Literature*[45] (this text was published after his death in 1941).

In *On Literature*, Kuki sees the essence of literature, and poetry in particular, in temporality (in this sense this work is connected to his examination of time during his period studying overseas). According to *On Literature*, time in poetry is not quantitative time that can be measured but rather qualitative time. A "pure duration or flow" is said to proceed there. This is based on Bergson's understanding of "pure duration." Kuki states that, in poetry, "one element of diversity gets inside another, and they invade each other."[46]

Kuki also finds the foundations of rhyme in poetry. There is a poem by Takahashi no Mushimaro included in the *Man'yōshū* (vol. 6, 971) that reads, "When the hilly paths of the Tatsuta Road are redolent with red azaleas, and when the cherry blossoms bloom . . ." Here rhyming occurs when the "red" of "red azaleas" and the "red" of "redolent," or the "bl" of "blossoms" and the "bl" of "bloom," interpenetrate and permeate each other.[47] Here time is not simply time that flows away as an amount. There is time that persists through memory, layering and interpenetrating itself. Time is multilayered. As an example of multilayered time, Kuki examines a poem by Bashō: "Tachibana tree, lesser cuckoo in the field; I do not know when."

> The past resurrects as the present with exactly the same form.
> Here there are two presents that are exactly the same, a present
> with infinite depth. We can say that time repeats and is tinged
> with recurrence, and we can also say that an eternal present
> actually exists.[48]

If learning is situated in the past and morality in the future, art "is situated in the present." This "present," however, is by no means a single point on a straight line. It is a present with depth in which various times are interlayered. In this sense, literature and poetry can be described as a "small universe" that reflects the greater universe. The present can possess infinite past and infinite future while remaining the present. It can also be described as an "eternal now with infinite depth."[49] Rhyme realizes an "eternal now" by "repeating the present tinged with recurrence" or by "stopping a poem at the place of the same present and making it stand still."

Within *On Literature*, Kuki put the greatest effort into an essay entitled "Rhyme in Japanese Poetry."[50] Of course, he had not only become interested in the topic of rhyme at the end of his life. While living in Paris in 1929 he had written an essay called "Concerning Rhyme,"[51] which was submitted to *Bright Star* (owing to this magazine's discontinuation, however, it did not actually appear in print). This demonstrates that Kuki had a profound interest in the potential of Japanese poetry from early in his career.

In "Rhyme in Japanese Poetry," Kuki examines the question of whether or not rhyme is possible in Japanese verse. It is generally said that rhyme is not suited to Japanese poetry. Kuki rejected this kind of understanding, however, as a view based on insufficient knowledge of the richness of the Japanese language and the sensibility of Japanese people. Classical poetry clearly shows that Japanese people had "superb ears of the mind that heard the music of the universe in the movement of heavenly bodies, and acute perception that secretly imparts intoxication even to rustling rhymes."[52] The Japanese language expresses this sensibility, and is amply equipped with structures capable of opening up "a realm of contingency and freedom that emerges, beautifully and as though in a dream, on the other side of the real world in which we are bound by desires." What Kuki tried to argue in "Rhyme in Japanese Poetry" was that it was now necessary to develop this potential toward realization through rhyme and musicality and thereby elevate Japanese poetry to a global standard.[53]

3. Watsuji Tetsurō

(1) THE DEVELOPMENT OF WATSUJI'S THOUGHT

As noted in chapter 2, Raphael von Koeber played a major role in the history of Japanese philosophy, and the two Japanese philosophers most influenced by him (along with Kuki Shūzō, as discussed in the previous section) were Watsuji Tetsurō and Abe Jirō. Koeber believed strongly in the fertile potential of "*Philologie*," that is, the study of literature, and Watsuji continued this tradition with a paradigmatic approach. While on the one hand writing about the history of philological criticism of Homer's *Iliad* and *Odyssey*, on the other hand he also took a profound interest in Japan's ancient culture. In his *Ancient Temple Pilgrimage*,[54] published in 1919, Watsuji describes the Bodhisattva Ekadaśamukha statue in Nara's Shorinji Temple.

> Its entire body seems enveloped in the rich atmosphere of Tang China, the pinnacle of Far Eastern culture and the forge in which various cultures were melded that let all things flower fully in

> its voluptuousness. It . . . is an object that aims to crystallize
> the mystery of human existence all at once in a single form.[55]

It is clear from this passage that in ancient Japanese Buddhist art Watsuji found an acme of beauty created by the fusion of various Eastern and Western cultures.

He followed this text with one major work after another, including *Japan's Ancient Culture*[56] (1920) and *Studies in the Intellectual History of Japan*[57] (1926). Having displayed great talent in the domain of the history of Japanese culture, Watsuji was invited to teach a course on ethics by faculty members at Kyoto University, including Nishida Kitarō and Hatano Seiichi. At first Watsuji demurred, saying he was not suited to such a systematic discipline as ethics, but after repeated urging from Nishida and others he eventually took up a position at Kyoto University in 1925. In 1927 he went to Germany to study abroad until the following year, and in 1934 he moved to the University of Tokyo where he laid the foundations for its ethics course. In the year he moved to Tokyo he published *Ethics as the Study of Human Beings*,[58] and in 1937 he published the first volume of his *Ethics* (the second volume was published in 1942, and the third and final volume in 1949). These two books are Watsuji's most important works. He continued to write prolifically even after reaching the statutory retirement age and leaving the University of Tokyo in 1949, publishing works such as *National Isolation*[59] (1950), *The History of Japanese Ethical Thought*[60] (1952), *Kabuki and Jōruri*[61] (1955), and *Katsura Imperial Villa*[62] (1955). He passed away in 1960.

(2) Climate

One of the by-products of Watsuji's having gone to study in Germany was *Climate and Culture*[63] (1935). This work is thought to have been inspired by the various climates he encountered during his journey to Europe by ship, but it was also greatly influenced by Heidegger's *Being and Time*, a copy of which Watsuji acquired during his time studying abroad. In a sense it can be described as a work born out of his critique of Heidegger. Watsuji writes about this in its preface.

> I found [Heidegger's] attempt to grasp the structure of human
> existence as temporality extremely interesting. The problem for
> me, however, was why, when temporality is employed as the
> structure of subjective existence in this way, spatiality is not

also employed in the same way as the fundamental structure of existence. . . . . temporality that does not conform to spatiality is not yet true temporality.[64]

To begin with, it is important to clarify what Watsuji meant by the word "climate." At the beginning of the first chapter of *Climate and Culture*, he writes, "Here 'climate' is a general term for various aspects of a particular area, such as its weather and climate, the quality, nature, and form of its soil, and its scenery or landscape. . . . I have good reason, however, for trying to think about this as 'climate' rather than addressing it as 'nature.' "[65] "Climate" overlaps with what is generally called "nature," but it is not the same as "nature." It is distinguished by the fact that it has not been separated from humanity. What Watsuji sought to address through this theory of climate was not so-called nature, but on the contrary humanity, the "subjective existence of human beings."

The "subjective existence of human beings" is not human beings observed objectively from the outside but living human beings themselves as the subjects of their own lives. Watsuji aimed to address climate as one moment of this "subjective human existence." As a result, he did not address nature as simply an object of observation or the objective circumstances of human life; to put it another way, he did not consider nature as the environment that determines the lives of human beings. Nor was he trying to examine how nature as this kind of object regulates human ways of living in an objective manner. Watsuji's interest was always focused on "subjective human existence." To give a concrete example, when we feel cold in the winter, we figure out how to make warm clothes, how to build homes suited to cold weather, and how to grow crops in order to deal with this coldness. Only weather or landscapes imbued with this kind of "movement of self-understanding" of "subjective human existence" is "climate" in Watsuji's sense of the word.

At the root of this kind of understanding was a critique of the European view of nature and humanity that saw nature as an objective target of study and treated nature and human activity or nature and human culture as opposing concepts. By considering culture and nature not as opposing concepts but rather in the context of a necessary relationship, Watsuji attempted to examine culture—for example, religion and art—within a broad perspective that had never been employed before.

In *Climate and Culture*, Watsuji addresses various types of climate, and the relationship between climate and human beings, from this kind of perspective. He also attempts to describe what kind of human beings have been created within this context. Watsuji sets out three main types of climate: monsoon, desert, and pasture. Monsoon climates, characterized by a "combination of heat and humidity," produce rich blessings for humanity but also involve violent bouts of heavy rain, flooding, and drought. This kind of climate spawns "receptive, forbearing" people. In the desert, nature appears as a menace, threatening human beings with death. Humans must therefore do battle with nature. To this end they must also unite with other people. These strongly united groups must fight not only against nature but also against other groups seeking scarce natural resources. This creates people who are "submissive" within their own group and "belligerent" toward the outside world. In contrast, the climate in Europe is mild, easily acceding to human control once cultivated. Regular patterns will be found everywhere in this kind of mild climate. In such a climate, human beings necessarily become "rational." A stance of discovering the laws of nature and using them to even better control the natural environment emerges.

This theory of climate put forward by Watsuji received various critiques. One of them was Abe Yoshishige's claim[66] that "along with the materials of its argument being subjectively limited, in order to reach definite conclusions this view is unable to escape subjective limitations." In contrast, the French geographer Augustin Berque (b. 1942), author of texts such as *Vivre l'espace au Japon* (1982) and *Le Sauvage et l'artifice: Les Japonais devant la nature* (1986), enthusiastically praised Watsuji's theory of climate. In *Le Sauvage et l'artifice*, drawing on Watsuji's understanding of "climate," Berque employs the fascinating concepts "trajective" and "*trajet.*" He describes the particular dimension of Watsuji's "climate" that is subjective and at the same time objective, natural and at the same time artificial, as "trajective," and the state of this climate, whose essential nature is trajectivity and which is neither simply subject nor object, as *trajet.* Assigning this kind of meaning to the French word *trajet,* which normally means "journey," Berque argues that subject and object, nature and culture, and the individual and society, all of which are normally seen as fixed oppositional pairs in the modern way of looking at things, are by no means fixed dualities in climate, asserting that on the contrary they engage in "reciprocal genesis" and can travel a "reversible path."[67]

(3) The Ethics of "Relationships"

Watsuji's greatest contribution was laying the foundations of ethics in Japan through his *Ethics as the Study of Human Beings* and his three-volume *Eth-*

ics.[68] What sort of science did Watsuji understand ethics to be? In *Ethics as the Study of Human Beings* he defines it as follows. "Ethics is the science that tries to elucidate the order or reasoning that forms the roots of human relationships and therefore of human communities."[69] In other words, ethics is the science that clarifies the laws of human morality as the correct logic of human relationships. It was thus neither the study of subjective moral consciousness nor of its inculcation (moral training).

When he made this declaration that ethics is not the study of individual consciousness, Watsuji had in mind the traditional ethics of the West. In Kant, for example, there is the question of autonomy versus heteronomy; do we make the substantial content obtained as the result of an action, that is, "happiness," the grounds for decision-making, or, out of "respect" for the laws of morality that are the laws of reason, do we ground our decision-making in these laws themselves? In contrast, Watsuji thought ethics cannot be reduced to this kind of individual-level question of on what grounds a particular individual is to determine their own will.

This understanding of ethics was deeply tied to how Watsuji understood human beings. Criticizing the modern Western view of humanity that tried to see human beings primarily as individuals, he addressed the problem of the "dual structure of human existence." In other words, according to Watsuji, a human being is a human being when they relate to another human being, that is, in their relationships with other people, and a human being cannot be considered in isolation from human relationships or society. Based on this understanding, Watsuji defines the concept of "human being" as follows. "Human beings are both 'the world' itself [as relationships between human beings] and 'people' in the world. 'Human beings' are thus neither simply [individual] people nor society; both are dialectically unified in 'human beings.' . . . Thinking of 'Mensch [person]' and 'Gemeinschaft [community]' as distinct entities of some kind is not permitted in our conception of 'human beings.' "[70] Being at the same time both *Mensch* and *Gemeinschaft* is what Watsuji describes as the "dual structure of human existence."

The title *Ethics as the Study of Human Beings* refers to the study of human existence in this sense. Human beings are always relating to other human beings, forming the particular "relationships" within which they live. The study of the order or logic that governs these "relationships" is what Watsuji understood ethics to be.

Watsuji views these relationships not simply as static relationships, such as being parent and child from the moment of birth or being husband and wife under the law, but rather as "active relationships." "Relationships," in Watsuji's understanding, are, first and foremost, composed of "those who are relating acknowledging each other in practice as active subjects." He puts it this way because "recognizing [the other party] as an individual subject" is necessarily tied to action. In concrete terms, because I recognize the other party as a friend, I put my trust in them and conversely try to earn the trust they put in me. In other words, when I recognize the other party as an ethical subject, this understanding does not stop at understanding but at the same time is also connected to action. That is not to say, however, that "relationships" first arise through action. On the contrary, Watsuji believed that the "relationship" exists first, and actions are then carried out as its concretization or objectivization.

Watsuji asserts that "relationships" are "active relationships" in this sense. The idea that human beings cannot be considered without taking into account these "active" relationships that arise between the self and the other can be described as the starting point of Watsuji's ethics. From this perspective, in his *Ethics* Watsuji analyzes the structure of various human relationships, namely, the family, the ethnic group, and the nation, and the structure of solidarity among individuals, that is, how they are bound together in these groupings.[71]

(4) Criticism of Watsuji's Ethics

Various critiques of Watsuji's approach have since been made. Utsunomiya Yoshiaki (1931–2007), for example, raises the following point in his *Ethics and [Relationships] Between Human Beings* (1980).[72] Watsuji begins by focusing on the relationships between individuals and believes that this is the place where ethics emerge, but soon shifts from "relationships" that arise between individuals to relationships between the individual and society or the individual and the whole. When it comes to the individual and society or the individual and the whole, while Watsuji asserts that both sides form the dual structure of human existence, the emphasis is always placed on the whole rather than on the individual, and the shape of this dual structure thus becomes distorted.[73]

Another important critique of Watsuji's ethics has been made by Kaneko Takezō (1905–1987), his successor as teacher of the ethics course at the University of Tokyo. Watsuji begins with the idea that the order that governs human existence, the laws of morality, lies in the places where human beings are concretely situated and live their lives. He then focuses on "relationships" and tries to bring out the order that is found in them and governs them. The order thus discovered, however, is only ever a "fact."

And "values," "norms," and "what ought to be" cannot be derived from "facts." In other words, "existence" cannot lead to "ethics." This is Kaneko's critique.[74] Of course, as we have already seen, it can be said that Watsuji saw "relationships" as "active relationships" not relationships of static positions, and these included elements that were not limited to "facts" and involved values. Nevertheless, there are aspects of Kaneko's criticism that "facts" and "values" are not clearly distinguished in Watsuji that warrant consideration. How these weaknesses can be overcome while pursuing Watsuji's aim of transcending Western individualistic ethics is a question that remains to be addressed.

4. The Development of the Study of Aesthetics

(1) THE DEVELOPMENT OF THE STUDY OF AESTHETICS IN JAPAN

While aesthetics as a field of study had been known in Japan since the Meiji period through works such as Fenollosa's *True Theory of Art* (1881), Nakae Chōmin's translation of Eugène Véron's *L'esthetique* (*Aesthetics of Mr. Véron*, in two volumes, 1883–1884), and Mori Ōgai and Ōmura Seigai's 1899 translation[75] of Eduard von Hartmann's *Die Philosophie des Schönen* (1887), original scholarship in this field did not begin until around the end of the Meiji and start of the Taishō periods. Great contributions to the development of this field were then made by Ōtsuka Yasuji, who taught at the University of Tokyo, and Fukada Yasukazu (1878–1928), who was in charge of the history of art and aesthetics at Kyoto University. Examples of achievements in the study of aesthetics during this period include Abe Jirō's *Aesthetics* and Ōnishi Yoshinori (1888–1959)'s *Principles of Aesthetics* (both published in 1917). Abe's *Aesthetics* addresses the fundamental questions of aesthetics from the perspective of sympathy or emotional projection[76] developed in Theodor Lipps (1851–1914)'s *Ästhetik* (1903). Ōnishi's *Principles of Aesthetics* also took as its foundation the psychological aesthetics of philosophers such as Lipps, Johannes Volkelt (1848–1930), and Gustav Fechner (1801–1887) and discussed the elements and qualities of the "sense of beauty" as well as the principles that compose it. Their scholarship can be said to have laid the foundations for the study of aesthetics in Japan.

Fukada Yasukazu, like Kuki and Watsuji, studied under Koeber. Koeber's influence can be seen in Fukada's most prominent works, such as "The Beautiful Soul."[77] He published no books during his lifetime, but after his death *The Complete Works of Fukada Yasukazu*[78] was published in four volumes (1930–1931). His scholarship was multifaceted, spanning ancient and modern periods and incorporating the history of art, the philosophy of art, and art criticism. The lecture entitled "Art in General"[79] that he delivered to the Kyoto Education Association in 1924 can also be cited as a representative work in which he clearly lays out his understanding of art (it was published as *A Theory of Beauty and Art*[80] in 1971). In this text, Fukada discusses what art is while comparing it to science and morality, and asserts there is something completely different in art from the "effort" to seek something or realize something. Drawing on *Die Spiele der Tiere* (1896) and *Die Spiele der Menschen* (1899) by the German philosopher of aesthetics Karl Groos (1861–1946), he argues that the play instinct is the wellspring of art, and that by its nature this instinct opens up a "special, free, and completely different world"[81] that is distinct from the worlds of science and morality.

(2) Ōnishi Yoshinori

Ōnishi Yoshinori replaced Ōtsuka and took charge of the course on aesthetics and art history at the University of Tokyo in 1930. After taking up this post he published *A Study of Kant's* Critique of Judgment[82] (1931) and *The Aesthetics of the Phenomenology School*[83] (1937). The latter was the first proper introduction in Japan of the new phenomenological school of aesthetics that had arisen after Lipps and Volkelt. In particular, it introduced Rudolf Odebrecht (1888–1945)'s "theory of aesthetic value," which played a particularly important role in this school of aesthetics and added a critical examination of this approach.

Later Ōnishi turned his attention to senses of beauty unique to Japan, publishing works such as *Yūgen and Aware* (1939),[84] *On Refined Taste: A Study of "Sabi"*[85] (1940), and *The Feeling of Nature in the* Man'yōshū[86] (1943). Ōnishi's systematic theory of aesthetics was presented in detail in the posthumously published *Aesthetics* (in two volumes, 1959–1960). In the second volume of this work, *A Theory of Aesthetic Categories*,[87] Japanese aesthetic concepts such as *yūgen* and *aware*[88] are considered from a systematic perspective. According to Ōnishi, "aesthetic categories" are types of "beautiful things" and their forms of value, but this topic had not necessarily been given sufficient attention in recent approaches such as that of phenomenological aesthetics. If aesthetics was to be a systematic discipline, however, Ōnishi believed it was obvious that consideration of aspects and categories of beauty must be one of the central tasks undertaken. Another assertion Ōnishi makes in *On Categories of Beauty* is that to further develop aesthetics, which had originally been built on Western art and Western conceptions of beauty, it was necessary to take into consideration the art and understanding of beauty found in the East.

In addressing these topics, while drawing on the aesthetics of German Idealism and Hermann Cohen (1842–1918)'s *Ästhetik des reinen Gefühls*, Ōnishi begins by proposing "beauty," "sublimity," and "humor" as aesthetic categories. As derivative forms he then adds "elegant beauty," "tragic beauty" and "comical beauty" from a Western perspective and *aware, yūgen,* and *sabi* from an Eastern perspective.

Regarding *aware,* Ōnishi describes it as an aesthetic feeling or intuition that has permeated the foundations of metaphysics and expanded into a kind of worldview. *Yūgen* is a concept that was given particular emphasis in the discussion of poetry, and in cases in which an indescribable "mood" floats behind the words of a poem it was used to refer to this "aesthetic feeling." The term *sabi* comes from the verb *sabu* meaning "fall into disorder or ruin," and originally it referred to a state of desolation or having been worn by the passage of time. The category of beauty called *sabi,* however, emerges when this negative quality is turned into something positive through the refined mental state attained by the long practice of tea ceremony and *haikai* poetry. Ōnishi points out that this includes moments of "humor," as seen in the *shōfū* style of *haikai* poetry developed by Matsuo Bashō and his disciples.[89]

Ōnishi thus developed a theory of aesthetic categories based on Japanese conceptions of beauty, but his intention in doing so was not simply to emphasize or enhance the distinctiveness of the Japanese sense of beauty. He distinguished fundamental and derivative aesthetic categories and placed categories of beauty specific to Japan among the latter. As can be seen from this approach, the defining characteristics of his theory are to be found in his intension to reexamine Japanese conceptions of beauty from a universal perspective. This is where the great significance of the thought of Ōnishi's later period lies. As Tanaka Kyūbun puts it, Ōnishi "aimed to liberate Japanese traditional aesthetics from its closed perspective and elucidate its significance in the context of its relationship to universal aesthetics."[90]

(3) The Reception of Konrad Fiedler's Aesthetics

The aesthetic thought of Konrad Fiedler (1841–1895) left a large imprint on the history of the development of aesthetics and the study of art in Japan. Fiedler was an independent researcher operating outside of the academy, but as the author of works such as *Ursprung der künstlerischen Tätigkeit* (1887) he became an influential figure in the formation of modern art theory in Germany.

In *Ursprung der künstlerischen Tätigkeit*, Fiedler begins by viewing our reality as something that is unclear, constantly changing, and without fixed form. He then states that there are two ways to grasp this reality as "incessant play." One is to apprehend it through language, the other is to take hold of it as something visible through visual perception. Language is characterized by giving clear form to that which is constantly changing and unclear. At the same time, however, it adds a definitive transformation of our experience or constantly changing reality. In contrast, by taking the second path, that is, the method of grasping our target as that which is visible through our visual perception, we can avoid introducing this kind of veil that covers reality. But we are always in the midst of change with this approach, too, because what we see with our eyes quickly disappears. Nevertheless, if we fully concentrate on our organs of visual perception (Fiedler calls this *reines Sehen* [pure seeing]), the possibility arises of developing to a higher level what the eyes give the consciousness. In other words, visual perception can activate a physical mechanism of the human body and facilitate the expression of what this perception gives us. Fiedler saw the artist's act of drawing or molding something as the development of the process of visual perception in this sense. Fiedler indeed finds the essential characteristic of the artist in "the ability to independently develop the process of perception through the eyes toward visible expression."

The first to focus on Fiedler's understanding of art in Japan was Nishida Kitarō. In section 19 (published in 1915) of his *Intuition and Reflection in Self-Awareness* he touches on Fiedler's concept of "pure seeing," writing, "Konrad Fiedler says that when we focus purely on our visual perception, we immediately sense the developmental potential of visual representation and naturally move on to the act of expression."[91] Nishida endorses this understanding of art, that is, Fiedler's understanding that the act of artistic creation becomes possible through visual representation "moving on to the act of expression." Moreover, he then suggests that all experience—not only the act of artistic creation, but every kind of experience—can be seen as this kind of development.

> I suspect what these people [Fiedler and the Fauvist painter Henri Matisse] say about artistic intuition can also be said about the

> true nature of all experience. . . . I think all experience arises
> according to the process laid out above, and reality is this kind
> of creative system.[92]

This text shows that while Nishida held Fiedler's understanding of art in high regard, at the same time there was a major difference between their views. While Fiedler thought of the development from the act of seeing to expression as unique or particular to artistic activity, Nishida tried to view all forms of experience as this kind of development (in his words, as a "creative system"). To Nishida, the act of artistic creation was merely one example of experience with this kind of structure. To put it another way, this meant that in Nishida's case the question of art was considered within the broader question "what is reality?"

(4) Ueda Jyuzō's Studies in Aesthetics and Art History

Ueda Jyuzō (1886–1973) studied under Fukada Yasukazu, and after Fukada passed away took over as teacher of the aesthetics and art history course in 1930. During his time as an assistant, he participated in the editing of the *Journal of Philosophical Studies*, the journal of the Kyoto University Philosophy Society, and he was strongly influenced not only by Fukada but also by Nishida. His intense interest in Fiedler was presumably sparked by the latter. Ueda developed his own theory of art while being strongly influenced by both of these philosophers. One of the results of his efforts was *The Structure of Visual Perception* (1941).[93] In this text he does not touch on Fiedler's thought directly, but topics inspired by it become the focus of his own theory of art. Ueda placed the problem of "visual perception" at the core of his own theory. When we look at the outside world, we distinguish various colors and shapes. For us to be able to do this, there must already be something that enables this distinguishing. He calls this "visual perception" or "visuality." Our seeing various colors and shapes in nature is "visuality seeing its own shadow in nature."[94] Ueda made "the pursuit of the meaning of this 'visual perception'" his life's work. Specifically, he addressed the questions of what kind of transcendental structure our visual perception has,[95] how this structure operates in the creation and appreciation of classical Japanese artwork, and what sort of universal structures exist there.

"What makes art art?" This was also an important question to Ueda. He persistently viewed art as "an aesthetic fact." In other words, we acknowledge a work as a work of art when we see "that which is beautiful" being given form through it. Of course, it is possible for this to include various intentions, for example religious or moral aims. Ueda rejected the understanding that we only grasp a work as a work of art when we understand the various intentions surrounding "that which is beautiful" as a fatal error. His view was that what makes something a work of art is nothing apart from its "nature as art."

In saying this, Ueda adopted a stance that clearly differed from that of Nishida. In *Art and Morality*[96] (1923), Nishida writes, "I think art arises anticipating morality, and artistic creation anticipates moral development."[97] Nishida believed art that is not involved in the realization of moral ideals is nothing more than play. In contrast, Ueda believed that art arises as art and has value as art because it has "that which is beautiful." This can also be seen as the assertion that art possesses its own unique meaning and value that cannot be replaced by other cultural undertakings.

(5) The Beauty of Handicrafts

In the first section of this chapter I noted that the year after the publication of *An Inquiry into the Good* Takahashi Satomi released the first academic critique of this work, "The Fact of Phenomena of Consciousness and Their Significance: Reading Nishida's *An Inquiry into the Good*." In that same year Yanagi Muneyoshi (1889–1961), who would later promote the folk art movement, published an essay entitled "Revolutionary Painters"[98] (1912) in which he discussed Nishida's theory of "pure experience." Yanagi's focus on Nishida from such an early period was a result of his having had the opportunity to interact with him in person during his third year at Gakushūin High School (Nishida had transferred there from the Number Four High School to teach German for a year). After this encounter they continued to exchange ideas. From the "Interview with Yanagi's Wife Kaneko" appendix to Mizuo Hiroshi's *Critical Biography of Yanagi Muneyoshi*, we can also see that Yanagi had a deep reverence for both Nishida and Suzuki Daisetsu.

Yanagi's understanding of beauty and art forms a sharp contrast to that of Okakura Tenshin discussed in chapter 2. Okakura's view was that the role of artists lay in leading people to refinement as "the world's luminaries," and in this regard they were clearly distinguishable from artisans and craftspeople. Yanagi, on the other hand, asked whether "beauty" was not indeed present in the works produced by artisans and craftspeople, and whether "handicrafts" were truly of little value in comparison to pure art.

Ever since art and handicrafts had been distinguished from each other in the early modern period, art had been placed in a higher position thanks to the "purity" of being for the sake of beauty, and handicrafts had been placed in a lower position because of the "impurity" of being for the sake of daily life. In his *Handicraft Culture* (1942),[99] however, Yanagi rejected this view as one-sided. The handicrafts produced by unsung artisans did not possess intense beauty and did not include the kinds of distinctive, extraordinary works produced by artistic geniuses, but they did have what he called "uneventful beauty"[100] or "ordinary beauty."[101] While unremarkable, have handicrafts not enriched people's daily lives? Is it not this "ordinary beauty" that in a true sense makes people happy? Yanagi's arguments can be said to have posed these sorts of questions.

If the beauty produced by great artistic geniuses were a road, it would be a steep path ordinary people could never tread. The beauty possessed by handicrafts, in contrast, would be a level road accessible to all. In this sense, Yanagi argues that the beauty produced by a genius is a "side street," while the beauty of handicrafts is a "main thoroughfare."[102]

5. The Philosophy of Religion

The first solid foundations for the study of religion as an academic discipline in Japan were laid by the introduction of university courses on this topic, first at the University of Tokyo in 1905 (thirty-eighth year of the Meiji period) and then at Kyoto University in 1907. Anesaki Masaharu (1873–1949) taught the first religious studies course at the University of Tokyo. Anesaki left a legacy of many writings on the history of religion, including *The History of Religion in India*[103] (1897) and *On the History of Buddhist Sacred Texts*[104] (1899). The course at Kyoto University was taught by Matsumoto Bunzaburō (1869–1944) in the form of a supplement to his course on the history of Indian philosophy. Nishida Kitarō taught this course for a year in 1913, but it wasn't until Hatano Seiichi (1877–1950) took over in 1917 that the position of religious studies was finally solidified. Hatano continued in this role for twenty years, during which time he published *The Essence of the Philosophy of Religion and Its Fundamental Questions*[105] (1920) and *The Philosophy of Religion*[106] (1935). Along with others written after his retirement such as *Introduction to the Philosophy of Religion*[107] (1940) and *Time and Eternity*[108] (1943), these writings made a major contribution to the philosophy of religion as an academic discipline.

(1) Hatano Seiichi's Philosophy of Religion

Hatano Seiichi was another philosopher who studied under Raphael Koeber and was greatly influenced by both his scholarship and his personality. When Koeber died, Hatano published an essay entitled "Reminiscences," in which he writes, "I felt that Sensei [Koeber] both summoned and satisfied a thirst for things elevated and pure."[109] Hatano directly inherited this idealism and the Greek freedom and Christian piety that were deeply rooted in Koeber.

Not long after graduating from university, Hatano was baptized by Uemura Masahisa and became a Christian, and the Christian faith he received from Uemura was always at the root of his scholarship as it developed from that point on. His thought, however, was not confined to the framework of Christianity. His aim can be said to have been the philosophy of religion as a field of study with broad universality.

On the other hand, as can be seen by looking at the "Hatano trilogy" beginning with *The Philosophy of Religion*, he consistently emphasized the importance of religious experience. According to *The Philosophy of Religion*, the philosophy of religion includes the study of religion's essence, typology, and philosophical anthropology. Hatano believed that these three areas of inquiry interact, and it is only through this complementary interaction that a philosophical understanding of religion is possible. Regarding this kind of anthropology, he writes, "While always taking religious experience as a premise, it must earnestly listen to what this experience is trying to say."[110]

From this perspective, Hatano criticized the rationalist understanding of religion for taking as its starting point ideas or concepts rather than experience. In *Introduction to the Philosophy of Religion*, along with this rationalist perspective Hatano also cites supernaturalism that emphasizes the transcendency of the divine and the dialectic theology that was popular at the time as "mistaken philosophies of religion." He contrasts these "mistaken philosophies of religion" with the "correct philosophy of religion," which, as he puts in it *Time and Eternity*, is "philosophy that takes as its object *religion itself*, not the *objects of religion*."[111] In other words, a philosophy that takes as its starting point not a transcendent being as an object of faith but rather religious experience, that is, a philosophy "that takes as its object religion as a human undertaking."[112] "Correct philosophy of religion . . . emerges as reflective self-understanding of religious experience and theoretical retrospection on it."[113] This, of course, does not mean adopting the stance of positivism. Positivism inevitably descends into relativism, and as a result can never become a correct philosophy of religion.

In *The Philosophy of Religion*, Hatano sees the essential characteristic of religion as not being limited to existing facts, but "negating, symbolizing, and therefore giving meaning to natural reality."[114] The world of religion arises through ideality and conceptuality. In order to accurately grasp religion, we must first adopt the stance of idealism. Idealism, however, cannot approach the reality of the object of faith itself, which forms the central characteristic of religion. Idealism must therefore transition to mysticism. Mysticism often employs the word "nothingness" in referring to the higher-level reality that is this object of faith as "that with neither name nor form." This is not "nothingness" as a concept or an object of consciousness, but rather as something "to whose power we must surrender, and into whose depths we must cast ourselves."[115] But "the content of these depths, the deep reality that symbolizes nothingness" itself is never revealed. Hatano says that as a result mysticism must thoroughly transform itself into personalism.

"Personalism" means "a commitment to unreservedly accepting the reality of 'the other' (other selves)." According to Hatano, this means adopting the "standpoint of 'love.'" In other words, it meant entering a "community of life with the other."[116] What Hatano tries to show in *Time and Eternity* is that we can only obtain eternality when we bind ourselves to a "new communion" in this community of life. Interestingly, Hatano says that it is through the lens of temporality that this light of eternality refracts and manifests itself in the world. He writes that "the communion of holy love is only realized as human community."[117] In other words, "love" is perfected and realized by being made concrete through holy person-to-person communion—"holy communion (communio sanctorum)" in the language of Christianity. It is notable, however, that this "love" is by no means pure community. "First and foremost, it is the struggle for community and yearning for the other. Its starting point is a lack of community."[118] Here the effort to begin from human experience characteristic of Hatano's philosophy of religion is plainly evident.

(2) Suzuki Daisetsu's "Logic of Is/Not"

Suzuki Daisetsu (1870–1966)[119] did not concern himself with philosophy or the philosophy of religion as an academic pursuit. He was a practitioner of Zen Buddhism and a scholar of Buddhism and Zen thought. The "logic of is/not"[120] that he would eventually advocate, however, was deeply connected to and interwoven with Nishida Kitarō's "logic of contradictory self-identity." Suzuki met Nishida after entering the Ishikawa Prefecture Specialty School,[121] which later became the Number Four Middle and High School.

Suzuki himself used the expression "childhood friends," but the two maintained a close relationship throughout their lives. Suzuki practiced Zen Buddhism under Kamakura Engakuji Temple's Shaku Sōen (1890–1919), and at Shaku's recommendation went to America in 1897 and took a position at the Open Court Publishing Company. While working for this company he continued to pursue the study of Buddhism on the side and published works such as an English translation of *Awakening of Faith in the Mahāyāna*. After twelve years in America, he returned to Japan in 1909 and later taught at Gakushūin University and Shinshū Ōtani University (now Ōtani University). During his time in America, Suzuki sent Nishida information about the publication of William James's *The Varieties of Religious Experience* and a copy of James's essay "A World of Pure Experience." From letters addressed to Suzuki it is clear that Nishida was greatly impressed by these texts.

In his early writings, when discussing the nature of Buddhism, Suzuki emphasized above all else that it is fundamentally different from philosophy and logic. To give one example, in *The First Principle of Zen* Suzuki asserts that while philosophy is formed on the basis of analyzing or breaking down living things, Zen is characterized by trying to become things themselves and understand them from the inside, a process that does not involve "the slightest bit of discriminating reason." Eventually, however, his attention turned to the question of the logic at the root of Zen. This may well have been because of the influence of Nishida Kitarō.

This change was also manifested in Suzuki's later years when he repeatedly spoke of the "Eastern perspective," and in relation to it emphasized that even Zen requires philosophy. In an essay entitled "The Mission of Eastern Scholars,"[122] Suzuki stresses that in the East there is a particularly Eastern way of thinking with its own distinctive characteristics, and writes, "I cannot help wanting to emphasize the 'Eastern perspective.' "[123] These words, however, were not intended to one-sidedly assert the superiority of the Eastern way of looking at things. In the essays "The Eastern Perspective," "That Which Lies at the Root of Eastern Culture,"[124] and "The Japanese Mind,"[125] Suzuki acknowledges that Western thought based on a dualistic way of thinking is superior when it comes to "generalizing, logicizing, and deriving principles," and that this has formed the foundations of Western culture and its great achievements. At the same time, he also repeatedly states that this element is lacking in Eastern thought and that "thoroughgoing duality" is needed in the East. He also repeatedly criticizes the irrationality or sentimentality found in Eastern thought. He writes, for example, "What stands out as something that can be seen as a weakness in the Japanese mind is a lack of emphasis on rationality. . . . This shortcoming emerges clearly in sentimental irrationality."[126]

Having thus acknowledged the importance of logical thinking (rationality), Suzuki then states that if we remain mired in dualistic thinking, that is, the standpoint of rationality, we can never grasp things as they are. Contrasting both approaches, Suzuki expresses the difference between them. "In the West, thinking proceeds with things being divided in two as its foundation. The East, on the contrary, starts from an earlier point where they are indivisible."[127] Eastern thinking begins before things have been broken down by dualistic thought, or, in Suzuki's words, from "an earlier point where they are indivisible."

When an English translation of Nishida's *An Inquiry into the Good* was published, Suzuki contributed a foreword for it entitled "How to Read Nishida" in which he writes as follows.

> In the East, nothingness or emptiness or the self-identity of contradictions has nothing to do with analysis or abstraction, it is purely an experience personally gone through. In other words, the West starts intellectually with a dualistic world, whereas the East keeps the feet firmly on the ground of emptiness, which is a world of concrete existentialism and not a logical framework of abstraction.[128]

Along with such assertions, Suzuki also acknowledges that Eastern thinking and Zen also have major weaknesses. He criticizes these approaches for stopping at experience and not developing thought. For example, in the essay "The Philosophy of Zen," published after the Second World War in the journal *Philosophy East and West*, he asserts that experience can only become experience when we give it logical expression, bluntly stating that "Zen too must have its philosophy."

From this perspective, Suzuki focused on the "logic of is/not" found in the *Diamond Sutra* (*Vajracchedikā Prajñāpāramitā Sūtra*).[129] The *Diamond Sutra* is one of the prajñāpāramitā sutras thought to have been put together in its original form around year zero of the Common Era, and it includes the following passage. "Buddha taught perfect wisdom; this is not directly perfect wisdom; it is named perfect wisdom." Suzuki takes this to mean "the perfect wisdom taught by the Buddha is not directly perfect wisdom, therefore it is named perfect wisdom." Suzuki expresses this in English as "Being is Being because Being is not Being" or as "A is not-A and therefore A is A." This is the "logic of is/not."

The "logic of is/not" is of course not simply a form of logic, such as, for example, rules for thinking without falling into contradiction. It is instead something connected to how we are to understand the true nature of things. In other words, it is something spoken of in relation to the fundamental thought of Buddhism that views the truth of things as "emptiness" or "true emptiness with no being."[130] Nishida was keenly aware that the "logic of absolute contradictory self-identity" he contemplated in his later years and Suzuki's "logic of is/not" shared a common foundation. For example, in "Logic and Mathematics"[131] (1944), one of his last essays, he writes as follows.

> I believe on the contrary we can discover the logic of nothing-ness in philosophy of the mind or Buddhist philosophy that takes as its object the self itself. . . . my logic of contradictory self-identity is a formalization of this logic. . . . There must be similarities to Suzuki Daisetsu's "logic of is/not."[132]

Chapter 7

The Disciples of Nishida and Tanabe

1. The Zen Tradition—Hisamatsu Shin'ichi and Nishitani Keiji

In this chapter I discuss the thought of disciples of Nishida Kitarō and Tanabe Hajime. Disciples of Nishida in his early period include Amano Teiyū, Hisamatsu Shin'ichi, Yamauchi Tokuryū, Mutai Risaku, Tsuchida Kyōson, Miyake Gōichi, and Miki Kiyoshi. Tanabe Hajime left Tohoku University and came to Kyoto University as an assistant professor in 1919, and those who then studied under both Nishida and Tanabe include Kōsaka Masaaki, Kimura Motomori, Nishitani Keiji, Tosaka Jun, Yanagida Kenjūrō, and Shimomura Toratarō. Notable students enrolled during Nishida's final years at Kyoto University include Karaki Junzō, Kōyama Iwao, and Shin'ichi Funayama. Disciples from the period after Nishida retired and Tanabe became a full professor include Noda Matao, Kuno Osamu, Takeuchi Yoshinori, Mutō Kazuo, Ōshima Yasumasa, and Tsujimura Kōichi.

(1) Hisamatsu Shin'ichi

As has often been pointed out, at the root of Nishida Kitarō's thought was his long-standing practice of Zen Buddhism. Nishida did not make Zen itself the subject of his inquiry, but evidence of its powerful influence on him is found throughout his writings. Hisamatsu Shin'ichi (1889–1980) and Nishitani Keiji (1900–1990) were two disciples who inherited this aspect of Nishida's approach and delved deeply into the world of Zen in their philosophy. In this section I focus on their thought.

At heart, Hisamatsu was a devotee of Zen, but at the same time he was also a scholar of Buddhism and a philosopher of religion. Even as a philosopher of religion, however, his thought was always grounded in his experience of Zen. Takeuchi Yoshinori, who knew him at Kyoto University, writes, "Hisamatsu's philosophy of religion, from start to finish, was unwaveringly rooted in his experience of Rinzai Zen."[1] Here I will examine Hisamatsu's thought based on his experience of Zen by focusing on his first book, *Eastern Nothingness*[2] (1939), and in particular its first essay, "The Metaphysical Element of the East."[3]

Things that exist concretely in reality, while of course having the characteristic of "being," at the same time confront "nothingness"; they are simultaneously "being" and "nothingness." "Being" and "nothingness" compose the positive and negative aspects of things that exist in reality. From ancient times, people have thought of something "metaphysical" as the foundation, or as the cause or idea, of things that exist in reality. This has occurred in both the West and the East. But these "metaphysical elements" are always in contrast to us, that is, they are always "objective elements." Various approaches to the contemplation of such "objective elements" have been undertaken in Western metaphysics. Those engaging in contemplation have done so from the perspective of "being" as something that exists in reality. Hisamatsu says, "In the West it is not known that there is such a thing as escaping the standpoint of that which exists in reality and ceasing to be a being."[4] In contrast to this view, he then asserts the possibility of a standpoint that transcends the standpoint of something that exists in reality. We can dismantle the self as something that exists, and when we do so all determinations and contradictions disappear and we become "nothing." But this of course does not mean a state in which there is nothing whatsoever; according to Hisamatsu, "a free body that has escaped from all determination and contradiction"[5] will be present there. Takeuchi's claim that Hisamatsu's "experience of Zen" lies at the root of his philosophy of religion can be thought of as referring to this kind of understanding. Hisamatsu also expresses this as the "presencing of free flowing and unhindered great action"—a great working that operates with nothing to impede it. Here Hisamatsu emphasizes that "nothingness" is "subjective and existential."

This is what he calls the "metaphysical element of the East." It is characterized as "Eastern," but Hisamatsu claims it is not limited to the East. It is described this way because it happens to have been discovered in the East, but in fact it possesses a universal character; he argues that it "has the right to demand recognition as something genuinely metaphysical in the West as well."[6]

(2) Nishitani Keiji

As we have just seen, Hisamatsu emphasized that "nothingness" is "subjective and existential," and this focus on the "subject" was shared by Nishitani Keiji. This is evident in his most important prewar text, *The Philosophy of Originary Subjectivity* (1940). As the title of this work suggests, the core of Nishitani's thought can be expressed in the phrase "originary subjectivity."

In the preface to this book, Nishitani presents its key assertion as follows.

> The ultimate root of our "I am" is bottomless. At the origin of our being alive there is a place with nothing for us to stand on; it is indeed because we stand in a place where there is no foothold that life is life. And it is from the self-awareness of this kind of baselessness that a new subjectivity emerges as something that runs consistently through religious wisdom, reason, and natural life.[7]

This way of being of the self that holds in its view the fact that there is nothing to serve as a foothold for its own existence, and the new subjectivity that emerges from this self-awareness—this is "originary subjectivity."

Nishitani believed this "originary subjectivity" takes two forms. One is European medieval mysticism. Through the "absolute negation of self-will (the old essence of the self) by God . . . the originary subjectivity of the self can emerge as one with the subjectivity of God."[8] A new will is born, and a new self "sheds the old self." Here we see one form of "originary subjectivity." The other form is seen in modern people. This is "originary subjectivity" as the "human subjectivity" found in Fichte, in which the classical idea of God as "substance" is rejected in favor of a moral "world order" in the debate over atheism. Nishitani also expresses this as "originary subjectivity manifested in the ego." Here self-will is negated by adopting the standpoint of universality. In this regard Nishitani believed there was something in this standpoint of natural reason that transcended medieval mysticism. But here people inevitably get stuck within their own egos and cannot truly reject their "I." They are unable to reach the "bottomless self-awareness" of there being "nothing to stand on."

Nishitani says that an "absolute change" is needed to transcend the limits of the ego and allow a new subjectivity to emerge. Only by absolutely negating the ego is "originary subjectivity as egoless subjectivity able to emerge."[9] According to Nishitani, this is nothing other than adopting the "standpoint of absolute nothingness."[10] The phrase "absolute nothingness" of course suggests the influence of Nishida Kitarō, but here Nishitani was also strongly influenced by the standpoint of mysticism. To reach "bottomless subjectivity," "subjectivity of the ego must completely and subjectively combine with the subjectivity of the absolute other that is its absolute negation."[11] The "standpoint of absolute nothingness" is said to have mysticism "as its forerunner." Here a characteristic of Nishitani's thought not found in Nishida can be clearly discerned.

However, this "standpoint of absolute nothingness" does not stop at the standpoint of medieval mysticism. This can be seen in Nishitani's assertion that the "standpoint of absolute nothingness" does not reject the standpoint of reason. On the contrary, it includes within itself a return toward this standpoint. It incorporates reason within itself and operates as one with it. Nishitani says that this allows us to once again make good use of the "improving/progressive nature" of reason. Not only that, but this egoless originary subjectivity is also present inside the "naturalness that lies at the end of reason."[12] The natural life that had been tied to the ego and given rise to drives and desires is liberated and incorporated into an egoless subjectivity as neutral naturalness. This is what is being referred to in the preface when originary subjectivity is described as "something that runs consistently through religious wisdom, reason, and natural life."

2. Phenomenology, the Philosophy of History, and the Theory of Social Existence—Yamauchi Tokuryū, Kōsaka Masaaki, and Mutai Risaku

(1) Yamauchi Tokuryū's "Logic of Analogia"

As noted in chapter 4, the foundation of the study of phenomenology in Japan was laid by Yamauchi Tokuryū (1890–1982) in works such as *A Discourse on Phenomenology*[13] (1929). Yamauchi's having begun by studying phenomenology had a significant influence on his understanding of philosophy. Both Nishida Kitarō and Tanabe Hajime had placed the dialectic at the foundation of their thought, but Yamauchi was always skeptical and critical of this stance of his mentors.

As is evident in texts such as "Dialectic and Phenomenology,"[14] included in *System and Evolution*[15] (1937), Yamauchi was strongly sympathetic to phenomenology and its emphasis on the differences possessed by things that exist in reality. In classical logic, based on the law of the excluded middle it was assumed there could be nothing between p and not-p. The dialectic, too, viewed the opposition of p and not-p as a paradox, or relationship of mutual exclusion, and sought to address its sublation. In concrete reality, however, things with various differences coexist rather than mutually exclude each other; countless middle terms can be conceived between two opposing poles. It was Yamauchi's understanding that viewing these differences as differences was phenomenology. In "The Departure of Philosophy,"[16] another essay included in *System and Evolution*, he addresses the criticism that phenomenology, which does nothing but describe facets of things as they appear to us in particular instances, always maintains a partial perspective, can never grasp the whole, and can never be systematic. In response to this criticism, Yamauchi asserts that phenomenology is by no means fixated on a partial perspective, but rather by looking at parts attempts to glimpse the whole. Conversely, he argues, an approach that tries to address the whole from a point of view that is always comprehensive lacks concreteness and falls into an abstract perspective.

In relation to this understanding, in *System and Evolution* Yamauchi also discusses the "logic of mixture" and "analogic thought." Mixture is generally rejected as something nonscientific that indicates the immaturity of logic, but Yamauchi argues that even within mixture there is a kind of order and set of relationships. Mixture is positioned in contrast to synthesis; while in the latter elements fuse to become one, in the former elements maintain their independence and form relationships while being bound to each other. This manner of relating Yamauchi calls the "logic of mixture," and he finds that which makes this possible in the "idea of analogia." According to Yamauchi, logical logos that aims at synthesis is not the only way of combining things; we can also conceive of a logos (analogos) that binds elements together in a state of mixture. In other words, we can conceive of a "logic of analogos" that does not look outside of a plurality of things to find a single thing to oppose them, but rather seeks this unity within the plurality. The contemplation of this kind of union of things is "analogic thought." Interestingly, this "analogic thought" is connected to the "logic of lemma" Yamauchi formulated in his later years (see chapter 10, section 3).

(2) Kōsaka Masaaki's Philosophy of History

Kōsaka Masaaki (1900–1969) was the disciple who best took up and developed Nishida's and Tanabe's understanding of history. He published his first work, *The Historical World: A Phenomenological Essay*,[17] in 1937, and this was followed by *Historical Philosophy and Political Philosophy* (1939)[18] and *Introduction to Historical Philosophy*[19] (1943). In a letter to his disciple Mutai Risaku, Nishida Kitarō later wrote, "I have someone for the philosophy of history. For the logic of place, I rely on your efforts,"[20] and here "I have someone for the philosophy of history" is undoubtedly referring to Kōsaka.

Of course, in *A Self-Aware System of the Universal* (1930), Nishida had already discussed "the historical world" and the "irrationality" at its roots. In *The Self-Aware Determination of Nothingness* (1932), he states that "the historical world" is "the world in which we are placed as an active self"[21] and that this is the concrete world of actual existence. Miki Kiyoshi had also published a text entitled *The Philosophy of History*[22] in 1932. In this text he addresses historical questions by introducing interesting concepts such as the "social body" and "historical anthropology."

Kōsaka's *The Historical World* drew on the understanding of history found in Nishida and Miki. The concept of "the historical world" itself had been inherited from Nishida, but Kōsaka of course developed his own thought on this subject. He called that which supports history and forms its foundation "historical substance." Initially this refers to nature as the womb from which history is born, but nature is not only history's substance; at the same time, it is also an object on which history operates. Kōsaka describes this nature as an object by dividing it into "environmental nature" and "historical nature."

Here the question of how "the historical world" is born out of "historical substance" arises as a major problem, and Kōsaka begins by focusing on the "nation" as the center of "the historical world." The "nation," however, is the foundational part of history most closely connected to nature and involves irrational elements. For "the historical world" to be formed out of it, there must therefore be another center. Kōsaka says this is "culture." Culture is not bound by blood and soil, or, in other words, by a particular territory or people, and seeks to add universality to the nation. "The historical world" is formed when the "dark nature" (based on Schelling's "nature in God") of the nation is penetrated by the "freedom" found in "culture." Kōsaka thus understood "the historical world" in terms of the two "historical centers" of the nation and culture as places mediated by the practice of subjects.

In a reciprocal turn, Kōsaka's philosophy of history then influenced Nishida's historical understanding. In "Historical Understanding," the second chapter of *The Historical World*, Kōsaka writes, "In the historical world, the people who make history are themselves created by history. Moreover, they themselves are created in their individual uniqueness in the historical world they create. A cycle is thus formed in which, while it is human beings that create the historical world, these human beings are once again created by this world,"[23] and Nishida in his correspondence talks about having been strongly influenced by this understanding of "history." From *Philosophical Essays Volume 2* (1937) onward, Nishida often used the phrase "from that which is made to that which makes," and this was based on Kōsaka's understanding. Its members' thought having been formed in extremely close relationship to each other is one of the major characteristics of the Kyoto School, and Kōsaka and Nishida's understanding of history is a prime example of this.

(3) Mutai Risaku's "On Social Existence"

In examining Mutai's scholarship, I will begin by focusing on his *On Social Existence* (1939). As is evident from the titles of its fourth and fifth parts, "Species-Type Society" and "The Structure of Species-Type Society," it is a work highly conscious of Tanabe Hajime's "logic of species." The year it was published, Maruyama Masao's review of this book appeared in the *Journal of the Association of Political and Social Sciences*,[24] in which he writes, "With Professor Tanabe's theory of social existence yet to be presented in a single volume, this book has great significance as the first complete account of 'the logic of species.' "[25]

However, Mutai also draws on Nishida's concept of "action-intuition" and takes the "active subject" as his starting point. *On Social Existence* was thus a book heavily influenced not only by Tanabe but also by Nishida. This kind of "action" is only possible in the "real world," and Mutai thinks of "species-like substance" as the "substance" that allows for the mutual determination of the individual and the world. Mutai addresses the relationship between these three elements, the individual, species-type society, and the world, in part 5. Unlike Tanabe, however, to avoid getting involved in the question of the nation, Mutai keeps his explanation speculative. Maruyama hits on this point in the review cited above, adding the criticism that "when philosophical contemplation skips over the results obtained from the perspective of social *science* and ties itself directly to the *object* of social science, there is a risk of the realization or politicization of philosophy in a bad sense."[26]

Mutai followed up this work with *Expression and Logic*[27] in 1940 and *The Logic of Place*[28] in 1944. As noted above, Nishida wrote "I have someone for the philosophy of history. For the logic of place, I rely on your efforts" in a 1942 letter to Mutai. From this it is clear that Nishida expected Mutai to carry on and develop the "logic of place." *The Logic of Place* can be described as an attempt to fulfill this expectation.

In *Problems of Japanese Culture*, published in 1940, Nishida writes that while the shoots of something that might be called the "logic of the mind" exist in Buddhism, they have not yet been developed into logic beyond direct experience. Mutai says something similar in *The Logic of Place*, arguing that the development of these shoots into "logic as a science" is a task for the present era.

Mutai draws on Nishida's theory of "place" in taking up this task, but while Nishida expresses the relationship between the whole and the individual with the terms "place" and "that which is emplaced," Mutai describes this as the relationship between "that which envelops" and "that which is enveloped." He then describes it as "the relationship in which that which envelops reflects that which is enveloped within itself, and conversely that which envelops is projected within that which is enveloped" or a relationship in which "each penetrates the other, and this reflecting relationship thus inverts." Shortly after receiving this book, Nishida sent a reply in which he praised it, writing, "With *The Logic of Place*, I think you have created something that can be called your own."

(4) The Establishment of the Study of Philosophy at Taihoku Imperial University

The two texts discussed above were published during Mutai's time at Tokyo Bunrika University, but prior to this post Mutai had held a teaching position at Taihoku Imperial University, which had been established in Taiwan in 1927. During his time there he focused mainly on the study of Hegelian philosophy. The results of this work were published as *A Study of Hegel*[29] immediately after his return to Japan. While the new philosophy of Husserl and Heidegger was garnering considerable attention at the time, there was also an upsurge in interest in the study of Hegel. During the years surrounding the hundredth anniversary of Hegel's death in 1931, a movement to revive Hegel arose in Germany, and this wave then swept over all of Europe and eventually Japan. Contributions to this movement in Japan included Tanabe Hajime's *Hegel's Philosophy and Dialectic* (1932) and Mutai's *A Study of Hegel*. The quality of Hegelian studies in Japan can be said to have been greatly elevated by these two works.

It is also worth noting that the study of Japanese philosophy took root in Taiwan during Mutai's time there.[30] After studying philosophy at the University of Tokyo, Hong Yaoxun (1902–1986) returned to Taiwan shortly after the establishment of Taihoku Imperial University, where he served as subassistant (and later assistant) in the Faculty of Letters and Politics' philosophy department.

In his first article, "Philosophical Problems Today"[31] (1934), Hong presents his own thoughts on Heidegger's understanding of "existence" while drawing on Kuki Shūzō's introduction to Heidegger's philosophy. While expressing agreement with the conception of Heidegger's fundamental ontology, in "Philosophical Problems Today (Continued)"[32] (1934) he criticizes Heidegger from a Hegelian perspective, writing, "There is clearly no manifestation of the contradiction or negativity that is a necessary condition for the dialectic."[33] This argument seems to have been inspired by Mutai Risaku's scholarship. It is notable, however, that while thus displaying sympathy for Hegelian philosophy, at the same time Hong also criticized it. In "Philosophical Problems Today (Continued)," he says that in Hegel "flesh and blood human beings grounded in real life" are not addressed, and as a result "contradiction" in its true sense is not grasped. Here too he seems to have drawn inspiration from Mutai. In *A Study of Hegel*, while expressing strong sympathy for Hegelian philosophy, Mutai adds, "I myself could never be satisfied with Hegel's concept of spirit." Hong's understanding of "being" also seems to have been influenced by the criticism that Hegel keeps his focus on grasping the world spirit, and the "self-consciousness" that enters and forms this spirit and its "reality as a subjective individual"[34] are not sufficiently understood. In addition to the above, Hong addresses Nishida Kitarō's question of "I and you" in "Philosophical Problems Today (Continued)" (1934), Tanabe Hajime's "species-type substance" in "Art and Philosophy (Specifically in Relation to Historical Society)" (1936), and Watsuji Tetsurō's "climate" and Mutai's "expressive world" in "A Climate View of Culture: In Relation to the Climate of Taiwan" (1936).

3. The Logic of Imagination—Miki Kiyoshi

As noted in chapter 4, after moving to Tokyo in 1927 Miki Kiyoshi (1897–1945) became a prominent figure in critical circles, but in 1930 he was arrested on suspicion of having given financial support to the Japanese Communist Party, which had been ruled illegal at the time, and resigned from his position at Hōsei University.[35] His focus then shifted to questions regarding the philosophy of history (in 1932 he published *The Philosophy of History*[36]). A series of articles he published beginning in 1937 was then collected in *The Logic of Imagination Part One*[37] (1939) and *The Logic of Imagination Part Two*[38] (1946, published posthumously). This work became his magnum opus. In 1945 he was arrested on suspicion of hiding and aiding the escape of suspected violators of the Peace Preservation Law, and he died in Toyotama Prison in September 1945, shortly after the war had ended.

The Logic of Imagination was written over a long period and was not published in a complete form; at the end of its final chapter (chapter 4, "Experience") Miki gives a preview of the next chapter in which he will address "language." It is thus an unfinished work, but this does not change the fact that it is of enormous significance in the development of Miki's thought. To begin with, *The Logic of Imagination* includes an attempt to solve a problem that had been unresolved in his work up to that point. Briefly stated, this was the problem of "the unification of logos and pathos."[39] Miki discusses this in the preface to *The Logic of Imagination Part One*.

> After the publication of *The Philosophy of History*, I was dogged by the question of how the subjective and the objective, the rational and the irrational, and the intellectual and the emotional might be unified. At the time I formulated this as the problem of the unification of logos and pathos, and to abstract logical and pathetic elements from all that is historical and discuss their dialectical unity has since become my main undertaking.[40]

He proceeds to reflect on the fact that this approach was "too formal" and was unable to elucidate where the unity of the logical and the pathetic "was to be found" in concrete terms. He then adds, "Recalling that Kant had recognized the function of unifying understanding and sensibility in the imagination, I arrived at the logic of imagination."[41]

Here it should be noted that Miki's diverse previous studies flowed into his theory of the logic of imagination. In concrete terms, his theories of humanity, logos/pathos, technology, poesis (production), the body, history, and literature were all utilized in the writing of *The Logic of Imagination*. The writing of this text can thus be seen as a continuation of these studies and as signifying an attempt to synthesize them. It should also be noted that these diverse ideas packed into *The Logic of Imagination* are pregnant with many possibilities. For example, a stance that views people as physical rather than simply intellectual beings is consistent throughout *The Logic of Imagination*. In other words, issues concerning action, production (poesis), technology, and so on are discussed from the perspective of human beings as physical or pathetic beings. It is also interesting that Miki focuses on the great significance of the formation of images in his discussion of action, production, and poesis. Moreover, these images—Miki also refers to them as "forms"—are not raw facts, but rather fictions, that is, something that is created. That it is within such fictions that reality is to be found, however, is the assertion Miki emphasizes most strongly in *The Logic of Imagination*. Here we can see the liveliness of Miki's thought that remains bracingly fresh even today.

Miki's intentions in addressing "the logic of imagination" can be gleaned from the opening passage of chapter 1, "Myth." Citing phrases such as Alexander Baumgarten (1714–1762)'s "logic of imagination"[42] and "logic of fantasy,"[43] Pascal's "logic of the heart,"[44] and French psychologist Théodule Ribot (1839–1916)'s "logic of the emotions,"[45] he poses the question of whether "a logic distinct from the logic of abstract thinking" or "a logic different from the logic of reason" exists, and presents this question as the central focus of his book. In other words, "the logic of imagination" is, to begin with, "a logic distinct from the logic of abstract thinking."

As for why a logic differing from the logic of abstract thinking or formal logic must be addressed, Miki answers this question as follows.

> We encounter things themselves, things in their materiality, with our bodies. We encounter things as things. If we call the body in its subjectivity "pathos," then the logic of things must presumably involve not only logos-type logic but at the same time also something pathetic.[46]

What Miki is seeking is not merely logic as rules for thinking, but a logic or philosophy that takes as its object human beings as beings who possess a body and act through the mediation of the body, and the reality that is encountered in the place of action. In this sense the "logic of imagination" is not simply a "logic of knowledge" but a "logic of action."

Before he began releasing essays on the "logic of imagination," from 1933 to 1937 Miki worked on preparing the publication of *Philosophical Anthropology* (he rewrote and revised it many times, but it was not actually published). In it he had already taken up the questions discussed here. In its first chapter, "The Concept of Anthropology," Miki states that anthropology differs from other sciences; its defining characteristic lies not in taking up the domain of the workings of human beings and through it seeking to understand them, but rather in addressing human beings in their entirety, which, first and foremost, means "not abstracting human beings from the physical body." "Not abstracting human beings from the physical body" means, in other words, not reducing human beings to simply consciousness or spirit, but rather viewing them as physical beings. Conversely, however, this body is of course not the body abstracted from human beings or the body as simply the object of objective analysis. Miki expressed this body that is inseparable from human beings as the "body 'animated by the mind (*beseelt*[47]).' "[48] Human beings are moved by various emotions (pathos) harbored in the mind, and the body attempts to express these externally. In other words, it is a "subjective" body. In *Philosophical Anthropology*, Miki emphasizes that the workings of this subjective physical body form the foundation of various workings of consciousness, and discarding or abstracting them and reducing the mental workings of human beings to simply intellectual workings is impossible.

At the same time, Miki also asserts that human beings cannot escape their own inner world and become "subjects of action," or, in other words, "express" themselves, with pathos alone. Quoting Georg Simmel (1859–1919)'s phrase "turn toward the idea,"[49] Miki states that it is only by "seeing the idea," that is, by connecting to logos, that the pathetic becomes able to "express" itself externally. It would seem, however, that Miki believed it was impossible to properly address this "turn toward the idea," or, in other words, the unification of pathos and logos, within the framework of "philosophical anthropology." To this end he began to think it was necessary to consider "imagination."[50]

In chapter 1, "Myth," of *The Logic of Imagination*, Miki addresses the question of why it is necessary to examine "imagination" in the form of a critique of the French social thinker Georges Sorel (1847–1922). He quotes from Sorel's *Réflexions sur la Violence*: "Strictly speaking, it is not imagination that causes action; but hope and fear, likes and dislikes, appetite, passion, the stirrings of selfishness and self-love."[51] He then responds to Sorel's assertion as follows.

> We cannot think about imagination abstracted from physicality. Imagination is indeed what binds together things such as hope and fear, likes and dislikes, appetite, passions and stirrings; this is why Descartes and Pascal deemed it a source of error. Imagination is bound to emotions and creates images from within

them. Through imagination, emotions can be transformed into something objective, strengthened as such, and made permanent.[52]

As is evident from this passage, Miki understood human actions not as simple expressions of emotions, passions, and urges, but rather as the undertaking of creating images from them, or, in other words, the undertaking of giving form to that which is formless. Here he is of course drawing on the original meaning of *Einbildungskraft* (imagination), "image making capacity." Imagination is nothing other than the capacity to transform pathos into something with form by unifying it with something logos-like. Miki believed that what makes human action truly human action is its not simply expressing pathos but rather giving it a new order through imagination. By doing so, pathos is not only expressed externally but "strengthened and made permanent." Miki's concrete examples of the formation of images include "myths" and "social systems," discussed in chapters 1 and 2 of *The Logic of Imagination*, respectively.

The "logic of imagination" was presented as an attempt to grasp the human undertaking of transforming pathos into images or that which has form, and was also referred to as the "logic of form and image."[53] At the stage of the writing of chapter 1, "Myth," there was a chance it could have fallen into "irrationalism or subjectivism," but Miki says that "from the time I began considering 'social systems,' it gradually became clear that the logic of imagination I was considering was in fact the 'logic of form.'"[54] From a subjective perspective he expressed his own stance as the "logic of imagination," but he was aware that from an objective perspective it was the "logic of form." He also notes that it was with Nishida's philosophy as a backdrop that he arrived at this understanding.

Miki thus acknowledged having approached Nishida's philosophy through his contemplation of the "logic of imagination," but this did not mean the unification of their thought. Miki's "logic of imagination" can be described as an attempt to surpass Nishida's philosophy, which he believed emphasized the importance of logos, did not give sufficient consideration to the pathetic, and was incapable of fully understanding the meaning of action. Miki expresses this as follows.

Imagination has almost always been thought of as simply an artistic activity. Form has also almost always been thought of from the standpoint of contemplation. I am now freeing imagination from these constraints and connecting it to action in general. What is important in this case is for it to be understood not as a matter of abstract will as in the subjectivist realism of the past, but rather as making something. In a broad sense all actions are making something, that is, they have the meaning of production. The logic of imagination is this kind of logic of production.[55]

It is also notable, however, that in a letter to his friend Sakata Tokuo (1898–1984), written just before his arrest in 1945, Miki writes:

> Thinking I must first fundamentally reexamine my understanding of Nishida's philosophy and create a foundation to surpass it, I am now engaged in this undertaking. Nishida's philosophy can perhaps be called the perfection of Eastern realism, but along with its great strengths, does this Eastern realism not have serious weaknesses? . . . In any case, I do not think it is possible for the new Japanese philosophy of the future to emerge without fundamentally confronting Nishida's philosophy. This task is as important as it is difficult.[56]

On the one hand Miki intensely criticized Nishida's philosophy for having a tendency to stop at impressions without addressing objects in reality, while on the other hand he felt a keen need to fundamentally engage with this philosophy. Only after this had been done did he believe a "new Japanese philosophy of the future" could be born. This continues to be an "important task," not only for Miki but also for the philosophers of today.

4. Encounters with Marxism—Tosaka Jun and Kakehashi Akihide

(1) Tosaka Jun's "Scientific Spirit"

Inspired by thinkers such as Miki Kiyoshi, at the end of the 1920s Tosaka Jun (1900–1945) became deeply interested in the writings of Marx and began his own serious study of materialism. In 1931 he took up a position as a lecturer at Hōsei University as a replacement for the departing Miki, and the following year, together with Oka Kunio and Saigusa Hiroto, he organized the Association for the Study of Materialism,[57] the journal of which, *Materialism Studies*,[58] was published until 1938. In 1935 he was dismissed from Hōsei University for "disruptive thought," and from then on dedicated his efforts to the activities of the Association for the Study of Materialism and the publication of *Series of Books on Materialism*.[59] In 1937 he was ordered to stop writing, and the following year he was arrested. He was initially released on bail, but in 1944 he was taken into custody and in August of the following year he died in Nagano Prison.

Tosaka had begun by studying Kant and the Neo-Kantian School, and at the root of his thought there is a spirit of "criticism" inherited from this approach. Even in his first book, *On Scientific Methodology* (1929), he says that what makes science exist as science is its scientific nature. As for the question of what this nature is, Tosaka believed it could be answered from the perspective of the end to which science is pursued. He asserted this aim was "obtaining truth," and wrote that "obtaining truth is only possible through criticism."[60] Tosaka thus sought the scientific nature of science in "radical criticism," but he also argued that this criticism had to be extended beyond science to become a "way of life." He writes that "science itself must be the method for living and for the social/practical world."[61] This radical criticism was not limited to philosophy and science but was also focused on the society that was their foundation and the various ideologies that supported the views of the day.

Tosaka's criticism was made concrete in *On Japanese Ideology: A Critique of Japanism, Fascism, Liberalism, and Other Thought in Contemporary Japan*. Its targets were not only fascist thought and the proponents of Japanism such as Kanokogi Kazunobu and Kihira Tadayoshi, but also thinkers who adopted the stance of liberalism such as Nishida Kitarō and Tanabe Hajime.

The first essay of its second part, "A Critique of Liberalism and Its Fundamental Principles," is titled "Modern Idealism in Disguise: On Principles for the Critique of 'Philosophy of Interpretation,'" and in it Tosaka sees Nishida's philosophy as idealism that has donned the guise of "philosophy of interpretation." The original aim of interpretation was to follow facts and ultimately alter them, but "philosophy of interpretation" has lost sight of this aim. It addresses the meaning of facts but divorces it from the facts themselves, and "relying only on interconnections between meanings themselves, constructs a *world of meaning*."[62] This replaces reality with a "world of meaning" and avoids all real problems, and Tosaka took issue with this "disguise." In "The Formation of Tanabe's Philosophy," included in *Lectures* on *Contemporary Philosophy*[63] (1934), Tosaka also criticizes Tanabe Hajime, under whom he had studied, from the same perspective. He praises Tanabe for attempting to bind and mediate life and logic, which are by nature difficult to bring together, through "moral practice." Tanabe's understanding of "practice," however, does not get beyond the "concept" of practice, and can never attain the conception of *practice*. Tanabe's philosophy is a "philosophy of interpretation" capable of addressing only "practice based on interpretation," and Tosaka criticizes him for having remained an idealist in this sense.

Tosaka's books *The Philosophy of Technology*[64] (1933) and *On Science*[65] (1935) and articles "What Is the Scientific Spirit?"[66] and "What Is the Technological Spirit"[67] (both 1937) can be said to have been based on the criticism outlined above. In *The Philosophy of Technology*, in the context of the Great Depression that had begun in 1929 and the profound economic, political, and cultural crises faced by capitalist countries around the world (and against the backdrop of Japan having set out on the path to war following the Mukden Incident in 1931), Tosaka points out the emergence of an environment in which people have begun to discuss the limits of material civilization and to oppose it with spiritual civilization or "Eastern metaphysics." In this work, Tosaka sought to reexamine the role technology should play in constructing society under these circumstances in which there was talk of transcending the limits of material civilization through spiritualism.

It was not until slightly later, but Miki Kiyoshi also became deeply interested in the issue of technology. After touching on this topic in *Introduction to Philosophy* (1940), he published *Technology Philosophy*[68] in 1942. One characteristic of Miki's view of technology was his attempt to address "technology" within an extremely wide field of view. In this regard it was diametrically opposed to Tosaka Jun's approach. Tosaka saw technology exclusively as "production technology," and vehemently opposed any wider interpretation on the grounds that an excessively broad interpretation of "technology" would create "endless confusion" ("What Is the Technological Spirit?"). Miki, on the other hand, did not agree that only the technology of material production was "technology," and believed that nature, too, could be technological. This was because nature is "formative," that is, it creates things with "form." The "form of living creatures," for example, can be thought of as having been created by nature. Looked at another way, this meant that Miki viewed that which creates things with form as "technology." He may have been drawing on Nishida's assertion in *Logic and Life*[69] (1936) that "nature is an ingenious engineer."

(2) Kakehashi Akihide's "Total Natural History Process"

Kakehashi Akihide (1902–1996), influenced by both Miki and Tosaka, elected to pursue the study of Marxism. According to one of his essays written after the war, "Prison and the Military,"[70] in the 1920s Marxism had been received in Japan as purely social science or economics, and from a Marxist perspective philosophy was disregarded as simply idealism. In this context, it was Miki Kiyoshi who led the way in addressing Marxism from a new vantage point. Many students were drawn to this approach. In this essay Kakehashi writes of these circumstances as follows.

> When Miki, equipped with a rich education in philosophy, set out to crack this academic shell from the inside, that is, when rather than abandoning philosophy and moving into economics in order to be a Marxist he pioneered an approach in which it was precisely being an active philosopher that allowed him to be a Marxist, it was no wonder I chose to follow him down this path. [71]

In 1934, Kakehashi published the results of his studies on Marxism as *A Philosophical Concept of Matter*, in which he proposes the concept of a "total natural history process."[72] The "total natural history process" was "the process of the transformation of the form of matter in stages" or "the process of the dialectical development of nature." In concrete terms, this was a comprehensive process that included the three stages of historical development: material objects, living beings, and society. Here society was seen as a "specific form of matter."[73] Kakehashi viewed this process of the development of nature as "self-movement." In other words, matter was viewed not simply as an objective entity, but as something with subjectivity that creates life and consciousness. Matter was said to be "subjective history."[74] An attempt was made to view nature and matter from an interesting perspective, but the meaning of this "subjectivity" was not made clear.

As I have just noted, Kakehashi was strongly influenced by Miki Kiyoshi, but eventually he began to articulate a fundamental criticism of Miki's philosophy. In the preface to *A Philosophical Concept of Matter*, he states that the starting point of the theoretical endeavor undertaken in this text was a critique of Miki's philosophy. In an essay entitled "The Fascist Form of Miki's Philosophy," with Miki's *Philosophy of History* in mind he argues that while Miki tries to work out a general theory of the conception of history common to both the materialist view of history and the idealist view of history held by thinkers such as Hegel, this effort is merely the product of formal logic-style thinking, turning a blind eye to the "contradictions of actual existence" and thereby serving to conceal them.[75]

5. Development in Diverse Fields—Kimura Motonori, Kōyama Iwao, Tsuchida Kyōson, and Shimomura Toratarō

(1) Kimura Motonori's Theory of the Body/Expression

Kimura Motonori (1895–1946) entered Kyoto University in 1920 and studied under Nishida Kitarō. He is known as the translator of Fichte's *Grundlage der gesamten Wissenschaftslehre* and as the author of *Fichte,* published as one of the volumes in the "Western Philosophy Series"[76] (Kōbundō Shobō), but after moving from Hiroshima Arts and Science University[77] to Kyoto University's Faculty of Letters and taking charge of the pedagogy and teaching methods course in 1933, the focus of his research gradually shifted to pedagogy and art theory. His books on pedagogy include *Culture and Education in the Nation*[78] (1946), and in his 1939 essay "Body and Spirit"[79] he discusses "expression," a topic with great significance in the domain of art (this text was included in *Expressive Love*, also published in 1939). This essay is known for having been praised by Nishida, who sent Kimura a postcard on which he wrote, "I was grateful to receive 'Body and Spirit.' Kimura. This essay is good. It felt as though I were holding hands with you."

As the title suggests, in this essay Kimura begins by addressing "the body."

> What is the body? Whether we conceive of it as mere natural matter or even as a biological entity, the body's essence cannot be grasped. Human beings are essentially formative expressive entities. They are beings who are situated outside to in turn possess an inside; they are spiritual-qua-material entities. The body is nothing other than the dialectical moment of this kind of dialectical entity, concretely making possible its formative realization.[80]

According to Kimura, a human being is not only a body in a material sense but also a spiritual being. When he says "spiritual," Kimura focuses his attention mainly on "expression." Human beings express the fruits of their spiritual or intellectual activities outside of themselves. In other words, they form a self outside of themselves. To use Kimura's phrase, they "are situated outside to possess an inside." It is in this sense that Kimura describes human beings as "essentially formative expressive entities."

Particularly worth noting here is that Kimura understood this activity, that is, expressing the results of one's spiritual or intellectual activities outside oneself, as a two-way rather than one-way interaction. For expression to be possible, there must first be stimulation from the outside. Receiving this stimulation, a human being carves their own spiritual activities in the material objects of the outside world. In other words, they "are situated outside to possess an inside." In this sense Kimura understood human beings as "spiritual-qua-material entities," or, in other words, "dialectical entities." According to him it is "the body" that makes possible this kind of dialectical formation and expression; the body is an essential moment that undergirds the work of "formation" and "expression" carried out by human beings as dialectical entities.

Let us examine Kimura's understanding in a bit more detail. He uses the phrase "expressive life" to refer to the subject that carries out the work of "formation" and "expression." The core of this work is the "manifestation of the inside on the outside." But this is not simply displaying one's internal will to the outside world. Displaying the inside on the outside requires material. Only by working with material does it become possible for the inside to display itself on the outside. This material, however, is not simply material objects. According to Kimura, it is "something that speaks to the subject." This material being not simply a material object but "something that speaks to the subject" is a result of it being "that which has been historically created, or that which has been expressively made." The "outside" speaks to the "inside" as something of this nature. Soil and stones, too, are not merely soil and stones; as that which is expressively made, they "incite and speak to the human will." The "inside" then "responds" to this outside that calls out to it. In other words, it "takes the determination that is a call from the outside as the mediation to formatively determine the outside from the inside in return."[81] "Manifesting the inside on the outside" is nothing other than responding to this call from the outside as that which is made and determining it in turn by means of "formation."

Kimura can be said to have seen the essential nature of human beings in the carrying out of this kind of "formation," or, in other words, in being "formative expressive" entities. What supports the "formative nature" of this kind of "formative expressive" entity is "the body." Kimura defines the body as "a will that works its way into nature," and this phrase aptly expresses the character of Kimura's understanding of the body. He describes the body as "a will that works its way into nature" because while being a part of material nature, at the same time it also realizes the will of the subject as something belonging to it, and, in order to do so, thrusts itself into nature and "manifests the inside on the outside." Kimura believed it was this body as "a will that works its way into nature" that was responsible for carrying out the formative and expressive activities of human beings.

Interestingly, Kimura uses the term "historical nature" to describe the nature that, along with enabling these acts of formation of individual human beings, "moves and becomes on its own" through these same acts.[82]

He chose the phrase "historical nature" because Nishida Kitarō had used it in an essay entitled "Logic and Life"[83] (included in *Philosophical Essays Volume 2*) several years before "Body and Spirit" in 1936. There Nishida had written, "We, individuals, have developed out of the world of historical nature. As Aristotle says, 'nature makes' (ἡ φύσις ποιεῖ)[84] everything. Historical nature must be logical. . . . our bodies, too, must be understood from the world of historical reality."[85] Nishida called this nature found in the world of historical reality "historical nature," and believed that this nature, as Aristotle says in his *Politics*, is something that makes, and moreover something that makes logically, and that our bodies exist as the products of this nature's logical functioning.

Based on Nishida's understanding, along with calling that which subsumes the formative and expressive acts of individual human beings within itself and allows them to arise as "historical nature," Kimura states that "the body is the apex of the creative will that historical nature drives into its own material aspect."[86] Here it is understood that "historical nature" also drives this creative will into material nature, the apex of which is the human "body." This is the core of Kimura's understanding of the body. It was perhaps this point that lay behind Nishida's phrase "it felt as though I were holding hands with you" in his letter to Kimura.

(2) Kōyama Iwao's "Philosophy of World History"

Kōyama Iwao entered Kyoto University in 1925 and studied under Nishida Kitarō, Tomonaga Sanjyūrō, and Tanabe Hajime. Nishida left his position upon reaching retirement age in 1928, and Kōyama was thus a member of the last class to study under him for three years. In 1938 he became an associate professor in Kyoto University's Faculty of Letters, where he was responsible for the course on the spiritual history of Japan[87] and a special course on philosophy. Tanabe Hajime reached retirement age in 1945, and the following year Kōyama became professor of the philosophy course. He resigned in August of that year, however, following an order purging public officials. The purge of public officials was lifted in 1951, and Kōyama then took positions as a professor at several universities, including Kanagawa University, Nihon University, and Takushoku University. His writings include the explanatory guides to Nishida's philosophy *Nishida Philosophy*[88] and *Nishida Philosophy Part Two*,[89] *The Study of Cultural Types*,[90] *The Philosophy of World History*,[91] and *The Logic of Place and the Principle of Concordance*[92] (1951), in which he presents his own intellectual position.

From the time he was a university student, Kōyama showed a strong interest in Wilhelm Dilthey's method of human science that sought to pursue the individuality of experience and its generality in terms of similar types. He paid particular attention to Dilthey's concept of "type," and within it his effort to typify worldviews. *The Study of Cultural Types* (1939) was conceived by expanding on this approach. This work was inspired by Dilthey's study of worldviews and attempted to apply his concept of type to the cultures of various peoples. Kōyama's pursuit of this line of inquiry was tied to his having been in charge of the spiritual history of Japan course at Kyoto University. According to Kōyama, to engage in the study of cultural types was to extract essential elements and core structures from the cultures of various peoples, reconstruct them as ideal types, and by comparing these ideal types come to understand the spiritual or intellectual particularities of each people. Through this undertaking, Kōyama's ultimate aim was "to elevate the Japanese spirit to truly profound consciousness."[93]

In addition to these works, Kōyama published *Philosophical Anthropology* in 1938 and *The Philosophy of World History* in 1942. Their content harkened back to "The History of Philosophy and Types of Worldview: Hegel's Concept of the History of Philosophy and Dilthey's Concept of Worldview," an essay he had published in 1932. In it Kōyama refers to one of the dilemmas presented by philosophy: philosophy demands a system of knowledge with universal validity, but in reality it cannot escape historical relativity. This essay clearly shows that Kōyama perceived this antinomy between system and history as a major problem. Looking for a path to its solution, he focused on Hegel's history of philosophy and Dilthey's theory of worldview. But the former did not give sufficient consideration to history, and in Dilthey the systematic aspect was lacking. To overcome the deficiencies of both approaches and resolve the antinomy between system and history, Kōyama developed "philosophical anthropology" and the "philosophy of the history of philosophy." These approaches were concretely realized in the two works cited above.

Kōyama was in charge of both the course on the spiritual history of Japan and a special course on philosophy, and in the special course he took up various issues related to the philosophy of history, including "the one-time-only and universal nature of history" and "various aspects of historical time." The results of these inquiries are presented together in *The Philosophy of World History*. Kōyama expresses the basic idea of this work as "the philosophy of history must be the *philosophy of world history*."[94] What he had in mind when he said this was primarily a critique of the historical understanding in which Europe is considered equivalent to "the world." In Kōyama's understanding, Europe was one "modern world," but now a "contemporary world" with a different order and structure was emerging. He can be said to have attempted to establish a philosophy of history grounded in an understanding of this new "world." Relatedly, Kōyama also had in mind a critique of the naïve "world monism" that views the history of the world as something that moves and develops in accordance with a single principle (Kōyama saw this kind of approach in the Christian view of history as well as in the views of history of Hegel and Marx). In contrast, the "philosophy of world history," according to Kōyama, arises when we "emphasize that each historical world has its own completeness and incompleteness based on differences between regions and peoples, and remain profoundly conscious of the fact that the development and construction of world history is conducted through their mixing and interconnecting."[95]

(3) Tsuchida Kyōson

After studying at Kyoto University, Tsuchida Kyōson (1891–1934), while positioning himself outside of academia, engaged in diverse criticism on a variety of topics including philosophical thought, society, literature, and art. He was also involved in education at schools such as Shinano (Ueda) Free University,[96] an institution for the self-education of common people. When *Complete Works of Tsuchida Kyōson*[97] was published after Tsuchida's death, Nishida Kitarō, in an endorsement of this text entitled "A Thinker of the Streets,"[98] writes, "He was more a man of the streets than one who locked himself away in the ivory tower" and "his many skills and multiple talents made him fit to be called truly astounding."[99]

Tsuchida's scholarship did indeed span an extremely wide range of subjects and is difficult to survey in its entirety. Here I would like to focus on his unique perspective as a "thinker of the streets" who positioned himself as an outsider and engaged in various social activities and educational undertakings. The "value of life" was one of the concepts Tsuchida addressed from this point of view. Tsuchida saw himself as a "civilizational critic," and held criticism in high regard among human cultural pursuits. Before entering Kyoto University, while still a student at Tokyo Higher Normal School he had already published *Civilizational Intellectual Trends and New Philosophy*[100] (1914), which included the essay "High Criticism of Civilization."[101] In it he writes, "Natural science is the use of the materials of life, but philosophy is the discerning of the values of life. . . . knowledge is sufficient to make use of the materials of life, but criticism is required to discern the values of life."[102] He could not of course have seen his own future at the time, but Tsuchida can be said to have pursued criticism in this sense, that is, criticism based on philosophy that distinguishes the "values of life," throughout his career. In concrete terms, this was an effort to bring out the illness at the root of modern civilization, namely, "the various aspects of life progressing dividedly and individually, without a unified perspective having arisen,"[103] and look for ways to overcome it (see, for example, *Where Is Civilization Going?*[104] [1930]).

Another notable aspect of Tsuchida's legacy was his having introduced the history of Japanese philosophy in English. At the request of W. Tudor Jones, the general editor of Williams and Norgate's "Library of Contemporary Thought" series, *Contemporary Thought of Japan and China* was published in 1927. After having written this English manuscript, Tsuchida produced a Japanese version that was published one year earlier. In this text, in addition to introducing the thought of figures such as Nishida, Tanabe, Nishi Shin'ichirō (1873–1943), Kihira Tadayoshi, Sōda Kiichirō, Tanaka Ōdō, and Hasegawa Nyozekan (1875–1969), Tsuchida also surveyed Japanese socialist thought, and the English edition of this text had great significance as a detailed introduction to the philosophy of Japan that had been largely unknown outside its borders. It is also interesting to note that Tsuchida developed a critique of academic philosophy in this work. He criticized Japanese academic philosophy for being too individualistic and insufficiently concerned with actual society, and as a result completely incapable of presenting solutions to actual social problems. He was also critical of the emergence of a nationalistic character that made the state "the highest form of human ideals." Also notable is how this text prefigures something that can be thought of as the "history of East Asian philosophy." From what had initially been a mixture—Tsuchida uses the term "ragout"—of Western and Eastern elements, Japanese and Chinese philosophy had both progressed toward the establishment of a more logical and methodical philosophy. They were confronted, however, by the problem of how to navigate between the opposing concepts of tradition and universality. In this book, Tsuchida sets his sights on solving this problem and presents a history of philosophy written from a broad perspective. Writing a "history of East Asian philosophy" that fulfills Tsuchida's aim is a task that may one day be taken up.[105]

(4) Mathematics as "Spiritual History"—Shimomura Toratarō

Shimomura Toratarō (1902–1995)'s first book was *Leibniz* (1938), and he also had a deep interest in the philosophy of math and the philosophy of science. In his later years he published a long essay, "Pilgrimage to My Own Writings, or Praising My Own Work,"[106] in which he traces his own thought and writings. In it he writes that Tanabe Hajime's *Overview of Science*[107] and *A Study of the Philosophy of Mathematics*[108] were the start of his philosophical training. At the same time, he also writes as follows.

> For both Nishida and Tanabe, who were motivated by their confrontation with the epistemology of the Neo-Kantian School, logic was the fundamental problem. . . . They were logicians, not historians. But is it impossible for philosophers to be historians? . . . I came to think of myself as a historian rather than a logician, and this awareness gradually strengthened. Even when considering logic, I found myself turning toward the question of its historicity. The philosophy of mathematics and the philosophy of science, too, were in actuality the philosophy of the history of mathematics and the philosophy of the history of science. Not the history of mathematics and the history of science, but the philosophy of the history of mathematics and the philosophy of the history of science.[109]

In a note entitled "Fireside Ramblings,"[110] Shimomura also writes in regard to Nishida, "How can history arise in an 'eternal now'?" and in regard to Tanabe, "In Tanabe's philosophy historicity is the 'moment' that changes the past into the future. Here history that has scope—with persistence—is impossible in principle."[111] Shimomura's aim was indeed to be a "philosopher who is a historian"[112] capable of considering the historicity of logic.

Shimomura's most important prewar text was *The Philosophy of the History of Science*[113] (1941). He begins by acknowledging Europe as one of the "classics" (emerging in a particular society but at the same time having universal significance) of human cultural history. His aim was to clarify the character of "academic inquiry," one of the essential elements of this classic nature. Here he focused particularly on mathematics. According to Shimomura, the defining characteristic of European academic inquiry is that mathematics, science (natural science), and philosophy (metaphysics) form a trinitarian system, but he believed the conceptual formation of this academic inquiry only became possible with the establishment of mathematics. In this sense, Shimomura holds that the formation of mathematics as academic inquiry (pure mathematics) was a "world historical event"[114] rather than simply something that happened in Europe. In this book he addresses the origins, significance, and consequences of this event. Its emergence is not normally discussed in the history of mathematics as its existence is taken for granted. Shimomura, however, addresses the creation of mathematics. He also considers the creation of mathematics in relation to the history of philosophy and the history of science. His subject is not the "history of mathematics" but "history *toward* mathematics." He says this history is not the "natural history" of the environment in which mathematics was born, but purely "spiritual history." In other words, Shimomura addressed the nature of the spirit or mentality that formed mathematics, what this spirit became conscious of through mathematics, and what this spirit then created. By doing so, he attempted to elucidate the significance of the concept of European academic inquiry in intellectual history. One of Shimomura's great achievements was the establishment of this method of pursuing "spiritual history."

Chapter 8

The Kyoto School

1. What Was/Is the Kyoto School?

(1) Establishment of the Name "Kyoto School"

The philosophy of Nishida and Tanabe and the thought of their colleagues and disciples were examined in chapters 5 to 7, and these thinkers are generally referred to as the "Kyoto School." Here I would like to consider the nature of this school of philosophy. I will start with when this name first came to be used. As far as can be determined from the literature, Tosaka Jun, who studied under both Nishida Kitarō and Tanabe Hajime, was the first to use the phrase "Kyoto School" in his essay "The Philosophy of the Kyoto School,"[1] which was published in *Economic Comings and Goings*[2] in 1932.[3]

> Nishida's philosophy is developing into a Nishida School or Kyoto School. This is now a robustly formed social entity. It seems that blazing a trail from Nishida's philosophy to a Nishida School is an august undertaking that can only be entrusted to Tanabe Hajime.

From this passage we see that the term "Kyoto School" was used to describe circumstances in which Tanabe Hajime was becoming established as Nishida's successor. Tosaka's words "Nishida's philosophy is developing into a Nishida School" did not, however, simply express Tanabe being the successor of Nishida's philosophy. As we have already seen, in 1930, two years before they were written, Tanabe had published an essay entitled "A Request for

Professor Nishida's Thoughts" in which he had publicly criticized Nishida's thought. This can also be seen as having been Tanabe's declaration of independence from Nishida. Indeed, it was from that point on that his thought was referred to as "Tanabe philosophy." It was presumably in the context of this development that Tosaka recognized the formation of a "social entity" that could no longer be described as "Nishida philosophy" but could nevertheless be subsumed within a single school.

It is important to note here that Tosaka did not employ the term "Kyoto School" in positively evaluating or agreeing with the philosophy of Nishida and Tanabe. In this essay, Tosaka took the clearly critical view that Nishida's and Tanabe's philosophy was impractical philosophy that had no connection to concrete society. "Kyoto School" was first used in this kind of critical context. Naturally, therefore, Tosaka did not position himself within it; on the contrary, he was clearly conscious of being "outside" it. The name "Kyoto School" was thus first given from the "outside."

(2) What Was/Is the "Kyoto School"?

Thereafter the phrase "Kyoto School" became widely known, but this did not mean there was a great deal of scholarship on the thought and philosophy of the Kyoto School. Books and articles dealing with it directly were far fewer than those discussing the philosophy of Nishida Kitarō, for example. When the disciples of Nishida and Tanabe are included in this school, their direct involvement and thus inability to take sufficient distance to relativize this thought can be considered one reason for this. The lack of clarity about the scope of this school also made discussing it difficult. The "Kyoto School," unlike normal philosophical schools, was not a group that arose through criticism of a previous school, or, in other words, a group that began by asserting a particular thesis. Instead, it was a group that naturally emerged in the period during which Japanese philosophy, which had begun by receiving Western philosophy, was starting to take its own path, and as such its assertions and scope had no clear outline.

In recent years, however, there have been efforts to put forward common characteristics, engage in definition, and establish who belonged to this school. Examples of this include John C. Maraldo's article "The Identity of the Kyoto School: A Critical Analysis."[4] Maraldo proposes the following six criteria to establish the borders of the "fuzzy set" known as the Kyoto School: "a connection with Nishida"; "an association with Kyoto University"; "a stance toward Japanese and Eastern intellectual traditions"; "a stance toward three interrelated matters: Marxism, the nation-state, and the Pacific war"; "a stance toward the Buddhist tradition, and religion in general"; and "a stance toward the notion of absolute nothingness."

This strong interest in the question of the identity of the "Kyoto School" among scholars overseas can be thought of as stemming from their understanding that the commonality of the members of this school, whether Nishida and Tanabe or their disciples, is stronger than their differences (and of course holding up a mirror for comparison with Western philosophy). From the perspective of comparison with Western philosophy, what first stands out is the concept of "nothingness." In Maraldo's article there is a particular focus on "absolute nothingness," and this is presumably owing to his interest in what kind of contribution thought based on "absolute nothingness" makes to philosophy from this original perspective distinct from Western philosophy.[5] Interest in the identity of the "Kyoto School" can be seen as deriving from this focus.

However, it is not easy to come up with a quality or characteristic that applies to Nishida, Tanabe, and all of their disciples. This is related to the already noted fact that the "Kyoto School" was not a group that began by advancing a particular doctrine or theory. Consequently, there was almost no understanding of what the "Kyoto School" was among the people "inside" this school themselves.[6] As I noted above, when Tosaka used this phrase for the first time it was as a label applied from the "outside." Later characterizations of the "Kyoto School" can also be said to have mostly been made from the "outside."

As can be seen from these formative circumstances, it is not easy to lay out several qualities or criteria to define the "Kyoto School." In actuality, a diverse array of figures were inspired by Nishida and Tanabe. Tosaka Jun, who took a Marxist stance, was one of them, but there were also those such as Miyake Gōichi and Shimomura Toratarō who produced outstanding work in the fields of the philosophy of science and cultural history. It is nearly impossible to formulate criteria that would apply to all of them.[7]

(3) The "Kyoto School" as an Intellectual Network

One notable attempt to define the "Kyoto School" that takes a different approach from Maraldo's method of proposing common characteristics is that of Takeda Atsushi. In his "Shimomura Toratarō: The Path Toward 'Intellectual History' "[8] he defines the "Kyoto School" as "the whole intellectual network, centering around the two figures of Nishida and Tanabe, intimately and reciprocally formed . . . by those who received the influence of both *directly*, both academically and personally."[9]

Takeda uses the phrase "intimately and reciprocally formed," and there were in fact extraordinarily "intimate" connections between Nishida, Tanabe, and their disciples. They engaged in discourse on the same problems and strongly influenced each other. These were two-way relationships rather than one-way transmissions from teacher to student. Nishida and Tanabe themselves criticized each other, and the stimulation this gave them was a driving force in the ongoing formation of their thought. It was also not uncommon for their disciples to influence them. For example, Miki Kiyoshi's thought concerning history and the body and Shimomura Torataro's scholarship on Leibniz and the philosophy of science gave significant inspiration to Nishida and Tanabe (the case of Nishida and Kōsaka Masaaki discussed in the previous chapter is another example of this). These kinds of reciprocal relationships in which its members stimulated each other is one of the characteristics of the Kyoto School.

In his "Commentary" in *Kimura Motomori: The Praxis of Beauty*,[10] Iwaki Ken'ichi likens the Kyoto School to an artist's workshop, referring to it as a "philosophical workshop," and in doing so he can be said to have accurately grasped the relationships found in this school. He then notes that, unlike today, the issue of intellectual priority was not given much importance within this group.

For the mentors, a disciple publishing thought similar to their own using the same concepts was not plagiarism, but rather evidence of the power of their own ideas, and they used the new thought of their disciples as grist to bolster the persuasiveness of their own arguments.[11]

Nishida was by no means a systematic thinker. When one of his disciples, Kōyama Iwao, wrote an exegetical text entitled *Nishida Philosophy*[12] in 1935, Nishida was asked to write its preface. In it he writes, "I am only ever a miner." As this phrase aptly expresses, Nishida's style of contemplation was something like extracting ore from a lode or cutting rough lumber from raw wood. He did very little along the lines of carefully following the thought of philosophers of the past from start to finish. He did not engage in such work as translating and faithfully interpreting individual texts or tracing the process of the intellectual development of individual thinkers and writing general overviews. Such tasks he actively entrusted to his disciples. A prime example of this was the *Western Philosophy Series*, which was supervised by Tanabe Hajime and edited by the likes of Shimomura Torataro, Kimura Motomori, and Kōsaka Masaaki. Its having adopted this kind of organic division of labor was presumably another reason the Kyoto School was likened to an artist's workshop. However, the relationship between its members was not like that in an artist's workshop in which people simply collaborate to produce new works. Criticizing each other was a frequent occurrence.

There were those who engaged in open criticism of Nishida Kitarō and Tanabe Hajime and others who made only the most restrained critiques, but in either case, by criticizing Nishida and Tanabe they developed their own thought. For example, Miki Kiyoshi, Yamauchi Tokuryū, Nishitani Keiji, and Miyake Gōichi all formed their own independent thought with criticism of Nishida and Tanabe as their impetus. Their mentors, too, tried to address this criticism head on. For example, shortly after the publication of Tanabe's "A Request for Professor Nishida's Thoughts," Nishida wrote as follows to his disciple, Mutai Risaku: "Regarding Tanabe's essay, I very much hope that this truly sincere attitude and atmosphere continues to flourish in academia. If not, there is no way for academic inquiry in our country to progress."[13] Nishida did in fact then deepen his own thought regarding the issues Tanabe had addressed regarding "action" and "history." This kind of connection that allows for criticism can also be cited as one of the main characteristics of the Kyoto School. The term "network" aptly expresses this relationship between its members.

Nonetheless, there are several things that must be added to Takeda's definition. When he says "those who received the influence of both [Nishida and Tanabe] *directly*," he is presumably thinking mainly of the relationship between Nishida, Tanabe, and their disciples such as Nishitani Keiji, Shimomura Toratarō, and Mutai Risaku, and does not have in mind Kuki Shūzō and Watsuji Tetsurō. But I think we must consider the "Kyoto School" to include those such as Hatano Seiichi, Fukada Yasukazu, Kuki Shūzō, and Watsuji Tetsurō who taught at Kyoto University during the same period as Nishida and Tanabe, and who, albeit to a differing degree, also influenced each other intellectually.

When Takeda says "the whole intellectual network . . . intimately and reciprocally formed," he seems to exclude people who were critical of Nishida's and Tanabe's thought. Tosaka Jun, whose name I have just mentioned, was one of Nishida and Tanabe's disciples who intensely criticized their views, but he was also someone whose thought was formed amid the academic influence of these two thinkers. The discourse of figures such as Tosaka and Kakehashi Akihide also had considerable influence on Nishida and Tanabe.[14] In this sense I would argue that both Tosaka and Kakehashi can be added to the Kyoto School, although when he coined the phrase "Kyoto School" I am quite certain Tosaka did not expect to one day be included in it.

Another addition I would like to make to Takeda's understanding of the Kyoto School is that it seems perfectly plausible to include not only those "directly" influenced by Nishida and Tanabe but also those of later generations who were influenced by them when we think about this school. This would of course differ from the intimate relationships formed by those who were "personally" influenced by them directly, but being "academically" influenced is possible even at a later time. In other words, carrying on the philosophy of Nishida and Tanabe, or critically examining and developing it, is something that can be done by later generations, and indeed can be described as one of the tasks they must address. It is presumably possible to consider the "Kyoto School" as including such figures.

(4) The Philosophy of "Nothingness"

While several points thus need to be examined further, the definition of the "Kyoto School" as an "intellectual network" aptly characterizes its nature. Insofar as it does not touch on the philosophical content of this school, however, this definition can of course be said to have a major failing. This is the case because interest in the philosophy of the Kyoto School does not stop at historical interest but is also ultimately tied to the question of what can be extracted from it, or, in other words, what kind of contribution it has made to philosophy. When the "Kyoto School" is addressed from this perspective its intellectual characteristics naturally become the topic of inquiry. Such interests can be assumed to have lain behind the focus on the concept of "absolute nothingness" in the article by Maraldo discussed above.

As we have seen, Nishida believed there is a "self-awareness of absolute nothingness" at the root of all beings. In his *Philosophy as the Way of Repentance*, Tanabe Hajime also viewed the transformation he experienced through the thoroughgoing self-awareness of the impotence of his own philosophy as "nothingness that is love," or the "great negation that is great mercy" of "absolute nothingness." Contemplation of this kind of "nothingness" was then taken up by philosophers such as Hisamatsu Shin'ichi and Nishitani Keiji. It is thus of course possible to characterize the philosophy of the Kyoto School as the "philosophy of absolute nothingness." On the other hand, taking this stream of thought to be directly equivalent to the philosophy of the Kyoto School is also problematic; it is indeed one stream passed on from Nishida to his disciples, but does not encompass the entirety of this school's thought. The intellectual undertakings of the members of this school were extremely diverse in scope, encompassing such fields as the philosophy of history, the philosophy of math, the philosophy of science, aesthetics, cultural history, and pedagogy. Producing results in such diverse areas of inquiry is also one of the major characteristics of the Kyoto School. Describing the philosophy of the Kyoto School as the "philosophy of absolute nothingness" runs the risk of excluding such results from our field of view.

As I have noted above, however, "nothingness" as something fundamentally alien to the philosophy of the West seems to have attracted particularly intense interest from the perspective of Western philosophy. It is precisely through this kind of dialogue between distinct ideas that new developments in philosophy arise, and from this perspective it is indeed fruitful to view the philosophy of the Kyoto School as the "philosophy of nothingness."

2. Overcoming Modernity

(1) The Critiques of the "Overcoming Modernity" and "Japan and the Perspective of World History" Symposia

There are two symposia that are often discussed in relation to the Kyoto School's responsibility for the war. One was a symposium called "Overcoming Modernity." Held in July of 1942, it was organized by a coterie of intellectuals, including Kawakami Tetsutarō (1902–1980), Kamei Katsuichirō (1907–1966), Kobayashi Hideo (1902–1983), and Nakamura Mitsuo (1911–1988), connected to *The Literary World*[15] for a special issue of this journal, and invitees included Nishida Kitarō's disciples Nishitani Keiji and Shimomura Toratarō, as well as Suzuki Shigetaka, who taught Western history at Kyoto University. The other was a three-part symposium held around the same time as "Overcoming Modernity" by Nishitani and Suzuki along with Kōsaka Masaaki and Kōyama Iwao. The records of this symposium were initially presented in the journal *Central Review*[16] and in 1943 were published by Chūō Kōron Sha as a book entitled *Japan and the Perspective of World History*.[17]

After the war, the significance of the debate surrounding "overcoming modernity" was highlighted by Takeuchi Yoshimi (1910–1977). In his essay "Overcoming Modernity," Takeuchi states that as a trendy phrase or "magic words" this expression was deeply connected to the "Greater East Asia War" and served as one of its symbols.[18] He describes the influence of this symposium as "dominant." The phrase "overcoming modernity" was in fact seen by most intellectuals as a slogan justifying the war in Asia and the Pacific, and there were undoubtedly many young men who went to the front having been persuaded by these words.[19]

Around the same time as Takeuchi's critique, Odagiri Hideo (1916–2000) published an essay entitled "Regarding 'Overcoming Modernity'" in which he characterizes this symposium as follows.

> Forming one wing of the "intellectual war" that was an organic part of the militaristic regime's "all-out war," the debate on "overcoming modernity" that took place during the Pacific War was an intellectual campaign undertaken in order to eliminate modern, democratic systems of thought and demands for [modern] ways of life.[20]

While this criticism was not directed exclusively at the Kyoto School, this group was presumably one of its targets. More recently, in his book *Discourses on "Overcoming Modernity": A Fragmentary Reflection on the Intellectual History of the Showa Period* [21] Hiromatsu Wataru (1933–1994) criticizes the Kyoto School's approach to "overcoming modernity" for having fallen into an abstract theory lacking an analysis of the social and historical foundations of "modernity."[22] In *What Is 'Overcoming Modernity'?*, Koyasu Nobukuni asserts that the historical philosophical arguments made by the Kyoto School in the symposia on "Overcoming Modernity" and "Japan and the Perspective of World History" attempted to provide a moral rationale for Japan's wars, or, in other words, "the actions of Japan to advocate for a new Asian order in response to the existing European world order" and fire up the citizenry.[23]

(2) A Symposium that Became a Free-for-all Discussion

"Overcoming Modernity" was organized by the coterie of the *Literary World* at the beginning of 1942, that is, shortly after the start of the war in the Pacific. In his "Conclusion" to this symposium, Kawakami says, "That this meeting . . . was undertaken in the midst of the intellectual angst and turmoil within a year after the war had started is a fact that should not be covered up,"[24] and there was clearly an intention to give meaning to this war in one way or another.

But why was the theme "overcoming modernity" chosen? Behind it lay the powerful sense of stagnation of this era shared by everyone at the time. Most people sought the cause of this sense in Japan's modernization that had begun in the Meiji period. They believed the stagnation of the era could be broken through by in some manner transcending "modernity." This transcending of "modernity" was then easily equated with negating the "West" from which "modernity" had originated and the fight against the great powers of Europe and America that had begun in the real world. To give one example, in "Memorandum Concerning the Contemporary Spirit,"[25] an article submitted for the symposium, Kamei Katsuichirō writes as follows.

> The war we are fighting at present is externally to destroy Anglo-American influence, but internally it is to fundamentally cure the illness of the spirit caused by modern culture. These are two sides of a holy war, and if either is neglected the war effort will surely flounder.[26]

The intention to try to give meaning to and justify this war (and, while it was not directly discussed at the symposium, to justify the invasion of Asia) by arguing it was not a conflict between imperialist nations unfolding in the era of "modernity," but rather a war to transcend "modernity" itself, can be said to have been packed into the phrase "overcoming modernity." This expression thus took on a life of its own as "magic words" that captivated many hearts and minds.

However, regarding the content of this symposium itself, Takeuchi Yoshimi asserts it was "intellectually devoid of content to a strange degree"[27] such that it could not even constitute an ideology of war and fascism, and "aiming at the formation of ideas, the result was the loss of ideas."[28] According to Takeuchi, the cause of this was to be found in the fact that the "aporia of modern Japanese history," that is, the aporia that arises from the fundamental axis of the opposing ideas "restoration and innovation," "nationalism and civilizational enlightenment," and "East and West" that was the driving force behind this symposium, was not looked at directly despite being an issue that should have been addressed.

Of course, not everything discussed at the symposium was meaning-less rhetoric. There was interesting discourse on questions such as "What is Western modernity?," "What is science?," and "What is the significance of thinking in Japanese?" But there is a strong impression that the diversity of the themes addressed made it hard to tell what the central question was, and more importantly that the arguments of the participants did not mesh with each other. In his "Conclusion" cited above, Kawakami Tetsutarō expresses this as the specializations of the participants being different and their discourse "like tapping on the walls to talk to comrades in adjoining cells." Ultimately the participants each developed their own ideas without there ever being a focus on the questions of what "modernity" was, why it had to be overcome, and what direction this transcending of modernity should take. Without any discussion of these differences, the symposium ended up, to use Kawakami's phrase, as simply a "free-for-all discussion."

Significant issues were also raised. For example, in his essay "Doubts About 'Modernity,' "[29] Nakamura Mitsuo points out that the topic of "overcoming modernity" was originally addressed in Europe and expresses doubt about whether this phrase is appropriate to describe the situation being faced in Japan. "What most concerns me is the conceptual nature this topic [overcoming modernity] has for us. Does this phrase 'overcoming modernity' resonate for us with the same strong feeling and clear content with which it undoubtedly resonates for modern Europeans?"[30] Along with pointing out the conceptual nature of the title of the symposium, Nakamura discusses the "injudicious paradox" of borrowing Western concepts to oppose the West. Despite such concrete issues having been raised, they were not discussed at greater depth within the symposium.

The understanding of the participants differed widely not only regarding "overcoming modernity" but also how "modernity" was to be viewed in the first place. Most were in agreement that the modernization of Japan from the Meiji period onward had brought with it various harms. For example, Kamei Katsuichirō made the following statement at the symposium. "As one of the characteristics of post-Meiji civilization, what I feel most acutely is, in a phrase, the loss of wholeness as human beings."[31] Here the harm wrought by modernization is expressed with the words "loss of wholeness as human beings," and in an article contributed to the symposium, "Memorandum Regarding the Modern Spirit," this is expressed with the phrase "decline of receptivity"[32] that emerges from the orientation toward the rational. In a somewhat different vein, Nakamura Mitsuo discusses the "mental deformity"—I will return to this phrase later—that arises through the process of modernization. In contrast to this, Shimomura Toratarō clearly opposes emphasizing only the negative aspects of modernity—when Shimomura uses "modernity" he refers not only to Japanese modernity but modernity in general—or, in other words, considering modernity as simply an "unhappy era." This raises another important issue, but here too the gaps in understanding could not be filled in.

(3) "Modernity" as the Self and "Modernity" as the Other

Looking at the "Overcoming Modernity" symposium as a whole, two broad understandings regarding the nature of "modernity" stood in contrast to each other. The first understanding rests on the idea that the harms brought by modernization—often seen as identical with modernity itself—did not originally belong to Japan. Building on this assumption, it was asserted that in order to expunge such harmful influences it was necessary to return to "pure" Japanese things. For those who took this view, "overcoming modernity" was nothing other than a return to that which is pure and Japanese. Here "modernity" can be said to have been regarded as something essentially alien to oneself as a Japanese person. According to the second understanding, on the other hand, "modernity" was by no means something belonging to others, but rather a problem belonging to Japanese people themselves and the place in which they currently existed. It tried to look directly at the "self" that the first understanding had overlooked or misapprehended.

The first understanding can be seen in Kawakami's "Conclusion" to the symposium "Overcoming Modernity" when he writes, "We intellectuals have indeed long been very unsatisfied on a personal level owing to the conflict between our Japanese blood that functions as the true driving force behind our intellectual activities and the Western thinking that has awkwardly imposed a system on it." Here "Japanese blood" is contrasted with "Western thinking that has awkwardly imposed a system on it." "Japanese blood" was presumably equivalent to what Kawakami described in the symposium as "the true nature of Japanese people." It was claimed that since the Meiji period Japanese people had used "Western thinking" to express themselves, but this expression was full of cracks and contradictions. The "true nature" of Japanese people and this expression of it were thus taken to be clearly distinguishable and of different origin. Here we find the assertion that behind the Western thinking that awkwardly imposed its system on this "true nature," that is, behind "modernity," there was a pure Japanese nature, and if the Western thinking that had covered it were stripped away, a return to this "true nature" would be possible. "Modernity" was thought of as being like a coat given to the Japanese by someone else, and its harmful effects were thus not their own responsibility.

Nakamura Mitsuo can be cited as an example of someone who had this second understanding. Nakamura had indeed used the phrase "overcoming" modernity in his previously mentioned essay "Doubts About 'Modernity.'"

He addressed this problem because Japanese modernity had a "sad underbelly." He also expressed this "sad underbelly" with the phrase "spiritual deformity." Quoting a passage from Natsume Sōseki (1867–1916)'s novel *And Then*[33] in which the protagonist likens Meiji Japan, a society trying to digest Western culture as quickly as possible and compete with the West, to "a frog competing with a bull" and warns, "Careful now or you'll split your belly," Nakamura describes the "spiritual deformity" Japan had to undergo beginning in the Meiji period. "Intent only on 'hastily' conforming to the superficial trends of the times, we have lost the habit of thinking about things for ourselves."[34] In Nakamura's view, having lost the habit of thinking about things for ourselves was the greatest problem concomitant with Japanese "modernity."

In his understanding, however, this was the result of Japan's own modernization and the responsibility of Japanese people themselves rather than someone else. "Assuming that having fallen into this confusion as a result of the particular influence of the West is our responsibility, trying to expunge Western culture at this point will not remove this malign effect at its root."[35] Nakamura, unlike Kawakami, understood himself as being right in the middle of a distorted modernity. According to Nakamura, this distortion of the spirit existed within those who advocated the expulsion of Western culture and a return to the Japan of the past. They too were people who had "lost the habit of thinking about things for themselves." Critical of their efforts, he writes, "I cannot believe that a project as serious as the cultural awakening of a nation can be accomplished through such facile spiritual undertakings."

(4) Shimomura Toratarō's "Modernity"

Among all of the participants in the "Overcoming Modernity" symposium, it was Shimomura Toratarō who most clearly asserted that "modernity" was not something belonging to others but the environment in which Japanese people themselves existed. Shimomura did not submit an article for the symposium, but when *Overcoming Modernity* was published as a book by Sōgensha in 1943 it included his essay "The Direction of Overcoming Modernity."[36] In it he writes, "Modernity is us. Overcoming modernity is overcoming ourselves. To somehow criticize it as though it were someone else's problem can only be described as facile."[37] These words convey a deep-seated antipathy toward those who argued about "modernity" as though it were something alien that essentially had nothing to do with them. Shimomura recoiled from the pronouncements of such people as "shameless blather." Here he was undoubtedly referring to the remarks made at the symposium by Kawakami and Kamei.

Profoundly connected to this understanding of "modernity," Shimomura's thoughts regarding the issue of "overcoming modernity" also differed greatly from those of the other participants. On the one hand, he addresses it not as a specifically Japanese issue but rather as first a European or indeed a universal problem. According to his remarks at the "Overcoming Modernity" symposium, the problem of "overcoming modernity" as a universal problem was nothing other than the problem of the gap between external "civilization" achieved through science, technology, and machines and internal "culture." It was the problem of a spirit that could not fully adapt to the development of "civilization." Shimomura spoke of this problem of "overcoming modernity" as one that lay not in rejecting "civilization" and smashing its machines but "on the contrary, in culture actively chasing down civilization and taking control of it."[38] To attempt to expunge modernity as an "evil era" was simply to try to avert one's eyes from reality, a stance Shimomura found unacceptable. What Shimomura thought of as "overcoming modernity" was overcoming the problems latent in modernity based on having recognized its "positive nature."

To Shimomura, this was a universal problem and at the same time a Japanese problem. In "The Direction of Overcoming Modernity" he writes, "Our predecessors and we ourselves have in fact worked to adopt the modern West and have grown by doing so." He then continues, "Today we are in the position of reflecting on and critiquing what was received, how, and to what extent. This is all that the question of overcoming modernity means for us."[39] To Shimomura, the question of "overcoming modernity" involved examining the results of receiving modernity, bringing their problematic aspects into relief, and considering the issues thus raised. There was thus an aspect in which it had the character of a "confrontation with modern Europe." This was not, however, a process of replacing European modernity with something Japanese or something premodern and "pure."

As for how this overcoming was to be carried out, unfortunately in this essay Shimomura offers only broad suggestions. He goes no further than speaking of the "vegetative character" of the Japanese intellect and the need for the construction of a "theory of intellectual improvement" in the modern era on the model of Spinoza.[40] What he meant by the words "vegetative character" and "theory of intellectual improvement" is not revealed in this essay, but after the war in 1946 he published an essay entitled "Theory of

Intellectual Improvement" in the newly established journal *Outlook*.[41] This text provides insight into what Shimomura meant by "intellectual improvement." He begins by explaining the "vegetative character" of the Japanese intellect through its relationship to nature. According to him, Japanese people have "extremely sensitive and delicate senses, feelings, and wisdom" regarding nature. "Diverse and changeable" nature had compelled "minute observation and prompt action." While this stance also includes "prompt action," fundamentally it is characterized by a "passivity" that tries to "obey" a nature that is diverse and displays surprising, unpredictable changes. This had indeed created a delicate sensitivity and detailed understanding of nature. However, this was completely "passive, empirical knowledge" and not "active, constructive knowledge that seeks to actively operate on nature and make it conform to our will."[42] Shimomura called this character of the Japanese intellect "vegetative."

In contrast to this, modern science and technology, or "modernity," was based on active, constructive knowledge that seeks to make nature conform to our will. To put it in terms of the question of "what was received, how, and to what extent" cited above, Japanese modernization had not reached the point of adopting this "active, constructive" attitude. Shimomura's "theory of intellectual improvement" can be thought of as improving an "obeying" intellect into an "active, constructive" intellect. Shimomura understood the problem of "overcoming modernity" in Japan as overlapping with intellectual improvement in this sense.

(5) What Came Out of the "Overcoming Modernity" Symposium

As we have seen, the symposium's participants differed greatly when it came to their understanding of "modernity" and how to think about "overcoming" it. But genuine debate over these differences was not joined. In this sense the symposium cannot be considered a success. Nevertheless, "overcoming modernity" became "magic words" that came to hold great power. They acquired this power because they created an image that was key to justifying the war. The symposium itself may have been simply an empty shell that failed at the "formation of ideas," but through this image devoid of content it served to cover up the true nature of a war that involved competition by imperialist great powers and the invasion of Asian countries. The symposium whose results were published as *Japan and the Perspective of World History* also played this kind of role. This is plainly evident in Kōyama Iwao's remarks at the third symposium, "The Philosophy of Total War." "It must be said that this war is a change in thought concerning order, in short, a change in worldview."[43] In *Japan's Task and World History*, published immediately after *Japan and the Perspective of World History*, Kōyama expresses this more clearly. "The Great East-Asian War is a war to change the global order. It is not a war within the modern world, but an epochal conflict to emerge beyond the modern world. This is ultimately the root cause of the Great East-Asian War being a total war."[44]

The debate at this symposium on "overcoming modernity" may have been empty, with no substantial content having been conferred by these discussions. It played a major role, however, by providing a "container" in which those involved could insert their own meaning. In this sense, this symposium actively supported the war ideology of the governing system.

Part III

The Period of Development—
Postwar Philosophy

Chapter 9

Starting from Defeat

1. The Issues of "Modernity" and "Subjectivity"

(1) Immature Modernity

In 1945 Japan experienced a pivotal change in its thought and value systems as a result of its defeat in the war. What Maruyama Masao pointed out during this period was the "immaturity of modernity" in the path taken by Japanese history. In "Modern Thinking,"[1] an essay published in the first issue of *Culture Conference*,[2] a mimeograph magazine put out by a small group of intellectuals called "Youth Culture Conference"[3] (members of which also included Noma Hiroshi and Uchida Yoshihiko), Maruyama writes with a combination of irony and self-mockery.

> If I compare the atmosphere of the last few years, in which the predominant discourse among the scholars, writers, and critics we are supposed to respect was one in which the modern mind-set was notorious and treated as though it were the ultimate source of all contemporary evils, or, failing that, "modernity" was allowed to have simply played a role in the past and the only question—even, or indeed uniquely, in this country—was to "overcome" it, with today's Japan that is learning the ABCs of modern civilization from Douglas MacArthur, I cannot help but feel a deep emotion in which our misery and ridiculousness are intermingled.[4]

"Overcoming modernity," needless to say, refers to the symposium discussed in chapter 8. As noted in that chapter, Kawakami Tetsutarō and most of the other participants advocated expunging the Western thinking that had imposed an ill-fitting system on Japanese intellectual activity since the Meiji period—in other words, "modernity"—and returning to Japan's "true nature." In contrast, Maruyama questions whether a "modernity" to be overcome had existed in Japan in the first place. In "Modern Thinking," he writes, "The fact that in our country modern thinking had not even been truly acquired, let alone reached the point of being 'overcome,' has at last become clear in the eyes of all. As a result, when studying our modern intellectual history, the need to begin by tiresomely repeating this basic proposition as in the past has for the moment greatly diminished."[5]

In opposing "overcoming" modernity, however, Maruyama did not take the view that modernity was "irrelevant" in Japan. He opposed the simplistic equating of modern and Western, or modern thought and Western thought, and on the contrary looked for instances of the "autonomous emergence of modern thought" within the path Japanese thought had taken in the past. One such era he focused on was the Edo period. He expressed a desire to make the task of "searching for the wellspring of modernity as it trickles out in obscure, subtle ways" in the intellectual history of the Tokugawa period his own. Maruyama's *A Study of the History of Japanese Political Thought*[6] was published in 1952, but preparations for it are thought to have begun during the war, and this work is presumably what he had in mind when he made this statement.

The concerns about "immature modernity" raised by Maruyama were broadly shared by writers and social scientists after the war. For example, in an essay entitled "Creating a Modern Type of Human Being"[7] included in *Human Foundations of Modernization*[8] (1948), Ōtsuka Hisao (1907–1996) argues that to democratically rebuild the economy we must begin with the modernization/democratization of the human subject, or the formation of a modern/democratic type of human being. The phrase "the enormous undertaking of establishing a modern character" also appears in Maruyama's "Modern Thinking," and it is clear that he and Ōtsuka shared an awareness of the establishment of modern human beings who would undertake modernization within social systems as an important issue.

For Maruyama, the task of establishing democracy was not simply a matter of adopting a system in which the people hold and exercise power, but rather one that could only be realized by constantly providing this system with authenticity through the establishment of this kind of modern character. This is the case because, particularly in a society in which the formation of diverse, autonomous groups, free discussion within them, and competition between them through debate that constitutes the foundation of democracy is not sufficiently mature, such a system is constantly being eroded and "cemented" by premodern morals. From this perspective, in a speech entitled " 'Being' and 'Doing' " he makes the following assertion.

> Democracy can only come to life when the people are on constant guard against the system's becoming an end in itself—its fetishization—and adopt a stance of constantly monitoring and criticizing the system's actual workings.[9]

Maruyama's understanding that genuine democracy is only realized and can only survive when there is constant democratization through an independent character played an important role in democracy putting down its roots in postwar Japan.

But this of course does not mean that there were not areas in which this approach was inadequate. For example, it fails to address the people who were made to suffer various hardships under Japan's colonial rule prior to its defeat. Tajiri Yūichirō (born in 1954) writes, "With few exceptions such as Takeuchi Yoshimi, there was little interest in how we should share history with our Asian neighbors." Regarding people in Asian countries having been made to suffer under Japanese colonial rule, he writes, "Without addressing this fact, Japan's rebirth runs the risk of being full of self-deception. But the point of view of postwar democratic intellectuals was limited to Japanese domestic affairs in a narrow sense, and did not include the idea of deepening our self-improvement (democratization) as Japanese by addressing the people subjected to colonial rule."[10]

(2) Criticism of "Modernism"

A controversy referred to as the "subjectivity debate"[11] that occurred among writers in Japan after the war also drew in philosophers, and it too involved the question of the establishment of the modern subject discussed above. Leaders on one side included Ara Masahito (1913–1979) and Honda Shūgo (1908–2001), who wrote mainly for *Modern Literature*. In an article entitled "A Literary Image of Humanity,"[12] Ara writes of those responsible for the proletarian literary movement, "While they may be overcoming modernity in their worldview and political activities, when it comes to the aspects of ethics, truth, and perception that support this as the bottom of the iceberg they remain mired in the premodern." In other words, he points out that while intellectually gazing out on "tomorrow" (a socialist society), physically they remained caught up in "yesterday" (premodernity). On this basis, he argues that the goal of the democratic revolution was in fact "catching up to modernity," writing, "To begin with, what is needed is the establishment of ourselves as a modern . . . petit bourgeoisie intelligentsia."[13] Here too the establishment of the modern self is emphasized as a pressing task.

On the other hand, Maruyama and Ōtsuka, as well as *Modern Literature* writers such as Ara and Honda, were heavily criticized as "modernists" by the Marxists who had become the leading figures in the postwar public discourse. In "Modernism and Its Overcoming" (1948) published in the journal *Vanguard*, for example, Kurahara Korehito (1902–1991) criticizes "modernism," writing that by "promoting individualism, weakening the spirit of social solidarity among the general public and between the general public and the intelligentsia, and rejecting the social and moral responsibility of artists" it "causes a loss of confidence in the establishment of a new, rational society."[14]

Ultimately, the critique of those writing from a Marxist perspective was that by talking about the establishment of the modern individual, the "modernists" had stealthily replaced the issue of class with the issue of the independence of the individual and averted people's eyes from the realities of class warfare. Conversely, however, those who criticized "modernists" in this way averted their own eyes from the problem of how to overcome the individual mode of thinking and premodern nature of human relationships still present in the postwar period and failed to address it directly. It may also be fair to say that they mistook this modernity that was in fact not fully realized for something that had already been overcome or surpassed.

(3) The Subjectivity Debate

The problem of subjectivity was first raised from within the domain of philosophy by Umemoto Katsumi (1912–1974). Umemoto had studied under Watsuji Tetsurō and had been a teacher at Mito High School before the war, but after Japan's defeat he was highly conscious of the fact that in the face of fascism "I had no retort . . . [I experienced] intellectual defeat" and gradually began to approach Marxism. During this process he wrote "Materialism and Humanity: Marxism and Religious Elements"[15] (1947). In this essay, after stating that "the scientific truth which sheds light on the material conditions of human liberation and the existential pillars of the human beings that are thereby liberated must remain in constant contact with each other,"[16] Umemoto points out that this unity has not been consciously reflected on within Marxism and has not been given its proper place within Marxist theory; in other words, there is a "gap" between theory and practice or between scientific truth and human subjectivity. This claim drew a sharp response from Marxists, sparking what came to be known as the "subjectivity debate."

Umemoto's theory of subjectivity was an attempt to answer the questions raised by Tanabe Hajime, who had begun to speak out actively on political issues after the war on the basis of "repentance" (see the next chapter). In 1946 Tanabe published essays such as "Urgent Matters for Political Philosophy"[17] and "Between the Socialist Party and the Communist Party"[18] and discussed the role political philosophy should play in the new era. But in the same year he also published "Christianity, Marxism, and Japanese Buddhism: Anticipating a Second Reformation"[19] and argued for a new form of religion in which religious liberation was at the same time social liberation. Citing the paradoxical contradiction that exists between the rational system of scientific socialism and practical subjectivity, in this work he discusses the negative mediation of this contradiction between necessity and freedom by "nothingness."[20]

Umemoto raises the issue of subjectivity again in "The Logicality of Nothingness and Factiousness"[21] (1948), writing, "How can we authentically be ourselves amid objective historical necessity? How can that which is understood, rather than simply understanding, combine with the deepest roots of our existence?"[22] As a means of answering this question, he turns to Tanabe Hajime's "dialectic of nothingness," which involves the "death and resurrection" of the individual. But there were two sides to Umemoto's assessment of Tanabe. While on the one hand he accepts the significance of "nothingness" Tanabe describes in the context of the subject arising through self-consciousness, on the other hand he criticizes this for having the potential for metaphysical substantiation.

Umemoto's subjectivity and "gap" theories sparked a wide-ranging, lively debate at the time. Tairako Tomonaga (born in 1951) divides participants in this debate into four groups: those, such as Shimizu Ikutarō (1907–1988) and Miyagi Otoya (1908–2005), who asserted a scientific basis for the concept of subjectivity; those, such as Maruyama Masao and Mashita Shin'ichi (1906–1995), who tried to reinterpret Umemoto's concept of subjectivity through their own worldviews and methodologies; writers and critics at *Modern Literature*; and orthodox Marxists such as Matsumura Kazuto (1905–1977).[23]

In "Revisionism in Philosophy: On the Perspective of Umemoto Katsumi"[24] (1948), Matsumura asserts that Umemoto understands Marxism objectively and does not understand its subjective aspect correctly. According to Matsumura, the subjective aspect of Marxism is nothing other than "the interests of the working class, the necessity of its liberation, the class consciousness that is formed amid joint struggle, and the consciousness of solidarity,"[25] but Umemoto does not address this, focusing instead on the "fundamental self-interest" inside human beings and looking for the emergence of the subject where the "essence of the self" is obtained by negating this selfishness. In Matsumura's view, this was an attempt to ethically sanctify the subject, and this stance adopted by Umemoto amounted to Marxist ethical revisionism. Regarding the "gap" between theory and practice, Matsumura argues that Marxism is essentially practical in its stance, aiming at the liberation of the working classes, and the "gap" Umemoto posits does not exist—"the 'gap' is not in Marxism, but in those who feel there is a 'gap' in Marxism."[26]

Mashita Shin'ichi put together a collection of essays entitled *The Subjectivity Debate*[27] in 1948 in order to refocus this debate that had developed in such diverse directions and give "subjectivity" a clear conceptual definition. While fundamentally adopting a Marxist perspective, Mashita did not understand materialism as simply a logic of existence or something understood objectively from a scientistic perspective; he emphasized that it was the true task of the era to take up the "question, unavoidable for every human being who thinks and acts, of how to live," for oneself, and to "understand thoroughly one's views of the world and of life to their depths."[28]

(4) Takeuchi Yoshimi's Critique of Modernism

Takeuchi Yoshimi criticized modernism from a completely different perspective than Marxism. What he called "modernism" was a way of thinking in which Westernization was progress or a step forward for Japan (this included Marxism). In Takeuchi's understanding, Europe was by nature expansionist, so its invasion of the East was inevitable. The East had "resisted" this invasion, fallen back, and been defeated. In this "resistance," however, the East had truly been the East. Japan had not known "resistance" to this invasion (in this sense it was not part of the East). Without knowing "resistance," Japan had not had "the desire to preserve itself." It had always sought new things outside itself. Through these new things it had indeed realized progress. But this was progress in which it abandoned itself, the "progress of a slave."[29] In other words, here Japan had no "subjectivity." This lack of subjectivity was criticized by Takeuchi.

Takeuchi thus criticized modernity for lacking "subjectivity," and in "The Problem of Modernism and the Problem of Ethnicity,"[30] published in *Literature* in 1951, he explains this in relation to "ethnicity." On the one hand, Takeuchi acknowledges the role modernism played in the postwar cultural vacuum. But modernists steered clear of "blood-soaked nationalism"; "they made nationalism becoming ultra [nationalism] an event outside of their own responsibility." They were therefore unable to fully illuminate the "dark expanse" that stretched below it. But the "ethnicity" that dwells in these dark corners has a legitimate voice, and "this is also connected to the 'correct' nationalism in Asian countries other than Japan."[31] To avoid abandoning ourselves and to prevent dark forces from rising again, Takeuchi believed we had no choice but to stare into this dark expanse.

2. Toward the Realization of Peace

(1) Efforts Toward the Realization of Peace

The war, in which the Japanese people had left cruel scars on many as perpetrators of violence and had also experienced horrors themselves, had ended, and based on profound reflection on these circumstances the first intellectual tasks addressed in the postwar period were the establishment of democracy and the realization of peace. One of the figures who played a major role regarding the latter was Yoshino Genzaburō (1899–1981). Yoshino is known as the author of *How Do You Live?*,[32] originally published as a volume in the *Japan Young Citizen Library*[33] in 1937, but in 1946 he became the first editor-in-chief of the magazine *The World*,[34] and through this position and other activities, such as organizing a working group on the issue of peace, dedicated himself to opposing war and promoting peace.

Amid global tensions that were rising once again after the Second World War and inspired by "An Appeal for Peace by Social Scientists: A Statement by Eight UNESCO Social Scientists Regarding Causes of Tension That Lead to War," a statement issued by UNESCO in July of 1948[35] (*The World*, January 1949), Yoshida organized a "Roundtable on the Issue of Peace" and suggested to writers who contributed essays to *The World* that along with undertaking the study of peace they should issue a joint statement with an eye to its realization. Those who agreed—including Abe Yoshishige, Ōuchi Hyōe, Shimizu Ikutarō, Maruyama Masao, and Kuno Osamu, as well as Watsuji Tetsurō, Amano Teiyū, and Noda Matao—released a "Statement by Japanese Scientists Regarding War and Peace"[36] in December of 1948. This declaration made several strong assertions: through nuclear weapons war could lead to an extinction crisis for humanity; peace was to be realized not simply by maintaining the status quo but by the active improvement of the current circumstances; what was needed in concrete terms was the elimination of inequality and the realization of social justice; and science and education had an important role to play in solving the various problems facing society.[37] On this basis, the following year the Tokyo Peace Working Group and Kyoto Peace Working Group were organized, and amid ongoing debate subsequent declarations were issued, such as the "Peace Working Group Statement on the Issue of Peace"[38] (1949) and, following the outbreak of the Korean War, "The Third Statement on Peace"[39] (1950).

Building on the activism of the peace working groups, in 1958 a constitutional issues working group was organized. In response to the government having begun planning constitutional reform and establishing a constitution examination committee under the auspices of the cabinet, the eight members of the working group, including Ōuchi Hyōe, Kaya Seiji, Yanaihara Tadao, and Yukawa Hideki, argued that the members of the government committee were biased and did not represent the broader public will and common sense, and called for the constitution to be examined from the perspective of defending its fundamental principles of peace and freedom (Maruyama Masao, Mutai Risaku, Tanikawa Tetsuzō, Kuno Osamu, and Kuwabara Takeo also participated). Confronted by the rise of a campaign to support the constitution centered around the activities of this working group, the movement for constitutional reform was forced into retreat.

While initially the movement to realize peace was carried out mainly by academics, eventually it developed into a form involving ordinary citizens. Tsurumi Shunsuke (1922–2015), known for having introduced American pragmatism to Japan, and author Oda Makoto (1932–2007) played a major role in this development. Tsurumi's intellectual starting point after the war was *The Science of Thought*,[40] a magazine he founded in May of 1946 along with Taketani Mitsuo, Takeda Kiyoko, Tsuru Shigeto, and Maruyama Masao.[41] One of its slogans was "the people's philosophy." This magazine aimed to make intellectual activity available to individual ordinary citizens rather than limit it to groups of experts. Its goals were for ideas to be held by individuals rather than groups, and for people to weave philosophical thought into the activities of daily life as participants in these activities rather than in isolation from them. Tsurumi also emphasized thought being tied to action, and his active involvement in civil movements included organizing the Association of the Silent Voices[42] together with political scientist Takabatake Michitoshi (1933–2004) and artist Kobayashi Tomi (1930–2003) in opposition to the revision of the Japan–U.S. Security Treaty in the 1960s, as well as its offshoot, the Japan "Peace for Vietnam!" Committee,[43] together with Oda Makoto and Kaikō Takeshi (1930–1989) in 1965.

Ethicist Moritaki Ichirō (1901–1994), himself an atomic bomb survivor, organized the World Conference Against Atomic and Hydrogen Bombs, and the image of him staging hunger strikes in Hiroshima Peace Memorial Park when nuclear tests were carried out and appealing for the abolition of nuclear weapons is etched in our memories. Natural scientists also played a major role in efforts to promote peace after the war. Yukawa Hideki was a signatory to the Russell-Einstein Manifesto issued in 1955, and together with Tomonaga Shin'ichirō (1906–1979) from 1957 he played an important role in organizing the Pugwash Conferences, an initiative that aimed to realize the spirit of this Manifesto. Beginning in 1962, he and Tomonaga organized the Kyoto Scientists' Conference, to which they invited scholars in the humanities and social sciences such as Tanikawa Tetsuzō, Kuwabara Takeo, and Nanbara Shigeru, and argued for the necessity of efforts to abolish nuclear weapons and war and the magnitude of scientists' responsibility.

(2) Thought Concerning Peace

One text that can be cited as a theoretical examination of peace is Kuno Osamu's essay "The Logic of Peace and the Logic of War" (1949). In his "Commentary" to volume 4 of the *Postwar Japanese Thought Series*, *Thought on Peace* (1968), Tsurumi Shunsuke praised Kuno for this essay that, at a time when it was vociferously argued that the theory of peace should be subordinate to revolutionary thought, asserted the relative independence of these pursuits and demonstrated that the path of building a system of thought that begins with the demand for peace was open.[44] According to Kuno, the only way for a "logic of peace" to oppose the "logic of war" (the idea that war is inevitable as long as humanity has the instinct to fight, and the only way to oppose organized violence by groups utilizing tactics and strategy is with similar violence) is to overcome the temptation to violence and rely as much as possible on nonviolent resistance. In other words, in facing the challenge of violence the only way forward was to adhere to an attitude of thorough disobedience and noncollaboration.[45] In order to maintain this mentality of "passive resistance," it was necessary to begin by having "a sense of active loathing for war." On this basis, we must understand the "anti-value" of war and make sure that this sense of loathing is not clouded by a way of thinking that distinguishes between just war and unjust war. In addition, we must also strive to ensure that the right to oppose war is guaranteed in law, and along with clarifying the conditions that give rise to war (social psychology conditions, economic conditions, and so on) work to resolve them.[46] Kuno thus laid out a path toward the formulation of a "logic of peace" in contrast to the "logic of war."

In response to talk of peace or attempts to pursue it, the criticism was constantly being made that while this is indeed a worthy ideal, in the real world where military might holds sway it amounts to nothing more than empty theorizing. Pacifism is one of the principles on which the Constitution of Japan is based. Its preamble states, "We, the Japanese people, desire peace for all time and are deeply conscious of the high ideals controlling human relationship." It then continues, "We have determined to preserve our security and existence, trusting in the justice and faith of the peace-loving peoples of the world."[47] This stance can be said to rest on a unilateral belief in the justice and good faith of other countries. The criticism that this is merely empty idealism can also be made. In "The Path Beyond Power Politics" (1966), however, Sakamoto Yoshikazu (1927–2014) asserts that this view contains "high wisdom." He explains this with the following metaphor: "It contains the philosophy and wisdom of the idea that the various peoples [of the world] may or may not be wolves, but until someone takes the first step of betting that they are not wolves they all will be wolves."[48] From a realist perspective, unilateral trust in others may seem an irrational choice, but it expresses the wisdom to pursue an ideal society founded on trust in humanity, and can be said to include "high-level rationality." The fact that peace has been preserved, however imperfectly, in the seventy years since the war can be described as a manifestation of this wisdom. Today, with confrontations and conflicts involving military force constantly arising, the need to solidify this wisdom can be said to be greater than ever.

As we have seen, while not necessarily voluminous, there was a significant body of thought on the issue of peace. In contrast to this, however, very little consideration of note was conducted regarding responsibility for the war, a premise on which this discourse on peace was based. In his "Commentary" to *Thought on Peace*, the fourth volume of the *Postwar Japanese Thought Series*, Tsurumi Shunsuke identifies this as one of the biggest problems in postwar thought. One of the few exceptions was Ienaga Saburō's *Responsibility for War* (1985). Ienaga took up this issue because various undesirable outcomes in the postwar period had arisen because the responsibility of the Japanese people for the ravages of the war had not been made clear, and because he believed that the examination of this responsibility would lead to avoiding future crises and preserving world peace and human security.[49] From this perspective, in this book Ienaga discusses in detail the horrors caused internationally (particularly in Asian countries) by the fifteen years of conflict from the Sino-Japanese War to the Second World War and responsibility for them, as well as the damage suffered by the Japanese people and responsibility for it. It is a work to which we must constantly return when discussing the issue of peace.

3. New Perspectives in the Postwar Era

(1) An Era of Popularization

The failure of the movement to stop the revision of the Japan-U.S. Security Treaty that marshalled great enthusiasm in the 1960s[50] gave rise to major changes in Japan's intellectual environment. The statements made by intellectuals on the topics of peace and democracy lost their efficacy, and many people tried to stay away from politics. Behind this lay the major changes Japanese society underwent as it charged headlong into what came to be known as the period of high economic growth. People's focus shifted from society and politics to their own daily lives, from the future as an ideal to being comfortable in the present, and from production to consumption. The character of daily life can be said to have gone from a life based on a sense of duty to a life grounded in desire.

The advent of the era of popularization meant the absence of a receptive audience for the opinions of intellectuals. How did intellectuals take this? An example of their response can be seen in Maruyama Masao. In "August 15th and May 19th: The Historical Significance of Japanese Democracy,"[51] published in 1960, Maruyama discusses "the becoming 'private' of the 'people.'" According to him, the postwar period had begun as a return from being "vassals" to being "the people," but this reversion had split into two directions, one toward "the making 'private' of the 'people,'" and another toward an "active reform movement." In other words, most of the "people" had moved toward "an increased focus on their own economic interests" and "enjoying their private lives."[52] To use Maruyama's phrasing from an earlier work, *The World of Politics*[53] (1952), the number of " '*members of the general public like grains of sand*' that are losing their distinctive individuality and unity of personality and becoming a uniform stereotype in their lives, in their judgments, and in their hobbies and tastes" was steadily growing.[54] Of course, Maruyama did not take a completely negative view of the becoming "private" of the "people." He had high hopes for the growth of interaction between the two types of "people" and the roots of democracy being cultivated. He expected postwar history to mark a turning point. But reality did not develop in accordance with his expectations. On the contrary, a scenario unfolded in which mutual understanding became more difficult.

Another figure who, as we have just seen in Maruyama, addressed the issue of how intellectuals view the general public was Yoshimoto Takaaki (1924–2012). In "What Is an Intellectual?"[55] (1960), Yoshimoto argues that in this impoverished and deformed society, the common people or general public are forced to have "daily experiences in which there are many complex resistances," and these "experiences of daily life" run counter to the culture and ideology dispensed by intellectuals as fictions and have the potential to transcend them.[56] From this perspective, in "What Are the Circumstances? 2 The Myth of the Postwar Intellectuals,"[57] included in *An Independent Intellectual Footing*[58] (1966), Yoshimoto criticizes Maruyama as follows.

> What is embossed on the way of thinking adopted by Maruyama Masao is in no sense a progressive stance but in fact a return to the prewar method of intellectuals confining themselves to their own circles, both intellectually and as a political group, and abandoning the task of "constantly drawing the original image of the general public into one's own thought" that is their responsibility and the greatest lesson taught by the war.[59]

In this way Yoshimoto can be described as having sought to destroy the "from intellectuals to the general public" way of thinking. Whether Yoshimoto was indeed able to approach the "original image of the general public" himself or whether his invocation of it was also a false representation is of course a question that must be asked.

(2) The Perspective of Citizens Living Ordinary Lives

Tsurumi Shunsuke, unlike Maruyama, tried to take a more positive view of the era of popularization. As already noted, from the start, *The Science of Thought*,[60] which Tsurumi founded along with like-minded editors, was grounded in the idea that thought is to be undertaken by each individual as they go about their daily life. When the sixth iteration of this journal launched in 1972, the following passage was included in the "On the Start of Publication" section in which the members of the editorial committee were listed.

> We view thought, first and foremost, as something that lives and works in people's daily lives. We aim to use the method of the "science of thought" to create independent thought rooted in daily life that, while critically confronting everydayness that is being managed and manipulated, distinguishes the richness of life that lies beneath this rigidity.[61]

Here it is claimed there is a rich life underlying an everydayness that is managed and manipulated, and that it is from this source that free thought will emerge. The "we" that is being addressed here is not the "we" of the general public as a lump lacking in individuality. It is individual people living their daily lives. *The Science of Thought* aimed to ground itself in the life underlying this everydayness. Tsurumi's focus on popular culture and "marginal art," that is, art made and enjoyed by people who are not experts (such as senryu poems, folk songs, and tea ceremonies), in works such as *On Marginal Art*[62] (1967) and *The History of Popular Culture in Postwar Japan*[63] (1984) can also be said to have been based on this stance.

In this era of popularization, Kuno Osamu advocated "citizenism."[64] This was based on the view that politics should not operate through power and orders, but rather should be supported by open groups in which people gather freely, debate freely, and out of this discussion seek direction in their actions, or by a society created by such groups.[65] Kuno calls citizens who participate in politics in this way "political citizens." These are people who are not involved in politics as a profession, but rather purely as citizens (as "apolitical" people). That is not to say, however, that such groups are concretely defined. Kuno's claims align with the question or reflection, "Does the greatest poverty of Japanese politics and culture perhaps arise from the absence of the capacity for self-governance?"[66] This is precisely why he sought to cultivate the capacity for self-governance in citizen movements.

This self-governing capacity cannot be developed by leaving thinking up to groups or leaders. "Individuals" must be independent, and each must be a subject that freely engages in debate. What is required here is "intellectual dialogue" in which "relying on each other's rationality, each party conveys to the other their true feelings and point of view. Each conveys to the other on which points and on what basis they agree and sympathize or disagree and do not sympathize."[67] What Kuno expected from philosophy was the "rational logic and rhetoric" to support this dialogue. He called this "citizen philosophy."

Chapter 10

The Postwar Kyoto School

1. The Development of Tanabe's Philosophy

(1) Critique of the Kyoto School

Kuki Shūzō passed away in 1941, Nishida Kitarō succumbed to illness in 1945, and in that same year both Tosaka Jun and Miki Kiyoshi died in prison. Kimura Motomori died suddenly in 1946, and with Japan's defeat in the war the Kyoto School reached a major turning point. Tanabe Hajime, who had been in charge of the philosophy course at Kyoto University, reached retirement age in 1945 and secluded himself in a mountain cottage in Kitakaruizawa, Gunma Prefecture. Kōyama Takao was barred from public office for statements he had made during the war, and Nishitani Keiji was barred from teaching.[1]

The Kyoto School thus lost its central figures one after another following the end of the war. On top of these losses, intense criticism was also leveled at statements Nishida, Tanabe, and their disciples had made during the war. A major characteristic of scholarship concerning Nishida's and Tanabe's philosophy that appeared immediately after the war was a stream of writings criticizing their views of history and the nation for being unscientific and providing an intellectual rationalization for Japan's wars of aggression. This includes, for example, writings by Nagata Hiroshi, Hayashi Naomichi, Yamazaki Ken, Yamada Sakaji, and Takeuchi Yoshitomo. The most vigorous criticism was developed by Nagata Hiroshi (1904–1947). In his *Philosophy and Democracy: A Critique of the Philosophy of Nishida and Tanabe*[2] (1948), Nagata finds the origins of Nishida's unscientific thinking in his idealistic character. In concrete terms, he points out that by confusing the contemplative process and the formative process of actual existence, or, in other words, by actualizing logical universals and understanding their "self-determining" as the creative process of actual existence, he could not help falling into a hollow understanding of history.

After the war, intense criticism was also directed toward the previously discussed "Overcoming Modernity" symposium and *The World Historical Perspective and Japan*, a collection of the results of symposia involving figures such as Nishitani, Suzuki Shigetaka, and Kōsaka Masaaki. For example, in "Modern Thought"[3] (1946), his first essay after demobilization, Maruyama Masao strongly criticizes intellectuals who "bowed their heads before the 'world historical' significance of fascism" before and during the war. In *A Critique of Nishida Philosophy*[4] (1949) Hayashi Naomichi also strongly condemns philosophers of the Kyoto School such as Kōsaka for having given the war a philosophical foundation, or, in other words, for "beautifying and sacralizing wars of invasion and trying to serve up ethical content for the aggressive framework of the East Asia Co-prosperity Sphere."[5]

Entering the 1950s, criticism of statements actively supporting the situation at the time by members of the Kyoto School became less prominent, while at the same time a tendency to avoid directly discussing Japanese philosophy from the prewar and wartime periods emerged. Of course, it goes without saying that it is important to consider what these philosophers said and with what intentions, what role this discourse played in history, why they were swept along by the trends of their era without being able to oppose them, and other such questions. However, it is also important to elucidate and consider, alongside or in addition to such questions, the significance of their philosophy itself—on the one hand its historical significance, and on the other its significance in relation to us today and the problems of our era. With steady efforts to this end having been made, forty or fifty years after the war ended Nishida's philosophy and the philosophy of the Kyoto School at last became subjects of objective study, freed from the emotional attachment of people of the same era and the antipathy they had faced in the postwar period. This pivot was led by the Nishida studies produced by Nakamura Yūjirō and Ueda Shizutaru in the 1980s and 1990s. In the afterword to 1994's *Collection of Writings Commemorating Fifty Years Since His Death: Nishida's Philosophy*,[6] its editor, Ueda Shizutaru, writes, "The long time frame required to consider 'that which is unchanging in Nishida's philosophy' has at last begun to be reached."[7] These words aptly express this turning point in the study of Nishida and his philosophy.

(2) Tanabe Hajime's "Philosophy as the Way of Repentance (Metanoetics)"

After Japan's defeat in the war, the Kyoto School received intense criticism as described above, but its members of course continued their philosophical undertakings in various forms. Here I would like to examine how this unfolded.

As has already been noted, Tanabe left his position upon reaching the age of retirement in 1945 and shut himself away in a mountain cottage in Kitakaruizawa, foregoing all public appearances. He remained active as a writer, however, and continued to have a significant influence after the war. He had left Kyoto, but in this sense the figure at the center of the postwar Kyoto School can be said to have been Tanabe Hajime. The starting point of Tanabe's postwar thought was *Philosophy as the Way of Repentance* (1946). Tanabe came to describe his own stance during this period using the words of this title, calling it "the way of repentance" or "the philosophy of the way of repentance." Tanabe's prewar thought was characterized by "the logic of species," but his postwar thought was characterized by this phrase of his own invention, "the way of repentance." Tanabe began speaking of "repentance" in 1944, and here I will begin by examining what he understood by this term.

In a lecture entitled "The Way of Repentance: Metanoetics" (1944), while on the one hand saying, "As a person, I feel indignation at the irrational things happening in this country," on the other hand Tanabe states that, unable to find measures to address this in the midst of a war, he was in a state of "not simply saying that I am powerless to act, but feeling that I am also profoundly powerless in terms of knowledge [philosophy]."[8] At the root of this sense of impotence was his having been swept along by the tide of the times, ultimately unable to actively resist limitations on academic freedom and freedom of speech, and his own philosophy having failed to provide the foundation for such resistance. Shame regarding this powerlessness, along with feelings of guilt for his own role in sending students to the battlefield, seems to have been what drove Tanabe to "repentance." This repentance, for Tanabe, did not stop at merely regretting his own mistakes or feeling shame at his own powerlessness; it meant "despairingly discarding oneself."[9] This "self" included the philosophical undertakings to which he had been devoted, which he called "self-powered philosophy" in the sense of philosophy supported by the autonomous power of reason. Tanabe experienced for himself the impotence of this approach.

At the same time, he also experienced a change or transformation. At the limit of self-awareness and the thorough examination of his own powerlessness, he experienced an encounter with another power that transcends the self and makes its life and actions possible. Tanabe states that this power is called "love" in Christianity and "mercy"[10] or "great compassion"[11] in Buddhism. He also describes this entire process of transformation, which involves the encountering of another power that transcends the self and is formed on the basis of the discarding of the self and being reborn, as "death and resurrection" and "the transformation of living while dying, living while being resurrected."[12] This is what Tanabe calls the "way of repentance."

Tanabe's new philosophical path began from this point. Not philosophy based on reason itself, but philosophy "another power lets me . . . carry out." Tanabe used the phrase "philosophy that is not philosophy" to describe this philosophy that is not philosophy in the ordinary sense. He uses the expression "*that is not philosophy*" because it is something that emerges after philosophy has been discarded. He describes it as "*philosophy* that is not philosophy," however, because it has passed through the negation of philosophy and become "something that satisfies the desire for thorough self-awareness and ultimate contemplation that is the aim of philosophy."

Tanabe also uses the term "metanoetics" to describe this "way of repentance" as "philosophy that is not philosophy." This coinage was inspired by the Greek word *metanoia* (μετάνοια) as spoken by John the Baptist in the Gospel of Matthew. Metanoia is made up of the words *meta* (after) and *noien* (see, think), and means to look back and consider one's actions or to regret. Tanabe overlaid his own idea of repentance on this term. At the same time, another reason he used this word is that "metanoetics" can also include the meaning of surpassing or going beyond expressed by the German word *Noetik*. The term *Noetik*, still occasionally used today, is derived from *noien*, and means science or scholarship related to knowledge or thinking. Tanabe presumably saw within this the *noien* functioning of *nous* (intelligence, reason), or, in other words, the "philosophy of reason" that characterizes Western philosophy. (Tanabe uses the Japanese Buddhist term *rikan*,[13] which means to directly observe universal truth and is composed of Chinese characters meaning "logic/reason" and "see/observe"). "Metanoetics" means something that goes beyond this; "meta-noetik," that is, "beyond *rikan*" or "beyond the philosophy of reason." In other words, with the term metanoetik Tanabe sought to express both a sense of regret or repentance and something that surpasses the philosophy of reason. He can be seen as having used this term in conjunction with the phrase "the way of repentance" to make up for what it does not adequately express on its own.

The main element of this "philosophy as the way of repentance," as indicated by the phrases "beyond *rikan*" and "beyond the philosophy of reason" quoted above, was a critique of reason or rational philosophy. Of course, philosophy can be said to have already included the criticism of reason within its domain of inquiry. The prime example of this is Kant's critique of reason. Tanabe himself acknowledges this. According to him, however, Kant did not make the reason that engages in this critique itself the target of criticism. In this sense Kant's critical philosophy did not criticize reason in its entirety. Tanabe sought a thorough critique of reason that does not place the reason that is the agent of criticism beyond its purview but rather includes it as an object of criticism. Tanabe calls this thoroughgoing critique of reason "absolute criticism." In Tanabe's understanding, it is only when a critique of reason reaches the thoroughness of an absolute critique that it can become a genuine critique of reason. Engaging in an "absolute critique" in this sense can be described as the central task of the way of repentance.

Based on this understanding, in this text Tanabe engages in a critique of the thought of philosophers such as Kant, Hegel, Schelling, Nietzsche, Heidegger, and Eckhart, and attempts its "dismantling." This was not, however, an effort to simply negate or reject their ideas. Tanabe's intention was on the contrary to "revive and develop [them] using the approach of the way of repentance."[14] His aim was to impart concrete content to "philosophy as the way of repentance" through this "critical dismantling."

In the final chapter of *Philosophy as the Way of Repentance*, Tanabe discusses "The Religious View of Society as an Outlook of the Way of Repentance." This chapter title aptly expresses one of the characteristics of the way of repentance. Namely, the way of repentance is by no means individual self-awareness or something closed off within the self. On the contrary, it is open to others and to society. It is in the "standpoint of social cooperation" that it truly becomes concrete.

As noted above, Tanabe describes the other power that enables a transformation at the limit of repentance as both "love" and "great mercy," and the work of this power is not complete with the "death and resurrection" of the self. On the contrary, it requires those who have achieved rebirth to work for the benefit of those who have not yet experienced it and demands the mediation of the work of salvation of the absolute. "The saving of oneself becomes genuine through its transformation into the saving of others. Becoming the intermediary of absolute nothingness-that-is-love and leading others to salvation on the basis of love in this way is philosophy. This can therefore be called the 'path of enlightenment-that-is-the path of evangelizing.'"[15]

Tanabe's attention then turned to the task of realizing a *society* based on this "guidance toward salvation on the basis of love." He describes the establishment of a "society that achieves equality in its order through people coexisting, cooperating, and leading each other to salvation"[16] as being a "demand of history." From the introduction to *Existence, Love, and Practice*[17] (1947) it is evident that Tanabe took a great interest in Christianity from this perspective. This was the result of his belief that Christianity provided a clearer and more concrete guide to the realization of this kind of society than Buddhism. This view can also be found in *Apology for Christianity* (1948), his follow-up to *Existence, Love, and Practice*.

(3) The Philosophy of Death

The most important work in Tanabe Hajime's late thought is "Ontology of Life or Dialectic of Death?,"[18] an essay begun in 1957 and completed in 1958. (It was published in part as "Todesdialektik" in *Martin Heidegger zum siebzigsten Geburtstag, Festschrift* in 1959).

This work covers a wide range of topics, but running through it is an awareness of the modern era as a "century of death" symbolized by nuclear weapons as the pinnacle of science and technology. Tanabe asserts that what is needed in the present era is a turning away from the "philosophy of life," which is deeply bound to science and technology and aims to provide a grounding for the direct appreciation of life, toward a "philosophy of death" that directly confronts the fact that the modern era is an "era of death." In an essay published during this period entitled "Memento Mori," he emphasizes the necessity of breaking through the impasse of the "philosophy of life," which has banished the death that is the flipside of life from its sight and sought only the extension of life, by bringing this death that underlies life within its field of view.

This conception of the "philosophy of death" was also closely tied to the task of confronting Heidegger. Seeing Heidegger's philosophy as the "philosophy of life" of course requires explanation, because death was an important theme for him as well. Tanabe, who had studied at the University of Freiberg in the 1920s and attended Heidegger's lectures, was well aware of this. He criticizes the "self-conscious ontology of Heidegger's lectures" for merely "taking the possibility of decisive death as a conceptual sign and developing analytically the self-conscious existence of life in linguistic interpretation by relying on its mediation."[19] He says that in Heidegger, "death" is only addressed as a "conceptual sign" leading to the self-consciousness of "life." For example, Tanabe rejects Heidegger's position, presented in *Holzwege*, that "to be grateful for the blessing of existence, sacrifice the self, and obtain the noble freedom to serenely give up all things"[20] is the mission of human beings as a stance of separating oneself from actual society and the problems it faces. He argues that this "idealistic idealism" lacks the power to "transcend objective paradox." Tanabe's "philosophy of death" can indeed be said to have confronted this kind of Heideggerian philosophy.

Tanabe viewed "death" not only as a problem common to the era, but also as an individual problem, the problem of an individual being. For Tanabe, the problem of death, first and foremost, was something that concerned death in the second person, that is, the death of "you." Moreover, this was not simply the death of "you," but the problem of death in the *relationship* between you and me. More precisely, he addressed death as a problem of the *relationship* between you who are dead and me as someone who yet lives. Here we find one of the characteristics of Tanabe's "philosophy of death."

Normally we think of your death as bringing about the end of my interaction with you. Death is the conclusion of our relationship. However, not everything ends with it. Death seeps into life. Through this process, a new relationship is created. A new horizon of relating opens up. Death is not something that extinguishes our relationship; on the contrary, it is something that can also create it. Here death is viewed not as simply external, or as the limit of life, but rather as something that makes its way into life and forms a relationship with it. It is this kind of new relationship with a dead person created in this way that Tanabe seeks to address.

What makes this kind of relationship with the dead possible, in Tanabe's understanding, is love. In "Ontology of Life or Dialectic of Death?," he writes, "The love of the dead person, who during their life had wished the living person to be like this or like that, is renewed again and again for the living person even after their death, and this love, operating ceaselessly through the mediation of the love of the living person for the dead person, realizes death and resurrection as the reciprocal existential cooperation of love."[21] Here Tanabe coins the phrase "existential cooperation" to express a reciprocal relationship, made possible by love and transcending life and death, between a person who is dead and a person who is alive.

"Existential cooperation" is this kind of relationship formed on the foundation of the love of the person who has died for the person who is alive and the love of the person who is alive for the person who has died.

However, this does not mean a closed-off relationship between only you and me as people who love each other. Tanabe understands it on the contrary as a relationship open to others. From this perspective he looked toward Zen. He focused, for example, on the relationship between the master and the disciple seen in the koan "Daowu's Condolence Call" included in the *Blue Cliff Record*'s 55th Case. It involves a master trying to convey the truth to his disciple through his own death and leading him to enlightenment—a typical example of what is called "transfer of merit" (*pariṇāmanā*)[22] in Buddhism. Tanabe uses the term "monadological existential cooperation" to refer to the relationship seen here in which "the individual self-denyingly offers themselves to the whole while maintaining their individuality, . . . themselves allowing other individuals to live."[23]

Tying this even more closely to Buddhist tradition, Tanabe also refers to it as the "bodhisattva path." In Mahāyāna Buddhism, a bodhisattva is a being who, while having attained what is required to become a buddha, abandons this aim and instead turns their energy to the salvation of other living things, and the "bodhisattva path" refers to such actions, what they allow to live in others, and this being conveyed from one individual to another so that this relationship expands without limit.

In the introductory section of "Ontology of Life or Dialectic of Death?," regarding the "dialectic of death" Tanabe writes, "Surely this is nothing other than the Eastern thinking of Zen, which must break through the impasse of Western thinking."[24] What he presumably had in mind here was the realization of "monadological existential cooperation" through the "bodhisattva path" described above. Tanabe sought the possibility of "breaking through the 'era of death' " in "renewing human groups as species" through the realization of this kind of opened relationship.

2. The Development of the Philosophy of Nothingness (Emptiness)

(1) Hisamatsu Shin'ichi's "Atheism"

As noted in chapter 7, in his prewar work *Eastern Nothingness*, Hisamatsu Shin'ichi poses the question of what can be described as uniquely Eastern when confronting the Western philosophical tradition and expresses this unique element with the phrases "the metaphysical element of the East" and "Eastern nothingness." In *Atheism*[25] (1981), one of his major postwar works, he expresses it with this title—"atheism."

After the war, Hisamatsu continued his criticism of Western thought (see, for example, "The Character of Eastern Nothingness" in *The Way of the Absolute Subject* [1948]), but circumstances had arisen in which it was no longer possible to develop this critique by simply positioning Eastern thought in opposition to Western thought. It was an environment in which European history had become "world" history, in a manner of speaking, and Japan had been incorporated into this history in such a way that it could no longer be understood in terms of a simple East/West schema. Hisamatsu instead tried to view it from a perspective that transcended the modernity into which Japan had been incorporated, an approach he described as "postmodern." It was from this kind of perspective that he spoke about "atheism."

In "Atheism" (first published in 1949), an essay included in *Atheism*, Hisamatsu attempts to elucidate the characteristics of his own conception of "atheism" while comparing it to medieval and modern religion. He characterizes medieval religion as heteronomous religion centered on a god who is positioned as a transcendental deity. Modern religion, in contrast, is an autonomous religion centered on human beings—in a sense, an atheistic religion. Here, however, people seek to extend themselves without limit and fall into crisis. Hisamatsu expresses this with the phrase "fundamental crisis of human nature." The horizon of the postmodern religion Hisamatsu contemplates opens up where this crisis is overcome. How can the "anthropocentrism" of the modern era be overcome without going back to heteronomous religion? According to Hisamatsu, this can only be accomplished by thoroughly negating the autonomous self. He asserts that through this negation the true self "comes back to life." As he puts it in *Eastern Nothingness*, a "free body liberated from all limitations and contradictions" is born. People "awaken" to themselves as this kind of "free body." In this sense, Hisamatsu says that postmodern religion is not a religion of "faith" but a religion of "awakening."[26] Hisamatsu expresses his own postwar stance with this term, "awakening."[27] Moreover, it is not only the chosen few who are awakened; everyone becomes (or can become) a god or Buddha. No heteronomous god or Buddha exists. In this sense Hisamatsu calls his own stance "atheism" or "thoroughgoing atheism."

(2) NISHITANI KEIJI

After the war, Nishitani Keiji devoted most of his energies to the problem of nihilism. In *Nihilism*, published in 1949, he discusses nihilism from the perspective of philosophical history, addressing mainly the thought of Nietzsche, Stirner, and Heidegger, while in *What Is Religion?*, published in

1961, he examines the issue of nihilism in relation to the circumstances of the times in which we are living.

Modernity, according to Nishitani, is an era in which mechanization has progressed in all aspects of daily life through the remarkable development of science and technology. This has brought us a great number of conveniences. At the same time, however, it has also driven us to pursue unlimited desires. Nishitani says that an abyss of meaninglessness and purposelessness yawns beneath these desires. Human beings are placed in a state of desperately striving to produce ever more things ever more quickly without being able to find meaning in their efforts. This is what Nishitani calls nihilism.

According to Nishitani, this is not the "emptiness" in a normal sense that people experienced in the past. He describes the nihilism we are facing in the modern era as follows. "This emptiness extends to the place where god exists, becoming abyssal, and above this abyssal emptiness of no god, all life, that is, not only biological life and souls, but even spiritual, personal life, wears a mien of fundamental meaninglessness."[28] This kind of emptiness cannot be overcome simply by contraposing religion or ethics. If so, the only path that remains is not to avert our eyes from nihilism but rather confront it directly and overcome it from the inside. Nishitani expresses this as "overcoming nihilism through nihilism."[29]

With this focus on nihilism, Nishitani's thought possesses a unique character in the history of Japanese philosophy. He directs his gaze toward questions not posed by Nishida and Tanabe, and the philosophy of the Kyoto School can be said to have begun a new chapter in its development through his examination of this topic.

In thinking about "overcoming nihilism through nihilism," Nishitani draws on the concept of "emptiness" in Mahayana Buddhism. Of course, if the doctrine of "emptiness" is presented just as it is found in the Mahayana Buddhism of the past, it will not prove effective within the context of the abyssal nihilism of modernity. How the path to overcoming modern nihilism can be found while utilizing this concept is precisely the question Nishitani addresses in *What Is Religion?*, in which he speaks of "the standpoint of emptiness." Rather than simply accepting "emptiness" dogmatically, he attempts to incorporate it into his own way of living.

Here another viewpoint is layered on top of the way of looking at things that has become predominant in the modern era—the way of looking at things in which everything is judged from the usability perspective of what benefits it can bring. Nishitani expresses this with the term "double exposure."

> There is a Zen phrase, "skulls scattered across a field," and
> this field can be, for example, Ginza Street. . . . Ginza, while
> remaining the opulent Ginza of today, can be seen as a field of
> grass. It can be looked at like a "double exposure" photograph.
> It is in fact this kind of double exposure that reflects the truth.
> The truth is double layered. . . . a living person walking cheer-
> fully down the street can at the same time be seen in a double
> exposure as a dead person.[30]

The truth, or reality, is found where a grand avenue in a major city and
a field of grass touched by nothing but the wind, or life and death, are
superimposed on each other. "The standpoint of emptiness" is a stance in
which this superimposition of life and death is accepted as literal reality.

In *What Is Religion?*, Nishitani argues it is this kind of "standpoint of
emptiness" that can reveal the way forward for human beings who have fully
become agents of desire and mark the path to liberation from the nihility
that stretches below them. This is not, of course, an attempt to argue that the
path to overcoming nihilism is to be found in this kind of "double exposure"
theoretically. What is addressed is always the adopting of this kind of stance
oneself. In this sense Nishitani emphasizes "realization." He also describes
this with a Japanese term that means "understanding through experience"[31]
and the phrase "realization-that-is-understanding through experience." This
is not simply understanding "emptiness" on an intellectual level, but "taking
a step beyond the place of consciousness and reason" and understanding
it at the most fundamental level of life. In this sense, the "standpoint of
emptiness" is the "understanding through experience" of "emptiness." This
is where Nishitani sought the path to overcoming nihilism.

(3) Ueda Shizuteru

Ueda Shizuteru (1926–2019) studied under Nishitani and succeeded
Nishitani and Takeuchi Yoshinori as head of the religious studies course at
Kyoto University. Initially he studied German mysticism, particularly the
thought of Meister Eckhart, but at the foundation of his contemplation
was a profound understanding of Zen. Ueda developed his own distinctive
thought in the place where German mysticism and Zen thought overlap.
In writings collected in volume 8, *Non-Mysticism: Eckhart and Zen*,[32] of *The
Ueda Shizuteru Collection*,[33] Ueda extracts the fundamental experience shared

by the Eastern and Western traditions of Zen and Eckhart and expresses it with the fascinating phrase "nonmysticism."

Ueda begins by seeing the most notable characteristic of mysticism in "one." Mysticism aims to break through the normal way of being of the self and realize a state of "being one with god." Ueda, however, does not view this "one" as simply "unity," but rather as "unity-that-is-detachment."[34] Moreover, here he is asserting not merely that "unity" has the characteristic of "detachment" or arises out of "detachment," but rather that a movement or kinesis "from unity to detachment"[35] can be recognized. On the one hand, Eckhart speaks of the need to thoroughly abandon the self and become "one" with God. On the other hand, however, in order to abandon what can be described as the "attachment to the self" that remains in human beings in a unity with God, he requires even the "discarding of God." He says that it is only by "God returning to nothingness, and the human being also returning to nothingness" that a unity between God and the self can arise in a true sense. Ueda believed that what is being sought here is not simply "unity" but at the same time also an emergence or breaking free from that state.

In the case of Zen, the phrase "all things return to one" appears in Case 45 of *Blue Cliff Record*,[36] a famous collection of kōans. In the phenomenal world, all things are distinct and differentiated, but in the true world they are equal and inseparable. After it is said that "all things return to one," however, the question "to where does one return?" is then posed. Ueda believed that when such questions are asked, the world in which Zen demonstrates its true character appears before us.[37] In other words, in Zen "one" is not established as an absolute, and freely emerging from it is to be sought. This is where Zen's true worth lies. Ueda used the phrase "nonmysticism" to express this dynamism of freely leaving this "one" instead of remaining stuck in it found in both Zen and mysticism.

The study of Nishida's philosophy in Japan made great progress in the 1980s and 1990s, and laying the foundations for this was one of Ueda's major achievements. Drawing on Zen here as well, Ueda viewed Nishida's philosophy as having emerged from throwing himself into the gap between philosophy as reflective inquiry and the Zen approach of noncontemplation and self-consciously addressing the question of "Zen and philosophy." It was Ueda's understanding that within the melting pot of Nishida, so to speak, circumstances arise in which "faced with Zen, philosophy questions the fundamentality of its principles; faced with philosophy, Zen questions the logicality and concreteness of its world structure."[38] In works such as *Reading Nishida Kitarō*[39] (1991), Ueda lucidly describes Nishida's thought surrounding "pure experience" that emerged from the interweaving of these two forms of inquiry.

(4) The Spread of the Philosophy of "Nothingness"

After the war, the philosophy of "nothingness (emptiness)" inherited from Nishida and Nishitani also attracted the attention of many foreign scholars and was discussed in various forms, both as an approach capable of providing a perspective that differs from Western philosophy and as an undertaking with the potential to pioneer new philosophical possibilities through dialogue with its own unique ideas. Works such as Hans Waldenfels's *Absolutes Nichts*, James Heisig's *Philosophers of Nothingness*, and Bernard Stevens's *Topologie du néant* emerged out of this kind of interest.[40] Heisig criticizes the Kyoto School for lacking concrete understanding of social and historical issues and being incapable of being sufficiently critical on such matters, but at the same time also expresses hope that through its uniqueness (for example, its understanding of "self-awareness") this school of thought can make a positive contribution to "world philosophy."

Of course, notable research on the connection between the thought of the Kyoto School philosophers and Buddhist, particularly Zen, thought was carried out in Japan as well. For example, *Zen and the Kyoto Philosophy*,[41] published under the supervision of Ueda Shizuteru, focused mainly on Zen and discussed the thought of six philosophers: Nishida, D. T. Suzuki, Hisamatsu, Nishitani, Morimoto Shōnen (1889–1983), and Kataoka Hitoshi (1902–1993). This collection of essays focuses mainly on "Zen and philosophy," that is, the connection between Zen centered on "the practice of noncontemplation"[42] and philosophy, "the high-level contemplative activity of reflecting on reflection," and while it does not address the Kyoto School directly, it is nevertheless an important text in understanding the connection between this school's thought and that of Zen Buddhism.

The Kyoto School's concept of "absolute nothingness" has been examined not only from a Buddhist but also from a Christian perspective. A symposium on "The Kyoto School and Christianity" was organized by the Nanzan Institute for Religion and Culture in 1980, and the results were published the following year as *Absolute Nothingness and God: The Philosophical Tradition of Nishida and Tanabe and Christianity*.[43] This text aimed to create a dialogue between Christianity and the Kyoto School, which was attempting to give Eastern religious traditions, particularly Mahayana Buddhism, new life in the modern era. This of course raises the question of whether the Kyoto School faithfully represents the thought of Mahayana Buddhism, and this was one of the issues addressed by the symposium. In *Absolute Nothingness and God: The Philosophy of the Kyoto School*,[44] Onodera Isao attempts to lay out a Japanese approach to Christian theology through dialogue with the philosophers of the Kyoto School.[45]

There has also been great interest in the Kyoto School's tradition of the philosophy of religion and the philosophy of "absolute nothingness" in the Chinese-speaking world. For example, Taiwan's Ng Yu-Kwan (born in 1946) studied not only Nishida and Tanabe but also Hisamatsu Shin'ichi, Nishitani Keiji, Abe Masao (1915–2006), and Ueda Shizuteru, and, from the perspective of "absolute nothingness" being the most deeply rooted aspect of East Asian thought and spirituality, produced numerous writings on this subject, including *The Philosophy of the Kyoto School: Hisamatsu Shin'ichi*, *The Philosophy of Absolute Nothingness—Introduction to the Philosophy of the Kyoto School*, and *Seven Lectures on the Philosophy of the Kyoto School*.[46] The emergence of research comparing the thought of the Kyoto School to that of New Confucian scholars such as Xiong Shili (1885–1968) and Mou Zongsan (1909–1995) is also worthy of note.[47]

3. The Diverse Development of the Kyoto School

As discussed in the previous section, "nothingness (emptiness)" was one of the important themes of the postwar Kyoto School, but there were also disciples of Nishida and Tanabe who became active in a wide range of other fields of inquiry. In this section I would like to touch on some examples of this diversity.

(1) Nishida's Disciples

Yamauchi Tokuryū was appointed professor in charge of the history of classical and medieval philosophy course in Kyoto University's Faculty of Letters in 1931, and following the war, after Kōyama Iwao had been banned from public office, in 1946 he was made professor of the philosophy course, thereby coming to occupy a central position in the study of philosophy at Kyoto University. As discussed in chapter 7, however, he was thoroughly critical of the philosophical perspectives of Nishida and Tanabe that were grounded in the dialectic.

Late in his life, Yamauchi published a book called *Logos and Lemma*[48] (1974), and after his death a posthumous manuscript entitled *The Philosophy of Fundamental Desires (Anuśaya)*[49] was published in 1993. In this text, drawing on thought from before the war, he develops a logic that acknowledges differences that exist in reality as differences. In doing so he utilizes the concept of lemma (λῆμμα), the origins of which can be traced to ancient Indian logic. Lemma, a word derived from the verb *lambáno* (λαμβάνω; I take), means "grasping things concretely and directly."[50] The four modes of existence known as *catuṣkoṭi* in ancient Indian logic, that is, A, not A, A and not A, neither A nor not A, are called the "tetralemma." There Yamauchi found a logic that acknowledged not only the binary of affirmation and negation but also an intermediary between them.

Yamauchi tried to see these four lemmata not simply as an enumeration of the ways of being of entities, but rather as a systematic logic based on principles. To this end, drawing on the thought of Nāgārjuna, he replaced the third and fourth lemma with the negation (dual negation) and affirmation (dual affirmation) of the first two, respectively. He believed that the "middle" domain Nāgārjuna spoke of could be opened through both affirmation and negation being negated by the third lemma. The fourth lemma then indicates "a new world" created there. Yamauchi called this logic that centered around the third lemma as a turning point the "logic of lemma." Here the problem becomes how the third lemma transitions to the fourth lemma. Yamauchi thought this was not a matter of reasoning but rather something grasped intuitively or experienced directly. In this sense he says that the "logic of lemma" is "immediate logic."[51] In his later years Yamauchi added observations concerning this "immediate logic" from various perspectives—with a particular focus on the "grounding" of existence—in the essays collected in the posthumously published *The Philosophy of Fundamental Desires*, but his main ideas can be said to have already been articulated in *Logos and Lemma*.

Mutai Risaku radically changed his philosophical worldview after the war. This shift was triggered by the events surrounding the suicide of Kan Sueharu (1917–1950). After studying philosophy at Tokyo Bunrika University and Kyoto University's graduate school, Kan had been conscripted into the army and interned in the Soviet Union after the war. Upon returning to Japan, he had been accused in the Diet on suspicion of being a secret agent for the Soviets or the Communist Party of Japan and ultimately took his own life. Mutai's task then became "establishing the principles of a humanism that can fight fascism."[52] In *Humanism Today*,[53] published in 1961, after defining humanism as "a spirit that respects human life, human values, human cultivation, and human creativity, and seeks to protect and further enrich them"[54] he then divides it broadly into three categories: renaissance humanism, early modern civil society individualistic humanism, and the humanism of modern humanity/socialist humanism. Mutai's aim was the final, "third humanism," and along with being an approach that intellectually opposes the negation of human nature and adopts a "standpoint of humanity" that recognizes the value of all human beings, it is also a "humanism of the whole human being" that seeks to restore people from their state of alienation and realize whole human beings. At the same time, Mutai also asserts that this must be a "practical humanism" that realizes its thought through action without being limited to ideas. The goal of this, according to Mutai, is neither the establishment of a personal, subjective ethics nor an objective ethics that adopts the perspective of a society or nation, but rather the construction of an "ethics of humanity" that desires the peace and happiness of all humankind.

For Mutai, this shift toward a perspective of humanism also signified a confrontation with Nishida's philosophy. In "memories of a scholar," Mutai criticizes Nishida's philosophy for "not having been able to see through the fearsome power of fascism that lay behind the nationalism of the era and crushed the freedom of the individual."[55] He also criticizes Nishida's thought for not grasping the relationships between individuals and society and individuals and humanity as something concrete because of having placed "absolute nothingness" at its foundation. "Rather than mediating issues of humanity through direct absolute nothingness or negative species," Mutai changed course toward "starting from the aspect of social conditions, and, amid the *task of humanizing* them, reacknowledging the importance of the issues of the individual, existence, and humanity."[56] This was the substance of what he called "humanism."

Miyake Gōichi (1895–1982) entered Kyoto University in 1916, between Mutai Risaku and Miki Kiyoshi. After studying under Husserl at the University of Freiberg, in 1938 he took a position as an assistant professor in Tōhoku University's Faculty of Science (later becoming a professor in the Faculty of Law and Literature in 1946) and in 1954 he returned to Kyoto University as a replacement for the retiring Yamauchi Tokuryū. His major works include *The Formation of Science and the Natural World: The Historical Study of Western Philosophy* (1940)[57] and *The Intellectual History of the Philosophy of Mathematics* (1947).[58] His most significant postwar achievement was *Human Ontology*,[59] published in 1966. Philosophy has a long history as the study of existence in general, but in this work Miyake poses the question of whether it has brought sufficient clarity to the reality of human beings and our existence itself. He focuses in particular on the relationship between human beings and nature (including issues related to the body) and the historicity of human existence (including issues related to actions and social systems). From this perspective he attempts to view human beings not simply as objective beings but as beings who live subjectively within their relationships to nature and history.

At the end of *Human Ontology*, Miyake includes a specific critique of Nishida in a chapter entitled "Nishida's Philosophy: Tradition and Philosophy." There he criticizes Nishida for thoroughly adopting the stance of "the self-consciousness of a mind contemplating history"[60] and failing to grasp the world of actual history itself. In "Reality and History,"[61] an essay included in *The Philosophy of Empirical Reality*[62] (1980), he writes, "I see reality as an empirical reality, a reality given to our experience, and I would like to consider it in relation to the understanding of history as empirical science,"[63] and this stance is profoundly connected to his criticism of Nishida.

Kōyama Iwao received a sentence of exclusion from public office in 1946, and, unable to emerge in public venues until this ban was lifted in 1951, devoted himself to contemplation and the writing of many texts, including *Reason, Spirit, and Existence*[64] (1948). Among these, a work that is particularly notable for seeking to present Kōyama's own position is *The Logic of Place and the Principle of Call and Response*[65] (1951). Here he of course touches on the philosophy of Nishida Kitarō, but Kōyama criticizes Nishida's logic for being fundamentally the logic of "absolutely contradictory self-identity" and nevertheless failing to actively express the substantial relationship between these contradictory elements themselves. In this context, Kōyama tries to discover personal, reciprocal relationships between those who call out and those who respond, as well as creative relationships that give rise to new things. In contrast to Nishida, Tanabe advocated the "logic of species" and addressed the issues of absolute negation and absolute mediation between genus, species, and individual. In this sense he attempted to examine substantial content. According to Kōyama's understanding, however, in Tanabe these relationships of absolutely negative mediation are not grasped in their entirety, that is, in their "indivisibility." Kōyama tried to express this "indivisible state of affairs" with the phrase "identity of call and response."

In chapter 7, I noted that in his most significant prewar text, *The Philosophy of the History of Science*, Shimomura Toratarō presents his view that the conception of European learning was mediated by the establishment of mathematics and discusses the history of the creation of this field. Shimomura does not address mathematics as an established field of inquiry but rather focuses on the "spirit (mentality)" that created it and attempts to trace the formation of mathematics from this starting point. After the war, building on this foundation he sought to grasp the history of science as "spiritual (intellectual) history." In "On the History of Science as Spiritual History," published in 1955, Shimomura argues that it is the task of this "history of science as spiritual history" to "investigate how the spirit [that was behind or at the root of science] formed science, determined its character, and fostered its development."[66]

Shimomura began by examining the establishment of mathematics and science within the framework of "spiritual history" in this way, but his focus later shifted to the history of culture (the turning point for this shift was his trip to Europe in 1956). Beginning with *Leonardo da Vinci* (1961) and *Saint Francis of Assisi* (1965), he wrote book after book in this vein, including *The Renaissance Image of Humanity* (1955). In chapter 7, I stated that Shimomura thought of himself as a "historian," and as can be seen from these works his postwar activities clearly demonstrate that this was indeed his essential character.

Near the end of his life, Shimomura published a major work entitled *The World of Burckhardt: Art Historian, Cultural Historian, and Philosopher of History*[67] (1983). This text sought to understand Burckhardt in his entirety, and "systematically reform all of his thought."[68] Shimomura saw the appeal of Burckhardt particularly in his being an "art historian who gave form to culture." According to Shimomura, the Italian Renaissance only began *to exist* after Burckhardt wrote *Renaissance Culture in Italy*.[69] In other words, this was when it began to display a clear form. In particular, Shimomura holds Burckhardt in high regard for thus being "a formative artist by means of his pen," and Shimomura's own diverse undertakings after the war can perhaps be said to have been spawned by his desire to be an "artist who gives form to culture."

(2) Tanabe's Disciples

Like Nishida, Tanabe also fostered many distinguished scholars who were important members of the Kyoto School. Here I will discuss a few of them.

Karaki Junzō (1904–1980) entered Kyoto University in 1924 and studied under Nishida Kitarō, but he was also strongly influenced by Tanabe

Hajime, then an assistant professor. In 1940 he founded the publishing company Chikuma Shobō with Usui Yoshimi and Furuta Akira, acquaintances from his hometown, and maintained deep ties to Tanabe after working with this publishing house as an advisor and editor of the journal *Outlook*. The publication of Tanabe's *Introduction to Philosophy: Fundamental Philosophical Problems*[70] (1949, three books of supplemental writings 1949–1952), which became a bestseller, came in response to Karaki's entreaties. Karaki himself chose the path of criticism, penning many excellent works including *Literature of the Middle Ages*[71] (1954), *Transience*[72] (1964), and *The History of the Japanese Mind: Focusing on Changes in the Perception of Beauty in the Seasons*[73] (parts 1 and 2, 1970–1972). In "An Attempt at Modern History: Forms, Individuality, and Existence,"[74] an essay published shortly after the war in *An Attempt at Modern History*[75] (1949), Karaki views modern history as the history of "the loss of forms," an approach inspired by Mori Ōgai's 1918 essay "A Complaint About Manners."[76] In this essay Mori laments a state of affairs in which, while existing meanings and forms were all being separated and forms of all kinds were being destroyed through the awakening of the critical spirit, "new forms capable of bearing the old meanings" were nowhere to be found. After the Mukden Incident, the military took the initiative and mechanically absolutized the nation, the "path of contemplation" disappeared completely from view, and a "single form" lacking universality was imposed on everyone, but eventually this pattern was destroyed along with the nation. What then appeared was the naked form of "existence," the "completely independent individual" lacking both a vertical thread connecting it to universality and horizontal ties to other people. In Mori's case, clear forms still existed within himself, but "today's formlessness is true formlessness" and "something uprooted."[77] Karaki's "An Attempt at Modern History" ends with the question of how the "loss of forms" can be remedied. His subsequent thought can perhaps be seen as an attempt to answer this question.

Noda Matao (1910–2000) was one of Tanabe Hajime's early disciples when the latter succeeded Nishida as professor of the philosophy course at Kyoto University. In a lecture entitled "Nishida's Philosophy and Tanabe's Philosophy: A Recollection"[78] delivered in his later years, along with recalling Tanabe's "A Request for Professor Nishida's Thoughts," discussed in chapter 5, being published shortly after he had entered university and his own surprise at the intensity of its criticism, Noda states that this criticism became an opportunity for both of these mentors to advance their thought in different directions, and by doing so paradoxically created an intellectual closeness between them. For example, in their later years both Nishida and Tanabe turned their attention to the issue of "action." But Noda points out that their approaches were quite different; while Nishida understood "action" centered around poesis, Tanabe emphasized praxis, or, in other words, moral practice.

Noda engaged in scholarship on a wide range of topics, including the thought of Descartes, Pascal, and Kant, but his own distinctive character is best expressed in *Three Traditions of Philosophy*[79] (1974). In this book he gives an overview of how philosophy that tries to attach meaning to the world and life from the stance of reason took shape in the ancient world and developed up to the present day and attempts to paint a portrait of this phenomenon as a whole. According to him, the philosophical traditions that took shape in Greece, India, and China had almost the same level of sophistication until the medieval period, but beginning in the modern period in the West the topic of understanding the world was objectively reinterpreted on the basis of a mechanical view of nature, and this led to a leap forward in development. In Noda's understanding, however, the task of adding new reflections on the meaning of life from this perspective had not been adequately addressed.

Takeuchi Yoshinori (1913–2002) was the disciple who most closely followed Tanabe Hajime's understanding of philosophy centered on Hegel, but he demonstrated his own distinctive character in his philosophical study of the Japanese Buddhist monk Shinran, who taught that salvation can be achieved by entrusting everything to the absolute power of Amida Buddha (an "other power" outside the self). In *Philosophy as the Way of Repentance*, Tanabe sought to walk the path of repentance in the domain of philosophy with the path Shinran "walked in religion" as a point of reference and reframe philosophy as the "way of repentance," and one resource upon which he drew in doing so was Takeuchi's *The Philosophy of Kyōgyōshinshō*[80] (1941). In this text Takeuchi attempts to elucidate a logic running through the entire *Kyōgyōshinshō* with the "three vow transition" at its core. The "three vow transition" is an understanding in which the religious states spoken of in vows nineteen, twenty, and eighteen of the forty-eight vows of Hōzō Bodhisattva for the salvation of mankind extolled in the Great *Sukhāvatīvyūha Sūtra* are viewed as a process of transitioning from a stage of attachment to one's own power to a religious awareness of a genuine other power. Tanabe undertook his own philosophical reading of the *Kyōgyōshinshō* on this basis.

After the war, Takeuchi dedicated himself to the philosophical explication of Pure Land thought and primitive Buddhism with a focus on Shinran, but it is notable that in this endeavor he was strongly influenced by existentialist philosophy. This is particularly apparent in *Shinran and the World Today*[81] (1974). In this text he considers the question of faith from the perspective of human limitations, that is, our awareness of our own mortality and fallibility. In the "transdescendental" awareness of falling endlessly and despairingly at the bottom of the self and the extreme misery of this "descent," a human being encounters things from the future brought before their eyes in the present. Takeuchi believed it is the intimate relationship between the voice of the absolute other heard calling out there and the religious resolve that seeks to answer it that makes salvation possible.

Mutō Kazuo (1913–1995) studied under Tanabe Hajime, and after holding several positions, including as a teacher at the Number Three High School, he was put in charge of the Christian studies course in Kyoto University's Faculty of Letters. As indicated by the title of his major work, *Between Theology and the Philosophy of Religion*[82] (1961), while on the one hand he sought to understand the essence of Christianity from the inside, that is, from the standpoint of faith, he also aimed to adopt a thoroughly academic perspective and elucidate the essence and history of this religion from a broader rational perspective. This can be described as an effort to place himself "between" the two, or, in other words, in a dynamic position that they reciprocally delimit. In this sense he left behind an important legacy.

Ōshima Yasumasa (1917–1989) studied under Tanabe for three years beginning in 1937 and later taught at the Tokyo University of Literature and Science (later known as the Tokyo University of Education and today as the University of Tsukuba). His most important work is *The Historical Positioning of Existential Ethics: God-Man and Man-God*[83] (1956). Beginning with Greek tragedy, its wide-ranging scope includes Old Testament thought, Kantian philosophy, and modern nihilism, so why is it called "The Historical Positioning of Existential Ethics"? According to Ōshima, his use of the term "positioning"[84] is based on Jaspers's concept of the "limit situation." In other words, it refers to the fundamental situation of a human being standing in the historical present, confronting their own self-negating crisis, and attempting a transition to transcendence and the overcoming of this crisis. In this book Ōshima attempts to relive this kind of transition and mediation that has occurred in the past. Unlike Jaspers, who looked to construct an existential system, Ōshima refers to the aim of his undertaking as "existential ethics" because of a deep-seated desire to orient himself toward existence that is thoroughly subjective and investigate the contradictions that arise between social and historical circumstances and individual limit states strictly as contradictions.

Tsujimura Kōichi (1922–2010) visited the University of Freiberg from 1956 to 1959 where he studied under Heidegger. He was one of the Japanese philosophers most strongly influenced by Heidegger. He not only gave a detailed interpretation of the intellectual path Heidegger followed from his early period to late period, but also contributed greatly to Heideggerian studies in Japan by publishing translations of *Sein und Zeit* (1967) and a Japanese edition of *The Complete Works of Martin Heidegger* beginning in 1985. His interpretation of Heidegger's philosophy is notable for having focused on its relationship to Zen thought. In "The Question of Being and Absolute Nothingness,"[85] included in *The Essence of Zen and Human Truth*[86] (Hisamatsu Shin'ichi and Nishitani Keiji, eds., 1969), Tsujimura attempts to compare Heidegger's fundamental question, the "question of being," that is, the question "what is the meaning of being?" that concerns the "truth [true nature]" of being, and the Zen perspective. According to Tsujimura, the "and" in the expression "being and time" that displays the fundamental standpoint of the question of being must, in its true manifestation, inevitably boil down to the "true face of the self" understood in Zen, which he interprets as the "absolute nothingness" that had been addressed by members of the Kyoto School beginning with Nishida Kitarō.

(3) Thought Related to the Kyoto School—Nakai Masakazu, Hayashi Tatsuo, Hanada Kiyoteru, and Suzuki Tōru

Next I would like to focus on those who were not direct disciples of Nishida or Tanabe but were nevertheless directly or indirectly influenced by them or their disciples in developing their own unique thought.

After the war, Nakai Masakazu served in various positions, such as assistant director of the National Diet Library and chair of the board of directors of the Japan Library Association, and devoted himself to developing cultural activities through the venue of libraries before passing away from illness in 1952. His best-known work, *Introduction to Aesthetics*[87] (1951), was published the year before his death. In this text he divides beauty into three categories. One is the beauty found in nature. This is the beauty we perceive when we are enfolded in nature, or the order of the universe, and find ourselves fascinated by it and directly resonating with it. It is the beauty Bashō may have felt when he wrote, based on a verse by Chéng Hào, "If you look quietly, all things understand themselves [they are where they should be and as they should be]." Next, Nakai finds beauty in craftsmanship and technology. Speaking of the beauty of a Japanese blade, for example, he says, "When the function of cutting is purely realized, this order reaches the point of surpassing the beauty of nature." He then addresses the beauty present in art. This beauty emerges when people attempt to create something solely for beauty's sake, devoid of any practical use. Such beauty is of course not easy to produce. Here a "writhing toward freedom" is needed. But it is in this world that differs from natural and technological beauty, the "world that takes a great leap forward"[88] that opens up here, that Nakai identifies the distinctive character of artistic beauty.

Like Nakai, Hayashi Tatsuo (1896–1984) studied aesthetics at Kyoto University. After the war, he was involved in editing the journal *Thought* and compiling the *World Encyclopedia*[89] (Heibonsha) and published numerous works of incisive political and cultural criticism, such as "The Ironic Spirit"[90] (1946), "Communistic Humanity: 20th Century Political Folklore"[91] (1951), and "Intellectual History: A Discourse on the Method"[92] (1969). If one constant can be said to run through all of his works, it would presumably be "the critical spirit." During the war, this took the form of "the ironic spirit."

In his "Commentary" in volume 1, *Cicerone [Guide] to Art*,[93] of *The Collected Writings of Hayashi Tatsuo*,[94] Katō Shūichi writes as follows.

> The intense pressure applied beginning in the 1930s caused a "conversion" in left-wing intellectuals. From the mid-1930s to the end of the war, a compromise with power was struck by a broad spectrum of intellectuals. This compromise was half externally imposed and consciously adhered to, half internally generated and carried out unconsciously. The internal, unconscious compromise showed the weak relationship between people and thought, people and knowledge, and people and language among Japanese intellectuals.[95]

Amid these circumstances in which thinkers were faced with harsh choices, whether they compromised or stood up in opposition, Hayashi was exceptional in maintaining a "quiet courage." He remained completely silent from the outbreak of the Pacific War to the end of this conflict. This silence was broken by the essay "The Ironic Spirit," published in the journal *New Tide*[96] in June of 1946. In it he describes his own considerations regarding "strategy and tactics in intellectual warfare" during this difficult reactionary period. In the midst of despair, so to speak, he thought about the "tactics of despair." This is where Hayashi Tatsuo's "critical spirit" and "ironic spirit" are most clearly manifested. He discusses these tactics in "Descartes' Politique"[97] (1939), and he bravely delivered the lecture "The New Order and the Direction of Philosophy"[98] (quoted in "The Ironic Spirit") at a time when the imperial rule assistance movement held enormous power throughout Japan. He sought the possibility of the "tactics of despair" in the "ironic conformism" (*conformisme ironique*) of Socrates, who, while pretending to adopt an understanding in line with that of the majority, mercilessly dismantled commonly held beliefs or authority that lacked substance or legitimacy, and in the approach of Descartes, who wrote *Discourse on the Method* rather than presenting a cosmology in light of the Roman Inquisition's treatment of Galileo, and who practiced "disguising conformism" (*conformisme déguisé*)[99] by laying out his own philosophical principles in the guise of a textbook for Jesuit schools in his *Principles of Philosophy*.

Hanada Kiyoteru (1909–1974) is known for his works of criticism featuring exceptional rhetoric published after the war in books such as *The Spirit of the Era of Reconstruction*[100] (1946) and *The Logic of Derangement*[101] (1947). He also devoted his energies to advancing new artistic and cultural movements in the postwar period through works such as *Avant-Garde Art* (1954). These activities were far removed from philosophy, but Hanada had a deep interest in philosophy regarding the process of the formation of his thought. He had been drawn to Nishida's philosophy as a student at the Number Seven High School in Kagoshima, and after studying philosophy as an auditing student at Kyūshū University, in 1929 he entered Kyoto University as a nonregular student majoring in English literature. Nishida had already left his position, having reached the age of retirement the previous year, but Hanada presumably had opportunities to attend his lectures and talks. He may already have acquired a critical view of Nishida's philosophy, however, at the point of choosing to major in English literature. In an essay published in 1938 entitled "Flag" (included in the essay collection *Self-Evident Principles*), while he does not mention it by name, he clearly has *An Inquiry into the Good* in mind when he writes as follows.

> It was called our nation's first book of original philosophy. Original? It was indeed unmistakably original. It was original because its author skillfully utilizes our nation's feudal ideology while "criticizing" various European civil philosophies. It was a monumental work that emerged as a reflection of the process of

the semifeudal governing regime adroitly adapting itself to civil development. And it was indeed original in the same way that our nation's capitalism was original.[102]

Another point of connection between Hanada Kiyoteru and the philosophy of the Kyoto School was that in 1959 he published a collection of essays entitled *Overcoming Modernity*. This collection itself was nothing more than a book of essays written during this period, but his deep interest in this problem of "overcoming modernity" can be seen from the essay entitled "The Anachronism of the Modernists" he had published the preceding year. Touching on the *Literary World* roundtable, he writes, "While it may seem a statement from a standpoint contrary to my own, from then until now it is just the standpoint that is different, and I too have always aimed to 'overcome modernity.'"[103]

Suzuki Tōru (born in 1919) entered the philosophy program at Kyoto University as a nonregular student in October 1944, and attended Tanabe Hajime's final lecture. In *Existence and Labor*,[104] published in 1958, Suzuki attempted to build a bridge between the existentialist and Marxist perspectives using the original concept of "labor existence,"[105] and in *The Echo Existence World*,[106] published in 1967, he tried to give the assertions made in *Existence and Labor* a logical grounding using the concept of "echo existence."[107] At the same time, from early in his career he had a profound interest in Nishida's philosophy, and the results of his study of it are presented in *The World of Nishida Kitarō*[108] (1977). He also takes up Nishida's philosophy in a later work, *Seeking a Grounding for Living* (1982), in which on the one hand he praises Nishida for having clarified the relationship of absolutely contradictory self-identity between finite and infinite, relative and absolute, and time and eternity and established the perspective of the dialectic of place, while on the other hand he criticizes this perspective as being limited to the spatial and static and lacking in process-oriented moments. Suzuki also understood the relationship of correspondence between finite and infinite as being a one-way transmission from infinite to finite and emphasized that in this respect his understanding was different from that of Nishida.[109]

(4) Expansion Beyond Philosophy

The influence of the Kyoto School thus rippled outward in concentric circles, and this expansion included diverse developments that went beyond the framework of philosophy. This wide-ranging influence can also be described as one of the major characteristics of the postwar period.

Physicist Yukawa Hideki (1907–1981), for example, graduated from the Number Three High School and entered Kyoto University's Faculty of Science, and later reflected on his time in high school in *Traveler: Reminiscences of a Physicist* (1958), a book of autobiographical essays.

> At first, what I read with passionate intensity in the Number Three High library were works of philosophy. My interest shifted from the Chinese philosophy of Laozi and Zhuangzi to Western philosophy. The Neo-Kantian School was at its height. Bergson's philosophy was also popular. Like most young people at the time, however, I was drawn most strongly to Nishida's philosophy.[110]

He also records not missing any of Nishida's introduction to philosophy lectures.

Imanishi Kinji (1902–1992) graduated from Number Three High School a year ahead of Yukawa and entered Kyoto University's Department of Agriculture. An ecologist known for the "theory of habitat segregation," Imanishi was nevertheless greatly influenced by the philosophy of Nishida and Tanabe in the process of forming his own thought. He is said to have always been in the front row whenever Nishida returned to give a lecture at Kyoto University after his retirement and has stated that he repeatedly read "Logic and Life" (1936),[111] an essay included in Nishida's *Second Collection of Philosophical Essays*.[112]

Imanishi's fundamental understanding regarding life, living things, and nature is discussed in *The World of Living Things*[113] (1941), and the influence of Nishida's thought on matters such as life, the body, and the environment expressed in "Logic and Life" is evident in this work. For example, Nishida says that life and the environment are intertwined in ways that make them difficult to separate, writing, "along with life changing the environment, the environment changes life," and together they compose "dialectically one world."[114] Drawing on this understanding, Imanishi states that living things are not merely constrained by the environment through bodies that are, in a manner of speaking, extensions of it, but also at the same time operate on the environment through their bodies and express their own wills in it. In this sense, he asserts that living things and the environment create "a single, organically unified whole."[115] Based on this understanding, Imanishi develops an original theory of evolution that, in contrast to Darwin's theory, which only considers how the environment acts on living things, asserts that how living things adapt to the environment in which they are placed, or, in other words, how living things act on their environment, is also an important factor in evolution.

In *Theory of Living Things Society*, published in 1949, Imanishi posits "species societies (specia)" as the ultimate units that compose the natural world of living things and develops a sociological theory of living things with "species" at its core. In *Proposal for the Study of Nature* (1948), in addition to stating that the natural world of living things is made up of the three layers of individuals (individual species), species societies, and the society of living things as a whole, he emphasizes that species societies are neither simply containers of individuals nor conceptual frameworks, but "real, recognizable things that have their own agency."[116] This positioning of "species" is clearly based on Tanabe Hajime's "logic of species" (although Imanishi himself makes no mention of it). Of course, there are also major differences between their understandings of "species." Based on his theory of habitat segregation, Imanishi postulates a principle of harmony between species societies, while Tanabe positions species as an "irrational direct form."[117] It was this irrationality Tanabe aimed to overcome through the "logic of species."

Kimura Bin (1931–2021) specialized in psychopathology but was heavily influenced by the tradition of the Kyoto School in developing his own theories in this field. His thought was not limited to psychopathology in a narrow sense, as can be seen in his having tackled topics such as "*mono* and *koto*,"[118] "the self and the other," "life," and "reality and actuality" in various works including *Time and Self*[19] (1982), *Between*[120] (1988), and *The Truth and Poetry of Schizophrenia*[121] (1998). In the process of addressing these topics, Kimura was profoundly influenced by elements of Kyoto School thought such as Nishida's understanding of the "self" and the "other," Tanabe's "logic of species," and Watsuji Tetsurō's theory of climate. I will discuss Kimura's understanding of "the concrete and the abstract" and "the self and the other" in the next chapter, but here I would like to examine his views regarding "life."

Kimura began to display a deep interest in the topic of "life" around the second half of the 1980s. The trigger of this interest was sympathy with the view of "life" expressed by the German medical scholar Viktor von Weizsäcker (1886–1957). In one of his most well-known works, *Der Gestaltkreis* (1940), which Kimura and one of his colleagues translated into Japanese, Weizsäcker focuses on the fact that while both organisms and the environment are constantly changing, a relationship with a fixed order nevertheless arises between them, and he dubs this connection that possesses a certain consistency "coherence" (*Kohärenz*).[122] He furthermore points out that this "coherence" is maintained by the circular connection (*Kreis*) between the perceptions and movements of living organisms, and he refers to this structure as a whole as *Gestaltkreis*. Weizsäcker then describes the principle that undergirds this "coherence" with the term "subject." In *Between*, Kimura understands this "subject" overlaid with what Nishida called "historical life." According to Nishida, on the one hand this is "something made" in the real world bearing the weight of history, but on the other hand it is also something that realizes itself through its own body and "makes" the world. Nishida expresses the reciprocal relationship between subject and object that arises there with the term "action-intuition," and this relationship, according to Kimura, is the same circular structure Weizsäcker refers to as *Gestaltkreis*.[123]

Chapter 11

The Diverse Development of Postwar Japanese Philosophy

1. Being and Knowledge

(1) Being and Cognition

As we saw in chapter 5, Nishida Kitarō argued that true existence is "pure experience" in which subject and object are not distinguished, and from this perspective he rejected views of existence in which subjectivity and objectivity are arbitrarily assumed to be distinct and independent. According to Nishida, "pure substance" posited before any perception is "the furthest thing from the true landscape of existence." There are many points at which this understanding of Nishida's overlaps with the thought of Ōmori Shōzō (1921–1997), who developed his own philosophy in the postwar period while drawing on advances in analytic philosophy and the philosophy of science and made a significant mark on the world of Japanese philosophy.

Ōmori was a philosopher who repeatedly reexamined and deepened his thought regarding the same themes, and many changes in his approach can be seen over time. Here, however, I will give only a broad overview of his thought. In "On the Spirit of Language" (1973),[1] an essay included in *Things [Mono] and the Mind* (1976),[2] Ōmori sharply criticizes the dualistic view that distinguishes between perceptions and things, or between representations and objects. In a thoroughly dualistic schema, perceptions and thoughts (recollection and imagination) are all considered manifestations of "objects," that is, "representations," and "objects" are pushed behind the curtain of these "representations" that conceal them. We cannot look directly at the other side of this curtain. Adopting this dualistic view, therefore, means inevitably falling into agnosticism or skepticism. To avoid getting stuck in this narrow path, Ōmori proposes the concept of "emergence."[3] He calls that which corresponds to perceptual representation "perceptual emergence of the object" and that which corresponds to intellectual representation "intellectual emergence of the object." In contrast to a dualistic schema in which "objects" only manifest *through* "representations," in Ōmori's monistic approach, "the 'object' emerges *directly*, without any intermediary such as 'representation.'"[4] There is no "object" lying behind this "emergence," nor is there any "representation" mediating an "object." Ōmori believed an "emergence" always emerges *directly*.

This "emergence" was not simply emergence in the perceptual world limited to the here and now. In "The 'Mono-Goto' of the Landscape of Space"[5] (1975), included, like "On the Spirit of Language," in *Things [Mono] and the Mind*, Ōmori uses the interesting expression "emergence in four-dimensional space." If we think about the experience of being overwhelmed by the majestic form of Mount Fuji, for example, Ōmori says that this mountain is not manifested simply hanging in empty space.

> The impressive Mount Fuji seen on that day is merely emerging as a single vivid episode; the "main body," so to speak, of the emergence is the Mount Fuji that persists over the thousands or tens of thousands of years that stretch blackly before and after this emergence as a single fragment of it. Naturally, the landscape that enfolds this Mount Fuji is the landscape of four-dimensional space-time. [6]

Mount Fuji emerges as an entity with an expanse that transcends space and time. As such, Mount Fuji emerges with various meanings or various expressions. In "The Mind/Body Problem: One Proposed Solution"[7] (1979), included in *Flow and Stagnation: Philosophical Fragments*[8] (1981), Ōmori writes, "The world is always emerging with emotional coloring."[9] "Encountering Myself-Consciousness Is the Root of the Evil That Separates a Person from the World," an article published in the *Asahi Shimbun* newspaper on November 12, 1996, three months before his death, includes the following passage.

> In reality, the world itself is already something emotional. The world is emotional, and the world itself is a gladdening world

and a saddening world. What is mistaken for an emotion in my own heart is in fact no more than a tiny foregrounding of the emotion of the world as a whole. . . . simply stated, the world is emotional, and heaven and earth have feelings. We human beings who are adjacent to this heaven and earth, too, take part in this having of feelings as miniscule elements of its foreground.[10]

Ōmori's understanding of the world as "heaven and earth having feelings" is deeply connected to Nishida Kitarō's understanding of "pure experience." Nishida asserts that true existence, that is, pure experience, is "a state of consciousness fusing intellect, emotion, and volition that eclipses subject and object," and giving the example of Heine's poem that likens stars in the night sky to "golden nails," he expresses this with the phrase "our world is constructed on the basis of our feelings."[11]

Ōmori criticizes the dualism of perception and thing, or representation and object, and asserts the monism of "emergence," but how are dualistic views positioned within this monism he takes as a premise? We have the difficult-to-escape conception that it is things that are the primary entities, while our perceptions are nothing more than their reflection or projection. We think of the scientific depiction of the world through concepts like atoms, elementary particles, and electromagnetic fields as its true depiction, and the landscape we perceive as merely a secondary projection. Ōmori, in contrast, argues for a fundamental inversion of this understanding. In an article entitled "The Perceptual Landscape and the Scientific Image of the World"[12] (1969) included in *Language, Perception, and the World*[13] (1971), he asserts that it is in fact the perceptual landscape that is the fundamental premise of the scientific depiction. "The place (positional coordinates) where physical objects (for example, elementary particles and electromagnetic fields) exist, and therefore also their form and size, is defined by and within the perceptual landscape."[14] In other words, the scientific depiction can only have meaning in conjunction with the perceptual landscape. In "The Mind/Body Problem: One Proposed Solution" he uses the phrase "superimposition" in summarizing this assertion.

The objective world and subjective image of the world in a dualistic structure are expressed in a monistic structure as the "superimposition" of the everyday depiction and scientific depiction. Accordingly, the "thing/mind relationship" of "source (objective world)—its image (subjective image of the world)" or

> "cause-effect" found in the dualistic structure must also be jetti-
> soned. A relationship of "A-that-is-B" through "superimposition"
> then appears in its place.[15]

The scientific depiction is merely an expression of the perceptual landscape in a different form, and there is no relationship of "original thing and representation" or "cause and effect" between them. Both, on the contrary, are in fact the same thing. In *The Construction of the Intellect and the Spell It Casts*[16] (1994), Ōmori expresses this with the phrase "one mind, one body co-habitation of 'thing' and 'perceptual image.'"[17] Here we find "living nature," that is, nature as "something vibrantly alive." Modern science had adopted a dualistic perspective, expelled "psychological matters" from the domain of truth, leaving only "things," and "deanimated" the natural world, and Ōmori's aim can be said to have been to "revitalize" this dead nature.

Ōmori Shōzō used the term "landscape" to explain "emergence," writing "when we '*see*' something, a landscape '*is seen*,' a landscape *exists* there,"[18] and Sawada Nobushige (1916–2006) sought to bring this word to the fore in developing his own thought. In *The Landscape of Cognition* (1975), Sawada explains that his intention in focusing on the word "landscape" is to elucidate what has been overlooked by theories of knowledge that start from the fragmentary matter of "sensory perception" by drawing on the more concrete and comprehensive "perceptual landscape" and "environmental landscape" in contrast to empiricism and sensualism. In concrete terms, this means focusing on the place—the "environmental landscape"—where sensory perceptions are given with a concrete form and function. Of course, this landscape is thoroughly "my landscape, a landscape for me." I am not, however, locked inside myself there. The "environmental landscape" of which Sawada speaks is not like a screen inside our heads on which the world is projected. It is "something that allows me to purposively insert myself into environmental nature of which I am a part."[19] There I choose the actions that should be taken and realize them. In this sense, the "environmental landscape" can be described as the "most fundamental place where I determine how I will live."[20]

When Ōmori Shōzō criticizes dualism that distinguishes things from perceptions and asserts a monism of "emergence," how is this "emergence" described? While the "subject-predicate" form of expression we use in daily life may be suitable for describing a dualistic image of the world, it is not necessarily an appropriate expression from a monistic perspective that does not assume "objects." In *Language, Perception, and the World*, Ōmori asserts that in regard to such forms of description, while the scope of its application may not be wide, a "depiction of circumstances in a spatial location" should be possible. Depictions of pain such as "it hurts on my right side" are examples of this. Greek philosophy scholar Fujisawa Norio (1925–2004) was one of those who opposed the approach of assuming a "thing"-like substance and explaining perception in a cause-and-effect manner, and in *Greek Philosophy and Modernity: The Aspects of Worldview* (1980) he discusses a "depiction of place" approach to description from this kind of perspective. Drawing on "feature-placing statements" that express a particular feature being seen in a particular place, such as "it is raining here now," focused on by leading British ordinary language philosopher Peter Frederick Strawson (1919–2006), Fujisawa asserts that while a statement like "this is a desk" formally adopts the "subject-predicate" pattern, the "this" in this sentence can be interpreted as a word designating the place where the perceptual image appears, and therefore "this is a desk" can be interpreted as "here is seen a desk" or "the perceptual image called 'desk' has appeared in this place."[21] In this book he attempts to reinterpret Plato's theory of ideas from the perspective that this "depiction of place" approach to describing things is the "method of description that conforms to the most fundamental way of being of the world."

During the twentieth century, traditional metaphysics and ontology were subjected to intense criticism. Logical positivism, for example, asserted that any proposition for which no method of verification can be given is meaningless. Watanabe Jirō (1931–2008) is one of those who, on the basis of the main thrust of this criticism, adopted the understanding that the true role of philosophy is to grasp the actual state of existence revealed to us through experience and sought to reexamine questions of "being" and "experience of being." According to Watanabe, it is through "refining our experience of being" that we are able to acquire "understanding of the self and understanding of the world" and construct a foundation for all human undertakings. Of course, there are limits to human cognition. But Watanabe claims that it is only through an ongoing attempt to grasp "the entire meaning of the existence of the self and the world" while immersing ourselves in the "fathomless depths of existence" that a foundation for life can be secured.[22]

(2) *Mono* and *Koto*

Mono and *koto* are Japanese words that can both be translated as "thing." Broadly speaking, *mono* refers to "thing" in a more tangible sense, that is, an object that has a shape, while *koto* refers to "thing" in a more intangible sense, including, for example, an action or event.

After the war, an attempt to examine the problem of existence from the perspective of *mono* and *koto* was undertaken by Yamauchi Tokuryū and Hiromatsu Wataru (1933–1994). Their approaches to this topic had been preceded by a contrasting view taken before the war by Watasuji Tetsurō. Regarding language, in "The Japanese Language and Philosophical Questions,"[23] an essay included in *Continued Studies in the Intellectual History of Japan*[24] (1935), drawing on the work of Wilhelm von Humboldt (1767–1835), Watsuji writes, "The spiritual character and linguistic formation of an ethnic group are closely integrated."[25] According to Watsuji, the structure of a language reflects the intellectual character of an ethnic group. Or it may even be said that it is this character itself. From this perspective, he ties the particular grammatical qualities of Japanese, which does not distinguish gender or number, to the intellectual character of Japanese people who show more interest in morality and art than rational understanding. He not only conducts this kind of analysis but attempts to engage in his own thought based on the sense of a "pure Japanese language," in order to demonstrate the potential of the Japanese language to develop in a logical direction. Specifically, he takes up the question "What sort of thing [*koto*] is what is referred to as 'to be'?" Watsuji was thus one of the few thinkers who considered the particular traits of the Japanese language in connection with philosophical questions, and having done so he also made concrete efforts to expand its potential.

According to Watsuji, the question "What sort of thing [*koto*] is what is referred to as 'to be'?" includes four issues. First "thing [*koto*]," second "what is referred to," third "who refers to 'what is referred to,'" and fourth, "to be." In relation to the first issue, he begins by examining the difference between *koto* and *mono*. For example, if we consider the "thing" (*koto*) that is referred to as "to move" (*ugoku*), on the one hand "moving" (*ugoku-koto*) is that which makes a moving "thing" (*mono*) a thing that "moves," and in this sense provides the foundation or basis for a "moving thing" (*ugoku-mono*). At the same time, however, it also belongs to a "moving thing" (*ugoku-mono*) as the "moving" (*ugoku-koto*) of a "moving thing" (*ugoku-mono*). In this sense, *koto* is the foundation that makes a *mono* what it is and at the same time belongs to a *mono*. *Koto*, when written with a specific Chinese character, can also mean "language" or "words,"[26] and as such "reveals" matters. By doing so it discovers "things" (*mono*). On the other hand, at the same time this *koto* (words) is based on the self-understanding nature of the "person" (*mono*) who produces it. In this sense *koto* is indeed the foundation of *mono*, but on a more fundamental level is itself based on *mono*. Watsuji focused on this kind of interplay between *mono* and *koto*.

Yamauchi Tokuryū also focused on these views expressed by Watsuji. In *The Metaphysics of Meaning*,[27] published in 1967, he addressed the question of whether what things are should be referred to as *mono* or *koto*. Unlike Watsuji, Yamauchi asserts that *mono* can only become what they are by being some kind of *koto*, and "along with being the basis that makes *mono* whatever sort of '*mono*' that they are, '*koto*' are also the source of the various ways of being of '*mono*.'"[28] He also focused on the idea that *mono* that are made *mono* by *koto* in this way do not simply exist but also express themselves. In short, *mono* that are made *mono* by *koto* possess "meaning." In other words, they are "semantic beings." What Yamauchi tries to argue in *The Metaphysics of Meaning* is that what things are can only be grasped in this "semantic world."

Hiromatsu Wataru taught the philosophy of science at the University of Tokyo, and he too considered the relationship between *mono* and *koto* and developed his own worldview. He expressed this with the phrase "from a *mono* worldview (image of the world) to a *koto* worldview." This approach was developed in works such as *The Intersubjective Ontological Structure of the World*[29] (1972, Keisō Shobō), *Outpost to the Koto Worldview*[30] (1975, Keisō Shobō), and *Being and Meaning: Cornerstone of the Koto Worldview*. In *Being and Meaning*, Hiromatsu explains that in a *koto* worldview, substance does not first exist in itself and then secondarily enter into relationships; this is a relationist ontological view in which it is relationships that are the primary existence, and what is commonly called "substance" is nothing more than a "nodule" stipulated by them. In contrast, he believes the "*mono* worldview (*mono* image of the world)" arises out of reifying these primary existence relationships and misidentifying the "substance" thus established as primary existence. In *The Ontological Structure of the Cognitive World*,[31] volume 1 of *Being and Meaning*, Hiromatsu argues that the "subjective-objective" schema is established on the basis of this substantist image of the world and gives rise to aporias in epistemology. He then sets out to strip away this schema, elucidate the "four limbed structure" of the epistemic world, and "grant rights to the so-called intersubjective validity of cognition."[32] The "four-limbed structure" refers to phenomena having a two-limbed structure in both their subjective and objective aspects. We are not only conscious of things in terms of sensory data; to give an easy-to-understand example, in addition to sensory data regarding its appearance, I am also aware that what I am looking at right now is a pencil. These two elements (manifesting data[33] and semantic understanding[34]) are the two limbs of a phenomenon's objective aspect. On the other hand, I do not see what is in front of me as a "pencil" as a unique individual, or as "me as me"; I see it with the awareness that it being a "pencil" is presumably a "fact" with universal validity among other people as well. I see it, so to speak, from a universal, communal subjective perspective. Here I am "me beyond me" or "me as someone." These two elements (the particular person who perceives[35] and the generic someone who understands[36]) are the two limbs of a phenomenon's subjective aspect. Hiromatsu believed that the phenomenal world constitutes the linked form of the four-limbed structure of these four moments (it is phenomena of this linked form that are *koto.*) He emphasizes that these four moments do not first exist and then reciprocally relate to each other but rather can only exist as the terms of the functional relationship of this linked form of a four-limbed structure. It was his understanding that the substantist image of the world held in the past had arisen from mistakenly thinking of these moments as though they existed independently.[37]

(3) Reality and Actuality

Kimura Bin (1931–2021), who had many accomplishments in the domain of psychiatry as well as a deep interest in philosophical questions, also discussed the issue of *mono* and *koto.* Based on the *mono-koto* discourse of Watsuji and Hiromatsu described above, he discusses this topic from the perspective of psychopathology with fascinating results. In concrete terms, what he presents is the issue of *mono* and *koto* in relation to the symptoms of patients suffering from depersonalization.

One of the works in which Kimura discusses depersonalization is *The Psychopathology of Self-Awareness: What Is Called the "Self"*[38] (1978). Here he records the complaints of a twenty-four-year-old woman. "I cannot feel 'myself.' 'Myself' has disappeared. . . . no matter what I do, I do not feel as though 'myself' is doing it. All 'emotion' has vanished." Patients with depersonalization have this sense of a loss of self. At the same time, this patient also describes her own condition as follows. "Depth, distance and proximity have disappeared, and everything seems lined up on a single plane. . . . Even when I look at something made of iron it doesn't seem heavy, and paper cuttings don't seem light."[39] The sense of objects really existing is also lost. In *Time and Self,*[40] published in 1982, Kimura views this loss of the sense of the real existence of both the self and external objects as the disappearance of *koto*.

For example, if a person with depersonalization holds a lump of iron in their hand, they perceive it as a lump of iron. They have no problem in this regard. But this is simply a *mono*, and the "expression" it ought to have is missing. At the sites of our experience where we concretely see and hear something present alongside us, normally this thing does not only exist objectively as a *mono* completely unrelated to our own existence; if we pick up a lump of iron, for example, we feel its weight and the fear that we may drop it. Things being experienced by us in this way, the world appearing to us in this way—this is *koto*. Here *mono* are filled with "expression." *Mono* can be said to coexist with *koto*. In patients with depersonalization, this co-existing *koto* is lost. In *Time and Self* Kimura writes, "The *koto*-type sensations that provide a rich backdrop for the *mono*-type perceptions of the world in everyday life when a person is healthy completely disappear, and the world loses its expression."[41]

In the 1990s Kimura began to use the terms "reality" and "actuality" to express this issue of *mono* and *koto*. In *The Psychopathology of Chance*[42] (1994) he writes that reality is "spoken of regarding the existence of real objects that comprise reality from the perspective of recognizing and confirming them," while actuality "is spoken of regarding the workings of actions operating on reality themselves."[43] In other words, actuality is the "reality" of things we are conscious of in the midst of acting when we try to operate on reality. In "Reality and Actuality,"[44] an essay published in 1997 (and included in *The Poetry and Truth of Schizophrenia*[45] in 1998), drawing on Bergson's understanding of memory and Gilles Deleuze (1925–1995)'s interpretation of Bergson (*Le Bergsonisme*, 1966), Kimura writes about his idea of "actuality" as follows.

> The actuality of meaning creates itself ceaselessly from the latency of memory that is in all respects private . . . as a "womb," and realizes itself as a constant self-realization from virtuality, in the state of a generator, at the point of intersection with the world, in the manner of developing itself in material reality.[46]

This is an understanding in which an actuality that is one with material reality is created through the active involvement of memory, something that is latent (virtual). To put it in terms of the depersonalization described above, in patients with this condition this actuality realized in material reality "in the state of a generator" falls away, and reality thus laid bare, so to speak, is perceived just as it is.

Kimura's doubts about the state of modern psychopathology and psychiatry were presumably what lay behind his focus on actuality and its differences from reality. Along with notable advances in the scientific study of the central nervous system, the trend toward attempting to reduce all mental activities and mental illnesses to material processes in the brain was gaining strength, but it was Kimura's understanding that genuine psychiatry emerges where we encounter states of mind that cannot be addressed by mechanically measuring or quantifying them. In *Thinking About the Pathology of the Mind* (1994), Kimura writes about his intentions in addressing the topic of actuality.

> Science has no idea how to handle this actuality, because actuality cannot be fixed, even for an instant. Only reality that can be fixed in the perfect tense can be the object of science. The "life sciences," therefore, do not study actual life but only biological material. We, on the other hand, are always living in the present continuous tense. To observe the actual, immaterial life of the present continuous tense, we require a gaze that is outside of science. For psychiatry that aims to treat people with mental illness who struggle to live in actual interpersonal situations, the importance of looking at things from a point of view outside of science cannot be overstated.[47]

This assertion of Kimura's can be seen as having been aimed not only at psychiatry but at our scientistic way of looking at things in general. It is a claim that has great significance when we try to grasp our reality itself.

(4) Phenomenology

One of the fields that attracted a lot of attention from scholars after the Second World War was phenomenology. Of course, as has already been mentioned, Nishida Kitarō had discussed Husserl in the 1910s, and the foundations of the study of phenomenology in Japan had been laid in the 1930s by scholars such as Yamauchi Tokuryū and Takahashi Satomi who had studied under Husserl in the 1920s. Heidegger's philosophy had also been introduced in the 1920s—even before the publication of *Being and*

Time—by philosophers such as Tanabe Hajime and Miki Kiyoshi, and had come to be widely known. But it was not until after the war that writings on phenomenology were introduced in detail and debated in earnest. Great contributions to this development were made by scholars such as Watanabe Jirō and Tatematsu Hirotaka (1931–2016), who translated Husserl's writings on phenomenology, and Takiura Shizuo (1927–2011) and Kida Gen (1928–2014), who introduced the thought of Maurice Merleau-Ponty. Regarding the study of Heidegger in Japan, a significant role was played by the publication of *The Complete Writings of Heidegger* by several scholars, including Tsujimura Kōichi and Kayano Yoshio (1925–2016).

There has been a significant body of scholarship on phenomenology, but Nitta Yoshihiro's *Nishida's Philosophy as a Contemporary Inquiry*[48] (1998) is particularly notable for its relationship to Japanese philosophy. Nitta states that Nishida's theory of pure experience, that is, an attempt to place "experience" at the foundation of all knowledge as the only true existence and explain everything on this basis, or, to put it another way, an attempt to seek the foundation of knowledge in experience, must face a significant problem. Namely, in order for it to be possible to make experience the foundation of knowledge and ground all knowledge on it, grounds for making all knowledge knowable must already exist in experience itself. This is a difficult problem, because the fact that these grounds are the grounds of knowledge means that they themselves cannot be the object of knowledge. While being that which makes knowledge arise, with the emergence of knowledge they fade into the background. In other words, at the site of the emergence of knowledge there is a "simultaneous occurrence of appearance and disappearance." In other words, the apparent world has the character of the "appearance of what is not apparent."[49]

Phenomenology is also focused on the same kind of situation. Husserl, for example, says in his later period that the existence of the world is not confirmed in the manner of direct sensory perception, but is rather given in the form of a constant underlying foundation. In other words, he asserts that the fact that there is a world is always tacitly affirmed from the start as a passive belief before the objects of perception are posited. Nitta, however, believed that the difficult problem just described could not be completely overcome through Husserl's methodological approach of "reflection," because what is at issue are the very grounds that make reflection itself possible. He asserts that the methodological approach of reflection itself "blocks the path to properly resolving this situation."[50] The question then becomes how philosophical contemplation can "return to within its own workings themselves" or "reach its own roots" without relying on reflection, and on this point Nitta says that "a change in the direction of contemplation itself" is required. Moreover, he argues that this must not be a horizontal change in direction such as that found in reflection, but rather a shift in vertical orientation.

From this perspective Nitta focuses on Nishida's thought, particularly that of his later period. In 1944, right at the end of his life, Nishida published an essay entitled "Space,"[51] in which he writes as follows about the "world of true existence," that is, the world in which we are situated and in which we act. "The world is a world that expresses itself thoroughly without foundation, a world that reflects itself in itself, and a world that forms itself self-expressively."[52] Here the term "expression" is used, but it does not simply mean something being transferred to a different place. Nor does it simply mean something latent being made manifest. The relationship between the world and its self-expression cannot be understood as this kind of relationship between the latent and the manifest. Instead, what Nishida refers to is, in Nitta's words, the "simultaneous occurrence of appearance and disappearance." The "world that expresses itself" must "always have all its relationships apparent, and furthermore be something that does not appear, something that self-negatingly manifests itself."[53] While being something that does not appear as itself, "always something that does not appear," the world nevertheless expresses itself through self-negation. This manner in which Nishida addresses "the totality of the structure of experience of the world and human beings" through examining the living relationship between the dimensions of objectness and nonobjectness was highly regarded by Nitta.

2. The Self and the Other

(1) THE RECEPTION OF EXISTENTIALISM

The intellectual movement of existentialism became a major trend in Japan after the Second World War. French existentialist thought, such as the work of Jean-Paul Sartre (1905–1980) and Albert Camus (1913–1960), was introduced and had a broad influence not only on philosophy but also on other domains such as literature. Sartre's assertion that human beings do not simply exist like things but "project" themselves toward the future and that this "existence precedes essence" had a major influence on Japanese thinkers searching for the direction society should take. At the same time, thinkers who sought to address the question of "existence" also emerged out of the philosophical tradition following Kierkegaard. The Jaspers Association was founded in 1951 by Mutai Risaku and Kaneko Takezō and the Kierkegaard Association was founded in 1950 by Masuda Keisaburō (1904–1990) and Iijima Munetaka (1920–1987). The Existentialism Association was established in 1957 as a successor to these groups, and activities along similar lines were later taken up by the Existential Thought Association in 1985.

Works of excellent scholarship concerning existentialism, such as Kaneko's *The Philosophy of Existential Reason: Based on Jaspers' Philosophy* (1953), appeared from a comparatively early date. The high level of interest in Jaspers' philosophy during this period was related to the large number of thinkers who saw the task of existentialism as looking unflinchingly at the irrational elements found inside human beings, such as hatred and desire. Underlying this was the sympathy many philosophers had for Jaspers' understanding of "reason" that did not discard rational cognition or the scientific view of things, but while including such elements at the same time turned its attention to elements that transcend them. Kaneko, too, as he indicates in the title of his book, established his own standpoint from the perspective of an "existential reason" that had this sort of character.

(2) REAL EXISTENCE AND EMPTY EXISTENCE—THE "I" AND THE SELF

In *Place: Existence in a Twofold World*[54] (1992), Ueda Shizuteru, who was discussed in the previous chapter, contrasts "real existence" and "empty existence" as human ways of being and engages in a fascinating examination of this theme. According to Ueda—drawing on a Buddhist worldview and Nishida's philosophy—the place where we exist is twofold; in terms of Nishida's distinction, it is both the "place of being" and the "place of absolute nothingness." We not only exist in the world (are "beings in the world") but are also at the same time situated in "an infinite, void-like opening." We cannot directly see this "world/void" duality, but when this duality is the place of the being in question, the self of this subject is no longer closed off within self identity but rather opens itself toward this place as a "self that is not self." Ueda says that the void appears within this kind of self like the border of the world. This was Ueda's distinctive understanding of the self. In other words, when a self is not closed off within itself but open to the place in which it is situated, this self is negated and becomes "not I" ("empty existence"). When "the opening of place becomes light that illuminates the self," the self of this I-that-is-not-I becomes itself again. Ueda understands the self as this whole process of "leaving the self and returning to the self." He also describes the self as being "the awareness that 'I, losing I, am I.'"[55] Ueda expresses this way of being of the self within the "world/void" duality with the phrases "real existence/empty existence," that is, "real existence that is empty existence, empty existence that is real existence."

In *What Am I?*, published in 2000, Ueda calls the "I" that is closed off within the self, and therefore the "I" in which obsession with the self begins to operate, the "ego,"[56] and the I that rejects itself and tries to open itself up to the outside the "self."[57] He expresses the self-understanding when the "ego" driven by "I-ness" says "I am me" as "self-consciousness," and in contrast views the opening of the "self" to the place in which it is situated and "knowing the I" that is illuminated by the opening of this place as "self-awareness." Ueda says that at the start of the birth of self-awareness there is "awareness," an event in which the husk of the old self is stripped away. As these terms suggest, this "awareness" being verbalized and the understanding of the self being established is "self-understanding." He also says there is development of this "self-awareness" in a different dimension, namely, the dimension in which the state of "self-awareness" is reexamined within the "understanding of the self and the world" of the self as a "being in the world." Ueda considers this entire process to be "self-awareness."[58]

Izutsu Toshihiko (1914–1993) also discusses the difference between the "ego" and the "self" in *To the Depths of Meaning: The Water Level of Eastern Philosophy*,[59] published in 1985. As I will discuss in relation to language in the next section, Izutsu explores the domain of the deep layer of consciousness that undergirds its surface layer while drawing on the psychology of Carl Jung (1875–1961). If that which lies at the center of the surface layer consciousness is the "ego," that which "forms the core of a truly integrated subjectivity in the deep layer of consciousness"[60] is the "self." Modern people in a globalized society have been made uniform and average. They cannot help living only as "egos" on the surface layer of consciousness, and through "ego" being enlarged in this way, that is, through the surface layer of consciousness becoming thicker, the "self" is covered over and hidden. In contrast to this, the various intellectual traditions of the East have been developed with a focus on the "self" found in the deeper layer. Izutsu maintains that the "investigation of the true self" that has been thus obscured has been the "starting point, foundation, and central topic of philosophical inquiry" in the East. According to Izutsu, the defining characteristic of Eastern thought is to be found in its attempting to understand human existence as a "multilayered structure" including the "self" of the deep layer, and at the same time also in its aiming to understand this "self" not simply conceptually, but "people who are philosophers beginning by pursuing the true 'self' subjectively to the depths of their own being and living it themselves."[61] Izutsu refers to a subject capable of living in this way with the phrase "Eastern subjectivity." This is also related to the "originary subjectivity" discussed by Nishitani Keiji discussed in chapter 7.

(3) The Self and the Other

Kimura Bin's study of psychopathology, as can be seen from the titles of works such as *Time and Self* and *Schizophrenia and the Other*[62] (1990), was profoundly connected to issues of the self and the other. He was particularly focused on the "self" in relation to the depersonalization discussed in the previous section. The major characteristic of depersonalization is indeed the sense of a loss of self in which patients "truly cannot feel the thing called 'self.'" To express this in terms of *mono* and *koto*, where normally both exist overlapping each other, here *koto*, that is, meaning and expression, has been stripped away from experience. Looked at from the other side, this describes a "self" that is understood not as a substantial being that maintains an unchanging identity, in other words, a *mono*, but only as *koto*.

In *Time and Self*, Kimura says that the "self" does not simply refer to a *mono* that exists here and now, but to a state in which the *koto* of thinking and speaking now is tied to various experiences and thoughts from the past and events that are expected to occur in the future and is fulfilled by the countless meanings that arise through these relationships. In other words, the "self" can be described as the *koto*, or network between *koto* and *koto*, imbued with this richness of expression. The sense of a loss of self experienced by patients with depersonalization is thought to be caused by this "rich expanse" of *koto* having been lost or stripped away from their "I," leaving only a *mono* that exists here and now. When he understands *koto* and the "self" in this way, Kimura can be seen as drawing on Nishida's understanding of "experience." In this work he quotes a passage from Nishida's "Introduction" to *From That Which Acts to That Which Sees*, "At the root of Eastern culture, something like seeing the shape of that which has no shape and hearing the voice of that which has no voice lies submerged," and states that the "that which has no shape" and "that which has no voice" Nishida refers to are indeed nothing other than *koto*.

In his essay "Pathology of the Self and the 'Absolute Other' "[63] (included in *Questions for Nishida's Philosophy*,[64] edited by Ueda Shizuteru, 1990), Kimura engages in a fascinating examination of "the other" while tying it to issues in psychopathology. Specifically, he discusses "the other" seen in schizophrenia in conjunction with "the absolute other" Nishida Kitarō discusses in his essay "I and You"[65] (included in *The Self-Aware Determination of Nothingness*,[66] 1932). According to Kimura, "the other" seen in patients with schizophrenia appears not outside the self, but rather in the most interior, core part of the self. It moreover appears in a manner that causes fundamental doubt about the selfness of the being of the self. This other is not a concrete other like that seen in paranoid delusions, but an unknowable other lacking concreteness. Schizophrenic patients experience their minds being read and their wills being controlled by this unknowable other. Unlike in the case of paranoid delusions, this other is not an other conceived on the foundation of the self or as a projection of the self; on the contrary, here it is the other that is the foundation, and the concrete contents of the self emerge as its self-realization. Kimura expresses the otherness of this foundational other as "absolute otherness."[67] Kimura tried to understand the "other" with these characteristics experienced by schizophrenia patients by superimposing it on the "absolute other" described by Nishida.

Of course, these two conceptions of "the other" cannot be thought of as exactly the same. Nishida says, "I am me through acknowledging you, and you are you through acknowledging me," but in such cases he is thinking of reciprocal acknowledgment with a concrete other. Here he envisions a reciprocal relationship in which not only are you the foundation of my self-awareness, but at the same time I am the root of your self-awareness. In the case of patients with schizophrenia, in contrast, the other is one-sidedly the foundation of the self. Conversely, in Nishida's case the "I-you" relationship is a reciprocal, twofold relationship. It goes without saying, however, that they have in common a focus on the absolute "otherness" of "the other."

(4) RELATIONSHIPS AND THE BINOMIAL RELATIONSHIP OF "I" AND "YOU"

In *Between Person and Person: A Psychopathological Study of Japan*[68] (1972), Kimura Bin includes a chapter entitled "The Japanese Language and the Humanity of Japanese People" in which he points out that compared to European languages, Japanese has many more first- and second-person pronouns, and argues that this is closely connected to the nature of self-other relationships. Within Japanese-speaking society, who the self, the speaking subject or agent, and its interlocutor are is not unambiguously determined from the start but rather can only be established through concrete interpersonal relationships. The relationship between the two parties is more significant than the identity of the self and its interlocutor, and words to represent each are chosen on this basis. Kimura expresses this with the phrase "supremacy of relationships."[69]

When Kimura speaks in this way, he is drawing on Watsuji Tetsurō's concept of "relationality" and the ethics he constructed based upon it. According to Watsuji, before human beings are individuals they are already living in relationships with others. Ethics is the order or logic that runs through these relationships, and human beings are living with this ethics from the moment their existence begins. To put it another way, ethics is always present within human existence itself. Kimura highlighted the connection between this way of being in which the relationship to the other has fundamental significance and the Japanese language's distinctive use of multiple first- and second-person pronouns.

In *Experience and Thought*[70] (1977), Mori Arimasa (1911–1976) points out that the relationship with the other possesses critical significance for Japanese people. He begins with the view that "experience" is the "accumulation of sensations." These are gradually organized, ordered, and come to reveal universal modes of existence, and their ultimate form is "thought." Defining "experience" and "thought" in this way, Mori discusses the unique character of the "experience" of Japanese people in contrast to what is found in the West. According to Mori, the distinctive character of Japanese "experience" lies in the difficulty of its deepening, that is, the difficulty of ripening it into "thought." He argues that "experience," for Japanese people, "cannot be analyzed as one's own individual experience." "For Japanese people, 'experience' does not define a single individual but rather multiple people, or, in concrete terms, a relationship formed by two people."[71] Mori's phrasing is idiosyncratic and difficult to understand, but simply stated he asserts that within Western experience the individual or the subjectivity of the individual arises out of "experience," but in the case of Japanese people this subjectivity of the individual does not emerge. "I" am always connected to "you." "You" exist first, and "I" can only be anything insofar as I am facing "you." He refers to this kind of relationship in which "I" am defined by "you" as a "binomial relationship"[72] or "binomial composite system."[73] Moreover, "I" am always closed off inside this relationship. This is what Mori says impedes the "deepening of experience." Experience arising atop a binomial relationship means that experiences cannot be separated from their contexts. Experiences only have meaning within this relationship, and this prevents them being universalized. Experience arising out of binomial relationships implies the formation of a closed-off space. In order to maintain this closed-off space, that which is strange or unknown is excluded from it and only accepted after having been transformed into something conducive to its maintenance. Mori refers to this "experience" lacking in openness with the word *taiken* (personal, closed experience).[74] He asserts that Japanese people's "experiences" have a strong tendency to transform into *taiken* before they can ripen into "thought."[75]

(5) Roles and Masks

An emphasis being placed on relationality as described above, or on the relationships we form with specific individuals in particular instances, also means an emphasis being placed on the "roles" we play in these situations.

In *Between Person and Person*, Kimura Bin argues that Japanese people have a strong aptitude for "melancholy affinity." Kimura had held a symposium with Wolfgang Blankenburg (1928–2002), best known as the author of *Der Verlust der natürlichen Selbstverständlichkeit* (1971). Blankenburg argued that while in Western societies, in which consciousness of self-identity is very strong, there is an emphasis on "I-identity" (*Ich-Identität*), in Japanese society, in which there is an emphasis on relationships, a consciousness of taking on a certain role, that is, "role-identity" (*Rollenidentität*), occupies a supreme position, and overly identifying with a particular role can lead to melancholy.[76]

Watsuji Tetsurō's "Mask and Persona"[77] (1935) is a widely known study of the issue of "roles." Comparing sculpture and Noh theater masks, he asserts that the latter have a characteristic not found in the former. To express humanity, Noh masks strip away all else and leave only the face. This disembodied face, however, has the power to freely restore its limbs. In the case of a Noh mask, this power permeates the limbs and entire body of the performer and underpins this body's movement during the performance. After having presented this view, Watsuji then discusses the polysemic nature of the word "persona" based on this characteristic of Noh masks. "Persona" originally referred to masks used in dramas. It then came to signify the roles performed in these dramas. According to Watsuji, it was through the power of masks described above, that is, the power of a mask to absorb a performer's limbs and actions within itself, that this transition became possible. A mask does not stop at the actor's face it covers, but permeates their entire body and the role they are performing. This is what enabled the shift in the meaning of "persona" from mask to role. Based on this shift, in this essay Watsuji discusses "persona" having come to have various meanings (grammatical person, divine persona, persona in the sense of a person's character or personality, and so on).

Sakabe Megumi (1936–2009) was another thinker who engaged in a fascinating examination of this topic of "masks." As can be seen from his 1976 work *The Anxiety of Reason: The Genesis and Structure of Kant's Philosophy*,[78] Sakabe took the study of Kant as his starting point. From the perspective that a vague uneasiness that threatened the continued existence of the traditional "reason" of the West lay at the root of Kant's thought, and that this may indeed have been the driving force behind his inquiry, in this work Sakabe attempts to examine the significance of Kant's philosophy from a hidden substratum that had gone almost entirely unexamined. At the same time, however, Sakabe was also interested in developments in modern thought such as structuralism and the characteristics and structure of the Japanese language, and in the same year he also published *The Hermeneutics of Masks*,[79] a work in which he tied these interests together.

When we speak of masks, as is evident from the Japanese word for "mask" that literally means "temporary face," we are thinking of something temporary or transient. To put this in terms of "roles," we temporarily play a certain role in a certain situation, and our true selves are elsewhere. In other words, we think reality lies in our "bare face" beneath the mask. In *The Hermeneutics of Masks*, Sakabe reveals doubts about this view. He points out that this way of looking at things is a specifically modern perspective, that is, a way of looking at things grounded in categorizing all things based on the logic of identity and viewing their opposition as fixed. Sakabe represents "mask" and "face" with the Japanese word *omote*. In normal use this word means "surface" or "top," but it originated as a contraction of a phrase meaning "front side," the opposite of which is "back side" (*urate*). Which of two opposing sides was "front" and which was "back" in this sense is relative, and it is not as though which is original or essential and which is fake or temporary were determined a priori. Both can be described as reciprocally convertible. In other words, both "front" (*omote*) and "back" (*urate*) can reciprocally change into each other (they are metamorphosable). In the modern era, however, at the hands of the logic of self-identity the relationship between them has generally come to be seen as fixed. That it thus deprives us of this sense of "metamorphosis," Sakabe argues, is indeed one of the evils of modernity.

According to Sakabe, this means that the "bare face," or that which is thought of as reality beneath the "mask," is also in its essence "the other (or 'the other of the other')." In other words, a "pure self with no attachment to otherness" does not exist anywhere. This means that what we call "I" manifests only as a certain concrete "grammatical person = persona," or as a "mask = persona." On this basis, Sakabe writes, "It is equally valid to consider the bare face a metaphor for the mask (not some sort of 'original model') as to consider the mask a metaphor for the bare face."[80]

What is thus referred to as *omote* is neither a mask separated from the bare face nor a "façade" or "phenomenon" distinguished from reality. Sakabe says that on the contrary it can be seen as a "gap" or "intervening space." In other words, he asserts it is the boundary surface on which "the cosmos possessing meaning emerges from the instability of chaos" and "the boundary surface of the 'original person' in which the unobjectified predicate side [Nishida's terminology] . . . within its autonomous transformation begins 'to speak' and 'to acquire concrete form' and 'self' and 'self' emerge face to face [*omote* to *omote*]."[81] *Omote*, in terms of its position, does not belong to either an inside or outside in fixed opposition to each other, but on the contrary exists at their border and autonomously transforms. Here Sakabe goes beyond "masks" and "roles" to engage in a fascinating investigation of the nature of the "self."

3. Language

(1) Experience and Language

From the 1970s to the 1980s, along with other parts of the world Japan saw a flourishing of interest in the topic of language, with the study of the linguistics of figures such as Ferdinand de Saussure being undertaken by Japanese scholars such as Maruyama Keizaburō (1933–1993) and the introduction of *The Linguistic Turn* (1967), a seminal text edited by Richard Rorty (1931–2007). The idea that language is what secures a path to reality for human beings had already been put forward by thinkers such as Wilhelm von Humboldt and Ernst Cassirer (1874–1945), but through this postwar examination of issues related to language there was a clear departure from the perspective that language gives names to already distinguished objects and concepts and constitutes a list of such elements. It came to be clearly asserted that language as our framework for understanding and interpreting events and objects that arise in the world is involved in our experience right from the start, and that without it experience itself is impossible.

Indeed, as the discourse surrounding language in recent years has shown, there is undeniably a profound connection between experience and language. However, experience is not expressed in language just as it is. In "The Science of Experience,"[82] an essay published in 1939, Nishida Kitarō writes as follows concerning the fundamental limitations of language.

> For example . . . when we say, "there is a horse over there," our experience becomes fixed. . . . it is determined by some kind of static thing instead of action. Language separates several bundles from the living main body and causes them to congeal. This is useful, but results in something completely different from experience. Regarding experience, language possesses its own essential limitations.[83]

Nishida's warning regarding the danger of the difference between language and experience being overlooked still has great significance today. We cannot look back before language, but it cannot be said that language is experience just as it is. The problem lies between these two elements, that is, between language and experience.

In *The Existence of Language: Zen and Literature* (1997),[84] for example, Ueda Shizuteru attempts to examine experience by viewing it in terms of the duality of experience itself and our self-understanding of it through language. Experience possessing this duality can be understood in two ways depending on which aspect is emphasized. On the one hand, the view can be taken that it is only with self-understanding through language that experience can be experience, and on the other hand, because language can only exist as individual languages that are "limited to a designated lexical sphere and specific segmental organization," the view that experience itself will forever remain beyond the understanding of language can also be advanced.[85]

Ueda, however, does not understand language with either of these one-sided approaches, and instead views experience and its self-understanding as a single, sequential process. To begin with, in experience itself the framework for understanding the world we already possess is broken through. In other words, language is taken away. Here, however, experience appears as "primitive emotional reaction sounds." Ueda interprets these sounds as "root words." They are not yet language. They are the language before language, the first event in what will lead to language. Ueda expresses this series of actions in which language is taken away and then sought once again with the phrase "departing from language and emerging into language." A state in which both subjectivity and objectivity had been undifferentiated at the start is segmented and separated out into subject and object. Ueda breaks this process of segmentation into a primary segment and a secondary segment. Even within the primary segment, things are expressed in terms of an "A is B" relationship between subject and object. Here, however, "at the same time a reflection toward the undifferentiated state that is the source of 'subject and object' will be superimposed on this relationship."[86] A is B because of being brought back to "undifferentiated nothingness" in which A is not B. The primary segment is thus a segment in which "A is B" and "A is not B" arise simultaneously. Here the development toward verbal expression at the site of differentiated intellect is rejected by a turn toward "undifferentiated nothingness." (In Zen, for example, things in this dimension are expressed with the words "mountains are mountains, and mountains are not mountains, therefore they are mountains"). In the secondary segment, in contrast, a state of affairs emerges from this kind of dimension and is analyzed, understood, and explained as the relationship between subject and object arising at the place of differentiated intellect. This secondary segment is also thought of as the dimension of the self-development of "undifferentiated nothingness." In this way Ueda attempts to understand the relationship between experience and language as experience with undifferentiated subject and object in which language is taken away and the self-development of this experience toward primary and secondary segments, or as "a three-dimensional, dynamic connection that spans three levels or dimensions."[87]

Sakabe Megumi, as noted in the previous section, had a deep interest in the Japanese language and undertook an intriguing examination of terms such as *omote* (front, face), *kage* (shadow, something hidden), and *shirushi* (sign, omen). (Here we can see the influence of Tokieda Motoki [1900–1967]'s discourse on Japanese grammar and view of language referred to as "language process theory" and Watsuji Tetsurō's attempt to engage in philosophy through the Japanese language.) In 1972 Sakabe published an essay entitled "The Logic and Thought of Western Languages and the Japanese Language,"[88] in which he attempted to elucidate the logic or structural characteristics of Western languages and the Japanese language based on instances of concrete language usage that are placed outside the field of view of logic in a narrow sense. His interest in language continued, and he went on to publish *The Poetics of Persona: Narration, Behavior, and Mind* in 1989 and *Narration* in 1990. In a chapter of the former entitled

"Narration and Silence," Sakabe views the act of *katari* (narration) or *kataru* (to narrate) as something positioned between the top-down vertical speech act of *noru* (impart from on high) and the bottom-up vertical speech act of *utau* (to sing) or *tonaeru* (to chant), and understood this place where *katari* emerges as a middle ground sandwiched between "*shijima* [silence] as condensed silence" above and "the chaotic abyss of silence as the simple absence of language" below. He then inserts this understanding of "narration" or "language" into the context of Nishida's philosophy. "Starting from here, I would like to understand things like 'the face of the transcendental predicate' and 'the place of nothingness' as this kind of rich '*shijima* [silence]' in which 'language' and 'narration,' including symbolic expression, arise."[89] Here too we can find important clues to understanding the connection between experience and language.

(2) The Creativity of Language

On the one hand, language is something that is institutionalized within society and has a fixed framework (for example, the domain of meaning of individual words is determined by the language in question). Our experience is understood after having been inserted into this framework, and this creates a worldview as a way of looking at or seeing the world. On the other hand, language also tries to break down this kind of fixed framework and approach matters themselves. This creative power of language has been addressed in various ways.

For example, in "Language: Its Power of 'Fiction,' "[90] an essay included in *The Existence of Language: Zen and Literature*, Ueda Shizuteru focuses on language's "power of 'fiction.'" Normally, we express things that have actually occurred through language in a form without logical contradictions. In this sense language normally has a "real" character. Sometimes, however, we say "impossible 'things [*koto*]' that in reality could never happen or constitute logical contradictions,"[91] not simply as a slip of the tongue but with the active intention of doing so. For example, in poems we may describe things that could not occur in reality. But this is not simply an expression of imaginary or fantastical things. Here expression is given to "things" grasped by "their slipping free of the limitations of perception by 'me' and expanding into unbounded places."[92] Through such expressions of "fiction" we try to approach "things" themselves that cannot be grasped within the existing framework of language. To give a different example, in Zen there are sayings such as "when a person is crossing over a bridge, the bridge is flowing while the river is not." What is being expressed could never occur in reality. But far from being meaningless, in order to express "things" understood through the experience of Zen, things we normally experience or the logic running through them are inverted. By actively upending the logic of our ordinary experience, "things" are pushed to the fore. In this way language does not stop at being a rigid framework for understanding the world but also has the power to express that which transcends such constraints. Ueda calls this function of language, an advanced function of which nothing else is capable, language's "power of 'fiction.'"

Sasaki Ken'ichi (born in 1943), who has published many works in the field of aesthetics, focuses on the creative nature of rhetoric. In "Rhetoric as the Art of Discovery: Figure and Imagination,"[93] published in *Thought*, Sasaki argues that figure as rhetorical expression has a kind of "substantiveness." This is "literary style" or the ornamentation of language, but it is not simply decoration; like deeply impressive rhetoric that remains in its original form in one's memory, it possesses "evident figure-ness." It has an "absoluteness" that cannot be reduced to anything else. This kind of expression possessing substantiveness that remains in the memory "regulates new understanding and provides the nucleus for new expression."[94] In this sense, figure has a creative function. As a facilitator of the activities of the imagination, it is a driving force in new figures being given. In other words, it functions as "ars inveniendi (the art of discovery or invention)." In this sense rhetoric can be said to possess substantiveness and creativeness.

While Ueda asserted that language has the "power of 'fiction,'" biblical scholar Yagi Seiichi (born in 1932) speaks on the contrary of the reality of language (particularly religious language) in works such as *Religion and Language/Religious Language*[95] (1993). Yagi views religious language as expressing "things that really exist," albeit in a different sense than the "descriptive language" that objectively describes the things and events that exist before our eyes. Of course, even in Yagi's understanding, religious language is not something that describes objective facts shared by speaker and listener that anyone can verify. On the contrary, it expresses things experienced within the speaker themselves and can thus be characterized as "expressive language." It cannot be verified, but it does not express "fiction" with no basis. For example, Socrates is said to have spoken of "a kind of divine, supernatural sign" (*daimonion*) that had appeared to him from the time he was a small child, and while it is not clearly specified, this phrase can be understood as describing his experience of something that approached him in a way that was difficult to oppose and that he could not help accepting with a sense of awe. That such a thing could be experienced is something other people can understand, and here a kind of rationality can be sought. An inescapable reality can be said to exist in religious language spoken on the basis of "the experience of a working that transcends both humanity and nature and breathes life into our entire personality." Yagi believes that here the "understandable, verifiable reality most fundamental to our lives" is expressed.[96]

In his book *One Life: Hints for Living Well*,[97] haiku poet and scholar of German idealist philosophy Ōmine Akira (1929–2018) invokes Friedrich Hölderlin's (1770–1843) understanding that poems are human beings' reply to the summons of "being" and writes about the nature of poetry as follows.

> Because poetry is work that takes as its materials neither color nor sound but language, something that lacks substance and cannot be seen, it is different from other arts, and forms the domain in which language displays its purest function. As for where this poetry that is the working of pure language comes from, it emerges as a reflection of the infinite. The pure language we call "poetry" can only be created in the innocent place where the human mind in some way interacts with the infinite.[98]

In Ōmine's view, poetry is pure language that emerges into being illuminated in the light of the infinite and can thus be described as language filled with reality that addresses infinity.

Hase Shōtō (born in 1937) asserts there is an "image reality" in religious statements that differs from the reality of things. For example, in the *Longer Sukhāvatīvyūha Sūtra*, one of the core scriptures of Pure Land Buddhism, there is an account of the king of a certain country who left home and became a Boddhisattva called Dharmākara. Seeing people in anguish, Dharmākara vowed to save all living beings, and after endless contemplation of how this salvation might be accomplished, he hit upon a method of doing so and transformed from a Bodhisattva into a Buddha called Amitābha. While there are those who seek to exclude such stories from the teachings of this religion as too fantastical or as myths that would weaken the veridicality of Buddhism, Hase opposes this kind of demythologization as an approach that will on the contrary lead to a rejection of Buddhist (Pure Land) teachings. Of course, he does not claim that this story is a historical fact. While not a historical fact, it is not merely a fairy tale but rather "something that expresses a wish or demand that lies buried at the root of the lives of all human beings in the form of a story, and brings about self-awareness."[99] Hase believes this kind of story possesses reality as the raising to self-awareness of a fundamental desire of human beings. The power to save people originates in this reality. Hase expresses this as "image reality."

(3) THE DYNAMISM OF LANGUAGE—SURFACE STRUCTURE AND DEEP STRUCTURE

In one aspect, language can be described as a fixed social system of conventional symbols that bear conventional meanings, but rather than view language as this kind of superficial "gaunt system of meanings," Izutsu Toshihiko focused on its deeper layers and tried to understand it as something plastic and dynamic. In doing so he drew on the concept of *ālaya-vijñāna* (repository consciousness) addressed in the Buddhist philosophical tradition of Yogācāra.

In most cases, Buddhism divides the workings of human knowledge, consciousness, or the mind into six categories (eye, ear, nose, tongue, body, and thoughts). On top of this foundation, Yogācāra adds *mānas-vijñāna* (mind consciousness; it can also be described as the fundamental consciousness of self-attachment) and *ālaya-vijñāna* (repository consciousness). According to Yogācāra, all human experiences project a reflection on the depths of consciousness and then disappear. In other words, they leave traces. Their traces immediately or over some span of time gather together and transform into *bīja* (seeds). Just as sprouts emerge from seeds, various beings and representations of beings then emerge from these *bīja*. The place where these *bīja* that are the source of *sarva-dharma* (all that exists) are stored is the *ālaya-vijñāna* (repository consciousness).

In "Culture and Linguistic Ālaya-Consciousness: On the Possibility of Intercultural Dialogue,"[100] an essay included in *To the Depths of Meaning: The Water Level of Eastern Philosophy*, Izutsu contemplates a "linguistic *ālaya*-consciousness" by incorporating the concept of *ālaya-vijñāna* into his theory of language ("extending it in the direction of linguistic theory"[101]). In short, he conceived of this "linguistic *ālaya*-consciousness" as the storehouse of language as "latent meaning" that has not yet been incorporated into language as an established social system. This storehouse is the domain below consciousness where "bodies of potential meaning" that have not yet been segmented or come to acquire a clear meaning are created. There countless "bodies of potential meaning" struggle to emerge into the light of the surface of consciousness, jostling and tangling with each other. The system of conventional symbols that can be called "external language" arises with the "lively activity of this kind of semantic mandala filled with creative energy"[102] as its underpinning. Eventually, if the right conditions are put in place, this kind of potential meaning floats up to the surface of consciousness as actual meaning. The traces of experience formed there then come together once again in the *ālaya*-consciousness to create new *bīja*. Izutsu's understanding of language is thus characterized by its attempt to grasp language not only in terms of its surface structure but as a complete dynamic structure that includes the "deep layer of language" found in the *ālaya*-consciousness.

Maruyama Keizaburō is known as a scholar of Saussure's theory of language, but in his understanding of language he follows the approach of Izutsu seen above. Saussure understood language as *langage*, the universal linguistic capacity (symbolizing activity) possessed by all human beings, viewed in terms of two aspects: *langue*, a language that has been systematized in a society, and *parole*, the individual speech acts of individual people. Drawing inspiration from Izutsu's understanding of language, Maruyama introduced the concepts of surface layer and deep layer and distinguished between *langage* that has been turned into *langue* at the surface level of consciousness and *langage* that has not undergone this conversion at the deep level of consciousness. Moreover, he understood these elements not as separated in a dichotomous manner but as existing in circular motion. In other words, on the one hand *langage* as "the fertility of darkness" is actualized at the surface level of consciousness, becomes *langue* as a tool, and supports its order, while at the same time it also dismantles itself and returns to the deep layer of consciousness.[103] Maruyama understood language as this kind of process of circular motion.

(4) Translation

If, as we have seen, when we try to understand things, language is involved from the start, and how the world appears and ought to be, in other words, our worldview, is determined by the language we speak, the question then arises of whether it is possible to step outside this framework through which we understand the world. We may also ask whether the language spoken inside the birdcage that is the world created by our language can be transferred to another birdcage, whether we can understand and be understood by people in another cage, and how this mutual understanding can be achieved. To address such questions directly means the creation of something that might be called "translation studies." Much remains to be done, however, before this can be established as an independent field. In his article mentioned above, "Culture and Linguistic Ālaya-Consciousness: On the Possibility of Intercultural Dialogue," Izutsu Toshihiko states, "When it comes to an understanding of an *ālaya*-consciousness foundation of meaning in which 'bodies of potential meaning' emerge, we must seriously question the extent to which mutual understanding is possible, and indeed even whether something like mutual understanding can exist in the first place."[104] On the other hand, various attempts have been made to establish translation studies in the sense described above. Eugene A. Nida (1914–2011)'s *Toward a Science of Translating* (1964) is well known in the United States, and works such as Jean-René Ladmiral (born in 1942)'s *Traduire: Théorèmes pour la Traduction* (1979) have been published in France. In Japan, Yanabu Akira (1928–2018) published many works related to translation, including *The Logic of Translation Words: The Structure of Japanese Culture Seen in Language*[105] (1972) and *What Is Translation? Japanese and Translation Culture*[106] (1976).

Particularly notable in Yanabu's theory of translation is his focus on the "cassette effect" of translation words, that is, words used as translations of foreign terms such as *jiyū* (freedom) or *kenri* (right). Here "cassette" is used in the sense of the French word meaning "small box (usually containing precious objects such as jewelry)," and its salient characteristic is that people cannot see inside it. Seeing such a beautiful box, one is led to think it must be full of even more beautiful things. Yanabu believed such jewelry boxes and new translations of foreign words have something in common. The content of freshly coined translations is not clearly understood. They have a fresh resonance, however, and the words themselves fascinate people, creating the impression that they contain new, heretofore inaccessible knowledge. Yanabu calls this effect created by new translations the "cassette effect." For example, Fukuzawa Yukichi translated "society" using Japanese words such as *kōsai* (relationships), *ningen kōsai* (human relationships), and *majiwari* (association), and in most cases translated "individual" as *hito* (person). He strove to keep his writing as easy to understand as possible. In contrast, translations of "individual" as jinmin kakko (each individual citizen) or ikko jinmin (an individual citizen) (Nakamura Masanao) can give the impression of conveying content that cannot be understood using ordinary language or of containing deep meaning that cannot be easily discerned at a glance.[107]

Presumably with such an effect in mind, the technical terminology and specialist jargon created in Japanese in the Meiji period actively employed new words made from Chinese characters rather than native Japanese terms. Chinese studies were largely displaced by the influx of Western studies, but words using Chinese characters themselves were widely introduced and expanded from the Meiji period onward. These terms found favor because they made it easier to create the "cassette effect." Yanabu discusses this in *Circumstances of the Establishment of Translation Words*.[108]

> Translation words are words with different meanings and different origins that have entered the context of the mother tongue. There are always some aspects of such heterogenous terms whose meaning is not understood. The feel of the word is somehow off. It is in fact better for such terms to be like this, feeling off and not precisely understood. . . . words that seem somehow incongruous are better than words that feel solidly familiar in the mother tongue.[109]

It was words that had this sense of incongruity and clearly felt like translations that took hold as the standard Japanese rendering of foreign terms. Instead of *kōsai* or *majiwari*, it is Fukuchi Ouchi (1841–1906)'s *shakai*, a term whose meaning cannot be readily discerned at first sight, that remains with us today as the Japanese translation of "society."

Here, of course, a major issue remains. In the case of both "society" and "individual," these terms were not originally purely academic jargon, but rather words embedded in daily life that have been handed down through history. They have been rendered as *shakai* and *kojin* in Japanese without the meaning thus formed being conveyed, and these words have since been used as both academic terms and everyday words.

The Japanese words *shakai* and *kojin* have come to be used not only as academic terms but also more widely in ordinary life, but most technical terms (particularly philosophical jargon) have not become rooted in everyday language and have been used only in the academic world or a narrow, specialized domain. There is a wide gap between the language of the world of concrete experience and these translated terms. In "The Japanese Language and Philosophical Questions,"[110] an essay included in *Continued Studies in the Intellectual History of Japan*, Watsuji Tetsurō points out that there is a wide chasm between "language that expresses concepts and language that expresses experience," and in *Circumstances of the Establishment of Translation Words* Yanabu discusses this as follows.

> In the fields of scholarship and philosophical thought, Chinese character-heavy expressions that are suitable as translations, on the

> other hand, have put to one side and stripped away expressions in everyday language derived from native Japanese terms that are not suitable as translations . . . Japanese philosophy has put to one side and stripped away the meaning we live in our daily lives. This is indeed contrary to the fundamental stance taken by Descartes 350 years ago when he ventured to write his *Discours de la méthode* in French rather than in Latin.[111]

Those who engage in philosophy must seriously address this issue raised by Yanabu. On the other hand, it is nearly impossible to express philosophy created through abstract thought with everyday or traditional language. The problem is that almost all of the words used in abstract thinking are not words created from words that convey concrete everyday meaning, but words created with no relation to everyday language. While their meaning may not be sufficiently clear, they nevertheless stand on their own as concepts that have been firmly established. Both those who write using abstract language and those who read such texts abandon any consideration of the difference between these words and reality and defer to existing concepts.[112] Thought assembled using Chinese character-heavy technical jargon always comes with the risk that we will abandon the work of deepening and enriching it. This is a danger against which we must remain vigilant.

4. Looking at the Body

(1) What Is the Body?

For much of its history, philosophy sought to explain various phenomena on the basis of rational principles and to discover universal truths. In the process, however, it excluded from its purview examination of the irrational and the contingent that falls outside of what is universal. As a result, it did not give sufficient attention to phenomena such as sensibility and emotion, the body, and language. From the late nineteenth century to the middle of the twentieth century, however, through figures such as Bergson and Merleau-Ponty, philosophy began to turn its attention to the workings of the body that support our perception and cognition at their roots, and the body became one of the main topics addressed by philosophy.

While discourse on the body did not flourish in Japan until the thought of philosophers such as Merleau-Ponty became known after the war, Miki Kiyoshi had focused on the problem of the "body" from an early period. As noted in chapter 7, Miki viewed the body not only as something physical and objective, but as the "body 'animated by the mind (*beseelt*).'" Miki saw human beings as beings with impulses, desires, and feelings who are moved by pathos and interact with things, and he created the "logic of imagination" as a logic through which to understand such beings.

After the war, the discourse on the body was led by figures such as Ichikawa Hiroshi (1931–2002) and Yuasa Yasuo (1925–2005). Drawing on the theories of the body of thinkers such as Bergson and Merleau-Ponty, they examined distinctively Eastern understandings of the body and interaction between the mind and the body. In this context, Nakamura Yūjirō (1925–2017) shed new light on the problem of the body from the perspective of sensus communis and pathos and undertook the "recombination" of existing knowledge.

Ichikawa's theory of the body is presented in works such as *The Body as Mind*, published in 1975, and *The Structure of "Mi* [body, flesh],*" published in 1984. Behind the seemingly paradoxical title of the former lay Ichikawa's view that the life we actually lead cannot be expressed by either the word "mind" or the word "body." We normally think of "the mind" and "the body" as having clearly distinct, fixed domains, but this is nothing more than a preconception; our concrete lives have a "distinctive structure that is neither mind nor body." Ichikawa says that it is this distinctive structure with both mind and body that is fundamental, and "mind" and "body" are no more than aspects or conceptual limits that arise when this structure is abstracted.

To begin with, Ichikawa understands the "body as mind" possessing this distinctive structure as "body as subject." This is not the body that is seen or objectified, but the body we live from the inside and of which we are directly conscious. This forms the "substratum of our acting" and is not something we can grasp in and of itself. Ichikawa describes the nature of this kind of "body as subject" as "not our *having* a body but our *being* a body."[113] On the other hand, we are also conscious of the body as a "body as object." That is, we also understand our body from the outside as something with a form. This is the body viewed as an object, but it is not the same as the body addressed by science. The body addressed by science has been stripped of all "meaning," but the "body as object" is not simply the body as a target of observation; it is my own body I encounter in my concrete life as a being actually living in the world. A distinction or separation arises between this body with a clear form and "I" who look at it and touch it. Rather than being a body, here instead we "*have* a body."

Ichikawa also addressed the issue of the "body as an entangled body." The world in which we live does not consist only of the level of consciousness or the things of which we are conscious. Things that were not realized but had the possibility of being realized, and which give meaning to things that were realized from the background, are one of the elements that comprise reality. If reality that has been realized is an "actual unity," then this can be referred to as a "latent unity." The body is not only the actual body; there is also a latent body that, while hidden by the body as an actual unity, underlies it, supports it, and gives it meaning. Drawing on Paul Valéry (1871–1945)'s concept of *implexe*, Ichikawa calls this an "entangled body."[114] This entangled body lies beyond analysis, but its existence can be negatively confirmed through some kind of abnormality (such as the phenomena of phantom limbs or asomatognosia). The body as an actual unity is an incidental manifestation of this kind of body as an entangled body hidden in the background.

Ichikawa thus strove to elucidate the "distinctive structure that is neither mind nor body" of our lives, and in doing so he focused on the word *mi*[115] (body, flesh) as an expression of its concrete structure. This is examined in detail in *The Structure of Mi*. The word *mi* has multiple definitions and is used with a diverse range of meanings. It refers to both flesh without life and bodies with life, and it can also refer to life itself and people engaged in concrete ways of life in society or their engagement in daily life. Unlike the word *karada*[116] (body) that abstracts the life and mental activities of human beings, *mi* is used to refer to the human being as a whole, including these elements. Ichikawa focused on *mi* as a term capable of aptly expressing "the dynamics of the body we are concretely living"[117] and demonstrating the potential to transcend the framework of a dichotomous mind-object (body) understanding.

Ichikawa's use of the concept of *miwake*[118] (bodily distinction) in relation to *mi* is also fascinating. We insert divisions into continuous, undivided objects of perception through language and construct the "world" through segmentation, but prior to this segmentation we have already engaged in segmenting the world at the level of the body. This is related to our being a self-organizing entity. We distinguish between what has meaning and what does not have meaning for self-organization and segment the world accordingly. To take mites as a concrete example, most species understand the world around them using three senses: an olfactory sense that responds to butyric acid emitted by their prey, a thermal sense that detects the warmth of their prey, and a tactile sense that allows them to search for areas of their prey's skin without hair. This means that the world is segmented into objects recognized by these three senses. Conversely, however, it also means that the *mi* (body) segments itself—in the case of the example just given, into organs of olfactory sense, thermal sense, and tactile sense. The segmentation of the world and the segmentation of the *mi* itself are interrelated. Ichikawa expresses the "concurrent event" of both kinds of segmentation as *miwake* (bodily distinction). This *miwake* is not limited to the level of sensation; if we view *mi* as the mental or psychological self, the attachment of meaning or value to the world that arises together with self-formation and self-organization at this level can also be thought of as being included in *miwake*.

Another interesting aspect of Ichikawa's understanding of the body is his examination of "predicative unity." While it goes without saying that the body that engages in *miwake* is not the "body as object" but the "concrete, lived body," Ichikawa maintains that the sensations, emotions, and moods experienced by this body are not *mine* but "partly belong to the world, or arise out of the world." Here there is only "adhesive intuition from the place [world],"[119] and neither the subject nor object of perception is substantiated. Ichikawa expresses this state of affairs with this phrase "predicative unity." Of course, the body immediately centers itself, distinguishes the things around it from itself, and topicalizes and nominalizes them. The situation is understood as the relationship between this nominalized subject and the various qualities it possesses. This is "subjective unity." The modern way of looking at things deems subjective unity legitimate and discards predicative unity as illegitimate or irrational, and here Ichikawa asks whether this may cause our view of the situation to become obscured.

Sakabe Megumi's interest in the experience of "touching" in *The Philosophy of "Touching"* (1983)[120] can be said to have derived from touching this kind of "predicative unity." Sakabe says that touching "does not presuppose a fixed division, and on the contrary is an experience prior to division"[121] and here there is a "super-logos quality and super-segmentation quality." "Touching" is of course profoundly related to the sense of touch, but is not limited to it; on the contrary, as seen in the Japanese expression "to be touched by people's eyes" meaning "to receive public attention," it can be thought of as extending to all of the senses or existing in all of their substrata. Here the distinction between inside and outside, self and other has not been made, and these remain a unity; people do not simply "touch" but "contact." Sakabe believes they "overflow the self and come into contact with and enter the life of an other."[122] Ichikawa's "predicative unity" can presumably be seen as extending to this kind of "contact of lives" of the self and the other.

(2) Sensus Communis, Pathetic (Emotional) Knowledge, and Clinical Knowledge

One of those who focused in particular on "that which exists in the substrata of all senses" discussed above was Nakamura Yūjirō (1925–2017). In *A Theory of Sensus Communis: Towards a Reassembly of Knowledge*[123] (1979) he made sensus communis the axis of his inquiry. (He had previously engaged in wide-ranging activities as a writer, but according to his own account it was during this period that he established his own perspective.) The phrase "sensus communis" originates in Aristotle, and others had focused on this concept before Nakamura. Nakai Masakazu makes reference to it in "The Problem of Mediation in Art"[124] (1931), and touching on Aristotle's concept of "sensus communis (κοινὴ αἴσθησις)" in "Artistic Creation as a Historical Act of Formation"[125] (1941), Nishida Kitarō writes, "The historical, physical perspective of viewing the world immanently I have stated can also be described as the perspective of Aristotle's sensus communis."[126] Nishitani Keiji also discusses this concept in detail in *Essays on Aristotle*[127] (1948).

Nakamura encountered this concept in the process of examining Descartes' theory of emotions in *The Awakening of Sensibility* (1975). Adopting a stance of mind-body dualism, Descartes asserted that the workings of the two were connected in the pineal gland, which was the site of the "sensus communis" that connected and gave order to our many senses, and Nakamura believed that this conception of "sensus communis" contained important ideas that needed to be developed. This view was concretely presented in *A Theory of Sensus Communis*. This book was given the subtitle "For the Recombination of Knowledge." As this suggests, Nakamura sought to recombine knowledge that in the past had been undergirded by "reason and logic" through "sensus communis and language."

One of the inspirations behind Nakamura seeking a clue to reexamining knowledge from a new perspective in "sensus communis" was the focus on this topic in the approach to psychopathology of Kimura Bin (as well as that of Wolfgang Blankenburg). In an article entitled "Depersonalization"[128] (included in *Self/In-between/Time*,[129] 1981) published in 1976, Kimura sought the cause of patients suffering from depersonalization receiving "the world" as simply "a bundle of sensory stimulations" or "chaos that pierces the surface of perception" in the inadequate function of their sensus communis, the unified sensory capacity that enables the formation of connections between human beings and the world.[130]

Drawing on Kimura's idea of a receptive capacity that lies at the root of and unifies a human being's various functions involved in interacting with the world such as sensation, emotion, and intellect, Nakamura also focused his attention on the sensus communis. This led to a reexamination of the modern understanding of perception, that is, the understanding of perception that positions visual perception as something that unifies all other kinds of perception. In contrast to this vision-centric understanding of perception, Nakamura viewed the most fundamental unity of all forms of perception as a "somatosensory" unity.[131] The "somatosensory system" refers to perceptions obtained through the skin such as touch or pain and the deep sensation that senses things like the movement of muscles, and Nakamura believed that along with unifying all of the other senses and supporting the activities of the body it also opens up the "horizon" that enables us to interact with other people and nature.

Along with this approach, by viewing "sensus communis" as that which "while taking the body as its foundation and incorporating physical, perceptual, and image-like elements, unifies these elements in words = reason"[132] Nakamura also reexamined the existing understanding of language. Nakamura's theory of "sensus communis" can also be described as an attempt to transcend the logic of analytic reason through language that restores the image-like and physical elements this kind of logic excludes.

In *The Knowledge of Pathos: Developing a Sensus Communis Portrait of Humanity* (1982), Nakamura focused on the "knowledge of pathos" based on this approach. The "knowledge of pathos" is the polar opposite of the one-sided, active knowledge that aims to logically grasp its object upon which philosophy has been based. It is the knowledge related to our manner of existence in which, because we are equipped with a body, we are unavoidably being acted upon by others and at the same time interacting with others on the basis of this passivity. This way of thinking itself had already been discussed in *The Awakening of Sensibility*. In this earlier work, Nakamura turns his attention to the "world of pathos" that has been suppressed by philosophy from a rationalist perspective, a "world of pathos" undergirded by physicality and the unconscious, which it takes as its foundations, and describes his intention to bring philosophy closer to its essential wholeness and fundamentality.[133] This way of thinking was of course not new. As we saw in chapter 7, in *Philosophical Anthropology* and *The Logic of Imagination*, Miki Kiyoshi argued that the mental activity of human beings cannot be reduced to simply intellectual workings and is on the contrary underpinned by pathos. Miki believed that the workings of our minds are supported by the body not only as a passive site but as an "active" body that tries to express the pathos that arises within us on the outside. Nakamura's theory of pathos can be said to have directly adopted Miki's understanding.

As noted above, in *A Theory of Sensus Communis* Nakamura sought to undertake a "recombination of knowledge" around the axis of the concept of "sensus communis," and most of his later writings can be described as efforts to make this recombination concrete. *What Is Clinical Knowledge?*, published in 1992, can be characterized as a work that once again discusses this undertaking. Since the scientific revolution of the eighteenth century, modern science has based its theories on "universality," "rationality," and "objectivity," at the same time making these principles the basis of its efforts to persuade other people, but here Nakamura raises the question of whether the "reality" before our eyes can be fully grasped through them. This is also the question of what is dismissed or excluded by modern science that upholds these three principles. Nakamura argues that modern science dismisses or excludes the fact that things and experience occur at specific times and places that cannot be reduced to universality, the fact that they have multiple meanings and various aspects that cannot be explained by a one-track cause and effect relationship of a single cause and effect, and the fact that they are not isolated and independent as objective objects but always exist in the midst of relationships with subjects. Nakamura refers to "an approach that, at individual times and places, grasps a phenomenon in the midst of interacting with it while giving sufficient consideration to the polysemic nature of the object"[134] as "clinical knowledge."

This way of thinking shares commonalities with what Nishida Kitarō tried to express in his later thought using concepts such as "action-intuition" and what Miki Kiyoshi tried to assert through contrasting the "logic of imagination" with the logic of abstract contemplation. Nakamura's thought was significant, however, insofar as through making sensus communis its axis it gave a clear structure to the issues these thinkers had in common. Taking this as a guide it clarified the meaning of the knowledge of magic and drama, and, in addition to what had been addressed in the past, it took up the examination of questions of cutting-edge medicine in a literally clinical setting.

(3) Eastern Theories of the Body

In Western or modern knowledge, it goes without saying that there is an emphasis on objective knowledge, that is, knowledge that is based on careful observation and clearly expressed through language. Science and technology are constructed on the basis of a way of looking at things that emphasizes this kind of knowledge. In the tradition of Eastern knowledge, in contrast, what is addressed is nonverbal, nonobjective knowledge. Yuasa Yasuo focused on Eastern knowledge and in particular theories of the body from this perspective.

According to *The Body: An Attempt to Establish an Eastern Mind-Body Theory*[135] (1977), one of Yuasa's most important works, the body, and the relationship between the body and the mind, has a two-layer structure. On the one hand there is so-called sensation centered in the cerebral cortex—the domain of motor circuits, the external perception and motor sensation that are functionally connected to them, and the "consciousness" that arises out of intellectual activity. On the other hand, there are the internal organs governed by the autonomic nervous system and the emotions and internal organ sensations that are functionally connected to them. Yuasa calls the former the "surface structure of the mind-body relationship" and the latter the "base structure of the mind-body relationship."[136] Part of the base structure appears in the domain of consciousness in the form of "emotions," but most of it belongs to the domain of the "unconscious." This greater part does not normally reveal itself, but it can become manifest in dreams or hypnotic states, for example, or in neurosis or mental illness (this is similar to the "entangled body" described by Ichikawa Hiroshi). Based on this understanding, Yuasa asserts that while Western mind-body discourse tends to focus only on the "surface structure" without paying sufficient attention to the "base structure," the Eastern discourse on this topic places its emphasis instead on the latter structure. In order to discuss Eastern views of the body and the relationship between the body and the mind, we must focus on this two-layer structure of the mind-body relationship and the "base structure" in particular.

For example, "meditation" has been emphasized in traditional Eastern religions as a method of spiritual training or self-discipline. Conscious activities (workings at the surface level of the mind-body relationship) connected to the cerebral cortex or its functions play a central role in our daily lives, but meditation can be thought of as something that seeks to suppress these higher functions and activate the workings of the mind and body at the base level. By engaging in meditation, practitioners aim to bring to the surface, release, and dissolve the fundamental emotions and passions submerged in the unconscious and to control their own minds and bodies. According to Yuasa, this is something meditation has in common with treatment methods such as psychotherapy used by therapists, but the two are not the same.

In treatment the aim is to recover a state of health from a state of illness, but in meditation the aim is to separate ourselves from an everyday way of being in which we are moved by our emotions and passions and reach an essential self (called "*samādhi*" in Buddhism) that exists beyond it.

When Yuasa compares Eastern thought and Western philosophy, he finds the distinctive nature of the former in *shugyō* (spiritual training or self-discipline, *sādhanā*) including meditation. In other words, he believed the distinctive character of Eastern thought lay in its viewing knowledge not simply as something logically apprehended from the analysis of an object, but as something grasped through "learning by experience" or "recognizing through experience" using the entirety of one's own body and mind. From this perspective, Yuasa defines *shugyō* as "a practical attempt to acquire true knowledge through experience using one's entire mind and body."[137] The idea that the body is deeply involved in knowledge can be found in the traditional thought of the East.

Nishitani Keiji addresses the same topic in his essay entitled "What Is Known as '*Gyo* [actions or austerities with spiritual or religious connotations]'" (1960). In it he states that in the modern era "the dimension of knowledge in which the examination of objects and the self-examination of the subject are an inseparable whole has been closed off." Describing this kind of knowledge, Nishitani writes, "Differing from objective knowledge facing only outward such as scientific knowledge, it is the kind of knowledge in which facing outward and facing inward are both distinct and identical."[138] This is the kind of knowledge in which to learn or master something is not merely to grasp an object but at the same time also to know oneself and thereby change oneself from the inside. Nishitani focuses on this kind of knowledge always being tied to "the body," or, in other words, being "self-knowledge of the entire body and mind" tied to action.

In "What Is Known as '*Gyō*,'" Nishitani says that to engage in *gyō* is to limit oneself to a *kata* (form or mold) and discipline the self that tries to escape. In this sense *gyō* has the character of a method of understanding *hō* (the universal law or nature of reality, dharma). Interestingly, however, Nishitani says that *gyō* (such as the seated meditation practiced in Zen Buddhism) is not simply a means, skill, or technique. *Gyō* is instead something created by *hō*. Expressed from the perspective of *hō*, *gyō* can be described as the delimiting of how human beings should be by *hō*. Human beings realize *hō* by fitting themselves inside a "form" through *gyō*. Nishitani asserts that in this sense "form" is not something devised by human beings for our own convenience but "something human beings have discovered from the nature of their own existence itself."[139] In *The Body*, Yuasa similarly asserts that *shugyō* is putting one's body in a certain *katachi* (shape, form) and thereby steering the state of one's mind in the right direction. He writes, "Instead of the mind controlling the body, the starting point of *shugyō* is adopting a stance in which the state of the body controls the state of the mind."[140]

As Nishitani and Yuasa point out, in the Eastern understanding of body and mind the body is regulated through *kata* and the state of the mind is in turn regulated through this regulated body. One of those who focused on this kind of *kata* was Minamoto Ryōen (1920–2020). According to *Kata*,[141] which Minamoto published in 1989, the Japanese word *kata* (型) originally meant the outer frame of a mold made of earth. The "开" part of the character, originally written as "井," refers to the *katachi* (shape, form) delimiting this outer frame. The word *katachi* (形) adds "彡," and this "彡" refers to the presence of color or sheen. In other words, *katachi* refers to the beautiful, finished object that has been separated from the frame of the mold. Today, *kata* is still used to mean "mold," but it also refers to fixed, predetermined movements of the body, often with aesthetic elements. Leading examples of this are the *kata* found in Noh and Kabuki theater, but the term also refers to the fixed routines used in the process of learning a *kata* in this sense. Minamoto distinguishes between the two types by calling the former "fundamental, simple *kata*" and the latter "complex *kata*."[142] *Kata* in the latter sense, having been emphasized in aspects of Japanese culture such as the performing arts, martial arts, and the tea ceremony, can be connected to the Eastern understanding of mind and body discussed above in which there is a directionality of "from the body to the mind."

We have just seen that *katachi* means a finished, molded object, but as it can also refer to external shape or form, it can also be used with nearly the same meaning as *kata*. Yanagi Muneyoshi (1889–1961), known for having promoted the folk-art movement, takes a fascinating approach to contrasting the difference in meaning between these two terms. In an essay entitled "Thinking about Tea Ceremony,"[143] he writes about *kata* as follows.

> If the right utensils are used in the right place at the right time, [all things] naturally return to the *hō* [universal law, dharma]. When one arrives at the least wasteful manner of using something, this becomes a fixed *kata*. A *kata* can be described as the crystallized form of a manner of use. When it is boiled down all the way, the essence of a thing is reached. This is the *kata* or the way.[144]

When the way of using something is "boiled down all the way" and settles into a place with no waste whatsoever, this state of affairs is a *kata*. Here the particular "someone" who came up with it is of no significance.[145] On the contrary, this manner of use is inevitable. Here there is no unnecessary action whatsoever; there is only the most natural manner. However, people tend to be captivated by the *katachi* that can be seen from the outside. Tea ceremony is often said to be "mired in '*kata*,'" and Yanagi strongly rejects being tied to *kata* as a misunderstanding of "tea." Of course, it is not as though people can acquire natural *kata* straight away. It is precisely toward this end that the "complex *kata*" spoken of by Minamoto Ryōen are required.

(4) Bioethics and Environmental Ethics

In recent years, questions of bioethics and environmental ethics have been vigorously debated. Before the term "bioethics" became widely known, most of these issues were discussed within the framework of "medical ethics." The creator of this foundation for discussion in Japan was Omodaka Hisayuki. Beginning in 1941, Omodaka taught a course called Introduction to Medical Science[146] at Osaka University for many years, and he was succeeded in this role by Nakagawa Yonezō (1926–1997). Nakagawa published the results of his research in works such as *The Ethics of Medicine*[147] (1977), and these writings focus mainly on issues such as the right to health, that is, health as a fundamental right that all human beings should share, the proper relationship between doctors and patients, and the relationship between medicine and economics.

Behind the transition from this "ethics of medicine" to bioethics lay the rapid development of the life sciences. In concrete terms, it was largely precipitated by the emergence of the possibility of manipulating genes. Questions such as whether such actions are ethically permissible, whether they are safe, and what sort of laws or regulations should be put in place regarding them came to be debated. Another factor behind the focusing of attention on bioethics was the vigorous development of various human rights movements, such as the civil rights movement and women's liberation movement in America in the 1960s and 1970s, and alongside them the advancement of a movement to protect the rights of patients in medical settings in which patients' "right to self-determination" (and the "informed consent" this requires) were strongly advocated. In this context, bioethics was established with the "right to self-determination" as one of its main pillars.

Among those who introduced American bioethics to Japan and argued for the need to further develop this discourse were Katō Hisatake (born in 1937) and Yonemoto Shōhei (born in 1946). In works such as *The Foundations of Bioethics: On Western "Bioethics"*[148] (coedited with Iida Nobuyuki, 1988), Katō introduced debates surrounding "bioethics" in Europe and America, and through works such as *What Is Bioethics?*[149] (1986) and *For Those Studying Bioethics*[150] (coedited with Kamo Naoki, 1998) he laid the foundations for academic discourse in this field. In "The Way of Thinking of Modern Bioethics,"[151] included in *For People Studying Bioethics*, Katō expresses the fundamental principle of bioethics as "adults with the capacity for judgment have the right of self-determination, to the extent that they do not harm others, regarding 'their own things' including their body and quality of life, even if this may lead to a senseless result for the person in question when viewed rationally,"[152] and points out that this principle based on liberalism is problematic insofar as it is too widely permissive of human behavior and thus cannot provide grounds for necessary regulation.

Yonemoto Shōhei's *Bioethics*[153] also played an important role in a relatively early period as a text that offered an easy-to-understand description of the issues confronted in bioethics. Particularly notable are Yonemoto's assertions that scientists have a duty to speak out to society at large regarding issues such as the safety of gene recombination experiments and that science journalists are responsible for not simply reporting scientists' statements but ferreting out what lies behind them (including the significance of what they leave unsaid) and critically commenting on them. In *Biopolitics: What Does It Mean to Control the Human Body?*[154] (2006), Yonemoto also points out that the existing bioethics that emerged in America with the "right of self-determination" as its foundation is now facing difficult problems, such as, for example, the commodification of human tissue (including genetic information). Individual people may make erroneous judgments in the places where this tissue is bought and sold. On the basis of such circumstances, Europe has been moving toward establishing laws and regulating such issues. The term "biopolitics" refers to this kind of situation, and going forward these issues also seem certain to become topics of debate.

There have been remarkable developments in technology, which has become unified with science, not only in the fields of the life sciences and bioengineering but more broadly. In *Where Is Cutting-Edge Technology Going?*[155] (1987) Sakamoto Kenzō (1931–1991) anticipates the arrival of an era in which human beings serve technology (including economics, states, and religions), an epoch he refers to as the "era of high technology."[156] The surprising developments in artificial intelligence we see today show that we are indeed heading down the path Sakamoto foresaw. When we reach the destination he described, the era in which we must seriously confront the question of whether a path to interfacing with technology as active subjects can be found will have arrived.

In America, the movement to protect nature has a long history going back to the end of the nineteenth century, but starting in the 1960s the environmental protection movement began to gain steam, with people like Rachel Carson (1907–1964) raising the alarm regarding increasingly severe pollution and destruction of the environment, and at the same time debate over the intellectual grounds on which to support such a movement flourished. This led to the establishment of the field of environmental ethics. Katō Hisatake introduced the thought of prominent environmental ethicists such as Kristin Shrader-Frechette (born in 1944) and Hans Jonas (1903–1993) and spurred the discussion of environmental ethics in Japan. In *Introduction to Environmental Ethics*,[157] published in 1991, he divided the assertions of environmental ethics into three categories: "the problem of nature's right of survival," "the problem of intergenerational ethics," and "Earth totalitarianism."[158]

On the basis of human interactions with the environment and the manner of existence of human beings having undergone drastic changes with the development of science and technology, Imamichi Tomonobu (1922–2012) advocated what he called "eco-ethica." Imamichi argued that today, when the scope of ethics has expanded to include not only the people around us but nature and the environment, and the ethical nature of not only individuals but also states and corporations has been called into question, the ethics of the past must transform into an "ethics that thinks on the scale of humanity's biosphere."[159]

5. The Perspective of Comparison

When philosophy was first brought to Japan in the Meiji period, people were undoubtedly interested in the similarities and differences between the newly introduced Western philosophy and traditional thought, and the comparison of the two quickly became a topic to be addressed. For example, as noted in chapter 2, Western logic was positively received at the start of the Meiji period, and scholarship attempting to elucidate the differences and commonalities between it and the traditional Buddhist logic known as "*inmyō* (*hetuvidyā*)" immediately emerged. Kira Kōyō, introduced in chapter 2, was one of the leading figures in this field, and Ōnishi Hajime also referenced both approaches in *Logic*[160] (1883). In contrast to Kira, who emphasized the strong points of *inmyō*, Ōnishi points out the glaring deficiencies of this approach in terms of induction logic.

As was also discussed in chapter 2, Inoue Enryō constructed a history of philosophy out of the two traditions of Eastern and Western philosophy, and in *Philosophical Trifles* Miyake Setsurei discusses the debate between the Confucian and Buddhist tradition and Western philosophy in detail and expresses a belief that new possibilities will arise from it. One of the defining characteristics of Meiji philosophy can be found in attempting to view philosophy from this kind of broad perspective.

(1) Nakamura Hajime's Attempt at an "Intellectual History of the World"

After the war, while there were not necessarily many thinkers examining Eastern and Western philosophy from this kind of broad perspective, Nakamura Hajime (1912–1999) and Izutsu Toshihiko can be cited as examples of those who took this approach.

In *On Comparative Thought*[161] (1960), Nakamura includes a section called "the dream of universal intellectual history"[162] in which he discusses the state in which the world has been placed with all its disturbances and confusion and how difficult it is to realize peace and happiness for humanity as a whole. To reach this elusive goal, he argues, mutual understanding between peoples is required. In order to achieve this, he asserts that Indian philosophy should not be studied within the framework of Indian philosophy; what is needed instead is scholarship that includes all philosophical and intellectual approaches within its field of view. From this perspective, in *Selected Writings of Nakamura Hajime*[163] Nakamura plots out an *Intellectual History of the World*[164] (*Selected Writings*, volumes 17–23). In the appended "Introduction: Outline of a Universal Intellectual History," after discussing approaches to history in the West (such as those of Hegel and Windelband) that exclude ancient Indian and Chinese thought from the history of philosophy as merely precursors or run-ups to the emergence of philosophy, Nakamura argues against this as follows. Whether in the East or in the West, all philosophers address the same matters concerning human beings and the universe and debate the same questions. Many similarities can be found in their accounts, and they can be said to share several philosophical theses in common. In other words, "Most philosophical problems are universal to humanity, and should not be treated simply historically but also from a purely philosophical point of view. Truth must be found in all peoples and all religions."[165]

From this perspective, in this "intellectual history of the world" Nakamura does not stop at "philosophy" as a system of scholarly knowledge; focusing his attention on "human contemplation itself," he attempts to elucidate what common problems are found there and how they are discussed. While on the one hand this involves singling out common problems, at the same time, given that the results of contemplating these problems are not necessarily the same, this is also an attempt to clarify their differences and identify the unique characteristics of different philosophical approaches. By doing so, Nakamura aimed to clarify the significance of each approach and position them within his "intellectual history of the world."

(2) Izutsu Toshihiko's "Synchronic Structuring" of Eastern Thought

The scope of Izutsu Toshihiko's scholarship ranges from Greek philosophy to Islamic philosophy, Jewish thought, Indian philosophy, Taoist thought, Confucianism, and Buddhism, especially Zen. He was a thinker who realized the comparison of East and West in one person, and among his fascinating undertakings was the "synchronic structuring" of Eastern thought.

In *Consciousness and Essence: Searching for the East in an Intellectual Context*,[166] published in 1983, Izutsu refers to various philosophical traditions of the East together with the phrase "Eastern philosophy," but raises the question of whether this can be seen as a "single, unified body possessing coherence" that can be contrasted with "Western philosophy." While it is referred to with a single word, the "East" encompasses both a long history and an extensive geographical area. There are things in it that have survived for a long time, and things that have already gone extinct. Here there is neither coherence as a whole nor a unified structure. Are there not merely numerous traditions existing alongside each other? If these coexisting approaches could be brought together in an organic, unified whole, however, would it not be possible, within the current intellectual circumstances of the world, to look toward the future and produce something that "could become a creative starting point for philosophical contemplation"? Izutsu set himself this task. "Syncretic structuring" was conceived as an action to be undertaken to this end.

This undertaking began with a process of moving the major philosophical traditions of the East to a single conceptual plane, recombining them paradigmatically and repositioning them spatially, and "artificially creating a single intellectually connected space that structurally envelops all of them." This is of course a "multipolar, multilayered structure," but by analyzing it, several "fundamental thought patterns" emerge. These have the character of "root patterns governing the philosophical contemplation of Eastern people at a deep level." Izutsu attempted to "take up within myself and subjectivize" this system of root patterns of Eastern philosophy and "standing on this foundation, work out what might be called my own Eastern philosophical perspective."[167]

Izutsu artificially attempted this kind of theoretical manipulation because he felt that "to study the various traditions of Eastern thought only academically or philologically" was insufficient. He had a strong sense that what was needed at that moment was "to create a new philosophy in a global context" within the magnetic field created by internalizing these traditions of Eastern thought within himself.[168] His subsequent works such as *To the Depths of Meaning: The Water Level of Eastern Philosophy* (1985), *Cosmos and Anti-Cosmos: For the Sake of Eastern Philosophy* (1989), and *The Metaphysics of Consciousness: The Philosophy of "Awakening of Faith in the Mahāyāna"* (1993) can be described as attempts to make this grand vision concrete.

(3) THE POSSIBILITY OF THE STUDY OF COMPARATIVE PHILOSOPHY (THOUGHT)

The emergence of comparative study from various perspectives was one of the characteristics of postwar Japanese philosophical scholarship, both regarding individual themes such as logic and experience, language, and beauty and broader fields such as philosophy, intellectual history, and the study of religion and Buddhism with concrete targets of comparison such as the West and the East or India/China and Japan. One factor that encouraged the development of this comparative scholarship was the establishment of the Japanese Association for Comparative Philosophy by Nakamura Hajime and other scholars in 1974. In his opening remarks at the association's founding conference, "The Futurity of the Study of Comparative Philosophy," Nakamura points out that sectionalism has emerged along with the subdivision of scholarship in the humanities and emphasizes the need to break down these barriers and create a new form of inquiry from a global perspective.[169]

When philosophy (or thought more generally) is made the target of comparative study, this inquiry can take various forms. For example, multiple philosophical approaches can be lined up beside each other and the existence of elements common among them pointed out, or, regarding a certain philosophical approach, its particular qualities and characteristics can be brought into relief through comparison to other philosophical approaches that have arisen in different cultural traditions. There can also be scholarship that elucidates the influences different philosophical approaches have on each other. Many doubts have emerged, however, regarding such undertakings.

For example, attempts to point out common elements among different philosophical approaches have been criticized for failing to go beyond superficial, incidental similarities in most cases, and it has been suggested that the essence of the philosophy or thought in question may be distorted by singling out only one of its aspects and ignoring the assumptions that underlie it. Even if similarities and differences can be made clear, doubt has also been expressed about whether this itself constitutes genuine philosophical inquiry.[170]

Is it not possible, however, to find unique significance in the act of "comparison" that differs from thinking only within a particular tradition? "Comparison" is by no means limited to pointing out superficial similarities and includes various forms of inquiry. For example, the following approaches can be taken.

a. Lay out multiple facts (often expressed in the form of writings) and discover and enumerate the commonalities and differences between them (and in some cases their influence on each other).

b. Engage in the explication and comparison of the climatic, social, and historical backgrounds of these similarities and differences.

c. From such undertakings, extract the essence of various phenomena and elucidate their individual qualities and universal principles.

Through this kind of inquiry, comparison can allow us to turn our gaze on things that could not be discovered when only a particular philosophical approach was being considered. The characteristics and limitations of each approach can be elucidated both by comparing them to other worldviews and senses of value and by comparing the climatic and social backdrops against which they are established. By using heterogeneous thought as a mirror, so to speak, many things become visible in reflection. "Comparison" can be an effective means of enabling this. By engaging in it, we may be able to transcend the limitations of individual philosophical approaches and broaden our intellectual horizon. In this sense, "comparison" has great significance. It can also be said, however, that comparison itself is not the ultimate goal; beyond it the further development of each philosophical or intellectual approach must be considered.

Afterword

Along with reflecting on how "philosophy" was received in Japan after having been introduced as an academic field in the Meiji period, the form in which original Japanese philosophy emerged based on this received thought, and how this philosophy then developed, this book was also written with the aim of looking forward toward the future of Japanese philosophy. In presenting all of this in concrete terms, I faced several difficult questions, such as from what perspective and in what form to discuss the long history of Japanese philosophy. Here I would like to lay out the approach I have taken in addressing these challenges.

In recent years, the work of Japanese philosophers such as Nishida Kitarō, Tanabe Hajime, Kuki Shūzō, and Watsuji Tetsurō has attracted considerable attention, not only in Japan but around the world, with many translations of their writings and academic texts being published. Almost all of this domestic and overseas scholarship, however, has been limited to the study of Nishida Kitarō and Tanabe Hajime or the Kyoto School, and a full portrait of Japanese philosophy has not been drawn. In this book, in contrast, I have aimed to elucidate the characteristics and significance of Japanese philosophy as a whole. It goes without saying, however, that this is far from easy. After first grasping this subject in its entirety, I then had to draw a clear portrait of it, and the topics of inquiry involved, such as ethics, art, and religion, were wide-ranging and complex. There was more than could possibly be addressed in one book. I have nevertheless endeavored to discuss as many thinkers as possible and present the diverse development of Japanese philosophy. In doing so, I have not addressed the thought of each philosopher separately and simply lined them up in a row, but rather sought to grasp the thought of each period, whether Meiji, Taishō, or Shōwa, as a whole and discuss each individual philosophical approach within the context of this understanding.

One of the issues that must be faced when discussing Japanese philosophy is the distinction between "philosophy" and "thought." Traditionally they have been separated and each given their own niche. Of course, it is not as though there has been no interaction between them. Traditional thought such as that of Buddhism and Confucianism has flowed into the philosophy developed in Japan, giving it its unique qualities and characteristics. If the history of Japanese philosophy were to be strictly separated from this thought and the latter excluded from it, the resulting account would be greatly impoverished. In this book I have traced the history of the development of philosophy in Japan while considering that which surrounds and underlies it. I have taken this approach because I believe it allows for a richer depiction of the history of philosophy. Of course, when a traditional Western conception of "philosophy" is assumed, it may be asked whether traditional Japanese or Eastern thought can be called "philosophy," and there is also the question of whether "thought" prior to the Edo period can be included in a discussion of the history of philosophy. For my thoughts on these matters, see the preface.

As noted above, rather than present individual philosophical approaches separately, in this book I have focused on overall intellectual trends, but I have also touched on the relationships between earlier philosophy and the philosophy that succeeded it and between various philosophical approaches of the same era. I took this approach because I believed it would allow me to elucidate the context in which each philosopher developed their thought.

While the subject of this book is of course the formation and development of Japanese philosophy, rather than limit the object of consideration to Japanese philosophy or the intellectual undertakings of Japanese philosophers and give an account purely within this framework, I sought to break down such strictures and address topics such as experience and language, the self and the other, and action and history in an expanse that transcends them, or, in other words, in a universal intellectual space. What is important for philosophy as an intellectual undertaking is pursuing matters themselves, not erecting frameworks. Consequently, while I was not able to devote many pages to such discussions for reasons of space, where necessary I have also touched on the Western philosophy drawn on by Japanese philosophers and their reception of it.

One thing of which I became keenly aware through the writing of this book is that the work of Japanese philosophers is based on understandings of nature, history, and human beings shaped within a long history, and this has provided one of the major characteristics of Japanese philosophy. I do not think this is a negative thing for philosophy, because I believe that comparing thought created on the basis of different cultural traditions and finding things in common or searching for directions of development in different approaches is a very meaningful undertaking for this field. This illustrates the importance of "dialogue" to philosophy as an intellectual undertaking. Through engaging in this kind of dialogue, I have no doubt that philosophy based on Japanese cultural traditions can make a significant contribution. This is another reason I have sought to pursue thought in an open space rather than establish a closed-off framework.

I first had the idea of publishing this book twenty years ago. Amid a broad reform of Japanese universities and graduate schools at the time, Japanese philosophy courses were introduced by Kyoto University's Faculty of Letters in 1995 and Graduate School of Letters the following year. This book was inspired by my having taught these courses. This occurred exactly fifty years after the end of the Second World War. The establishment of these courses can be seen as having been precipitated by circumstances in which there was enough distance to objectively evaluate the philosophy of Nishida Kitarō and Tanabe Hajime, who played a central role in the history of Japanese philosophy, including their statements and those of their disciples during the war. In other words, these courses were created because sufficient distance had emerged to allow for this thought and the role it played in its era to be evaluated on its own terms without any lingering emotional attachment or antipathy toward it.

I first conceived of this book because of the pressing need I felt, when I began lecturing on this topic, for a text giving an overview of the history of Japanese philosophy. Right around the same time, I was asked to write a complete history of Japanese philosophy by Suzuki Ryōichi, the editor-in-chief of Shōwadō, publisher of the journal *Japanese Philosophy* on which I had worked as an editor, and my plan to write such a text became concrete. This book, however, did not come together right away. It took more than twenty years to write. This caused a lot of trouble for Shōwadō, and I remain profoundly grateful for their patience. On the other hand, these more than twenty years and the lectures I gave and seminars I led during that time were very useful in introducing me to many texts and deepening my understanding. Writings I made at various opportunities in line with this plan formed the foundation of this book. In this sense, I do not think this time was wasted.

Of course, the discussion in this book is wide-ranging and complex, and I fear it may have many flaws. I hope I have the chance to produce something much better in the future on the basis of readers' criticisms.

May 3, 2018

Postscript to the English Edition

In this book, I trace the path of what Japanese thinkers contemplated from when they first encountered Western "philosophy" in the Meiji period until the present era and what was born out of their undertakings. I am very pleased that this English version will allow readers in the English-speaking world to follow this path as well. I hope that through its publication, dialogue between philosophical approaches will occur in an unprecedented form, and new developments in philosophy will result. I am indebted to Robert Chapeskie for his work in preparing this English version. Translating technical terms originating in Buddhism and original expressions used by Nishida Kitarō and Tanabe Hajime is not easy, but thanks to his extraordinary Japanese ability and deep understanding of the field of philosophy these barriers have been overcome. Helpful advice on a variety of matters in the preparation of this text was also provided by Bret Davis. I would like to express my deep gratitude once again to both for their efforts.

Fujita Masakatsu
Kyoto, Japan
November 8, 2024

Notes

Introduction

1. *Ri* (理) is a key term in Chinese and Japanese thought prior to the advent of Western philosophy. It has been translated simply as "principles" here, but it can be thought of as encompassing both the laws of nature and the principles and logic governing various aspects of human life and thought [trans.].

2. In Hori Tatsunosuke's *Pocket English-Japanese Dictionary* (Yōsho Shirabesho, 1862), "philosophy" is translated as *rigaku* (理学, study of *ri*) while "natural philosophy" is translated as *kyūrigaku* (究理学, thorough study of *ri*). The Japanese terms *rigaku* (理学, the study of *ri*), *riron* (理論, theory of *ri*, used today to mean "logic"), and *rika* (理科, "workings of *ri*," used today to mean "natural science") are given in Shibata Masakichi and Koyasu Takashi's *English and Japanese Dictionary* (Nisshūsha, 1873). As translations of "science," the former gives *gakumon* (学問, academic inquiry) and *gigei* (技芸, craft, technique), the latter *gakugei* (学芸, study of technique), *gakumon* (学問, academic inquiry), *chie* (知恵, wisdom), *chishiki* (知識, knowledge), and *hakugaku* (博学, erudition). The more modern terms *rigaku* (理学) and *kagaku* (科学) were not yet being used.

3. Nishi Amane, *Nishi Amane zenshū* [西周全集; Collected works of Nishi Amane], 4 vols., ed. Ōkubo Toshiaki (Munetaka Shobō, 1960–1981), vol. 1, 31.

4. 聖希天賢希聖士希賢

5. 通書

6. See Fujita Masakatsu, *Zen no kenkyū no hyakunen—sekaihe/sekaikara* [『善の研究』の百年──世界へ/世界から; A hundred years of an inquiry into the good: To the world / from the world] (Kyoto University Press, 2011), 369–81.

7. *Les Philosophes Célèbres*, published under the direction of Maurice Merleau-Ponty (L. Mazenod, 1956).

8. Maurice Merleau-Ponty, *Signes* (Gallimard, 1960), 161.

9. Georg W. F. Hegel, *Werke in zwanzig Bänden*, ed. E. Moldenhauer and K. M. Michel, 20 vols. (Suhrkamp Verlag, 1971), vol. 18, 15. English translation

by E. S. Haldane, *Hegel's Lectures on the History of Philosophy* (Routledge and Kegan Paul, 1955), xiv.

10. Merleau-Ponty, *Signes*, 161.

11. Edmund Husserl, *Die Krisis der europäischen Wissenschaften und die transzendentale Phänomenologie*, trans. David Carr, *The Crisis of European Sciences and Transcendental Phenomenology* (Northwestern University Press, 1970), 16.

12. Merleau-Ponty, *Signes*, 161.

13. Thomas S. Kuhn, *The Structure of Scientific Revolutions* (University of Chicago Press, 1962).

14. Karl R. Popper, *The Myth of the Framework*, ed. M. A. Notturno (Routledge, 1994), 35–36.

15. 民約訳解

16. 理学鉤玄

17. 理学沿革史

18. 一年有半

19. Nakae Chōmin, *Nakae Chōmin zenshū* [中江兆民全集; Collected works of Nakae Chōmin], 17 vols. and supplementary volume (Iwanami Shoten, 1983–1986), vol. 10, 155. "Swallow the fruit without tasting it" is a Zen proverb in which "the fruit" represents another person's theory or doctrine.

20. 中国哲学史大綱

21. Works on "the history of Japanese philosophy" in English have tended to include pre-Meiji "thought" as well as modern "philosophy" inspired by the West, and in order to avoid any confusion I have therefore added the word "modern" to the English title of this book.

22. 日本倫理思想史

23. Watsuji Tetsurō, *Watsuji Tetsurō zenshū* [和辻哲郎全集; Collected works of Watsuji Tetsurō] (Iwanami Shoten, 1961–1978), vol. 12, 11.

24. *Japanese Philosophy: A Sourcebook*, ed. James W. Heisig, Thomas P. Kasulis, and John C. Maraldo (University of Hawai'i Press, 2011).

25. 自由の理

26. 社会平権論

27. A detailed account of the history of the history of philosophy in Japan is given in Shibata Takayuki's *Testugaku shi seiritsu no genba* [哲学史成立の現場; The site of the formation of the history of philosophy] (Kōbundō, 1997).

28. 百学連環

29. 致知学

30. 理体学

31. 生性発蘊

32. George Henry Lewes, *A Biographical History of Philosophy* (London: C. Knight, 1845–1846).

33. George Henry Lewes, *Comte's Phlosophy of the Sciences* (London: Bohn, 1853).

34. Albert Schwegler, *Handbook of the History of Philosophy.* trans. J. H. Stirling, 2nd ed. (Edinburgh: Edmondston, 1868).

35. Albert Schwegler, *Geschichte der Philosophie im Umriß* (Stuttgart: C. Conradi, 1847).

36. Francis Bowen, *Modern Philosophy from Descartes to Schopenhauer and Hartmann* (New York: Charles Scribner's Sons, 1877).

37. 訳解近世哲学

38. Victor Cousin, *Cours de l'histoire de la philosophie moderne* (Paris: Didier, 1841–1846).

39. Victor Cousin, *Course of the History of Modern Philosophy*, trans. O. W. Wight, 2 vols. (New York: Appleton, 1852).

40. 近代哲学宗統史

41. Heinrich Moritz Chalybäus, *Historical Survey of Speculative Philosophy from Kant to Hegel*, trans. from the 4th edition of the German by Alfred Tulk (Andover, MA: Longmans,1854).

42. Heinrich Moritz Chalybäus, *Historische Entwickelung der speculativen Philosophie von Kant bis Hegel* (Dresden/Leipzig: Ch. F. Grimmer'sche Buchhandlung, 1837).

43. 独逸哲学英華

44. 理学沿革史

45. Alfred Fouillée, *Histoire de la philosophie* (Paris: Ch. Delagrave, 1875).

46. 希臘古代理学一斑

47. 西洋哲学講義

48. 哲学要領前編

49. 哲学涓滴

50. Kuno Fischer, *Geschichte der neuern Philosophie*, 6 vols. (Mannheim/Heidelberg: Basserman, 1854–1877).

51. *Kiyozawa Manshi zenshū* [清沢満之全集; Complete works of Kiyozawa Manshi], vol. 5 (Iwanami Shoten, 2002–2003).

52. 西洋哲学史

53. 東京専門学校

54. 西洋哲学史 完

55. 大西博士全集

56. Ōnishi Hajime, *Ōnishi hakase zenshū* [大西博士全集; Collected works of Professor Ōnishi], rev. ed. (Keiseisha, 1924–1927), vol. 3, 8.

57. 六合雑誌

58. Hegel (1971), vol. 18, 49.

59. Hegel (1971), vol. 18, 49.

60. Hegel (1971), vol. 18, 61.

61. Hegel (1971), vol. 18, 46.

62. Albert Schwegler, *Geschichte der Philosophie im Umriß*, 14th ed (Stuttgart, 1887), 7.

63. Schwegler, *Geschichte der Philosophie im Umriß*, 2.

64. Wilhelm Windelband, *Lehrbuch der Geschichte der Philosophie*, 3rd ed. (Tübingen/Leipzig: J.C.B. Mohr, 1903), 9.

65. 哲学史とは何ぞや

66. Ōnishi (1924–1927), vol. 7, 58.

67. Ōnishi (1924–1927), vol. 7, 59.

68. Ōnishi (1924–1927), vol. 7, 60.

69. Ōnishi (1924–1927), vol. 7, 61.

70. 岩波講座倫理学

71. 尊皇思想とその伝統

72. 献身の道徳とその伝統

73. 日本倫理思想史

74. Hegel (1971), vol. 12, 72.

75. Ōnishi (1924–1927), vol. 3, 4.

76. Ienaga Saburō's *Nihon shisō shi gaku no hōhō* [日本思想史学の方法; Methodology of the study of the history of Japanese thought] (Meicho Kankōkai) is a text that discusses the methodology of "the study of the history of thought." In it, Ienaga deals with the third type of inquiry into the history of thought described here, and while fundamentally acknowledging that material relationships of production form a base structure that then constrains the intellectual production of human beings, he points out that it is not as though the base determines all aspects of the superstructure. The thought of Shinran (親鸞), for example, was undoubtedly constrained by the fundamental socioeconomic structures of thirteenth-century Japan, but Ienaga argues that while these can therefore be said to have been necessary conditions for the creation of Shinran's thought, they cannot be described as having been sufficient. See *Nihon shisō shi gaku no hōhō* [日本思想史学の方法; Methodology of the study of the history of Japanese thought] (Meicho Kankōkai, 1993), 52.

77. 西田幾多郎の哲学-その哲学体系

78. Sueki Takehiro, *Nishida Kitarō no tetsugaku—Sono tetsugaku taikei* [西田幾多郎の哲学 ——その哲学体系; The philosophy of Nishida Kitarō: His philosophical system], 4 vols. (Shunjūsha, 1983–1988), vol. 1, 4.

79. 善の研究

80. 西田幾多郎——人間の生涯ということ

81. Ueda Shizuteru, *Ueda Shizuteru shū* [上田閑照集; Collected works of Ueda Shizuteru] (Iwanami Shoten, 2001–2003), vol. 1, 41–42.

Chapter 1

1. Hubert Cieslik, "Funai no korejiyo—Ōtomo Sōrin kiten yon hyaku shūnen niyosete" [府内のコレジョ——大友宗麟帰天四百周年によせて; Funai Collegio: The 400th anniversary of the death of Ōtomo Sōrin], in *Kirishitan kenkyū* [キリシタン研究; Christian Studies], vol. 27, 101.

2. A theology course was later begun at the Funai Collegio in 1585. The courses in philosophy and theology in Funai were mainly led by a Spanish Jesuit priest named Pedro Gomes (1535–1600), and the text he employed was long thought to have been lost. It was discovered in the twentieth century, however, in the Vatican library (among materials donated by Queen Christina of Sweden, a friend of René Descartes) by the German Jesuit priest Joseph Schütte. See Joseph Schütte, "Drei Unterrichtsbücher für Japanische Jesuitenprediger aus dem XVI Jahrhundert," *Archivum Historicum Societas Iesu* 8 (1939). The book Gomes used in his course was written in 1592–1593 and entitled *Compendium catholicae Veritatis, in gratiam Japonicorum fratrum Societatis Iesu.*

3. *Sanctos no Gosagveo no vchi Nvqugaqi* [サントスの御作業の内抜書; Excerpts from hagiographies] (Benseisha, 1976).

4. *Sanctos no Gosagveo no vchi Nvqugaqi* [サントスの御作業の内抜書; Excerpts from hagiographies], print ed. (Benseisha, 1976), vol. 2, 328–29; transliterated ed. (Benseisha, 1979), vol. 2, 318–19. See also the "Commentary" by Saigusa Hiroto in the "Philosophy Section" of *Nihon tetsugaku shisō zensho* [日本哲学思想全書; Encyclopedia of Japanese philosophy and thought], vol. 1, 3 (Heibonsha, 1957), and Kayano Yoshio, "Kindai nihon no tetsugaku to doitsu kannenron" [近代日本の哲学とドイツ観念論; Modern Japanese philosophy and German idealism], in *Doitsu kannenron to nihonkindai* [ドイツ観念論と日本近代; German idealism and Japanese modernity], ed. Kayano Yoshio (Minerva Shobō, 1994), 12.

5. *Okamoto Sanemon hikki* [岡本三右衛門筆記; The writings of Okamoto Sanemon].

6. *Shūmon no shomotsu* [宗門之書物; Religious writings].

7. The Cabinet Library is a collection of old documents in the National Archives of Japan under the jurisdiction of the Cabinet Office.

8. "Shinajina no gakumon no koto" [品々ノ学文[学問]ノ事; On various forms of academic inquiry].

9. *The Writings of Okamoto Sanemon* is included as one of the materials related to *Seiyō kibun* [西洋紀聞; An account of the West] in Arai Hakuseki's *Shintei seiyō kibun* [新訂西洋記聞; Revised account of the West] (Heibonsha, Tōyōbunko no. 113, 1968), 344.

10. *Seiyō kibun* [西洋紀聞; An account of the West].

11. Arai Hakuseki (1968), 13, 16–17.

12. The doctrine of *taiji* (太極; supreme pole) holds that in the beginning, the contrasting elements of *yin* and *yang* emerged out of a single, undifferentiated "supreme pole" and everything in the universe has arisen out of their changing and combining with each other.

13. *Bunken manroku, daiichi* [聞見漫録、第一; Jottings on things seen and heard, part one].

14 学師

15. Watanabe Kazan, Takano Chōei, Sakuma Shōzan, Yokoi Shōnan, and Hashimoto Sanai [渡辺崋山・高野長英・横井小楠・橋本左内], *Nihon shisō taikei*

[日本思想大系; Series on Japanese thought], vol. 55 (Iwanami Shoten, 1971), 205.

16. 論理学

17. 知理義学

18. 倫理学

19. 法教

20. 格物窮理学

21. 数学

22. Watanabe Kazan, Takano Chōei, Sakuma Shōzan, Yokoi Shōnan, and Hashimoto Sanai (1971), 210. It is not known what writings Takano used as the basis for his Seiyō gakushi no setsu [西洋学師ノ説; Teachings of Western scholars].

23. 哲学

24. *Ra po nichi jiten* [Latin-Portuguese-Japanese dictionary] (Amakusa Gakurin, 1595).

25. Nishi Amane (1960–1981), vol. 1, 16.

26. Seiriron [性理論; Philosophical theory] (Misuzu Shobō, 2001).

27. Nishi Amane (1960–1981), vol. 1, 13.

28. 希哲学

29. Hyakugaku renkan [百学連環; Network of All Studies (Encyclopedia)] was a course or series of lectures given by Nishi Amane at Ikueisha [育英舎], his private school. Quotations from Network of All Studies throughout this book are taken from a record of these lectures set down by Nagami Yutaka, one of Nishi's disciples. This record is included in vol. 4 of *The Collected Works of Nishi Amane* [Nishi Amane zenshū [西周全集], 4 vols., ed. Ōkubo Toshiaki] (Munetaka Shobō).

30. "Seisei hatsuun" [生性発蘊; To clarify human nature].

31. 聖希天賢希聖士希賢

32. Tōng shū [通書].

33. *Tengai dokugo* [天外独語; Monologue of Tengai (Tsuda)].

34. 求聖学

35. Tsuda Mamichi, *Tsuda Mamichi zenshū* [津田真道全集; Collected works of Tsuda Mamichi], 2 vols, ed. Ōkubo Toshiaki, Kuwabara Shinsuke, and Kawasaki Masaru (Misuzu Shobō, 2001), vol. 1, 73, 20.

36. See Saitō Tsuyoshi, *Meiji no kotoba—Higashi kara nishi he no kakehashi* [明治のことば——東から西への架け橋; Meiji words: A bridge from East to West] (Kōdansha, 1977), 348.

37. 理学

38. 性理学

39. The first detailed introduction to Western academic inquiry published in China was *Xī xué fán* [西学凡, Summary of Western studies], a book written by the Jesuit missionary Giulio Aleni (1582–1649), and here too "philosophy" is translated as 理科 [Chinese *lǐkē*, Japanese *rika*, subject of principles (*ri*)]" and 理学 [Chinese *lǐxué*, Japanese *rigaku*, study of principles (*ri*)]. See Saito Takeshi (1977), 317–20.

40. *Fukubōshisho* [復某氏書, Reflections on a certain person].

41. 希賢学

42. 百一新論

43. It is thought that Nishi also lectured on *A New Theory That Unites All Theories* when he opened a private school in Kyoto and began a course on foreign learning the year after he returned from the Netherlands. It is not known, however, whether he was already using *tetsugaku* as a translation of "philosophy" at this time. In contrast to Nishi, who mainly used *tetsugaku* from his Network of All Studies lectures onward, Tsuda was using *kitetsugaku* even in his essay "Discourse on Methods of Advancing Enlightenment" [開化ヲ進ル方法ヲ論ス] published in *Meiji Six Journal* [明六雑誌] no. 3 in 1874 (Tsuda Mamichi [2001], vol. 2, 306). Tsuda may have thought that this term that preserved the original sense of "philosophy" was more appropriate.

44. Nishi Amane (1960–1981), vol. 1, 289.

45. A department of science [理科, *rika*] was established along with departments of law, letters, and the armed services in the Daigaku Nankō, a predecessor to the University of Tokyo, and this was then succeeded by what came to be called the "faculty of science [理学部, *Rigaku-bu*]." A field of study called *seiri* (principles [*ri*] of nature and humanity) that corresponded to philosophy was established within Daigaku Nankō's Faculty of Letters.

46. *Tetsugaku jii* [哲学字彙; Dictionary of philosophy].

47. 批評理学

48. 実践理学. In *Tetsugaku jii* [哲学字彙; Dictionary of philosophy] "science" is translated as *rigaku, kakaku* [理学、科学; the study of principles (*ri*), the study of subjects].

49. 理学沿革史

50. 理学鉤玄

51. 理論

52. Nishi had translated "theology" as shinrigaku [神理学; study of divine principles (*ri*)] and "metaphysics" as chōrigaku [超理学; study of super-principles (*ri*)] in "To Clarify Human Nature" [生性発蘊], and it was not the case that he did not employ the concept of "principles (*ri*)" itself.

53. *Kaidai mon* [開題門; Introductory exegesis].

54. Nishi Amane (1960–1981), vol. 1, 19. In the original Japanese "philosophy" is not translated but rather transliterated as 斐鹵蘇比 (pronounced *hirosohi*), indicating that *Kaidai mon* [開題門, Introductory exegesis] was begun during Nishi's time in the Netherlands. See Hasunuma Keisuke, "Nishi Amane's Introductory Notes on a Comparative Philosophy: A Re-examination," *Kobe Law Journal* 30, no. 2 (September 1980): 439–52.

55. Nishi Amane (1960–1981), vol. 4, 181.

56. 名教学

57. Nishi Amane (1960–1981), vol. 4, 160.

58. Nishi Amane (1960–1981), vol. 4, 169.

59. Itō Jinsai, *Rongo kogi* [論語古義, Ancient meaning of *The Analects*], revised by Sato Masanori (Rokumeikan, 1909), general remarks, 6.

60. Nishi Amane (1960–1981), vol. 4, 182.

61. Nishi Amane (1960–1981), vol. 4, 182–83.

62. Meiji tetsugaku kai no kaiko [明治哲学界の回顧; Reflections on the world of Meiji philosophy].

63. 大日本帝国憲法

64. See "Meiji tetsugakukai no kaiko" [明治哲学界の回顧; Reflections on the world of Meiji philosophy] in *Iwanami kōza: Tetsugaku* [岩波講座 哲学; Iwanami course: Philosophy] (Iwanami Shoten, 1932), 6–9.

In *Meiji tetsugakushi kenkyū* [明治哲学史研究; Studies in the history of Meiji philosophy] (Minerva Shobō, 1959), Funayama Shin'ichi divides the history of Meiji philosophy into five periods. First there was the "transplantation of positivism" period, which lasted until 1882 (the fifteenth year of the Meiji period). Next came the "differentiation of idealism and materialism" period, which lasted until 1889 (the twenty-second year of the Meiji period). This was followed by the "establishment of Japanese idealism" period, which lasted until 1905 (the thirty-eighth year of the Meiji period). After that came the "promotors of philosophical enlightenment" period, which ran from 1895 to 1911 (the forty-fourth year of the Meiji period) and·thus partially overlapped with the third period. Finally, there was the "flourishing of Japanese idealism" period, which ended in 1926 (the final year of the Taishō period).

65. "Nishida Kitarō Sensei" [西田幾多郎先生; My teacher Nishida Kitarō].

66. Karaki Junzō, "Nishida Kitarō sensei—Shōwa nijyū nen roku gatsu no nōto kara" [西田幾多郎先生――昭和二十年六月のノートから; Nishida Kitarō Sensei: From notes taken in June of 1945], included in *Nihon no kokoro* [日本の心; The Japanese mind]. Karaki Junzō, *Karaki Junzō chosakushū* [唐木順三著作集; Collected writings of Karaki Junzō], expanded edition in 19 vols. (Chikuma Shobō, 1981–1982), vol. 4, 422.

67. 蕃書調所

68. Kōsaka Shiro, "Atarashii sekai wo motomete—Nishi Amane to oranda to no deai" [新しい世界を求めて――西周とオランダとの出会い; Seeking a new world: The encounter between Nishi Amane and the Netherlands], included in University of Shimane Nishi Amane Research Group, ed., *Nishi Amane to Nihon no kindai* [西周と日本の近代; Nishi Amane and Japanese modernity] (Perikansha, 2005), 62–64. The original text is included in Gerhart Vissering, *De Troonbestijging van den Kaizer van Japan. De relation in ouden tijd van Holland tot Japan* (Amsterdam), 6–8.

69. Nishi Amane (1960–1981), vol. 2, 141–142.

70. "Hyakugaku renkan" [百学連環; Network of All Studies (Encyclopedia)].

71. *Bankoku kōhō* [万国公法; Law of many nations].

72. *Shinrigaku* [心理学; Study of the principles of the mind]. In today's Japanese *shinrigaku* (心理学) has become the standard word for "psychology."

73. See Hasunuma Keisuke, *Nishi Amane ni okeru tetsugaku no seiritsu* [西周に於ける哲学の成立; The formation of philosophy in Nishi Amane] (Yūhikaku, 1987), 119–27.

74. *Jinsei sanpō setsu* [人生三宝説; On the three treasures of life].

75. Nishi Amane (1960–1981), vol. 1, 51.

76. Nishi Amane (1960–1981), vol. 4, 181.

77. "Seisei hatsuun" [生性発蘊; To clarify human nature].

78. 統一の観

79. Nishi Amane (1960–1981), vol. 1, 36.

80. Nishi Amane (1960–1981), vol. 4, 23–24.

81. The phrases "theological stage," "metaphysical stage," and "positive stage" in this quote are written in English in the original Japanese text [trans.].

82. Nishi Amane (1960–1981), vol. 4, 62–63.

83. In "Introductory Exegesis," a text believed to have been begun during Nishi's time in the Netherlands, "philosophy" is not translated but rather represented phonetically with the Chinese characters "斐鹵蘇比." See Keisuke Hasunuma, "Kaidaimon no seiritsu jijyō" [開題門の成立事情; Circumstances of the formation of "Introductory Exegesis"], *Kōbe Law Journal* 30, nos. 2 and 3 (1980).

84. Nishi Amane (1960–1981), vol. 1, 19. For a detailed examination of "Introductory Exegesis," see Koizumi Takashi, *Nishi Amane to ōbei shisō to no deai* [西周と欧米思想との出会い; The Encounter between Nishi Amane and Western thought] (Sanrei Shobō, 1989), 54–63.

85. Nishi Amane (1960–1981), vol. 4, 61. In "Shōhaku sakki" [尚白箚記, Unfinished essays] Nishi criticizes Confucianism as follows. "To extol a universal principle [天理] in regard to everything, to hold that there is a fixed universal principle that covers everything from nature and weather to humanity and morality without exception, and to stipulate that to deviate from it is to go against the laws of the universe, may lead to gross misapprehension, and from here one may fall into great error, reaching the point of delusion at which it is declared that particular droughts, floods, or eclipses of the sun or moon are connected to human politics." See Nishi Amane (1960–1981), vol. 1, 170.

86. Nishi Amane (1960–1981), vol. 1, 20.

87. "Kaikoku" [開国; Opening of the country].

88. Maruyama Masao, *Maruyama Masao zenshū* [丸山真男全集; Collected works of Maruyama Masao], 8 vols. (Iwanami Shoten, 1995–1997), vol. 8, 49.

89. 文明開化

90. Nishimura Shigeki includes this quote from Mori Arinori in his *Ōjiroku* [往事録; Reminiscence]. See *Meiji keimō shisō shū* [明治啓蒙思想集; Meiji enlightenment thought], in *Meiji bunkagu zenshū* [明治文学全集; Collection of Meiji literature], vol. 3 (Chikuma Shobō, 1967), 412.

91. *Meiroku Zasshi* [明六雑誌, Meiji 6 Journal].

92. *Meiji keimō shisō shū* (1967), 412.

93. Fukuzawa Yukichi, *Fukuzawa Yukichi zenshū* [福沢諭吉全集; Collected works of Fukuzawa Yukichi] (Iwanami Shoten, 2nd ed., 1969–1971), vol. 19, 555.

94. *Bunmeiron no gairyaku* [文明論之概略; An outline of a theory of civilization].

95. Fukuzawa Yukichi (1969–1971), vol. 4, 19.

96. Fukuzawa Yukichi (1969–1971), vol. 4, 17.

97. Fukuzawa Yukichi (1969–1971), vol. 4, 146.

98. Fukuzawa Yukichi (1969–1971), vol. 4, 147.

99. Fukuzawa Yukichi (1969–1971), vol. 3, 79.

100. *Gakumon no susume* [学問のすゝめ, An encouragement of learning].

101. Fukuzawa Yukichi (1969–1971), vol. 3, 121.

102. Fukuzawa Yukichi (1969–1971), vol. 3, 125.

103. Fukuzawa Yukichi (1969–1971), vol. 4, 24.

104. Fukuzawa Yukichi (1969–1971), vol. 4, 145–46.

105. *Fukuō jiden* [福翁自伝, Autobiography of Fukuō (Fukuzawa)].

106. Fukuzawa Yukichi (1969–1971), vol. 7, 167–68

107. Fukuzawa Yukichi (1969–1971), vol. 4, 161.

108. Fukuzawa Yukichi (1969–1971), vol. 4, 163.

109. Fukuzawa Yukichi (1969–1971), vol. 4, 163.

110. 修己安人

111. 修身斉家

112. 道

113. "Fukuzawa ni okeru 'jitsugaku' no tenkai—Fukuzawa Yukichi no testugaku kenkyū josetsu" [福沢における「実学」の転回——福澤諭吉の哲学研究序説; "The 'practical learning' turn in Fukuzawa: An introduction to the philosophy of Fukuzawa Yukichi].

114. See Maruyama Masao (1995–1997), vol. 3, 114.

115. Fukuzawa Yukichi (1969–1971), vol. 4, 162.

116. Fukuzawa Yukichi (1969–1971), vol. 4, 49.

117. Fukuzawa Yukichi (1969–1971), vol. 4, 160.

118. "Seitai sanshu setsu" [政体三種説; A theory of three types of government].

119. "Seigo jyūni kai" [西語十二解; An explanation of twelve foreign words].

120. *Nihon Dōtoku Ron* [日本道徳論; A theory of Japanese morality].

121. *Meiji keimō shisō shū* [明治啓蒙思想集; *Meiji Enlightenment Thought*], in *Meiji bunkagu zenshū* [明治文学全集; *Collection of Meiji Literature*] (Chikuma Shobō, 1967), 370.

122. *Meiji keimō shisō shū* (1967), 378.

123. *Seiri sōdan* [政理叢談; Writings on political theory], in [政理叢談; Journal of Futsu Gaku Jyuku] (1882–1883).

124. *Minyaku yakkai* [民約訳解; Annotated translation of *Du Contrat Social*].

125. *Rigaku enkaku shi* [理学沿革史; History of philosophy (*Rigaku*)].

126. *Rigaku kōgen* [理学鉤玄; Digging up the hidden and profound truths of philosophy (*Rigaku*)].

127. 理学

128. 窮理

129. *Yì Jīng* [易経; Book of Changes].

130. Nakae Chōmin (1983–1986), vol. 7, 13.

131. *Sekkaden* [説卦伝]

132. 格物窮理

133. 空理

134. 実理

135. Nishi Amane (1960–1981), vol. 4, 52–53.

136. 虚学

137. 実学

138. "Kaika wo susumuru hōhō wo ronzu" [開化ヲ進ムル方法ヲ論ス; Discourse on methods of advancing enlightenment].

139. Tsuda Mamichi (2001), vol. 1, 306.

140. "Sakuron" [策論; Offering solutions].

141. Nakae Chōmin (1983–1986), vol. 1, 25.

142. *Ichinen yūhan* [一年有半; A year and a half].

143. Nakae Chōmin (1983–1986), vol. 10, 155.

144. Published in 1883–1884 by the Editorial Bureau of the Ministry of Education with the Japanese title *Ishi bigaku* [維氏美学; Aesthetics of Mr. Véron].

145. *Zoku ichinen yūhan* [続 一年有半; A year and a half continued].

146. 道理 [logic of the "way" in traditional Eastern thought].

147. Nakae Chōmin (1983–1986), vol. 10, 260.

148. Nakae Chōmin (1983–1986), vol. 1, 132.

149. Nakae Chōmin (1983–1986), vol. 1, 134.

150. 共和国

151. 自治の国

152. *Tōyō Jiyū Shimbun* [東洋自由新聞; *Eastern Liberty* newspaper].

153. Nakae Chōmin (1983–1986), vol. 11, 26.

154. Jean Jacques Rousseau, *Du contrat social et oevres politiques*, with an introduction by Jean Ehrard (Garnier, 1975), 236; English translation by G. D. H. Cole (London, 1913), 10.

155. Nakae Chōmin (1983–1986), vol. 14, 1.

156. Nakae Chōmin (1983–1986), vol. 14, 2.

157. Rousseau (1975), 247; English translation by G. D. H. Cole, 18.

158. In arriving at this understanding of liberty, Nakae may also have been influenced by Émile Acollas (1826–1891), a French legal scholar with whom he is thought to have had contact, and the *Dictionnaire des Sciences Philosophiques* compiled by Adolphe Franck (1809–1887). For more on this point, see Miyamura

Haruo's *Rigakusha Chōmin—Aru kaikokukeiken no shisōshi* [理学者 兆民——ある開国経験の思想史; Philosopher [Nakae] Chōmin: An intellectual history of the opening of the country]. Musuzu Shobō, 1989.

159. Rousseau 1975), 247; English translation by G. D. H. Cole, 19.

160. Nakae Chōmin (1983–1986), vol. 14, 2.

161. Nakae Chōmin (1983–1986), vol. 14, 410.

162. Nakae Chōmin (1983–1986), vol. 14, 48.

163. Nakae Chōmin (1983–1986), vol. 14, 2.

164. From the "Translator's Preface" to Nakae's *Annotated Translation of* Du Contrat Social, Nakae Chōmin (1983–1986), vol. 1, 134.

165. Nakae Chōmin (1983–1986), vol. 14, 10.

166. From the chapter "Gong Sun Chou" [公孫丑] in *Mengzi* [孟子; The writings of Mencius].

167. Nakae Chōmin (1983–1986), vol. 1, 166.

168. Nakae Chōmin (1983–1986), vol. 1, 26.

169. See Nakae Chōmin (1983–1986), vol. 10, 177.

170. Regarding this point, see chapter 9 of Matsunaga Shōzō's *Nakae Chōmin hyōden* [中江兆民評伝; A critical biography of Nakae Chōmin] (Iwanami Shoten, 1993).

171. 理

172. 理義

173. Nakae Chōmin (1983–1986), vol. 10, 209.

174. Nakae Chōmin (1983–1986), vol. 10, 177.

175. Nakae Chōmin (1983–1986), vol. 10, 262.

176. Nakae Chōmin (1983–1986), vol. 10, 273.

177. Nakae Chōmin (1983–1986), vol. 10, 292.

Chapter 2

1. The Tokyo Kaisei School was founded by the national government at the beginning of the Meiji period for the study and dissemination of Western learning. After the University of Tokyo was established in 1877, it was renamed Imperial University [帝国大学] in 1886 and Tokyo Imperial University [東京帝国大学] in 1897. To avoid confusion, throughout this book I refer to it simply as the University of Tokyo. I likewise refer to Kyoto Imperial University [京都帝国大学] as Kyoto University.

2. *Taijō* [大丞] was a civil service rank, generally the fourth highest position in a given ministry.

3. *Tonarigusa* [隣草; Tree peony].

4. *Rikken seitai ryaku* [立憲政体略; Summary of the constitutional system].

5. *Shinsei taii* [真政大意; Outline of the true politics].

6. *Kokutai shinron* [国体新論; New theory of the national body].

7. *Meiji keimō shisō shū* (1967), 164, 166.

8. *Jinken shinsetsu* [人権新説; A new doctrine of human rights].

9. *Jinken shinsetsu* [人権新説; A new doctrine of human rights], 174, 177.

10. *Minsen giin setsuritsu kenpakusho* [民撰議院設立建白書; White paper on the establishment of a people's legislative assembly].

11. Hopkins's *Theory of Man* (人論) is thought to refer to Mark Hopkins's *An Outline Study of Man, or, the Body and Mind in One System*, published in 1876. Joseph Haven's *Mental Philosophy* was published in 1857. As I mentioned in the previous chapter, this book was translated into Japanese by Nishi Amane under the title *Shinrigaku* (心理学) (literally "study of the principles of the mind"; this word has become the standard term for "psychology" in today's Japanese) and published in three volumes in 1875 and 1876. Regarding Syle's lectures, see Nishio Kōji, "Meiji zenki no Tōkyō daigaku gaikokujin tetsugaku kyōshi no shiryō chōsa—Nihon ni okeru seiyō tetsugaku no shoki jyuyō ni kansuru chōsa/bunseki no tameni" [明治前期の東京大学外国人教師の資料調査——日本における西洋哲学の初期受容に関する調査・分析のために; A survey of documents of early Meiji period foreign instructors at the University of Tokyo: for a survey/analysis of the early reception of Western philosophy in Japan] in Ōtani University, *Shinshū Sogo Kenkyūsho kenkyū kiyō* [真宗総合研究所研究紀要; Annual memoirs of the Otani University Shin Buddhist Comprehensive Research Institute], no. 29, 63–68.

12. 明治哲学界の回顧

13. "Meiji tetsugakukai no kaiko" [明治哲学界の回顧; Reflections on the world of Meiji philosophy] in *Iwanami kōza: Tetsugaku* [岩波講座 哲学; Iwanami course: Philosophy] (Iwanami Shoten, 1932), 92.

14. 大学今昔譚

15. Miyake Setsurei, *Daigaku konjaku tan* [大学今昔譚; Universities then and now] (Gakansha, 1946), 35–36.

16. See the preface by Fenollosa's widow Mary to his *Epochs of Chinese and Japanese Art: An Outline History of East Asiatic Design*, vol. 1 (William Heinemann, 1912), xiii.

17. 哲学雑誌

18. 社会平権論

19. 世態開進論

20. 学芸志林

21. 世態学

22. 日本における社会心理学の形成

23. Takahashi Tōru, "Nihon ni okeru shakai shinrigaku no keisei" [日本における社会心理学の形成; The formation of social psychology in Japan], in *Konnichi no shakai shinrigaku* [今日の社会心理学; Today's social psychology], vol. 1, *Shakai shinrigaku no keisei* [社会心理学の形成; The formation of social psychology] (Baifukan, 1965), 418.

24. Ernest Fenollosa, "Setai kaishin ron" [世態開進論; Theory of the advancement of the state of the world], in *Fenorosa shakai ronshū* [フェノロサ社会論集; Collection of writings on society by Fenollosa], ed. Seiichi Yamaguchi (Shibunkaku Shuppan, 2000), 148. This lecture is thought to have been given on October 19, 1878, immediately after Fenollosa's arrival in Japan (Collection of writings on society by Fenollosa, 116).

25. Kurihara Shin'ichi, *Fenorosa to meiji bunka* [フェノロサと明治文化; Fenollosa and Meiji culture] (Rikugei Shobō, 1968), 22–23; Yamashita Shigekazu, *Supensaa to Nihon kindai* [スペンサーと日本近代; Spencer and Japanese modernity] (Ochanomizu Shobō, 1983), 126; Yamaguchi Seiichi, *Fenorosa—Nihon bunka no senyō ni sasageta isshō* [フェノロサ——日本文化の宣揚に捧げた一生; Fenollosa: A life devoted to the enhancement of Japanese Culture] (Sanseidō, 1982), vol. 1, 28–29. A particularly detailed account of the circumstances of Fenollosa's having come to Japan and his courses at the University of Tokyo can be found in Yamaguchi Seiichi's *Fenollosa: A Life Devoted the Enhancement of Japanese Culture.*

26. Kiyozawa Manshi, *Kiyozawa Manshi zenshū* [清沢満之全集; Collected works of Kiyozawa Manshi], ed. Akegarasu Haya and Nishimura Kengyō (Hōzōkan, 1953–1957), vol. 2, 564.

27. Sakatani's imperfect English is quoted here verbatim. His manuscripts, including this passage, are held in the Constitutional Documents Room of the National Diet Library. The part of the manuscripts concerning Hegel was translated by Moritsu Takashi into Japanese and published in the fifteenth issue of *Studies in Hegelian Philosophy* [ヘーゲル哲学研究] under the title "Tetsugaku-shi—Hegel ron" [哲学史——ヘーゲル論; History of philosophy—on Hegel]. The *Journal of Philosophy*, edited by the Society of Philosophy (no. 260), article "Former Professor Fenollosa Passes Away" also includes the following passage. "His philosophy ran a wide gamut, including lectures on Mill and Spencer discussing British philosophy along with those on Kant, Fichte, Schelling and Hegel when teaching German philosophy. According to his way of thinking, metaphysics had reached its culmination in Hegel, and this Hegelian thought was consistent with the theory of evolution; the way forward for philosophy in the future could be found in the harmonious merging of Hegel's thought on metaphysics and the thought of [evolutionary philosophers such as] Spencer and others. . . . this should be the aim of scholars, to ultimately bring the two into agreement as one. This is what Mr. Fenollosa considered most important for philosophy."

28. Miyake Setsurei, *Daigaku konjaku tan* [大学今昔譚; Universities then and now], 129.

29. See Yamaguchi Seiichi (1982), vol. 1, 42.

30. 哲学字彙

31. 倫理学

32. 言語学

33. 絶対

34. 世界観

35. 人格

36. 現象即実在論の要領

37. Inoue Tetsujirō, "Genshō soku jitsuzairon no yōryō" [現象即実在論の要領; Main points of the philosophy of phenomenon-reality identity], in *Tetsugaku zasshi* [哲学雑誌; *Journal of Philosophy*], vol. 13, no. 123, 383.

38. Inoue Tetsujirō, "Meiji tetsugakukai no kaiko" [明治哲学界の回顧; Reflections on the world of Meiji philosophy], in *Iwanami kōza: Tetsugaku* [岩波講座 哲学; Iwanami course: Philosophy] (Iwanami Shoten, 1932), 75.

39. 円融相即

40. 円融実在論

41. Watabe Kiyoshi discusses the influence of Hara Tanzan on Inoue Tetsujirō, Inoue Enryō, whom I discuss later in this chapter, and other such thinkers in detail in "Bukkyō tetsugakusha toshite no Hara Tanzan to *Genshō soku jitsuzai* ron no kankei" [仏教哲学者としての原坦山と『現象即実在論』の関係; The relationship between Hara Tanzan as a Buddhist philosopher and *The Philosophy of Phenomenon-Reality Identity*], in *Jōchi daigaku tetsugakuka kiyō* [上智大学哲学科紀要; Record of the Philosophy Department of Sophia University] no. 24: 107–11; "Inoue Tetsujirō no tetsugaku taikei to bukkyō no tetsuri" [井上哲次郎の哲学体系と仏教の哲理; Inoue Tetsujirō's philosophical system and the philosophical principles of Buddhism], in *Jōchi daigaku tetsugakuka kiyō* [上智大学哲学科紀要; Record of the Philosophy Department of Sophia University], no. 25: 78–80, and "'Nishida tetsugaku' no shinkei" [「西田哲学」の真景; The true shape of "Nishida philosophy"], in *Nihon no tetsugaku* [日本の哲学; Japanese Philosophy], no. 8: 58–59.

42. 懐旧録

43. 井上哲次郎自伝

44. 真如

45. Inoue Tetsujirō, "Ninshiki to jitsuzai to no kankei" [認識と実在との関係; The relationship between cognition and reality], in *Sonken ronbun ni shū* [巽軒論文二集; Sonken essays part II] (Fuzanbō, 1901), 221. Sonken is Inoue Tetsujirō's pen name.

46. Inoue Katsuhito examines this point in detail in *Nishida Kitarō to meiji no seishin* [西田幾多郎と明治の精神; Nishida Kitarō and the Meiji spirit] (Kansai Daigaku Shuppanbu, 2011). See pages 164–68.

47. 日本陽明学派之哲学

48. 日本古学派之哲学

49. 日本朱子学派の哲学

50. 折衷学派

51. 独立学派

52. Inoue Tetsujirō, "Meiji tetsugakukai no kaiko" [明治哲学界の回顧; Reflections on the world of Meiji philosophy], 86.

53. Funayama Shin'ichi, *Meiji tetsugakushi kenkyū* [明治哲学史研究; Studies in the history of Meiji philosophy] (Minerva Shobō, 1959), 47, 79. In *Nishida Kitarō and the Meiji Spirit*, Inoue Katsuhito also addresses this issue raised by Funayama

and treats the examination of the substantial connection between Nishida and the Meiji-period "Philosophy of Phenomenon-Reality Identity" as an important topic of inquiry (see page 151).

54. Inoue Tetsujirō, *Sonken ronbun ni shū* [巽軒論文二集; Sonken essays Part II], 147. "Tertium quid" and "Wesen" are written in Latin and German in the original Japanese text.

55. *Zen no kenkyū* [善の研究]. Nishida Kitarō, *Nishida Kitarō zenshū* [西田幾多郎全集; Collected works of Nishida Kitarō] (new ed.), in 24 vols., ed. Takeda Atsushi et al. (Iwanami Shoten, 2002–2009), vol. 1, 43, 144.

56. 現象即実在論

57. 純粋経験に関 する断章

58. 仏教の大綱

59. The metaphor of water and waves is found in *Awakening of Faith in the Mahāyāna*.

60. 哲学一夕話

61. Inoue Enryō, *Inoue Enryō senshū* [井上円了選集; Selected works of Inoue Enryō], in 25 vols. (Tōyō Daigaku, 1987–2004), vol. 1, 35.

62. Nishida Kitarō talks about the large influence *An Evening of Philosophical Conversation* had on him in an interview in the magazine *Gendai* [現代, Modernity]. "Originally I hadn't considered doing philosophy. I'd been thinking about going into science, but then Inoue Enryō released a thin pamphlet called 'An Evening of Philosophical Conversation.' It fascinated and stimulated me, and I gradually started getting into philosophy." "Sekaiteki tetsugakusha Nishida Kitarō hakushi ni mono wo kiku" [世界的哲学者西田幾多郎博士に物を訊く, Interview with world-famous philosopher professor Nishida Kitarō], in Nishida Kitarō (2002–2009), vol. 24, 80

63. 仏教活論序論

64. Inoue Enryō (1987–2004), vol. 3, 370.

65. Inoue Enryō (1987–2004), vol. 3, 371.

66. Inoue Enryō (1987–2004), vol. 1, 354.

67. Inoue Enryō (1987–2004), vol. 1, 395.

68. Inoue Enryō (1987–2004), vol. 1, 396.

69. Inoue Enryō (1987–2004), vol. 1, 401.

70. 哲学会

71. 哲学館

72. 哲学館講義録

73. 哲学要領

74. 哲学ノ必要ヲ論ジテ本会ノ沿革二及ブ

75. Tetsugakukai zasshi [哲学会雑誌; Journal of Philosophy], vol. 1, no. 1: 8–9.

76. In an interview in the magazine *Gendai* [現代, Modernity], Nishida Kitarō states that at the time Hegelian philosophy was popular thanks to books like *Philosophical Trifles*, and talks about how he himself was influenced by this text. "Sekaiteki tetsugakusha Nishida Kitarō hakushi ni mono wo kiku" [世界的哲

学者西田幾多郎博士に物を訊く; Interview with world-famous philosopher Professor Nishida Kitarō], in Nishida Kitarō (2002–2009), vol. 24, 80.

77. 独断法の哲学

78. 懐疑法の哲学

79. 批判法の哲学

80. Miyake Setsuri, *Miyake Setsurei shū* [三宅雪嶺集; Collected works of Miyake Setsurei], in *Meiji bungaku zenshū* [明治文学全集; Collected works of Meiji-period literature] vol. 33 (Chikuma Shobō, 1967), 198.

81. The Japanese term *benshōhō* (弁証法) had previously been used as a translation of "discursive" in Nishi Amane's book on logic *Chichikeimō* [致知啓蒙; Logic enlightenment] published in 1874. See Kayano Yoshio, *Benshōhō nyūmon—Tadashii ninshiki wo motomete* [弁証法入門——正しい認識を求めて; Introduction to the dialectic: Seeking a correct understanding] (Kōdansha Gendai Shinsho, 1969), 247. Nakajima Rikizō was the first to translate Hegel's Dialektik as *benshōhō*. This term is used in the essay "*'Hegerushi' benshōhō*" [「ヘーゲル氏」弁証法; 'Mr. Hegel' dialektik] published in vol. 48 of *Tetsugakukai zasshi* [Journal of Philosophy] in 1890. In *Retsudentai seiyō tetsugaku shōshi* [列伝体西洋哲学小史; A short biographical history of Western philosophy], published in 1898, different terms (*benshōron* and *benshōhō*) are used to translate Kant's Dialektik and Hegel's Dialektik. On the history of translations of Dialektik, see Funayama Shin'ichi, *Meiji ronrigakushi kenkyū* [明治論理学史研究; Studies in the history of logic in the Meiji period] (Risōsha, 1966), 167–68.

82. Miyake translated Hegel's dialectic as *sandanhō* (三段法, three-stage method).

83. Miyake Setsurei (1967), 189.

84. Sakai Osamu attempts to trace the origins of this kind of formal, schematic understanding of the dialectic in the essay "Hegeru tetsugaku no honpō torai" [ヘーゲル哲学の本邦渡来, The arrival of Hegel's philosophy in Japan], published in *Tetsugaku kenkyū* [Journal of Philosophical Studies], vol. 555 (1990).

85. Miyake Setsurei (1967), 151.

86. 王陽明

87. Miyake Setsurei (1967), 198–90.

88. 宗教哲学骸骨

89. 国文学中謹話

90. Fujioka Sakutarō, *Kokubungakushi kōwa* [国文学史講話; Lectures on the history of Japanese literature] (Tokyo Kaiseikan/Osaka Kaiseikan, 1908), 355.

91. Kondō Jyungo, "Kyoshō no koe" [巨鐘の声; Voice of the great bell], in *Kiyozawa Sensei nijyūgo nenki kinen shuppan, Kiyozawa Manshi* [清沢先生二十五年忌記念出版 清沢満之; Kiyozawa Manshi Publication on the 25th anniversary of the death of Kiyozawa-Sensei] (Kanshōsha, 1928), 217–18.

92. Kiyozawa Manshi (Iwanami Shoten, 2002–2003), vol. 5, *Seiyō tetsugakushi kōgi* [西洋哲学史講義, Lectures on the history of Western philosophy], 126–27.

93. Kiyozawa Manshi (Iwanami Shoten, 2002–2003), vol. 5, 306.

94. Kiyozawa Manshi (Iwanami Shoten, 2002–2003), vol. 5, 313.

95. Kiyozawa Manshi (Iwanami Shoten, 2002–2003), vol. 5, 315.

96. Kuwaki Gen'yoku, *Tetsugaku gairon* [2002–哲学概論; Overview of philosophy], rev. ed. (Waseda Daigaku Shuppan, 1903), 126–27.

97. See Sakai Osamu, "Hegeru tetsugaku no honpō torai" [ヘーゲル哲学の本邦渡来, The arrival of Hegel's philosophy in Japan], *Tetsugaku kenkyū* [Journal of Philosophical Studies], vol. 555, 33–34.

98. Yamashita Shigekazu presents this note by Sakatani in "Fenorosa no Tōkyō daigaku kyōjyu jidai" [フェノロサの東京大学教授時代; Fenollosa's time as a professor at the University of Tokyo], Kokugakuin hōgaku [国学院法学; *Kokugakuin Journal of Law and Politics*], vol. 12, no. 4, 148.

99. Part of these notes taken by Kiyozawa are quoted in the Hōzōkan edition of *Kiyozawa Manshi zenshū* [清沢満之全集; Collected works of Kiyozawa Manshi] (1953–1957). See vol. 1, p. 616. Kiyozawa's notes regarding Hegel are translated and presented in *Hegeru tetsugaku kenkyū* [ヘーゲル哲学研究; Studies in Hegel's philosophy] (nos. 17, 19, and 21).

100. Albert Schwegler, *Handbook of the History of Philosophy*, trans. J. H. Stirling, 6th ed. (Edinburgh, 1877), 262.

101. Kiyozawa Manshi (Iwanami Shoten, 2002–2003), vol. 1, 6.

102. Kiyozawa Manshi (Iwanami Shoten, 2002–2003), vol. 1, 7.

103. 万物万化

104. 二項同体

105. Kiyozawa Manshi (Iwanami Shoten, 2002–2003), vol. 1, 9.

106. 東京専門学校

107. 哲学史

108. 論理学

109. 学原稿本

110. Nishi Amane (1960–1981), vol. 4, 148.

111. Nishi Amane (1960–1981), vol. 4, 197.

112. 致知啓蒙

113. 学原

114. 致知学

115. 演繹推理学

116. 論理学講義

117. 論理学

118. 因明

119. 真宗大谷派

120. 因明学協会

121. 因明大意

122. 因明活眼

123. 因明入正理論講義

124. 活用講述因明学全書

125. 因明学大意

126. 明治哲学史研究

127. Funayama Shin'ichi (1959), 18.

128. 帰納法論理学——真理研究之哲理

129. 帰納論理経世危言

130. 早稲田文学

131. 哲学雑誌

132. 大西祝全集 第一巻 論理学

133. Ōnishi Hajime, *Ōnishi hakase zenshū* [大西博士全集; Collected works of Professor Ōnishi], rev.ed. (Keiseisha, 1924–1927), vol. 1, 194–95.

134. Ōnishi (1924–1927), vol. 1, 271.

135. Ōnishi (1924–1927), vol. 1, 3–4.

136. 勅語衍義

137. 教育ニ関スル勅語

138. Kōsaka Masaaki, *Kōsaka Masaaki chosakushū* [高坂正顕著作集; Collected writings of Kōsaka Masaaki] (Risōsha, 1964–1970), in *Meiji tetsugaku shi* [明治思想史; History of Meiji thought], vol. 7, 234.

139. Ōnishi uses 批評主義 rather than 批判主義, the standard Japanese translation of "criticism" in the sense of critical philosophy (*Kritizismus*) [trans.].

140. 方今思想界の要務

141. Ōnishi (1924–1927), vol. 6, 18.

142. Ōnishi (1924–1927), vol. 6, 16.

143. Ōnishi translates Kant somewhat loosely, rendering his freie und öffentliche Prüfung as 公明正大なる試験 (fair and impartial examination). Here is a more direct English translation of this passage for comparison: "Religion through its holiness and legislation through its majesty commonly seek to exempt themselves from it (criticism). But in this way they excite a just suspicion against themselves, and cannot lay claim to that unfeigned respect that reason grants only to that which has been able to withstand its free and public examination" (Immanuel Kant, *Critique of Pure Reason*, trans. and ed. Paul Guyer and Allen W. Wood [Cambridge University Press, 1998], 101) [trans.].

144. Ōnishi (1924–1927), vol. 6, 636.

145. Ōnishi (1924–1927), vol. 6, 241.

146. The materials that served as the basis for *Ryoshin kigen ron* [良心起源論; On the origins of conscience], which are collected as vol. 5 of *Onishi hakushi zenshū* [大西博士全集; Collected works of Professor Ōnishi], had been written up as a graduate school thesis (although never actually submitted). Ōnishi later repeatedly revised and polished them, and released several supplemental essays in publications such as *Rikugō zasshi* [All-Encompassing Journal]. These writings were then brought together as *On the Origins of Conscience*.

147. Ōnishi (1924–1927), vol. 5, 145.

148. That Kanō had a great influence on his students can be seen, for example, in these words of Tanabe Hajime: "My mentor in scholarship was Professor Nishida, but my mentor in life was Professor Kanō." Kuno Osamu, *Sanjyū nendai no shisōka tachi* [三十年代の思想家たち; Intellectuals of the 1930s] (Iwanami Shoten, 1974), 13.

149. 徳育に就きて. Published in Number One High School's *Kōyūkai zasshi* [校友会雑誌; Magazine of Friends of the School Association], nos. 85 and 89, 1899.

150. Kanō's "Tokuiku ni tsukite" [徳育に就きて; On moral education] is included in part 2, "Selected Posthumous Writings," of Suzuki Tadashi's *Kanō Kōkichi no kenkyū* [狩野亨吉の研究; Studies of Kanō Kōkichi] (Minerva Shobō, 2013). See pages 327–28.

151. See Abe Yoshishige, *Senchū sengō* [戦中戦後; Wartime and postwar] (Hakujitsu Shoin, 1964), 212–13, and Kuno Osamu, *Sanjyū nendai no shisōka tachi* [三十年代の思想家たち; Intellectuals of the 1930s], 14.

152. 真営道

153. *Kanō Kōkichi ibun shū* [狩野亨吉遺文集; Collected posthumous writings of Kanō Kōkichi], ed. Abe Yoshishige (Iwanami Shoten, 1958), 26.

154. "Three Great Delusions of Humanity" was presented in the January 1932 edition of *Chūō kōron* as a talk given by Kanō Kōkichi and recorded by Watanabe Daitō. It is included in part 3, "Materials Related to Kanō Kōkichi," of Suzuki Tadashi's *Kanō Kōkichi no kenkyū* [狩野亨吉の研究; Studies of Kanō Kōkichi] (Minerva Shobō, 1970). See pages 581–82.

155. These "Ethics Lecture Manuscripts" are included in Suzuki Tadashi's *Kanō Kōkichi no kenkyū* [狩野亨吉の研究; Studies of Kanō Kōkichi]. See page 366.

156. Suzuki Tadashi (2013), 577–78.

157. 歴史の概念

158. 学生と歴史

159. *Kanō Kōkichi ibun shū* [狩野亨吉遺文集; Collected posthumous writings of Kanō Kōkichi], 123.

160. 美妙学説

161. Nishi Amane (1960–1981), vol. 1, 477. Here Nishi translates "aesthetics" as *bimyōgaku* (美妙学), but earlier he had translated it as *zenbigaku* (善美学) and *kashuron* (佳趣論). The first use of *bigaku* (美学), the current translation of "aesthetics," was by Nakae Chōmin. His Japanese translation of Veron's *L'esthétique* (1883–1884) was entitled *Ishi bigaku* [維氏美学].

162. 美麗

163. Nishi Amane (1960–1981), vol. 1, 492.

164. Nishi Amane, *Nishi Amane tetsugaku chosakushū* [西周哲学著作集; Collected philosophical works of Nishi Amane], ed. Asō Yoshiteru (Iwanami Shoten, 1933).

165. 美術真説

166. The largest group of artists in the history of Japanese painting, active from the Muromachi to Meiji periods.

167. Yamaguchi Seiichi (1982), vol. 1, 30.

168. Ernest Fenollosa, *Fenollosa bijutsu ronshū* [フェノロサ美術論集; Collection of Fenollosa's writings on art], ed. Yamaguchi Seiichi (Chūō Kōron Bijutsu, 1988), 9, 14–15.

169. Ernest Fenollosa (1988), 24.

170. Ernest Fenollosa (1988), 26.

171. 美学事始――芸術学の日本近代

172. Kanbayashi Tsunemichi, *Bigaku kotohajime—Geijutsu gaku no nihon kindai* [美学事始――芸術学の日本近代; The dawn of aesthetics: The study of art in modern Japan] (Keisō Shobō, 2002), 30.

173. フェノロサ――日本文化の宣揚に捧げた一生

174. Yamaguchi Seiichi (1982), 183. A vast number of Fenollosa's documents have been preserved at Harvard University, and their analysis is being undertaken in works such as Murakata Akiko's *Aanesuto Fenorosa bunsho shūsei—Honkoku/honyaku to kenkyū* [アーネスト・F・フェノロサ文書集成――翻刻・翻訳と研究; Earnest F. Fenollosa's documents: Reprinting/translation and study] (Kyoto University Press, 2000–2001). It is hoped that a fuller portrait of Fenollosa will emerge through this scholarship.

175. Ernest Fenollosa, *Epochs of Chinese and Japanese Art: An Outline History of East Asiatic Design* (Chūō Kōron Bijutsu, 1988), 156.

176. Ernest Fenollosa, *Epochs of Chinese and Japanese Art: An Outline History of East Asiatic Design* (Heinemann, 1912), vol. 1, xxiv.

177. 小説神髄

178. 小山正太郎

179. 東京師範学校

180. 洋技排斥例証及美術保護論草案

181. *Koyama Shōtarō sensei* [小山正太郎先生; Professor Koyama Shōtarō], Fudō-sha Kyūyū-kai [Old Friends of Fudō-sha Association] ed. Meguro Shoten, 1934), 233. The author of this "Draft on Examples of the Rejection of Western Techniques and the Protection of Art" is listed as Gijutsusha Dōmei [技術者同盟; Artists' Alliance], but in fact it was written by Koyama.

182. 書ハ美術ナラス

183. 東洋学芸雑

184. 書ハ美術ナラスノ論ヲ読ム

185. 日本美術史 (美術 及美術史)

186. Okakura Tenshin, *Okakura Tenshin zenshū* [岡倉天心全集; Collected works of Okakura Tenshin] (Heibonsha, 1979 1981), vol. 3, 11.

187. 美術家の覚悟

188. Okakura Tenshin (1979–1981), vol. 3, 279.

189. Okakura Tenshin (1979–1981), vol. 3, 279.

190. 鑑画会

191. Ernest Fenollosa (1988), 27.

192. Ernest Fenollosa (1988), 17.

193. Okakura Tenshin (1979–1981), vol. 4, 5.

194. Okakura Tenshin (1979–1981), vol. 4, 167.

195. 大日本美術新報

196. Okakura Tenshin (1979–1981), vol. 3, 22.

197. Ernest Fenollosa, *Epochs of Chinese and Japanese Art* (1912), vol. 1, 1.

198. Here Okakura is perhaps referring to the entire Nara period (710–794).

199. 泰東巧芸史

200. Watsuji Tetsurō, *Watsuji Tetsurō zenshū* [和辻哲郎全集; Collected works of Watsuji Tetsurō] (Iwanami Shoten, 1961–1978), vol. 17, 352.

201. 古寺巡礼

202. 太政大臣

203. 左大臣・右大臣

204. This proposal is recorded as "Opinion on Guiding the Development of the People's Hearts and Minds" in *Biography of Inoue Kowashi* [井上毅伝], Historical documents part 1 (Kokugakuin University Library, 1966). See page 251 of this text.

205. 明治二四、五年頃の東京文科大学選

206. Nishida Kitarō (2002–2009), vol. 10, 410.

207. 明治時代哲学界

208. Kuwaki Gen'yoku, *Meiji no tetsugakukai* [明治の哲学界; Philosophical community in the Meiji period] (Chūō Kōron Sha, 1943), 44–45.

209. *Metaphysik und Erkenntniskritik*

210. Ludwig Busse, *Philosophie und Erkenntnistheorie* [Metaphysics and the theory of knowledge]. Erste Abteilung. Erster Teil. *Metaphysik und Erkenntniskritik* [Part 1. Volume 1. Metaphysics and the critique of knowledge] (Leipzig: S. Hirzel, 1894), S. VI.

211. *Philosophie des Unbewußten*

212. See Inoue Tetsujirō, *Inoue Tetsujirō Jiden* [井上哲次郎自伝; Autobiography of Inoue Tetsujirō] (Fuzanbō, 1973), 25.

213. *Schopenhauer's Erlösungslehre.*

214. *Das philosophische System Eduard von Hartmann's.*

215. ケーベル先生の 追懐

216. Nishida Kitarō (2002–2009), vol. 13, 176.

217. 教養

218. ホメーロス批判

219. 枕草子

220. 日本精神史研究

221. 原始仏教の実践哲学

222. On the other hand, in his essay "Youth Without Youth" [青春なき青春], collected in *Shomotsu to seken* [書物と世間; Writings and the world] (Shunjūsha-shōhakukan, 1943), Kuwaki Gen'yoku writes, "While respectfully submitting to

Professor Koeber, I chafed against his mystical approach to scholarship and felt a profound desire for purely rational philosophy" (311–12).

Chapter 3

1. 将来之日本
2. 経済雑誌社
3. 平民主義
4. 民友社
5. 国民之友
6. 国民新聞社
7. 国民新聞
8. 政教社
9. 日本人

10. The terms *kokusuishugi* (国粋主義, excellence/refinement of the nation-ism) and *kokuminshugi* (国民主義, people of the nation/nationality-ism) were both used at the time with a similar meaning and have been translated as "nationalism." In both cases they were originally used to express the need to preserve the culture and traditions of Japan while taking what was best from those of other nations [trans.].

11. Kōsaka Masaaki, *Kōsaka Masaaki chosakushū* [高坂正顕著作集; Collected writings of Kōsaka Masaaki] (Risōsha 1964–1970), vol. 7, 280.

12. "Meiji tetsugakukai no kaiko" [明治哲学界の回顧; Reflections on the world of Meiji philosophy] in *Iwanami kōza: Tetsugaku* [岩波講座 哲学; Iwanami course: Philosophy] (Iwanami Shoten, 1932), 92.

13. 第十九世紀日本ノ青年及其教育

14. Tokutomi Sohō, *Shin Nihon no seinen* [新日本之青年; The youth of a new Japan], in *Meiji bungaku zenshū* [明治文学全集; Collected works of Meiji-period literature], (Chikuma Shobō, 1974), vol. 34, 118.

15. 時務一家言

16. 蘇峰自伝

17. Tokutomi Sohō, *Shōrai no Nihon* [将来之日本; The Japan of the future], in *Meiji bungaku zenshū* [明治文学全集; Collected works of Meiji-period literature], vol. 34, 56.

18. Tokutomi Sohō, *Shōrai no Nihon* [将来之日本; The Japan of the future], 78.

19. Shiga Shigetaka, " 'Nihonjin' ga kaihō suru tokoro no shigi wo kokuhaku su" [「日本人」が懐抱する処の旨義を告白す; Declaration of the significance of what "Japanese people" hold dear], in *Meiji bungaku zenshū* [明治文学全集; Collected works of Meiji-period literature], vol. 37, 101.

20. Regarding the preceding quotations, see *Nihon no meicho* [日本の名著, Japanese masterpieces], 37, *Kuga Katsunan・Miyake Setsurei* [陸羯南・三宅雪嶺; Kuga Katsunan・Miyake Setsurei] (Chūō Kōron Sha, 1971), 446–48.

21. 真善美日本人

22. Miyake Setsurei (1967), 201.

23. Miyake Setsurei (1967), 200–201.

24. 国民主義

25. Kuga Katsunan, *Kuga Katsunan zenshū* [陸羯南全集; Complete works of Kuga Katsunan], in 10 vols. (Misuzu Shobō, 1968–1985), vol. 2, 3.

26. 政海一片の黒雲

27. Kuga Katsunan (1968–1985), vol. 1, 357.

28. Kuga Katsunan (1968–1985), vol. 2, 3.

29. Kuga Katsunan (1968–1985), vol. 2, 375.

30. Kuga Katsunan (1968–1985), vol. 2, 3.

31. Kano Masanao, "Shinmin·shimin·kokumin" [臣民·市民·国民; Subjects, citizens, nationality (*kokumin*)], in *Kindai Nihon shisōshi taikei* [近代日本思想史大系; Intellectual history of modern Japan series], editorial supervisors Miyazawa Toshiyoshi and Ōkouchi Kazuo, vol. 3, ed. Hashikawa Bunsō and Matsumoto Sannosuke, *Kindai Nihon seiji shisōshi I* [近代日本政治思想史I; History of modern Japanese political thought I] (Yūhikaku, 1971), 245–46.

32. 国会開設の勅諭

33. Kuga Katsunan (1968–1985), vol. 2, 7.

34. 日本国民 ハ明治二十二年二月十一日を以て生れたり

35. 近時政論考

36. 国民論派

37. Kuga Katsunan (1968–1985), vol. 1, 66.

38. 大日本膨脹論

39. Tokutomi Sohō, *Dai Nippon bōchō ron* [大日本膨張論; On the expansion of great Japan], in *Meiji bungaku zenshū* [明治文学全集; Collected works of Meiji-period literature], vol. 34, 255, 261.

40. 時事小言

41. Fukuzawa Yukichi, *Fukuzawa Yukichi zenshū* [福沢諭吉全集; Collected works of Fukuzawa Yukichi], 2nd ed. (Iwanami Shoten, 1969–1971), vol. 5, 187.

42. Fukuzawa (1969–1971), vol. 9, 195–96.

43. 大日本膨脹論

44. 独逸哲学英華

45. 近代哲学宗統史

46. 支那論

47. 兵火にあらずんば文明を清国に伝ふる能はず

48. Takekoshi Yosaburō, *Shinaron* [支那論; On China] (Minyūsha, 1894), 97.

49. Kuga Katsunan, *Kuga Katsunan zenshū* [陸羯南全集; Complete works of Kuga Katsunan] (Misuzu Shobō, 1968–1985), vol. 6, 19–20.

50. Okakura Tenshin, *Okakura Tenshin zenshū* [岡倉天心全集; Collected works of Okakura Tenshin] (Heibonsha, 1979–1981), vol. 1, 142.

51. 東洋の理想

52. Okakura Tenshin (1979–1981), vol. 1, 112–13.

53. Okakura Tenshin (1979–1981), vol. 1, 15.

54. 東京専門学校

55. 想世界

56. 内部生命論

57. Kitamura Tōkoku, *Tōkoku zenshū* [透谷全集; Collected works of Tōkoku], rev. ed. (Iwanami Shoten, 1973–1975), vol. 2, 248.

58. 丁酉倫理会. *Teiyū* (*hinototori*) is a traditional name for a year in a large sequence, in this case referring to 1897 (this organization grew out of the Teiyū Discussion Society, which had been founded in that year).

59. 修養主義

60. 忠君愛国

61. Teiyū rinri kai kōen shū [丁酉倫理会講演集; Collected lectures of the Teiyū Ethics Society] 1 (Dai Nippon Tosho, 1900), 2–3.

62. 日本精神史の課題

63. Miyakawa Tōru, *Nihon seishinshi no kadai* [日本精神史の課題; Issues in Japanese intellectual history] (Kinokuniya Shoten, 1980), 127.

64. 人格の力――修養の方法

65. 教育者の人格修養

66. 精神主義

67. 精神界

68. Kiyozawa Manshi, *Kiyozawa Manshi zenshū* [清沢満之全集; Collected works of Kiyozawa Manshi], ed. Akegarasu Haya and Nishimura Kengyō (Hōzōkan, 1953–1957), vol. 8, 296.

69. Kiyozawa Manshi (Hōzōkan, 1953–1957), vol. 6, 92.

70. Katō Genchi, "Jyōshikishugi to seishinshugi" [常識主義と精神主義; Common sense-ism and spiritualism], in *Shin Bukkyō* [新仏教; New Buddhism], vol. 2, no. 3, 1901, 115.

71. 欧州倫理思想史

72. 春秋倫理思想史

73. 悲哀の高調

74. 病間録

75. "Wretchedness" is written in English in the original Japanese text [trans.].

76. 悲哀の秘儀

77. 予が見神の実験

78. Tsunashima Ryōsen, "Yo ga kenshin no keiken" [予が見神の経験; My experience of seeing God], in *Meiji bungaku zenshū* [明治文学全集; Collected works of Meiji Literature], vol. 46, *Niijima Jyō, Uemura Masahisa, Kiyozawa Manshi, Tsunashima Ryōsen* [新島襄・植村正久・清沢満之・綱島梁川] (1977), 354.

79. 梁川、樗牛、時勢、新自我

80. Shimamura Takitarō, *Kindai bungei no kenkyū* [近代文芸之研究; A study of modern literature] (Waseda Daigaku Shuppanbu, 1909), 456.

81. Nishida (2002–2009), vol. 19, 83–84.

82. Abe Yoshishige, *Iwanami Shigeo den* [岩波茂雄伝; Biography of Iwanami Shigeo] (Iwanami Shoten, 1957), 44.

83. 教育ト宗教ノ衝突

84. 近代日本の形成とキリスト教

85. Sumiya Mikio, *Kindai Nihon no keisei to Kirisutokyō* [近代日本の形成とキリスト教; The formation of modern Japan and Christianity], in *Sumiya Mikio chosakushū* [隅谷三喜男著作集; Collected writings of Sumiya Mikio], in 9 vols. (Iwanami Shoten, 2003), vol. 8, 107.

86. 近代精神とその限界

87. 理想団

88. In the Meiji period, harmful substances released by the Ashio Copper Mine caused significant environmental pollution. This incident has received considerable attention as the first environmental disaster of its kind in Japan.

89. 聖書之研究

90. 無教会

91. 我の改革法

92. 真理の説言

93. Ienaga Saburō, *Kindai seishin to sono genkai* [近代精神とその限界; The modern spirit and its limits], in *Ienaga Saburō shū* [家永三郎集; Inenaga Saburō collection], in 16 vols. (Iwanami Shoten, 1997–1999), vol. 4, 145.

94. 自由の衰退

95. 洗礼晩餐廃止論

96. Uchimura Kanzō, *Uchimura Kanzō zenshū* [内村鑑三全集; Collected works of Uchimura Kanzō], in 40 vols. (Iwanami Shoten, 1980–1984), vol. 9, 53.

97. 労役者 の組合

98. 労働者の声

99. Kōsaka Masaaki (1964–1970), vol. 7, 305.

100. 村井知至

101. 安部磯雄

102. 片山潜

103. 幸徳秋水

104. 木下尚江

105. 西川光二郎

106. 社会主義

107. Murai Tomoyoshi, *Shakaishugi* [社会主義; Socialism] (Rōdō Shinbunsha, 1899), in *Kindai Nihon Kirisutokyō meichosenshū* [近代日本キリスト教名著選集; Collection of important modern Japanese Christian writings], vol. 30, *Shakaishugi/Kirisutokyō to shakaishugi* [社会主義 / 基督教と社会主義; Socialism/Christianity and socialism] (Nihon Tosho Sentā, 2004), 129–30.

108. 社会主義者となるまで——安部磯雄自叙 伝

109. See Abe Isoo, *Abe Isoo chosakushū* [安倍磯雄著作集; Collected writings of Abe Isoo], in 6 vols. (Gakujyutsu Shuppankai, 2008), vol. 6, *Shakaishugi sha to narumade* [社会主義者となるまで; Until becoming a socialist], 144.

110. Heimin-sha (平民社) was an association of thinkers who advocated against war in the late Meiji period.

111. 平民新聞

112. Kōtoku Shūsui, *Kōtoku Shūsui shū* [幸徳秋水集; Kōtoku Shūsui collection], *Kindai Nihon shisō taikei* [近代日本思想大系; Series on modern Japanese thought], vol. 13 (Chikuma Shobō, 1975), 154–155.

113. 余が思想の変化(普通選挙に就て)

114. Kōtoku Shūsui (1975), 291.

115. In what is referred to as the "High Treason Incident" (大逆事件), Kōtoku and many other socialists were prosecuted for alleged involvement in a plot to assassinate the emperor.

116. Two months after Kōtoku Shūsui was arrested in June of 1910, Ishikawa Takuboku is known to have written an essay entitled "The Current State of Occlusion of the Era" (時代閉塞の現状)." The phrase "occlusion of the era" aptly describes the state of affairs during this period.

117. 退社に際し涙香兄に贈りし覚書

118. 日清戦争の義

119. 義戦

120. 時勢の観察

121. Uchimura Kanzō (1980–1984), vol. 3, 233.

122. Uchimura Kanzō (1980–1984), vol. 2, 406.

123. 戦争廃止論

124. Uchimura Kanzō (1980–1984), vol. 2, 296.

125. Uchimura Kanzō (1980–1984), vol. 2, 405.

126. Uchimura Kanzō (1980–1984), vol. 2, 409.

127. Kōtoku Shūsui (1975), 185.

Chapter 4

1. 読書遍歴

2. 読書と人生

3. Miki Kiyoshi, *Miki Kiyoshi zenshū* [三木清全集; Complete works of Miki Kiyoshi], in 20 vols. (Iwanami Shoten, 1966–1986), vol. 1, 389–90.

4. 大正哲学史研究

5. Funayama Shin'ichi, *Taishō tetsugakushi kenkyū* [大正哲学史研究; Studies in the history of Taishō philosophy] (Hōritsu Bunka Sha, 1965), 40.

6. "Capacities" and "Personality" are written in English in the original Japanese text [trans.].

7. "Self-realization" is written in English in the original Japanese text [trans.].

8. 人格

9. 教育的倫理学講義

10. Nakajima Rikizō, *Kyōiku teki rinri gaku kōgi* [教育的倫理学講義; Lectures on educational ethics] (Kōdōkan, 1912), 142.

11. 中学修身教科書

12. Inoue Tetsujirō, *Chūgaku shūshin kyōkasho* [中学修身教科書; Middle school moral training textbook], in 5 vols. (Kinkōdō Shoseki, 1902), vol. 5, 56–58.

13. Inoue Tetsujirō, "Nakajima Rikizō hakase wo tsuiokusu" [中島力造博士を追憶す; Remembering professor Nakajima Rikizō], in *Teiyū Rinri kai kōen shū* [丁酉倫理会講演集; Collected lectures of the Teiyū Ethics Society], no. 436 (Dai Nippon Tosho, 1903), 81.

14. 人格主義

15. Abe Jirō, *Jinkaku shugi* [人格主義; Personality-ism] (Iwanami Shoten, 1922), 56.

16. 序論—理想主義

17. Abe Jirō (1922), 9.

18. 君主人

19. Abe Jirō (1922), 157.

20. 三太郎の日記

21. 修養主義

22. 教養主義

23. 追懐

24. ケーベル博士随筆集

25. See Raphael von Koeber, *Keiberu Hakase zuihitsu shū* [ケーベル博士随筆集; Collected essays of Professor Koeber], trans. and ed. Kubo Masaru, 26th printing (Iwanami Shoten, 1963), 194.

26. 学生叢書

27. 学生と教養

28. Kawai Eijirō, ed., *Gakusei to kyōyō* [学生と教養; Students and cultivation] (Nippon Hyōron Sha, 1936), 2.

29. 現代史への試み

30. Karaki Junzō, *Gendaishi he no kokoromi* [現代史への試み; An attempt at modern history], new ed. (Chikuma Shobō, 1963), 46–47.

31. 黎明会

32. Yoshino translated democracy as *minponshugi* (民本主義; people-based-ism) rather than the widely used *minshushugi* (民主主義; people-ruling-ism) [trans.].

33. Sōda Kiichirō, "Bunkashugi no ronri" [文化主義の論理; The logic of culturism], in *Sōda Kiichirō zenshū* [左右田喜一郎全集; Complete works of Sōda Kiichirō], (Iwanami Shoten, 1930), vol. 4, 9.

34. Kuwaki Gen'yoku, *Bunka shugi to shakai mondai* [文化主義と社会問題; Culturism and social problems] (Shizendō Shoten, 1920), 178–79.

35. 文化主義と社会問題

36. 文化主義原論

37. 文化主義の研究

38. 文化哲学 叢書

39. 自然科学と歴史学

40. 文化の概念

41. Funayama Shin'ichi (1965), 4.

42. カント著作集

43. カントと現代の哲学

44. カントの平和論

45. カントの実践哲学

46. カントの目的論

47. Tomonaga Sanjyūrō, *Kanto no heiwaron* [カントの平和論; Kant's theory of peace] (Kaizōsha, 1922), 59.

48. Tomonaga Sanjyūrō, *Kanto no heiwaron*, 69.

49. 経済哲学の諸問題

50. 文化価値と極限概念

51. 認識論に於ける論理主義の限界――マールブルヒ派とフライブルヒ派の批評

52. For a detailed discussion of this point, see my "Nishida Tetsugaku to Tanabe Tetsugaku—Sōzō teki taiwa no hitotsu no katachi" [西田哲学と田辺哲学――創造的対話の一つの形; Nishida's philosophy and Tanabe's philosophy: One form of constructive dialogue] (*Shisō* [思想; Thought], no. 1099, 2015), 9.

53. 生命

54. 生命の拡充

55. 生命の創造

56. 三太郎の日記

57. "16, Individuality, Art, Nature" [一六、個性、芸術、自然], 1913.

58. Suzuki Sadami, "What Is 'Taishō Life-ism'?," in *Taishō seimeishugi to gendai* [大正生命主義と現代; Taishō life-ism and modernity], ed. Suzuki Sadami (Kawade Shobō Shinsha, 1995), 3.

59. ベルグソンの哲学的方法論

60. ベルグソンの純粋持続

61. Nishida (2002–2009), vol. 1, 254.

62. ベルグソンと現代思潮

63. ベルグソン

64. ベルグソンの哲学

65. 創造的進化

66. 創造的進化

67. Kuki Shūzō, *Kuki Shūzō zenshū* [九鬼周造全集; Complete works of Kuki Shūzō] in 11 vols. and supplementary volumes (Iwanami Shoten, 1980–1982), vol. 1, 437. The English translation of this passage from "Bergson au Japon" given here is based on the Japanese translation by Sakamoto Kenzō [trans.].

68. 自然科学と歴史学

69. 美的生活を論

70. ニイチェ 研究

71. Watsuji Tetsurō, *Watsuji Tetsurō zenshū* [和辻哲郎全集; Collected Works of Watsuji Tetsurō] (Iwanami Shoten, 1961–1978), vol. 1, 8.

72. See Ukita Yūichi, "Kindai Nihon tetsugaku to puragumatizumu" [近代日本とプラグマティズム; Modern Japan and pragmatism], in *Nihon Dyūi gakkai kiyō* [日本デューイ学会紀要; Bulletin of the John Dewey Society of Japan], no. 25 (1984): 97.

73. プラグマティズムに就て

74. Kuwaki Gen'yoku, *Seikaku to tetsugaku* [性格と哲学; Personality and philosophy] (Hidaka Yūrindō, 1906), 156.

75. 書斎から街頭に

76. 徹底個人主義

77. 創造と享楽

78. 哲学の改造

79. Funayama Shin'ichi (1965), 39.

80. In "Taishō demokurashii no tōgō to bunkyoku" [大正デモクラシーの統合と分極; Taishō democracy's unity and polarity], Koyama Hitoshi describes Taishō period cultivationism as "one form of expression of Taishō liberalism" and sees it as overlapping with Taishō democracy. Furuta Hikaru, Sakuta Keiichi, and Ikimatsu Keizō, eds., *Kindai Nihon shakai shisōshi* [近代日本社会思想史; The history of modern Japanese social thought], vol. 2 (Yūhikaku, 1971), 13–14.

81. Matsuo Takayoshi, *Taishō demokurashii no gunzō* [大正デモクラシーの群像; Portraits of people during the Taishō democracy era] (Iwanami Shoten, 1990), 2.

82. 憲政の本義を説いて其有終の美を済すの道を論ず

83. 中央公論

84. Yoshino Sakuzō, *Yoshino Sakuzō shū* [吉野作造集; Yoshino Sakuzō collection], in *Kindai Nihon shisō taikei* [近代日本思想体系; Modern Japanese thought system], vol. 17 (Chikuma Shobō, 1976), 69.

85. See Yoshino Sakuzō (1976), 77.

86. See the "Commentary" by Matsuo Takayoshi in Yoshino Sakuzō (1976), 468.

87. An incident in which socialists and anarchists such as Kōtoku Shūsui were arrested on suspicion of plotting to assassinate the Meiji Emperor. Twelve of those arrested were executed.

88. 貧乏物語

89. 大阪朝日新

90. 社会問題研究

91. In the "Explanatory Notes" appended to the Iwanami Bunko edition of *Binbō monogatari* [貧乏物語, Poverty story] (1947), Ōuchi Hyōe writes that this book "raised world historical questions in Japan" along with Yoshino Sakuzō's view of "the essential meaning of constitutional government and how it can be brought to perfection," and that with it the "splendor of the scattering of social thought appeared in Japan" (177).

92. 我等 (Warera)

93. 社会主義研究

94. 近世経済思想史論

95. 唯物史観研究

96. 資本主義経済学の史的発展

97. マルクス学に於ける唯物史観の地位

98. 社会主義は闇に面するか光に面するか——河上博士著『資本主義経済学の史的発展』に関する一感想

99.『櫛田民蔵全集』第一巻

100. 経済学批判の方法論

101. 唯物史観と中間派史観

102. See Fukumoto Kazuo, *Yuibutsu shikan to chūkanha shikan* [唯物史観と中間派史観; Historical materialism and the centrist view of history] (Kibōkaku, 1926), 177.

103. In Kawakami's later *Jijoden* [自叙伝; Autobiography] he writes that in response to this criticism from Kushida and Fukumoto he "indulged himself" and embarked on a "new journey from economics to philosophy." Kawakami Hajime, *Jijoden* [自叙伝; Autobiography], vol. 1 of 3 vols. (Iwanami Shoten, 1989), 214–15.

104. Ishikawa Kōji, "Nishida tetsugaku to keizaigaku" [西田哲学と経済学; Nishida's philosophy and economics], in *Nishida Kitarō zenshū* [西田幾多郎全集; Complete works of Nishida Kitarō] (Iwanami Shoten 1965–1966), "Monthly Report." This report is included in *Nishida Kitarō—Dōjidai no kiroku* [西田幾多郎——同時代の記録; Nishida Kitarō: Contemporaneous records], ed. Shimomura Toratarō (Iwanami Shoten, 1971), 132.

105. See Bian Chongdao, "Chūgoku no tetsugaku to nihon no tetsugaku tono taiwa" [中国の哲学と日本の哲学との対話; Dialogue between Chinese philosophy and Japanese philosophy], in *Shiriizu: Kindai Nihon no chi* [シリーズ・近代日本の知; Series: Modern Japanese thought], vol. 1, ed. Fujita Masakatsu, *Chi no zahyō jiku* [知の座標軸; Coordinate axes of thought] (Kōyō Shobō, 2000), 255–57. Bian Chongdao's "Higashi Ajia ni okeru kindai Nihon tetsugaku no igi—Meiji tetsugaku wo chūshin toshite" [東アジアにおける近代日本哲学の意義——明治哲学を中心として; The significance of modern Japanese philosophy in East Asia: Focusing on Meiji philosophy], is included in *Higashi Ajia to tetsugaku* [東アジアと哲学; East Asia and philosophy], ed. Fujita Masakatsu, Bian Chongdao, and Kōsaka Shirō (Nakanishiya Shoten, 2003).

106. Lu Xudong, "Honyaku kara mita nijyū seiki Chūnichi bunka kōryū" [翻訳から見た二十世紀中日文化交流; Twentieth-century Chinese-Japanese cultural exchange from the perspective of translation], trans. Akioka Hideyuki, in *East Asia and Philosophy*, ed. Fujita, Bian, and Kosaka, 379–80.

107. Legal scholar Takigawa Yukitoki spent two years studying in Germany beginning in 1922, and when he was staying in Frankfurt he often visited a friend in Heidelberg. Recalling this time, he writes, "One day I went to a lecture, either on philosophy or the history of philosophy, to see Rickert's face, and there were

several black-haired Japanese heads lined up in the second-to-front row." *Thoughts and Recollections* [随想と回想] (Yūhikaku, 1949), 142.

108. *Kritik der reinen Vernunft*.

109. Hermann Glockner, *Heidelberger Bilderbuch* (Bonn, 1969), 232. In his essay entitled "Reading Wanderings" (読書遍歴) Miki Kiyoshi writes of Germany at the time that the record postwar inflation allowed visiting Japanese students to "experience being a millionaire," while for Germans it was on the contrary a "hellish period." It was owing to these circumstances that Rickert gladly accepted work as a private instructor. It is said that Rickert was only able to maintain his household finances thanks to the gratuity Kuki paid him in British pounds. Miki also received private instruction from several scholars including Eugen Herrigel (1884–1955), Glockner, and Karl Mannheim (1893–1947) during his time in Heidelberg and from Karl Löwith (1897–1973) and Hans-Georg Gadamer (1900–2002) after moving to Marburg.

110. Miki Kiyoshi, *Miki Kiyoshi zenshū* [三木清全集, Complete Works of Miki Kiyoshi (Iwanami Shoten, 1966–1986), vol. 1, 414.

111. カントの目的論

112. Tanabe Hajime, *Tanabe Hajime zenshū* [田辺元全集; Complete works of Tanabe Hajime], in 15 vols. (Chikuma Shobō, 1963–1964), vol. 3, 9.

113. ラスクの論理

114. *Die Logik der Philosophie und die Kategorienlehre*

115. *Lehre vom Urteil*

116. 場所

117. *Ideen zu einer reinen Phänomenologie und phänomenologischen Philosophie. Erstes Buch*, in *Husserliana, Gesammelte Werke*, bk. 3, ed. Walter Biemel (Den Haag, 1950).

118. *Jahrbuch für Philosophie und phänomenologische Forschung*

119. *Méditations cartésiennes*

120. *Die Krisis der europäischen Wissenschaften und die transzendentale Phänomenologie*, in *Husserliana, Gesammelte Werke*, bk. 6, ed. Walter Biemel (Den Haag, 1954). English translation: *The Crisis of European Sciences and Transcendental Phenomenology*, trans. David Carr (Northwestern University Press, 1970).

121. 認識論に於ける純論理派の主張に就て

122. 現代に於ける理想主義の哲学

123. Itō Kichinosuke translated Husserl's *Philosophie als strenge Wissenschaft* in 1915 and published it under the title "Philosophy as Science" [学としての哲学] in the *Journal of Philosophy* [哲学雑誌].

124. When Husserl died, Mutai Risaku published an essay entitled "Edmund Husserl" [エドムンド・フッセル] in the magazine *Thought* [思想] in which he mourned his passing. He records Husserl inviting him and Takahashi to his house and speaking passionately about phenomenology. Regarding Husserl's lectures, he writes, "Halfway through the term the audience that had at first nearly filled the stairs had

dwindled to a third; only the Japanese students who always sat at the front did not diminish in number." Mutai Risaku, *Hyōgen to ronri* [表現と論理; Expression and logic] (Kōbundō, 1940), 324.

125. フッセルの現象学——特にその現象学的還元

126. フッセルの現象学

127. 現象学叙説

128. 現象学概論

129.「いき」の構造

130. See Fujita Masakatsu, *Kuki Shūzō—Richi to jyōnetsu no hazama ni tatsu <kotoba> no tetsugaku* [九鬼周造——理知と情熱のはざまに立つ＜ことば＞の哲学; Kuki Shūzō: A philosophy of 'language' standing between reason and passion] (Kodansha, 2016), 85–89.

131. Ontologie (Hermeneutik der Faktizität)

132. 現象学に於ける新しき転向——ハ イデッガーの生の現象学

133. 種の論理の意味を明にす

134. 生の存在学か死の弁証法か

135. 解釈学的現象学の基礎概念

136. *Sein und Zeit* (Tübingen, 2001).

137. パスカルに於ける人間の研究

138. Miki Kiyoshi (1966–1986), vol. 1, 429.

139. Die Selbstbehauptung der deutschen Universität

140. Miki Kiyoshi (1966–1986), vol. 10, 320.

141. 時間の問題——ベルグソンとハイデッガー

142. ハイデッガーの哲学

143. 実存の哲学

144. *Unterwegs zur Sprache* (Pfullingen, 1959).

145. Watsuji Tetsurō (1961–78), vol. 8, 1–2.

146. *Die Stellung des Menschen im Kosmos*

147. *Die Stufen des Organischen und der Mensch*

148. 人間学

149. The commonly accepted English translation "nothingness" has been used for the Japanese word *mu* (無) throughout this book, but the implication of abstractness conveyed by "-ness" may be misleading. Other possible translations include "nonbeing" and simply "nothing" [trans.].

150. 場所の自己限定としての意識作用

151. Nishida (2002–2009), vol. 5, 89.

152. 哲学の根本問題

153. 人間学の立場

154. 思想

155. 神話

156. 構想力の論理

157. 哲学的人間学

158. *Geschichte und Klassenbewußtsein*

159. *Herrn Eugen Dührings Umwälzung der Wissenschaft*

160. *Ludwig Feuerbach und der Ausgang der klassischen deutschen Philosophie*

161. *Die deutsche Ideologie*

162. *Ökonomisch-philosophische Manuskripte aus dem Jahre 1844*, in *Marx-Engels Gesamtausgabe*, Abteilung 1, Bd. 3 (Berlin, 1932).

163. 人間学のマルクス的形態

164. マルクス主義と唯物論

165. プラグマチズムとマルキシズムの哲学

166. 唯物史観と現代の意識

167. Miki Kiyoshi (1966–1986), vol. 3, 3.

168. Regarding this point, see Tomonaga Tairako, "Shōwa shisōshi ni okeru Marukusu mondai—'Doitsu ideorogii' *to Miki Kiyoshi*" [昭和思想史におけるマルクス問題——『ドイツ・イデオロギー』と三木清; The issue of Marx in Shōwa intellectual history: *Die deutsche Ideologie* and Miki Kiyoshi], in *Nihon no tetsugaku* [日本の哲学; Japanese Philosophy], no. 11 (2010), 92–94.

169. 唯物論研究

170. 物質の哲学的概念

171. 一般者の自覚的体系

172. Tosaka Jun, *Tosaka Jun zenshū* [戸坂潤全集; Complete works of Tosaka Jun] (Keisō Shobō, 1966–1967), vol. 3, 172–73.

173. The German word einseitig is used in the original Japanese text.

174. Nishida (2002–2009), vol. 21, 121.

175. Tanabe Hajime (1963–1964), vol. 3, 9.

176. A military action undertaken in the northeastern region of China known as Manchuria by Japan's Kwantung Army. It led to the Second Sino-Japanese War and ultimately the Pacific War.

177. 労農派

178. 人民戦線事件

179. This expression is a reference to an incident in ancient China in which people hid books in their walls to protect them after Emperor Qin Shi Huang ordered their burning to clamp down on critical discourse.

180. 教学刷新評議会

181. 日本諸学振興委員会

182. "Undercurrent" is written in English in the original text.

183. 刑法講義

184. 刑法読本

185. 委員会の論理

186. 無批判性

187. 無協同性

188. 審議性

189. 代表性

Chapter 5

1. For example, Yamada Munemutsu considers Nishida's *An Inquiry into the Good* to be "the philosophization of Tokoku's 'Theory of Inner Life' " (*Nishida Kitarō no tetsugaku* [西田幾多郎の哲学; The philosophy of Nishida Kitarō] (San-Ichi Shobō, 1978), 68. Furuta Hikaru views Nishida's philosophy as "philosophy that takes as its starting point the search for the spiritual pillars of the 'modern individual' in Japan" and focuses on the Fukuzawa Yukichi-Tsunashima Ryōsen-Nishida lineage ("Nihonteki kannenron tetsugaku no seiritsu" [日本的観念論哲学の成立; The formation of Japanese idealist philosophy], in *Kindai Nihon shisōshi* [近代日本思想史; The history of modern Japanese thought], ed. Tōyama Shigeki et al. (Aoki Shoten, 1956), vol. 2, 418. "Nishida Kitarō" in *Kindai shakai shisōshiron* [近代社会思想史論; Essays on the history of modern social thought], ed. Mutai Risaku et al. (Aoki Shoten, 1959), 353, 355, 363. Ueyama Shunpei has discussed the connection between Nishida, Nakae Chōmin, and Kanō Kōkichi: see *Nihon shisō—Dochaku to ouka no keifu* [日本思想——土着と欧化の系譜; Japanese thought: Genealogy of nativity and Westernization] (Saimaru Shuppankai, 1971), chapters 1–4. In "Kindaiteki seikaikan no tetsugakuteki Keisei" [近代的世界観の哲学的形成; The philosophical formation of the modern worldview], Hashimoto Mineo positions Nishida's *An Inquiry into the Good* in the context of the "philosophy of the organism" of thinkers such as Inoue Enryō, Inoue Tetsujirō, and Miyake Setsurei: Furuta Hikaru, Sakuta Keiichi, and Ikimatsu Keizō, eds., *Kindai Nihon shakai shisōshi I* [近代日本社会思想史I; The history of modern Japanese social thought I] (Yūhikaku, 1968), 297.

2. As we saw in chapter 2, Funayama Shin'ichi saw Nishida's theory of "pure experience" as having "developed and expanded" Inoue's "philosophy of phenomenon-reality identity" (Funayama Shin'ichi, 1959), 79. On the other hand, in " 'Nishida tetsugaku' no shinkei" [「西田哲学」の真景; The true picture of 'Nishida philosophy']" (published in *Nihon no tetsugaku* [日本の哲学; Japanese Philosophy], no. 8, 2007), Watanabe Kiyoshi emphasizes the connection between Nishida's thought, Inoue Tetsujirō's "philosophy of phenomenon-reality identity," and the thought of *Awakening of Faith in the Mahayānā* on which Inoue had drawn, and asserts that when it came to Nishida "there was almost no originality in the content of his thought" (71).

3. 自覚における直観と反省

4. 働くものから見るものへ

5. 場所

6. 弁証法的一般者

7. 行為的直観

8. Nishida (2002 2009), vol. 1, 3.

9. 西田哲学

10. Nishida (2002–2009), vol. 11, 281.

11. Nishida (2002 2009), vol. 1, 9.

12. Nishida (2002–2009), vol. 1, 11.

13. Nishida (2002–2009), vol. 1, 157.

14. Nishida (2002–2009), vol. 1, 34.

15. 版を新にするに当つて

16. Nishida (2002–2009), vol. 1, 4. See Gustav Theodor Fechner, *Die Tages-ansicht gegenüber der Nachtansicht* (Leipzig: Breitkopf and Härtel, 1879), 1.

17. Nishida (2002–2009), vol. 1, 50.

18. Nishida (2002–2009), vol. 15, 99. *Rot* is written in German in the original text [trans.].

19. Nishida (2002–2009), vol. 1, 71.

20. Nishida (2002–2009), vol. 1, 67.

21. Nishida (2002–2009), vol. 1, 52.

22. Henri Bergson, *Introduction à la métaphysique* in *Œvres,* annotated by André Robinet (Presses universitaires de France, 1959), 1408.

23. Nishida (2002–2009), vol. 1, 255.

24. Nishida (2002–2009), vol. 1, 261.

25. 場所

26. 西田哲学の方法に就いて——西田博士の教を乞ふ

27. Sōda Kiichirō, "Nishida tetsugaku no hōhō ni tsuite—Nishida hakuse no oshie wo kou" [西田哲学の方法に就いて——西田博士の教を乞ふ; On the method of Nishida philosophy: Seeking the teaching of Professor Nishida], (*Tetsugaku kenkyū* [哲学研究; Philosophy Studies], no. 127, 3), ed. Fujita Masakatsu, *Nishida tetsugaku senshū* [西田哲学選集; Essays on Nishida philosophy], supplemental vol. 2 (Tōeisha, 1998), 45.

28. 働くもの

29. Nishida (2002–2009), vol. 3, 479.

30. Nishida (2002–2009), vol. 8, 255.

31. 自覚に於ける直観と反省

32. Nishida (2002–2009), vol. 11, 281.

33. Nishida (2002–2009), vol. 3, 325.

34. Nishida (2002–2009), vol. 7, 221. In the original Japanese text the words "the Reality" are included in English following the Japanese word 実在 (reality, that which is real) and the word "ὑποκείμενον" is included in Greek following the Japanese word 基体 (hypokeimenon, substance) [trans.].

35. Nishida (2002–2009), vol. 3, 327.

36. Nishida (2002–2009), vol. 3, 397.

37. Nishida (2002–2009), vol. 3, 351.

38. Nishida (2002–2009), vol. 3, 350.

39. Nishida (2002–2009), vol. 3, 350–351.

40. In the original Japanese text Nishida writes 実体 (substance) in Japanese followed by "οὐσία" in Greek [trans.].

41. Nishida (2002–2009), vol. 7, 221.

42. 基体

43. Nishida (2002–2009), vol. 3, 419.

44. Nishida (2002–2009), vol. 3, 424.

45. Nishida (2002–2009), vol. 3, 436.

46. 措定判断に就て

47. 数理哲学研究

48. 科学概論

49. カントの目的論

50. ヘーゲル哲学と弁証法

51. カントの目的論

52. Tanabe Hajime, *Tanabe Hajime zenshū* [田辺元全集; Complete works of Tanabe Hajime] (Chikuma Shobō, 1963–1964), vol. 3, 8.

53. 認識論と現象学

54. Tanabe Hajime (1963–1964), vol. 4, 22.

55. 現象学に於ける新しき転向——ハイデッガーの生の現象学

56. The German word *Sachlichkeit* is included in the original Japanese text [trans.].

57. Tanabe Hajime (1963–1964), vol. 4, 22.

58. The German words *Selbstauslegung* and *hermeneutische Phänomenologie* are included in the original Japanese text [trans.].

59. Tanabe Hajime (1963–1964), vol. 4, 29.

60. 弁証法の論理

61. ヘーゲル哲学と弁証法

62. Tanabe Hajime (1963–1964), vol. 3, 9.

63. ヘーゲル哲学と弁証法

64. Tanabe Hajime (1963–1964), vol. 3, 77–78.

65. 行為と歴史、及び弁証法のこれに対する関係

66. 弁証法

67. Tanabe Hajime (1963–1964), vol. 3, 78.

68. ヘーゲル哲学と絶対弁証法

69. Tanabe Hajime (1963–1964), vol. 3, 166.

70. "Shu no ronri no imi wo akirakani su" [種の論理の意味を明にす; Elucidating the meaning of the logic of species], in Tanabe Hajime (1963–1964), vol. 6, 465.

71. 行為と歴史、及び弁証法のこれに対する関係

72. 西田先生の教を仰ぐ

73. Tanabe Hajime (1963–1964), vol. 3, 338–39.

74. Tanabe Hajime (1963–1964), vol. 3, 355.

75. Tanabe Hajime (1963–1964), vol. 3, 355.

76. Tanabe Hajime (1963–1964), vol. 3, 369.

77. Tanabe Hajime (1963–1964), vol. 3, 366–67.

78. Tanabe Hajime (1963–1964), vol. 3, 230.

79. Tanabe Hajime (1963–1964), vol. 4, 309

80. Tanabe Hajime (1963–1964), vol. 4, 311.

81. Tanabe Hajime (1963–1964), vol. 4, 312.

82. Tanabe Hajime (1963–1964), vol. 4, 315.

83. 無の自覚的限定

84. Nishida (2002–2009), vol. 5, 3.

85. Nishida (2002–2009), vol. 5, 9.

86. Nishida (2002–2009), vol. 4, 301.

87. Nishida (2002–2009), vol. 4, 357.

88. Nishida (2002–2009), vol. 5, 7.

89. Nishida (2002–2009), vol. 4, 326.

90. Tanabe Hajime (1963–1964), vol. 3, 361.

91. 行為と歴史、及び弁証法のこれに対する関係

92. Tanabe Hajime (1963–1964), vol. 3, 227.

93. Tanabe Hajime (1963–1964), vol. 3, 223.

94. 私と汝

95. *Phänomenologie des Geistes*

96. Hegel, *Werke in Zwanzig Bänden. Bd. 3. Phänomenollogie des Geistes* (Suhrkamp, 1970), 29.

97. Hegel, *Werke in Zwanzig Bänden*, 145.

98. Nishida (2002–2009), vol. 5, 295.

99. Nishida (2002–2009), vol. 5, 306.

100. Nishida (2002–2009), vol. 5, 280.

101. 哲学の根本問題 続編

102. 形而上学序論

103. Nishida (2002–2009), vol. 6, 50.

104. Nishida (2002–2009), vol. 6, 171.

105. Nishida (2002–2009), vol. 6, 46.

106. Nishida (2002–2009), vol. 7, 101.

107. Nishida (2002–2009), vol. 7, 143.

108. Nishida (2002–2009), vol. 8, 47.

109. 場所的論理と宗教的世界観

110. Nishida (2002–2009), vol. 10, 331.

111. Nishida (2002–2009), vol. 8, 485–86.

112. Nishida (2002–2009), vol. 10, 314.

113. 煩悩具足

114. *Jōdo shinshū seiten (chūshaku-ban)* [浄土真宗聖典（註釈版）; Jōdo Shinshū sacred texts, annotated version], ed. Shinshū Sacred Texts Compilation Committee (Hongwanji Publishing, 1988), 266.

115. 歎異抄

116. Nishida (2002–2009), vol. 10, 314.

117. Nishida (2002–2009), vol. 10, 344.

118. 逆対応

119. 社会存在の論理——哲学的社会学試論

120. 種の論理と世　界図式——絶対媒介の哲学への途

121. 種の論理の意味を明にす

122. For a more detailed account, see my article " 'Shu no ronri' ha donoyouni shite seiritsu shita no ka—Tanabe tetsugaku no seiritsu he no michi" [「種の論理」はどのようにして成立したのか——田辺哲学の成立への道; How was the 'logic of species' formed? The path toward the formation of Tanabe's philosophy], (*Shisō* [思想; Thought], no. 1093, 2015.

123. 綜合と超越

124. 人間学の立場

125. 図式「時間」から図式「世界」へ

126. *Kant und das Problem der Metaphysik.*

127. Tanabe Hajime (1963–1964), vol. 6, 9.

128. Tanabe Hajime (1963–1964), vol. 4, 349.

129. Tanabe Hajime (1963–1964), vol. 4, 349.

130. 種の論理に対する批評に答ふ

131. Tanabe Hajime (1963–1964), vol. 6, 399.

132. Tanabe Hajime (1963–1964), vol. 6, 454.

133. 日本精神

134. 日本精神の哲学

135. 日本主義

136. Based on what he had heard directly from Kuno Osamu, who had been involved in the incident as a student, Ienaga Saburō writes that the Taki-gawa Incident held great significance for Tanabe. "The Takigawa Incident seems to have been the first time Tanabe was forced to directly confront the trend toward fascism that had been rapidly progressing since the start of the Fifteen Years' War [1931–1945]." Ienaga Saburō, *Tanabe Hajime no shisōshi teki kenkyū* [田辺元の思想史的研究; Studies in Tanabe Hajime from the perspective of intellectual history] (Hōsei University Press, 1974), 47.

137. 哲学通論

138. Tanabe Hajime (1963–1964), vol. 6, 176–77.

139. The Japanese word for "tribe" (種族) contains the character for "species" (種).

140. Tanabe Hajime (1963–1964), vol. 6, 449.

141. Throughout this book, Tanabe's 民族 is translated as "nation" in the sense of a people or ethnic group with a shared culture and language, while his 国家 is translated as "state" in the sense of a political body. 民族国家 is therefore translated as "nation-state" [trans.].

142. The Japanese word for "humanity" or "humankind" (人類) contains the character for "genus" (類) [trans.]

143. Tanabe Hajime (1963–1964), vol. 6, 69.

144. Tanabe Hajime (1963–1964), vol. 6, 133.

145. Nishida (2002–2009), vol. 7, 248.

146. Tanabe Hajime (1963–1964), vol. 6, 202.

147. 世界の自己同一と連続

148. Nishida (2002–2009), vol. 7, 71.

149. Tanabe Hajime (1963–1964), vol. 6, 195.

150. Tanabe Hajime (1963–1964), vol. 6, 202.

151. Tanabe Hajime (1963–1964), vol. 6, 202–3.

152. 哲学論文集第二

153. 種の生成発展の問題

154. 論理と生命

155. Nishida (2002–2009), vol. 8, 91.

156. Tanabe Hajime (1963–1964), vol. 7, 36.

157. Tanabe Hajime (1963–1964), vol. 7, 91.

158. 応現

159. Tanabe's serious attempts to point the correct way forward for the state in difficult circumstances drew the attention not only of philosophers but also scholars of political science. Nanbara Shigeru discusses Tanabe's "logic of species" in his 1942 text *Kokka to shukyō—Yōroppa seishinshi no kenkyū* [国家と宗教——ヨーロッパ精神史の研究; State and religion: A study of the spiritual history of Europe]. What he highlights there, however, is the possibility of the "logic of species" providing a grounding for the "divinity" of the actual state.

160. 国家の道義性

161. 思想報国の道

162. 実存概念の発展

163. 懺悔道 としての哲学; translated as *Philosophy as Metanoetics* by Takeuchi Yoshinori with Valdo Viglielmo and James W. Heisig (University of California Press, 1986).

164. 死生

165. Tanabe Hajime (1963–1964), vol. 8, 260.

Chapter 6

1. 意識現象の事実と其意味——西田氏著『善の研究』を読む

2. 高橋(里美)文学士の拙著『善の研究』に対する批評に答ふ

3. フッセルの現象学、特にその現象学的還元

4. フッセルにおける時間と意識流

5. フッセルの現象学

6. This is a direct translation of the Japanese translation of the German *Einfühlung* (感情移入), which is often translated as simply "empathy" in English [trans.].

7. Takahashi Satomi, *Takahashi Satomi zenshū* [高橋里美全集; Complete works of Takahashi Satomi], in 7 vols. (Fukumura Shuppan, 1973), vol. 4, 32–37.

8. 全体の立場

9. 体験と存在

10. 歴史と弁証法

11. 包弁証法

12. Takahashi Satomi (1973), vol. 1, 86.

13. Takahashi Satomi (1973), vol. 1, 87. In his "Commentary" appended to Takahashi Satomi's *Zentaisei no genshōgaku* [全体性の現象学; Phenomenology of totality] in (*Kyōto tetsugaku sensho* [京都哲学選書; Selected writings of Kyoto philosophy], vol. 17 (Tōeisha, 2001)), Noe Keiichi states that this stillness as the totality of development was "a bright thread running throughout Takahashi's philosophy." He also points out, however, that concepts such as "development," "totality," and "stillness" are given only abstract, formal definitions (404).

14. Takahashi Satomi (1973), vol. 4, 78.

15. 現象学的還元 の可能性——付、中和変様の導来

16. 西田哲学について

17. Takahashi Satomi (1973), vol. 4, 214.

18. Kuki Shūzō, *Kuki Shūzō zenshū* [九鬼周造全集; Complete works of Kuki Shūzō] (Iwanami Shoten, 1980–1982), vol. 1, 437.

The English translation of this passage from "Bergson au Japon" given here is based on the Japanese translation by Sakamoto Kenzō [trans.].

19. Henri Bergson, "Introduction à la Métaphysique," in *Œvres*, annotated by André Robinet (Presses universitaires de France, 1959), 1408.

20. 回想のアンリ・ベルグソン

21. 形而上学的時間

22. 人間と実存

23. 時間論

24. 回帰的時間

25. 輪廻

26. 劫波

27. 「いき」の構造

28. Kuki Shūzō (1980–1982), vol. 1, 3.

29. Kuki Shūzō (1980–1982), vol. 1, 8.

30. 会得

31. 媚態

32. 意気地

33. 諦め

34. 霊化

35. 偶然性の問題

36. 偶然の諸相

37. 驚きの情と偶然性

38. Kuki Shūzō (1980–1982), vol. 2, 9.

39. Kuki uses the phrase "If p then p" to express a cause and effect relationship in which a certain cause necessarily leads to a separate effect.

40. 浄土論

41. Kuki Shūzō (1980–1982), vol. 2, 317.

42. 巴里心景

43. 巴里の窓

44. 明星

45. 文芸論

46. Kuki Shūzō (1980–1982), vol. 4, 18.

47. This is an English analogue of the "rhymes (押韻)" cited in the original poem. The Japanese text is "竜田道の岡辺の道に丹躑躅のにほはむ時 の桜花咲きなむ時に . . . ," and the "rhymes" are "ニツツジノのニ" and "ニホハムトキノの ニ" in the first instance and "サクラバナのサ" and "サキナムトキニのサ" in the second [trans.].

48. Kuki Shūzō (1980–1982), vol. 4, 22.

49. Kuki Shūzō (1980–1982), vol. 4, 33.

50. 日本詩の押韻

51. 押韻に就いて

52. Kuki Shūzō (1980–1982), vol. 4, 448.

53. For a detailed discussion of this point, see my *Kuki Shūzō—Richi to jyōnetsu no hazamani tatsu "kotoba" no tetsugaku* [九鬼周造—— 理知と情熱のはざまに立つ＜ことば＞の哲学; Kuki Shūzō: A philosophy of "words" in the space between intellect and passion] (Kōdansha, 2016), 212–13.

54. 古寺巡礼

55. Watsuji Tetsurō, *Watsuji Tetsurō zenshū* [和辻哲郎全集; Collected works of Watsuji Tetsurō] (Iwanami Shoten, 1961–1978), vol. 2, 44.

56. 日本古代文化

57. 日本精神史研究

58. 人間としての倫理学

59. 鎖国

60. 日本倫理思想史

61. 歌舞伎と操り浄瑠璃

62. 桂離宮

63. 風土——人間学的考察; translated as *Climate and Culture* by Geoffrey Bownas (Greenwood Press, 1988).

64. Watsuji Tetsurō (1961–1978), vol. 8, 2–3.

65. Watsuji Tetsurō (1961–1978), vol. 8, 7.

66. Abe Yoshishige, *Watsuji kun no Fūdo* [和辻君の『風土』; Watsuji's climate], in *Sōyashū* [草野集; Essay collection 'Sōya'] (Iwanami Shoten, 1936), 367.

67. Augustin Berque, *Le sauvage et l'artifice, les Japonais devant la nature* (Gallimard, 1986), 150.

68. 倫理学

69. Watsuji Tetsurō (1961–1978), vol. 9, 13

70. Watsuji Tetsurō (1961–1978), vol. 9, 20

71. Thought that focuses on "relationships" as Watsuji does is also found in Western ethics. Karl Löwith (1897–1973)'s *Das Individuum in der Rolle des Mit-*

menschen can be cited as a leading example. This text was published in 1929, and Watsuji may have drawn on it in writing his *Ethics as the Study of Human Beings.* In the introduction to *Ethics* (vol. 1), Watsuji praises this work for "not taking up the 'person' as an individual, but rather the relationship between self and other, that is, the reciprocal interactions between human beings" (*Ethics*, vol. 10, 19), but there are differences between their approaches. In contrast to Löwith's emphasis on the relative independence of the individual within "relationships" and the individual's initiative, in Watsuji the emphasis is placed on the connections between people and structures of solidarity within the groupings of family, society, and nation.

72. 人間の間と倫理

73. See Utsunomiya Yoshiaki, *Ningen no aida to rinri* [人間の間と倫理; Ethics and [relationships] between human beings] (Ibunsha, 1980), 98–101.

74. See Kaneko Takezō, "Taikei to hōhō" [体系と方法; System and method], in *Hito to shisō: Watsuji Tetsurō* [人と思想・和辻哲郎; Person and thought: Watsuji Tetsurō], ed. Yuasa Yasuo (San-Ichi Shobō, 1973), 205.

75. *Shinbi kōryō* [審美綱領; Outline of the aesthetics]

76. *Einfühlung.* See note 6 in chapter 6, section 1 [trans.].

77. 美しき魂

78. 深田康算全集

79. 芸術一般

80. 美と芸術の理論

81. Fukada Yasukazu, *Bi to geijutsu no riron* [美と芸術の理論; A theory of beauty and art] (Hakuhōsha, 1971), 278.

82. カント「判断力批判」の研究

83. 現象学の美術

84. 幽玄とあはれ

85. 風雅論——「さび」の研究

86. 万葉集の自然感情

87. 美的範疇

88. These terms are difficult to translate and can have varying meanings depending on the context. Very simply stated, *yūgen* (幽玄), often used in discussing poetry, refers to that which is too subtle or profound to be directly expressed in words, while *aware* (あはれ) refers to the pathos of impermanence or evanescence [trans.]

89. See Ōnishi Yoshinori, "Biteki hanchūron" [美的範疇論; A theory of aesthetic categories], in *Bigaku* [美学, Aesthetics] (Kōbundō, 1960), vol. 2, 452.

90. Tanaka Kyūbu, "Onishi Yoshinori ni okeru Nihonbi no kōzō—'Aware' 'yūgen' 'sabi'" [大西克礼における日本美の構造——「あはれ」・「幽玄」・「さび」; The structure of Japanese beauty in Ōnishi Yoshinori: 'Aware,' 'Yūgen,' and 'Sabi'], in *Shisōkan no taiwa* [思想間の対話; Dialogue between intellectual traditions], ed. Fujita Masakatsu (Hōsei University Press, 2015), 260.

91. Nishida (2002–2009), vol. 2, 95.

92. Nishida (2002–2009), vol. 2, 95–96.

93. 視覚構造. Iwaki Ken'ichi's "Shikaku no ronri—Ueda Jyuzō" [視覚の論理——植田寿蔵; The logic of visual perception: Ueda Jyuzō] discusses this theory of art centered on "visual perception." See Tsunetoshi Sōzaburō, ed., *Nihon no tetsugaku wo manabu hito no tame ni* [日本の哲学を学ぶ人のために; For people learning Japanese philosophy] (Sekaishisōsha, 1998), 197–98.

94. Ueda Jyuzō, *Shikaku kōzō* [視覚構造; The structure of visual perception] (Kōbundō Shobō, 1941), 10.

95. Ueda's interest in this question may have been sparked by Nishida's understanding of art. For example, in "Bi no honshitsu" [美の本質; The essence of beauty], an essay included in *Geijutsu to dōtoku* [芸術と道徳; Art and morality], Nishida writes, "The act of visual perception is an internal relationship in which color itself distinguishes color, and an a priori on which the experience of color is based" (Nishida (2002–2009), vol. 3, 10.

96. 芸術と道徳

97. Nishida (2002–2009), vol. 3, 309.

98. 革命の画家

99. 工芸文化

100. 無事の美

101. 尋常の美

102. See Yanagi Muneyoshi, *Kōgei bunka* [工芸文化; Handicraft culture] (Iwanami Bunko, 1985), 163.

103. 印度宗教史

104. 仏教聖典史論

105. 宗教哲学の本質及其根本問題

106. 宗教哲学

107. 宗教哲学序論

108. 時と永遠

109. Hatano Seiichi, *Toki to eien: Hoka hachi hen* [時と永遠 他八篇; Time and eternity: Eight other texts] (Iwanami Bunko, 2012b), 410.

110. Hatano Seiichi, *Shūkyō tetsugaku joron / Shūkyō tetsugaku* [宗教哲学序論・宗教哲学; Introduction to the philosophy of religion / the philosophy of religion], two works in one volume (Iwanami Bunko, 2012a), 168.

111. Hatano Seiichi (2012b), 280.

112. Sadamichi Ashina, "Kaisetsu" [解説, Commentary], in Hatano Seiichi (2012a), 532.

113. Hatano Seiichi (2012b), 84.

114. Hatano Seiichi (2012a), 246.

115. Hatano Seiichi (2012a), 297.

116. Hatano Seiichi (2012a), 360.

117. Hatano Seiichi (2012b), 199.

118. Hatano Seiichi (2012b), 199.

119. Often referred to as D. T. Suzuki outside of Japan [trans.].

120. 即非の論理

121. 石川県専門学校

122. 東洋学者の使命

123. Suzuki Daisetsu, *Suzuki Daisetsu zenshū* [鈴木大拙全集; Complete works of Suzuki Daisetsu], new enlarged ed. in 40 vols. (Iwanami Shoten, 1999–2003), vol. 20, 217.

124. 東洋文化の根柢にあるもの

125. 日本人の心

126. Suzuki Daisetsu (1999–2003), vol. 20, 307.

127. Suzuki Daisetsu (1999–2003), vol. 20, 221.

128. Suzuki Daisetsu, "How to Read Nishida," in Nishida Kitarō, *A Study of Good,* trans. V. H. Viglielmo (Japanese Government Printing Bureau, 1960), iii.

129. See book 5, "Zen of the Diamond Sutra" [金剛経の禅], in *Japanese Spirituality* [日本的霊性], published in 1944.

130. For a more detailed discussion, see my "Suzuki Daisetsu to Nishida Kitarō" [鈴木大拙と西田幾多郎; Suzuki Daisetsu and Nishida Kitarō], included in Ōtani Daigaku Shūkyō Gakkai, ed., *Shūkyō gakkai hō* [宗教学会報; Religious Studies Association Bulletin], no. 13.

131. 論理と数理

132. Nishida (2002–2009), vol. 10, 69.

Chapter 7

1. Takeuchi Yoshinori, "Sei wo koeru mono" [聖を超えるもの; That which transcends the sacred], in *Takeuchi Yoshinori chosakushū* [武内義範著作集; Collected writings of Takeuchi Yoshinori], in 5 vols. (Hōzōkan, 1999), vol. 5, 163.

2. 東洋的無

3. 東洋的に形而上的なるもの

4. Hisamatsu Shin'ichi, *Hisamatsu Shin'ichi chosakushū* [久松真一著作集; Collected writings of Hisamatsu Shin'ichi], enlarged edition in 9 vols. and a supplementary vol. (Hōzōkan, 1994–1996), vol. 1, 20.

5. Hisamatsu Shin'ichi (1994–1996), vol. 1, 27.

6. Hisamatsu Shin'ichi (1994–1996), vol. 1, 15.

7. Nishitani Keiji, *Nishitani Keiji chosakushū* [西谷啓治著作集; Collected writings of Nishitani Keiji], in 26 vols. (Sōbunsha, 1986–1995), vol. 1, 3.

8. Nishitani Keiji (1986–1995), vol. 1, 65.

9. Nishitani Keiji (1986–1995), vol. 1, 77.

10. Nishitani Keiji (1986–1995), vol. 1, 77.

11. Nishitani Keiji (1986–1995), vol. 1, 78.

12. Nishitani Keiji (1986–1995), vol. 1, 85.

13. 現象学叙説

14. 弁証法と現象学

15. 体系と展相

16. 哲学の出発

17. 歴史的世界——現象学的試論

18. 歴史哲学と政治哲学

19. 歴史哲学の序説

20. Nishida (2002–2009), vol. 23, 8.

21. Nishida (2002–2009), vol. 5, 277.

22. 歴史哲学

23. Kōsaka Masaaki, *Rekishitekiseka—Genshōgakuteki shiron* [歴史的世界——現象学的試論; The historical world: Phenomenological essays] (Iwanami Shoten, 1937), 142–43.

24. 国家学会雑誌

25. Maruyama Masao, *Maruyama Masao zenshū* [丸山真男全集; Collected Works of Maruyama Masao] (Iwanami Shoten, 1995–1997), vol. 1, 113.

26. Maruyama Masao (1995–1997), vol. 1, 114.

27. 表現と論理

28. 場所と論理学

29. ヘーゲル研究

30. Taihoku Imperial University was the seventh imperial university to be established and had been preceded by Keijō (Seoul) Imperial University in 1924. Abe Yoshishige and Miyamoto Wakichi (1883–1972) were in charge of the latter institution's Philosophy/History of Philosophy program. Many future philosophers studied under them, including Park Chong-Hong (1903–1976). See Kōsaka Shirō, *Higashi Ajia no shisō taiwa* [東アジアの思想対話; Intellectual dialogue in East Asia] (Perikansha, 2014), 191–94.

31. 今日に於ける哲学の問題

32. 今日に於ける哲学の問題（承前）

33. Hong Yaoxun, "Konnichi ni okeru tetsugaku no mondai (shōzen)" [今日に於ける哲学の問題（承前）; Philosophical problems today (continued)], in *Taiwan kyōiku* [台湾教育; Taiwan Education], March 1934, 21.

34. Mutai Risaku, *Mutai Risaku chosakushū* [務台理作著作集; Collected writings of Mutai Risaku], in 9 vols. (Kobushi Shobō, 2000–2002), vol. 2, 9.

35. After being detained for six months, Miki was found guilty and given a suspended sentence. Following his release he dedicated himself mainly to writing.

36. 歴史哲学

37. 構想力 第一

38. 構想力 第二

39. Miki recognized two tendencies or aspects within pathos. On the one hand, in keeping with the meaning of the Greek word πάθος (pathos), which is derived from the word πάσχω (paskho), meaning "to undergo or be subjected to something," he understood it as the passivity of our receiving something and as a

result being put in a certain mood or emotional state. The place where this pathos as "affectivity" (Befindlichkeit) arises is the body. In this sense the body is called the "place of passivity." Pathos is thus a certain "affectivity" that arises in this "place of passivity." At the same time, however, Miki also finds in pathos a "root source activity." Transformation of the "affectivity" that arises in the "place of passivity" does not stop at being a transformation but has the power to express itself in the outside world. In other words, pathos has an "impulsive" character. It drives us to action through the body. It is because of this activity of pathos underlying the body that it can be described as "a body in its subjectivity" and not simply a physical object. This is the sense in which "pathos" and "pathetic" are used in Miki's thought.

40. Miki Kiyoshi, *Miki Kiyoshi zenshū* [三木清全集, Complete works of Miki Kiyoshi], (Iwanami Shoten, 1966–1986), vol. 8, 4.

41. Miki Kiyoshi (1966–1986), vol. 8, 5.

42. Logik der Einbildungskraft

43. Logik der Phantasie

44. Logique du cœur

45. Logique des sentiments

46. Miki Kiyoshi (1966–1986), vol. 8, 15

47. The word beseelt (animate, having a soul) is included in German in the original Japanese text.

48. Miki Kiyoshi (1966–1986), vol. 18, 149.

49. Wendung zur Idee

50. Einbildungskraft

51. Georges Sorel, *Réflexions sur la violence*, 6th ed. (M. Rivière, 1925), 45. The English translation used here is from *Reflections on Violence*, ed. Jeremy Jennings (Cambridge University Press, 1999), 28 [trans.]. As Miki notes, this is a quotation from John Henry Newman's "An Essay in Aid of a Grammar of Assent."

52. Miki Kiyoshi (1966–1986), vol. 8, 49.

53. 形像の論理

54. Miki Kiyoshi (1966–1986), vol. 8,6.

55. Miki Kiyoshi (1966–1986), vol. 8, 6–7.

56. Miki Kiyoshi (1966–1986), vol. 19, 453.

57. 唯物論研究会

58. 唯物論研究

59. *Series of Books on Materialism* (唯物論全書) was a series of books on materialist thought published by Mikasa Shobō beginning in 1935. Tosaka Jun's *On Science* was one volume in this series.

60. Tosaka Jun (2001), vol. 1, 36.

61. Tosaka Jun (2001), vol. 1, 39.

62. Tosaka Jun (2001), vol. 2, 332.

63. 現代哲学講話

64. 技術の哲学

65. 科学論

66. 科学精神とは何か

67. 技術精神とは何か

68. 技術哲学

69. 論理と生命

70. 牢獄と軍隊

71. Kakehashi Akihide, "Rōgoku to guntai—Sengo rondan ni okeru futatsu no kūseki ni kaiso suru ichi seishinteki eiyōshicchō kanja no memorandamu toshite" [牢獄と軍隊——戦後論壇に於ける二つの空席に回想する一精神的栄養失調患者のメモランダムとして; Prison and the military: As a memorandum of someone with spiritual malnourishment remembering two empty seats in postwar critical circles], in *Kaisō no Tosaka Jun* [回想の戸坂潤; Recollections of Tosaka Jun], ed. Tanabe Hajime et al. (San-ichi Shobō, 1948), 62.

72. 全自然史的過程

73. Kakehashi Akihide, *Kakehashi Akihide keizaitetsugaku chosakushū* [梯明秀経済哲学著作集; Collected writings on the philosophy of economics by Kakehashi Akihide], in 5 vols. (Miraisha, 1982–1987), vol. 1, 107.

74. Kakehashi Akihide (1982–1987), vol. 1, 329.

75. Kakehashi Akihide (1982–1987), vol. 2, 248.

76. 西哲叢書

77. 広島文理科大学

78. 国家に於ける文化と教育

79. 身体と精神

80. Fujita Masakatsu, ed., *The Philosophy of the Kyoto School*, trans. Robert Chapeskie and revised by John W. M. Krummel (Springer, 2018a), 119.

81. Fujita Masakatsu, ed. (2018a), 115.

82. Fujita Masakatsu, ed. (2018a), 119.

83. 論理と生命

84. This phrase is included in Greek in the original Japanese text [trans.].

85. Nishida Kitarō (2002–2009), vol. 8, 26.

86. Fujita Masakatsu, ed. (2018a), 120.

87. The "Spiritual History of Japan" course was established at Kyoto University in response to a demand from the Ministry of Education for "Japanese national polity theory" courses to "theoretically grasp and academically ground the national polity as the basic framework of national existence."

88. 西田哲学

89. 続西田哲学

90. 文化類型学

91. 世界史の哲学

92. 場所的論理と呼応の原理

93. Kōyama Iwao, *Kōyama Iwao chosakushū* [高山岩男著作集; Collected writings of Kōyama Iwao] (Tamagawa University Press, 2007–2009), vol. 3, 27.

94. Kōyama Iwao (2007–2009), vol. 4, 23.

95. Kōyama Iwao (2007–2009), vol. 4, 84.

96. 信濃(上田)自由大学

97. 土田杏村全集

98. 街頭の思索者

99. Nishida Kitarō (2002–2009), vol. 11, 304.

100. 文明思潮と新哲学

101. 文明の高等批評

102. Tsuchida Kyōson, *Tsuchida Kyōson zenshū* [土田杏村全集; Complete works of Tsuchida Kyōson], in 15 vols. (repr. ed., Nihon Tosho Center, 1982), vol. 8, 16.

103. Tsuchida Kyōson (1982), vol. 2, 422.

104. 文明は何処へ行く

105. For a text that considers such issues, see Shimizu Masayuki's "Higashi Ajia kindai tetsugakushi no kanōsei—Tsuchida Kyōson no kokoromi ni miru" [東アジア近代哲学史の可能性——土田杏村のこころみにみる; The potential of modern East Asian philosophy: Seen in the efforts of Tsuchida Kyōson], in *Shisōkan no taiwa—Higashi Ajia ni okeru tetsugaku no jyuyō to tenkai* [思想間の対話——東アジアにおける哲学の受容と展開; Dialogue between thoughts: The reception and development of philosophy in East Asia], ed. Fujita Masakatsu (Hōsei University Press, 2015).

106. 著作遍路或いは自画自賛

107. 科学概論

108. 数理哲学研究

109. Shimomura Toratarō, *Shimomura Toratarō chosakushū* [下村寅太郎著作集; Collected writings of Shimomura Toratarō], in 13 vols. (Misuzu Shobō, 1988–1999), vol. 13, 344.

110. 炉辺空語

111. Shimomura Toratarō (1988–1999), vol. 3, 565.

112. "Historian" is written in English in the original text [trans.].

113. 科学史の哲学

114. Shimomura Toratarō (1988–1999), vol. 1, 144.

Chapter 8

1. 京都学派の哲学

2. 経済往来

3. Tosaka Jun (2001), vol. 3, 175. Tsuchida Kyōson's *Contemporary Thought of Japan and China* (1926) was mentioned in the previous chapter, and while he does not use the term "Kyoto School" (京都学派) in this text he does employ the similar phrase "young philosophers descended from Nishida known as the 'Kyoto Faction [京都派]'" (page 117 of the original 1926 edition, *Nihon shina gendai sisō kenkyū* [日本支那現代思想研究; Studies of contemporary thought of Japan and China] Daiichi Shobō, 1926)).

4. John C. Maraldo, "The Identity of the Kyoto-School: A Critical Analysis," in Maraldo, *Japanese Philosophy in the Making 2: Borderline Interrogations* (Chisokudō, 2019), 293–317.

5. This interest can also be clearly seen in J. W. Heisig's essay "Nihon tetsugaku no basho—Ōbei kara mita" [日本哲学の場所——欧米から見た; The place of Japanese philosophy: Seen from the West] (included in *Nihon no tetsugaku* [日本の哲学; *Japanese Philosophy*] no. 3).

6. Evidence for this is seen when Takeda Atsushi, who studied under and was strongly influenced by Shimomura Toratarō, writes, "I have no recollections of Shimomura actively addressing the topic of the 'Kyoto School,'" in "Shimomura Toratarō: The Path Toward 'Intellectual History,'" ed. Fujita Masakatsu (2018a), 194.

7. In "Shimomura Toratarō: The Path Toward 'Intellectual History,'" Takeda Atsushi writes, "How meaningful is the conceptualization itself of this kind of grouping of human beings that, to put it in commonly used terms, includes individuals from both the 'Left' and the 'Right'?" (Fujita Masakatsu [2018a], 193).

8. 下村寅太郎——「精神史」への軌跡

9. Fujita Masakatsu (2018a), 193.

10. 木村素衞・美のプラクシス

11. Kimura Motomori (2000), *Kimura Motomori—Bi no purakushisu* [木村素衛——美のプラクシス; Kimura Motomori: Beauty and praxis], ed. Iwaki Ken'ichi (Tōeisha, 2000), 260.

12. 西田哲学

13. Nishida (2002–2009), vol. 20, 399.

14. Notable recent studies from this perspective include Hattori Kenji's *Nishida tetsugaku to saha no hitotachi* [西田哲学と左派の人たち; Nishida's philosophy and people on the left] (Kobushi Shobō, 2000) and Yoshida Masatoshi's *Kindai Nihon shisō ron* [近代日本思想論; Modern Japanese thought], vol. 2, *"Kyōto gakuha" no tetsugaku—Nishida, Miki, Tosaka wo chūshin ni* [「京都学派」の哲学——西田・三木・戸坂を中心に; The philosophy of the Kyoto School: Centered on Nishida, Miki, and Tosaka] (Ōtsuki Shoten, 2011).

15. 文学界

16. 中央公論

17. 世界史的立場と日本

18. "Overcoming Modernity," 274. Takeuchi's essay "Overcoming Modernity" was first published in 1959 in *Kindai Nihon shisōshi kōza* [近代日本思想史講座; History of modern Japanese thought course], vol. 7, *Kindaika to dentō* [近代化と伝統; Modernization and tradition], ed. Kamei Katsuichirō and Takeuchi Yoshimi (Chikuma Shobō). It was also included in *Kindai no chōkoku* [近代の超克; Overcoming modernity] (1979), a volume in *Fuzanbō hyakka bunko* [富山房百科文庫; Fuzanbō encyclopedia]. Quotes from this essay and remarks made at the symposia are taken from this text and are cited in the notes as "Overcoming Modernity"

followed by the page number. These quotations have been translated from the cited Japanese text, but for a complete English translation see *Overcoming Modernity: Cultural Identity in Wartime Japan*, ed. and trans. Richard Calichman (Columbia University Press, 2008).

19. For an idea of how young people at the time received this symposium, see, for example, Nina Makoto "Jyūnenme—'Gendai Nihon no chiteki unmei' wo megutte" [十年目——「現代日本の知的運命」をめぐって; The tenth year: Concerning "Japan's intellectual destiny"], (*Shin Nihon Bungaku* [新日本文学; New Japanese Literature], June 1952.

20. *Bungaku* [文学; Literature], April, 1958, 111.

21. 〈近代の超克〉論——昭和思想史への一断想

22. Hiromatsu Wataru, 〈*Kindai no chōkoku*〉*ron—Shōwa shisōshi he no ichi dansō* [〈近代の超克〉論——昭和思想史への一断想; Discourses on "overcoming modernity": A fragmentary reflection on the intellectual history of the Shōwa period] (Asahi Shuppansha, 1980). Republished as 〈*Kindai no chōkoku*〉*ron—Shōwa shisōshi he no ichi shikaku* [〈近代の超克〉論——昭和思想史への一視角; The Theory of "overcoming modernity": A viewpoint toward the intellectual history of the Shōwa period] (Kōdansha Gakujyutsu Bunko, 1989).

23. Koyasu Nobukuni, *"Kindai no chōkoku" to ha nanika* [「近代の超克」とは何か; What is "overcoming modernity"?] (Seidosha, 2008), 77.

24. "Overcoming Modernity," 166.

25. 現代精神に関する覚書

26. "Overcoming Modernity," 15.

27. "Overcoming Modernity," 275.

28. "Overcoming Modernity," 288.

29. 『近代』への疑惑

30. "Overcoming Modernity," 150–51.

31. "Overcoming Modernity," 233.

32. "Overcoming Modernity," 9.

33. それから

34. "Overcoming Modernity," 163.

35. "Overcoming Modernity," 164.

36. 近代の超克の方向

37. "Overcoming Modernity," 113.

38. "Overcoming Modernity," 114.

39. "Overcoming Modernity," 112.

40. "Overcoming Modernity," 116–17.

41. 展望

42. Shimomura 22, 169.

43. Kōsaka Masaaki et al., *Sekaishiteki tachiba to Nihon* [世界史的立場と日本; The perspective of world history and Japan] (Chūō Kōron Sha, 1943), 280.

44. Kōyama Iwao, *Nihon no kadai to sekaishi* [日本の課題と世界史; Japan's task and world history] (Kōbundō, 1943), preface, 1–2.

Chapter 9

1. 近代的思惟
2. 文化会議
3. 青年文化会議
4. Maruyama Masao (1995–1997), vol. 3, 3.
5. Maruyama Masao (1995–1997), vol. 3, 4.
6. 日本政治思想史研究
7. 近代的人間類型の創出
8. 近代化の人間的基礎
9. Maruyama Masao, " 'De aru' koto to 'suru' koto" [「である」ことと「する」こと; "Being" and "doing"], in *Nihon no Shisō* [日本の思想; Japanese thought] (Iwanami Shinsho, 1961), 156.
10. Tajiri Yūichirō, "Sengo minshushugi" [戦後民主主義; Postwar democracy], in *Gaisetsu Nihon shisōshi* [概説日本思想史; Outline of Japanese intellectual history], ed. Satō Hiroo (Minerva Shobō, 2005), 278.
11. 主体性論争
12. 文学的人間像
13. Ara Masahito, *Makeinu—Bungei hyōronshū* [負け犬――文芸評論集; Loser: Collected literary criticism] (Shinbisha, 1947), 89, 98.
14. Kurahara Korehito, "Kindaishugi to sono kokufuku" [近代主義とその克服; Modernism and its overcoming] (1948), in *Kindaishugi hihan* [近代主義批判; Modernism criticism], ed. Izu Kimio (Dōyūsha, 1948), 229.
15. 唯物論と人間――マルクシズムと宗教的なるもの
16. Umemoto Katsumi, *Umemoto Katsumi chosakushū* [梅本克己著作集; Collected writings of Umemoto Katsumi], in 10 vols. (San-ichi Shobō, 1977–1978), vol. 1, 34.
17. 政治哲学の急務
18. 社会党と共産党の間
19. キリスト教とマルクシズムと日本仏教――第二次宗教改革の予想
20. See Tanabe Hajime (1963–1964), vol. 10, 279.
21. 無の論理性と党派性
22. Umemoto Katsumi (1977–1978), vol. 1, 69.
23. Tairako Tomonaga, "Nihon ni okeru Marukusushugi jyuyō no tokushusei to shutaisei ronsō no igi" [日本におけるマルクス主義受容の特殊性と主体性論争の意義; The significance of the subjectivity debate and the uniqueness of the reception of Marxism in Japan], in *Nihon no tetsugaku* [日本の哲学; Japanese Philosophy], no. 16 (2015): 89.

24. 哲学における修正主義——梅本克己の立場について

25. Matsumura Kazuto, *Yuibutsuron to shutaiseiron* [唯物論と主体性論; Materialism and subjectivity theory] (Nippon Hyōronsha, 1949), 53.

26. Matsumura Kazuto (1949), 81.

27. 主体性論争

28. Mashita Shin'ichi, ed., *Shutaisei ronsō* [主体性論争; The subjectivity debate] (Hakuyōsha, 1949), 235–36.

29. Takeuchi Yoshimi, "Kindai toha nanika (Nihon to Chūgoku no baai)" [近代とは何か（日本と中国の場合）; What is modernity? (the case of Japan and China)], (first published as "Chūgoku no kindai to Nihon no kindai——Rojin wo tegakari toshite" [中国の近代と日本の近代——魯迅を手掛かりとして; Modern China and modern Japan: Lu Xun as a hint]), in *Takeuchi Yoshimi zenshū* [竹内好全集; Complete works of Takeuchi Yoshimi], in 17 vols. (Chikuma Shobō, 1980–1982), vol. 4, 148.

30. 近代主義と民族の問題

31. Takeuchi Yoshimi (1980–1982), vol. 7, 34.

32. 君たちはどう生きるか

33. 日本少国民文庫

34. 世界

35. 平和のために社会科学者はかく訴える——戦争をひきおこす緊迫の原因に関して、ユネスコの八人の社会科学者によってなされた声明

36. 戦争と平和に関する 日本の科学者の声明

37. See Abe Yoshishige, et al., "Sensō to heiwa nikansuru Nihon no kagakusha no seimei" [戦争と平和に関する日本の科学者の声明; Statement by Japanese scientists regarding war and peace], in *Kindaishugi* [近代主義; Modernism], ed. and commentary by Hidaka Rokurō, *Gendai Nihon shisō taikei* [現代日本思想大系; Modern Japanese thought series] (Chikuma Shobō, 1964), vol. 3, 369–73.

38. 講和問題についての平和問題談話会声明

39. 三たび平和について

40. 思想の科学

41. After several stops and restarts, the *Science of Thought* ceased publication after its June 1996 issue.

42. 声なき声の会

43. ベトナムに平和を！市民連合（べ平連）

44. Tsurumi Shunsuke, ed., *Heiwa no shisō* [平和の思想; Thought on peace], "Kaisetsu" [解説; Commentary] by Tsurumi Shunsuke, *Sengo Nihon shisō taikei* [戦後日本思想大系; Postwar Japanese thought series], (Chikuma Shobo, 1968), vol. 4, 11.

45. See Kuno Osamu, *Heiwa no ronri to sensō no ronri* [平和の論理と戦争の論理; The logic of peace and the logic of war] (Iwanami Shoten, 1972), 8.

46. See Kuno Osamu, *Heiwa no ronri to sensō no ronri*, 18, 21–22.

47. Quoted directly from the English translation of the Constitution of Japan on the website of the prime minister of Japan and his cabinet, https://japan.kantei.go.jp/constitution_and_government_of_japan/constitution_e.html [trans.].

48. Sakamoto Yoshikazu, "Kenryoku seiji wo koeru michi" [権力政治を越える道; The path beyond power politics], ed. Tsurumi Shunsuke (1958), 214. First published in *Sekai* [世界; The World], June 1966.

49. See Ienaga Saburō, *Sensō sekinin* [戦争責任; Responsibility for war] (Iwanami Shoten, 1968), 1–2.

50. While the 1960 revision of the Japan-U.S. Security Treaty gave Japan greater autonomy than it had enjoyed under the existing treaty signed after the Second World War, it was strongly opposed by those who wanted Japan to take a more neutral position in the context of the Cold War.

51. 八・一五と五・一九──日本民 主主義の歴史的意味

52. Maruyama Masao (1995–1997), vol. 8, 372.

53. 政治の世界

54. Maruyama Masao (1995–1997), vol. 5, 188.

55. 知識人とは何か

56. See Yoshimoto Takaaki, *Yoshimoto Takaaki zenshū* [吉本隆明全集, Complete works of Yoshimoto Takaaki], (Shōbunsha, 2014–2024), vol. 6, 160–61.

57. 情況とは何か── 2 戦後知識人の神話

58. 自立の思想的拠点

59. Yoshimoto Takaaki (2014–2024), vol. 9, 269.

60. 思想の科学

61. *Shisō no kagaku* [思想の科学; The science of thought] (6th iteration), April 1972, 1.

62. 限界芸術論

63. 戦後日本の大衆文化史

64. 市民主義

65. See Kuno Osamu, *Seijiteki shimin no fukken* [政治的市民の複権; The restoration of the political citizen] (Ushio Shuppansha, 1975), 213.

66. Kuno Osamu, *Shiminshugi no seiritsu* [市民主義の成立; The formation of citizenism] (Shunjūsha, 1996), 222.

67. Kuno Osamu, *Shiminshugi no seiritsu*, 75.

Chapter 10

1. "Bans from public office (公職追放)" referred to those who had encouraged militarism or nationalism during the war being prohibited from holding public office under orders from the American authorities in postwar Japan (GHQ/SCAP). "Bans from educational employment (教職追放)" referred to a separate process in which individuals were barred from serving as educators in schools of all levels, from elementary schools to universities, for the same reason through the deliberation of the teacher qualification examination committee.

2. 哲学と民主主義──西田・田辺哲学批判のために

3. 近代的思惟

4. 西田哲学の批判

5. Hayashi Naomichi, *Nishida tetsugaku hihan* [西田哲学批判; Critique of Nishida philosophy] (Kaihōsha, 1948), 182.

6. 没後五十年記念論文集 西田哲学

7. Ueda Shizuteru, ed., *Botsugo gojyūnen kinen ronbunshū, Nishida tetsugaku* [没後五十年記念論文集 西田哲学; Collection of writings commemorating fifty years since his death: Nishida's philosophy] (Sōbunsha, 1994), 442.

8. Fujita Masakatsu, ed., *Tanabe Hajime tetsugakusen II, Zangedō tosite no tetsugaku* [『田辺元哲学選』II『懺悔道としての哲学』; Tanabe Hajime philosophy selection II, philosophy as the way of repentance] (Iwanami Bunko, 2010), 16.

9. Tanabe Hajime (1963–1964), vol. 9, 4.

10. 慈悲

11. 大悲

12. Tanabe Hajime (1963–1964), vol. 9, 40.

13. 理観

14. Tanabe Hajime (1963–1964), vol. 9, 10.

15. Tanabe Hajime (1963–1964), vol. 14, 423.

16. Tanabe Hajime (1963–1964), vol. 9, 265.

17. 実存と愛と実践

18. 生の存在学か死の弁証法か

19. Tanabe Hajime (1963–1964), vol. 13, 528.

20. Tanabe Hajime (1963–1964), vol. 13, 541.

21. Tanabe Hajime (1963–1964), vol. 13, 575.

22. 回施

23. Tanabe Hajime (1963–1964), vol. 13, 190.

24. Tanabe Hajime (1963–1964), vol. 13, 529.

25. 無神論

26. Hisamatsu Shin'ichi, *Hisamatsu Shin'ichi chosakushū* [久松真一著作集; Collected writings of Hisamatsu Shin'ichi], enlarged edition in 9 vols. and a supplementary vol. (Hōzōkan, 1994–1996), vol. 2, 69.

27. 覚

28. Nishitani Keiji (1986–1995), vol. 10, 104.

29. Nishitani Keiji (1986–1995), vol. 20, 192.

30. Nishitani Keiji (1986–1995), vol. 10, 58.

31. 体認

32. 神秘主義——エックハルトと禅

33. 上田閑照集

34. 合一即脱自

35. Ueda Shizuteru (2001–2003), vol. 8, 37.

36. 碧巌録

37. See Ueda Shizuteru (2001–2003), vol. 8, 6.

38. Ueda Shizuteru, "Zenbukkyō to seiyōtetsugaku—Nishida Kitarō" [禅仏教と西洋哲学——西田幾多郎; Zen Buddhism and Western philosophy: Nishida Kitarō], in *Kindai Nihon shisō no kiseki—Seiyō to no deai* [近代日本思想の軌跡——西洋との出会い; Tracks of modern Japanese thought: Encounter with the West], ed. Noda Matao (Hokuju Shuppan, 1982), 131.

39. 西田幾多郎を読む

40. Hans Waldenfels, *Absolutes Nichts: Zur Grundlegung des Dialogs zwischen Buddhismus und Christentum* (Herder, 1976); James Heisig, *Philosophers of Nothingness: An Essay on the Kyoto School* (University of Hawai'i Press, 2001); Bernard Stevens, *Topologie du néant: Une approche de l'école de Kyoto* (Éditions Peeters, 2000). There has also been new scholarship released in Japan, such as Hosoya Masashi's *Tanabe tetsugaku to Kyōto gakuha—Ninshiki to sei* [田辺哲学と京都学派——認識と生; Tanabe philosophy and the Kyoto School—understanding and life] (Shōwadō, 2008) that attempts to interpret the "philosophy of absolute nothingness" of the Kyoto School with "recognition and life" as its key terms.

41. *Zen to Kyōto Tetsugaku* [禅と京都哲学; Zen and the Kyoto philosophy], supervised by Ueda Shizuteru, ed. Kitano Hiroyuki and Mori Tetsurō (Tōeisha, 2006). Sueki Fumihiko's *Kindai Nihon to Bukkyō* [近代日本と仏教; Modern Japan and Buddhism] (Transview, 2004) includes an essay entitled "Kyōto gakuha to Bukkyō" [京都学派と仏教; The Kyoto School and Buddhism]; Hanaoka Eiko's *Zettaimu no tetsugaku—Nishida tetsugaku kenkyū nyūmon* [絶対無の哲学——西田哲学研究入門; The philosophy of absolute nothingness: Introduction to the study of Nishidean philosophy] (Sekai Shisōsha, 2002) discusses the thought of philosophers such as Nishida, Tanabe, and Nishitani while focusing on the concept of "absolute nothingness."

42. 非思量

43. 絶対無と神——西田・田辺哲学の伝統とキリスト教

44. 絶対無と神——京都学派の哲学

45. Onodera Isao, *Zettaimu to kami—Kyōto gakuha no tetsugaku* [絶対無と神——京都学派の哲学; Absolute nothingness and God: The philosophy of the Kyoto School] (Shunpūsha, 2002). Other such texts have been published, including Fritz Buri's *The Buddha-Christ as the Lord of the True Self: The Religious Philosophy of the Kyoto School and Christianity* (Mercer University Press, 1997).

46. Ng Yu-Kwan, 京都学派哲学——久松真一 [The philosophy of the Kyoto School: *Hisamatsu Shin'ichi*] (Taiwan, Wenchin Shubanshe, 1995); 絶対無的哲学——京都学派哲学導論 [The philosophy of absolute nothingness; Introduction to the philosophy of the Kyoto School] (Taiwan, Commercial Press, 1998); and 京都学派哲学七講 [Seven lectures on the philosophy of the Kyoto School] (Taiwan, Wenchin Shubanshe, 1998). Texts published in China include Liu Jichen's 京都学派哲学 [The philosophy of the Kyoto School] (Guangming ribao chuban she, 1993). Here what is considered the "Kyoto School" of course differs from that in

Ng's scholarship, and the focus is placed on Nishida, Tanabe, Miki, and Tosaka, philosophers who adopted a Marxist perspective.

47. For example, Lin Zhenguo has published 空性与现代性——从京都学派新儒家到多音的仏教詮释学 [Emptiness and modernity: From the Kyoto School and New Confucianism to multivocal Buddhist hermeneutics] (Taiwan, Lixu Wenhua, 1999). Asakura Tomomi's *"Higashi Ajia ni tetsugaku ha nai" no ka—Kyōto gakuha to shinjuka* [「東アジアに哲学はない」のか——京都学派と新儒家; Is there "no philosophy in East Asia"? The Kyoto School and New Confucianism] (Iwanami Shoten, 2014).

48. ロゴスとレンマ

49. 随眠の哲学

50. Yamauchi Tokuryū, *Rogosu to renma* [ロゴスとレンマ; Logos and lemma] (Iwanami Shoten, 1974), 68.

51. Yamauchi Tokuryū, *Rogosu to renma*, 307.

52. "Gakkyū no omoide" [学究の思い出; Memories of a scholar], in Mutai Risaku, *Mutai Risaku chosakushū* [務台理作著作集; Collected writings of Mutai Risaku] (Kobushi Shobō, 2000–2002), vol. 5, 289–90.

53. 現代のヒューマニズム

54. Mutai Risaku (2000–2002), vol. 6, 174.

55. Mutai Risaku (2000–2002), vol. 5, 301.

56. "Shakai to jitsuzonteki kojin [社会と実存的個人; Society and the existential individual], Mutai Risaku (2000–2002), vol. 5, 345.

57. 学の形成と自然的世界——西洋哲学の歴史的研究

58. 数理哲学思想史

59. 人間存在論

60. Miyake Gōichi, *Ningen sonzairon* [人間存在論; Human ontology] (Keisō Shobō, 1966), 237.

61. 現実と歴史

62. 経験的現実の哲学

63. Miyake Gōichi, *Keikenteki genjitsu no tetsugaku* [経験的現実の哲学; Philosophy of empirical reality] (Kōbundō, 1980), 133.

64. 理性・精神・実存

65. 場所的論理と呼応の原理

66. Shimomura Toratarō (1988–1999), vol. 2, 404.

67. ブルクハルトの世界——美術史家・文化史家・歴史哲学者

68. Shimomura Toratarō, *Shimomura Toratarō chosakushū* [下村寅太郎著作集; Collected writings of Shimomura Toratarō] (Misuzu Shobō, 1988–1999), vol. 9, 635.

69. イタリアにおけるルネサンスの文化

70. 哲学入門 ——哲学の根本問題

71. 中世の文学

72. 無常

73. 日本人の心の歴史——季節美感の変遷を中心に

74. 現代史への試み──型と個性と実存

75. 現代史への試み

76. 礼儀小言

77. Karaki Junzō, *Shinban, Gendai shi heno kokoromi* [新版 現代史への試み; New edition: An attempt at modern history] (Chikuma Sōsho, 1963), 16.

78. 西田哲学と田辺哲学──一つの回想

79. 哲学の三つの伝統

80. 教行信証 の哲学. *Kyōgyōshinshō* is the abbreviated title of *Kenjōdo Shinjitsu Kyōgyōshō Monrui* [顕浄土真実教行証文類; A collection of passages revealing the true teaching, practice and realization of the Pure Land way], Shinran's most important text.

81. 親鸞と現代

82. 神学と宗教哲学との間

83. 実存倫理の歴史的境位──神人と人神

84. 境位

85. 有の間と絶対無

86. 禅の本 質と人間の真理

87. 美学入門

88. Nakai Masakazu, *Nakai Masakazu hyōronshū* [中井正一評論集; Collected criticism of Nakai Masakazu], ed. Osada Hiroshi (Iwanami Bunko, 1995), 240, 246.

89. 世界大百科事典

90. 反語的精神

91. 共産主義的人間──二十世紀政治のフォークロア

92. 精神史───一つの方法序説

93. 芸術へのチチュローネ

94. 林達夫著作集

95. Hayashi Tatsuo, *Hayashi Tatsuo chosakushū* [林達夫著作集; Collected writings of Hayashi Tatsuo], vol. 1, *Geijutsu he no chichurōne* [芸術へのチチュローネ; Cicerone to art] (Heibonsha, 1971), and Katō Shūichi, "Kaisetsu" [解説; Commentary], 371.

96. 新潮

97. デカルトのポリティーク

98. 新秩序と哲学の動向

99. Hayashi Tatsuo, *Hayashi Tatsuo hyōronshū* [林達夫評論集; Collected criticism of Hayashi Tatsuo], ed. Nakagawa Hisayasu (Iwanami Bunko, 1982), 132–33.

100. 復興期の精神

101. 錯乱の論理

102. Hanada Kiyoteru, *Hanada Kiyoteru zenshū* [花田清輝全集; Complete works of Hanada Kiyoteru], in 15 vols. and 2 supplementary vols. (Kōdansha, 1979–1980), vol. 2, 13–14.

103. Hanada Kiyoteru (1979–1980), vol. 7, 78.

104. 実存と労働

105. 労存

106. 響存的世界

107. 響存

108. 西田幾多郎の世界

109. See Suzuki Tōru, *Ikiru konkyo wo motomete* [生きる根拠を求めて; Seeking a grounding for living] (Sanichi Shobō, 1982), 176–77.

110. Yukawa Hideki, *Tabibito—Aru butsurigakusha no kaisō* [旅人——ある物理学者の回想; Traveler: Reminiscences of a physicist] (Kōdansha, 1966), 191–92.

111. 論理と生命

112. 哲学論文集第二

113. 生物の世界

114. Nishida (2002–2009), vol. 8, 15.

115. Imanishi Kinji, *Imanishi Kinji zenshū* [今西錦司全集; Complete works of Imanishi Kinji], in 13 vols. and a supplementary vol. (Kōdansha, 1993–1994), vol. 1, 47.

116. Imanishi Kinji (1993–1994), vol. 9, 61.

117. 非合理的な直接態

118. *Mono* and *koto* are Japanese words that can both be translated as "thing." Broadly speaking, *mono* refers to "thing" in a more tangible sense, that is, an object that has a shape, while *koto* refers to "thing" in a more intangible sense, including, for example, an action or event. In ordinary usage both can refer to concrete things, but Kimura thought of *koto* as things that are concrete or directly experienced and *mono* as things that are abstracted from them [trans.].

119. 時間と自己

120. あいだ

121. 分裂病の詩と真実

122. Viktor von Weizsäcker, *Der Gestaltkreis: Theorie der Einheit von Wahrnehmen und Bewegen*, 4th ed. (Stuttgart: Thieme, 1950), 9, 18, 116, 165.

123. Kimura Bin, *Kimura Bin chosakushū* [木村敏著作集; Collected writings of Kimura Bin], in 8 vols. (Kōbundō, 2001), vol. 6, 147, 179.

Chapter 11

1. ことだま論

2. 物と心

3. 立ち現れ

4. Ōmori Shōzō, *Ōmori Shōzō chosakushū* [大森荘蔵著作集; Collected writings of Ōmori Shōzō], in 10 vols. (Iwanami Shoten, 1998–1999), vol. 4, 132.

5. 宇宙風景の「もの—ごと」

6. Ōmori Shōzō (1998–1999), vol. 4, 205.

7. 心身問題、その一答案

8. 流れとよどみ——哲学断章

9. Ōmori Shōzō (1998–1999), vol. 5, 168.

10. Ōmori Shōzō (1998–1999), vol. 9, 382. Itō Katsuhiko quotes this passage and discusses it in detail in *Tenchiujyō no tetsugaku—Ōmori Shōzō to Mori Arimasa* [天地有情の哲学——大森荘蔵と森有正; The philosophy of heaven and earth having emotions: Ōmori Shōzō and Mori Arimasa] (Chikuma Gakugei Bunko, 2000), 14–16.

11. Nishida (2002–2009), vol. 1, 50.

12. 知覚風景と科学的世界像

13. 言語・知覚・世界

14. Ōmori Shōzō (1998–1999), vol. 3, 289–90.

15. Ōmori Shōzō (1998–1999), vol. 5, 176.

16. 知の構築とその呪縛

17. Ōmori Shōzō (1998–1999), vol. 7, 160.

18. Ōmori Shōzō (1998–1999), vol. 4, 27.

19. Sawada Nobushige, *Ninshiki no fūkei* [認識の風景; The landscape of understanding] (Iwanami Shoten, 1975), 157.

20. Sawada Nobushige, *Ninshiki no fūkei*, 46.

21. See Fujisawa Norio, *Girishia tetsugaku to gendai—Sekaikan no arikata* [ギリシア哲学と現代——世界観のありかた; Greek philosophy and modernity: The aspects of worldview] (Iwanami Shoten, 1980), 115–19.

22. Watanabe Jirō, "Gendai ni okeru sonzai no mondai" [現代における存在の問題; The problem of existence in the modern era] (2003), in *Watanabe Jirō chosakushū* [渡邊二郎著作集; Collected writings of Watanabe Jirō], in 9 vols. (Chikuma Shobō, 2011), vol. 9, 614, 616.

23. 日本語と哲学の問題

24. 続日本精神史研究

25. Watsuji Tetsurō, *Watsuji Tetsurō zenshū* [和辻哲郎全集; Collected Works of Watsuji Tetsurō] (Iwanami Shoten, 1961–1978), vol. 4, 506.

26. In ancient times it was said that "things" (事, *koto*) were one with "words" (言, *koto*) and "words" had the power to make "things" come true.

27. 意味の形而上学

28. Yamauchi Tokuryū, *Imi to keijijyōgaku* [意味と形而上学; Meaning and metaphysics] (Iwanami Shoten, 1967), 307.

29. 世界の共同主観的構造

30. 事的世界観への前哨

31. 認識的世界の存在構造

32. See Hiromatsu Wataru, *Sonzai to imi—Koto teki sekai kann no teiso* [存在と意味——事的世界観の定礎; Being and meaning: Cornerstone of the koto worldview] (Iwanami Shoten, 1982), xii.

33. 現相的所与

34. 意味的所識

35. 能知的誰某

36. 能識的或者

37. Hiromatsu's relationist view of ontology was deeply connected to Nishida Kitarō's understanding of "experience." This can be seen in *"Kindai no chōkoku" ron—Shōwa shisōsi he no ichidansō* [<近代の超克>論——昭和思想史への一断想; The theory of "overcoming modernity": A fragmentary thought toward an intellectual history of the Shōwa period] (Asahi Shuppansha, 1980), in which, while strongly criticizing the abstractness of the "overcoming modernity" theory of Nishida's disciples, Hiromatsu nevertheless writes as follows about Nishida himself. "While Nishida's philosophy was formed in several stages of development, from its early period it was positioned in the *phase prior to* the so-called 'subjective–objective distinction,' and in this sense it can be said to have taken a stance of breaking away from the schema of *classical* modern philosophy" (240–41).

38. 自覚の精神病理——自分ということ

39. Kimura Bin, *Kimura Bin chosakushū* [木村敏著作集; Collected writings of Kimura Bin], in 8 vols. (Kōbundō, 2001), vol. 1, 212.

40. 時間と自己.

41. Kimura Bin (2001), vol. 2, 146–47.

42. 偶然性の精神病理

43. Kimura Bin (2001), vol. 7, 62.

44. リアリティとアクチュアリティ

45. 分裂病の詩と真実

46. Kimura Bin (2001), vol. 7, 313.

47. Kimura Bin (2001), vol. 6, 261.

48. 現代の問いとしての西田哲学

49. *Gendai no toi toshite no Nishida tetsugaku* [現代の問いとしての西田哲学; Nishida's philosophy as a contemporary inquiry] (Iwanami Shoten, 1998), 105.

50. *Gendai no toi toshite no Nishida tetsugaku*, 16.

51. 空間

52. Nishida (2002–2009), vol. 10, 165.

53. Nishida (2002–2009), vol. 10, 158.

54. 場所——二重世界内存在

55. Ueda Shizuteru *Ueda Shizuteru shū* [上田閑照集; Collected works of Ueda Shizuteru], (Iwanami Shoten, 2001–2003), vol. 9, 151.

56. 自我

57. 自己

58. See Ueda Shizuteru (2001–2003), vol. 10, 131–134.

59. 意味の深みへ——東洋哲学の水位

60. Izutsu Toshihiko, *Imi no fukami he—Tōyō tetsugaku no suii* [意味の深みへ——東洋哲学の水位; To the depths of meaning: The water level of Eastern philosophy] (Iwanami Shoten, 1985), 15.

61. Izutsu Toshihiko, *Imi no fukami he Tōyō tetsugaku no suii*, 27.

62. 分裂病と他者

63. 自己の病理と「絶対の他」

64. 西田哲学への問い

65. 私と汝

66. 無の自覚的限定

67. Kimura Bin (2001), vol. 2, 394–95.

68. 人と人との間――精神病理学的日本論

69. Kimura Bin (2001), vol. 3, 260.

70. 経験と思想

71. Mori Arimasa, *Mori Arimasa zenshū* [森有正全集; Complete works of Mori Arimasa], in 14 vols. (Chikuma Shobō, 1978–1982), vol. 12, 62.

72. 二項

73. 二項結合方式

74. 体験

75. See Mori Arimasa (1978–1982), vol. 12, 94, 107.

76. *Jiko—Seishin igaku to tetsugaku no kanten kara* [自己――精神医学と哲学の観点から; The self: From the viewpoints of psychiatry and philosophy], Japan–Germany Symposium (Kawai Institute for Culture and Education, 1986), 66.

77. 面とペルソナ

78. 理性の不安――カント哲学の生成と構造

79. 仮面の解釈学

80. Sakabe Megumi, *Kamen no kaishakugaku* [仮面の解釈学; The hermeneutics of masks] (University of Tokyo Press, 1976), 83.

81. Sakabe Megumi, *Kamen no kaishakugaku*, 21–22.

82. 経験科学

83. Nishida (2002–2009), vol. 8, 434.

84. ことばの実存――禅と文学

85. See Ueda Shizuteru, *Kotoba no jitsuzon—Zen to bungaku* [言葉の実存――禅と文学; The existence of language: Zen and literature] (Chikuma Shobō, 1997), 83–84.

86. Ueda Shizuteru, *Kotoba no jitsuzon—Zen to bungaku*, 50.

87. Ueda Shizuteru, *Kotoba no jitsuzon—Zen to bungaku*, 56.

88. 欧米語と日本語の論理と思考

89. Sakabe Megumi, *Perusona no shigaku—Katari furumai kokoro* [ペルソナの詩学――かたり ふるまい こころ; The poetics of persona: Narration, behavior, and mind] (Iwanami Shoten, 1989), 20.

90. ことば――その「虚」の力

91. Ueda Shizuteru (2001–2003), vol. 2, 347.

92. Ueda Shizuteru (2001–2003), vol. 2, 353.

93. 明証的な形象性

94. "Hakkenjyutsu toshite no retorikku—*Figyūru to sozō ryoku*" [発見術としてのレトリック――フィギュールと想像力; Rhetoric as the art of discovery: Figure and imagination], in *Shisō* [思想; Thought], no. 706 (April 1984): 68–69.

95. 宗教と言語・宗教の 言語

96. Yagi Seiichi, "Gengo to shūkyō—Shūkyō no kotoba toha doiumono ka" [言語と宗教——宗教の言葉とはどういうものか; Language and religion: What is the nature of religious words?], *Anjali* (アンジャリ), no. 15 (Center for Shin Buddhist Studies, 2008), 29.

97. 命ひとつ——よく生きるヒント

98. Ōmine Akira, *Inochi hitotsu—Yoku ikiru hinto* [命ひとつ-よく生きるヒント; One life: Hints for living well] (Shogakukan 101 Shinsho, 2013), 52–53.

99. Hase Shōtō, *Yokubō no tetsugaku—Jyōdokyō sekai no shisaku* [欲望の哲学——浄土教世界の思索; The philosophy of desire: The thought of the world of Pure Land Buddhism] (Hōzōkan, 2003), 299. See Hase Shōtō, "Yōgen no sekai toshite no shūkyō—Kōsōryoku wo megutte" [影現の世界としての宗教——構想力をめぐって; Religion as the world of manifestation: Regarding imagination], *Nihon no Tetsugaku* [日本の哲学; Japanese Philosophy], no. 2 (2001): 90.

100. 文化と言語アラヤ識——異文化間対話の可能性をめぐって

101. Izutsu Toshihiko, *Imi no fukami he—Tōyō tetsugaku no suii* [意味の深みへ——東洋哲学の水位; To the depths of meaning: The water level of Eastern philosophy] (Iwanami Shoten, 1985), 77.

102. Izutsu Toshihiko (1985), 80.

103. See Maruyama Keizaburō, *Yokudō* [欲動; Drive (Trieb)] (Kōbundō, 1989), 137, 153.

104. Izutsu Toshihiko (1985), 81.

105. 翻訳語の論理——言語にみる日本文化の構造

106. 翻訳とはなにか——日本語と翻訳文化

107. See Yanabu Akira, *Honyakugo seiritsu jijyō* [翻訳後成立事情; Circumstances of the establishment of translation words] (Iwanami Shinsho, 1982), 33.

108. 翻訳語成立事情

109. Yanabu Akira (1982), 186–87.

110. 日本語と哲学の問題

111. Yanabu Akira (1982), 124.

112. See Yanabu Akira, *Honyakugo no ronri—Gengo ni miru Nihon bunka no kōzō* [翻訳語の論理——言語に見る日本文化の構造; The logic of translation words: The structure of Japanese culture seen in language] (Hōsei University Press, 1972), 45–46.

113. Ichikawa Hiroshi, *Seishin toshite no shintai* [精神としての身体; The body as spirit] (Keisō Shobō, 1975), 8.

114. 錯綜体

115. 身

116. 体

117. Ichikawa Hiroshi, *<Mi> no kōzō* [＜身＞の構造; The structure of <Mi>] (Seidosha, 1984), 37.

118. 身分け

119. 身分け, 18.

120. 「ふれる」ことの哲学

121. Sakabe Megumi, *"Fureru" koto no tetsugaku* [「ふれる」ことの哲学; The philosophy of "touching"] (Iwanami Shoten, 1983), 31.

122. Sakabe Megumi, *"Fureru" koto no tetsugaku,"* 27.

123. 共通感覚論——知の組みかえのために

124. 芸術における媒介の問題

125. 歴史的形成作用としての芸術的創作

126. Nishida (2002–2009), vol. 9, 284.

127. アリストテレス論攷

128. 離人症

129. 自己・あいだ・時間

130. Kimura Bin (2001), vol. 5, 324.

131. See Nakamura Yūjirō, *Kyōtsū kankaku ron* [共通感覚論; A theory of sensus communis] (Iwanami Shoten, 1979), 131, 284.

132. Nakamura Yūjirō, *Kyōtsū kankaku ron*, 199.

133. See Nakamura Yūjirō, *Kansei no kakusei* [感性の覚醒; The awakening of sensibility] (Iwanami Shoten, 1975), 11.

134. Nakamura Yūjirō, *Rinshō no chi toha nanika* [臨床の知とは何か; What is clinical knowledge?] (Iwanami Shinsho, 1992), 9.

135. 身体——東洋的身心論の試み

136. Yuasa Yasuo, *Shintai—Tōyōteki shinshi nron no kokoromi* [身体——東洋的心身論の試み; The body: An attempt to establish an Eastern mind–body theory] (Sōbunsha, 1977), 251.

137. Yuasa Yasuo (1977), 16.

138. Nishitani Keiji, *Nishitani Keiji chosakushū* [西谷啓治著作集; Collected writings of Nishitani Keiji], (Sōbunsha, 1986–1995), vol. 20, 45.

139. Nishitani Keiji (1986–1995), vol. 20, 58.

140. Yuasa Yasuo, *Shintai—Tōyōteki shinshin ron no kokoromi* [身体——東洋的心身論の試み; The body: An attempt to establish an Eastern mind-body theory] (Sōbunsha, 1977), 151.

141. 型

142. Minamoto Ryōen, *Kata* [型; Form] (Sōbunsha, 1989), 9–10.

143. 茶道を想ふ

144. Yanagi Muneyoshi, *Yanagi Muneyoshi sadō ronshū* [柳宗悦茶道論集; Yanagi Muneyoshi collected essays on tea ceremony], ed. Kumakura Isao (Iwanami Bunko, 1987), 15–16.

145. Minamoto Ryōen expresses the distinctive character of this kind of *kata* with the term "anonymity." Minamoto Ryōen (1989), 15.

146. 医学概論

147. 医の倫理

148. バイオエシックスの基礎——欧米の「生命倫理」論

149. バイオエシックスとは何か

150. 生命倫理学を学ぶ人のために

151. 現代生命倫理学の考え方

152. Katō Hisatake and Kamo Naoki, eds., *Seimei rinri gaku wo Manabu hito no tame ni* [生命倫理学を学ぶ人のために; For people studying bioethics] (Sekaishisōsha, 1998), 13.

153. バイオエシックス

154. バイオポリティクス——人体を管理するとはどういうことか

155. 先端技術のゆくえ

156. Sakamoto Kenzō, *Sentan gijutsu no yukue* [先端技術のゆくえ; Where is cutting–edge technology going?] (Iwanami Shinsho, 1987), 165.

157. 環境倫理学のすすめ

158. See Katō Hisatake, *Kankyō rinri gaku no susume* [環境倫理学のすすめ; Introduction to environmental ethics] (Maruzen, 1991), 1–12.

159. Imamichi Tomonobu, *Ekoetika—Seiken rinri gaku nyūmon* [エコエティカ——生圏倫理学入門; Eco–ethica—Introduction to biosphere ethics] (Kōdansha Gakujutsu Bunko, 1990), 17.

160. 論理学

161. 比較思想論

162. 普遍的思想史の夢

163. 中村元選集

164. 世界思想史

165. Nakamura Hajime, *Nakamura Hajime senshū* [中村元選集, Selected works of Nakamura Hajime], in 23 vols. (Shunjyūsha, 1961–1977), vol. 17, 11.

166. 意識と本質——精神的東洋を索めて

167. Izutsu Toshihiko, *Ishiki to honshitsu—Seishin teki tōyō wo motomete* [意識と本質——精神的東洋を索めて; Consciousness and essence: Searching for the East in an intellectual context] (Iwanami Shoten, 1983), 429.

168. Izutsu Toshihiko, *Ishiki to honshitsu—Seishin teki tōyō wo motomete*, 430.

169. See Nakamura Hajime, "Hikaku shisō kenkyū no miraisei" [比較思想の研究の未来性; The futurity of studies in comparative philosophy], *Hikaku shisō kenkyū* [比較思想研究; Studies in Comparative Philosophy], no. 1, 11.

170. These kinds of issues have been raised by Fukui Fumimasa in works such as "Hikaku kenkyū no mondaiten ni tsuite" [比較研究の問題点について; On problems with comparative studies], in *Hikaku shisō kenkyū* [比較思想研究; Studies in Comparative Philosophy], no. 3, and "Hikaku kenkyū no genkai" [比較研究の限界; The limits of comparative studies], in *Shisō* [思想; Thought], no. 539.

Bibliography

Abe Isoo. (2008). *Abe Isoo chosakushū* [安倍磯雄著作集; Collected writings of Abe Isoo]. Gakujyutsu Shuppankai.

Abe Jirō. (1918). *Santarō no nikki* [三太郎の日記; The diary of Santaro]. Iwanami Shoten.

Abe Jirō. (1922). *Jinkaku shugi* [人格主義; Personality-ism]. Iwanami Shoten.

Abe Yoshishige. (1924). *Kanto no jissen tetsugaku* [カントの実践哲学; Kant's practical philosophy]. Iwanami Shoten.

Abe Yoshishige. (1957). *Iwanami Shigeo den* [岩波茂雄伝; Biography of Iwanami Shigeo]. Iwanami Shoten.

Abe Yoshishige. (1964). *Senchū sengo* [戦中戦後; Wartime and postwar]. Hakujitsu Shoin.

Andō Shōeki. (2006). *Kōhon shizen shineidō* [稿本自然真営道; The way of the enterprise of natural truth]. Edited and annotated by Yasunaga Toshinobu. Heibonsha.

Ara Masahito. (1947). *Makeinu—Bungei hyōron shū* [負け犬――文芸評論集; Loser: Collected literary criticism]. Shinbisha.

Arai Hakuseki. (1968). *Shintē seiyō kibun* [新訂西洋記聞, Revised account of the West]. Heibonsha.

Ariga Nagao. (1884/1885). *Yakukai kinsei tetsugaku* [訳解近世哲学; Translation of modern philosophy with commentary]. Translation of F. Bowen's *Modern Philosophy from Descartes to Schopenhauer and Hartmann*. Kōdō Shoin.

Asakura Tomomi. (2014). *"Higashi Ajia ni tetsugaku ha nai" no ka—Kyōto gakuha to shinjuka* [「東アジアに哲学はない」のか――京都学派と新儒家; Is there "no philosophy in East Asia"? The Kyoto School and New Confucianism]. Iwanami Shoten.

Bergson, Henri. (1959). *Introduction à la métaphysique. Œuvres*. Texts annotated by André Robinet. Presses universitaires de France.

Berque, Augustin. (1986). *Le sauvage et l'artifice, les Japonais devant la nature*. Gallimard.

Berque, Augustin. (1992). *Fūdo no nihon* [風土の日本; Japan and climate]. Translated by Shinoda Katsuhide. Chikuma Shobō.

Blue Cliff Record [碧巌録]. (1992–1996) Translated and annotated by Iriya Yoshitaka et al., 3 vols. Iwanami Bunko.

Bosanquet, Bernard. (1895). *The Essentials of Logic*. London.

Bowen, Francis. (1877). *Modern Philosophy from Descartes to Schopenhauer and Hartmann*. New York.

Buri, Fritz. (1997). *The Buddha-Christ as the Lord of the True Self: The Religious Philosophy of the Kyoto School and Christianity*. Translated by Harold H. Oliver. Mercer University Press.

Busse, Ludwig. (1894). *Philosophie und Erkenntnistheorie* [Metaphysics and the theory of knowledge]. Erste Abteilung. Erster Teil. Metaphysik und Erkenntniskritik [Part 1. volume 1. Metaphysics and critique of knowledge]. Leipzig.

Chalybäus, Heinrich Moritz. (1837). *Historische Entwickelung der speculativen Philosophie von Kant bis Hegel*. Dresden/Leipzig.

Chalybäus, Heinrich Moritz. (1854). *Historical Survey of Speculative Philosophy from Kant to Hegel*. Translated from the 4th ed. of the German by Alfred Tulk. Andover.

Cieslik, Hubert. (1987). "Funai no korejiyo—Ōtomo Sōrin kiten yon hyaku shūnen niyosete" [府内のコレジョ――大友宗麟帰天四百周年によせて; Funai Collegio: The 400th anniversary of the death of Ōtomo Sōrin]. *Kirishitan kenkyū* [キリシタン研究; Christian Studies], vol. 27.

Cohen, Hermann. (1912). *Ästhetik des reinen Gefühls*. 2 vols. Berlin: B. Cassirer.

Comte, Auguste. (1830–1842). *Cours de philosophie positive*. Paris.

Cousin, Victor. (1841–1846). *Cours de l'histoire de la philosophie moderne*. Paris.

Cousin, Victor. (1852). *Course of the History of Modern Philosophy*. Translated by O. W. Wight. 2 vols. New York.

Daijō kshin ron. (1994). [大乗起信論; Awakening of faith in the Mahāyāna]. Translated and annotated by Ui Hakujyu and Takasaki Jikidō. Iwanami shoten.

Davis, Bret, ed. (2020). *The Oxford Handbook of Japanese Philosophy*. Oxford University Press.

Fechner, Gustav Theodor. (1879). *Die Tagesansicht gegenüber der Nachtansicht*. Leipzig.

Fenollosa, Ernest. (1882). *Bijyutsu shinsetsu* [美術真説; True theory of art]. Ryūchi-kai.

Fenollosa, Ernest. (1912). *Epochs of Chinese and Japanese Art: An Outline History of East Asiatic Design*. Vol. 1. William Heinemann.

Fenollosa, Ernest. (1978–1981). *Toyō Bijyutsu Shi Kō* [東洋美術史綱; An outline of the history of East Asiatic art]. Translated by Mori Tōgo. Tokyō Bijyutsu.

Fenollosa, Ernest. (1988). *Fenollosa bijyutsu ronshū* [フェノロサ美術論集; Collection of Fenollosa's writings on art]. Edited by Yamaguchi Seiichi. Chuō Kōron Bijyutsu.

Fenollosa, Ernest. (2000). *Fenorosa shakai ronshū* [フェノロサ社会論集; Collection of writings on society by Fenollosa]. Edited by Seiichi Yamaguchi. Shibunkaku Shuppan.

Fichte, Johann Gottlieb. (1931). *Zen Chishiki gaku no kiso* [全知識学の基礎; The foundation of the entire study of knowledge]. Translated by Kimura Motomori. Iwanami Shoten. Translation of Fichte's *Grundlage der gesamten Wissenschafts-lehre*. Leipzig, 1794/1795.

Fiedler, Konrad. (1887). *Ursprung der künstlerischen Tätigkeit*. Leipzig.

Fischer, Kuno. (1854–1877). *Geschichte der neuern Philosophie*. 6 vols. Mannheim/Heidelberg.

Fouillée, Alfred. (1875). *Histoire de la philosophie*. Paris.

Fujioka Sakutarō. (1908). *Kokubungakushi kōwa* [国文学史講話; Lectures on the history of Japanese literature]. Tokyo Kaiseikan/Osaka Kaiseikan.

Fujisawa Norio. (1980). *Girishia tetsugaku to gendai—sekaikan no arikata* [ギリシア哲学と現代——世界観のありかた; Greek philosophy and modernity: The aspects of worldview]. Iwanami Shoten.

Fujita Masakatsu, ed. (2000). *Shiriizu: kindai Nihon no chi* [シリーズ・近代日本の知; Series: Modern Japanese thought], vol. 1, *Chi no zahyō jiku* [知の座標軸; Coordinate axes of thought]. Kōyō Shobō.

Fujita Masakatsu, ed. (2001). *Kyoto gakuha no tetsugaku* [京都学派の哲学; The philosophy of the Kyoto School]. Shōwadō.

Fujita Masakatsu. (2011). *Nishida kitaō noshisaku sekai—jyunsui keiken kara sekai ninshiki e* [西田幾多郎の思索世界——純粋経験から世界認識へ; Nishida Kitarō's world of thought—from pure experience to world recognition]. Iwanami Shoten.

Fujita Masakatsu, ed. (2011). *Zen no kenkū no hyakunen—sekaie / sekaikara* [『善の研究』の百年——世界へ／世界から; A hundred years of *An Inquiry into the Good*: To the world / from the world]. Kyoto University Press.

Fujita Masakatsu, ed. (2015). *Shisōkan no taiwa* [思想間の対話; Dialogue between intellectual traditions]. Hōsei University Press.

Fujita Masakatsu. (2016). *Kuki Shūzō—Richi to jyōnetsu no hazama ni tatsu <kotoba> no tetsugaku* [九鬼周造——理知と情熱のはざまに立つ＜ことば＞の哲学; Kuki Shūzō: A philosophy of 'language' standing between reason and passion]. Kodansha.

Fujita Masakatsu. (2018). *Nihon tetsugaku shi* [日本哲学史; The history of modern Japanese philosophy]. Shōwadō.

Fujita Masakatsu, ed. (2018). *The Philosophy of the Kyoto School*. Translated by Robert Chapeskie and revised by John W. M. Krummel. Springer.

Fujita Masakatsu. (2024). *Nihon tetsugaku nyūmon* [日本哲学入門; Introduction to Japanese philosophy]. Kōdansha.

Fujita Masakatsu, Bian Chongdao, and Kōsaka Shirō, eds. (2003). *Higashi Ajia to tetsugaku* [東アジアと哲学; East Asia and philosophy]. Nakanishiya Shoten.

Fujita Masakatsu and Bret Davis, eds. (2000). *Sekai no naka no Nihon no tetsugaku* [世界のなかの日本哲学; Japanese philosophy in the world]. Shōwadō.

Fukada Yasukazu. (1971). *Bi to geijutsu no riron* [美と芸術の理論; A theory of beauty and art]. Hakuhōsha.

Fukumoto Kazuo. (1926a). *Keizaigaku hihan no hōhōron* [経済学批判の方法; On the methodology of economic criticism]. Hakuyōsha.

Fukumoto Kazuo. (1926b). *Yuibutsu shikan to chūkanha shikan* [唯物史観と中間派史観; Historical materialism and the centrist view of history]. Kibōkaku.

Fukuzawa Yukichi. (1872–1876). *Gakumon no susume* [学問のすゝめ; An encouragement of learning]. Fukuzawa Yukichi.

Fukuzawa Yukichi. (1875). *Bunmeiron no gairyaku* [文明論之概略; An outline of a theory of civilization]. Publisher unknown.

Fukuzawa Yukichi. (1899). *Fukuō jiden* [福翁自伝; Autobiography of Fukuō (Fukuzawa Yukichi)]. Jiji Shinpō Sha.

Fukuzawa Yukichi. (1969–1971). *Fukuzawa Yukichi zenshū* [福沢諭吉全集; Collected works of Fukuzawa Yukichi]. 2nd ed. Iwanami Shoten.

Funayama Shin'ichi. (1959). *Meiji tetsugakushi kenkyū* [明治哲学史研究; Studies in the history of Meiji philosophy]. Minerva Shobō.

Funayama Shin'ichi. (1965). *Taishō tetsugakushi kenkyū* [大正哲学史研究; Studies in the history of Taishō philosophy]. Hōritsu Bunka Sha.

Funayama Shin'ichi. (1966). *Meiji ronrigakushi kenkyū* [明治論理学史研究; Studies in the history of logic in the Meiji period]. Risōsha.

Glockner, Hermann. (1969). *Heidelberger Bilderbuch*. H. Bouvier.

Green, Thomas Hill. (1883). *Prolegomena to Ethics*. Oxford.

Hanada Kiyoteru. (1979–1980). *Hanada Kiyoteru zenshū* [花田清輝全集; Complete works of Hanada Kiyoteru], in 15 vols. and two supplementary vols. Kōdansha.

Hanaoka Eiko. (2002). *Zettaimu no tetsugaku—Nishida tetsugaku kenkyū nyūmon* [絶対無の哲学——西田哲学研究入門; The philosophy of absolute nothingness: Introduction to the study of Nishidean philosophy]. Sekai Shisōsha.

Hartmann, Eduard von. (1869). *Philosophie des Unbewussten*. Berlin.

Hase Shōtō. (2003). *Yokubō no tetsugaku—Jyōdokyō sekai no shisaku* [欲望の哲学——浄土教世界の思索; The philosophy of desire: The thought of the world of Pure Land Buddhism]. Hōzōkan.

Hasunuma Keisuke. (1987). *Nishi Amane ni okeru tetsugaku no seiritsu* [西周に於ける哲学の成立; The formation of philosophy in Nishi Amane]. Yūhikaku.

Hatano Seiichi. (2012a). *Shūkyō tetsugaku joron, Shūkyō tetsugaku* [宗教哲学序論・宗教哲学; Introduction to the philosophy of religion, The philosophy of religion]. Iwanami Bunko

Hatano Seiichi. (2012b). *Toki to eien: Hoka hachi hen* [時と永遠 他八篇; Time and eternity: Eight other texts]. Iwanami Bunko.

Hattori Kenji. (2000). *Nishida tetsugaku to saha no hitotachi* [西田哲学と左派の人たち; Nishida's philosophy and people on the left]. Kobushi Shobō.

Hayashi Naomichi. (1948). *Nishida tetsugaku hihan* [西田哲学批判; Critique of Nishida philosophy]. Kaihōsha.

Hayashi Tatsuo. (1971–1987). *Hayashi Tatsuo chosakushū* [林達夫著作集; Collected writings of Hayashi Tatsuo]. Heibonsha.

Hayashi Tatsuo. (1982). *Hayashi Tatsuo hyōronshū* [林達夫評論集; Collected criticism of Hayashi Tatsuo]. Edited by Nakagawa Hisayasu. Iwanami Bunko.

Hegel, Georg W. F. (1955). *Hegel's Lectures on the History of Philosophy*. Translation by E. S. Haldane. Routledge and Kegan Paul.

Hegel, Georg W. F. (1971). *Werke in zwanzig Bänden*. Edited by E. Moldenhauer and K. M. Michel. Suhrkamp.

Heidegger, Martin. (1950). *Holzwege*. Vittorio Klostermann.

Heidegger, Martin. (1959). *Unterwegs zur Sprache*. Neske.

Heidegger, Martin. (2001). *Sein und Zeit*, 18. Aufl. Max Niemeyer.

Heisig, James W. (2001). *Philosophers of Nothingness: An Essay on the Kyoto School*. University of Hawai'i Press.

Heisig, James W., Thomas P. Kasulis, and John C. Maraldo, eds. (2011). *Japanese Philosophy: A Sourcebook*. University of Hawai'i Press.

Hikaku shisō kenkyū. (1974). [比較思想研究; Studies in comparative philosophy], edited by the Japanese Association for Comparative Philosophy.

Hiromatsu Wataru. (1980). 〈*Kindai no chōkoku*〉 *ron—Shōwa shisōshi he no ichi dansō* [〈近代の超克〉論――昭和思想史への一断想; Discourses on "overcoming modernity": A fragmentary reflection on the intellectual history of the Shōwa period]. Asahi Shuppansha.

Hiromatsu Wataru. (1982). *Sonzai to imi—Koto tek isekai kann no teiso* [存在と意味――事的世界観の定礎; Being and meaning: Cornerstone of the Koto worldview]. Iwanami Shoten.

Hisamatsu Shin'ichi. (1981). *Mushinron* [無神論; Atheism]. Hōzōkan.

Hisamatsu Shin'ichi. (1994–1996). *Hisamatsu Shin'ichi chosakushū* [久松真一著作集; Collected writings of Hisamatsu Shin'ichi]. Enlarged edition in 9 vols. and supplementary vol. Hōzōkan.

Hisamatsu Shin'ichi and Nishitani Keiji, eds. (1969). *Zen no honsitsu to ningen no sinri* [禅の本質と人間の真理; The essence of Zen and human truth]. Sōbunsha.

Hong Yaoxun. (2019). *Collected Writings of Hong Yaoxun*. Edited by Liao Qinbin. Taiwan University Press Center.

Hori Tatsunosuke. (1862). *Eiwa taiyaku shūchin jisho* [英和対訳袖珍辞書; Pocket English-Japanese dictionary]. Yōsho Shirabesho.

Hosoya Masashi. (2008). *Kyōto gakuha—Ninshiki to sei* [田辺哲学と京都学派――認識と生; Tanabe's philosophy and the Kyoto School: Recognition and life]. Shōwadō.

Husserl, Edmund. (1950). *Ideen zu einer reinen Phänomenologie und phänomenologischen Philosophie. Erstes Buch*. In *Husserliana. Gesammelte Werke*, book 3, edited by Walter Biemel. Den Haag.

Husserl, Edmund. (1954). *Die Krisis der europäischen Wissenschaften und die transzendentale Phänomenologie*. In *Husserliana, Gesammelte Werke*, book 6, edited by

Walter Biemel, Den Haag. English translation: *The Crisis of European Sciences and Transcendental Phenomenology*, translated by David Carr. Northwestern University Press, 1970.

Hu Suh. (1919). *Chūgoku tetsugaku shi taikō* [中国哲学史大綱; Overview of the history of Chinese philosophy]. *Commercial Press* (China).

Ibsen, Henrik. (1913). *Ningyō no ie* [人形の家; *A Doll's House*]. Translated by Shimamura Hōgetsu. Waseda Daigaku Shuppanbu.

Ichikawa Hiroshi. (1975). *Seishin toshite no shintai* [精神としての身体; The body as spirit]. Keisō Shobō.

Ichikawa Hiroshi. (1984). *<Mi> no kōzō* [<身>の構造; The structure of <mi>]. Seidosha.

Ienaga Saburō. (1968). *Sensō sekinin* [戦争責任; Responsibility for war]. Iwanami Shoten.

Ienaga Saburō. (1974). *Tanabe Hajime no shisōshi teki kenkyū* [田辺元の思想史的研究; Studies in Tanabe Hajime from the perspective of intellectual history]. Hōsei University Press.

Ienaga Saburō. (1993). *Nihon shisō shi gaku no hōhō* [日本思想史学の方法; Methodology of the study of the history of Japanese thought]. Meicho Kankōkai.

Ienaga Saburō. (1997–1999). *Ienaga Saburō shū* [家永三郎集; Inenaga Saburō collection], 16 vols. Iwanami Shoten.

Imamichi Tomonobu. (1990). *Ekoetika—Seiken rinri gaku nyūmon* [エコエティカ——生圏倫理学入門; Eco-ethica: Introduction to biosphere ethics]. Kōdansha Gakujutsu Bunko.

Imanishi Kinji. (1993–1994). *Imanishi Kinji zenshū* [今西錦司全集; Complete works of Imanishi Kinji], in 13 vols. and a supplementary volume. Kōdansha.

Inoue Enryō. (1886). *Tetsugaku isseki wa* [哲学一夕話; An evening of philosophical conversation]. Tetsugaku Shoin.

Inoue Enryō. (1886–1887). *Tetsugaku yōryō* [哲学要領; Key points in philosophy]. 2 vols. Reichikai.

Inoue Enryō. (1887). *Bukkyō katsuron jyoron* [仏教活論序論; An introduction to a discourse to revitalize Buddhism]. Tetsugaku Shoin.

Inoue Enryō. (1909). *Tetsugaku Shinan* [哲学新案; A new conception of philosophy]. Kōdōkan.

Inoue Enryō. (1987–2004). *Inoue Enryō senshū* [井上円了選集; Selected works of Inoue Enryō], 25 vols. Tōyō Daigaku.

Inoue Katsuhito. (2011). *Nishida Kitarō to meiji no seishin* [西田幾多郎と明治の精神; Nishida Kitarō and the Meiji spirit]. Kansai Daigaku Shuppanbu.

Inoue Kowashi den. (1966). [井上毅伝; Biography of Inoue Kowashi]. Edited by the Editorial Committee of Biography of Inoue Kowashi, Historical Documents Part One. Kokugakuin University Library.

Inoue Tetsujirō et al., eds. (1881). *Tetsugaku jii* [哲学字彙; Dictionary of philosophy]. University of Tokyo Three Faculties Printing.

Inoue Tetsujirō. (1891). *Chokugo engi* [勅語衍義; Explanation of imperial edicts]. Keigyōsha.

Inoue Tetsujirō. (1893). *Kyōiku to shūkyo tono shōtotsu* [教育ト宗教ノ衝突; The collision of education and religion]. Keigyōosha.

Inoue Tetsujirō. (1900). *Nihon yōmei gaku ha no tetsugaku* [日本陽明学派之哲学; The philosophy of the Japanese Yangming School]. Fuzanbō.

Inoue Tetsujirō. (1901). *Sonken ronbun ni shū* [巽軒論文二集; Sonken essays part II]. (Sonken is Inoue Tetsujirō's pen name.) Fuzanbō.

Inoue Tetsujirō. (1902a). *Chūgaku shūshin kyōkasho* [中学修身教科書; Middle school moral training textbook]. 5 vols. Kinkōdō Shoseki.

Inoue Tetsujirō. (1902b). *Nihon kogaku ha no tetsugaku* [日本古学派之哲学; The philosophy of the Japanese Ancient Learning School]. Fuzanbō.

Inoue Tetsujirō. (1905). *Nihon shushi gaku ha no tetsugaku* [日本朱子学派之哲学; The philosophy of the Japanese Cheng-Zhu School]. Fuzanbō.

Inoue Tetsujirō. (1932). "Meiji tetsugaku kai no kaiko" [明治哲学界の回顧; Reflections on the world of Meiji philosophy], in *Iwanami Kōza Testugaku* [岩波講座 哲学; Iwanami lecture series on philosophy]. Iwanami Shoten.

Inoue Tetsujirō. (1943). *Kaikyū roku* [懐旧録; Reminiscences]. Shunjyūsha.

Inoue Tetsujirō. (1973). *Inoue Tetsujirō jiden* [井上哲次郎自伝; Autobiography of Inoue Tetsujirō]. Fuzanbō.

Inoue Tetsujirō and Ariga Nagao. (1883–85). *Seiyō tetugaku kogi* [西洋哲学講義; Lectures on Western philosophy]. Sakagami Hanshichi.

Itō Jinsai. (1909). *Rongo kogi* [論語古義, Ancient meaning of the Analects]. Revised by Sato Masanori. Rokumeikan.

Itō Katsuhiko. (2000). *Tenchi ujyō no tetsugaku—Ōmori Shōzō to Mori Arimasa* [天地有情の哲学——大森荘蔵と森有正; The philosophy of heaven and earth having emotions: Ōmori Shōzō and Mori Arimasa]. Chikuma Gakugei Bunko.

Itō Tomonobu et al., ed. (1982). *Kindai nihon tetugaku shisōka jiten* [近代日本哲学思想家辞典; Dictionary of modern Japanese philosophers and thinkers]. Edited by Nakamura Hajime and Takeda Kiyoko. Tōkyō Shoseki.

Izu Kimio, ed. (1948). *Kindai shugi hihan* [近代主義批判; Modernism criticism]. Dōyūsha.

Izutsu Toshihiko. (1983). *Ishiki to honshitsu—Seishin teki tōyō wo motomete* [意識と本質——精神的東洋を索めて; Consciousness and essence: Searching for the East in an intellectual context]. Iwanami Shoten.

Izutsu Toshihiko. (1985). *Imi no fukami he—Tōyō tetsugaku no suii* [意味の深みへ——東洋哲学の水位; To the depths of meaning: The water level of Eastern philosophy]. Iwanami Shoten.

Jiko—Seishin igaku to tetsugaku no kanten kara. (1986). [自己——精神医学と哲学の観点から; The self: From the viewpoints of psychiatry and philosophy] Japan-Germany Symposium, Kawai Institute for Culture and Education.

Jōdo shinshū seiten (chūshaku-ban). (1988). [浄土真宗聖典（註釈版）; Jōdo Shinshū sacred texts, annotated version]. Edited by Shinshū Sacred Texts Compilation Committee. Hongwanji Publishing.

Kaisō no Tosaka Jun. (1948). [回想の戸坂潤; Recollections of Tosaka Jun]. Edited by San-ichi Shobō editorial department. San-ichi Shobō.

Kakehashi Akihide. (1982–1987). *Kakehashi Akihide keizaitetsugaku chosakushū* [梯明秀経済哲学著作集; Collected writings on the philosophy of economics by Kakehashi Akihide]. 5 vols. Miraisha.

Kanbayashi Tsunemichi. (2002). *Bigaku kotohajime—Geijutsu gaku no nihon kindai* [美学事始──芸術学の日本近代; The dawn of aesthetics: The study of art in modern Japan]. Keisō Shobō.

Kaneko Takezō. (1953). *Zitsuzon risei no tetsugaku—Yasupāsu tetsugaku ni sokusite* [実存理性の哲学──ヤスパース哲学に即して; The philosophy of existential reason: Based on Jaspers' philosophy]. Kōbundō.

Kanō Kōkichi. (1958). *Kanō Kōkichi ibun shū* [狩野亨吉遺文集; Collected posthumous writings of Kanō Kōkichi]. Edited by Abe Yoshishige. Iwanami Shoten.

Kanokogi Kazunobu. (1931). *Nihon seishin no tetsugaku* [日本精神の哲学; Philosophy of the Japanese spirit]. Naobinomusubi Shuppanbu.

Kant, Immanuel. (1956). *Kritik der reinen Vernunft,* Riga, 1781. Immanuel Kant, *Werke,* Theorie-Werkausgabe, books 3–4. Suhrkamp.

Karaki Junzō. (1963). *Shinban, Gendai shi heno kokoromi* [新版 現代史への試み; An attempt at modern history, new edition]. Chikuma Shobō.

Karaki Junzō. (1981–1982). *Karaki Junzō chosakushū* [唐木順三著作集; Collected writings of Karaki Junzō]. Expanded edition in 19 vols. Chikuma Shobō.

Katō Hiroyuki. (1868). *Rikken seitai ryaku* [立憲政体略; Summary of the constitutional system]. Taniyamarō.

Katō Hiroyuki. (1870). *Shinsei taii* [真政大意; Outline of the true politics]. Taniyamarō.

Katō Hiroyuki. (1874). *Kokutai shinron* [国体新論; New theory of the national body]. Taniyamarō.

Katō Hisatake. (1991). *Kankyō rinr igaku no susume* [環境倫理学のすすめ; Introduction to environmental ethics]. Maruzen.

Katō Hisatake and Kamo Naoki, eds. (1998). *Seimei rinri gaku wo Manabu hito no tame ni* [生命倫理学を学ぶ人のために; For people studying Bioethics]. Sekaishisōsha.

Kawai Eijirō, ed. (1936). *Gakusei to kyōyō* [学生と教養; Students and cultivation]. Nippon Hyōron Sha.

Kawai Eijirō, ed. (1940). *Gakusei to rekishi* [学生と歴史; Students and history]. Nippon Hyōron Sha.

Kawakami Hajime, ed. (1919–1930). *Shakai mondai kenkyū,* [社会問題研究; Social problems studies]. Kōbundō.

Kawakami Hajime. (1947). *Binbō monogatari* [貧乏物語; Poverty story] Edited with commentary by Ōuchi Hyōe. Iwanami Shoten.

Kawakami Hajime. (1989). *Jijoden* [自叙伝; Autobiography]. 3 vols. Iwanami Shoten.

Kayano Yoshio. (1969). *Benshōhō nyūmon—Tadashii ninshiki wo motomete* [弁証法入門——正しい認識を求めて; Introduction to the dialectic: Seeking a correct understanding]. Kōdansha.

Kayano Yoshio, ed. (1994). *Doitsu kannenron to nihonkindai* [ドイツ観念論と日本近代, German idealism and Japanese modernity]. Minerva Shobō.

Kihira Tadayoshi. (1906). *Jinkaku no chikara—Shūyō no hōhō* [人格の力——修養の方法; The power of character: A method of personal cultivation]. Dōbunkan.

Kihira Tadayoshi. (1930). *Nihon Seishin* [日本精神; The Japanese spirit]. Iwanami Shoten.

Kimura Bin. (2001). *Kimura Bin chosakushū* [木村敏著作集; Collected writings of Kimura Bin]. 8 vols. Kōbundō.

Kimura Motomori. (1939). *Hyōgenai* [表現愛; Expressive love]. Iwanami Shoten.

Kimura Motomori. (1946). *Kokka ni okeru bunka to kyōiku* [国家に於ける文化と教育; Culture and education in the nation]. Iwanami Shoten.

Kimura Motomori. (2000). *Kimura Motomori—Bi no purakushisu* [木村素衛——美のプラクシス; Kimura Motomori: Beauty and praxis]. Edited by Iwaki Ken'ichi. Tōeisha.

Kindai Nihon seiji shisōshi I. (1971). [近代日本政治思想史I; History of modern Japanese political thought I], edited by Hashikawa Bunsō and Matsumoto Sannosuke. In *Kindai Nihon shisōshi taikei* [近代日本思想史大系; Intellectual history of modern Japan series], edited by Miyazawa Toshiyoshi and Ōkouchi Kazuo, vol. 3. Yūhikaku.

Kindai Nihon shakai shisōshi. (1971). [近代日本社会思想史; The history of modern Japanese social thought], edited by Furuta Hikaru, Sakuta Keiichi, and Ikimatsu Keizō, vol. 2. Yūhikaku.

Kindai Nihon shisōshi. (1956–1957). [近代日本思想史; The history of modern Japanese thought], 3 vols., edited by Tōyama Shigeki et al. Aoki Shoten.

Kindai no chōkoku. (1979). [近代の超克; Overcoming Modernity], *Fuzanbō hyakka bunko* [富山房百科文庫; Fuzanbō encyclopedia]. Fuzanbō.

Kindai shakai shisōshiron. (1959). [近代社会思想史論; Essays on the history of modern social thought]. Edited by Mutai Risaku et al. Aoki Shoten.

Kindaika to dentō. (1959). [近代化と伝統; Modernization and Tradition], edited by Kamei Katsuichirō and Takeuchi Yoshimi. In *Kindai Nihon shisōshi kōza* [近代日本思想史講座; History of modern Japanese thought course], vol. 7. Chikuma Shobō.

Kindaishugi. (1964). [近代主義; Modernism]. Edited with commentary by Hidaka Rokurō. In *Gendai Nihon shisō taikei* [現代日本思想大系; Modern Japanese thought series], vol. 3. Chikuma Shobō.

458 | Bibliography

Kira Kōyō. (1881). *Inmyō taii* [因明大意; Outline of Inmyō]. Kira Kōyō.

Kira Kōyō. (1884a). *Inmyō katsugan* [因明活眼; Insights into Inmyō]. Kira Kōyō.

Kira Kōyō. (1884b). *Inmyō nisshōriron kōgi* [因明入正理論講義; Lectures on the introduction to the logic of Inmyō]. Hōzōkan.

Kitamura Tōkoku. (1973–1975). *Tōkoku zenshū* [透谷全集; Collected works of Tōkoku], rev. ed. Iwanami Shoten.

Kitano Hiroyuki and Mori Tetsurō, eds. (2006). *Zen to Kyōto Tetsugaku* [禅と京都哲学; Zen and the Kyoto philosophy]. Supervised by Ueda Shizuteru. Tōeisha.

Kiyono Tsutomu. (1883). *Kakuchi tetsugaku (shoron)* [格致哲学（緒論）; Philosophy of logic (introduction)]. Maruzen Shōsha.

Kiyono Tsutomu. (1889). *Kinōhō ronri gaku—Sinri kenkyu no tetsuri* [帰納法論理学——真理研究之哲理; Inductive logic: Philosophy of the study of truth], parts 1 and 2. Tetsugaku Shoin.

Kiyono Tsutomu. (1890). *Kinōhō ronri keisei kigen* [帰納論理経世危言; Inductive logic and harsh opinions on politics and economics]. Tetsugaku Shoin.

Kiyozawa Manshi. (1892). *Shūkyō tetsugaku gaikotsu* [宗教哲学骸骨; Skeleton of a philosophy of religion]. Hōzōkan.

Kiyozawa Manshi. (1953–1957). *Kiyozawa Manshi zenshū* [清沢満之全集; Collected works of Kiyozawa Manshi]. Edited by Akegarasu Haya and Nishimura Kengyō. Hōzōkan.

Kiyozawa Manshi. (2002–2003). *Kiyozawa Manshi zenshū* [清沢満之全集; Complete works of Kiyozawa Manshi]. Edited by Ōtani University. Iwanami Shoten.

Kiyozawa Sensei nijyūgo nenki kinen shuppan, Kiyozawa Manshi. (1928), [清沢先生二十五年忌記念出版 清沢満之; Kiyozawa Manshi: Publication on the 25th anniversary of the death of Kiyozawa-Sensei]. Edited by Kanshōsha. Kanshōsha.

Koeber, Raphael von. (1881). *Schopenhauer's Erlösungslehre*. Berlin.

Koeber, Raphael von. (1884). *Das philosophische System Eduard von Hartmann's*. Breslau.

Koeber, Raphael von. (1963). *Keiberu Hakase zuihitsu shū* [ケーベル博士随筆集; Collected essays of Professor Koeber], translated and edited by Kubo Masaru, 26th printing. Iwanami Shoten.

Koizumi Takashi. (1989). *Nishi Amane to ōbei shisō to no deai* [西周と欧米思想との出会い; The encounter between Nishi Amane and Western thought]. Sanrei Shobō.

Kōsaka Masaaki. (1937). *Rekishitekisekai—Genshōgakuteki shiron* [歴史的世界——現象学的試論; The historical world: Phenomenological essays]. Iwanami Shoten.

Kōsaka Masaaki et al. (1943). *Sekaishiteki tachiba to Nihon* [世界史的立場と日本; The perspective of world history and Japan]. Chūō Kōron Sha.

Kōsaka Masaaki. (1964–1970). *Kōsaka Masaaki chosakushū* [高坂正顕著作集; Collected writings of Kōsaka Masaaki]. Risōsha.

Kōsaka Shirō. (2014). *Higashi Ajia no shisō taiwa* [東アジアの思想対話; Intellectual dialogue in East Asia]. Perikansha.

Kōtoku Shūsui. (1903). *Shakaishugi Shinzui* [社会主義神髄; The essence of socialism]. Chōhōsha.

Kōtoku Shūsui. (1975). *Kōtoku Shūsui shū* [幸徳秋水集; Kōtoku Shūsui collection]. Chikuma Shobō. In *Kindai Nihon shisō taikei* [近代日本思想大系; Series on modern Japanese thought], vol. 13.

Kōyama Iwao. (1935). *Nishida Tetsugaku* [西田哲学; Nishida's philosophy]. Iwanami Shoten.

Kōyama Iwao. (1938). *Tetsugaku teki ningen gaku* [哲学的人間学; Philosophical anthropology]. Iwanami Shoten.

Kōyama Iwao. (1943). *Nihon no kadai to sekaishi* [日本の課題と世界史; Japan's task and world history]. Kōbundō.

Kōyama Iwao. (2007–2009). *Kōyama Iwao chosakushū* [高山岩男著作集; Collected writings of Kōyama Iwao]. Tamagawa University Press.

Koyama Shōtarō sensei. (1934). [小山正太郎先生; Professor Koyama Shōtarō]. Edited by Fudō-sha Kyūyū-kai [Old Friends of Fudō-sha Association]. Meguro Shoten.

Koyasu Nobukuni. (2008). *"Kindai no chōkoku" to ha nanika* [「近代の超克」とは何か; What is "overcoming modernity"?]. Seidosha.

Kuga Katsunan (1968–1985). *Kuga Katsunan zenshū*, [陸羯南全集; Complete works of Kuga Katsunan]. Misuzu Shobō.

Kuga Katsunan, Miyake Setsurei. (1971) [陸羯南・三宅雪嶺; Kuga Katsunan, Miyake Setsurei]. In *Nihon no meicho* [日本の名著, Japanese masterpieces], vol. 37. Chūō Kōron Sha.

Kuhn, Thomas S. (1962). *The Structure of Scientific Revolutions*. University of Chicago Press.

Kuki Shūzō. (1928). *Propos sur le temps*. Philippe Renouard.

Kuki Shūzō. (1930). *"Iki" no kōzō* [「いき」の構造; The structure of "iki"]. Iwanami Shoten.

Kuki Shūzō. (1980–1982). *Kuki Shūzō zenshū* [九鬼周造全集; Complete works of Kuki Shūzō]. Iwanami Shoten.

Kuno Osamu. (1972). *Heiwa no ronri to sensō no ronri* [平和の論理と戦争の論理; The logic of peace and the logic of war]. Iwanami Shoten.

Kuno Osamu. (1974). *Sanjyū nendai no shisōka tachi* [三十年代の思想家たち; Intellectuals of the 1930s]. Iwanami Shoten.

Kuno Osamu. (1975). *Seijiteki shimin no fukken* [政治的市民の複権; The restoration of the political citizen]. Ushio Shuppansha.

Kuno Osamu. (1996). *Shiminshugi no seiritsu* [市民主義の成立; The formation of citizenism]. Shunjūsha.

Kurihara Shin'ichi. (1968). *Fenorosa to meiji bunka* [フェノロサと明治文化; Fenollosa and Meiji culture]. Rikugei Shobō.

Kuwaki Gen'yoku. (1903). *Tetsugaku gairon* [哲学概論; Overview of philosophy]. Rev. ed. Waseda Daigaku Shuppan.

Kuwaki Gen'yoku. (1906). *Seikaku to tetsugaku* [性格と哲学; Personality and philosophy]. Hidaka Yūrindō.

Kuwaki Gen'yoku. (1917). *Kanto to gendai no tetsugaku* [カントと現代の哲学; Kant and modern philosophy]. Iwanami Shoten.

Kuwaki Gen'yoku. (1920). *Bunka shugi to shakai mondai* [文化主義と社会問題; Culturism and social problems]. Shizendō Shoten.

Kuwaki Gen'yoku. (1943a). *Meiji no tetsugakukai* [明治の哲学界; Philosophical community in the Meiji period]. Chūō Kōron Sha.

Kuwaki Gen'yoku. (1943b). *Shomotsu to seken* [書物と世間; Writings and the world]. Shunjūsha-shōhakukan.

Ladmiral, Jean-René. (1979). *Traduire: Théorèmes pour la traduction*. Payot.

Lask, Emil. (1911). *Die Logik der Philosophie und die Kategorienlehre*. J.C.B. Mohr.

Lask, Emil. (1912). *Lehre vom Urteil*. J.C.B. Mohr.

Lévy-Bruhl, Lucien. (1910). *Les fonctions mentales dans les sociétés inférieures*. Félix Alcan.

Lewes, George Henry. (1845–1846). *A Biographical History of Philosophy*. London.

Lewes, George Henry. (1853). *Comte's Philosophy of the Sciences*. London.

Lin Zhenguo. (1999). 空性与现代性——従京都学派新儒家到多音的仏教詮釈学 [Emptiness and modernity: From the Kyoto School and New Confucianism to multivocal Buddhist hermerneutics]. Taiwan, Lixu Wenhua.

Lipps, Theodor. (1903/1906). *Ästhetik*. 2 vols. Leopold Voss.

Liu Jichen. (1993). *Kyoto gakuha tetsugaku* [京都学派哲学; The philosophy of the Kyoto School]. China, Guangming ribao chuban she.

Löwith, Karl. (1928). *Das Individuum in der Rolle des Mitmenschen*. Munich: Drei Masken Verlag.

Maruyama Keizaburō. (1989). *Yokudō* [欲動; Drive (trieb)]. Kōbundō.

Maruyama Masao. (1961). *Nihon no Shisō* [日本の思想; Japanese thought]. Iwanami Shinsho.

Maruyama Masao. (1995–1997). *Maruyama Masao zenshū* [丸山真男全集; Collected works of Maruyama Masao]. Iwanami Shoten.

Marx, Karl. (1859). *Zur Kritik der politischen Ökonomie*. Berlin.

Marx, Karl. (1932). *Ökonomisch-philosophische Manuskripte*, in: *Marx-Engels-Gesamtausgabe*. Abteilung 1, Bd. 3. Marx-Engels Verlag.

Mashita Shin'ichi, ed. (1949). *Shutaisei ronsō* [主体性論争; The subjectivity debate]. Hakuyōsha.

Matsumura Kazuto. (1949). *Yuibutsuron to shutaiseiron* [唯物論と主体性論; Materialism and subjectivity theory]. Nippon Hyōronsha.

Matsunaga Shōzō. (1993). *Nakae Chōmin hyōden* [中江兆民評伝; A critical biography of Nakae Chōmin]. Iwanami Shoten.

Matsuo Takayoshi. (1990). *Taishō demokurashii no gunzō* [大正デモクラシーの群像; Portraits of people during the Taishō democracy era]. Iwanami Shoten.

Matsushima Kō. (1881–1884). *Shakai heiken ron* [社会平権論; Social equal rights theory]. Hōkokusha. Translation of Spencer's *Social Statics.*

Meiji keimō shisō shū. (1967). [明治啓蒙思想集; Meiji enlightenment thought]. In *Meiji bunkagu zenshū* [明治文学全集; Collection of Meiji literature], vol. 3. Chikuma Shobō.

Meiroku Zasshi. (1874–1875). [明六雑誌; *Meiji 6 Journal*], vols. 1–43. Meirokusha.

Merleau-Ponty, Maurice, éd. (1956). *Les philosophes célèbres.* L. Mazenod.

Merleau-Ponty, Maurice. (1960). *Signes.* Gallimard.

Miki Kiyoshi. (1966–1986). *Miki Kiyoshi zenshū* [三木清全集, Complete works of Miki Kiyoshi]. Iwanami Shoten.

Mill, John Stuart. (1859). *On Liberty.* London.

Minamoto Ryōen. (1989). *Kata* [型; Form]. Sōbunsha.

Miyakawa Tōru. (1980). *Nihon seishinshi no kadai* [日本精神史の課題; Issues in Japanese intellectual history]. Kinokuniya Shoten.

Miyake Gōichi. (1966). *Ningen sonzairon* 「人間存在論; Human ontology]. Keisō Shobō.

Miyake Gōichi. (1980). *Keikenteki genjitsu no tetsugaku* [経験的現実の哲学; Philosophy of empirical reality]. Kōbundō.

Miyake Setsurei. (1889). *Tetsugaku kenteki* [哲学涓滴; Philosophical trifles]. Bunkaidō.

Miyake Setsurei. (1893). *Ō Yōmei* [王陽明; Wang Yangming]. Seikyōsha.

Miyake Setsurei. (1946). *Daigaku konjaku tan* [大学今昔譚; Universities then and now]. Gakansha.

Miyake Setsurei. (1967). *Miyake Setsurei shū* [三宅雪嶺集; Collected works of Miyake Setsurei]. In *Meiji bungaku zenshū* [明治文学全集; Collected works of Meiji-period literature], vol. 33. Chikuma Shobō.

Miyamura Haruo. (1989). *Rigakusha Chōmin—Aru kaikoku keiken no shisōshi* [理学者 兆民——ある開国経験の思想史; Philosopher [Nakae] Chōmin: Intellectual history of an experience of the opening of the country]. Musuzu Shobō.

Mizuo Hiroshi. (1992). *Hyōden Yanagi Muneyoshi* [評伝 柳宗悦; Critical biography of Yanagi Muneyoshi]. Chikuma Shobō.

Mori Arimasa. (1978–1982). *Mori Arimasa zenshū* [森有正全集; Complete works of Mori Arimasa]. Chikuma Shobō.

Murai Tomoyoshi. (1899). *Shakaishugi* [社会主義; Socialism]. In Rōdō Shinbunsha, *Kindai Nihon Kirisutokyō meichosenshū* [近代日本キリスト教名著選集; Collection of important modern Japanese Christian writings], vol. 30, *Shakaishugi/ Kirisutokyō to shakaishugi* [社会主義／基督教と社会主義; Socialism / Christianity and socialism]. Nihon Tosho Sentā, 2004.

Murakami Senshō. (1891). *Katsuyō kōjyutsu Inmyō gaku zensho* [活用講述因明学全書; Complete collection of practical lectures on Inmyō logic]. Tetsugaku Shoin.

Murakami Senshō. (1897). *Inmyōgaku taii* [因明学大意; Outline of the study of Inmyō]. Kōyūkan.

Murakata Akiko. (2000–2001). *Aanesuto Fenorosa bunsho shūsei—Honkoku/honyaku to kenkyū* [アーネスト・F・フェノロサ文書集成――翻刻・翻訳と研究; Ernest F. Fenollosa's documents: Reprinting/translation and study]. Kyoto University Press.

Mutai Risaku. (1940). *Hyōgen to ronri* [表現と論理; Expression and logic]. Kōbundō.

Mutai Risaku. (2000–2002). *Mutai Risaku chosakushū* [務台理作著作集; Collected writings of Mutai Risaku]. Kobushi Shobō.

Mutō Kazuo. (1961). *Shingaku to shūkyō tetsugaku tono aida* [神学と宗教哲学との間; Between theology and the philosophy of religion]. Sōbunsha.

Nagata Hiroshi. (1948). *Tetsugaku to minshushugi—Nishida Tanabe tetsugaku hihan no tameni* [哲学と民主主義――西田・田辺哲学批判のために; Philosophy and democracy: A critique of the philosophy of Nishida and Tanabe]. Komeiji Shoten.

Nakae Chōmin. (1882–1883). *Minyaku yakukai* [民約訳解; Annotated translation of *Du Contrat Social*]. Futsugakujyuku.

Nakae Chōmin. (1883–1884). *Ishi bigaku* [維氏美学; Aesthetics of Mr. Véron]. Monbushō. Translation of Eugene Véron's *L'Esthétique*.

Nakae Chōmin. (1886a). *Rigaku enkaku shi* [理学沿革史; The history of philosophy]. Monbushō.

Nakae Chōmin. (1886b). *Rigaku kōgen* [理学鉤玄; Digging up the hidden and profound truths of philosophy]. Shūseisha.

Nakae Chōmin. (1901a). *Ichinen yūhan* [一年有半; A year and a half]. Hakubunkan.

Nakae Chōmin. (1901b). *Zoku ichinen yūhan* [続 一年有半; A year and a half continued]. Hakubunkan.

Nakae Chōmin. (1983–86). *Nakae Chōmin zenshū* [中江兆民全集; Collected works of Nakae Chōmin]. Iwanami Shoten.

Nakagawa Yonezō. (1977). *I no rinri* [医の倫理; The ethics of medicine]. Tamagawa University Press.

Nakai Masakazu. (1995). *Nakai Masakazu hyōronshū* [中井正一評論集; Collected criticism of Nakai Masakazu]. Edited by Osada Hiroshi. Iwanami Bunko.

Nakajima Rikizō. (1898). *Retsudentai seiyō tetsugaku shōshi* [列伝体西洋哲学小史; A short biographical history of Western philosophy]. Fuzanbō.

Nakajima Rikizō. (1911). *Kyōiku sha no jinkaku shūyō* [教育者の人格修養; Educators' personal cultivation of character]. Meguro Shoten.

Nakajima Rikizō. (1912). *Kyōiku teki rinri gaku kōgi* [教育的倫理学講義; Lectures on educational ethics]. Kōdōkan.

Nakamura Hajime. (1960). *Hikaku shisō ron* [比較思想論; On comparative thought]. Iwanami Shoten.

Nakamura Hajime. (1961–1977). *Nakamura Hajime senshū* [中村元選集; Selected works of Nakamura Hajime]. 23 vols. Shunjyūsha.

Nakamura Masanao. (1871). *Jiyū no ri* [自由之理; The principles of liberty]. Kihira Ken'ichirō. Translation of J. S. Mill's *On Liberty*.

Nakamura Yūjirō. (1975). *Kansei no kakusei* [感性の覚醒; The awakening of sensibility]. Iwanami Shoten.

Nakamura Yūjirō. (1979). *Kyōtsū kankaku ron* [共通感覚論; A theory of sensus communis]. Iwanami Shoten.

Nakamura Yūjirō. (1982). *Patosu no chi—Kyōtsū Kankaku teki ningenzō no tenkai* [パトスの知——共通感覚的人間像の展開; The knowledge of pathos: Developing a sensus communis portrait of humanity]. Chikuma Shobō.

Nakamura Yūjirō. (1992). *Rinshō no chi toha nanika* [臨床の知とは何か; What is clinical knowledge?]. Iwanami Shinsho.

Nakazawa Rinsen. (1914). *Beruguson* [ベルグソン; Bergson]. Jitsugyō no Nihonsha.

Nanbara Shigeru. (1942). *Kokka to shukyō—Yōroppa seishinshi no kenkyū* [国家と宗教——ヨーロッパ精神史の研究; State and religion: A study of the spiritual history of Europe]. Iwanami Shoten.

Natsume Sōseki. (2017). *Sorekara* [それから; And Then]. In *Teihon Sōseki Zenshū* [定本漱石全集; The complete works of [Natsume] Soseki, definitive edition], vol. 6. Iwanami Shoten.

Neske, Günthe, ed. (1959). *Martin Heidegger zum siebzigsten Geburtstag, Festschrift*. Neske.

Ng Yu-Kwan. (1995). *Kyoto gakuha tetsugaku—Hisamatsu Shin'ichi* [京都学派哲学——久松真一; The philosophy of the Kyoto School: Hisamatsu Shin'ichi]. Taiwan, Wenchin Shubanshe.

Ng Yu-Kwan. (1998). *Kyoto gakuha tetsugaku shichikō* [京都学派哲学七講; Seven lectures on the philosophy of the Kyoto School]. Taiwan, Wenchin Shubanshe.

Ng Yu-Kwan. (1998). *Zettai mu teki tetsugaku—Kyoto gakuha tetsugaku dōron* [絶対無的哲学——京都学派哲学導論; The philosophy of absolute nothingness: Introduction to the philosophy of the Kyoto School]. Taiwan, Commercial Press.

Nida, Eugene A. (1964). *Toward a Science of Translating*. Brill.

Nihon no tetsugaku. (2000–2017). [日本の哲学; Japanese philosophy]. 18 vols. Shōwadō.

Niijima Jyō, Uemura Masahisa, Kiyozawa Manshi, Tsunashima Ryōsen. (1977). [新島襄・植村正久・清沢満之・綱島梁川], *Meiji bungaku zenshū* [明治文学全集; Collected works of Meiji literature], vol. 46.

Ningen gaku kōza. (1938–1939) [人間学講座; Anthropology course]. 5 vols. Risōsha.

Nishi Amane. (1865). *Fisseringu shi bankoku kōhō* [畢洒林氏万国公法; International law by Mr. Vissering]. Imai Kihei.

Nishi Amane. (1874a). *Chichikeimō* [致知啓蒙; Logic enlightenment]. Kawachiya Kichibē.

Nishi Amane. (1874b). *Hyaku ichi shinron* [百一新論; A new theory that unites all theories]. Yamamoto Kakuma.

Nishi Amane. (1875–1876). *Shinri gaku* [心理学; Mental philosophy]. Monbushō. Translation of Joseph Haven's *Mental Philosophy*. Boston, 1857.

Nishi Amane. (1933). *Nishi Amane chosakushū* [西周哲学著作集; Collected philosophical writings of Nishi Amane]. Edited by Asō Yoshiteru. Iwanami Shoten.

Nishi Amane. (1960–1981). *Nishi Amane zenshū* [西周全集; Collected works of Nishi Amane], 4 vols., edited by Ōkubo Toshiaki. Munetaka Shobō.

Nishi Amane to Nihon no kindai. (2005). [西周と日本の近代; Nishi Amane and Japanese modernity]. Edited by University of Shimane Nishi Amane Research Group. Perikansha.

Nishida Kitaro. (2002–2009). *Nishida Kitaro zenshu* [西田幾多郎全集; Collected works of Nishida Kitaro] (new ed.), 24 vols., edited by Takeda Atsushi et al. Iwanami Shoten.

Nishimura Shigeki. (1887). *Nihon Dōtoku Ron* [日本道徳論, A theory of Japanese morality]. Nishimura Kinji.

Nishitani Keiji. (1986–1995). *Nishitani Keiji chosakushū* [西谷啓治著作集; Collected writings of Nishitani Keiji]. Sōbunsha.

Nitta Yoshihiro. (1998). *Gendai no toi toshite no Nishida tetsugaku* [現代の問いとしての西田哲学; Nishida's philosophy as a contemporary inquiry]. Iwanami Shoten.

Noda Matao. (1974). *Tetsugaku no mittsu no dentō* [哲学の三つの伝統; Three traditions of philosophy]. Chikuma Shobō.

Noda Matao, ed. (1982). *Kindai Nihon shisō no kiseki—Seiyō to no deai* [近代日本思想の軌跡――西洋との出会い; Tracks of modern Japanese thought: Encounter with the West]. Hokuju Shuppan.

Nomura Waihan. (1914). *Beruguson to gendai sichō* [ベルグソンと現代思潮; Bergson and modern thought]. Daidōkan Shoten.

Nomura Waihan. (1921). *Bunka shugi no kenkyū* [文化主義の研究; Culturism studies]. Daidōkan Shoten.

Okakura Tenshin. (1979–1981). *Okakura Tenshin zenshū* [岡倉天心全集; Collected works of Okakura Tenshin]. Heibonsha.

Ōmine Akira. (2013). *Inochi hitotsu—Yoku ikiru hinto* [命ひとつ――よく生きるヒント; One life: Hints for living well]. Shogakukan 101 Shinsho.

Ōmori Shōzō. (1998–1999). *Ōmori Shōzō chosakushū* [大森荘蔵著作集, Collected writings of Ōmori Shōzō]. Iwanami Shoten.

Ōnishi Hajime. (Publication date unknown). *Seiyō tetsugaku shi, kan* [西洋哲学史 完; History of Western philosophy (complete)]. Tokyō Senmon Gakkō.

Ōnishi Hajime. (1924–1927). *Ōnishi hakase zenshū* [大西博士全集; Collected works of Professor Ōnishi]. Rev. ed. Keiseisha.

Ōnishi Yoshinori. (1939). *Yūgen to Aware* [幽玄とあはれ; Yūgen and aware]. Iwanami Shoten.

Ōnishi Yoshinori. (1940). *Fūga ron—"Sabi" no kenkyu* [風雅論――「さび」の研究; On refined taste: A study of "Sabi"]. Iwanami Shoten.

Ōnishi Yoshinori. (1943). *Man'yōshū no shizen kanjō* [万葉集の自然感情; The feeling of nature in the Man'yōshū]. Iwanami Shoten.

Ōnishi Yoshinori. (1959–1960). *Bigaku* [美学, Aesthetics]. 2 vols. Kōbundō.

Onodera Isao. (2002). *Zettaimu to kami—Kyōto gakuha no tetsugaku* [絶対無と神――京都学派の哲学; Absolute nothingness and god: The philosophy of the Kyoto School]. Shunpūsha.

Ōshima Yasumasa. (1956). *Jitsuzon rinri no rekishiteki kyōi—Shinjin to jinshin* [実存倫理の歴史的境位——神人と人神; The historical positioning of existential ethics: God-man and man-god]. Sōbunsha.

Ōtsuka Hisao. (1948). *Kindaika no ningen teki kiso*[近代化の人間的基礎; Human foundations of modernization]. Hakujitsu Shoin.

Ozaki Yukio. (1882). *Eneki suiri gaku* [演繹推理学; Logic of deduction]. Self-published.

Plessner, Helmuth. (1928). *Die Stufen des Organischen und der Mensch*. Walter de Gruyter.

Popper, Karl R. (1994). *The Myth of the Framework*. Edited by M. A. Notturno. Routledge.

Raponichi jiten. (1595). [拉葡日辞典; Dictionarivm Latino-Lvsitanicvm, ac Iaponicvm]. Amakusa Gakurin.

Raponichi taiyaku jisho. (1979). [羅葡日対訳辞書; Latin-Portuguese-Japanese dictionary]. Benseisha.

Rousseau, Jean-Jacques. (1975). *Du contrat social et oevres politiques*. Introduction by Jean Ehrard. Garnier.

Saigusa Hiroto and Shimizu Ikutarō, eds. (1955–1957). *Nihon tetsugaku shisō zensho* [日本哲学思想全書, Encyclopedia of Japanese philosophy and thought]. 20 vols. Heobonsha.

Saito Tsuyoshi. (1977). *Meiji no kotoba—Higashi kara nishi he no kakehashi* [明治のことば——東から西への架け橋; Meiji words: A bridge from East to West]. Kōdansha.

Sakabe Megumi. (1976a). *Kamen no kaishakugaku* [仮面の解釈学; The hermeneutics of masks]. University of Tokyo Press.

Sakabe Megumi. (1976b). *Risei no fuan—Kanto tetugaku no seisei to kozō* [理性の不安——カント哲学の生成と構造; The anxiety of reason: The genesis and structure of Kant's philosophy]. Keisō Shobō.

Sakabe Megumi. (1983). *"Fureru" koto no tetsugaku* [「ふれる」ことの哲学; The philosophy of "touching"]. Iwanami Shoten.

Sakabe Megumi. (1989). *Perusona no shigaku—Katari furumai kokoro* [ペルソナの詩学——かたり ふるまい こころ; The poetics of persona: Narration, behavior, and mind]. Iwanami Shoten.

Sakamoto Kenzō. (1987). *Sentan gijutsu no yukue* [先端技術のゆくえ; Where is cutting-edge technology going?]. Iwanami Shinsho.

Sanctos no Gosagveo no vchi Nvqugaqi. (1976). [サントスの御作業の内抜書, Excerpts from hagiographies] Print ed. Benseisha.

Sanctos no Gosagveo no vchi Nvqugaqi. (1979). [サントスの御作業の内抜書, Excerpts from hagiographies] Transliterated ed. Benseisha.

Satō Hiroo, ed. (2005). *Gaisetsu Nihon shisōshi* [概説日本思想史; Outline of Japanese intellectual history]. Minerva Shobō.

Satō Keiji. (1929). *Genshōgaku gairon* [現象学概論; Outline of phenomenology]. Waseda Daigaku Shuppanbu.

Sawada Nobushige. (1975). *Ninshiki no fūkei* [認識の風景; The landscape of understanding]. Iwanami Shoten.

Scheler, Max. (1928). *Die Stellung des Menschen im Kosmos*. Otto Reichl.

Schütte, Joseph. (1939). "Drei Unterrichtsbücher für Japanische Jesuitenprediger aus dem XVI Jahrhundert." *Archivum Historicum Societas Iesu* 8.

Schwegler, Albert. (1877). *Handbook of the History of Philosophy*. Translated by J. H. Stirling. 6th ed., Edinburgh.

Schwegler, Albert. (1887). *Geschichte der Philosophie im Umriß*. Stuttgart, 1847, 14th ed., Stuttgart.

Seikyō-sha bungaku shu. (1980). [政教社文学集; Collected literary works of Seikyō-sha]. In *Meiji bungaku zenshū* [明治文学全集; Collected works of Meiji-period literature], vol. 37. Chikuma Shobō.

Seiri sōdan. (1882–1883). [政理叢談; Writings on political theory]. Journal of Futsu Gaku Jyuku.

Shibata Masakichi and Koyasu Takashi. (1873). *Fuon sōzu eiwa jii* [附音挿図 英和字彙; English and Japanese dictionary with pronunciation and illustrations]. Nisshūsha.

Shibata Takayuki. (1997). *Testugaku shi seiritsu no genba* [哲学史成立の現場; The site of the formation of the history of philosophy]. Kōbundō.

Shimamura Takitarō. (1909). *Kindai bungei no kenkyū* [近代文芸之研究; A study of modern literature]. Waseda Daigaku Shuppanbu.

Shimomura Toratarō, ed. (1971). *Nishida Kitarō—Dōjidai no kiroku* [西田幾多郎——同時代の記録; Nishida Kitarō: Contemporaneous records]. Iwanami Shoten.

Shimomura Toratarō. (1988–1999). *Shimomura Toratarō chosakushū* [下村寅太郎著作集; Collected writings of Shimomura Toratarō]. Misuzu Shobō.

Shinran. (1988). *Kyōgyōshinshō* [教行信証; A collection of passages revealing the true teaching, practice, and realization of the Pure Land way]. In *Jōdo shinshū seiten, chushaku-ban* [浄土真宗聖典（註釈版）; Jōdo Shinshū sacred texts, annotated version]. Hongwanji Publishing.

Shisō no Kagaku. (1946–1996). [思想の科学; The science of thought]. Edited by Tsurumi Shunsuke et al. Published by several publishers including Senku-sha, Kōdansha, and Chuō Kōron-sha.

Simmel, Georg. (1911). *Philosophische Kultur*. W. Klinkhardt.

Sōda Kiichirō. (1917). *Keizai tetsugaku no sho mondai* [経済哲学の諸問題; Issues in economic philosophy]. Satō Shuppanbu.

Sōda Kiichirō. (1922). *Bunka kachi to kyokugen gainen* [文化価値と極限概念; Cultural values and extreme concepts]. Iwanami Shoten.

Sōda Kiichirō. (1930–1931). *Sōda Kiichirō zenshū* [左右田喜一郎全集; Complete works of Sōda Kiichirō]. Iwanami Shoten.

Sorel, Georges. (1925). *Réflexions sur la violence*. 6th ed. M. Rivière.

Spencer, Herbert. (1851). *Social Statics*. London.

Spencer, Herbert. (1876–1896). *The Principles of Sociology: A System of Synthetic Philosophy*. vols. 6–8. London.

Stevens, Bernard. (2000). *Topologie du néant: Une approche de l'école de Kyoto*. Peeters.

Sueki Fumihiko. (2004). *Kindai Nihon to Bukkyō* [近代日本と仏教; Modern Japan and Buddhism]. Transview.

Sueki Takehiro. (1983–1988). *Nishida Kitarō no tetsugaku—Sono tetsugaku taikei* [西田幾多郎の哲学——その哲学体系; The philosophy of Nishida Kitarō: His philosophical system]. 4 vols. Shunjūsha.

Suematsu Kenchō. (1883). *Girisha kodai rigaku ippan* [希臘古代理学一斑; A part of ancient Greek philosophy]. Suematsu Kenchō.

Sumiya Mikio. (2003). *Sumiya Mikio chosakushū* [隅谷三喜男著作集; Collected writings of Sumiya Mikio]. 9 vols. Iwanami Shoten.

Suzuki Daisetsu. (1960). "How to Read Nishida." In Nishida Kitarō, *A Study of Good*, translated by V. H. Viglielmo. Japanese Government Printing Bureau.

Suzuki Daisetsu. (1999–2003). *Suzuki Daisetsu zenshū* [鈴木大拙全集; Complete works of Suzuki Daisetsu. New enlarged ed. in 40 vols. Iwanami Shoten.

Suzuki Sadami, ed. (1995). *Taishō seimeishugi to gendai* [大正生命主義と現代; Taishō life-ism and modernity]. Kawade Shobō Shinsha.

Suzuki Tadashi. (2013). *Kanō Kōkichi no kenkyū* [狩野亨吉の研究; Studies of Kanō Kōkichi]. Minerva Shobō.

Suzuki Tōru. (1958). *Jitsuzon to rōdō* [実存と労働; Existence and labor]. Minerva Shobō.

Suzuki Tōru. (1967). *Kyōzon teki sekai* [響存的世界; The echo existence world]. Gōdō Shuppan.

Suzuki Tōru. (1977). *Nishida Kitarō no sekai* [西田幾多郎の世界; The world of Nishida Kitarō]. Keisō Shobō.

Suzuki Tōru. (1982). *Ikiru konkyo wo motomete* [生きる根拠を求めて; Seeking a grounding for living]. Sanichi Shobō.

Takahashi Satomi. (1931). *Fusseru no genshōgaku* [フッセルの現象学; Husserl's phenomenology]. Daiichi Shobō.

Takahashi Satomi. (1973). *Takahashi Satomi zenshū* [高橋里美全集; Complete works of Takahashi Satomi]. Fukumura Shuppan.

Takahashi Satomi. (2001). *Zentaisei no genshōgaku* [全体性の現象学; Phenomenology of totality]. In *Kyōto tetsugaku sensho* [京都哲学選書; Selected writings of Kyoto Philosophy], vol. 17. Tōesha.

Takahashi Tōru et al., eds. (1965). *Shakai shinrigaku no keisei* [社会心理学の形成; The formation of social psychology]. In *Konnichi no shakai shinrigaku* [今日の社会心理学; Today's social psychology], vol. 1. Baifūkan.

Takekoshi Yosaburō. (1884a). *Doitsu tetsugaku eika* [独逸哲学英華; The excellence of German philosophy]. Hōkokudō.

Takekoshi Yosaburō. (1884b). *Kindai tetsugaku shūtō shi*, vol. 1 [近代哲学宗統史（巻之一）; General history of modern philosophy, volume 1], Maruzen. Translation of V. Cousin's *Cours de l'histoire de la philosophie modern*.

Takekoshi Yosaburō. (1894). *Shinaron* [支那論; On China]. Minyūsha.

Takeuchi Yoshimi. (1980–1982). *Takeuchi Yoshimi zenshū* [竹内好全集; Complete works of Takeuchi Yoshimi]. Chikuma Shobō.

Takeuchi Yoshinori. (1999). *Takeuchi Yoshinori chosaku shū* [武内義範著作集; Collected writings of Takeuchi Yoshinori]. Hōzōkan.

Takigawa Yukitoki. (1949). *Zuisō to kaisō* [随想と回想; Thoughts and recollections]. Yūhikaku.

Tanabe Hajime. (1924). *Kanto no mokuteki ron* [カントの目的論; Kant's teleology]. Iwanami Shoten.

Tanabe Hajime. (1933). *Tetsugaku Tūron* [哲学通論; Outline of philosophy]. Iwanami Shoten.

Tanabe Hajime. (1963–1964). *Tanabe Hajime zenshū* [田辺元全集; Complete works of Tanabe Hajime]. Chikuma Shobō.

Tanabe Hajime. (2010). *Tanabe Hajime tetsugakusen* [田辺元哲学選; Tanabe Hajime philosophy selection]. Edited by Fujita Masakatsu, 4 vols. Iwanami Bunko.

Tanaka Ōdō. (1911). *Shosai kara gaitō ni* [書斎より街頭に; From the study to the streets]. Kōbundō.

Tanaka Ōdō. (1918). *Tettei kojin shugi* [徹底個人主義; Thorough individualism]. Tenyūsha.

Tanaka Ōdō. (1921). *Sōzō to kyōraku* [創造と享楽; Creativity and pleasure]. Tenyūsha.

Teiyū rinri kai kōen shū. (1900). [丁酉倫理会講演集; Collected lectures of the Teiyū Ethics Society], vol. 1. Dai Nippon Tosho.

Tetsugaku Kenkyū. (1916–). [哲学研究; Journal of Philosophical Studies], edited by the Kyoto Philosophical Society.

Tetsugaku Zasshi (Tetsugaku Kai Zasshi). (1887–). [哲学雑誌（哲学会雑誌）; Journal of Philosophy], edited by the Society of Philosophy.

Toda Kindō. (1886). *Jyakuon shi ronrigaku* [惹穏氏論理学; Jevons' Logic]. Gangyokudō. 1st ed., *Rojiku* [論事矩; Logic], Miyajima Gisaburō. 1879. Translation of Stanley Jevons's *Logic* (Macmillan 1876).

Tokutomi Sohō. (1935). *Sohō jiden* [蘇峰自伝; Autobiography of [Tokutomi] Sohō]. Chuō Kōron Sha.

Tokutomi Sohō. (1974). *Tokutomi Sohō shū* [徳富蘇峰集; Collected Works of Tokutomi Sohō]. In *Meiji bungaku zenshū* [明治文学全集; Collected works of Meiji-period literature], vol. 34. Chikuma Shobō.

Tomonaga Sanjyūrō. (1922). *Kanto no heiwaron* [カントの平和論; Kant's theory of peace]. Kaizōsha.

Tosaka Jun. (1966–1967). *Tosaka Jun zenshū* [戸坂潤全集; Complete works of Tosaka Jun]. Keisō Shobō.

Tsuboi Kumezō. (1883). *Ronri gaku kogi* [論理学講義; Logic lectures]. Sakai Seziō.

Tsubouchi Shōyō. (1885–1886). *Shōsetsu Shinzui* [小説神髄; The essence of the novel]. Shōgetsudo.

Tsuchida Kyōson. (1921). *Bunka shugi genron* [文化主義原論; Fundamentals of culturism]. Naigai Shuppan.

Tsuchida Kyōson. (1926). *Nihon shina gendai sisō kenkyū* [日本支那現代思想研究; Studies of contemporary thought of Japan and China]. Daiichi Shobō.

Tsuchida Kyōson. (1927). *Contemporary Thought of Japan and China*. London.

Tsuchida Kyōson. (1982). *Tsuchida Kyōson zenshū* [土田杏村全集; Complete works of Tsuchida Kyōson]. Repr. ed. Nihon Tosho Center.

Tsuda Mamichi. (2001). *Tsuda Mamichi zenshū* [津田真道全集; Collected works of Tsuda Mamichi]. 2 vols, edited by Ōkubo Toshiaki, Kuwabara Shinsuke, and Kawasaki Masaru. Misuzu Shobō.

Tsukamoto Shūzō. (1878). *Ronrigaku* [論理学; Logic]. Monbushō. Translation of the entry on logic in *Chambers' Encyclopedia*.

Tsunashima Ryōsen. (1905). *Byōkanroku* [病間録; Record of a period of illness]. Kanao Bunendō.

Tsunashima Ryōsen. (1907). *Shunjyū rinri shisō shi* [春秋倫理思想史; The history of ethical thought in the spring and autumn period in China]. Waseda Daigaku Shuppanbu.

Tsunashima Ryōsen. (1909). *Ōshū rinri shisō shi* [欧州倫理思想史; A history of European ethical thought]. Waseda Daigaku Shuppanbu.

Tsunetoshi Sōzaburō, ed. (1998). *Nihon no tetsugaku wo manabu hito no tame ni* [日本の哲学を学ぶ人のために; For people learning Japanese philosophy]. Sekaishisōsha.

Tsurumi Shunsuke. (1967). *Genkai geijyutsu ron* [限界芸術論; On marginal art]. Keisō Shobō.

Tsurumi Shunsuke, ed. (1968). *Heiwa no shisō* [平和の思想; Thought on peace]. In *Sengo Nihon shisō taikei* [戦後日本思想大系; Postwar Japanese thought series], vol. 4. Chikuma Shobō.

Tsurumi Shunsuke. (1984). *Sengo nihon no taishū bunka shi* [戦後日本の大衆文化史; The history of popular culture in postwar Japan]. Iwanami Shoten.

Uchimura Kanzō. (1980–1984). *Uchimura Kanzō zenshū* [内村鑑三全集; Collected works of Uchimura Kanzō]. 40 vols. Iwanami Shoten.

Ueda Jyuzō. (1941). *Shikaku kozo* [視覚構造; The structure of visual perception]. Kōbundō Shobō.

Ueda Shizuteru, ed. (1990). *Nishida tetsugaku heno toi* [西田哲学への問い; Questions for Nishida's philosophy]. Iwanami shoten.

Ueda Shizuteru, ed. (1994). *Botsugo gojyūnen kinen ronbunshū, Nishida tetsugaku* [没後五十年記念論文集 西田哲学; Collection of writings commemorating fifty years since his death: Nishida's philosophy]. Sōbunsha.

Ueda Shizuteru. (1995). *Nishida Kitarō—Ningen no shōgai to iukoto* [西田幾多郎——人間の生涯ということ; Nishida Kitarō: The life of a man]. Iwanami Shoten.

Ueda Shizuteru. (1997). *Kotoba no jitsuzon—Zen to bungaku* [言葉の実存——禅と文学; The existence of language: Zen and literature]. Chikuma Shobō.

Ueda Shizuteru. (2001–2003). *Ueda Shizuteru shū* [上田閑照集; Collected works of Ueda Shizuteru]. Iwanami Shoten.

Ueyama Shunpei. (1971). *Nihon shisō—Dochaku to ouka no keifu* [日本思想——土着と欧化の系譜; Japanese thought: Genealogy of nativity and Westernization]. Saimaru Shuppankai.

Umemoto Katsumi. (1977–1978). *Umemoto Katsumi chosakushū* [梅本克己著作集; Collected writings of Umemoto Katsumi]. San-ichi Shobō.

Utsunomiya Yoshiaki. (1980). *Ningen no aida to rinri* [人間の間と倫理; Ethics and [relationships] between human beings]. Ibunsha.

Waldenfels, Hans. (1976). *Absolutes Nichts: Zur Grundlegung des Dialogs zwischen Buddhismus und Christentum.* Herder.

Watanabe Jirō. (2011). *Watanabe Jirō chosakushū* [渡邊二郎著作集; Collected writings of Watanabe Jirō]. Chikuma Shobō.

Watanabe Kazan, Takano Chōei, Sakuma Shōzan, Yokoi Shōnan, Hashimoto Sanai. (1971). [渡辺崋山・高野長英・横井小楠・橋本左内]. *Nihon shisō taikei,* [日本思想大系; Series on Japanese thought], vol. 55. Iwanami Shoten.

Watsuji Tetsurō. (1913). *Niiche Kenkyū* [ニイチェ研究; Nietzsche studies]. Uchida Rōkakuho.

Watsuji Tetsurō. (1919). *Koji jyunrei* [古寺巡礼; Ancient temple pilgrimage]. Iwanami Shoten.

Watsuji Tetsurō. (1926). *Nihon seoshin shi kenkyū* [日本精神史研究; On Japanese intellectual history]. Iwanami Shoten.

Watsuji Tetsurō. (1927). *Genshi bukkyō no jissen tetsugaku* [原始仏教の実践哲学; The practical philosophy of primitive Buddhism]. Iwanami Shoten.

Watsuji Tetsurō. (1946). Homērosu hihan [ホメーロス批判; A philological criticism of Homer]. Kaname Shobō.

Watsuji Tetsurō. (1952). *Nihon rinri shisōshi* [日本倫理思想史; The history of Japanese ethical thought]. Iwanami Shoten.

Watsuji Tetsurō. (1961–78). *Watsuji Tetsurō zenshū* [和辻哲郎全集; Collected works of Watsuji Tetsurō]. Iwanami Shoten.

Weizsäcker, Viktor von. (1950). *Der Gestaltkreis: Theorie der Einheit von Wahrnehmen und Bewegen.* 4th ed. Georg Thieme.

Windelband, Wilhelm. (1903). *Lehrbuch der Geschichte der Philosophie.* 3rd ed. J.C.B. Mohr.

Yagi Seiichi. (1995). *Shūkyō to gengo/ shūkyō no gengo* [宗教と言語・宗教の 言語; Religion and language/religious language]. Board of Publications of the United Church of Christ in Japan.

Yamada Munemutsu. (1978). *Nishida Kitarō no tetsugaku* [西田幾多郎の哲学; The philosophy of Nishida Kitarō]. San-Ichi Shobō.

Yamaguchi Seiichi. (1982). *Fenorosa—Nihon bunka no senyō ni sasageta isshō* [フェノロサ——日本文化の宣揚に捧げた一生; Fenollosa: A life devoted to the enhancement of Japanese culture]. Sanseidō.

Yamashita Shigekazu. (1983). *Supensaa to Nihon kindai* [スペンサーと日本近代; Spencer and Japanese modernity]. Ochanomizu Shobō.

Yamauchi Tokuryū. (1929). *Genshōgaku josetu* [現象学叙説; A discourse on phenomenology]. Iwanami Shoten.

Yamauchi Tokuryū. (1937). *Taikei to tensō* [体系と展相; System and evolution]. Kōbundō Shobō.

Yamauchi Tokuryū. (1967). *Imi to keijijyōgaku* [意味と形而上学; Meaning and metaphysics]. Iwanami Shoten.

Yamauchi Tokuryū. (1974). *Rogosu to renma* [ロゴスとレンマ; Logos and lemma]. Iwanami Shoten.

Yamauchi Tokuryū. (1993). Zuimen no tetsugaku [随眠の哲学; The philosophy of fundamental desires (anuśaya)]. Iwanami Shoten.

Yanabu Akira. (1972). *Honyakugo no ronri—Gengo ni miru Nihon bunka no kōzō* [翻訳語の論理——言語に見る日本文化の構造; The logic of translation words: The structure of Japanese culture seen in language]. Hōsei University Press.

Yanabu Akira. (1982). *Honyakugo seiritsu jijyō* [翻訳語成立事情; Circumstances of the establishment of translation words]. Iwanami Shinsho.

Yanagi Muneyoshi. (1985). *Kōgei bunka* [工芸文化; Handicraft culture]. Iwanami Bunko.

Yanagi Muneyoshi. (1987). *Yanagi Muneyoshi sadō ronshū* [柳宗悦茶道論集; Yanagi Muneyoshi, collected essays on tea ceremony]. Edited by Kumakura Isao. Iwanami Bunko.

Yonemoto Shōhei. (1985). *Baio esikkusu* [バイオエシックス; Bioethics]. Kōdansha Gendai Shinsho.

Yonemoto Shōhei. (2006). *Baio poritikusu—Jintai wo kanrisuru toha dōiu kotoka* [バイオポリティクス——人体を管理するとはどういうことか; Biopolitics: What does it mean to control the human body?]. Chuō Kōron Sha.

Yoshida Masatoshi. (2011). *Kindai Nihon shisō ron* [近代日本思想論; *Modern Japanese Thought*] II, *"Kyōto gakuha" no tetsugaku—Nishida, Miki, Tosaka wo chūshin ni* [「京都学派」の哲学——西田・三木・戸坂を中心に; The Philosophy of the Kyoto School: Centered on Nishida, Miki, and Tosaka]. Ōtsuki Shoten.

Yoshimoto Takaaki. (2014–2024). *Yoshimoto Takaaki zenshu* [吉本隆明全集, Complete works of Yoshimoto Takaaki]. Shōbunsha.

Yoshino Genzaburō. (1982). *Kimitachi ha dō ikiruka?* [君たちはどう生きるか; How do you live?]. Iwanami Bunko.

Yoshino Sakuzō. (1976). *Yoshino Sakuzō shū* [吉野作造; Yoshino Sakuzō collection], In *Kindai Nihon shisō taikei* [近代日本思想体系; Modern Japanese thought system], vol. 17. Chikuma Shobō.

Yuasa Yasuo, ed. (1973). *Hito to shisō: Watsuji Tetsurō* [人と思想・和辻哲郎; Person and thought: Watsuji Tetsurō]. San-Ichi Shobō.

Yuasa Yasuo. (1977). *Shintai—Tōyōteki shinshin ron no kokoromi* [身体——東洋的心身論の試み; The body: An attempt to establish an Eastern mind-body theory]. Sōbunsha.

Yukawa Hideki. (1966). *Tabibito—Aru butsurigakusha no kaisō* [旅人——ある物理学者の回想; Traveler: Reminiscences of a physicist]. Kōdansha.

Zettai mu to kami—Nishida/Tanabe tetsugaku no dento to kirisuto kyo. (1981). [絶対無と神——西田・田辺哲学の伝統とキリスト教; Absolute nothingness and god: The philosophical tradition of Nishida and Tanabe and Christianity]. Edited by Nanzan Institute for Religion and Culture. Shunjyūsha.

Zhou Dunyi. (1932). *Tsū sho* [通書; Penetrating writings on *The Book of Changes*]. Revised by Takamatsu Jintarō. Kontonsha.

Index